INFRASTRUCTURE
AND SERVICES

INFRASTRUCTURE AND SERVICES

A Historiographical and Bibliographical Guide

David O. Whitten
AND
Bessie E. Whitten,
EDITORS

HANDBOOK OF AMERICAN BUSINESS HISTORY,
VOLUME III

GREENWOOD PRESS
Westport, Connecticut • London

Library of Congress Cataloging–in–Publication Data

Handbook of American business history / David O. Whitten, editor,
  Bessie E. Whitten, assistant editor.
    p.   cm.
  Includes bibliographical references.
  Contents: v. 1. Manufacturing.
  ISBN 0–313–25198–3 (v. 1 : alk. paper)
  1. United States—Industries—History—Handbooks, manuals, etc.
  I. Whitten, David O.   II. Whitten, Bessie E. (Bessie Emrick)
  HC103.H19   1990
  338.0973—dc20   89–25921

British Library Cataloguing in Publication Data is available.

Library of Congress Catalog Card Number: 89–25921
ISBN: 0–313–25198–3 (vol. I)
ISBN: 0–313–25199–1 (vol. II)
ISBN: 0–313–25200–9 (vol. III)

First published in 2000

Greenwood Press, 88 Post Road West, Westport, CT 06881
An imprint of Greenwood Publishing Group, Inc.
www.greenwood.com

Printed in the United States of America

∞

The paper used in this book complies with the
Permanent Paper Standard issued by the National
Information Standards Organization (Z39.48–1984).

10 9 8 7 6 5 4 3 2 1

for Beatrice E. Whitten

CONTENTS

PREFACE

The twenty-one entries of *Handbook of American Business History, volume III, Infrastructure and Services: A Historiographical and Bibliographical Guide* represent business history from Z (zinc, Chapter 1—zinc, assigned to volume II, *Extractives*, but unavailable by deadline, has been attached to volume III) to A (administration, Chapter 21). Volume I, *Manufacturing: A Historiographical and Bibliographical Guide*, appeared in 1990; volume II, *Extractives, Manufacturing, and Services: A Historiographical and Bibliographical Guide*, in 1997; and volume III in 2000. The series was researched, written, edited, and published in the most fecund, rapidly changing decade in American business history.

Just as zinc came to the *Handbook* too late for volume II, several chapters were pledged but the contracts never fulfilled. The most lamentable omission is of the telephone industry. Although a considerable body of telephone industry literature can be found in volume I, Chapter 17, "Radio, TV, and Communications Equipment," and in volume III, Chapter 2, "Telegraph Communications," and Chapter 3, "Radio and Television Broadcasting," a separate study of the talking machine was not forthcoming. Electronic communication was not an established industry with a recognizable history when the *Handbook* project was launched. There is no chapter devoted to the industry's brief history, but Chapters 2 and 3 of volume III include references to electronic telecommunications and its literature.

The 1990s opened with Republican George Bush in the White House. His successful Persian Gulf War in 1991 firmly placed the president on the path to re-election, but a tax increase and the sluggish economy propelled William J. "Bill" Clinton into office. Racked with scandal, conflict, and controversy, the final presidency of the twentieth century suggests J. Rogers Hollingsworth's whirligig of politics. Clinton's failed health care reform, his impeachment, and the budgetary imbroglio with dominant Republicans that closed down the nation's government are all contretemps worthy of bringing down a president. Yet Clinton has been one of the most popular chief executives in American history—at least in terms of approval ratings gleaned by opinion pollsters. The secret of Clinton's success is the economy, arguably the most prosperous in American history, prosperous despite global depression and a nagging international trade deficit (the federal budget deficit bequeathed Democrat Clinton by Republican presidents Ronald Reagan and George Bush was eliminated early in Clinton's second term of office).

The power of a strong economy to overcome myriad difficulties and deficiencies and keep a president in office and popular is a measure of the strength of economics and business in the United States. Steady economic growth, full employment, rising productivity, and stable prices have reflected so well on business that the electorate has willingly tossed aside social welfare programs and regulatory systems that over the course of the twentieth century were built up to alleviate social and economic difficulties generated as by-products of profit seeking.

The three volumes of *Handbook of American Business History* epitomize the highs and lows of American business and economic history. The project was launched in the late 1980s, when scholars trekked to libraries and thumbed through card catalogs or bound copies of *Books in Print, Reader's Guide to Periodic Literature,* and the *Index to Economic Journals,* but was brought to conclusion in the late 1990s, when those same scholars reworked chapters—out-of-date from a decade's delay in getting to press—by sitting before computer monitors and collecting citations from around the world. Most of the work cited in the three volumes was written by scholars without benefit of copying machines, computers, fax machines, printers, e-mail, or the World Wide Web. The *Handbook* recalls an era of slow-paced scholarship, charming in retrospect but drudgery then. The end-of-era technology so fetching to those who grew up without it heralds not a conclusion but a fascinating future.

The *Handbook* closes one epoch of scholarship and opens another. Research will never again be limited to painstaking examination of antique books, newspapers, letters, journals, or receipts. A few fortunate students will continue to unearth original material, but most will have recourse to archives on-line, scanned into computer banks. Books like this one are likely to be available on-line early in the twenty-first century. Research will resemble more a video game than hide-and-seek. Notwithstanding, these chapters are a launching platform into the history of an American enterprise system that has generated world-changing technology and that promises to make the twenty-first century as different from the twentieth as the twentieth century was from the Middle Ages.

INTRODUCTION
DONALD R. STABILE

Handbook of American Business History, volume III, Infrastructure and Services: A Historiographical and Bibliographical Guide is a consolidated business history of the United States that addresses basic industries (mining, communications, electricity, and natural gas), trade, services (financial, personal, business, health, educational, and social), business organizations, and public administration. In volume I, *Manufacturing*, Mira Wilkins wrote a general history of business as an Introduction. This Introduction, like its counterpart in volume II, *Extractives, Manufacturing, and Services*, is a guide to the chapters in the current volume of the *Handbook*.

Andrea C. Dragon probes a seemingly mundane extractive industry, zinc (Chapter 1). Zinc-bearing iron ore was uncovered in Sussex County, New Jersey, in the eighteenth century. Efforts to separate the zinc were frustrated until the 1840s, when technological breakthroughs made the recovery of zinc oxide and the smelting of zinc slabs feasible. Aided by congressional mandate to the newly created Bureau of Standards to distribute standard weights made from brass (an alloy of copper and zinc), Dr. Samuel Fowler, a representative from New Jersey, formed the Sussex Zinc and Iron Mining Company in 1848 to apply the new technology to the zinc deposits he had inherited. After fifty years of patent suits over the use of the technology, the litigants resolved their differences through a merger that formed the New Jersey Zinc Company (NJZC) in 1897. NJZC purchased new deposits of zinc in the United States as soon as they were discovered. Production of zinc increased tenfold between 1885 and 1915, as new uses for the metal were developed. Zinc oxide is essential to the manufacture of ready-mix paint, for example, and NJZC took the lead in creating that industry. To enhance its productivity, the company built a large smelter in New Jersey and surrounded it with a company town, complete with hospital, sociolog-ical department, and a plan to Americanize foreign-born workers. During World War I the company expanded to meet the increased demand for zinc for armaments production. After the war, plastic and other materials sup-planted zinc, and new mines were developed abroad; NJZC declined in importance but remained viable by producing new zinc alloys.

Susan DuBrock Wendel details the saga of Western Union and the tele-graph industry (Chapter 2). Although schoolchildren in the United States learn that American Samuel F. B. Morse was granted a patent on the mag-netic telegraph in 1840, they do not read about Leonard D. Gale, Alfred Vail, and Francis O. J. Smith, men who helped develop and market the device. Morse and associates, though divided over how to exploit their innovation, established the Magnetic Telegraph Company in 1845. The firm suffered from internal disagreements, technical difficulties, ineffective management, and competition. Like enterprises in the Gilded Age, tele-graph companies cooperated to establish industry standards yet competed fiercely for markets. Pools and cartels did not ease the competitive struggle, so monopolization by merger followed. The Western Union Telegraph Company, incorporated in 1851 as the New York & Mississippi Valley Printing Telegraph Company, bought out its major competitors to become the first U.S. national monopoly in 1866, a quarter century before federal antitrust legislation. Bolstered by its monopoly position and a thriving busi-ness providing communications for railroads, a complacent Western Union missed an opportunity to purchase the fledgling telephone company based on Alexander Graham Bell's patents. Western Union survived competition from telephone and radio in the first half of the twentieth century but fell before the onslaught of computers and facsimile machines in the second half of the century. What survives of Western Union specializes in the elec-tronic transfer of money as a subsidiary of First Data Corporation, the world leader in financial processing.

In her chapter on radio and television broadcasting (Chapter 3), Carole E. Scott reexamines the history of an increasingly complex industry created by scientists, inventors, entrepreneurs, and regulators. The names associ-ated with the industry suggest the diverse talents needed to make it succeed. James Clerk Maxwell first explained the theory of electromagnetic energy; Guglielmo Marconi used it to communicate with Morse code. Marconi surrounded himself with experienced business executives, who protected his invention with patents and franchises of its users worldwide. Lee de Forest, the most prolific inventor in the industry, showed less business acu-men. His ideas spawned companies that grew into giants—Westinghouse, General Electric, RCA, NBC, and CBS—in the hands of entrepreneurs like David Sarnoff and William S. Paley. Radio broadcasting began in the 1920s; television, in the late 1930s. Technology drives industry: crystal radios were replaced by vacuum tube sets, which, in turn, were supplanted by transistorized equipment; television transmission advanced from local-ized stations to coaxial cable, satellite relays, video recordings, and fiber-optic cable. Government regulation of the industry began in 1904, when President Theodore Roosevelt set up the Interdepartmental Board of Wireless Telegraphy. The Radio Act of 1912 required a license to operate a broadcast transmitter. In 1927 Congress passed the Radio Act to regulate broadcast frequencies, to prohibit stations from interfering with competing signals, and to define radio waves as public property. The Communications Act of 1934 established the Federal Communications Commission (FCC) to monitor the broadcasting industry. The FCC regulated competition until deregulation in the 1980s quickened competition, fostering new networks and the development of satellite receiving systems and niche channels. As communications and computer technology advance, the broadcast industry, both audio and visual, will offer consumers a wide range of entertainment, information, and other services.

John L. Neufeld analyzes the electric services industry (Chapter 4). Al-though American involvement with electricity began with the legendary experiments of Benjamin Franklin, the general use of electricity remained impractical until Thomas Alva Edison invented the incandescent light bulb and generated the power to light private homes—his Pearl Street Gener-ating Station in New York City was the origin of the Consolidated Edison and General Electric Companies. Because he promoted direct current (DC) when alternating current (AC) was more practical, Edison's influence on the business of generating electricity was short-lived. In the early twentieth century, water-powered generation and long-range transmission of electric-ity initiated a consolidation of the industry into larger firms to take advan-tage of economies of scale. Samuel Insull, for example, used holding companies to build national electric corporations, albeit many of them sub-sequently failed in the stock market crash of 1929 and the Great Depres-sion. State governments began regulating electric generating companies as natural monopolies, and the federal government became a producer through its creation of the Tennessee Valley Authority in 1933 and the Rural Electrification Administration in 1935. By the 1950s electrification was complete. The energy crisis of the 1970s, the environmental movement, and declining public support for nuclear energy have changed the electric industry: households are using electricity more efficiently—appliances sold in the 1990s are more energy-efficient and serviceable than their 1960s counterparts—and states are experimenting with deregulation and more flexible regulation. The competition in the production and distribution of electricity that disappeared in the early twentieth century may resurge in the twenty-first century.

Eleanor T. von Ende and Klaus G. Becker survey the production and distribution of manufactured and natural gas (Chapter 5). Manufactured gas, a commercial product in Europe at the end of the eighteenth century, was sold in the United States as early as 1807 in Newport, Rhode Island, and 1816 in Baltimore, Maryland—the Gas Light Company of Baltimore, the first company organized for gaslights, operated street lamps in that city. When electricity replaced gas for lighting in the late nineteenth century, gas stoves and furnaces became the target markets for gas companies. The discovery of natural gas offered a better fuel than manufactured gas, but exploitation was delayed until the 1920s by backward pipeline technology. The pipeline boom (1920s into the 1950s), integration of the industry through holding companies, and duplication of services combined to invite regulation by city, state, and federal government. The federal Public Utility Holding Company Act of 1935 placed limits on integration, and the Natural Gas Act of 1938 gave the Federal Power Commission the authority to regulate the gas industry and set price ceilings. In the 1970s, when gas production declined and shortages developed, regulatory agencies were unable to correct market imbalances. In the 1980s deregulation was introduced to let competitive forces allocate a limited supply to a growing market. Von Ende and Becker's bibliographic essay is especially thorough.

In volume II, *Extractives, Manufacturing, and Services*, K. Peter Harder wrote on the forestry industry. In volume III he expands into lumber and other construction materials wholesaling (Chapter 6), another old-line industry—the first commercial sawmill in the United States was started in Maine in 1631. As the country expanded across the continent, the lumber industry shifted from New England to the Midwest, then moved south and west. Except for a few large firms such as Weyerhaeuser, the industry has remained decentralized, accommodating many small producers, wholesalers, and retailers. There has been some industry coordination through the activities of trade associations, and several branches of the industry function effectively despite antitrust cases brought against them; nevertheless, the lumber industry remains fragmented in the 1990s.

James L. Wiles describes the transformation in retail shoe stores (Chapter 7). The demand for footwear has been steady for centuries, but the production and distribution of shoes have been subject to remarkable change. In the United States shoe manufacturers sold to wholesalers, who resold to dry goods retailers. By 1900 specialized shoe stores and shoe sections in department stores had supplanted general retailers. As the twentieth century progressed, chain stores and discount stores with self-service shoe departments entered the competition. Independent shoe retailers lobbied Congress for the Robinson-Patman Act of 1936 and the Miller-Tydings Act of 1937, "fair trade" laws designed to protect shoe manufacturers' minimum retail prices. In the 1950s, however, discount shoe stores and shoe departments in discount stores began to dominate the shoe market. By the 1980s the growth of shopping malls had diminished the importance of downtown shopping districts and their independent shoe stores. A growing demand for athletic shoes further reduced the viability of independent shoe stores and encouraged industry concentration in the 1990s—the top four firms producing athletic shoes boasted 39 percent of sales. At the end of the century, shoe sales by catalog and Internet have created a new market. Will the new millennium bring the demise of face-to-face shoe sales, or will buyers balk at virtual fitting and persist in trying on shoes as they have done for centuries?

The U.S. Federal Reserve System (Chapter 8) is the most influential financial institution in the world. The Federal Reserve Act of 1913, which created the Fed, also established twelve District Reserve Banks, which were to be paid for by stock purchases required of member banks. Shaped by politics, wars, and recessions, the Fed has evolved over the course of the twentieth century (although not under direct government control, the Fed has, for most of its existence, cooperated with the U.S. Treasury on economic and fiscal policies). H. Bruce Throckmorton's chapter is distinguished from the usual description of the Fed by his sketches of the seven men, from Marriner S. Eccles to Alan Greenspan, who have chaired the Board of Governors.

Mutual savings banks (Chapter 9) are, Richard C. Schiming reminds us, owned by depositors. Originated in England and Scotland in the early nineteenth century, the mutual form of banking was soon transplanted to the United States: the Provident Institution for Savings in the town of Boston and the Philadelphia Savings Fund Society were chartered in 1816. Unlike the officers of commercial banks, who had never encouraged small depositors, the founders of these banks intended to encourage saving among the poor by accepting small deposit accounts. The early founders were altruistic part-time managers who invested bank assets conservatively, but the professional managers who replaced the founders during the 1840s took a more balanced view of investing and lending depositors' money. Even as the U.S. economy expanded during the Gilded Age, the mutuals remained concentrated in New England and the East Coast, losing market share to profit-seeking institutions. In the 1970s, however, mutual savings banks in Massachusetts pioneered interest payments on checking accounts. Banking deregulation in the 1980s liberalized chartering options for new mutual savings banks and allowed federally chartered mutuals to convert to stock ownership, blurring the distinction between mutuals and other financial intermediaries; fortunately, the mutuals' conservative lending policies helped them avoid the crisis that engulfed the savings and loan industry.

Hugh T. Rockoff introduces the unfamiliar world of clearinghouse associations (Chapter 10). Banks use clearinghouses to settle the debts they have with each other. Clearinghouses operated in London in the late eighteenth century but not in the United States until 1853, when the New York Clearing House Association was organized; bankers imitated its success in other major cities. Before the establishment of the Federal Reserve System in 1913, clearinghouses in the United States performed many functions of a central bank, monitoring banks to ensure that they followed the mandated practices and issuing clearinghouse certificates (private money) to shore up banks during panics. Beyond taking over these regulatory and monetary policy functions, the Fed provided banks with clearing services as well. Clearinghouses adapted to this environment by offering banks specialized services. As the twentieth century gives way to the twenty-first, clearinghouses, in concert with the Federal Reserve, will use their expertise in information technology to effect the checkless society.

One of my contributions to *Infrastructure and Services* recalls the important services provided by mortgage bankers and brokers (Chapter 11), financial intermediaries who channel funds from investors to borrowers of loans secured by real estate. U.S. mortgage banking originated in the post–Civil War era, when brokers loaned surplus funds secured from the eastern United States and Europe to farmers in the Midwest and Plains states. These brokers executed the mortgage and serviced it, collecting a fee and profiting from interest differentials. For security, the typical mortgage was of short duration and required a high down payment with interest and principal payable at the end of the loan term. Until the federal government began to guarantee loans later in the twentieth century, residential mortgages were written by a few mortgage bankers, mutual savings banks, or savings and loans. The Mortgage Bankers Association, the trade organization for the industry, was formed in 1914. While the industry grew in the 1920s, the real catalyst to its development was the federal government. To bolster the housing industry during the Great Depression, Congress passed the National Housing Act of 1934, establishing the Federal Housing Administration (FHA). Through its provision of mortgage insurance, the FHA enabled mortgagors to offer long-term loans amortized through monthly payments, an innovation that revolutionized the housing industry in the United States. The federal government further supported the mortgage industry with the formation of the Federal National Mortgage Association (Fannie Mae) in 1938, the Government National Mortgage Association (Ginnie Mae) in 1968, and the Federal Home Loan Mortgage Corporation (Freddie Mac) in 1970. Aided by these governmental units, mortgage banking expanded during the last half of the twentieth century, helping fund the boom in private-residence construction during the 1950s and branching into commercial real estate construction later. As other financial institutions entered the industry, competition increased, leading to a period of consolidation and merger. Competition and deregulation of banking in general resulted in new products such as adjustable rate mortgages and the reverse mortgage of the 1990s.

Medical service and health insurance (Chapter 12) have long been politically and economically controversial. Medical plans in the United States began as sickness insurance offered by commercial insurers to the business community and independent professionals, by fraternal societies to their members, and by unions or workers' funds in the industrial sector. The plans had achieved only limited acceptance as late as the 1920s, however, and Marvin N. Fischbaum reviews the economics literature on the theory of health insurance to explain why. Although earlier versions of this innovation existed, the Blue Cross movement, originating at Baylor University in 1929, changed the scope of health insurance by offering group enrollment in a plan that provided hospital services for a fixed payment. The American Medical Association (AMA) opposed these plans initially, fearing they would evolve into compulsory insurance. When state associations began offering medical plans, the AMA initiated its own Blue Shield program. During World War II, the War Labor Board, anxious to keep wages under control, decided that firms could offer fringe benefits such as health insurance to attract workers. Between 1940 and 1960 the number of persons covered by health insurance increased tenfold. Throughout the twentieth century proponents of national healthcare advocated a variety of plans, but only Medicare for retirees was enacted. As the century ended, federal and private insurance providers were caught between the demand for expanding healthcare coverage and the need to contain healthcare costs.

Although as old as travel, the lodging industry (Chapter 13) did not become an organized business until the nineteenth century. Travelers in the United States depended on small inns and taverns before the first hotel in the young republic opened in New York in 1794. Nevertheless, the Tremont House in Boston, dating from 1829, was the forerunner of the modern hotel complete with private rooms, bathing facilities, and food service. The Tremont was imitated in other cities, and a luxury hotel industry was born. As the economy expanded during the nineteenth century and business travel increased, midpriced hotels became common. To take advantage of modern business methods, hoteliers organized chains; E. M. Statler led the way, opening the Buffalo Statler in 1908 and repeating his success in city after city. The twentieth century has seen the expansion of hotel chains and the spread of the lodging industry to include thousands of motels along the nation's extensive highway systems. Spiro G. Patton's bibliographic essay on the lodging literature is especially useful for first-time scholars of the industry.

Margaret S. Bond's contribution on funeral service and crematories (Chapter 14) is a reminder that while death is certain, the ornate funeral common to the United States in the twentieth century is not. Religious and spiritual ceremonies commemorating the dead are antediluvian. Embalming during the Civil War spearheaded the growth of the funeral industry in the United States, however. Embalming made possible the open display of the deceased in an ornamental casket, and funerals evolved into costly displays of conspicuous consumption. The industry's more than 22,000 funeral establishments conduct about 2 million funerals per year. Since World War II, government regulators' increasing scrutiny of marketing practices en-sures that consumers can choose between ornate funerals and inexpensive burials or cremation. To attain economies of scale in the face of changing demand, the industry has begun consolidating and can be expected to continue to do so into the twenty-first century.

R. D. Peterson considers the development of advertising agencies (Chapter 15), organizations that contract on commission for the purchase of advertising space in all media. In the United States advertising dates to space bought in the May 1704 issue of the *Boston News-Letter*. By the nineteenth century, postmasters, newsdealers, and independent solicitors handled the placement of advertisements. Newspaper agents bargained for space for advertisers, space jobbers served as intermediaries in securing the purchase and sale of advertising, and space wholesalers purchased space for resale to advertisers. By the end of the century, advertising offered a wide array of services to clients, including advice, copy, and artwork. During the twentieth century, advertising agencies have expanded in step with changes in media technology and the development of new marketing channels. A group of agencies formed the American Association of Advertising Agencies in 1917 as a trade association to set standards of service. Agencies began offering marketing research and product development strategies in the 1930s. By the 1950s the large advertising agency, partially protected by barriers to entry, was sufficiently entrenched that it became enshrined in fictional writing and motion pictures. Peterson's bibliographic essay adroitly covers this genre, and his bibliography is broad-based. As the next century begins, the technology of computer graphics and the accessibility of the World Wide Web will add new dimensions to advertising.

Personal care facilities (Chapter 16) are key units of the nursing home industry. These organizations for medical care and residential living for the elderly and others existed as eleemosynary institutions or county poorhouses before the federal government began alleviating the poverty of senior citizens. Passage of the Social Security Act of 1935 gave older persons an income with which they could purchase personal care services. Legislation in the 1960s created the Medicare and Medicaid programs to provide insurance coverage for personal care. In response, not-for-profit and for-profit nursing homes multiplied. Total spending in the industry rose from $1.3 billion in 1965 to $72.3 billion in 1994. During this period of rapid growth, the industry was characterized by the poor quality of care provided and rapidly rising costs. Although profit-seeking firms manage the bulk of U.S. nursing homes, their revenue comes mainly from public funds, so competition is limited. The proliferation of nursing home chains in the 1990s further limits competition; nevertheless, alternatives such as home care providers and assisted-living facilities are emerging in response to the needs of an aging population. Joseph A. Giacalone's bibliographic essay is especially thorough, considering the newness of this industry.

Martin A. Strosberg traces the origin of health maintenance organizations (HMOs) (Chapter 17) from group medical practices in the 1890s. HMOs provide medical services to voluntary subscribers for set fees that are paid in advance. During the Great Depression, HMOs took the form of cooperatively owned health programs to provide medical care at consistently low fees for persons whose incomes had become uncertain. Labor unions supported the spread of HMOs, but the medical profession argued that HMOs infringed on the doctor–patient relationship, limited a patient's choice of physician, and violated medical ethics by seeking profits from medical work. The federal HMO Act of 1973 ended state restrictions on HMOs and set up pilot projects. During the 1980s health policy experts advocated their use to help contain rising medical costs, and the number of HMOs expanded significantly. The inability of HMOs to permanently reduce national spending on healthcare has limited their growth in the 1990s. Strosberg supplies an extensive bibliography on this new and controversial industry.

Despite their traditionally outspoken criticism of education services (Chapter 18), American citizens have always valued education, argues Joseph Finkelstein. Private and parochial education notwithstanding, from the colonial period to the present, public spending on schools has been the hallmark of education in the United States. From the American Revolution to the Civil War, however, the educational system assumed the general shape of the modern system funded and controlled by local governments. After the Civil War, the Morrill Act of 1863 helped create public universities (a second Morrill Act in 1890 established a college system for Afro-Americans). During the twentieth century, the structure of the system has been stable. Debates have raged, however, over its form and content. Starting with a curriculum that stressed basic skills and fundamental religious and democratic values, schools have taken up the progressive, pragmatic precepts of John Dewey, seeking to provide the vocational and technical training needed by business along with the scientific education required by citizens of the modern world. Higher education expanded through the G.I. Bill, eventually becoming more open with legislation prohibiting racial discrimination. Throughout the century, federal government support for education at all levels has increased. Finkelstein's chapter concludes with a comprehensive bibliography.

Joseph Finkelstein and Nadia Ehrlich Finkelstein review the growth of social services (Chapter 19). Although poverty is a constant in human history, remedies remain haphazard. Historically, the poor were helped, if at all, by family, friends, or charitable organizations. During the agrarian era in America, free or inexpensive land enabled some of the poor to eke out a living; although industrialization created greater pockets of poverty, government was slow to act. Professionalization of social work began in the 1890s. During the Great Depression of the 1930s, state and local governments provided most social services. The Social Security Act of 1935 signaled the federal government's determination to reduce poverty; President Lyndon B. Johnson's vision of a War on Poverty expanded that commitment in the 1960s. In the 1990s opponents of federal aid to the poor persuaded voters, evidence to the contrary, that social programs do more harm than good. So-called welfare reform has saved federal money in the 1990s while creating a cohort of working poor who are likely to draw heavily on expensive social services in decades to come.

Business and professional organizations, the topic of my contribution in Chapter 20, are a key component of the society that has emerged in the United States in the twentieth century. For the last 100 years, men and women have been joining organizations in increasing numbers in search of a greater voice, higher status, and social influence. Businesspeople aspire to enhance their economic well-being through organizations like the National Association of Manufacturers and the U.S. Chamber of Commerce or to improve the conditions in a particular industry through the activities of trade associations like the National Hardware Association. Industry trade associations benefited from government programs inaugurated first by Secretary of Commerce Herbert Hoover in the 1920s and later by President Franklin D. Roosevelt's National Industrial Recovery Act of 1933. Professional associations are combinations of trained practitioners who want to maintain and elevate their specialty by adopting standards of education, competence, and ethical behavior: the American Bar Association, American Economic Association, American Institute of Certified Public Accountants, and American Medical Association exemplify those goals. Practitioners who work alone use professional associations to concentrate their voices in society; those who work for large firms rely on them for bargaining power against the corporate institution. Although professional associations support the best interest of their membership, their efforts often benefit society at large.

Don M. Coerver establishes a link between public administration (Chapter 21) and the growth of big business in the United States. In the early years of the country, public administration was a small-scale activity. To be sure, the framers of the Constitution gave the federal government broad powers to regulate commerce, but most early regulation was at the state and local levels. The Civil War extended federal intervention in the economy through taxation and the regulation of national banks. The formation of the Interstate Commerce Commission in 1887 to regulate railroads marked the first federal effort to apply public administration to economic affairs. The Progressive Era in the first two decades of the twentieth century, capped by federal control of industry during World War I, broadened the scope of public administration. After a dormant decade in the 1920s, the ranks of public administrators grew apace with the New Deal programs and agencies and in response to the military needs of World War II. President Johnson's Great Society programs mark another upswing; since the

1980s, however, pressures for deregulation, privatization, and downsizing of the federal government have slowed the growth of public administration. The chapter includes a particularly useful bibliographic essay.

The twenty-one chapters of *Handbook of American Business History, volume III, Infrastructure and Services: A Historiographical and Bibliographical Guide* are a useful antidote to the world of perfect competition contained in most economics textbooks, for they accentuate the liabilities as well as the assets of competitive markets. Six authors—Dragon, Wendel, Scott, Neufeld, and von Ende and Becker—investigate industries dominated by large corporations that are characterized by managerial capitalism (as delineated by Alfred D. Chandler, Jr.) and require government regulation at the state or federal level. Five other contributors—Harder, Wiles, Patton, Peterson, and Bond—highlight industries that support the large number of firms associated with competition, and even in those markets competition did not always serve the consumer (the mortuary industry is a good example). Eight authors—Wendel, Scott, Neufeld, von Ende and Becker, Throckmorton, Stabile, and Coerver—suggest that the economy of the United States cannot function without the assistance of government, especially the federal government. Four—Strosberg, Giacalone, and Finkelstein and Finkelstein—describe vital services that cannot exist without government support. Moreover, three chapters on business and professional organizations—Rockoff, Fischbaum, and Stabile—cover businesses not usually examined in the standard economic theories of competition. Free market economists often overlook business and service organizations as alternatives to government's providing the same functions.

Historians following the school of new institutional economics have interjected the human factor into economic theory by exploring the rational formation of business policies, organizations, and techniques. Over the last decade, however, practitioners of experimental economics and psychological economics have demonstrated that economic actors are not as rational as standard theory has long insisted. Real human beings rely on custom, habits, and rules to make many decisions when the costs of rational decision making are too high, the benefits too low, or the entire approach of rationality impossible. They also make mistakes in judgment, miscalculate costs and benefits, and ignore the advice of economists that the past is a sunk cost. Business historians have always known the drawbacks of rational choice theory, engaged as they are with the decisions made by business practitioners under conditions of uncertainty and poor information. Managers have muddled through regardless, and while modern techniques of linear programming, statistical analysis, and formulaic finance add rigor to business decisions, managers will continue to muddle on.

At the end of the twentieth century, business enjoys a popularity not seen since the Great Depression tarnished its image. Prosperity, rooted in real economic growth and reflected in a roaring bull market, has permeated the

American electorate and made it vulnerable to pledges of even greater prosperity if regulations put into place before the average voter was born are removed. Because the studies constituting *Infrastructure and Services* offer insights into the behavior of unfettered business, they are a guide to what can be expected if public oversight of private enterprise is seriously reduced.

Volume III is the final number in the *Handbook of American Business History*. Volume I treats twenty-three industries in manufacturing; volume II, sixteen industries in extractives, manufacturing, and services; and volume III, twenty-one industries in infrastructure and services. Sixty chapters written by a community of scholars is a reservoir of information on American businesses—a reliable starting point for any study of American business history.

Part I

Metal Mining
ESIC 10.0

CHAPTER 1

ZINC, 10.3

ANDREA C. DRAGON

The Congress of the United States created the Bureau of Standards in 1838 to bring under federal control local regulation of weights and measures. Before the federalization of weights and measures, a pound of flour might be one weight in Massachusetts and another in Florida, or a bushel of apples might be one size in Maine and another in Ohio. The Constitution had given Congress power "to fix the standard of weights and measures," but for nearly fifty years Congress had done nothing to ensure that weights and measures were uniform across state lines, and interstate commerce suffered. At the urging of the business community, Congress ordered the Washington Arsenal to manufacture and distribute to each state a set of standard weights made of brass, a copper and zinc alloy.

The federal order was welcomed by Dr. Samuel Fowler, a New Jersey congressman who owned the only source of zinc in the United States. In the early 1800s his father-in-law had purchased, from the estate of an eccentric English neighbor, what would become the largest zinc mine in the United States, indeed one of the most productive in all the world.

Zinc had first been discovered in the United States in Sussex County, northwestern New Jersey, in the middle of the eighteenth century. The ore was found on a huge tract of land owned by the Englishman William Alexander, who called himself "Lord Stirling." He was a descendant (perhaps legitimate) of Sir William Alexander, earl of Stirling, a great friend of James I, king of England (1603–1625). The king had granted Sir William nearly all of Canada and most of northeastern America; but by the late 1700s the only lands remaining of the royal grant were those in the far northwestern corner of New Jersey that were now claimed by his namesake. Lord Stirling traveled to England in 1761 to assert his claim to the ancient title and all its perquisites. His claim rejected, he returned to New Jersey imbued with an abiding animosity toward England. Devoting himself to the patriot cause in America, Lord Stirling crossed the Delaware with George Washington and distinguished himself at the Battle of Trenton, eventually rising to the rank of general in Washington's army (*Webster's Biographical Dictionary* 1972).

The land belonging to Lord Stirling in northwest New Jersey contained, in addition to zinc, commercial quantities of iron ore, which he had mined for decades. Shortly before the Revolutionary War, Lord Stirling attempted to smelt the ore and recover metallic zinc. The zinc metal could not be separated from the ore-bearing rock that encased it; no matter what smelting method he employed, he was unable to obtain zinc metal from the ore. Lord Stirling had first tried smelting in 1774, but when this attempt failed, he shipped several tons of ore to England, hoping that mining experts there would have the answer. Unfortunately for Lord Stirling, the consensus of British mining experts was that it was impossible to recover zinc in commercial quantities from the unusual ore (Ingalls 1908). Not until much later did geologists realize why the zinc deposits of northwestern New Jersey refused to yield metal when smelted by standard commercial methods. The three zinc minerals of New Jersey—franklinite, which contains iron and manganese; willemite, a silicate of zinc; and zincite, a red oxide of zinc— are unique (*First Hundred Years* 1948). Everywhere else in the world zinc occurs as sphalerite (also called zinc blende, or blackjack), or smithsonite (called calamine in Europe), or hemimorphite. The existing smelting methods had been developed to separate metal from these ores, but the New Jersey ores demanded sophisticated technical adjustments to standard smelting processes.

Although unique to New Jersey, the zinc deposits were so extensive that in 1899, fifty years after commercial mining had begun, the remaining ore body was known to be over a half mile long and in some places over 200 feet thick. Early mine owners knew there was a vast quantity of zinc to be extracted, but were frustrated in their attempts to exploit it.

By the 1820s, when New Jersey Congressman Fowler inherited the Lord Stirling mines, the iron deposits were nearly depleted. Fowler must either find a method of extracting zinc in commercial quantities or resign himself to owning worthless land. He hoped the publicity generated by the casting of the official brass weights with zinc from his mines would entice investors with the capital necessary to develop both commercial mining and smelting methods. Because no one in the United States knew how to smelt zinc ore, the Washington Arsenal hired Belgian metallurgists, who built a furnace and smelted just enough of Fowler's ore to make the brass weights. They then returned to Belgium.

Fowler's patience was rewarded. In 1848 he founded the Sussex Zinc and Iron Mining Company and with it the pioneer era of commercial production of zinc in the United States. The zinc industry sprang primarily from two technological breakthroughs: the development of a process in the 1840s that recovered zinc oxide (not metallic zinc) from the franklinite ore, and the transfer of Belgian smelting technology that made it possible to recover metallic, or slab, zinc from the other New Jersey ores. The sophisticated Belgian technology was a multistep process in which zinc was distilled in a retort.

Sussex Zinc and Iron Mining Company had by 1897 expanded through mergers and acquisitions into the New Jersey Zinc Company. Despite protracted litigation to sort out patent claims associated with both smelting processes, New Jersey Zinc prospered during the last half of the nineteenth century by strategic acquisitions of zinc deposits outside the New Jersey area nearly as fast as these were discovered. Demand for zinc products, particularly zinc oxide for paint, increased dramatically during the last decades of the century. At the turn of the twentieth century, New Jersey Zinc was the world's largest producer of zinc.

ZINC IN THE EARLY TWENTIETH CENTURY

After the turn of the century, the United States produced over 32 percent of the world's supply of zinc (Smith 1918), and the lion's share came from mines owned by New Jersey Zinc. Total zinc production in the United States had increased dramatically since 1885, when output totalled 40,000 tons. Twenty years later, in 1905, production had increased to 200,000 tons and by 1915 had more than doubled to 446,000 tons (*Zinc*, March 1918).

Much of this increase was due to rapid growth at New Jersey Zinc. As other zinc deposits across the country were located, they were systematically purchased by New Jersey Zinc, but the original New Jersey mines continued to be the company's flagship as late as 1948. By 1915 New Jersey Zinc owned mines in Colorado, New Mexico, Illinois, Wisconsin, Alabama, Georgia, Virginia, Pennsylvania, and Nevada as well as five mines in Mexico. The company operated mills in twenty-four states; owned coal fields in Illinois, Arkansas, West Virginia, and Pennsylvania; and had acquired two railroads to carry ore to smelters. New Jersey Zinc was the seventy-third largest company in the United States, making it larger than Proctor & Gamble, Firestone Tire & Rubber, Inland Steel, or John Deere (Chandler 1977).

This remarkable growth built on increasing market demand as new applications for zinc evolved; one of the earliest was pigmenting ready-mix paint with zinc oxide. For many decades, New Jersey Zinc was the only U.S. producer of zinc oxide and is credited with helping to create the ready-mix paint industry. Later the company began molding spelter, or metallic zinc, which is used to make brass or melted to coat iron and steel in the process known as galvanizing. (There are other methods of zinc coating; technically, galvanizing is the correct term only if the zinc is electroplated onto the steel or iron.)

The technological breakthroughs that enabled commercial quantities of zinc to be extracted from the difficult Sussex County ores in the middle of the nineteenth century were the focus of a fifty-year legal dispute that began almost the day the Sussex Zinc and Iron Mining Company was founded in 1848. The claims and counterclaims of the true origins of a particular process and of patent infringement are recorded on thousands of pages of detailed testimony and depositions. The legal issues were resolved in 1897 the way these matters usually are: the financially exhausted litigants agreed to merge.

The resolution of the lawsuits at the end of the nineteenth century permitted New Jersey Zinc to expand rapidly and to dominate and control the production of zinc. Smelting capacity was increased to process ores from newly purchased mines in the Midwest and West, and railroads were acquired to haul ores to smelters. A corporate headquarters built in New York utilized every conceivable application of zinc.

It may be useful to examine in some detail the company's product line in 1915. Zinc oxide, recovered by an inventive process first employed at New Jersey Zinc in 1850, was the only commercial product the company could wrest from the stubborn franklinite ore. Although the quantities extracted had increased dramatically over the ensuing decades, the process itself had remained essentially unchanged since the mid-nineteenth century. Reduced in a furnace fired with ground coal, the franklinite was then blasted by hot air up through the furnace grate, where it combined with oxygen and was forced out through pipes into hundreds of muslin bags, each bag forty feet long and twenty inches in diameter. The "bag-houses" at the company's Palmerton smelter contained approximately sixty miles of these bags. Extraneous gases escaped through the muslin, freely polluting the surrounding environment, but a white powder—zinc oxide—remained in the bags (Bolles [1881] 1966; Ingalls 1902). Three hundred pounds of zinc oxide at a time were collected and packed into wooden barrels made in the company's own cooperage. Most of the powder bagged was purchased by manufacturers of ready-mix paint, who preferred to substitute zinc oxide for the more dangerous lead oxide. Zinc oxide was also a necessary ingredient in the manufacture of tires (automobile tires usually contain 5 percent zinc oxide) and other rubber products, especially those that needed to be whitened. Much smaller quantities of zinc oxide were added in cosmetic face powder.

Spelter, zinc cast in ingots or slabs for commercial use, was also produced in vast quantities by New Jersey Zinc from ores it mined in the Midwest and West. However, in 1915 the original New Jersey mines still supplied about one-fifth of all American slab zinc. The zinc oxide "bag" process had been an American innovation, but New Jersey Zinc adopted a "Belgian process" to make slab zinc. First, a mixture of ore and coal was placed in the lower chamber of clay pots (retorts) ten inches in diameter and five feet long. These were set in the top of a furnace so that only the lower chamber was exposed to the heat. A perforation between the lower and upper chambers of the retorts allowed zinc vapor to rise up and condense in the cooler upper chamber, leaving slag behind in the lower chamber. As it cooled, the vapor condensed into liquid zinc that was removed from the retorts and poured into ingots or slabs. Each furnace could hold up to 450 clay retorts: smelting capacity was measured by the number of retorts in each facility. On January 1, 1916, the entire smelting capacity of the United States was measured at 171,662 retorts, most of which were owned by New Jersey Zinc (*Zinc*, March 1916).

As the United States inched toward the war in Europe, industrial consumers, stimulated by suggestions from the marketing department of New Jersey Zinc, devised many applications for slab zinc. Zinc protects iron and steel against rust and corrosion; remelted slab zinc coats industrial and consumer products from nails to roofing. Reheated and rolled into sheets of various thicknesses, waterproof and corrosion resistant zinc is essential to the building trades. Zinc alloys are common: brass, for example, is zinc alloyed with copper. Molten zinc alloys are die-cast into many industrial and consumer products.

PRODUCING ZINC AND PRODUCING AMERICANS

Because New Jersey Zinc's mines were the only ones in the United States that could produce both zinc oxide and slab zinc, the company had invested heavily in constructing the world's largest smelter close to a source of coal across the border from New Jersey in the Lehigh Valley of Pennsylvania. The smelter was the focus of an entire town named for Steven Palmer, president of the company. Palmerton was constructed by the company from the ground up just after the turn of the century; by 1915, it was home to 8,000 people.

Over half the employees at Palmerton were foreign-born, and their acculturation became a continuing mission for the company. New Jersey Zinc wanted to produce Americans from the "raw material" of Eastern Europe much as it had produced commercial products from the raw ores of its mines.

A leader in a growing industry, the company was able to devote considerable attention to the Americanization of its immigrant workforce. Its markets were strong, and it enjoyed a steady source of labor from immigrants seeking employment in mining and industry. Earlier immigrants had dreamed of homesteading in the Midwest; the closing of the American frontier and the accompanying inflation in land prices combined to render such dreams all but impossible for these more recent arrivals. They settled instead for mining and industrial occupations. But these newer immigrants, from Central and Eastern Europe, were desirable industrial employees: for the most part, they were comfortable with hierarchical structures and accustomed to societies in which distinctions between social classes were clear and respected; even their Roman Catholic religion emphasized submission to authority. In exchange for their labor, New Jersey Zinc offered them reasonable wages for the times. Just as important, it offered them the opportunity to integrate into a new way of life. The passions aroused by World War I (many of the Eastern Europeans harbored grudges against Germans) provided a rallying point around which the company would focus efforts to Americanize its immigrant workforce.

Many Eastern Europeans emigrated to the United States believing the opportunities closed to them in the Old World would be open to them in the New World. Friends and relatives who remained behind would soon face depredation; but those who had been willing to compromise their national identity by working in the mines and smelters of New Jersey Zinc, enduring the twin hardships of culture shock and dangerous working conditions, would for the most part be safe from the ravages of war and its aftermath.

THE AMERICANIZATION PROCESS
AT NEW JERSEY ZINC

After the smelter at Palmerton began operation, the company opened a "Sociological Department," whose function was to organize social and recreational activities for the employees and their families. Mines and smelters were located far from population centers, and opportunities for recreation were limited. Nearly all who worked at the mines and smelters, even the Americans, were separated from extended family and childhood friends. The company was clearly concerned that lawlessness, drunkenness, and prostitution would become as prevalent as in the mining camps of the Old West. To check licentiousness, the company cultivated family formation by creating a "town" and subsidizing homeownership. Palmerton, built from scratch by the company, provided housing for 8,000 residents, a modern hospital, schools, clubhouses, even a golf course.

Working closely with the company's staff of nurses, the Sociological Department at Palmerton encouraged the foreign-born to adopt American values and habits. To this end, it established boys and girls clubs and organized playtime in the clubhouse gymnasium, where children and their mothers could interact in an environment of "proper toys, pure milk, water, fresh air, and laughter" (*Zinc*, May 1919, 186). The nurses trained the employees in healthy habits, introducing many to the concept of regular bathing. Personal hygiene proved more theoretical than practical, for the company-built workers' houses had running water but no bathtubs. A spokesman reasoned that "although the need of a bathtub from a sanitary and cleanly [sic] standpoint is clearly recognized, the foreigners who inhabit these houses very seldom use bathtubs for purposes other than unsanitary catchalls" (Zinc, March 1917, 79). To promote personal cleanliness among the residents of Palmerton, the company built public bathhouses, with showers only, which were open four days a week for men and two days a week for women.

The company provided (and required) annual physical exams for employees; those with continuing medical problems were examined monthly, and the nurses kept meticulous records on the incidence of disease. Of the 3,000 men and women on the Palmerton payroll in 1915, 11 percent were found to have "organic" heart disease, 7 percent suffered from "health problems due to tobacco or drink," and 10 percent had "some pulmonary" condition (Zinc, April 1916, 48). Children were regularly weighed and measured, and sickly ones were monitored by in-home nursing visits, all free of charge. Doctor-staffed well-baby clinics were held three days a week for the "foreign women."

The company-built hospital at Palmerton was so successful that by 1917 only one-sixth of its patients were New Jersey Zinc employees. The majority of patients traveled sometimes great distances from other parts of Pennsylvania to take advantage of the advanced medical care and low fees. All hospital operating costs were paid by the company, and nonemployees using the hospital were charged a nominal fee. By the end of the war, young women from all over eastern Pennsylvania were enrolling in the hospital's nascent school of nursing.

The medical staff at Palmerton did not limit its activities to physical health and hygiene. Often it was the company nurse who arrived first on the scene after an incident of domestic violence, and it was she who called the police and insisted that the miscreant be jailed. In Palmerton, "the nurse, upheld by our Chief of Police, is making wife-beating unpopular" (Zinc, March 1916, 9). The nurse, trained to deal with the "drug and dope fiend," each day received a list of those who had not reported for work. She promptly called at the worker's home to see if the cause was "too much drink." It was also the nurse who inspected backyards for refuse and urged residents to plant vegetable gardens.

Although employees and the surrounding communities no doubt benefited from these responsible policies, the company's primary mission was not to improve social welfare but to mine zinc at a profit. To that end, it wanted healthy, sober employees who could perform hard manual labor. The company, never reticent in voicing its opinion on the relationship between worker performance and lifestyle, considered good workers those whose lives were free from unwholesomeness of any sort, for "back of all poor workmanship and inefficiency lie the problems of unsuitable food, poor housing, late hours, and the wrong use of recreation time" (*Zinc*, March 1916, 10). To ensure that recreation time would be spent appropriately, the company organized frequent picnics, bowling parties, golf outings, lectures, musicals, balls, and dances. Schoolchildren could enroll free in a daily two-hour after-school program providing "wholesome" play and music and dancing lessons. A weekly dance for young people began at 6:00 P.M. and often continued until 4:00 A.M. Clubhouses supported extensive libraries, filled with books on popular subjects as well as the current literature on mining and metallurgy. The company also purchased subscriptions to newspapers in Russian, Slavic, and Hungarian for the clubhouse libraries. English was taught daily after work, and prizes were awarded to the best students in company-sponsored contests.

Management's philosophy on the company's obligation to its immigrant workforce is best summed up in a sentence from an in-house publication:

Thinking people have come to realize that a greatly needed step is to Americanize our own nation, and to accomplish this we have to seek ways and means for welding together vast numbers of people who are now divided into a great number of races and classes . . . with no common bond but the desire to get a livelihood out of America. (*Zinc*, March 1916, 83)

In "welding together" its workforce during the war years, the company increased the number of educational programs, expanded its libraries, offered additional classes in healthy living, organized workers into baseball teams, awarded prizes for the best vegetables and gardens, and installed troops of Boy Scouts and Campfire girls. To acquaint families with the pleasures of outdoor recreation, including the American pastimes of hunting and fishing (activities usually reserved in Eastern Europe for wealthy landowners), boys and girls were sent to the company-owned camp in the summer, and all employees had access to the company's superb 6,000-acre wilderness reserve.

Although New Jersey Zinc spent considerable sums to Americanize its immigrant workforce, cultural and social differences among the employees remained. Management was prepared to recognize those differences if it could gain an advantage by doing so. In 1917 the company created an "Employment Department" at Palmerton to centralize hiring and salary administration, and in July the head of that department outlined a selection process in which ethnicity was a qualification. The company preferred to hire Poles, Lithuanians, and Americans as "grinders"; the Americans applying for these jobs were to be told that the majority of grinders were Polish, but if they were willing to work with Poles, they could be hired. For "forgers," the company wanted men who were over 18 years old and "big-boned." They could be American or Polish but must be able to "work up to drop hammer." American or Italian girls over 16 could work as "finishers" but must be "neat about clothing, without cheap finery," and it was better if they lived at home and were "not flirty" (*Zinc*, July 1917, 177).

LIFE AND DEATH: THE WAR COMES
TO NEW JERSEY ZINC

Many years after the war ended, biologists discovered that zinc is essential to plant and animal life. In the human body it appears in high concentrations in the red blood cells, where it promotes critical biochemical reactions for metabolizing carbon dioxide. Zinc in the pancreas may aid in the storage of insulin, and researchers now know it is needed for protein digestion in the intestinal tract. But in 1915, a complete understanding of zinc's life-sustaining qualities was many years in the future. American chemists and metallurgists who knew nothing of the relationship between zinc and life knew too well the relationship between zinc and death.

Modern warfare depends not on swords and cavalry mounts but on devices of mass destruction—submarines, tanks, exploding shells. In short, modern warfare and zinc are made for each other. Rather quickly it became obvious to all concerned that the European war would last much longer than first expected and that there would be monumental consequences for New Jersey Zinc. The demand for metallic zinc would certainly exceed any the company had experienced. If the United States mobilized, the company could not maintain a workforce large enough to supply all the zinc for the War Department. Even before the United States declared war on Germany in 1917, immigrants employed by New Jersey Zinc were returning to Europe to enlist in armies already in the field. Once an American draft was instituted in 1917, the company's employees were exempted as workers in an essential industry; yet every month more and more employees voluntarily joined the army, and by June 1918 their numbers had grown to over 500.

To induce workers to remain in its employ rather than enlist in the armed forces, the company shortened the workweek from 57 hours to 52, with no reduction in pay. Management impressed upon the workers how vital zinc was to winning the war; their efforts to defeat the Germans were as necessary as the efforts of the men in uniform. The company did not exaggerate.

DEATH-DEALING DEVICES

The War Department authorized the manufacture of ordnance in quantities never before produced in the United States. All the combatants needed brass to make shell casings (30 percent zinc/70 percent copper); but European sources of zinc were now unavailable, and the Allies were dependent upon mines and smelters in places previously unknown to them, places like Palmerton, Pennsylvania, and Sussex County, New Jersey. The British situation was especially desperate in 1918; that September, one of their war heroes was sent to rally workers at Palmerton. Lieutenant-Colonel Evans had survived a German gas attack, albeit with reduced lung capacity, and had been bayoneted in close combat. He had traveled across the ocean to tell the zinc workers that the British Government would buy their entire output for the next six months; his Government would, however, want considerably more zinc each month than the company had ever been able to produce. Evans shouted to the assembled workers, "When the boys over there require 1,500 more tons per month from you, by God give them 5,000" (*Zinc*, October 1918, 327). The Poles, Hungarians, Russians, Lithuanians, and Americans in his audience sprang to their feet, stomping and cheering. Not once did the workers at Palmerton fail to meet their quota.

During the war, zinc from Palmerton was used to manufacture brass casings for explosive shells; in fact, nearly all of the zinc produced went directly to the war effort. In August 1918, a Palmerton official reported to workers, "I can safely say that from 85 to 90 pounds of every 100 pounds of zinc which is made at this plant goes into some death-dealing device" (*Zinc*, August 1918, 243). Thousands of tons of slab zinc were melted to rustproof millions of tons of iron and steel or to die-cast casings for shell fuses, grenades, land mines, and rocket bombs. The company even sold the army 300 tons of sheet zinc for uniform buttons. Zinc oxide, available solely from New Jersey Zinc, was used in hundreds of thousands of gallons of paint for ships and land vehicles, in thousands of tons of rubber for truck tires and tank treads—even in smoke-screen chemicals. Metallic zinc dust mixed with zinc oxide was added to the explosive in projectiles to create a white cloud of smoke on impact. Before the war, no pharmaceutical-grade zinc oxide had been manufactured in the United States; now the horrible burns from German mustard gas suffered by the British and French troops spurred the company to develop a zinc oxide salve for protecting the soldiers' skin.

Like war, mining demands explosives, and over seven decades the company had become expert in their manufacture and use. Nitrocellulose, waste cotton impregnated with nitric and sulfuric acid, had been readily available, for the smelting processes at New Jersey zinc gave off sulfuric acid. The increased smelter activity throughout the war yielded excess acid. Because nearly all military explosives of the day contained at least some sulfuric acid, the market demand was enormous. New Jersey Zinc became the world's largest supplier of that valuable by-product.

WOMEN REPLACEMENT WORKERS

Despite its efforts to retain male employees and recruit new ones, by the summer of 1918 the company had a serious labor shortage at several of their operations. Management decided to conduct an experiment to determine whether women were physically able to work in one of the more demanding areas at the company's smelter in Depue, Illinois. Despite the foreman's misgivings, eleven women were hired to work as a transfer crew in the pottery. Smelting zinc required thousands of ceramic retorts, which were manufactured on-site in the pottery. The transfer crew moved retorts into and out of a drying room: After baking at low temperatures in the drying room, the retorts were removed then loaded with zinc ore and placed in furnaces. The women were expected to do the same work as the men they had replaced and would receive the same rate of pay. Before the women were permitted to begin work, the company nurse examined each woman to uncover any physical problems then weighed her periodically throughout the experiment and investigated any weight loss. The eleven women selected for the trial ranged in age from sixteen to forty-five. A photograph taken of the women in their work overalls shows several stocky women, but the majority were of average size, and several weighed less than 120 pounds. The nurse's records indicate that none of the women lost any significant amount of weight during the three months on the job, and for several the hard work must have increased their appetites, as they gained a few pounds.

The results of the three-month experiment are what one would expect. None of the women complained about the hard work, nor did they suffer any problems caused by heavy lifting. The only drawback they perceived was wearing the company-issued overalls in public: being seen in masculine attire as they walked to and from the pottery afforded them considerable embarrassment. The foreman, who had initially doubted the women could do the heavy work, reported that the "crew of women, replacing the same number of men, has consistently done more and better work than the men. While maintaining speed, they exercise much greater care in handling the retorts with a consequent decrease in the number of vessels broken in transfer. This female crew holds the pottery record of transferring 920 retorts in four hours" (*Zinc*, December 1918, 377).

After the crew had worked in the pottery for a few weeks, one of the women was replaced (why is not stated) by a man who had previously been a member of the all-male pottery crew. His first day back on the job, he went home early, saying he was sick; his second day, he reported to the foreman at noon and asked to be transferred, for "he could not keep up with the women and therefore was ashamed to work with them" (*Zinc*, December 1918, 378).

FINAL THOUGHTS

When the war ended, the demand for slab zinc declined as stainless steel and plastic replaced some applications, and Canadian and Australian zinc mines began to compete with the American mines. The New Jersey Zinc

Company continued to develop technologically advanced zinc alloys in the 1950s and 1960s; but by the late 1970s, the company no longer dominated the world's production of zinc, and the New Jersey mines—which had first opened in 1838 and had provided the zinc for the country's first standardized weights—closed.

Some would argue that New Jersey Zinc's long history of success was a matter of having the right product at the right time, but that explanation is simplistic. Although the company had a near monopoly on a mineral resource vital for American industrial development, substitutes have been found for many materials once thought irreplaceable. Few American companies have survived 125 years while marketing essentially the same product, and for that accomplishment alone New Jersey Zinc deserves an honored place in the history of American industry. But there is another reason to champion this industrial pioneer. Today, when companies are bought and sold with abandon and employees are routinely considered just another cost, the employment practices of New Jersey Zinc stand as a beacon, illuminating one company for whom a diverse workforce of men and women was the norm and its concern for their development and well-being a corporate obligation.

BIBLIOGRAPHIC ESSAY

"The history of zinc in the United States is much less interesting than the history of lead" wrote Walter Renton Ingalls in 1908 as he began his discussion of zinc in *Lead and Zinc in the United States*. So little was known about zinc that despite the book's title, the portion devoted to zinc does not begin until page 259.

Researchers interested in zinc will find that the best source is *Zinc*, the house organ of the New Jersey Zinc Company. Published monthly from 1916 until 1956, *Zinc*'s earliest volumes are filled with "proprietary information," including the capacity of competitors' smelters as well as its own, and even articles on the technology of smelting. Perhaps the company realized it was publishing information valuable to the competition, for it soon shifted the magazine's focus; by the mid-1920s, *Zinc* had became a typical house organ filled with articles about company golf tournaments and retirement dinners.

By the time the company issued *The First Hundred Years of the New Jersey Zinc Company* (1948), its founding had been somewhat mythicized. Nevertheless, the publication is a solid primary source on an industry sorely lacking documentation.

Zinc has not been of much interest to industrial historians, and secondary source materials are disappointingly brief. During the formative years of the industry, the dominant New Jersey Zinc Company controlled the dissemination of information, and researchers without access to company archives were denied important documentation. Today, however, the Special

Collections of Alexander Library at Rutgers University holds extensive archival materials from the New Jersey Zinc Company. Examining this collection is the first step for anyone interested in the history of the American zinc industry.

BIBLIOGRAPHY

Bolles, Albert S. *Industrial History of the United States*. 3d ed. 1881. Reprint. New York: Augustus Kelly, 1966.

Chandler, Alfred D., Jr. "The Beginnings of 'Big Business' in American History." *Business History Review* 33 (Spring 1959): 1–31.

———. *Strategy and Structure: Chapters in the History of the Industrial Enterprise*. Cambridge: MIT Press, 1962.

———. *The Visible Hand: The Managerial Revolution in American Business*. Cambridge: Harvard University Press, 1977.

———. *Scale and Scope: The Dynamics of Industrial Capitalism*. Cambridge: Harvard University Press, 1990.

Colorado School of Mines. *Annotated Bibliography on Selected Mining Subjects*. Quarterly of the Colorado School of Mines, vol. 61, no. 2. Golden: Colorado School of Mines, Department of Mining Engineering, 1966.

"Copper and Brass Continue to Shine." *Purchasing* 118, no. 1 (January 12, 1995): 36B13–36B20.

Day, David T. *Report on Mineral Industries in the United States*. Eleventh Census of the United States, vol. 7. Washington, DC: U.S. Government Printing Office, 1892.

Duffy, Michael. "MSHA: Undermining Progress in Occupational Safety and Health." *Regulation 1995* 18, no. 1 (1995): 20–24.

The First Hundred Years of the New Jersey Zinc Company: A History of the Founding and Development of an Industry 1848–1948. New York: New Jersey Zinc, 1948.

Gent, Ernest V. *The Zinc Industry: A Mine to Market Outline*. New York: American Zinc Industries, 1949.

Hartman, Howard L., and Mark J. Waltch. *Bibliography of Theses on Mining in U.S. Institutions*. Quarterly of the Colorado School of Mines, vol. 51, no. 2. Golden: Colorado School of Mines, 1956.

Hughes, Florence. *Sociological Work, The New Jersey Zinc Co*. Palmerton, PA: New Jersey Zinc, 1914.

Ingalls, Walter Renton. *Production and Properties of Zinc*. New York: *Engineering and Mining Journal*, 1902.

———. *Lead and Zinc in the United States: Comprising Economic History of the Mining and Smelting of the Metals and the Conditions Which Have Affected the Development of the Industries*. New York: Hill, 1908.

International Lead and Zinc Study Group. *Principal Uses of Lead and Zinc, 1986–1991*. London: International Lead and Zinc Study Group, 1993.

Jensen, Vernon H. *Heritage of Conflict: Labor Relations in the Nonferrous Metals Industry up to 1930*. Industrial and Labor Relations Series. Ithaca, New York: Cornell University Press, 1950.

———. *Collective Bargaining in the Nonferrous Metals Industry*. West Coast Col-

lective Bargaining Systems. Berkeley: University of California, Institute of
Industrial Relations, 1955.

Linda Hall Library. *Mining and Metallurgy: A List of Books, Periodicals, and Documents in the Linda Hall Library.* Bibliographic Bulletin no. 11. Kansas City, MO: Linda Hall Library, 1955.

New Jersey Zinc Company Papers. Special Collections, Alexander Library, Rutgers University, New Brunswick, New Jersey.

Porter, Frank. *Zinc Handbook: Properties, Processing, and Use in Design.* New York: M. Dekker, 1991.

Smith, Ernest A. *The Zinc Industry.* Monographs on Industrial Chemistry, edited by Sir E. Thorpe. New York: Longmans, Green, 1918.

U.S. Department of Labor. Bureau of Labor Statistics. *Industrial Wage Survey* [pt. 1. iron ores, pt. 2. copper ores, pt. 3. lead and zinc ores, pt. 4. uranium, radium, and vanadium ores]. Washington, DC: U.S. Government Printing Office, summer-fall 1977.

U.S. Tariff Commission. *Lead and Zinc: Report to the Congress on Investigation no. 332–26 (Supplemental) Under Section 332 of the Tariff Act of 1930.* Washington, DC: U.S. Government Printing Office, 1960.

Webster's Biographical Dictionary. Boston: Merriam-Webster, 1972.

Zinc. New York: New Jersey Zinc Company, 1916–1956.

Zinc. Washington, DC: U.S. Department of the Interior, Bureau of Mines, 1990– . Annual.

Zinc Industry. Washington, DC: U.S. Department of the Interior, Bureau of Mines, monthly.

Part II

Communications
ESIC 48.0

CHAPTER 2

TELEGRAPH COMMUNICATIONS, 48.2

SUSAN DUBROCK WENDEL

Samuel F. B. Morse received a patent on the magnetic telegraph in 1840. Within thirty years, the Western Union Telegraph Company was the largest corporation in the United States with a monopoly in telegraphy. In 1987 Western Union underwent a major financial restructuring to stave off bankruptcy. The beneficiary of technological development in the nineteenth century had become the victim of technological advance and deregulation in the twentieth. Western Union survives, a much-changed company with new ownership.

After successfully testing a rudimentary prototype of the magnetic telegraph in 1836, Morse formed a partnership with Leonard D. Gale, professor of chemistry and a colleague of Morse's at New York University. Gale improved the electromagnet and the battery, and made other minor changes. Alfred Vail, a graduate student with interests in mechanical and metallurgical engineering, joined the partnership in 1837. His father was the owner of the Speedwell iron and brass works in New Jersey, a source of supply and financing. Vail was to fund, build, and operate the demonstration telegraph used in soliciting congressional support for building the first telegraph line. Vail further agreed to work on the development of the telegraph for no salary. Vail transformed the crude Morse telegraph into a finished mechanical device.

The fourth member of the original partnership was Francis O. J. Smith, chairman of the House Committee on Commerce, a wealthy risk taker of questionable reputation. Smith was to act for the partners as counsel, promoter, and publicity man and provide the funds for a trip to Europe to secure patent rights (Thompson 1947).

The original partnership agreement of March 1838 provided for the following distribution of ownership: domestic, Morse 9/16, Smith 4/16, Vail and his brother George 2/16, and Gale 1/16; foreign, Morse 8/16, Smith 5/16, Vail and his brother George 2/16, and Gale 1/16 (Thompson 1947, 14). Morse was shrewd enough to maintain majority interest in the patent, but his selection of partners was too diverse to yield a cohesive and enduring business operation. He needed financing and technological expertise. Smith was a problem from the start. The partnership split into two factions. Smith sought the greatest profits with the least attention to quality. The Morse, Vail, and Gale faction was represented by Amos Kendall, journalist and past successful postmaster general. The Kendall faction sought government ownership of the telegraph, a no-risk, immediate payoff to the patent holders (Harlow [1936] 1971; Thompson 1947).

The first few licenses granted to use the patent had a government purchase clause as part of the agreement. When the potential for government ownership fizzled, the partnership formally created the Magnetic Telegraph Company, May 15, 1845 (Thompson 1947).

The early telegraph was fraught with problems. Equipment failure was a common occurrence. Weather and vandalism were major problems. Convincing the public to use the system was no small matter. Demonstrations were staged in cities where the telegraph was to be built to secure investment capital and stimulate usage. Using the telegraph to transmit information locally was not cost-effective. Once the system spread long-distance, communication from city to city and state to state, usage increased. Business transmissions were first to dominate and continue to do so (Du Boff 1980). Usage by the press was important to the initial growth of the industry and gave rise to the Associated Press organization. Railroads were latecomers. It was 1860 before the railroads used the telegraph to regularly direct traffic and freight. Hundreds of companies were created to build telegraphs. Many went bankrupt (Brock 1981; Harlow [1936] 1971; Thompson 1947).

The Morse group granted use of their patent in exchange for stock usually amounting to 50 percent of the original issuance. This effectively gave control of the company to the patent holders, a control that was seldom exercised in the form of managing the company. When the telegraph companies were created, it was customary to let the construction contract to a company controlled by stockholders. As an example, $15,000 was secured through the sale of stock. The company was capitalized at $30,000, half to the Morse group in exchange for patent usage and half to the actual cash investors. Construction costs depended on the type of terrain crossed. A line 100 miles long could consume all of the company's capital. The construction company made a profit. Without money to cover the first months of operation, the telegraph company went bankrupt (Thompson 1947).

In the first years of its existence, the telegraph industry did not have full-

time management. The officers of the company were the investors. The
president was elected or was the principal shareholder. This was an investment, and the time devoted to running the organization was directly
related to the percentage of wealth invested in the enterprise. The Illinois
& Mississippi Telegraph Company was an example of part-time management, organized in 1850 and on the verge of dissolution in 1852. Through
the efforts of John Dean Caton, the line was saved. Judge Caton found
himself devoting more and more time to the organization to ensure its
success (Harlow [1936] 1971; Thompson 1947).

The Morse companies were not without competition. Royal E. House
invented a printing telegraph. Alexander Bain, a Scots scientist, invented a
system similar to the Morse system. Hugh Downing, a manufacturer of
wire cord for Henry O'Rielly's lines, used the House machine in the New
Jersey Magnetic Telegraph Company. The House machine was too complex
for sustained usage. Technology needed to advance before the House machine became a practical means of communication. When working, it captured a significant amount of business. It could transmit faster than the
Morse key, and there was no need for translation. The Bain machine was
a strong competitor. A patent infringement suit was brought against Bain
by the Morse group. The litigation took two years. Morse won, but the
financial loss was significant. Dividends fell from 9 percent to 2 percent
due to Bain's competition (Thompson 1947, 195).

The major stumbling block to a Morse monopoly was Smith. The dis-
sension in the original investor group continued until 1847, when Smith
and Kendall reached a nonintercourse agreement dividing up the United
States. Smith was to operate in New England, New York, and the old
Northwest—Wisconsin, Illinois, Michigan, Indiana, and Ohio. Kendall
took the rest of the country (Thompson 1947).

The industry grew rapidly. Between 1846 and 1852 over 22,000 miles
of telegraph wire had been strung, enough wire to cross the continental
United States almost six times. New York City had eleven lines of service;
undeveloped Ohio had 3,210 miles of line and fourteen operating companies (Thompson 1947, 240–43).

In 1851 the New York & Mississippi Valley Printing Telegraph Company was formed. It had several organizational merits. The officers were
full-time managers as well as investors. The investor group was small and
local. Its plans for expansion were primarily to take over existing lines
rather than perpetuate the current building frenzy that had resulted in duplication. It had the foresight to realize the importance of the railroads as
major customers, and it concentrated its efforts in the North, thereby limiting the impact of the Civil War. The acquisition of the Erie & Michigan
Telegraph Company in 1855 secured it a monopoly position in the states
of Ohio, Indiana, Illinois, Michigan, Wisconsin, and Iowa and the territory
of Minnesota. Control of the House and Morse patents in the West vir-

tually eliminated any competition. As part of the consolidation agreement, the New York & Mississippi Valley Printing Telegraph Company was to be reincorporated in New York as the Western Union Telegraph Company. Hiram Sibley of Rochester, New York, was the entrepreneur who led Western Union to a nationwide monopoly. He was helped by Anson Stager and Jeptha Wade, who secured the railroad contracts for Western Union (Harlow [1936] 1971; Thompson 1947).

The telegraph industry proved to be a natural for the development of pools, cartels, and alliances. These efforts were innovative based on the scale to which they were applied. O'Rielly,[1] of Rochester signed a contract with Kendall for a line of telegraphs from the East Coast to the Mississippi River and principal towns in the Great Lakes region. The Atlantic, Lake & Mississippi Telegraph Company came into existence during August 1845. It divided the territory to be covered into six sections with a separate company in each. It guaranteed the capital to complete the O'Rielly contract in exchange for a controlling voice in each of the companies and at least one-eighth interest in the issued stock. As a result of a protracted lawsuit over the O'Rielly contract, the Atlantic, Lake & Mississippi Telegraph Company failed in its efforts at coordination. Two of the sectional companies—the Atlantic & Ohio and the Pittsburgh, Cincinnati & Louisville—along with several other lines formed the National Lines system with James D. Reid as superintendent. Reid promoted monopoly through consolidation, but the individual companies were unable to reach agreement, and the pool collapsed (Thompson 1947).

In 1853 Kendall invited all the lines using the Morse equipment to meet in Washington. The American Telegraph Confederation was formed by the sixteen companies in attendance. The purpose was to improve through-traffic on messages, create uniformity in operation, and secure a central purchasing agent (Thompson 1947).

The Six Party Contract of July 1857 created a cartel. The members jointly purchased the patent rights to the Hughes printing telegraph, the invention of David E. Hughes, a music professor from Kentucky. The contract divided the country into six sections: the American Telegraph Company, builders of the transatlantic cable, held most of the East Coast; the New York, Albany & Buffalo received part of New York State, and the Atlantic & Ohio, most of Pennsylvania; Western Union dominated the Northwest, including parts of New York, Pennsylvania, and Virginia; the New Orleans & Ohio held the lower Mississippi Valley, and the Illinois & Mississippi, the upper Mississippi Valley. They agreed to exclusive rights within each territory, and any disputes were to be referred to an arbitrator. The Kendall interests were not included in this contract; however, Morse held stock in the American Telegraph Company (Thompson 1947).

The era of consolidation in the telegraph industry preceded that of the railroad industry by more than a decade. Three companies dominated the industry in the 1860s: American Telegraph, Western Union, and U.S. Telegraph. At the close of the Civil War, Western Union aggressively sought to purchase both of the other companies. They fell in 1866, making Western Union the first national monopoly in the United States and the largest corporation at the time (Harlow [1936] 1971; Thompson 1947).

Western Union has remained dominant to the present time as a regulated monopoly, overseen first by the Interstate Commerce Commission (ICC), then by the Federal Communications Commission (FCC). Challenges to its existence came mainly from other forms of communication. Even the Postal Telegraph Company, its only serious industry competitor, was eventually purchased in 1943. The invention of the telephone and the radio was a greater threat to the Western Union monopoly. In both instances, Western Union survived because it primarily serviced business customers. Only a small percentage of its usage was personal. Business was transacted over the telephone but confirmed by telegram or cablegram. Western Union could provide the privacy that an open radio channel could not (Du Boff 1980). Computers, along with fax machines and e-mail, have captured the word transmission function of Western Union.

Western Union, one of the oldest monopolies in the United States, has suffered from bureaucratic inertia and lack of foresight. Management's egocentric approach cost it the Bell Telephone patents and allowed it only peripheral involvement in the development of the radio. In 1877 the controlling shareholders of the Bell Telephone Company offered Western Union the entire company, including patents, for $100,000. The president of Western Union said no. The telephone was still in a crude stage of development and able to transmit only over short distances. Western Union displayed too much confidence and shortsightedness. Within two years, Western Union had awakened and challenged the Bell patents by establishing the American Speaking Telephone Company. Using Elisha Gray's patents, it embarked on an aggressive telephone sales campaign. The Bell forces sued for patent infringement. A settlement was reached in 1879. Western Union recognized the Bell patents as valid and agreed never to enter the voice transmission business. The Bell company agreed to stay out of the telegraph business, pay for the American Speaking system at the cost of construction, and pay Western Union 20 percent of its rentals for seventeen years. American Speaking Telephone turned over 56,000 working units (Brooks 1975; Harlow [1936] 1971).

The tables turned when AT&T bought a controlling interest in Western Union. The consolidation was beneficial. Western was not in the best of shape, and the results of being purchased by AT&T were increased earnings and greater power. In 1913, threatened by an antitrust suit, AT&T divested itself of Western Union (Brooks 1975).

Western Union was absent from the scene in developing the radio. Early radio was a new means of communicating from coast to coast, over the oceans, and from ship to ship or from ship to shore. Commercial radio was an outgrowth of the original use of the radio. The creation of the Radio Corporation of America (RCA) was in direct competition with Western Union. By 1923 RCA handled 30 percent of the transatlantic business and 50 percent of the transpacific (Aitken 1985).

The first radio networks came into existence in the early 1920s. When AT&T refused to carry the transmissions, RCA went to Western Union and Postal Telegraph to rent its lines. Initial tests were successful, but when the lines were used for extended coverage, the transmission degraded into garble (Bilby 1986).

Postal Telegraph Company had been organized in 1881 around Gray's patents for the harmonic telegraph and a new steel and copper wire produced by Chester Snow. In 1883 John W. Mackay, a Virginia City silver king, invested in the firm and was promptly made president. Mackay was interested in foreign communication. The American Telegraph Company began the transatlantic cable project in 1854. Success was reached in 1886. Western Union had absorbed American and held a monopoly on telegraphic traffic. The Commercial Cable Company came into existence to build a competing transatlantic cable, which was placed into service in 1884. Mackay and Gordon Bennett, publisher of the *New York Herald*, formed the Commercial Cable Company as a subsidiary to Postal to lay two new transatlantic cables. By 1886 Mackay lines serviced London, Paris, and the continental United States; by 1903 the Pacific cable reached Manila. ITT purchased Postal in 1928. Western Union absorbed Postal in 1943 (Brock 1981; F. Brown 1927; Dibner 1959; Harlow [1936] 1971).

The Western Union monopoly has been challenged several times: by the telephone, the AT&T takeover, radio, and subsequently the AT&T teletypewriter Exchange Service and most recently by the computer industry. The modern business corporation no longer relies on a confirmation by telegram. The cost has risen dramatically, and the use of facsimile equipment, computer data transmission, and voice message systems is more economical. Western Union lost its monopolistic edge to new and different technology. Western Union survived the restructuring of the 1980s, but the telegraph did not. The messages sent out were no longer tapped out by key and sent by wire. Satellites, radio waves, and microwaves carry the asynchronous and digital information from place to place. Western Union seldom traffics in words of greeting and news. Its business is money transfer. Its business is international and very successful. Western Union Financial Incorporated is one of the largest funds-transfer organizations in the world, a truly global enterprise. By emphasizing funds-transfer, Western Union has become a profitable enterprise. New Valley Corporation sold Western Union Financial to First Financial Management Corporation of Atlanta for $1.2 billion, including the underfunded pension plan in October 1994. In September 1995 the Federal Trade Commission approved the merger of

First Financial with First Data Corporation of Hackensack, New Jersey. Western Union Financial is now part of the largest financial processing corporation in the world. As a funds-transfer operation, Western Union Financial continues to flourish.

The distinctive yellow and black Western Union marque is still in use by Western Union Commercial Services Messaging, a company that specializes in mass mailing of messages. Because the Western Union name on the envelope conveys a sense of urgency, mailers can anticipate a high percentage of opened mailings. Western Union Messaging can be easily accessed via the Internet: http://www.wucs.com.

BIBLIOGRAPHIC ESSAY

The literature on the history of the telegraph industry is limited. Lewis Coe published *The Telegraph: A History of Morse's Invention and Its Predecessors in the United States* in 1993. This factual account of the development of the telegraph contains very good photographs. The literature of the telegraph industry that imparts a feel for what it was like and how it was done is still best represented by Robert L. Thompson's *Wiring a Continent: The History of the Telegraph Industry in the United States, 1832–1866* (1947) and Alvin F. Harlow's *Old Wires & New Waves* ([1936] 1971). These books provide insightful knowledge about the early history of the industry. The impact of new technologies is discerned from reading Hugh G. J. Aitken's *Continuous Wave: Technology and American Radio, 1900–1932* (1985), John Brooks' *Telephone: The First Hundred Years* (1975), Robert W. Garnet's *Telephone Enterprise: The Evolution of the Bell System's Horizontal Structure, 1876–1909* (1985), George David Smith's *Anatomy of a Business Strategy: Bell, Western Electric, and the Origins of the American Telephone Industry* (1985), and Erik Barnouw's trilogy on the broadcasting industry, especially volume 1, *A Tower in Babel: A History of Broadcasting in the United States to 1933* (1966). To view the twentieth-century history of the telegraph, one must look at the broader subject of communication and piece together what happened to Western Union. This will involve reading on the telephone and radio industries and the computer industry. The best place to start a review of the telegraph industry is on the Internet. Go to the National Museum of American History (U.S.) Archives Center at the Smithsonian Institution. It owns the records of the Western Union Telegraph Company. The *Register of the Western Union Telegraph Company Collection, 1848–1963* has been published and is available for purchase through the Internet. This collection contains much of the early literature along with the company records and a large collection of pictures and many telegraph instruments. Current information on the company's ownership and Western Union's success as a money-transfer organization can be found in periodicals. The story of its purchase and repurchase can be tracked through the *American Banker, Business Week*, the *Wall Street Journal*, and *Facts on File World News Digest*. These are available on *Infotrack*, a periodical search engine.

NOTE

1. "The various members of the O'Rielly family differed in their ideas as to the proper spelling of the name. Henry O'Rielly . . . modified the conventional spelling of 'O'Reilly,' and he mentions in his letters that Brother John signed himself as 'Captain John I. Rielly' " (Thompson 1947, 77 n.15). See also the Henry O'Rielly Papers, New York Historical Society Library.

BIBLIOGRAPHY

Adler, Stacy. "Telexes Can Bind Reinsurer to Risk, N.Y. Court Rules." *Business Insurance* 24, no. 9 (February 26, 1990): 3–4.
Administrative Management. New York: Geyer-McAllister, 1961–82. Monthly.
Advertising Age. Chicago: Crain Communications, 1930– .
Aitken, Hugh G. J. *The Continuous Wave: Technology and American Radio, 1900–1932*. Princeton, NJ: Princeton University Press, 1985.
Alabama. Legislature. Senate. *In the Legislature of Alabama, July Session, 1919: Senate Bills 303 and 363 Permitting Telegraph Companies to Condemn and Pay Just Compensation for the Space on the Margins of Railroads Which Is Now Occupied by Them*. 4 vols. Montgomery: Brown Printing, 1919.
Alabama Public Service Commission. *General Rules for Electric, Gas, Water, Telephone and Telegraph Utilities*. Birmingham, AL: Birmingham Print, 1930.
Albert, Arthur Lemuel. *Electrical Communication*. New York: Wiley, 1934.
ABA [American Bankers Association] Banking Journal. New York: Simmons-Boardman for American Bankers Association, 1979– .
American Bankers Association Journal. New York: American Bankers Association, 1924–1934. See also *Banking*, 1934–1979.
American Demographics. Ithaca, NY: American Demographics, 1979– .
American Import/Export Management. Philadelphia: North American, 1981– .
American Institute of Electrical Engineers Library. *Catalogue of the Wheeler Gift of Books: Pamphlets and Periodicals in the Library of the American Institute of Electrical Engineers* [includes bibliographies in telegraph and sympathetic telegraph]. 2 vols. New York: American Institute of Electrical Engineers [AIEE], 1909.
American Shipper. Jacksonville, FL: Howard, 1976– . Monthly.
Ankomah, Baffour. "Instant Money Transfer Arrives in Ghana." *African Business* no. 188 (May 1994): 34–35.
———. "The Money Transfer Revolution." *African Business* no. 203 (October 1995). 28.
Arend, Mark. "Welfare by Wire, or EBT, Heats Up." *ABA Banking Journal* 86 (April 1994): 46+ .
Arndorfer, Bob. "Messages by Wire Have Succumbed to the Net." *Gainesville (Florida) Sun*, June 10, 1996.

AT&T Bell Laboratories Technical Journal: A Journal of the AT&T Companies.
New York: AT&T, 1984. See also *Bell System Technical Journal* and *AT&T Technical Journal.*

AT&T Technical Journal. New York: AT&T, 1985– .

Atlantic, Lake & Mississippi Telegraph Company. *American Telegraph System: Great Central Range between the Atlantic and Mississippi, including the Ohio Valley and the Lake Country.* Atlantic, Lake & Mississippi Telegraph Company, 1845. Goldsmiths'-Kress Library of Economic Literature, no. 34425.2. Woodbridge, CT: Research Publications, 1980. Microfilm.

Atlas, Riva. "Now You See It, Now You Don't." *Forbes* 155, no. 9 (April 24, 1995): 44–45.

Aviation Week & Space Technology. New York: McGraw-Hill, 1960– . Weekly.

Baker, Thomas Thorne. *Wireless Pictures and Television: A Practical Description of the Telegraphy of Pictures, Photographs, and Visual Images.* New York: Van Nostrand, 1927.

Banking. New York: Simmons-Boardman, 1934–1979.

Banks, Michael A. *Understanding FAX and Electronic Mail.* Sams Understanding Series. Carmel, IN: H. W. Sams, 1990.

Barnouw, Erik. *A History of Broadcasting in the United States.* Vol. 1, *A Tower in Babel: A History of Broadcasting in the United States to 1933.* New York: Oxford University Press, 1966.

Baum, Joel A. C., Helaine J. Korn, and Suresh Kotha. "Dominant Designs and Population Dynamics in Telecommunications Services: Founding and Failure of Facsimile Transmission Service Organizations, 1965–1992." *Social Science Research* 24 (June 1995): 97–135.

Beirne, Joseph A. *Report on PTT Trade Union Educational Activities.* Brussels, Belgium: Postal, Telegraph and Telephone Workers' International, Communications Workers of America, 1966. Pamphlets in American History. Labor; L 2112. Sanford, NC: Microfilming Corp. of America, 1979. Microfiche.

Bell, Trudy E. "A Picture Is Worth 50 Words." *IEEE Spectrum* 32, no. 6 (June 1995): 17.

Bell System Technical Journal. Short Hills, NJ: American Telephone & Telegraph, 1922–1983.

Berliner, Uri. "Celebrate.Stop.The Telegram.Stop." *San Diego Union-Tribune,* May 27, 1994, E1.

Bikson, Tora K., and L. Schieber. *Relationships between Electronic Information Media and Records Management Practices: Results of a Survey of United Nations Organizations.* A Rand Note, N-3150-RC. Santa Monica, CA: Rand, 1990.

Bilby, Kenneth. *The General: David Sarnoff and the Rise of the Communications Industry.* New York: Harper & Row, 1986.

"BITELEX—Bilingual Communicator." *Telecommunications* 17 (May 1983): 66.

Blake, George Gascoigne. *History of Radio Telegraphy and Telephony.* London: Chapman & Hall, 1928. Reprint. New York: Arno Press, 1974.

Blondheim, Menahem. *News over the Wires: The Telegraph and the Flow of Public Information in America, 1844–1897.* Harvard Studies in Business History, no. 42. Cambridge: Harvard University Press, 1994.

Bodson, Dennis, Kenneth R. McConnell, and Richard Schraphorst. *FAX: Digital Facsimile Technology and Applications*. 2d ed. Boston: Artech House, 1992.

Bradli, Hank. "GOES: The New Weather Satellites." *Satellite Communications* 18, no. 10 (October 1994): 32–36.

Brady, Jasper Ewing. *Tales of the Telegraph: The Story of a Telegrapher's Life and Adventures in Railroad, Commercial, and Military Work*. New York: Doubleday & McCLure, 1899.

Brandon, George. "New Rules on Tap for Business Wire Transfers." *The Bankers Magazine* (Boston) 174 (March–April 1991): 35–38.

Bright, Charles. *Submarine Telegraphs: Their History, Construction, and Working*. London: C. Lockwood, 1898. Reprint. New York: Arno Press, 1974.

Brock, Gerald W. *The Telecommunications Industry: The Dynamics of Market Structure*. Harvard Economic Studies, vol. 151. Cambridge: Harvard University Press, 1981.

Brooks, John. *Telephone: The First Hundred Years*. New York: Harper & Row, 1975.

Brown, Bob. "AT&T Leapfrogs Foes with EasyLink Deal." *Network World* 7, no. 28 (July 9, 1990): 1, 54.

Brown, Frank J. *Cable and Wireless Communications of the World*. Bath, England: Sir Isaac Pitman & Sons, 1927.

Brown, Steven A. *Final Report of the National Agricultural Library Telefacsimile Evaluation Project*. Washington, DC: U.S. Department of Agriculture, National Agricultural Library, 1986.

Burndy Library. *Heralds of Science: As Represented by Two Hundred Epochal Books and Pamphlets in the Dibner Library, Smithsonian Institution*. 25th anniversary edition. Dibner Library Publication no. 2. Burndy Library Publication no. 34. New York: N. Watson Academic Publications for Burndy Library, Norwalk, CT, and Smithsonian Institution, Washington, DC, 1980.

Business Insurance. Chicago: Crain Communications, 1967– .

Business Japan. Tokyo: Nihon Kogyo Shimbun, 1971–1991. Monthly.

Business Marketing. Chicago: Crain Communications, 1983– . Monthly.

Buyers Laboratory. *Mid- and High-Volume Telefacsimile Machines: Introduction and Test Reports on 20 Models*. Library Technology Reports, vol. 27, no. 6. Chicago: American Library Association, 1991.

Byrne, John J. "Ready for the New Wire Transfer Rules?" *ABA Banking Journal* 87 (November 1995): 26+ .

Byte. Peterborough, NY: McGraw-Hill, 1975– .

Canadian Pacific Railway Company. *Rules and Wages for Commercial Telegraphers and Clerks, as Mutually Agreed to between the General Manager of Telegraphs and a Committee of Telegraphers, Effective June 1st, 1928*. N.p.: Canadian Pacific Railway Company, 1928. Pamphlets in American History. Labor; L 2088. Sanford, NC: Microfilming Corp. of America, 1979. Microfiche.

Carroll, Paul B. "Mexican Retailer Skirts Credit Crunch by Shedding Western Union Venture." *Wall Street Journal*, January 15, 1996, Eastern edition, A8.

Case, Brendan M. "Mexicans Send Dollars Home and U.S. Companies Profit." *New York Times*, September 14, 1996, A, 31:2.

Chain Store Age Executive with Shipping Center Age. New York: Lebhar-Friedman, 1975–1995. Monthly.

Chilton's Electronic News. New York: Chilton, 1990–1991. Weekly. See also *Electronic News.*

Coates, Vary T., and Bernard S. Finn. *A Retrospective Technology Assessment: Submarine Telegraphy: The Transatlantic Cable of 1866.* San Francisco: San Francisco Press, 1979.

Coe, Lewis. *The Telegraph: A History of Morse's Invention and Its Predecessors in the United States.* Jefferson, NC: McFarland, 1993.

———. *Wireless Radio: A Brief History.* Jefferson, NC: McFarland, 1996.

Commercial Space. New York: McGraw-Hill, 1985– . Quarterly.

Commercial Telegraphers' Union of America. *Rules and Wages for Commercial Telegraphers, Taking Effect July 1st, 1912.* N.p.: Commercial Telegraphers' Union of America, Canadian Pacific System, Division No. 1, 1912. Pamphlets in American History. Labor; L 2087. Sanford, NC: Microfilming Corp. of America, 1979. Microfiche.

———. *Report of the International President, Sixteenth Regular Convention, Chicago, September 9th 1935, Commercial Telegraphers' Union of North America.* Chicago: Commercial Telegraphers' Union of America, 1935. Pamphlets in American History. Labor; L 2084. Sanford, NC: Microfilming Corp. of America, 1979. Microfiche.

———. *The CTU and Why?* Washington, DC: Commercial Telegraphers' Union of America, 1943. Pamphlets in American History. Labor; L 2086. Sanford, NC: Microfilming Corp. of America, 1979. Microfiche.

———. *Contract and Seniority Record, March 1, 1949* [December 29, 1948, agreement between United Press Associations and United Press System Division No. 47, a subordinate unit of the Commercial Telegraphers' Union]. N.p.: Commercial Telegraphers' Union of America. United Press System. Division No. 47, 1949. Pamphlets in American History. Labor; L 2089. Sanford, NC: Microfilming Corp. of America, 1979. Microfiche.

"Communications: The Attention-Grabbing Telegram." *Inc.* 15 (June 1993): 47.

Communications News. Geneva, IL: Harcourt Brace Jovanovich, 1964– . Monthly.

Computerworld. Newton, MA: Computerworld, 1967– . Weekly.

Congressional Quarterly Weekly Report. Washington, DC: Congressional Quarterly, weekly.

Costigan, Daniel M. *Electronic Delivery of Documents and Graphics.* New York: Van Nostrand Reinhold, 1978.

Data Communications. New York: McGraw-Hill, 1972– .

Dewey, Patrick R. *Fax for Libraries.* Supplements to Computers in Libraries, 13. Westport, CT: Meckler, 1990.

Dibner, Bern. *The Atlantic Cable.* Norwalk, CT: Burndy Library, 1959. 2d ed. New York: Blaisdell, 1964. See Burndy Library.

Dorf, Philip. *The Builder: A Biography of Ezra Cornell.* New York: Macmillan, 1952.

Doyle, Philip. "A Quarter Century of Wage Gains for Telephone-and-Telegraph Workers." *Monthly Labor Review* 97, no. 7 (July 1974): 57–58.

Du Boff, Richard B. "Business Demand and the Development of the Telegraph in the United States, 1844–1860." *Business History Review* (Winter 1980): 459–79.

———. *Accumulation and Power: An Economic History of the United States*. Armonk, NY: M. E. Sharpe, 1989.

Eckerson, Wayne. "AT&T EasyLink Rolls Out Secure Bank Telex Software." *Network World* 8, no. 50 (December 16, 1991): 21, 42.

Editor & Publisher, the Fourth Estate. New York: Editor & Publisher, 1901– .

Electrical Communication. New York: International Western Electric Co., 1922–July 1925; International Standard Electric Corp., October 1925–April 1940; Standard Telephones and Cables Ltd., London, July–October 1940; International Telephone and Telegraph Corp., 194?–1986; Alcatel, NV, 1987–1992.

Electrical Review. Chicago: Electrical Review, 1917– .

Electrical Review: An Illustrated Weekly Journal of Scientific and Electrical Progress. New York: Electrical Review, 1898–1908.

Electrical Review and Western Electrician. Chicago: Electrical Review, 1908–1911. Weekly.

Electrical Review and Western Electrician with Which Is Consolidated Electrocraft. Chicago: Electrical Review, 1912–1917. Weekly.

Electrical World. New York: McGraw-Hill, 1883– .

Electronic Business. Boston: Cahners, 1975– . Monthly.

"An Electronic/Hard Copy Tariff." *American Shipper* 25 (June 1983): 22.

Electronic News. New York: Fairchild, 1956–1990.

Electronic News. New York: Electronic News, 1991– .

Electronic News Financial Fact Book & Directory. New York: Fairchild, Book Division, 1962– . Annual.

"Employee Medical Costs Rise under New Western Union Pact." *Business Insurance* 19 (September 30, 1985): 40.

Facsimile Users' Directory. New York: Monitor, 1989– . Semiannual.

Factory. New York: McGraw-Hill, 1959–1968; New York: Morgan-Grampian, 1971–1976.

Factory Management and Maintenance. New York: McGraw-Hill, 1933–1958. See also *Factory* and *Modern Manufacturing*.

Fagen, M. D. *A History of Engineering and Science in the Bell System* [the early years, 1875–1925; national service in war and peace, 1925–1975]. New York: Bell Telephone Laboratories, 1975.

Fahie, John Joseph. *A History of Wireless Telegraphy*. 1901. Reprint. New York: Arno Press and the *New York Times*, 1971.

———. *A History of Electric Telegraphy to the Year 1837*. London: E. & F. N. Spon, 1884. Reprint. New York: Arno Press, 1974.

Far Eastern Economic Review. Hong Kong: Review Publishing Co., 1946– .

Farr, Cheryl A. *Electronic Mail: A New Communications Alternative*. MIS Report, vol. 17, no. 10. Washington, DC: International City Management Association, Management Information Service, 1985.

Farwell, David C. "Decision Support for Human Rights: A Case Study" [Telegram Pledge Program, Amnesty International USA Urgent Action Network]. *Journal of Applied Business Research* 9, no. 2 (Spring 1993): 92–96.

Faulhaber, Gerald R. *Telecommunications in Turmoil: Technology and Public Policy.* Cambridge, MA: Ballinger, 1987.

Field, Henry Martyn. *The Story of the Atlantic Telegraph. History of the Atlantic Telegraph, to the Return of the Expedition of 1865.* New York: Scribner, 1866. Reprint. Technology and Society. New York: Arno Press, 1972.

Fischer, Jeffrey B. "Automating Wire and Cash Management Operations: A Boon for Smaller Banks?" *Bank Management* 67 (November 1991): 26–27.

Fitzgerald, Walter F., Jr. "DEA Recognizes Facsimile Technology." *Drug Topics* 138 (July 25, 1994): 53.

Fletcher, William B. *Summary of Trade and Tariff Information: Telephone and Telegraph Apparatus, Radio Navigational Aid, Radar, and Radio, Remote Control Apparatus. TSUS Items 684.62–684.64 and 685.60–685.61.* USITC Publication 841. Washington, DC: U.S. International Trade Commission, 1982.

Folio: The Magazine for Magazine Management. New Canaan, CT: Folio Magazine, 1972– .

Foner, Philip Sheldon. *Women and the American Labor Movement: From Colonial Times to the Eve of World War I.* New York: Free Press, 1979.

———. *Women and the American Labor Movement: From World War I to the Present.* New York: Free Press, 1980.

Frank, Jerome P. "A Facsimile Double Elephant Folio Gets the Acid Test from the Experts." *Publishers Weekly* 228 (November 1, 1985): 50–51.

Gabler, Edwin. *The American Telegrapher: A Social History, 1860–1900.* Class and Culture. New Brunswick, NJ: Rutgers University Press, 1988.

Gabrielson, Heidi. "Videofax: A Merger of Familiar Technologies." *The Office* 108 (September 1988): 32+ .

Garnet, Robert W. *The Telephone Enterprise: The Evolution of the Bell System's Horizontal Structure, 1876–1909.* Johns Hopkins/AT&T Series in Telephone History. Baltimore: Johns Hopkins University Press, 1985.

Goldman, Kevin. "Rival to Send Western Union a Message." *Wall Street Journal,* November 25, 1994, Eastern edition, B5.

Goldsmith, Alfred Norton, and John L. Callahan. *Radio Facsimile. An Assemblage of Papers from Engineers of the RCA Laboratories Relating to the Radio Transmission and Recorded Reception of Permanent Images.* New York: RCA Institutes Technical Press, 1938.

Graphic Arts Monthly and the Printing Industry. New York: Technical Pub., 1938– .

"Gridlock of Fed Wire Brings Call for Probe." *Pensions & Investment Age* 16 (February 22, 1988): 29–30.

Harlow, Alvin F. *Brass-Pounders: Young Telegraphers of the Civil War.* Denver, Sage Books, 1962.

———. *Old Wires & New Waves.* New York: D. Appleton-Century, 1936. Reprint. History of Broadcasting: Radio to Television. New York: Arno Press and the *New York Times,* 1971.

Hawks, Ellison. *Pioneers of Wireless.* London: Methuen, 1927. Reprint. New York: Arno Press, 1974.

Hindle, Brooke. *Emulation and Invention.* New York: New York University Press, 1981.

Holden, Alfred C. "How to Locate and Communicate with Overseas Customers." *Industrial Marketing Management* 20, no. 3 (August 1991): 161–68.

Holmes, James F. *Data Transmission and Data Processing Dictionary: A Compilation of Terminology in the Fields of Data Processing, Telephony, Telegraphy, Facsimile, and Data Transmission.* New York: J. F. Rider, 1965.

Holzmann, Gerar, J., and Bjorn Pehrson. *The Early History of Data Networks.* Los Alamitos, CA: IEEE Computer Society Press, 1995.

Horton, Liz. "Time Inc.'s Mag Net Attracts Digital Ads." *Folio: The Magazine for Magazine Management* 21 (January 1992): 32.

Inc. Boston: United Marine, 1979– . Monthly.

Industrial Management & Data Systems. Wembly, Middlesex, England: Embankment Press, 1980– . Monthly.

Industrial Marketing Management. New York: Elsevier, 1971– .

Infosystems. Wheaton, IL: Hitchcock, 1972– . Monthly.

"Ingersoll-Rand's Software Solution to Telex and Fax." *Communications News* 28, no. 8 (August 1991): 6–7.

Intriago, Charles A. "Bankers Challenge Proposed Wire Transfer Rules." *The Bankers Magazine* (Boston) 174 (July-August 1991): 55–59.

Irwin, Manley Rutherford. *Telecommunications America: Markets without Boundaries.* Westport, CT: Quorum Books, 1984.

Israel, Paul. *From Machine Shop to Industrial Laboratory: Telegraphy and the Changing Context of American Invention: 1830–1920.* Johns Hopkins Studies in the History of Technology, n.s., no. 14. Baltimore: Johns Hopkins University Press, 1992.

Joers, Richard V. "The Wire Function and Drug Money Laundering." *Issues in Bank Regulation* 13 (Fall 1989): 23–27.

Johnstone, Bob. "Microchip Messengers." *Far Eastern Economic Review* 156 (May 6, 1993): 38.

"Junk Fax' Bill Gets Panel OK." *Congressional Quarterly Weekly Report* 48 (May 19, 1990): 1554.

Kalow, Jay. "Facsimile: Universal Communications Link." *The Office* 115 (January 1992): 66.

Kenneally, James Joseph. *Women and American Trade Unions.* Monographs in Women's Studies. St. Albans, VT: Eden Press, 1978.

Kirchner, Jake. "FCC Blocks Electronic Mail Effort." *Computerworld* 13, no. 16 (April 16, 1979): 2.

Kittross, John M. *Documents in American Telecommunications Policy.* 2 vols. Historical Studies in Telecommunications. New York: Arno Press, 1977.

Knights of Labor, District Assembly No. 45, Executive Board. *Proceedings of the Executive Board, D.A. No. 45, Brotherhood of Telegraphers of the United States and Canada, Held at Cincinnati, Ohio, October 10–13, 1882.* Pittsburgh: J. H. Barrow, 1882. Pamphlets in American History. Labor; L 2022. Sanford, NC: Microfilming Corp. of America, 1979. Microfiche.

Kratochvil, D. *Satellite Provided Customer Premises Services: A Forecast of Potential Domestic Demand through the Year 2000: Final Report.* Vol. 4, Sensitivity Analysis. NASA Contractor Report, NASA CR 174662. Washington, DC: National Aeronautics and Space Administration, 1985. Microfiche.

Lasker, Timothy W. "Wirephotos and Color." *Editor & Publisher* 124, no. 39 (September 28, 1991): 2C, 36C.

Lawford, G. L., and L. R. Nicholson. *The Telcon Story*. London: Telegraph Construction and Maintenance, 1950.

Lebow, Irwin. *Information Highways and Byways: From the Telegraph to the 21st Century*. New York: IEEE [Institute of Electrical and Electronics Engineers] Press, 1995.

Lefton, Terry. "AT&T to Sell Line to Memorex." *Electronic News* 36 (April 16, 1990): 18.

Levin, Harvey J. *The Invisible Resource: Use and Regulation of the Radio Spectrum*. Baltimore: Johns Hopkins Press for Resources for the Future, 1971.

Limbacher, Patricia B. "PBGC [Pension Benefit Guaranty Corp.] Key in Bidding War: Agency Gets Say-So in New Valley Bankruptcy Sale." *Pensions & Investments* 22 (September 19, 1994): 2+ .

Lindley, Lester G. *The Constitution Faces Technology: The Relationship of the National Government to the Telegraph, 1866–1884*. Ph.D. diss., Rice University, 1971. Dissertations in American Economic History. New York: Arno Press, 1975.

———. *The Impact of the Telegraph on Contract Law*. Distinguished Studies in American Legal and Constitutional History, no. 16. New York: Garland, 1990.

Lodge, Oliver. *Lightning Conductors and Lightning Guards: A Treatise on the Protection of Buildings, of Telegraph Instruments and Submarine Cables, and of Electric Installations Generally, from Damage by Atmospheric Discharges*. London: Whittaker, 1892.

Maintenance Engineering, Chicago: McGraw-Hill, 1931–1933. Monthly.

Managing Office Technology. Cleveland, OH: Penton, 1993– . Monthly.

Marketing News. Chicago: American Marketing Association, 1967– . Biweekly.

Marshall, Jeffrey. "Money Order Game Gets a New Player." *United States Banker* 102, no. 6 (June 1992): 30–34, 44.

Marshall, Walter P. *Ezra Cornell, 1807–1874: His Contributions to Western Union and to Cornell University*. New York: Newcomen Society in North America, 1951.

Masini, Giancarlo. *Marconi*. New York: Marsilio, 1995.

Math, Irwin, and Hal Keith. *Morse, Marconi, and You*. New York: Scribner, 1979.

McDonald, Philip Bayaud. *A Saga of the Seas: The Story of Cyrus W. Field and the Laying of the First Atlantic Cable*. New York: Wilson-Erickson, 1937.

McFall, Russell W. *Making History by Responding to Its Forces* [Western Union Telegraph Company]. Newcomen address, 1971. New York: Newcomen Society in North America, 1971.

McLeod, Douglas. "Western Union Bid Includes Pensions." *Business Insurance* 28 (October 24, 1994): 2+ .

"Memorex Plans More Revamping, to Post Charge." *Wall Street Journal*, June 1, 1993, Eastern edition, A9A.

Miller, Frederick W. "Electronic Mail." *Infosystems* 25, no. 12 (December 1978): 35, 38–40.

Mills, Mike. "Nuisance Call Bill Clears Congress." *Congressional Quarterly Weekly Report* 49 (November 30, 1991): 3523.

Mini-micro Systems. Hudson, MA: Modern Data Services, 1976– . Monthly.

Modern Manufacturing. New York: Gilbert W. Chapman, Jr., 1968–1971.

Modern Office Technology. Cleveland, OH: Penton/IPC, 1983–1993. Monthly. See also *Managing Office Technology.*

Monthly Labor Review. Washington, DC: U.S. Department of Labor, Bureau of Labor Statistics, monthly.

Morehouse, H. G. *Equipment for Facsimile Transmission between Libraries: A Description and Comparative Evaluation of Three Systems.* Reno: University of Nevada, 1967.

Morgan, Alfred Powell. *Wireless Telegraphy and Telephony.* 4th ed. New York: Henley, 1912.

Nebenzahl, Israel D., and Eugene D. Jaffe. "Facsimile Transmission versus Mail Delivery of Self-Administered Questionnaires in Industrial Surveys." *Industrial Marketing Management* 24 (June 1995): 167–75.

Norman, Adrian R. D. *Electronic Document Delivery: The ARTEMIS Concept for Document Digitalisation and Teletransmission: A Study Prepared for the Directorate-General Information Market and Innovation, Commission of the European Communities.* Communications Library. White Plains, NY: Knowledge Industry, 1981.

Office Administration and Automation. New York: Geyer-McAllister, 1983– .

Operator and Electrical World [a journal for telegraphists, electricians, and electrical engineers]. New York: W. J. Johnston, 1883.

Order of Commercial Telegraphers. *Constitution of the Order of Commercial Telegraphers, Adopted at the First Session of the Grand Lodge, Held at Pittsburgh, Pennsylvania, November 26th, 1902.* St. Louis, MO: Order of Commercial Telegraphers, 1902. Pamphlets in American History. Labor; L 2090. Sanford, NC: Microfilming Corp. of America, 1979. Microfiche.

Order of Railroad Telegraphers (U.S.). *Information Which May Be of Benefit to You as Ready Reference on Certain Articles and Points of Various Schedules in Our Territory.* St. Louis, MO: Order of Railroad Telegraphers, 1916. Pamphlets in American History. Labor; L 2094. Sanford, NC: Microfilming Corp. of America, 1979. Microfiche.

Oslin, George P. *The Story of Telecommunications.* Macon, GA: Mercer University Press, 1992.

Parker, John R., and James M. Elford. *American Signal Book, or, The United States Telegraph Vocabulary: Being an Appendix to Elford's Marine Telegraph Signal Book . . . Adapted to the Use of the New Semaphoric Telegraph: To Which Is Added the Boston Harbor Signal Book.* Boston: From the Steam Power press office, W. L. Lewis, printer, 1832. Goldsmiths'-Kress Library of Economic Literature, no. 27822.9. Woodbridge, CT: Research Publications, 1980. Microfilm.

Penrose, Charles. *Newcomb Carlton, 1869–1953, of Western Union.* New York: Newcomen Society in North America, 1956.

Piirto, Rebecca. "Just the Fax, Ma'am." *American Demographics* 16 (November 1994): 6.

Plum, William Rattle. *The Military Telegraph during the Civil War in the United States.* Chicago: Jansen, McClurg, 1882. Reprint. Arno Press Telecommunications series. Introduction reprinted from "Union Signal Communications: Innovation and Conflict," *Civil War History* 9, no. 4, December 1963. New York: Arno Press, 1974.

Poje, Richard, and Bruce MacKenzie. "Wire Transfer Fraud: A Guide for Risk Averse Treasury Professionals." *TMA Journal 15* (September/October 1995): 4+ .

Prime, Samuel Irenaeus. *The Life of Samuel F. B. Morse.* New York: D. Appleton, 1875. Reprint. Telecommunications. Arno Press, 1974.

Prior, Frederick John. *Operation of Trains and Station Work and Telegraphy.* Chicago: F. J. Drake, 1919.

Public Utilities Fortnightly. Rochester, NY: Public Utilities Reports, 1929–1993; Arlington, VA: Public Utilities Reports, 1994– .

Purchasing. Boston: Cahners, 1979– . Monthly.

Quinn, Liam. "Dealing with the Invisible Disability." *Telemarketing Magazine* 11, no. 5 (November 1992): 24–26.

Radigan, Joseph, and Mark Borowsky. "Something Old, Something New in Deals." *United States Banker* 104 (October 1994): 8.

"Radio-Relay Antennas Tower over African Jungle as Links in Nigeria's Phone, Telex, TV Network." *Communications News* 23 (June 1986): 48.

Rafferty, James P. "Fax Servers Gain a Routing Standard." *Data Communications* 22 (September 1993): 53–54+ .

Ramirez, Anthony. "New $2 Billion Network Adapts Telegraph Tubes." *New York Times*, January 5, 1994, D, 6:5.

Rand McNally and Company. *Rand-McNally Indexed Pocket Map and Shippers' Guide of Alabama: Railroads, Electric Lines, Post Offices, Express, Telegraph and Mail Service . . . Population according to the Latest Official Census* [also published for other states]. Chicago: Rand McNally, 1917.

Reichert, Alan K., William Strauss, and Randall C. Merris. "An Economic Analysis of Short-Run Fluctuations in Federal Reserve Wire Transfer Volume." *Journal of Bank Research* 15 (Winter 1985): 222–28.

Reid, James D. *The Telegraph in America. Its Founders, Promoters, and Noted Men.* New York: Derby Brothers, 1879.

Robins, Margaret Dreier, and Emma Steghagen. *The Lot of the Woman Telegrapher: An Open Letter.* Chicago: National Women's Trade Union League of America, Women's Trade Union League of Illinois, 1907. Pamphlets in American History. Labor; L 2091. Sanford, NC: Microfilming Corp. of America, 1979. Microfiche.

Roesler, Paula. "AT&T [Export] Hot Line Offers World of Information." *Telephony* 222 (March 9, 1992): 22.

Rogers, Henry J., and Henry O'Reilly [O'Rielly]. *American Telegraph System, Semaphoric as well as Magnetic: American Semaphore or Marine Signals, Connected with the Electro-Magnetic Telegraph.* N.p., 1846. Goldsmiths'-Kress Library of Economic Literature, no. 34612.1. Woodbridge, CT: Research Publications, 1980. Microfilm.

Roget, Samuel Romilly. *A Dictionary of Electrical Terms, including Telegraphy, Telephony, and Wireless.* 3d ed., rev. and enl. London: I. Pitman, 1938.

Rosenberg, Jim. "Byso Screen Running at Two Sites." *Editor & Publisher, the Fourth Estate* 124, no. 12 (March 23, 1991): 34–37.

———. "How the European Reaches American Readers." *Editor & Publisher, the Fourth Estate* 124 (November 9, 1991): 32–33.

Ross, Mark. *Communication Access for Persons with Hearing Loss: Compliance with the Americans with Disabilities Act.* Baltimore: York Press, 1994.

Rossberg, Ehrhard A., and Helmut E. Korta. *Teleprinter Switching* (Fernschreib-Vermittlungstechnik). Princeton, NJ: Van Nostrand, 1960.

Ryan, Francis Milton, Jack Roderick Tolmie, and Roy Odell Bach. *Multiplex Radio Telegraphy and Telephony.* Seattle: Seattle University, 1920.

Ryan, Suzanne Alexander. "Memorex Telex Again Seeks Shield under Chapter 11." *Wall Street Journal*, February 14, 1994, Eastern edition, A11D.

Samuel, Margaret. "Non-Cash Alternatives and Money Laundering; An American Model for Canadian Consumers' Protection." *American Business Law Journal* 30 (September 1992): 169–222.

Schubert, Paul. *The Electric Word: The Rise of Radio.* New York: Macmillan, 1928.

Schultz, Ellen E. "Sending Money in Emergency Needn't Cost You Biggest Bucks." *Wall Street Journal*, June 26, 1991, C, 1:3.

"Seizing Wire Transfers." *Wall Street Journal*, September 20, 1993, Eastern edition, B8.

Sih, Philip C. W. *Fax Power: High Leverage Business Communications.* VNR Computer Library. New York: Van Nostrand Reinhold, 1993.

Smith, George David. *The Anatomy of a Business Strategy: Bell, Western Electric, and the Origins of the American Telephone Industry.* Johns Hopkins/AT&T Series in Telephone History. Baltimore: Johns Hopkins University Press, 1985.

Smith, Sydney F. *Telephony and Telegraphy: An Introduction to Instruments and Switching Systems (Electromechanical and Reed-Electronic).* 3d ed. London: Oxford University Press, 1978.

Smith, Willoughby. *The Rise and Extension of Submarine Telegraphy.* London: J. S. Virtue, 1891. Reprint. New York: Arno Press, 1974.

Southern Telegraph Companies. *Letter to Hon. J(ohn). H(enninger). Reagan, Post Master Gen'l. Containing Statement of Affairs.* Richmond, VA: Southern Telegraph Companies, 1862. Confederate Imprints, 1861–1865, reel 95, no. 2942. New Haven, CT: Research Publications, 1974.

Strauss, Paul R. "An '80s Facelift for a '30s Technology: AI Comes to Telex." *Data Communications* 17 (May 1988): 51–52+ .

Teinowitz, Ira. "Just the Fax, Ma'am, Latest Newspaper Refrain." *Advertising Age* 64 (April 26, 1993): S6.

Telephony. Chicago: Chambers-McMeal, 1901– . Weekly.

"Teletype Corp." *Telecommunications* 17 (November 1983): 660.

"Telex Corp." *Datamation* 34 (June 15, 1988): 117.

Thompson, Robert L. *Wiring a Continent: The History of the Telegraph Industry in the United States, 1832–1866.* Princeton, NJ: Princeton University Press, 1947.

"Towards the 3D Fax: Solid Geometry." *The Economist* 312 (August 19, 1989): 68+ .

Tribolet, Leslie Bennett. *The International Aspects of Electrical Communications in the Pacific Area.* Johns Hopkins University Studies in Historical and Political Science, extra volumes, n.s., no. 4. Baltimore: Johns Hopkins University, 1929. Reprint. New York: Arno Press, 1972.

United States Banker. Cos Cob, CT: Cleworth, 1977– .

Unrau, William E. *Tending the Talking Wire: A Buck Soldier's View of Indian Country, 1863–1866* [Hervey Johnson, 1839–1923]. University of Utah Publications in the American West, vol. 12. Salt Lake City: University of Utah Press, 1979.

U.S. Bureau of the Census. *Telephones and Telegraphs and Municipal Electric Fire-Alarm and Police Patrol Signaling Systems. 1912.* Prepared by William Mott Steuart, John W. Curry, and William A. Countryman. Washington, DC: U.S. Government Printing Office, 1915.

———. *Census of Electrical Industries. Telegraphs and Municipal Electric Fire-Alarm and Police-Patrol Signaling Systems.* Washington, DC: U.S. Government Printing Office, 1917–1919. Quinquennial.

———. *Census of Electrical Industries. Telegraphs.* Washington, DC: U.S. Government Printing Office, 1924–1930. Quinquennial.

———. *Census of Electrical Industries. Telephones and Telegraphs.* Washington, DC: U.S. Government Printing Office, 1932–1935. Quinquennial. [Statistics for telegraphs also issued separately as *Census of Electrical Industries 1917–1927. Telegraphs.*]

———. *Census of Manufactures. Industry Series. Telephone and Telegraph Apparatus, SIC 3661.* Washington, DC: U.S. Department of Commerce, Bureau of the Census, decennial.

———. *Current Industrial Reports. MA-36N. Selected Electronic and Associated Products, including Telephone and Telegraph Apparatus.* Washington, DC: U.S. Department of Commerce, Bureau of the Census, annual.

———. *Current Industrial Reports. MA36P. Communication Equipment, including Telephone, Telegraph, and other Electronic Equipment.* Washington, DC: U.S. Department of Commerce, Bureau of the Census, annual.

———. *Current Industrial Reports. MA36P. Communication Equipment and Other Electronic Systems and Equipment.* Washington, DC: U.S. Department of Commerce, Bureau of the Census, 1989– . Annual.

U.S. Bureau of Labor Statistics. *Wage Chronology: Western Union Telegraph Co. and the Telegraph Workers and the Communications Workers, 1943–76.* U.S. Bureau of Labor Statistics Bulletin—Bureau of Labor Statistics, 1927. [This bulletin replaces *Wage Chronology: Western Union Telegraph Co., 1943–67,* published as BLS Bulletin no. 1545, and incorporates the supplement covering the 1968–71 period.] Washington, DC: U.S. Department of Labor, Bureau of Labor Statistics, 1977.

———. *Earnings of Communication Workers 1951–59.* Washington, DC: U.S. Department of Labor, Bureau of Labor Statistics.

———. *Industry Wage Survey. Communications.* Washington, DC: U.S. Department of Labor, Bureau of Labor Statistics, 1960– .

U.S. Congress. House. Committee on Interstate and Foreign Commerce. *Communications Act of 1934, Section 214, Legislative Background.* 96th Cong., 1st sess., April 1979. Committee Print 96-IFC 18.

———. House. Committee on Energy and Commerce. Subcommittee on Telecommunications, Consumer Protection, and Finance. *Record Carrier Competi-*

tion Act of 1981. Hearings. 97th Cong., 1st sess., October 15, 1981. Serial 97–83.

———. House. *Record Carrier Competition Act of 1981: Report (to accompany H.R. 4927) (including Cost Estimate of the Congressional Budget Office).* 97th Cong., 1st sess., December 3, 1981. H. Rept. 97–356.

U.S. Congress. Senate. Committee on Railroads. *Railroad through Indian Territory: Proceedings before the Committee on Railroads of the United States Senate Relative to the Bill (S. no. 60) "Ratifying the Act of the General Council of the Choctaw Nation of Indians Granting to the Saint Louis and San Francisco Railway Company Right of Way for a Railroad and Telegraph Line through That nation."* Washington, DC: 1882. Pamphlets in American History. Indians; I 817. Glen Rock, NJ: Microfilming Corp. of America, 1978. Microfiche.

———. Senate. Committee on Commerce, Science, and Transportation. *Amending Section 222 of the Communications Act of 1934, as Amended; Report to Accompany S. 1866.* 95th Cong., 1st sess., 1977. S. Rept. 95–389.

———. Senate. Committee on Commerce, Science, and Transportation. Subcommittee on Communications. *International Record Carrier Competition Act of 1981.* Hearings on S. 271. 97th Cong., 1st sess., February 18, 1981. Serial 97–5.

———. Senate. Committee on Commerce, Science, and Transportation. *International Record Carrier Competition Act of 1981: Report (to Accompany S. 271).* 97th Cong., 1st sess., March 12, 1981. S. Rept. 97–25.

U.S. Department of the Interior. Census Office. *Report on the Agencies of Transportation in the United States: Including the Statistics of Railroad, Steam Navigation, Canals, Telegraphs, and Telephones.* Washington, DC: U.S. Government Printing Office, 1883.

U.S. Employment and Training Administration. *Career Opportunities in the Telephone and Telegraph Industries.* Washington, DC: U.S. Department of Labor, Employment, and Training Administration, 1977.

U.S. Federal Communications Commission. *Rules and Regulations. Volume 8* [see pt. 34, Uniform System of Accounts for Radiotelegraph Carriers; pt. 35, Uniform System of Accounts for Wire-Telegraph and Ocean-Cable Carriers]. Washington, DC: U.S. Federal Communications Commission, irregular.

U.S. Patent and Trademark Office. *Class 178: Telegraphy. Patent Classification Definitions.* U.S. Department of Commerce, Patent and Trademark Office, 1995.

U.S. Postal Service. *INTELPOST Service Directory and User's Guide.* USPS Publication 82 A. Washington, DC: U.S. Postal Service, 1992.

Vail, Alfred. *Description of the American Electro Magnetic Telegraph: Now in Operation between the Cities of Washington and Baltimore.* Washington, DC: J. & G. S. Gideon, 1845. Goldsmiths'-Kress Library of Economic Literature, no. 34159.25. Woodbridge, CT: Research Publications, 1980. Microfilm.

———. *Eyewitness to Early American Telegraphy.* New York: Hine Brothers, 1914. Reprint. New York: Arno Press, 1974.

Venture. New York: Venture Magazine, 1979–   .

Vogt, Ernest J. *Radio Technology: Telegraphy, Telephony, Television, Transcription, Facsimile.* New York: Pitman, 1949.

Weitzer, Bernard. "WU's New Digital Exchange System." *Telecommunications* 13, no. 1 (January 1979): 37–38, 40, 144.

Wells, P. L. *Narrow-Band Direct-Printing Radiotelegraphy: A State of the Art Survey.* OT Report 74–48. Washington, DC: U.S. Department of Commerce, Office of Telecommunications, sponsored by U.S. Maritime Administration, Institute for Telecommunication Sciences, 1974.

"Western Union Expanding to China." *Atlanta Constitution*, March 1, 1995, E, 1:2.

"Western Union Gains Concessions." *Monthly Labor Review* 108 (October 1985): 48.

Western Union Technical Review. New York: Western Union Telegraph Company, Committee on Technical Publication, 1947–1969. Quarterly.

Wiesner, Lothar. *Telegraph and Data Transmission over Shortwave Radio Links: Fundamental Principles and Networks* (Fernschreib- und Datenubertragung uber Kurzwelle: Grundlagen u. Netze. 4 Aufl.). 3d ed. Berlin: Siemens Aktiengesellschaft; Chichester, England: Wiley, 1984.

Williamson, John. "Text Transmission in Europe: Telex, Teletex and Facsimile All Share a Piece of the Pie." *Telephony* 214 (April 25, 1988): 26–27.

Wyatt, Edward. "A Lesson. This Time We've Got It on Tape." *New York Times*, December 10, 1995, Late New York edition, sec. 3, 1.

Yamada, Ken. "Motorola Readying Wireless Pagers." *Computer Reseller News* no. 703 (September 30, 1996): 26.

Ziegler, Bart. "MCI Takes on the Baby Bells—And Everyone Else." *Business Week* no. 3354, Industrial/Technology edition (January 17, 1994): 26–27.

Western Union Corp. Financial Woes and Reorganization—in the News 1974– (Arranged Chronologically)

Lyons, John F. "Western Union's Telegram—SOS." *Financial World* 141, no. 18 (May 1, 1974): 20–23.

Maremont, Mark. "How Western Union Went from Bad to Worse." *Business Week* no. 2878, Industrial/Technology edition (January 28, 1985): 110–16.

Chernoff, Joel, and Paul Dykewicz. "Western Union Falters." *Pensions & Investment Age* 14, no. 9 (April 28, 1986): 1, 68.

Norris, Floyd. "Major Test Looms at Western Union." *New York Times*, May 2, 1989, D, 12:3.

Bradsher, Keith. "Western Union's Debts May Force Bankruptcy." *New York Times*, March 22, 1990, D, 6:5.

Keller, John J. "Western Union to Propose Swap Offer to Note Holders to Avoid Chapter 11." *Wall Street Journal*, April 25, 1990, A, 3:2.

Ryan, Alan J. "Western Union: 'Send Money—Fast.' " *Computerworld* 24, no. 19 (May 7, 1990): 1, 111.

"ITT Increases Stake in Western Union, Becomes Big Holder." *Wall Street Journal*, May 8, 1990, C, 21:3.

Bradsher, Keith. "A.T.&T. Buying 3 Units of Western Union." *New York Times*, July 4, 1990, A, 43:3.

Karpinski, Richard. "AT&T Acquires WU's EasyLink." *Telephony* 219 (July 9, 1990): 8–9.

Norris, Floyd. "Western Union's Reorganization." *New York Times*, July 26, 1990, D, 8:3.

"Western Union and CWA [Communications Workers of America] Race Deadline for Strike." *Wall Street Journal*, August 7, 1990, C, 10:3.

"Western Union Strike Averted." *Wall Street Journal*, August 8, 1990, A, 5:2.

Western Union Corp. Locks Out Workers amid Contract Talks." *Wall Street Journal*, August 13, 1990, C, 15:6.

"Western Union Corp. Union People Replaced." *Boston Globe*, August 13, 1990, 9:5.

"Western Union Replaces Workers." *New York Times*, August 13, 1990, B, 3:5.

Poole, Shelia M. "Western Union Labor Dispute Leaves 100 Locked Out in Atlanta." *Atlanta Constitution*, August 14, 1990, C, 9:1.

"Western Union Debt Offer." *New York Times*, November 30, 1990, D, 5:3.

"Western Union Sells Units, Will Buy Back Junk Bonds." *Atlanta Journal Constitution*, January 1, 1991, F, 3:3.

"Western Union to Change Name for Publicity Reason." *Wall Street Journal*, April 3, 1991, A, 4:5.

"Western Union Corp." *Wall Street Journal*, April 11, 1991, A, 5:6.

"Western Union Debt Ratings Cut by Moody's." *Wall Street Journal*, April 15, 1991, C, 6:4.

Lazzareschi, Carla. "Western Union Tries to Save Its Good Name." *Los Angeles Times*, April 19, 1991, D, 2:1.

Sibley, Celestine. "Telegraphing the End of Old Western Union." *Atlanta Constitution*, April 19, 1991, C, 1:1.

"New Valley Corp. [formerly Western Union Corp.]." *Wall Street Journal*, June 17, 1991, C, 8:6.

Freedman, Alix M. "Western Union Plans Network to Cash Checks." *Wall Street Journal*, August 23, 1991, B, 1:3.

"New Valley Corp." *Wall Street Journal*, June 18, 1992, B, 4:4.

Woolley, Suzanne. "Western Union Banks on the Unbanked." *Business Week*, April 5, 1993, 71–72.

Hyatt, James C. "First Data Bids $480 Million for Parent of Western Union, Which Wants More." *Wall Street Journal*, May 26, 1994, Eastern edition, A9.

Adelson, Andrea. "A $430 Million Bid for Western Union Brings a Rejection." *New York Times*, May 27, 1994, Late New York edition, D4.

———. "First Data to Pay $95 Million for a Rival." *New York Times*, June 10, 1994, Late New York edition, D3.

Naik, Gautam. "New Valley to Sell Western Union Unit to First Data Corp. for $595 Million." *Wall Street Journal*, June 10, 1994, Eastern edition, B6.

Adelson, Andrea. "First Data Offer for New Valley Unit Topped." *New York Times*, June 16, 1994, Late New York edition, D5.

Naik, Gautam. "New Valley Accepts Forstmann Bid for Western Union, Ousting First Data." *Wall Street Journal*, June 16, 1994, Eastern edition, A4.

Adelson, Andrea. "First Data Raises Western Union Bid." *New York Times*, June 24, 1994, Late New York edition, D6.

Naik, Gautam. "First Data Raises Western Union Bid to $660 Million." *Wall Street Journal*, June 24, 1994, Eastern edition, C15.

Irvine, Martha. "First Data Gets FTC Clearance to Buy Western Union If It Wins Bidding War." *Wall Street Journal*, August 19, 1994, Eastern edition, B6E.

Byrd, Veronica. "Hello, Western Union? First Data Calling." *Business Week*, August 29, 1994, 78.

Thomas, Emory, Jr. "First Financial Management Has Plans to Bid for New Valley's Western Union." *Wall Street Journal*, August 30, 1994, Eastern edition, A4.

Bryant, Adam. "Bids Climb in Western Union Sale." *New York Times*, September 3, 1994, Late New York edition, 35+ .

Baker, Molly, and Robert Frank. "Bidders Offer as Much as $970 Million for New Valley's Western Union Unit." *Wall Street Journal*, September 6, 1994, Eastern edition, A4.

Antilla, Susan. "A Victor in Western Union Bids." *New York Times*, September 20, 1994, Late New York edition, D1+ .

Baker, Molly. "Judge Declares First Financial Winner in Three-Way Fight for Western Union." *Wall Street Journal*, September 20, 1994, Eastern edition, A3.

Thomas, Emory, Jr. "First Financial's CEO Is Victor in Western Union Battle: Thomas's Competitiveness Is Credited for Concern's Rise from Obscurity." *Wall Street Journal*, September 20, 1994, Eastern edition, B4.

"Western Union Sold for $1.19 Billion." *Washington Post*, September 20, 1994, C, 3:3.

Adelson, Andrea. "Western Union Buyer Ruled Not Liable for Pension Fund." *New York Times*, September 24, 1994, Late New York edition, 35.

"Bankruptcy Judge Approves Cash Bid for Western Union." *Wall Street Journal*, September 26, 1994, Eastern edition, B18.

Strom, Stephanie. "Pension Takeover Sought for Western Union." *New York Times*, October 18, 1994, Late New York edition, D4.

Freudenheim, Milt. "Buyer of Western Union Will Assume Pensions." *New York Times*, October 20, 1994, Late New York edition, D4.

Karr, Albert. "U.S. Announces Pension-Plan Pact for New Valley." *Wall Street Journal*, October 20, 1994, Eastern edition, A14.

"New Valley Accord to Fund Pension Plan Receives Approval." *Wall Street Journal*, October 24, 1994, Eastern edition, B5.

Baker, Molly. "New Valley Gets Set to Exit Chapter 11: Chairman LeBow Looks for Other 'Troubled Situations.' " *Wall Street Journal*, November 4, 1994, Eastern edition, A7A.

"United States: Mergers & Acquisitions." *Facts on File World News Digest*, 1994, 774 F2.

Fickenscher, Lisa. "1st Data, 1st Financial in Merger to Create $4B Electronic Processor." *American Banker* 1 (June 14, 1995): 2.

"First Data, First Financial Set Merger." *Facts on File World News Digest*, June 29, 1995. Reference: 1995, p. 468 C2.

"First Data to Sell Part of Unit to Ease F.T.C. Merger Concern." *New York Times*, August 29, 1995, Late New York edition, D4.

Jeffrey, Nancy Ann. "First Data Receives Approval to Shed Moneygram Unit." *Wall Street Journal*, November 6, 1996, B2.

CHAPTER 3

RADIO AND TELEVISION BROADCASTING, 48.3

CAROLE E. SCOTT

Modern broadcasting was shaped by scientists, inventors, and government: scientists generated and tested theories, inventors turned scientific creations into applicable devices, and government determined industry structure. The historical roots of broadcasting trace back to experiments on the spectrum by England's Sir Isaac Newton in 1666. In 1873 Scotsman James Clerk Maxwell published the modern concept of electromagnetic energy: light, radio waves, X-rays, and cosmic rays. These developments led to key inventions that include Italian Allessandro Volta's voltaic cell in 1794, Englishman Sir Charles Wheatstone's 1827 microphone, and American Samuel F. B. Morse's 1840 telegraph.

Voice transmission by wire was achieved in 1876 by America's Alexander Graham Bell. By 1895 European opera houses were equipped with either stereo or monophonic telephone systems. In 1893 in Budapest, Hungary, a wire system offered regular news and music programming up to twelve hours a day. A like service did not appear in the United States for another decade, although the Chicago Telephone Company broadcast local election returns by wire to more than 15,000 persons in 1894 (Sivowitch 1975, 18).

WIRELESS TELEGRAPHY

In 1886 Heinrich Hertz, a German, confirmed Maxwell's theory when he proved that electromagnetic waves can be transmitted through space at the speed of light and be reflected and refracted. Hertz did not believe these waves could be used for communication. Subsequently, Guglielmo Marconi proved they could. Marconi is widely recognized as being the first to prove that radio waves—then called Hertzian waves—could be used for communication. In the 1890s Marconi, who also invented the antenna, sent messages in Morse code over increasingly longer distances from his home in Italy.

The Italian minister of post and telegraph spurned Marconi's invention; so his Irish aristocrat mother took him to England. For the seafaring British, with their worldwide empire, wireless communication was attractive. The British Post Office's chief engineer of telegraphs had experimented with wireless and was interested in Marconi's device. On June 2, 1896, Marconi was granted a British patent for his wireless telegraph. A year later he obtained an American patent. With the help of British scientist Sir Oliver Lodge, Marconi developed a method for tuning wireless. The Italian navy also helped him with his experiments.

The first users of wireless were naval and merchant ships. Marconi gained worldwide recognition for his linking of Great Britain with the continent and its ships at sea. Newspaper publishers quickly recognized the advantages of wireless: in 1899, taking advantage of Marconi's wireless, the *New York Herald* reported the results of the America's Cup Race before the contestants returned to shore. Marconi also conducted successful tests for the U.S. War and Navy Departments. On December 12, 1901, using a kite antenna and a crude, spark-gap receiving unit, he was able to link continent with continent, transmitting the letter *S* from Signal Hill in the Canadian province of Newfoundland to Great Britain.

The twenty-three-year-old Marconi formed the Wireless Telegraph and Signal Company in 1897. Capitalized at £100,000, it had six directors, one of whom was Marconi, who held half the company's stock—the firm was later renamed Marconi's Wireless Telegraph Company. The inventor intended to create a worldwide monopoly in wireless communications, and to do so, his company refused to communicate with anyone using others' equipment. The failure of an international convention on wireless held in Berlin in 1903 is attributed to the uncooperative attitude of Marconi's company (Head 1956).

In 1899 the Marconi Wireless Company of America was incorporated in New Jersey with an authorized capital of $10 million. The parent company in England held 365,000 of its 2 million authorized shares—Marconi held 600,000 shares. Soon the American Marconi Company attracted competitors in a country concerned over a British monopoly of a national mania (Barnouw 1990). It took the American company six years to move out of red ink into black.

BREAKING THE BRITISH MONOPOLY

The U.S. Navy originated the name "radiotelegraph" and first used the term "broadcasting" for issuing orders to the fleet. As a wartime measure, in April 1917 the navy was given control of America's private wireless facilities—it held control until 1920. The navy argued that radio—whose primary use was marine—was vital and should not be left in private hands. Whether radio would be financed by the government, advertising, or the leasing of radios was an issue that raged into the 1920s. Unable to get the government to take over radio as a public monopoly, the navy suggested that an American-owned company be established to control the manufacture and marketing of wireless in the United States (Hybels and Ulloth 1978).

Citing the resolute opposition of the U.S. government to the control of the American Marconi Company by the British firm, in 1919 the American company was dissolved. The stock held by the British company was purchased for $2.5 million by the General Electric Company (GE). A condition of the sale was that the Marconi Company be allowed to buy Alexanderson alternators for use outside the United States.

GE's Ernst F. W. Alexanderson had developed an alternator that made reliable, long-distance radio communication possible. The U.S. Navy, which had purchased patent rights to the next-best radio energy generator, was afraid that Marconi would acquire the exclusive rights to the Alexanderson alternator and thus cement a worldwide British monopoly.

The Radio Corporation of America (RCA) was the American monopoly created by GE through one of its executives, Owen D. Young, to replace the American Marconi Company. RCA was a partnership (dominated by GE) of GE, Westinghouse, the American Telegraph Company (AT&T), and others (Hybels and Ulloth 1978, 52–53). The others included Western Electric, United Fruit Company, Wireless Specialty Apparatus Company, and International Radio Telephone Company. There were cross-licensing (pooling) agreements in 1919, 1920, and 1921 between GE, AT&T, Westinghouse, and their subsidiary RCA, which owned American Marconi's patents. By pooling their patents in RCA, the parent companies gave to RCA what none of them had, the ability to create a complete system. These firms sliced up the various radio-related markets among themselves: Westinghouse, GE, and RCA (the Radio Group) were authorized to sell receivers; AT&T and its subsidiary, Western Electric (the Telephone Group), controlled wire transmission and manufactured transmitters. Concerned about antitrust, AT&T sold its interest in RCA in 1923. In 1929 RCA purchased the Victor Talking Machine Company, which produced records. To settle an antitrust suit in 1930 GE and Westinghouse sold their stock in RCA.

For many years David Sarnoff and RCA were virtual synonyms. Sarnoff had begun his career at American Marconi as an office boy. Later, as a wireless operator, he gained fame and showed the importance of radio to shipping by picking up distress messages from the *Titanic*. He became president of RCA in 1930 and chairman of its board in 1947.

U.S. federal officials were dissatisfied with the near monopoly of radio by the British and moved to break it up. Subsequently, their concern turned to the U.S. monopoly their actions had created. RCA had expanded into practically every area of communications and electronics, and its extensive patent holdings gave it power over most competitors because these rivals were forced to pay royalties to use RCA patents; so, RCA's opponents could compete only if they were more efficient than RCA. Federal authorities were concerned that because none of RCA's numerous stockholders held a substantial portion of total shares, and because the firm had little debt, management was not answerable to any outsider.

RADIO GETS A VOICE

One of Marconi's competitors, Reginald Aubrey Fessenden, who formed the National Electric Signaling Company, had taught electrical engineering at the University of Pittsburgh and worked for Westinghouse. Unlike Marconi, who sent out an interrupted wave (Morse code) Fessenden sent out a continuous wave with the capacity to transmit music and voices. Fessenden's transmission on Christmas Eve 1906 was the first long-distance transmission of radio telephony and the birth of broadcasting (Head 1956, 103). That claim will be forever disputed by those who argue that Kentucky farmer Nathan B. Stubblefield previously broadcast a voice in a demonstration in 1892 (Hoffer 1975, 4). Fessenden sold equipment to the navy and to the United Fruit Company. United Fruit, which used the equipment to communicate with its plantations and ships, formed an equipment subsidiary. The subsidiary, which discovered that some crystals could detect radio waves and turn them into electric currents, specialized in "crystal detectors." Fessenden's company collapsed after a few years, and his patents were sold to Westinghouse (Barnouw 1990, 13).

Sir John Ambrose Fleming, a British consultant to Marconi, patented a two-element receiving tube in 1904 based on Thomas A. Edison's work. Called the Fleming valve, this electron tube controlled the flow of electricity as a water valve controls water and greatly amplified radio signals. Lee de Forest, a Yale Ph.D. whose first job was with Western Electric, improved on Fleming's device by adding a tube called the Audion (triode electron, or vacuum tube). It was the major component of a radio before the transistor was invented. De Forest also developed a method by which sound could be recorded on film in perfect synchronization with a moving picture.

The Audion's applications extended beyond radio, where it was used in generating, modulating, amplifying, and detecting radio energy. It was also important in the telephone industry, where it made possible coast-to-coast service for the first time via vacuum tube reamplifiers (repeaters). A specialized application of it is the television pickup and kinescope tubes. It also provided an amplification system for sound motion pictures.

In 1913 the American Marconi Company acquired the assets of de Forest's company, United Wireless, which went bankrupt after Marconi won a patent suit. This acquisition provided Marconi with a virtual monopoly on commercial wireless in America (Head 1956, 93).

Except during a World War I navy-decreed moratorium, when patent holders agreed to pool their patents, the first decades of radio were filled with litigation. In 1916 the courts ruled that de Forest had infringed on Fleming's patent on his valve and that the Marconi Company had infringed on de Forest's Audion. In 1934, after an expensive, twenty-year battle, the Supreme Court declared that de Forest, rather than Edwin Howard Armstrong, had invented the regenerative (feedback) circuit. AT&T brought an unsuccessful patent infringement suit against Armstrong over the superheterodyne circuit. The most controversial litigation was between four companies over the feedback circuit. (The vacuum tube was a basic component of a feedback circuit.) Twenty years later, in 1934, AT&T, which had purchased de Forest's patent on such a device, prevailed in the Supreme Court over General Electric, American Marconi, and the German Telefunken Company (Sivowitch 1975, 31, 101).

De Forest is credited with making the first news broadcast from High Bridge, New York, in 1906. His experimental station broadcast the returns of the Wilson-Hughes presidential election to a few amateur radio enthusiasts, signing off with the statement that Charles Evans Hughes would be the next president of the United States. In 1908 de Forest, who enjoyed music, broadcast phonograph music from the Eiffel Tower. In 1910 he broadcast the first opera, a low-quality broadcast of a Metropolitan opera featuring Enrico Caruso. In 1916 he set up an experimental radiotelephone station, broadcasting phonograph records and announcements. This was four years before a similar broadcast over an experimental station, KDKA (Pittsburgh), which is usually credited as having been the first regular broadcasting station (Sivowitch 1975, 102). Holder of more than 200 patents and considered by some to be the most imaginative inventor in the history of radio, de Forest fared poorly in business, for, unlike Marconi, he did not associate himself with men of sound business judgment (Maclaurin [1949, 87] 1971).

In 1919 Frank Conrad, a Westinghouse engineer, broadcast music in Pittsburgh. This breakthrough stimulated the sales of crystal sets and led to Westinghouse's creating KDKA on November 2, 1920. KDKA was the flagship of the Westinghouse Broadcasting Group (Group W). By providing an extremely simple and inexpensive rectifier of radio energy, the crystal set brought radio within reach of nearly everyone. A crystal set, which could be made at home, was composed of a tuning coil; a crystal detector; and a pair of earphones, the only component that cost more than a few cents. No battery or other electric source was required, as the crystal changed the high-frequency radio waves into weak electric currents made audible by the earphones. The sensitive spots on the crystal were located by the use of a "cat's whisker"—a thin piece of wire.

The invention that made broadcasting commercially feasible was the superheterodyne circuit invented by Armstrong (Maclaurin [1949, 103] 1971). It increased the sensitivity of receivers so much that an outdoor antenna was unnecessary. Patented in 1920, it was in general use by 1924.

Vying for dominance in broadcasting, the Telephone Group established WEAF. The Radio Group established WJZ. Each of these stations built up rival networks. AT&T licensed stations, charging them a fee to hook up to its long-distance lines, and it created the first broadcasting chain when it decided to give advertisers a discount on its stations.

KDKA began to broadcast prizefights and major league baseball in 1921. WEAF used telephone lines to broadcast the Chicago-Princeton football game from Stagg Field in 1922. In that year, too, it began selling advertising, scuttling plans for radio to be a nonprofit public service institution. Until the mid-1920s, a station's chief problem was keeping the station on the air.

While Conrad was creating KDKA, the *Detroit News* was operating what was to become WWJ. On August 20, 1920, it broadcast two records played on an Edison phonograph with a speaker horn directed toward a microphone connected to a de Forest transmitter. Soon stations were created by the *Kansas City Star, Milwaukee Journal, Chicago Tribune, Los Angeles Times, Louisville Courier-Journal, Atlanta Journal, Fort Worth Star-Telegram, Dallas News*, and *Chicago Daily News*. Such pioneer stations were more interested in entertaining the public than in providing news, which was simply gleaned from newspapers.

THE CREATION OF THE NETWORKS

According to AT&T's interpretation of cross-licensing agreements, the Radio Group—GE, Westinghouse, and their subsidiary, RCA—was barred from operating radio stations for profit. The Radio Group could not sell time to advertisers, and because AT&T refused access to its lines, the group's network had to depend on the inferior services of Western Union.

The Radio Group's rationale was to stimulate sales of the radio equipment it manufactured. The dominant Telephone Group's rationale was different. AT&T and its subsidiary, Western Electric, saw broadcasting as one-way telephony. Like its telephone service, AT&T's stations existed to provide others a facility for communicating. Broadcasting was the responsibility of AT&T's long-lines department, and advertising was called toll broadcasting. The first national radio advertising began in 1924, when Eveready Battery Company bought time on twelve stations. In contrast to the Radio Group, the Telephone Group left programming to others. By 1929 AT&T had made a national network possible by spanning the nation with radio lines.

By 1925 the chain headed by New York's WEAF (now WNBC) had twenty-six outlets stretching as far west as Kansas City. But broadcasting had taken AT&T away from its primary business, and its refusal to make its telephone lines available to rivals and its insistence on exclusive control of broadcast transmitters were bad for public relations. So in July 1926 AT&T agreed to get out of broadcasting in exchange for control of all forms of network relays. Broadcasting was reserved to RCA, and although RCA was permitted to compete with Western Electric in manufacturing transmitters, Western Electric was barred from manufacturing radio receivers.

RCA agreed to cease using the services of Western Union and to lease radio relay facilities from AT&T. AT&T agreed to sell WEAF to the Radio Group and was barred from reentering broadcasting without penalty. The previous May, AT&T had incorporated a subsidiary named the Broadcasting Company of America and transferred to it WEAF and its network operations. AT&T transferred it—as of November 1, 1926—to RCA for $1 million.

On September 26, 1926, RCA formed the National Broadcasting Company (NBC) to take over its network broadcasting business, including the properties acquired from AT&T. Sarnoff's RCA dominated the industry. Sarnoff anticipated the end of radio's novelty and a shift in public interest away from how broadcasts were received to the broadcasts themselves. Then "the task of reasonably meeting the public's expectations and desires will be greater than any so far tackled by any newspaper, theater, opera, or other public information or entertainment agency" (Archer 1939, 30–31).

Featuring humorist Will Rogers and the vaudeville team of Joe Weber and Lew Fields, NBC began broadcasting on November 15, 1926. RCA owned 50 percent of NBC's stock, GE 30 percent, and Westinghouse 20 percent. The Telephone Group's former chain became NBC's Red Network, and the Radio Group's chain became the Blue Network. Coast-to-coast network operations began in 1927.

In early 1927 only 7 percent of the nation's 737 stations were affiliated with NBC. In that year, a rival network, United Independent Broadcasters, was created by a talent-booking agent. The name was changed by an investment from a record company, and the new network became the Columbia Phonograph Broadcasting System, then Columbia Broadcasting System, and then CBS Inc. In 1928 Columbia was purchased and reorganized by a cigar company executive, William S. Paley. Paley's tenure with CBS ran well past a half century. In 1929 CBS showed a profit, and by 1934 it had 97 stations. NBC had 65 Red and 62 Blue stations. In 1938 CBS purchased the Columbia Record Company.

The *Chicago Tribune*'s WGN combined with other stations to form in 1934 the Mutual Broadcasting System. Unlike the big three networks, Mutual did not move into television. The Mutual network comprised four stations, two of which were clear channel stations. When Mutual encountered what it regarded as unfair competition, it filed a complaint with the Federal Communications Commission and thereby precipitated the sale by NBC of its weaker Blue Network to Edward J. Noble in 1943. The Blue was renamed the American Broadcasting Network (ABC) in 1945. Financially troubled Mutual was purchased by Amway Corporation in 1977.

NBC comedian Ed Wynn, vowing to bring theater to radio and limit commercials, in 1933 created the Amalgamated Broadcasting System. Despite its quick failure from lack of advertising revenues, by March 1934 plans existed for four additional networks. George Storer's group, called the American Broadcasting System, began broadcasts without advertisers in October 1934 on fourteen stations from New York to St. Louis. The network, but not its stations, failed in 1935.

Although 9 out of 10 radio stations were selling advertising time by 1930, in 1925 many owners' motive for running a station had been simply to advertise their businesses or generate publicity. In 1922 few stations sold advertisements. About a quarter of the nation's 500 stations were owned by radio-related firms. Another quarter were owned by manufacturers, retailers, and other firms, such as hotels and newspapers. Educational institutions, radio clubs, and civic groups and church, government, and military interests owned 40 percent of the stations. In 1939 more than a third of the nation's radio stations were running in the red. During World War II, an excess profits tax encouraged firms to spend money. Radio advertising nearly doubled, and by the end of the war, only 5 percent were in the red (Lichty and Topping 1975, 195–201).

Instead of making spot announcements, as they later did on television, radio advertisers sponsored entire shows. To avoid the high cost of production, local radio stations got most of their shows, other than news, from the networks—networks enjoyed economies of scale in production because their costs could be spread over the many stations airing their programming. Stations' revenues came from national and local advertisers. Their chief expense was personnel. The networks served as a distribution system for advertisements. Advertisers wishing to reach a national audience saved money by going to the networks instead of to hundreds of stations. A network affiliate was not bound to carry all network programming.

Radio's voracious appetite for broadcast material made it difficult for a station to pass up network affiliation, and by 1938, 40 percent of the 660 stations then in operation were network-affiliated. Because many non-network stations were low-power, part-time operations, 98 percent of prime nighttime programming was provided by network-affiliated stations (Federal Communications Commission 1941, 31). Network-owned stations were mostly located in the largest markets.

GOVERNMENT REGULATION

Government regulation of broadcasting began in 1904, when President Theodore Roosevelt organized the Interdepartmental Board of Wireless Telegraphy. The first radio legislation was the 1910 Wireless Ship Act, which required that all large ships have radios and operators. The impetus behind the Radio Act of 1912 was the government's desire to know who owned and controlled two-way communication equipment so that control of it could be gained in wartime. It mandated that a license must be obtained from the government in order to operate a transmitter. While the separation of frequencies was provided for, this was left more to operators than to the government. The number of stations that could be licensed by the secretary of commerce and labor was not limited. Eventually, a large number of stations, because they varied their frequencies and power, interfered— sometimes deliberately—with each other.

Industry representatives sought government aid in clearing up frequency-chaos. The Radio Act of 1927 solved the problem and helped the networks by reducing the number of stations permitted to broadcast. Under its authority, the Federal Radio Commission authorized fifty powerful, clear-channel stations. Stations on the same frequency as one of the authorized clear channels were not allowed to broadcast at night. Clear channels were supposed to allow some urban stations to reach distant rural areas that had no radio stations. Notwithstanding, broadcasters in small cities where a clear-channel station could be picked up opposed the creation and continued existence of clear-channel competition. By 1938 all but two of the clear-channel stations were either owned by, or affiliated with, a network. Because AM (amplitude modulation) stations were held to a maximum of 50,000 watts, their range and thus the size of their markets were limited— profitability is dependent on market size.

The Radio Act of 1927 established that radio waves were public property and that service must be equitably distributed. Broadcasting, though similar in some respects to other media, was said to be unique. Not everyone is entitled to use a channel; thus, only some of those who meet certain requirements would be granted licenses to use them. The act did declare, however, that radio is a form of expression protected by the First Amendment. The 1927 law also established the Federal Radio Commission with five members appointed by the president; a system of call letters; a systematic method of license renewal and equipment modification; and qualifications for station operators. It gave the government the power to revoke licenses, inspect station apparatus, and assign frequency power limits. It retained the 1912 act's provisions for ships.

The Communications Act of 1934 identified broadcasting as a separate entity apart from utilities and transportation and consolidated government authority over both wire and wireless communications systems. Like the

Radio Act of 1927, it expressed an intent to preserve competition. The 1934 legislation replaced the Federal Radio Commission with the Federal Communications Commission (FCC).

In 1941, in the *Mayflower* decision (the Mayflower Company owned WAAB), the Supreme Court outlawed broadcast editorials. However, it reversed this decision in 1949, creating what is called the *fairness doctrine*, which required that both sides of an issue be aired. The FCC required that controversial news and public affairs programs be broadcast and that individuals and organizations be given airtime to respond to editorials and commercials. To some congressmen's dismay, in 1987 the FCC voted to eliminate the fairness doctrine.

TELEVISION

"Television must stand as one of the least surprising inventions in human history," because, within only a few years of Bell's introduction of the telephone, popular artists were depicting its use in "everything from inter-office communication to coverage of foreign wars" (Greenfield 1977, 31). Television's roots, however, reach beyond Bell's day to 1839, when French physicist Alexandre Edmond Becquerel observed the electrochemical effects of light.

In 1842 Scotsman Alexander Bain proposed a facsimile device. Five years later an Englishman, F. C. Bakewell, constructed a copying telegraph that employed synchronous sequential scanning, which is the basis of analog television systems. In 1862 in France, Abbe Giacomo Caselli sent the first picture by wire over a long distance and operated stations that sent and received messages in handwriting. In 1877 a French physician, M. Senlecq, invented a "Telectroscope," which transmitted projected images. In 1884 a German scientist, Paul G. Nipkow, passed a turning disc with a spiral of holes in it over a picture to create a scanning effect. The light that came through each hole would be converted into electrical energy and transmitted to a receiver with a synchronized disc. In this way a crude picture with—as is the case with all motion pictures—a semblance of motion was achieved when the picture being scanned was changed rapidly.

By the 1920s crude pictures could be reproduced with high-intensity lighting. Maurice Leblanc developed a scanning method used in several mechanical television systems in the 1920s that was rivaled for simplicity only by Nipkow's device. In 1904 two Germans, Frankenstein and Jaworski, described a system for mechanical color television. Two Frenchmen, Rignoux and Fournier, devised a process that was the reverse of Nipkow's.

Not until January 27, 1926, were true television pictures sent by wire in a public demonstration by John Logie Baird of Great Britain. The quality of his mechanically produced pictures, however, was poor. In the 1930s his system was tested over radio wavelengths by the BBC. His financial backers ultimately decided that mechanical television could not survive without a higher-quality picture. In the United States, Charles Francis Jenkins' plans to produce sets and programming by 1930 were undone by the 1929 stock market crash (Lichty and Topping 1975, 47–51).

Mechanical television reappeared in the 1940s, when both CBS and RCA developed color systems. CBS's system utilized a spinning, three-color disc in front of a normal electronic scanner. In 1950 the FCC adopted the CBS system, but because it was mechanical and not compatible with existing monochrome standards—thus necessitating two systems—the industry was not willing to adopt it. An unsuccessful suit by RCA and the Korean War put color television on hold, and, faced with RCA, General Electric, Philco, Sylvania, Motorola, and even CBS planning to petition it to reconsider, on December 17, 1953, the FCC reversed itself and adopted RCA's system.

The foundation for electronic television was laid in 1907, when a Russian, Boris Rosing, built a cathode-ray tube. In 1908 A. A. Campbell-Swinton pretty much described an all-electronic system like the one Vladimir K. Zworykin would build in the 1930s. The breakthrough into electronic television was made by Zworykin, a Russian immigrant to the United States, and the American Philo Farnsworth. Zworykin, who had been Rosing's student and had worked for Westinghouse before transferring to RCA when it took over radio research, developed the iconoscope, a television pickup tube patented in 1923. He also invented the kinescope. The iconoscope was used for transmission, and the kinescope for reception.

In 1922, as a high school student, Farnsworth had outlined a scheme of electronic television. As an adult, Farnsworth, with his dissector tube, was RCA's strongest rival in the race to produce a commercially viable electronic television system. Ultimately, Farnsworth, who was financed by, among others, Philco, had more than 150 patents related to television, and in 1939 RCA capitulated and paid him royalties for the use of his technology.

Allen B. DuMont, who worked for Westinghouse in the 1920s, became interested in mechanical television while working for de Forest. DuMont contributed to the development of electronic television through his work on the cathode-ray tube and on synchronization techniques. In 1939 his company was the first to offer electronic sets to the public. Paramount Pictures, which was to merge with ABC in 1953, provided some of DuMont's financial backing. In 1944 he got his experimental television station licensed as WABD, and two years later he started the DuMont Television Network, which was the first to own an ultrahigh frequency (UHF) outlet. He was unable to make the network profitable and sold out to Metropolitan Broadcasting Company (Metromedia) in 1955.

In 1928 GE started the first experimental television station, WGY, in Schenectady, New York. In 1935 its signal range was only twenty-five miles, and passing planes and automobile ignitions caused static. By 1937 there were seventeen stations on the air. RCA's Sarnoff announced in 1938 that television sets would go on sale to the public when the World's Fair opened in New York in 1939.

In 1935 O. H. Caldwell, editor of *Electronics* magazine and former member of the Federal Radio Commission, asserted that the only thing holding back the development of television was money (*Broadcasting Magazine* 1982, 23). Some, however, were placing their bets on facsimile—the transmission to homes of fixed images on treated paper, which would enable advertisers to show the public their products. Some foresaw newspapers being delivered in this way by radio.

Coaxial cable, developed by AT&T for other purposes, made it possible for television stations to be hooked together into a network to broadcast special events, which is what they did for the opening of the New York World's Fair, the nominating conventions, and baseball and football games. AT&T enjoyed a near monopoly in the provision of television relay service. AT&T's dominance in the provision of this service was threatened by RCA's work on a radio relay system.

On an experimental basis, the first television network began on January 1, 1940. In 1941 the FCC approved a commercial license for the *Milwaukee Journal*'s station. Within a year nine more stations were licensed, but in 1942 the war caused the FCC to put a freeze on television's development, and it ceased to award licenses and halted the production of television receivers. Only six of the original ten stations survived the war. After the war, television grew rapidly. During 1948 the number of stations rose from seventeen to forty-one, and the number of cities with stations rose from eight to twenty-three. Beginning in 1947, radio set production and earnings declined.

DIVISION OF THE SPECTRUM

The Davis Amendment to the Communications Act required that stations be allocated among five radio zones under a quota system. This amendment was repealed on June 5, 1935. Thus, the FCC was empowered to license stations according to technical feasibility rather than population. "The FCC's allocations hearings stirred uneasiness among some broadcasters. To many, heavily invested in AM radio, FM loomed as an investment-devouring prospect of monstrous proportions" (*Broadcasting Magazine* 1982, 28).

Frequency modulation (FM) was invented in 1933 by Armstrong. Armstrong and John Bose in 1945 patented multiplexing, which allows one FM transmitting source to put out several signals at the same time over the same frequency. RCA, which had originally worked with Armstrong, who owned stock in RCA, lost interest in FM before World War II. FM development was frozen by the war and discouraged by the emergence of television. In 1945 FM development suffered another blow when the FCC moved FM to another part of the spectrum, which made existing FM receivers obsolete. The reason for this change was to open up more space for television. By 1950 there were 743 FM stations, a figure not exceeded for the next decade. Interest in FM increased in the 1970s because most AM frequencies had been taken, but many FM frequencies were still available. The development of stereo FM gave the medium another boost.

The shift of FM to higher frequencies provided for thirteen commercial, very high frequency (VHF) television channels. In 1948 channel 1, once assigned to FM, was assigned to nonbroadcast services, and channel allocations were frozen while the problem of possible interference and color television were studied. The freeze was not lifted until 1952, when a large slice of the spectrum was set aside for ultrahigh frequency (UHF) television. Of the 100 FM bands 20 were set aside for educational users. Since UHF stations could not stay on the air if people's sets could not pick up UHF signals, and consumers showed little interest in spending the money necessary to alter their sets to pick up UHF, the FCC required, starting in 1964, that all new sets have the capability to receive UHF signals.

Amplitude modulation (AM) refers to varying the amplitude of the radio wave to conform to the amplitude of the sounds broadcast. In contrast to AM, where the amplitude varies with the sounds transmitted, frequency modulation (FM) varies the frequency of the radio wave. Because atmospheric conditions affect amplitude, they do not create noise on FM broadcasts as they do on AM broadcasts. Thus, FM broadcasting is the better choice when sound quality is important. FM stations are allowed a wider band of frequencies, and this makes possible high-fidelity broadcasting. It also makes possible stereo broadcasting or the broadcasting of more than one program. Because FM is at higher frequencies than AM, FM travels in a straight line. There is no reflecting of FM waves back to Earth as is the case for AM; thus, FM waves do not travel as far.

UHF television is less subject than AM radio to static and less prone than VHF to "ghosts," reflected signals that cause receivers to pick up multiple images. However, UHF signals can be cut off by buildings and other obstructions that do not cut off VHF signals, and UHF signals must be stronger and receivers more sensitive.

Domestically, the FCC is responsible for allocating frequencies and preventing stations from interfering with one another. On the international level, this is the responsibility of a United Nations organization, the International Telecommunications Union (ITU).

RADIO'S GOLDEN AGE

In 1931 there were 608 radio stations serving 12 million of the nation's 30 million households. This was 570 more stations than there had been in

1921, but more than 100 fewer than in 1927, when the Radio Act had restored order to the radio spectrum. Radio editors reported that the most popular radio personalities were dance orchestra leaders Guy Lombardo and Paul Whiteman and singers Morton Downey, Bing Crosby, Rudy Vallee, Kate Smith, Ruth Etting, and Mildred Bailey (*Broadcasting Magazine* 1982, 4).

In 1932 the U.S. Senate, in the Couzens-Dill resolution, addressed advertising on radio and the feasibility of government ownership and operation of broadcasting facilities. The National Congress of Parents and Teachers and the National Committee on Education by Radio opposed the "American plan" (commercial) of broadcasting because it bypassed parents to influence children. Conflict begun earlier with the American Society of Composers, Authors and Publishers (ASCAP) continued to rage. A report that the manufacturer of Philco radios, Farnsworth, was conducting experiments with his new cathode-ray system of television apparently generated less concern than did issues such as the blame some newspapermen were placing on radio for their loss of advertising revenue and the fact that ASCAP was negotiating an increase in its royalties.

A CBS executive claimed that "Danger Number One lurks in Washington, in the form of congressional encroachment on the functions of the Federal Radio Commission" (*Broadcasting Magazine* 1982, 4). In Washington there were complaints of too much commercialism, monopoly in the radio industry, the domination of radio by the networks, newspaper ownership of stations, concentration of radio manufacturing, and widespread trafficking in broadcast licenses. Another complaint was that American-owned stations were serving the American market with powerful stations located in Cuba and Mexico. Supporters of educational radio, disturbed over the decline in the number of educational stations from ninety-five to thirty-nine since 1927, were opposing commercial broadcasting and demanding that more wavelengths be devoted to educational radio.

"The sporadic sniping of newspapers at radio broke into wide open warfare in 1933." One newspaper attacked commercial radio as being "venal, boorish, corrupt, tiresome" (*Broadcasting Magazine* 1982, 11). Joining in the attack on radio were ASCAP and the film industry, both of which blamed radio for their declining revenues. Radio people blamed poor revenues on the depression. Though they were to change their minds twenty years later, in the 1930s record producers, singers, and musicians feared that broadcasting their work would hurt record sales, and performers with shows on one network feared that their relationship would be damaged if their work was broadcast on another network.

Radio did not take these attacks lightly. On August 30, 1934, a suit encouraged by broadcasters was filed by the Department of Justice, which asked for the dissolution of ASCAP as an illegal monopoly under the Sherman Antitrust Act. Faced with this and a rival organization organized by broadcasters, ASCAP reduced its demands. Later, broadcasters were helped when, in 1940, a U.S. Court of Appeals ruled that when a broadcaster bought a record, he could do anything he wished with it.

Though early radio stations did not emphasize news, newspapers recognized radio's threat as a news competitor. The Associated Press (AP) in 1922 warned its members against broadcasting news it provided. Enforcement became difficult because so many stations were owned by newspapers, and the AP relaxed its position in 1925.

In 1930 NBC began offering a nightly news show featuring Lowell Thomas. Newspapers were becoming alarmed about being scooped by radio. An important story where radio got the scoop was the kidnapping of the Charles Lindbergh baby. In April 1933 the majority of the newspapers composing the AP voted to stop furnishing news to the networks, and stations owned by newspapers were required to pay an extra fee. The other two press associations, UP and INS, joined the boycott, so radio had to gather its own news or pirate it from early editions of newspapers, a practice AP sued to stop. Rising to the challenge, CBS formed the Columbia News Service, purchased the Dow-Jones ticker service, and set up news bureaus.

A compromise was reached in 1934. In exchange for the networks' ceasing to gather news, a Press-Radio Bureau would be formed that would present two five-minute newscasts daily on the networks from news supplied by the press associations. Bulletins covering extraordinary events would also be provided. Radio stations, however, wanted more news than this allowed for, and they started buying it from news agencies that quickly sprang up and came to eclipse the Press-Radio Bureau. Then UP and INS obtained releases from the Press-Radio Bureau agreement and began selling full news reports to radio stations. The AP then relaxed its position. In late 1934 radio won a victory when a federal judge ruled that once news had appeared in a newspaper, it could be broadcast without restriction. The Press-Radio Bureau stopped functioning in 1940, and newspapers resigned themselves to not being able to scoop radio.

In 1934, 60 percent of America's households had radios, and 1.5 million cars were equipped with radios. That year RCA recorded a first-quarter profit of $1,235,725 (a year earlier it had lost $478,164). CBS grossed $7,872,000, a 67 percent increase over the same period in 1933, and NBC grossed $13,599,354, a 34 percent increase—for the year, the two networks grossed $42,800,000. Radio that year earned 12.2¢ out of every dollar spent on advertising. However, some advertising money was turned away; for example, in 1935 NBC, CBS, and some independent stations refused to renew laxative accounts after the FCC sent out citations about commercials it deemed not in good taste.

NBC signed up Eddie Cantor and Al Jolson in the 1920s. During the 1930s radio mined vaudeville for stars and became a major source of entertainment for the nation. From vaudeville, which was destroyed, radio acquired the services of Fred Allen, Jack Benny, Edgar Bergen and Charlie McCarthy, George Burns and Gracie Allen, Bing Crosby, Jimmy Durante, Bob Hope, Groucho Marx, Fibber McGee and Molly, Red Skelton, Rudy Vallee, and Ed Wynn.

Few families missed two white men pretending to be blacks on *Amos 'n' Andy*. Serial dramas were introduced: radio's notable contribution to the "art of fiction" was the soap opera (Seldes [1950] 1970, 113). The so-called soaps began as short soap commercials with a touch of entertainment. Soaps were for Mom in the middle of the day; in the late afternoon, just before dinnertime, mystery and adventure shows were broadcast for children; and at night, variety shows, comedy, drama, mystery, and music entertained the whole family.

The Wagner Act of 1935 encouraged the organization of radio workers—in 1937 the American Guild of Radio Announcers and Producers was organized at CBS. Jurisdictional disputes were frequent. NBC and CBS agreed to a forty-hour week for their engineers. The American Federation of Musicians threatened a national strike unless stations employed more live musicians. A compromise was reached by network affiliates agreeing to spend $1.5 million more on staff musicians.

In 1938, fifty of fifty-two clear-channel stations were network affiliates. The networks' gross time sales rose 4 percent, the smallest gain since records had been kept. Ventriloquist Edgar Bergen and Charlie McCarthy's *Chase and Sanborn Hour* was the most popular show—the FCC was scandalized when stripper Mae West said Charlie, a dummy, had kissed her. Orson Welles' staging of an invasion from Mars on the *Mercury Theater of the Air* panicked some CBS listeners.

When Adolf Hitler's forces marched into Austria, it was reported by CBS, NBC, and Mutual by shortwave. CBS's H. V. Kaltenborn broadcast over a portable transmitter hidden in a haystack between Loyalist and Rebel forces to give listeners a firsthand account of action during the Spanish civil war. Radio brought Americans both the stirring oratory of Winston Churchill and the fiery demagoguery of Hitler, which was translated by anti-Nazi Kaltenborn. Kaltenborn, Boake Carter, Lowell Thomas, Edwin C. Hill, and Gabriel Heatter were the most popular news commentators. In 1937 CBS sent Edward R. Murrow, who was then an unknown, to Europe as its news chief. On March 12, 1938, Murrow in Vienna, his assistant, William L. Shirer in London, and newspapermen in Berlin, Paris, and Rome made the first multiple-pickup news broadcast. Murrow, who went on to become the nation's best-known news commentator, brought the war into the nation's living rooms with his "*This Is London*" broadcasts. George Hicks of ABC recorded a D-Day broadcast from a landing craft under fire.

News of Pearl Harbor first reached the nation by radio. The next day a record audience listened to President Franklin Roosevelt's message to Congress. NBC devoted less than 3 percent of its programming to news in 1937. By 1944 more than a quarter of its programming was news.

Variety shows were the most popular entertainment during the war, but the leading programs were news shows such as Lowell Thomas's *March of Time*, and Mutual's Heatter and Walter Winchell, whose reports were accompanied by the sound of a telegraph key. Radio's revenues more than doubled between the recession year of 1937 and 1945. In October 1945 there were 909 licensed commercial AM stations. Sixteen months later there were about 600 more stations either on the air or under construction.

In the mid-1940s CBS challenged NBC, by then shorn of its Blue Network, for the number one position. CBS's strategy was to delay the coming of television until it could gain the lead in programming. As part of this strategy, in 1948 it raided NBC for talent and succeeded in luring away Amos 'n' Andy (Charles Correll and Freeman Gosden), Jack Benny, Burns and Allen, Edgar Bergen, and Bing Crosby (Head 1956, 144). All of these performers abandoned radio for television.

THE TRIUMPH OF TELEVISION

Television made its breakthrough in 1948, the year when the value of national radio's time sales reached an all-time high. The transistor, which was to replace vacuum tubes, was developed. By 1948, too, RCA had developed the image-orthicon camera, which enhanced the possibility of using live pickups, and AT&T was extending the coaxial cable system, which preceded the microwave relay system later used for transcontinental broadcasting.

After 1947 radio had more revenue from local advertisers than network advertisers. In 1951 a transcontinental microwave relay was completed, and NBC broadcast the first regular, coast-to-coast, sponsored program, the *NBC Comedy Hour*. By then, Edward R. Murrow had moved from *Hear It Now* to *See It Now*. Television's first great star was NBC's Milton Berle, a seasoned comedian. In 1952 NBC created the first morning show, the *Today* show. By 1953 NBC and CBS were well along in switching their emphasis from radio to television. The 1953 Army-McCarthy hearings attracted a huge audience.

By 1955 television had surpassed radio and magazines in total advertising revenues. Television became the nation's number one advertising medium in 1956, although, due to their heavy local advertising, newspapers led in total advertising revenues. In 1959 half the shows were westerns like *Gunsmoke*. In the late 1950s a quiz show fad quickly faded when it was revealed that contestants were coached.

Walter Cronkite replaced Douglas Edwards, who had begun his career on radio, as CBS's star newsman. NBC's top stars were newscasters Chet Huntley and David Brinkley. In 1968 the still-running documentary *60*

Minutes began and soon attracted imitators. After 1965 television brought front-line war scenes from Vietnam into American homes, helping, many believed, fan antiwar sentiment.

In 1952 the Ford Foundation created the Educational Television and Radio Center, later renamed National Educational Television. Its function was producing programming. The first noncommercial, educationally licensed television station, KUHT in Texas at the University of Houston, went on the air in 1953. In 1967 the Public Broadcasting Act allocated funds for improving existing noncommercial stations and for building new ones and created the Corporation for Public Broadcasting, a quasi-governmental agency, to administer funds allocated to public broadcasting. Throughout its history public broadcasting has been largely dependent on audience contributions, grants from foundations and corporations, and government appropriations.

The number of AM and FM radio stations continued to rise after television displaced radio as the prime broadcast medium. Radio owed its survival to its low cost of reaching select audiences and to captive automobile listeners. The citizens band radio fad of the 1970s introduced competition for the automobile-bound audience that was taken up by audiotape players in the 1980s and compact disc players and cellular telephones in the 1990s. Color television monitors threaten to capture the attention of automobile passengers (sans driver) in the early years of the twenty-first century. Most of radio's post-television revenues came from local advertisers. The smallest share came from national network advertisers. The reverse was true of television stations.

Once filled with drama and comedy, by the 1950s radio had became a purveyor of news and music. Once dominated by network programming, radio switched to mostly independently produced material. Early radio was composed of live entertainment. Post-television radio was mostly taped. Prime time has moved to drive time, that is, early in the morning and late in the afternoon, when people are driving to and from work. Only in emergencies and power failures is radio a prime source of news. As low-wattage television sets operated on long-lasting batteries become less expensive and more popular, radio's emergency role will diminish. After an FCC ruling in 1967, the programming on half the FM stations in cities of 100,000 or more could not duplicate AM programming.

In 1959 radio was rocked by a payola scandal. Record companies had discovered that, to be highly successful, a record must get a lot of airtime; thus, they were paying disc jockeys to play their records. The payola and television quiz scandals led to amendments to the Communications Act of 1960 that require broadcasters to let their audiences know if they have taken payment in return for broadcasting material.

As a result of the payola scandal, stations quit letting disc jockeys choose what records were to be played; instead, station managers established their own programming to target chosen subsets of the population. Rather than focusing on music, a few stations became all talk. Phone-in talk shows were introduced in the 1970s. The typical station began depending on the wire services for news, which they provided in five-minute summaries. In the 1960s the FCC restricted one owner to seven AM, seven FM, and seven television stations, of which a maximum of five could be VHF, and prohibited ownership of CATV (community antenna) and television stations in the same market. Grandfathering in those exceeding the new maximum, in the top fifty markets three became the maximum number of such stations one person could own.

Satellite news gathering began just after World War II, when Westinghouse introduced Stratovision. Live television pictures were relayed 250 miles by bouncing them off airborne microwave equipment aboard a Constellation airplane. The first use of a satellite news vehicle (hauled by a tractor cab) took place during a vacation trip to Wyoming by President Jimmy Carter. Western Telecommunications Inc. used it to provide pool coverage of his trip for all three networks (Wold 1988).

The most important technological feat of the 1960s was news via Earth-orbiting satellites. AT&T's Telstar satellite was lunched on July 10, 1962. It permitted, for the first time, live transmissions between the United States and Europe. In 1963 the federally chartered Communications Satellite Corporation (COMSAT) was founded. Howard Hughes launched a satellite in 1964 with a synchronous orbit (positioned constantly over one point on Earth). In 1965 COMSAT put up the Early Bird satellite in synchronous orbit. This was followed by several launchings of Intelsat satellites. On July 1969 there was direct transmission from space of man's first steps on the moon.

A televised debate was a key element in the victory of John F. Kennedy over Richard Nixon for the presidency of the United States in 1960. An estimated 135 million people saw John Glenn's first manned orbital flight in 1962. The nation watched Jack Ruby on a live 1963 NBC pickup rushing forward to shoot and kill Lee Harvey Oswald, the alleged killer of President Kennedy. Lucille Ball's popular, long-running show, I Love Lucy, generated controversy when she appeared onscreen, in character, while obviously pregnant.

America's first superstation was begun by Ted Turner, who got into television in 1970, when he bought WTCG (now WTBS), a UHF station in Atlanta, Georgia. Turner was forced to learn about cable television because it was the only way many people could pick up his station without installing a special antenna. He discovered that cable offered a station the means to broadcast by satellite to cable systems across the country, and in 1976 he began doing this. Subsequently, he founded the Cable News Network (CNN). In 1988 WTBS and CNN were the second and third most popular cable channels.

Stations all across the country were soon complaining that programs they produced and aired were being picked up from WTBS via satellite and shown on local cable systems. To stop Turner, they wanted the FCC to reintroduce a recently abandoned rule known as syndex, which guaranteed exclusivity in its area to a station that had purchased a syndicated program. To lock in a source of programming, Turner tried to strike a friendly deal with the networks or Hollywood. Failing to do so, he mounted an unsuccessful hostile takeover of CBS. Then he purchased MGM/UA, ultimately selling all of it but its huge film library (Blair 1988). Turner's next move was in 1988, when he launched the Turner Network Television (TNT), enticing cable-system operators with an unprecedented four minutes an hour of local advertising (Mandese 1988).

THE COMPETITIVE ERA

Starting in the late 1970s, a belief that extensive government regulation was holding back the economy swept Washington. The resulting deregulation movement continued throughout the eight years of Ronald Reagan's presidency. Critics had long claimed that the supposed goals of FCC regulation were largely mythical. It was decided that the FCC's simply keeping the industry competitive might be a better way to regulate. Many of the changes in broadcasting experienced during the 1980s were the result of the FCC's reduced regulation.

Deregulation of television station ownership limits led many to attempt to build a network of independent television stations (Tell 1986). Independent television stations' audience share grew from 9 percent in 1972 to 21 percent in 1982. Their growth was attributed to several factors: the FCC's 1962 mandate that receivers be able to pick up UHF, its prime-time access rule, its rule banning networks from investing in programming or ownership of syndication rights, the wider coverage and better reception of cable television, and the improved quality of the syndicated programming that is so vital to the independents (Weisberg 1984).

Demand for syndicated programs was created by the FCC's 1971 prime-time access rule, which forced network affiliates to carry one half-hour of non-network in the evening (Schleier 1985). The FCC expected the requirement to stimulate local station productions that might well be innovative and superior to network alternatives. But stations turned to syndicated network shows and similar programs. The FCC also forbade the networks from engaging in domestic syndication of their own programs. By the 1980s advertisers had come to see syndicated shows, many of which were, due to a shortage of reruns, original programs, as an alternative to network shows (Rosenfeld 1986).

In the late 1970s the market share of the by then more evenly matched major networks—NBC, CBS, and ABC—began eroding. They experienced a 9 percent plunge in the 1987–1988 season alone, as viewers turned to alternatives such as cable television; Fox Broadcasting, a new, fourth network created by an international newspaper magnate known for his tabloids, Rupert Murdoch; and local, independent stations, which were providing live, syndicated specials and first-run series in prime time (Mahoney and Buckman 1988).

The networks attributed the decline in the ratings of their nightly news shows to the expansion of local affiliates' own news programs. Whereas in the past the news—perhaps enlivened by film clips—had been reported from the station, by the 1980s minicameras and microwave dishes had made it possible to report events live.

The FCC followed an open skies policy in the 1970s for satellite communications. It allowed any U.S. firm to launch and operate domestic satellites so long as minimum criteria were met. In the 1980s the FCC began a policy of deregulation of domestic satellite communications (Stoddard 1987). The International Telecommunications Satellite Organization (INTELSAT)—the largest nonprofit satellite cooperative—was disturbed by the American promotion of competition in the satellite field (Casatelli 1986). Starting in 1978, when the FCC began opening up the microwave spectrum, a like policy was followed for microwave communication. Owing to a fall in their price, the number of satellite dishes became so large that a significant number of households were receiving cable companies' programming without paying. This made necessary the scrambling of signals.

Starting in 1986, the FCC permitted citizens groups to participate in the broadcast licensing process. To keep groups from opposing their being granted a license, broadcasters began reaching agreements with them. As a result, the FCC proposed to outlaw the exchange of money for not pressing a petition (Burden 1987).

As Table 1 illustrates, by the 1980s on-the-air television was being challenged by cable and videocassette recorders (VCRs), both of which were growing at extraordinary rates.

By the 1980s foreign manufacturers had taken over the receiver and VCR markets. There was concern because Japan had a lead in the development of high-definition television. Homosexuality and other sexual deviations, nudity, explicit seductions, daring innuendos, profanity, and gutter language had become common themes in network programming, and material available on cassette tape and cable was even more explicit. Reduced federal funding for public television stations caused them to start accepting a few low-key advertisers. Scandalous personal behavior by some slashed the take of television evangelists, and television, which once had vainly sought major movie stars, was exporting television stars to the movies. Miniseries became very popular and expensive.

Table 1
Percentage of American Households with Radio Sets, Television Sets, Cable
Television, and VCRs, 1950–1987

% Households with	1950	1960	1970	1980	1987
Radio Sets	92.6	96.3	98.6	99.0	99.0
TV Sets	9.0	87.0	95.0	98.0	98.0
Cable TV				19.8	48.7
VCRs				1.1	48.7

Source: U.S. Bureau of the Census, Statistical Abstract of the United States, 1988 (Washington, DC: U.S. Government Printing Office, 1987), 523.

In 1984 the Bell System was broken up, exposing AT&T to competition from independents, like GTE, and its former operating companies, called the Baby Bells. By the late 1980s these companies offered a wide array of services utilizing fiber optics, a technology that apparently would not much longer suffer a cost disadvantage to copper cable, and the Baby Bells were agitating to be allowed to offer cable television to their telephone subscribers via fiberoptic cables. In January 1987 ABC saved 30 percent by moving its transmissions for *Nightline* from microwave links to an AT&T digital fiberoptic cable facility. However, the networks still primarily depended on analog satellite links. One reason was the cost of converting video and audio signals to the digital form necessary for fiberoptic transmission (Kemezis 1987).

Fiber optics is superior to copper cable because it resists magnetic interference, lasts fifty years, never corrodes, and carries many times more information (Slutsker 1988). Security and immunity to electromagnetic and atmospheric noise give fiber optics a competitive advantage over satellite communication; however, satellites offer advantages in reaching scattered or remote locations (Welter 1987).

In 1985 CBS recapitalized itself as a defense against the hostile junk bond-financed takeover bid by Turner Broadcasting System. A massive restructuring saw it sell off its holdings in such areas as toys, recordings, and software. ABC was sold in January 1986 to Capital Cities Television Corporation for $3,375 million, and in June GE reacquired RCA and its NBC subsidiary for $6.4 billion.

In *Quincy Cable TV v. FCC*, the Court rejected the scarcity rationale used to justify regulation of broadcasters. Quincy filed the case to challenge the twenty-year-old "must carry" rule, which forced cable systems to carry, on an uncompensated basis, local broadcasters. Despite this ruling, in 1986 and 1987 the FCC reimposed "must carry" rules (Glist 1987). Cases like this trap the broadcast industry in an endless policy loop consisting of an administrative decision, court appeal, court reversal, remand, and another administrative decision (Brotman 1988).

In 1985 MTV Networks was the largest supplier of cable programming ("MTV Tells Its Four" 1985). Cable had begun in the late 1940s as community antenna television (CATV). It served communities with poor reception. The FCC did not assert control over cable television until March 1966. Rules adopted in 1972 provided the basic regulatory framework until 1984, when the Cable Communications Act was passed. It essentially maintained the 1972 rules as the basis for dual federal-state or local regulation. By 1988 cable systems, franchised by local governments like a natural monopoly, served 23,000 communities. The largest system, Cox Cable, had about 279,200 subscribers. TCI, the largest multiple-system operator, had more than 5 million subscribers. Most cable systems obtained less than 5 percent of their gross revenues from advertising. Pay television, like Time Inc.'s Home Box Office (HBO), was on approximately 7,200 systems ("Short Course in Cable, 1988" 1988). Capital Cities/ABC owned the largest cable network, the Entertainment and Sports Programming Network (ESPN).

In the 1980s the networks faced competition from all sides. In addition to cable, home video rental stores provided a wide variety of movies and other programs to homes with VCRs. Consus, a satellite-linked consortium of nearly eighty local stations, generated and disseminated national news coverage. With the aid of Consus, Group W's Newsfeed, and Potomac Communication's service, local stations could replace the networks' national news programs ("TV News: Rapid Rise of Home Rule" 1988). Satellite Broadcast Networks (SBN), which provided network programs in rural areas after scrambling began, was feeding thousands of satellite dish owners network programming, bypassing local network affiliates. Although SBN pays copyright fees, the networks claim bypassing is illegal (Gardner 1988).

Along with cable and home video, the networks were also threatened by a currently small competitor, pay-per-view (PPV). Homeowners with PPV can push buttons on their remote-control units, and the PPV system's central computer will put the chosen programs on their screens and record the proper billing information. Another new competitor was interactive television. Consumers with this service can order products shown on their television screens or play blackjack by punching appropriate numbers on their telephones ("Big Boys' Blues" 1988). Monopoly has been replaced as the central issue in telecommunications by the question of which of the multivarious potential players will be allowed to compete.

In the 1990s broadcast media disappeared into telecommunications, and entertainment megacorps as giant mergers brought massive companies under single-umbrella control (Ramstad 1995; "Westinghouse Completes CBS Acquisition" 1995). Personal computers (PCs), originally envisioned as machines with great potential for business, not only outstripped expectations in the office but penetrated the home market as well. E-mail, known to a few in the 1980s, is a common means of communication around the world in the 1990s. Men and women who once considered computers machines restricted to billing offices spend hours surfing the World Wide Web for information, entertainment, and shopping. Two-way video communication via PC is likely to revolutionize personal communications in the early years of the twenty-first century ("World of Interest in Media Deals" 1995; Farhi 1996).

Television will shift from analog broadcasting to digital format in the first decade of the 2000s (Yang 1998). That change will progress in tandem with continuous advances in PC design. PCs were number crunchers for skilled users in the 1980s before manufacturers recognized and addressed the massive consumer market. The PC of the late 1990s requires no special skills yet permits access to information and processing unheard of even by experts ten years earlier. In 1999 the U.S. Internal Revenue Service encouraged Americans to file their annual returns via electronic technology. The PC of the late 1990s can link the user to other users around the globe, access libraries and other information repositories by the thousands, play high-quality stereo music from compact discs, and display a television program in one corner of the screen while the user works with data on the remainder.

Commerce, information, entertainment, and communications have converged in the PC. Not even science fiction writers can envision what the future holds ten years hence. After all, the realities of the late 1990s have exceeded much of the wildest speculation of the 1980s. The only certainty is change and the continued dominance of telecommunications in the changing technology of the third industrial revolution. When Benjamin Franklin began his experiments in electricity, he anticipated the vastness of the world he was peeking into. He would probably not be surprised at what has happened in the two centuries since his death, but he would surely be delighted.

BIBLIOGRAPHIC ESSAY

Without question, the single best history of the radio and television industry is Erik Barnouw's *Tube of Plenty: The Evolution of American Television* (1990), an updated condensation of his three-volume *History of Broadcasting in the United States* (1966–1970). Of exceptional value on the pioneering years of radio is Susan J. Douglas' 1987 *Inventing American Broadcasting, 1899–1922*.

The best source of current reporting on the activities of the industry is found in *Broadcasting Magazine*. In 1982 the editors of *Broadcasting Magazine* published *The First 50 Years of Broadcasting*, a volume of good retrospective reporting. Lawrence W. Lichty and Malachi C. Topping provide in *American Broadcasting: A Source Book on the History of Radio and Television* (1975) an excellent collection of insightful articles from a variety of sources about broadcasting history.

The best sources of information about some of the major figures in the industry are W. P. Jolly, *Marconi* (1972); Lawrence Lessing, *Man of High Fidelity: Edwin Howard Armstrong* (1956); Josephine Young Case and Everett Needham Case, *Owen D. Young and American Enterprise* (1982); and Kenneth Bilby, *The General, David Sarnoff and the Rise of the Communications Industry* (1986).

Government's hand in this industry is heavy; to understand the course it has followed, it is essential to consider politics and regulation. Good sources of this kind of information are Erwin G. Krasnow, Lawrence D. Longley, and Herbert A. Terry, *The Politics of Broadcast Regulation* (1982); Ellis W. Hawley, ed., *Herbert Hoover as Secretary of Commerce: Studies in New Era Thought and Practice* ([1974] 1981); and Harvey J. Levin, *Fact and Fancy in Television Regulation* (1980). The Cases' book about Owen Young is also helpful in this regard.

Broadcasting is an industry created by technology. Elliot Sivowitch's article "A Technological Survey of Broadcasting's 'Pre-History,' 1876–1920" in the *Journal of Broadcasting* (Winter 1970), provides an excellent overview. In *Emulation and Invention* (1981), Brookes Hindle provides a fine, more detailed, view of the relevant technology. Excellent coverage of radio technology can be found in *Invention and Innovation in the Radio Industry* ([1949] 1971) by W. Rupert Maclaurin. Lessing's *Man of High Fidelity* and Bilby's *General* are also good sources of information on the impact of technological change on the industry.

BIBLIOGRAPHY

Abramson, Albert. *Electronic Motion Pictures: A History of the Television Camera*. Berkeley: University of California Press, 1956.
———. *The History of Television, 1880–1941*. Jefferson, NC: McFarland, 1987.
———. *Zworykin, Pioneer of Television*. Urbana: University of Illinois Press, 1995.
Absher, Frank. "20 Years of Rock 'n Roll." *St. Louis Journalism Review* 26 (July 1996): 16.
Ace, Goodman. *Ladies and Gentleman—Easy Aces*. New York: Doubleday, 1970.
Ad Forum. New York: Agency File, 1980–1985. Monthly.
Advertising Age. Chicago: Crain Communications, 1930– . Weekly.
Alexander, Bobby Chris. *Televangelism Reconsidered: Ritual in the Search for Human Community*. AAR Studies in Religion, no. 68. Atlanta, GA: Scholars Press, 1994.
Allen, Fred. *Treadmill to Oblivion*. Boston: Little, Brown, 1954.
———. *Much Ado about Me*. Boston: Little, Brown, 1956.
Amador, Jorge. "Fairness Doctrine, R.I.P." *The Freeman*, June 1989, 226–31.
American Visions. Washington, DC: Visions Foundation, 1986– . Bimonthly.

Anderson, Christopher. *Hollywood TV: The Studio System in the Fifties*. Austin: University of Texas Press, 1994.

Anderson, Leland I. *Bibliography: Dr. Nikola Tesla (1856–1943)*. 2d ed., enl. Minneapolis: Tesla Society, 1956. See Ratzlaff, John T., and Leland I. Anderson.

Andrews, Robert Douglas. *Just Plain Bill, His Story*. Philadelphia: David M. Kay, 1935.

Appleby, Thomas. *Mahlon Loomis: Inventor of Radio*. Washington, DC: Loomis, 1967.

Archer, Gleason L. *History of Radio to 1926*. New York: American Historical Society, 1938.

———. *Big Business and Radio*. New York: American Historical Company, 1939.

Arnold, Frank A. *Broadcast Advertising: The Fourth Dimension*. Television Edition. New York: Wiley, 1933.

Aufderheide, Pat. "Dial Down to Jesus." *Technology Review* 90 (January 1987): 13–14.

Averson, Richard, and David Manning White. *Electronic Drama: Television Plays of the Sixties*. Boston: Beacon Press, 1971.

Bagdikian, Ben H. "How Technology Influences Journalism." *IEEE Spectrum* 21 (June 1984): 109–11.

Baker, Denise. "Taking a Trip Down Memory Lane: Telecommunications' National Policy Dates Back to the 1800s." *Nation's Cities Weekly* 17 (June 6, 1994): 5.

Baker, Robert K., and Sandra J. Ball. *Mass Media and Violence, Vol. 9: A Report to the National Commission on the Causes and Prevention of Violence*. Washington, DC: U.S. Government Printing Office, 1969.

Baker, Thomas T. *Wireless Pictures and Television: A Practical Description of the Telegraphy of Pictures, Photographs, and Visual Images*. London: Constable, 1926; New York: Van Nostrand, 1927.

Baker, W. J. *A History of the Marconi Company*. London: Methuen, 1970, New York: St. Martin's Press, 1971.

Balk, Mark, and Mark Newman. "He Became the Yankees." *Sporting News* 22 (July 1, 1996): 4.

Banning, William Peck. *Commercial Broadcasting Pioneer: The WEAF* [New York radio station] *Experiment 1922–1926*. Cambridge: Harvard University Press, 1946.

Bannister, Harry. *The Education of a Broadcaster*. New York: Simon & Schuster, 1965.

Barcus, Francis E. "Bibliography of Studies of Radio and Television Program Content, 1928–1958." *Journal of Broadcasting* 4 (fall 1960): 355.

———. *Saturday Children's Television: A Report of TV Programming and Advertising on Boston Commercial Television*. Newtonville, MA: Action for Children's Television, 1971.

———. *Television in the Afternoon Hours: A Study of Programming and Advertising for Children on Independent Stations across the United States*. Newtonville, MA: Action for Children's Television, 1975.

———. *Weekend Commercial Children's Television—1975*. Newtonville, MA: Action for Children's Television, 1975.

————. *Images of Life on Children's Television: Sex Roles, Minorities, and Families.* New York: Praeger, 1983.

Barcus, Francis E., and Rachel Wolkin. *Children's Television: An Analysis of Programming and Advertising.* New York: Praeger, 1977.

Barnouw, Erik. *Mass Communication: Television, Radio, Film, Press; The Media and Their Practice in the United States of America.* New York: Rinehart, 1958.

————. *A History of Broadcasting in the United States.* Vol. 1, *A Tower in Babel: A History of Broadcasting in the United States to 1933.* New York: Oxford University Press, 1966.

————. *A History of Broadcasting in the United States.* Vol. 2, *The Golden Web: A History of Broadcasting in the United States 1933–1953.* New York: Oxford University Press, 1968.

————. *A History of Broadcasting in the United States.* Vol. 3, *The Image Empire: A History of Broadcasting in the United States from 1953.* New York: Oxford University Press, 1970.

————. *International Encyclopedia of Communications.* New York: Oxford University Press and the University of Pennsylvania, Annenburg School of Communications, 1989.

————. *Tube of Plenty: The Evolution of American Television.* 2d rev. ed. New York: Oxford University Press, 1990.

————. *Media Marathon: A Twentieth-Century Memoir.* Durham, NC: Duke University Press, 1996.

Barrett, Marvin. *Survey of Broadcast Journalism 1968–1969.* New York: Grosset & Dunlap, 1969.

————. *Survey of Broadcast Journalism 1969–1970: Year of Challenge, Year of Crisis.* New York: Grosset & Dunlap, 1970.

————. *Survey of Broadcast Journalism 1970–1971: A State of Siege.* New York: Grosset & Dunlap, 1971.

————. *Survey of Broadcast Journalism 1971–1972: The Politics of Broadcasting.* New York: Thomas Y. Crowell, 1973.

————, ed. *Broadcast Journalism, 1979–1981.* Alfred I. duPont-Columbia University Survey; 8th. New York: Everest House, 1982.

Barrow, Roscoe L. et al. *Network Broadcasting: Report of the Network Study Staff to the Network Study Committee.* Washington, DC: Federal Communications Commission, 1957.

Baughman, James L. *Television's Guardians, the FCC and the Politics of Programming, 1958–1967.* Knoxville: University of Tennessee Press, 1985.

————. *The Republic of Mass Culture: Journalism, Filmmaking, and Broadcasting in America since 1941.* Baltimore: Johns Hopkins University Press, 1992.

Belz, Carl. *The Story of Rock.* New York: Oxford University Press, 1969.

Bennett, Tamara. "Benefits of Going Live." *Satellite Communications* 10 (October 1986): 49–50.

Benson, Thomas W. *Fundamentals of Television.* New York: Mancall, 1930.

Berg, Gertrude. *The Rise of the Goldbergs.* New York: Barse, 1931.

————. *Molly and Me.* New York: McGraw-Hill, 1961.

Berkman, Dave. "The Not Quite So Inevitable Origins of Commercial Broadcasting in America." *European Journal of Marketing* 21, no. 4 (1987): 34–43.

Bickel, Karl A. *New Empires: Newspapers and the Radio*. Philadelphia: J. B. Lippincott, 1930.

Bickel, Mary E. *Geo. W. Trendle, Creator and Producer of: The Lone Ranger, The Green Hornet, Sgt. Preston of the Yukon, The American Agent, and Other Successes. An Authorized Biography*. New York: Exposition Press, an Exposition-Banner Book, 1971.

"The Big Boys' Blues." *Time* (October 17, 1988): 56–62.

Bilby, Kenneth. *The General, David Sarnoff and the Rise of the Communications Industry*. New York: Harper & Row, 1986.

Billboard. New York: Billboard, 1963– . Weekly.

Bittner, John R., and Denise A. Bittner. *Radio Journalism*. Englewood Cliffs, NJ: Prentice-Hall, 1977.

Black Enterprise. New York: E. G. Graves, 1970– .

Blair, Gwenda. *Almost Golden: Jessica Savitch and the Selling of Television News*. New York: Simon & Schuster, 1988.

———. "Once More, with Cheek." *Business Monthly* 132 (July/August 1988): 30–38.

Blake, George Gascoigne. *History of Radio Telegraphy and Telephony*. London: Chapman & Hall, 1928. Reprint. New York: Arno Press, 1974.

Bliss, Edward, Jr. *Now the News: The Story of Broadcast Journalism*. New York: Columbia University Press, 1991.

———, ed. *In Search of Light: The Broadcasts of Edward R. Murrow 1938–1961*. New York: Knopf, 1967. Reprint. New York: Da Capo Press, 1997.

Bloch, Louis M., Jr. *The Gas Pipe Networks: A History of College Radio, 1936–1946*. Cleveland, OH: Bloch, 1980.

BloomBecker, J. J. Buck. "Captain Midnight and the Space Hackers." *Security MGMT* 32 (July 1988): 76–82.

Bluem, A. William. *Documentary in American Television: Form, Function, Method*. New York: Hastings House, Communication Arts Books, 1965.

Bluem, A. William, John F. Cox, and Gene McPherson. *Television in the Public Interest: Planning, Production, Performance*. New York: Hastings House, Communication Arts Books, 1961.

Blum, Daniel. *A Pictorial History of Television*. Dallas: Chilton, 1959.

BM/E: The Magazine of Broadcast Management/Engineering. New York: Mactier, 1965– . Monthly.

Boehlert, Eric. "AM Dial Offers Clear-Channel Choice: Listeners Will Travel 'Highway in the Sky.' " *Billboard* 105 (April 10, 1993): 66.

Bogart, Leo. *The Age of Television: A Study of Viewing Habits and the Impact of Television on American Life*. 3d ed., enl. New York: Frederick Ungar, 1972.

Bolt, Robert H., and Pier Mapes. "Point/Counterpoint Poll: Clutter Clatter; Thoughtful Therapy." *Marketing & Media Decisions* 23 (March 1988): 144–45.

Bouck, Zeh. *Making a Living in Radio*. New York: McGraw-Hill, 1935.

Bower, Robert T. *Television and the Public*. Holt, Rinehart & Winston, 1973.

Bracken, James K., and Christopher H. Sterling. *Telecommunications Research Resources: An Annotated Guide*. Telecommunications (Mahwah, NJ). Hillsdale, NJ: Lawrence Erlbaum Associates, 1995.

Briggs, Asa. *The History of Broadcasting in the United Kingdom.* 5 vols. New York: Oxford University Press, 1961–1995.

Broadcasting & Cable. New York: Cahners, 1993. Weekly.

Broadcasting & Cable Yearbook. 2 vols. New Providence, NJ: R. R. Bowker, 1993. Annual.

Broadcasting Cable Yearbook. Washington, DC: Broadcasting Publications, 1980–1981. Annual.

Broadcasting/Cablecasting Yearbook. Washington, DC: Broadcasting Publications, 1982–1988. Annual.

Broadcasting Magazine. Washington, DC: Broadcasting Publications, 1931– . Weekly. See also Editors, Broadcasting Magazine.

Brotman, Stuart N. "The Curious Case of the Must-Carry Rules: Breaking the Endless Policy Loop through Negotiated Rulemaking." *Federal Communications Law Journal* 40 (May 1988): 399–411.

Buehler, Ezra C. *American vs. British System of Radio Control.* The Reference Shelf, vol. 6, no. 10. Bronx, NY: H. W. Wilson, 1933.

Burden, Jared L. "Tying the Victim's Hands: Curbing Citizen Group Abuse of the Broadcast Licensing Process." *Federal Communications Law Journal* 39 (October 1987): 259–96.

Bushsbaum, Walter H. *Fundamentals of Television.* New York: J. F. Rider, 1964.

Buxton, Frank, and William Hugh Owen. *Radio's Golden Age.* New York: Easton Valley Press, 1966.

———, with Introduction by Henry Morgan. *The Big Broadcast—1920–1950.* Rev. and enl. edition of *Radio's Golden Age.* New York: Viking Press, 1972.

Cantor, Louis. *Wheelin' on Beale: How WDIA-Memphis Became the Story of the Nation's First All-Black Radio Station and Created the Sound That Changed America.* New York: Pharos Books, 1992.

Carter, Lee A., and John Kramer. "Radio Marketers Take a Fresh Look at Medium." *Advertising Age* 56 (August 1985): 26–27.

Carter, T. Barton. *Mass Communication Law in a Nutshell.* 4th ed. Nutshell Series. St. Paul, MN: West, 1994.

Carter, T. Barton, Marc A. Franklin, and Jay B. Wright. *The First Amendment and the Fifth Estate: Regulation of Electronic Mass Media.* 4th ed. Westbury, NY: Foundation Press, 1996.

———. *The First Amendment and the Fourth Estate: The Law of Mass Media.* 7th ed. Westbury, NY: Foundation Press, 1997.

Casatelli, Christine. "Intelsat's Richard Colino Candid on Competition." *Network World* 3 (October 6, 1986): 1, 42–44.

Case, Josephine Young, and Everett Needham Case. *Owen D. Young and American Enterprise.* Boston: David R. Godine, 1982.

Chakravarty, Subrata N. "An Exception to Murphy's Law?" *Forbes* 140 (August 1987): 36–38.

———. "He's a Constitutional Monarch Now." *Forbes* 142 (September 1988): 34–36.

Chappell, Matthew N., and Claude Ernest Hooper. *Radio Audience Measurement.* New York: Stephen Daye, 1944.

Charnley, Mitchell V. *News by Radio.* New York: Macmillan, 1948.

Chase, Francis. *Sound and Fury: An Informal History of Broadcasting*. New York: Harper & Brothers, 1942.

Cheney, Margaret. *Tesla, Man Out of Time*. Englewood Cliffs, NJ: Prentice-Hall, 1981.

Chervokas, John. "I'd Like to Own Everything." *Madison Avenue* 28 (June 1986): 24–28.

Chester, Edward W. *Radio, Television and American Politics*. New York: Sheed & Ward, 1969.

Coe, Douglass. *Marconi: Pioneer of Radio*. Englewood Cliffs, NJ: Julian Messner, 1943.

Coe, Lewis. *Wireless Radio: A Brief History*. Jefferson, NC: McFarland, 1996.

Cohen, Andrea. "Look Sharp, Suppliers: HDTV Will Be a Great Show." *Electronic Business* 14 (April 1988): 28, 30.

Cohn, Nik. *Rock from the Beginning*. New York: Stein & Day, 1969.

Cole, Barry. *Television*. New York: Free Press, 1970.

———. *Reluctant Regulators: The FCC and the Broadcast Audience*. Reading, MA: Addison-Wesley, 1978.

———. *Television Today: A Close-up View: Readings from TV Guide*. New York: Oxford University Press, 1981.

Coletti, Christopher. "Cable TV: Narrowcasters Gird for Program War with Big 3." *Advertising Age* 57 (December 1986): 58–59.

Colford, Paul D. *Howard Stern: The King of All Media*. New York: St. Martin's Press, 1996.

Collins, A. Frederick. *Experimental Television*. New York: Lothrop, Lee, & Shepard, 1932.

Collins, John Campbell. "TV Syndication—Living and Succeeding by the Rules of the Game." *Advertising Age* 56 (January 1985): 14–15.

Columbia Broadcasting System. *Network Practices*. New York: CBS, 1956.

———. *Radio in 1937*. New York: CBS, 1957.

Colvin, Geoffrey. "The Crowded New World of TV." *Fortune* 110 (September 1984): 156–66.

Communications & the Law. Westport, CT: Meckler, 1979– . Bimonthly.

Computer Networks and ISDN Systems. Amsterdam: Elsevier Science Publishers B.V. in association with the International Council for Computer Communication, 1965– .

Comstock, George A. *TV in America*. Sage Commtext Series, vol. 1. Beverly Hills, CA: Sage, 1980.

Contemporary Economic Policy. Huntington Beach, CA: Western Economic Association International, 1994– . Quarterly.

Contemporary Policy Issues. Long Beach, CA: Western Economic Association International; California State University, Long Beach, 1982–1993. Quarterly.

Cook, Philip S., Douglas Gomery, and Lawrence W. Lichty, eds. *The Future of News: Television-Newspapers-Wire Services-Newsmagazines*. Washington, DC: Woodrow Wilson Center Press; Baltimore: Johns Hopkins University Press, 1992.

Cooper, Isabella Mitchell. *Bibliography on Educational Broadcasting*. Chicago: University of Chicago Press, 1942.

Correll, Charles J., and Freeman F. Gosden. *All about Amos 'n' Andy and Their Creators Correll and Gosden*. New York: Rand McNally, 1929.

Cox, Kenneth A., and Nicholas Johnson. *Broadcasting in America and the FCC's License Renewal Process: An Oklahoma Case Study*. Washington, DC: Federal Communications Commission, 1968.

———. *Renewal Standards: The District of Columbia, Maryland, Virginia and West Virginia License Renewals (October 1, 1969)*. Washington, DC: Federal Communications Commission, 1969.

Crawley, Chewtode. *From Telegraphy to Television*. London: Warne, 1931.

Crosby, John. *Out of the Blue: A Book about Radio and Television*. New York: Simon & Schuster, 1952.

CTW Research Bibliography: Research Papers Relating to the Children's Television Workshop and Its Experimental Educational Series: "Sesame Street" and "The Electric Company"—1966–76. New York: Children's Television Workshop, Research Division, 1976.

Darrow, Ben H. *Radio Trailblazing: A Brief History of the Ohio School of the Air and Its Implications for Educational Broadcasting*. Columbus, OH: College Company, 1940.

Data Communications. New York: McGraw-Hill, 1972– .

Davis, Stephen. *The Law of Radio Communication*. New York: McGraw-Hill, 1927.

Day, James. *The Vanishing Vision: The Inside Story of Public Television*. Berkeley: University of California Press, 1995.

Decline and Fall of the Fairness Doctrine: A Work in Progress. Washington, DC: Broadcasting Book Division, 1987.

de Forest, Lee. *Television, Today and Tomorrow*. New York: Dial Press, 1942.

———. *Father of Radio: The Autobiography of Lee de Forest*. Chicago: Wilcox & Follett, 1950.

Domzal, Teresa J., and Jerome B. Kernan. "Television's New Technology: Hardware Plus Software Equal Segmentation Research." *Journal of Advertising Research* 23 (August/September 1983): 33–37.

Donahue, Hugh Carter. "The Fairness Doctrine Is Shackling Broadcasting." *Technology Review* 89 (November/December 1986): 45–52.

———. *The Battle to Control Broadcast News: Who Owns the First Amendment?* Cambridge: MIT Press, 1988.

Douglas, George H. *The Early Days of Radio Broadcasting*. Jefferson, NC: McFarland, 1987.

Douglas, Susan J. *Inventing American Broadcasting, 1899–1922*. Johns Hopkins Studies in the History of Technology. Baltimore: Johns Hopkins University Press, 1987.

"The Downsizing of CBS to Its Broadcasting Roots." *Mergers & Acquisitions* 22 (March/April 1988): 58–59.

Dreher, Carl. *Sarnoff, an American Success*. New York: Quadrangle; New York Times Book, 1977.

Dryer, Sherman H. *Radio in Wartime*. New York: Greenberg, 1942.

Dunlap, Orrin E. *Advertising by Radio*. New York: Ronald Press, 1929.

———. *Radio in Advertising*. New York: Harper, 1931.

———. *The Story of Radio*. New York: Dial Press, 1927, 1935.

———. *Radio's 100 Men of Science: Biographical Narratives of Pathfinders in Electronics and Television.* New York: Harper & Brothers, 1944.

———. *Understanding Television: What It Is and How It Works.* New York: Greenberg, 1948.

———. *Radio and Television Almanac.* New York: Harper & Brothers, 1951.

———. *Communications in Space, from Wireless to Satellite Relay.* New York: Harper & Row, 1964.

———. *Marconi: The Man and His Wireless.* New York: Macmillan, 1937. Reprint. History of Broadcasting, Radio to Television. New York: Arno Press, 1971.

———. *The Outlook for Television.* 1932. Reprint. New York: Arno Press, 1971.

Dunn, Joseph. "Cable Costs All over the Lot." *Marketing & Media Decisions* 18 (fall 1983): 55–60.

Durham, Richard. *Richard Durham's Destination Freedom: Scripts from Radio's Black Legacy, 1948–50.* Edited by J. Fred MacDonald. Media and Society Series. New York: Praeger, 1969.

Dygert, Warren B. *Radio as an Advertising Medium.* New York: McGraw-Hill, 1939.

Edel, Richard. "TV Syndication: Unwired Nets Share Marketers' Dollars." *Advertising Age* 59 (February 1988): 12.

Edelman, Murray. *Licensing of Radio Services in the United States: 1927–47.* University of Illinois Studies in the Social Sciences, vol. 31, no. 4. Urbana/Champaign: University of Illinois Press, 1950.

Editors, *Broadcasting Magazine. The First 50 Years of Broadcasting: The Running Story of the Fifth Estate.* Washington, DC: Broadcasting Publications, 1982.

Edmond, Alfred, Jr. "25 Years of Blacks in Media." *Black Enterprise* 25 (July 1995): 104.

Education on the Air . . . Yearbook of the Institute for Education by Radio. Columbus: Ohio State University, 1930–1934. See also MacLatchy, Josephine.

Elliott, William Y. *Television's Impact on American Culture.* East Lansing: Michigan State University Press, 1956.

Emery, Walter B. *National and International Systems of Broadcasting, Their History, Operation, and Control.* East Lansing: Michigan State University Press, 1969.

———. *Broadcasting and Government: Responsibilities and Regulations.* East Lansing: Michigan State University Press, 1961; revised 1971.

Endicott, R. Craig, Kristine Stiven, and Norma Green. "Leading Media Companies." *Advertising Age* 59 (June 1988): 51–53.

Engelman, Ralph. *Public Radio and Television in America: A Political History.* Thousand Oaks, CA: Sage, 1996.

Eoyang, Tsao. *An Economic Study of the Radio Industry in the United States of America.* New York: RCA Institute Technical Press, 1937. Ph.D. diss., Columbia University, 1936. Reprint. New York: Arno Press, 1974.

Erickson, Don V. *Armstrong's Fight for FM Broadcasting. One Man vs. Big Business and Bureaucracy.* University, AL: University of Alabama Press, 1973.

Evans, James F. *Prairie Farmer and WLS* [Chicago]:*The Burridge D. Butler Years.* Urbana/Champaign: University of Illinois Press, 1969.

Everson, George. *The Story of Television: The Life of Philo T. Farnsworth.* New York: W. W. Norton, 1949.

Fadde, Peter J., and James C. Hsiung. "Pay TV: A Historical Review of the Siphoning Issue." *Communications & the Law* 9 (April 1987): 15–26.

Fadiman, Clifton. *Prize Plays of TV and Radio, 1956.* New York: Random House, 1957.

Fagen, Herb. *White Hats & Silver Spurs: Interviews with 24 Stars of Film & Television Westerns of the Thirties through the Sixties.* Jefferson, NC: McFarland, 1996.

Fahie, John Joseph. *A History of Wireless Telegraphy, 1838–99.* Edinburgh, Scotland, UK: William Blackwood & Sons, 1899; American edition, 1901. Reprint. New York: Arno Press and the *New York Times,* 1971.

Farhi, Paul. "Media Giants' Bedfellowship Raises Questions about Competition." *Washington Post,* January 7, 1996, H1.

Federal Communications Bar Journal. Washington, DC: Federal Communications Bar Association, 1937–1976. See also *Federal Communications Law Journal.*

Federal Communications Commission. *Report on Chain Broadcasting.* Washington, DC: U.S. Government Printing Office, 1941.

———. *Public Service Responsibilities of Broadcast Licensees.* Public Notice 95462. Washington, DC: U.S. Government Printing Office, 1946.

———. *Federal Communications Commission Reports: Decisions, Reports, and Orders of the Federal Communications Commission of the United States.* Washington, DC: U.S. Government Printing Office, 1936–1986. Irregular.

Federal Communications Law Journal. Los Angeles: UCLA School of Law and the Federal Communications Bar Association, 1977– .

Federal Trade Commission. *Report of the Federal Trade Commission on the Radio Industry in Response to House Resolution 546.* [Radio Industry]. 67th Cong., 4th sess., December 1, 1923. Washington, DC: U.S. Government Printing Office, 1924.

Fessenden, Helen M. *Fessenden: Builder of Tomorrows.* New York: Coward-McCann, 1940.

Fielding, Raymond. *A Technological History of Motion Pictures and Television: An Anthology from the Pages of the Journal of the Society of Motion Picture and Television Engineers.* Berkeley: University of California Press, 1967.

FM Atlas and Station Directory. Adolph, MN: FM Atlas, 1972–1989.

Forrest, Jack E. "Advertising on PBS—Reality or Fantasy?" *Marketing & Media Decisions* 18 (October 1983): 146–52.

Fowler, Gene, and Bill Crawford. *Border Radio.* Austin: Texas Monthly Press, 1957.

Frantzich, Stephen E., and John Sullivan. *The C-SPAN Revolution.* Norman: University of Oklahoma Press, 1996.

The Freeman. Irvington-on-Hudson, NY: Foundation for Economic Education, 1950– . Monthly.

Freeman, Mike. "NATPE [National Association of Television Program Executives] at 30: Charting Syndication's Rising Star." *Broadcasting* 123 (January 25, 1993): 88.

Friendly, Fred W. *Due to Circumstances beyond Our Control . . .* New York: Random House, 1967.

Frost, S. E. *Education's Own Stations.* Chicago: University of Chicago Press for the Committee on Research of the National Advisory Council on Radio in Education, 1937. Reprint. New York: Arno Press and the *New York Times*, 1971.

Gardner, Laura. "Beam Me Up, Scrambled." *Venture* 10 (March 1988): 20–21.

Garratt, G.R.M. *The Early History of Radio: From Farady to Marconi.* London: Institution of Electrical Engineers, 1994.

Gastfreund, Irving, and Ervin G. Krasnow. *Political Broadcast Handbook: A Legal Guide for Broadcasters, Candidates, and Advertising Agencies.* 2d ed. Washington, DC: National Association of Broadcasters, 1984.

Gay, Verne. "The Way It Was: When the Upfront Was Smaller and the Tales Were Taller." *Adweek* 34, Eastern edition (June 7, 1993): TV30.

Gelman, Morrie. "75 Years of Pioneers." *Broadcasting & Cable* 125 (November 6, 1995): 80.

Gerster, Alec. "Television: New Programs and Profits? Clash!" *Marketing & Media Decisions* 19 (February 1984): 104–5.

Gilder, George F. *Life after Television.* The Larger Agenda Series. Knoxville, TN: Whittle Direct Books, 1990.

Ginsburg, Douglas H. *Regulation of Broadcasting: Law and Policy towards Radio, Television, and Cable Communications.* St. Paul, MN: West, 1979.

Glist, Paul. "Cable Must Carry—Again." *Federal Communications Law Journal* 39 (May 1987): 109–21.

Godfried, Nathan. *WCFL, Chicago's Voice of Labor, 1926–78.* Urbana: University of Illinois Press, 1997.

Gordon, George N. *The Communications Revolution: A History of Mass Media in the United States.* New York: Hastings House, Communication Arts Books, 1977.

Gordon, George N., and Irving A. Falk. *On the Spot Reporting: Radio Records History.* New York: Julian Messner, 1967.

Greenfield, Jeff. *Television, the First Fifty Years.* New York: Harry N. Abrams, 1977.

Gross, Ben. *I Looked and I Listened: Informal Recollections of Radio and TV.* New York: Random House, 1954. Reprint. New Rochelle, NY: Arlington House, 1970.

Hack, Henry E. "Tune In to Cable Theft." *Security MGMT* 32 (May 1988): 64–67.

Hagelin, Theodore M., and Kurt A. Wimmer. "Broadcast Deregulation and the Administrative Responsibility to Monitor Policy Change: An Empirical Study of the Elimination of Logging Requirements." *Federal Communications Law Journal* 38 (August 1986): 201–82.

Harlow, Alvin. *Old Wires and New Waves: The History of the Telegraph, Telephone and Wireless.* Englewood Cliffs, NJ: Appleton-Century, 1936. Reprint. History of Broadcasting: Radio to Television. New York: Arno Press and the *New York Times*, 1971.

Harmon, Jim. *The Great Radio Heroes.* New York: Doubleday, 1967.

———. *The Great Radio Comedians.* New York: Doubleday, 1970.

Harris, Michael David. *Always on Sunday—Ed Sullivan: An Inside View*. New York: Meredith, 1968.

Harvard University Graduate School of Business. *The Radio Industry: The Story of Its Development, As Told by Leaders of the Industry*. Chicago: A. W. Shaw, 1926. Reprint. New York: Arno Press, 1974.

Hawes, William. *The American Television Drama: The Experimental Years*. University, AL: University of Alabama Press, 1986.

Hawley, Ellis W., ed. *Herbert Hoover as Secretary of Commerce: Studies in New Era Thought and Practice*. Herbert Hoover Centennial Seminars, no. 2. West Branch, IA: Herbert Hoover Presidential Library Association, 1974, Iowa City: University of Iowa Press, 1981.

Hazlett, Thomas W. "Competition vs. Franchise Monopoly in Cable Television." *Contemporary Policy Issues* 4 (April 1986): 80–97.

———. "Wiring the Constitution for Cable." *Regulation* 12, no. 1 (1988): 30–34.

Head, Sydney W. *Broadcasting in America: A Survey of Television and Radio*. Boston: Houghton Mifflin, 1956. *Broadcasting in America: A Survey of Television, Radio, and New Technologies*. 4th ed. 1982. *Broadcasting in America: A Survey of Electronic Media*. 5th ed. 1987. *Broadcasting in America: A Survey of Electronic Media*. 6th ed. 1990.

———. *World Broadcasting Systems: A Comparative Analysis*. Belmont, CA: Wadsworth, 1985.

Hettinger, Herman S. *A Decade of Radio Advertising*. Chicago: University of Chicago Press, 1933. Reprint. New York: Arno Press, 1971.

Hettinger, Herman S., and Irvin Steward. *Radio: Selected A.A.P.S.S.* [American Academy of Political and Social Science] *Surveys, 1929–1941*. Reprint. New York: Arno Press, 1971.

Hickock, Eliza Merrill. *The Quiz Kids*. Boston: Houghton Mifflin, 1947.

Higby, Mary Jane. *Tune in Tomorrow; or, How I Found the Right to Happiness with Our Gal Sunday, Stella Dallas, John's Other Wife, and Other Sudsy Radio Serials*. New York: Cowles, 1968.

Hilbrink, W. R. *Who Really Invented Radio?* New York: G. P. Putnam's Sons, 1972.

Hill, George H., Lorraine Raglin, and Chas Floyd Johnson. *Black Women in Television: An Illustrated History and Bibliography*. Garland Reference Library of the Humanities, vol. 1228. New York: Garland, 1990.

Hill, Harold E. *The National Association of Educational Broadcasters: A History*. Urbana, IL: NAEB, 1954.

Hindle, Brookes. *Emulation and Invention*. New York: New York University Press, 1981.

Hirsch, Paul. *The Structure of the Popular Music Industry: The Filtering Process by Which Records Are Preselected for Public Consumption*. Ann Arbor: University of Michigan, Institute for Social Research, 1968.

Hoffer, Thomas W. "Nathan B. Stubblefield and His Wireless Telephone." In *American Broadcasting: A Source Book on the History of Radio and Television*, edited by Lawrence W. Lichty and Malachi C. Topping, 4. New York: Hastings House, 1975.

Howeth, L. S. *History of Communications—Electronics in the United States Navy*. Washington, DC: U.S. Government Printing Office, 1963.

Hubbell, Richard W. *4000 Years of Television, The Story of Seeing at a Distance.* New York: G. P. Putnam's Sons, 1942.
———. *Four Thousand Years of Television.* Edited by C. L. Boltz. London: George G. Harrap, 1946.
———. *Television Programming & Production.* 3d ed., rev. and enl. New York: Rinehart, 1956.
Hunt, Inez, and Wanetta W. Draper. *Lightning in His Hand: The Life Story of Nikola Tesla.* Denver: Sage Books, 1981. Reprint. Hawthorne, CA: Omni, 1984.
Husing, Ted. *Ten Years before the Mike.* New York: Farrar & Rinehart, 1935.
Husing, Ted, and Cy Rice. *My Eyes Are in My Heart.* New York: Random House, 1959; New York: Hillman, 1961.
Hutchinson, Thomas. *Here Is Television, Your Window to the World.* New York: Hastings House, 1946, 1950.
Hybels, Saundra, and Dana Ulloth. *Broadcasting: An Introduction to Radio and Television.* New York: D. Van Nostrand, 1978.
IEEE Spectrum. New York: Institute of Electrical and Electronics Engineers, 1964– . Monthly.
Inman, David. *The TV Encyclopedia: The Most Comprehensive Guide to Everybody Who's Anybody in Television.* New York: Perigee Books, 1991.
Institutional Investor. New York: Institutional Investor, 1967– . Monthly.
Ivey, Mark. "Sports on TV: Cable Is the Team to Watch." *Business Week*, August 22, 1988, 66–69.
Jacot, B. L., and D.M.B. Collier. *Marconi: Master of Space.* London: Hutchinson, 1935.
Johnson, Nicholas. "Broadcasting in America: The Performance of Network Affiliates in the Top 50 Markets." *Federal Communications Commission Reports* 42 F.C.C. 2d (August 10, 1973).
Jolly, W. P. *Marconi.* London: Constable, 1972; New York: Stein & Day, 1972.
Jome, Hiram L. *Economics of the Radio Industry.* Chicago: A. W. Shaw, 1925. Reprint. New York: Arno Press, 1971.
Journal of Advertising Research. New York: Advertising Research Foundation, 1960– . Bimonthly.
Journal of Broadcasting. Washington, DC: Broadcast Education Association, 1957–1984. Quarterly.
Journal of Broadcasting & Electronic Media. Washington, DC: Broadcast Education Association, 1985– . Quarterly.
Journal of Consumer Research. Gainesville, FL: American Association for Public Opinion Research, 1974– . Quarterly.
Jurgen, Ronald K. "High Definition Television Update." *IEEE Spectrum* 25 (April 1988): 56–62.
Kaltenborn, Hans von. *I Broadcast the Crisis.* New York: Random House, 1938.
———. *It Seems like Yesterday.* New York: G. P. Putnam's Sons, 1956.
Keillor, Garrison. *WLT: A Radio Romance.* New York: Viking, 1991.
Kemezis, Paul. "TV Codec Costs, Missing Standards Delay Use of DS-3 Fiber Optic Links." *Data Communications* 16 (December 1987): 70–74.
Kempner, Stanley. *Television Encyclopedia.* New York: Fairchild, 1948.

Kendrick, Alexander. *Prime Time: The Life of Edward R. Murrow.* Boston: Little, Brown, 1969.

Kenyon, Victor. "Ever Vigilant to Present 'the Preferred Angle.' " *Advertising Age* 67 (January 8, 1996): 22.

Kerr, Frances Willard. *Women in Radio: A View of Important Jobs in Radio Held by Women, Illustrated by Biographical Sketches.* Pamphlets in American History. Women; WO 423. Gerritsen Collection of Women's History, no. 1497. Glen Rock, NJ: Microfilming Corp. of America, 1978. Microfiche.

Kirby, Edward M., and Jack W. Harris. *Star-Spangled Radio.* Chicago: Ziff-Davis, 1948.

Klapper, Joseph T. *The Effects of Mass Communication.* Foundations of Communication Research, no. 3. Glencoe, IL: Free Press, 1960.

Klein, Frederick C. "Believe It or Not: The NFL Once Saw TV as a Bad Idea." *Wall Street Journal,* January 19, 1996, B8.

Knecht, Richard J., and Brian Grinonneau. "Challenging the Constitutionality of Must-Carry." *Communications & the Law* 8 (December 1986): 3–10.

Koenig, Allen E., ed. *Broadcasting and Bargaining: Labor Relations in Radio and Television.* Madison: University of Wisconsin Press, 1970.

Koenig, Allen E., and Ruane B. Hill. *The Farther Vision: Educational Television Today.* Madison: University of Wisconsin Press, 1967.

Krampner, Jon. *The Man in the Shadows: Fred Coe and the Golden Age of Television.* New Brunswick, NJ: Rutgers University Press, 1997.

Krasnow, Erwin G., and J. Geoffrey Bentley. *Buying or Building a Broadcast Station: Everything You Want—and Need—to Know, But Didn't Know Who to Ask.* Washington, DC: National Association of Broadcasters, 1982.

Krasnow, Erwin G., Lawrence D. Longley, and Herbert A. Terry. *The Politics of Broadcast Regulation.* 3d ed. New York: St. Martin's Press, 1982.

Krasnow, Erwin G., and Jill Abeshouse Stern. *The New Video Marketplace: A Regulatory Identity Crisis.* Cambridge: Harvard University, Center for Information Policy Research, Program on Information Resources Policy, 1985.

Kraus, Jeffrey. "The FCC's Microwave Rules Open New Spectrum Uses." *Telecommunications* 21 (June 1987): 79–86.

Kuriansky, Judy. "Sex Simmers, Still Sells." *Advertising Age* 66 (Spring 1995): 49.

Kurtz, E. B. *Pioneering in Educational Television.* Ames: Iowa State University Press, 1959.

Lackmann, Ron. *Remember Radio.* New York: G. P. Putnam's Sons, 1970.

———. *Remember Television.* New York: G. P. Putnam's Sons, 1971.

Lallande, Ann. "The Syndex Complex." *Marketing & Media Decisions* 23 (April 1988): 144, 146.

Lamb, Edward, with Foreword by Estes Kefauver. *No Lamb for Slaughter: An Autobiography.* New York: Harcourt, Brace, & World, 1963.

———. *Edward Lamb on "Trial by Battle," the Case History of a Washington Witch-Hunt.* Occasional Paper on the Free Society. Santa Barbara, CA: Center for the Study of Democratic Institutions, 1964.

Lang, Kurt, and Gladys Engle Lang. *Politics and Television Re-viewed.* Beverly Hills, CA: Sage, 1984.

Lange, David L., Robert K. Baker, and Sandra Ball-Rokeach. *Mass Media and Violence: A Report to the National Commission on the Causes and Preven-*

tion of Violence. NCCPV Staff Study Series, vol. 11. Washington, DC: U.S. Government Printing Office, 1969.

Larsen, Otto N. *Violence and the Mass Media*. New York: Harper & Row, 1968.

Lavin, Marilyn. "Creating Consumers in the 1930s: Irna Phillips and the Radio Soaps." *Journal of Consumer Research* 22 (June 1995): 75–89.

Lazarsfeld, Paul F. *Radio and the Printed Page*. New York: Duell, Sloan, & Pearce, 1940. Reprint. New York: Arno Press, 1971.

Lazarsfeld, Paul F., and Harry H. Field. *The People Look at Radio*. Chapel Hill: University of North Carolina Press, 1946; sponsored by National Association of Broadcasters.

Lazarsfeld, Paul F., and Patricia L. Kendall. *Radio Listening in America: The People Look at Radio—Again*. Englewood Cliffs, NJ: Prentice-Hall, 1948. Reprint. Perennial Works in Sociology. New York: Arno Press, 1979.

Lazarsfeld, Paul F., and Frank N. Stanton. *Radio Research*. New York: Duell, Sloan, & Pearce, 1941; Essential Books, 1942–43. Reprint. Perennial Works in Sociology. New York: Arno Press, 1979.

Lee, A. M., and E. B. Lee. *The Fine Art of Propaganda: A Study of Father Coughlin's Speeches*. San Diego: Harcourt, Brace, 1931.

Lerner, David. "Understanding Erosion." *Marketing & Media Decisions* 23 (June 1988): 112–16.

Lesser, Gerald S. *Children and Television: Lessons from Sesame Street*. New York: Random House, 1974.

Lessing, Lawrence. *Man of High Fidelity: Edwin Howard Armstrong*. Philadelphia: J. B. Lippincott, 1956.

Levin, Harvey J. *Broadcast Regulation and Joint Ownership of Media*. New York: New York University Press, 1960.

———. *The Invisible Resource: Use and Regulation of the Radio Spectrum*. Baltimore: Johns Hopkins University Press for Resources for the Future, 1971.

———. *Fact and Fancy in Television Regulation: An Economic Study of Policy Alternatives*. Publications of Russell Sage Foundation. New York: Russell Sage Foundation, 1980.

Lichty, Lawrence W. " 'The Nation's Station' ": A History of Radio Station WLW [Chicago]. Huntington Beach, CA, 1964. Ph.D. diss., Ohio State University. Ann Arbor, MI: University Microfilms, 1977. See also Perry, Dick.

Lichty, Lawrence W., and Malachi C. Topping, eds. *American Broadcasting: A Source Book on the History of Radio and Television*. Studies in Public Communication. New York: Hastings House, 1975.

Lipman, Andrew D. "CATV Case Challenges Legal Basis of All Rate Regulation." *Telephony* 209 (December 1985): 76–77.

Lipton, Amy. "Lights, Camera . . . Telaction!" *Supermarket Business* 43 (August 1988): 35–36.

Lohr, Lenox R. *Television Broadcasting: Production, Economics, Technique*. New York: McGraw-Hill, 1940.

Lutz, William W. *The News of Detroit: How a Newspaper and a City Grew Together*. Boston: Little, Brown, 1973.

Lyons, Eugene. *David Sarnoff: A Biography*. New York: Harper & Row, 1966.

MacDonald, J. Fred. *Don't Touch That Dial: Radio Programming in American Life, 1920–1960*. Chicago: Nelson-Hall, 1979.

———. "Radio: Medium Is Alive and Well in the Age of Video." *Advertising Age* 55 (September 1984): 11–13.

———. *Television and the Red Menace: The Video Road to Vietnam.* New York: Praeger, 1985.

———. *Blacks and White TV: Afro-Americans in Television since 1948.* 2d ed. Chicago: Nelson-Hall, 1992.

———. *One Nation under Television: The Rise and Decline of Network TV.* New York: Pantheon Books, 1990; Nelson-Hall Quality Paperback ed., updated and enl. Chicago: Nelson-Hall, 1994.

MacLatchy, Josephine. *Education on the Air.* Ohio State University, 1930–1944. Annual.

Maclaurin, W. Rupert, with technical assistance of R. Joyce Harman and Foreword by Karl T. Compton. *Invention and Innovation in the Radio Industry.* New York: Macmillan, 1949, New York: Arno Press and the *New York Times*, 1971.

Macnow, Glen. "NFL Films Is Scoring High." *Nation's Business* 76, no. 9 (September 1988): 44–47.

Madlin, Nancy. "Here's an Earful: Network Radio Is Hot!" *Madison Avenue* 28 (June 1986): 18, 20.

Magiera, Marcy. "TV Syndicators Want New Image, Old Quality." *Advertising Age* 58 (January 1987): 526–27.

Mahler, Richard. "Discussing Dollars Makes Sense/Networks Capitalize on Business." *Advertising Age* 55 (May 1984): 50–52.

Mahoney, William, and Adam Buckman. "Nets Battle Viewing Plunge." *Advertising Age* 59 (May 1988): 30.

Mandese, Joe. "Cable: Boom Time." *Marketing & Media Decisions* 23 (August 1988): 57–60.

———. "The Buying and Selling; Supply and Demand, 'Upfront,' Ratings Points, Media Fragmentation: Oh, How TV Has Changed." *Advertising Age* 66 (Spring 1995): 20.

Marconi, Degna. *My Father, Marconi.* New York: McGraw-Hill, 1962.

Marconi Review. Chelmsford, England: GEC-Marconi Electronics, 1926– . Irregular.

Marcus, Sheldon. *Father Coughlin: The Tumultuous Life of the Priest of the Little Flower.* Boston: Little, Brown, 1973.

Marketing & Media Decisions. New York: Decisions, 1979–1990.

Marketing Communications. New York: Media Horizons, 1985–1989. Monthly.

Masini, Giancarlo. *Marconi.* New York: Marsilio, 1995.

Mayer, Martin. *About Television.* New York: Harper & Row, 1972.

Mayo, John B. *Bulletin from Dallas: The President Is Dead; The Story of John F. Kennedy's Assassination as Covered by Radio and TV.* New York: Exposition Press, an Exposition-Banner Book, 1967.

McCarthy, Joe. *Fred Allen's Letters.* New York: Doubleday, 1965; New York: Pocket Books, 1966.

McDonough, John. "Bring Brands to Life: From Jack Benny to Ella Fitzgerald, the Presenter Can Seal the Deal." *Advertising Age* 66 (Spring 1995): 34.

———. "75-year Roller-coaster Ride." *Advertising Age* 66 (September 4, 1995): 22.

McGinniss, Joe. *The Selling of the President 1968*. New York: Trident, 1969; New York: Pocket Books, 1970.

Meisler, Andy. "Lucy Sure Didn't Start It, But She Stuck to It." *New York Times* 145, November 20, 1995, C5.

Mergers & Acquisitions. Philadelphia: MLR Enterprises, 1965– . Bimonthly.

Michael, Paul, and James Robert Parish. *The Emmy Awards: A Pictorial History*. New York: Crown, 1970.

Minow, Newton N. *Equal Time: The Private Broadcaster and the Public Interest*. Edited by Lawrence Laurent. New York: Atheneum, 1964.

Minow, Newton N., John B. Martin, and Lee M. Mitchell. *Presidential Television*. New York: Basic Books, a Twentieth Century Fund Report, 1973.

MIT's Technology Review. Cambridge: Association of Alumni and Alumnae of the Massachusetts Institute of Technology, 1997– . 8 no. a year. See also *Technology Review*.

Mitchell, Curtis. *Cavalcade of Broadcasting*. Chicago: Follett, a Benjamin Company/Rutledge Book, 1970.

Mitchell, Rodney, Jr. "Conjuring Up Data over CATV." *Network World* 4 (February 1987): 1, 35–36.

Morella, Joe, Edward Z. Epstein, and Eleanor Clark. *The Amazing Careers of Bob Hope: From Gags to Riches*. New Rochelle, NY: Arlington House, 1973.

Morgan, Edward P. *Clearing the Air*. Washington, DC: R. B. Luce, 1963.

Mosco, Vincent. *The Regulation of Broadcasting in the United States: A Comparative Analysis*. Ph.D. diss., Harvard University. Cambridge: Harvard University, Program on Information Technologies and Public Policy, 1975.

"MTV Tells Its Four Network Stories to the Madison Avenue Media Panel." *Madison Avenue*, December 1985, 99–105.

Murrow, Edward R. *This Is London*. Edited by Elmer Davis. New York: Simon & Schuster, 1941. Reprint. Witnesses to War. New York: Schocken Books, 1989.

Murrow, Edward R., and Fred Friendly, eds. *See It Now* [television program]. New York: Simon & Schuster, 1955.

National Broadcasting Company. *Broadcasting*. 4 vols. New York: NBC, 1935.

———. *NBC and You*. New York: NBC, 1944.

Nation's Business. Washington, DC: Chamber of Commerce of the United States, 1912– .

Nationwide Black Radio Directory. Atlanta, GA: Charles D. Edwards, 1979.

Nelson, Harold L., Dwight L. Teeter, and Frank Thayer. *Law of Mass Communications: Freedom and Control of Print and Broadcast Media*. 5th ed. Mineola, NY: Foundation Press, 1986. See also Thayer, Frank.

Nelson, Ozzie. *Ozzie*. Englewood Cliffs, NJ: Prentice-Hall, 1973.

Network World. Framingham, MA: CW Communications, 1986– . Weekly.

Newman, Mark. *Entrepreneurs of Profit and Pride: From Black-Appeal to Radio Soul*. Media and Society Series. New York: Praeger, 1988.

Nobel, Milton. *The Municipal Broadcasting System, Its History, Organization, and Activities* [New York radio station WNYC]. New York: MBS, 1953.

Noll, Roger G., Merton J. Peck, and John J. McGowan. *Economic Aspects of Television Regulation*. Studies in the Regulation of Economic Activity. Washington, DC: Brookings Institution, 1973.

North American Radio-TV Station Guide. Indianapolis: H. W. Sams, 1963– .

O'Connor, John E., ed., with Foreword by Erik Barnouw. *American History, American Television: Interpreting the Video Past*. Ungar Film Library. New York: Frederick Ungar, 1985.

Ogilvy, David. *Confessions of an Advertising Man*. New York: Atheneum, 1963; New York: Dell, 1964.

———. *Blood, Brains, & Beer: The Autobiography of David Ogilvy*. New York: Atheneum, 1978.

Oliver, John William. *History of American Technology*. New York: Ronald Press, 1956.

O'Malley, Beverly. "The 'Commercialization' of PBS." *Marketing & Media Decisions* 20 (October 1985): 96, 98.

O'Neill, John Joseph. *Prodigal Genius: The Life of Nikola Tesla*. New York: I. Washburn, 1944.

Papazian, Ed. "Learning from the Cable Network Experience." *Marketing & Media Decisions* 18 (October 1983): 82–86.

Paskowski, Marianne. "Outlook Remains Bullish for Independent TV." *Marketing & Media Decisions* 19 (September 1984): 62–63, 116, 118.

———. "Everybody Wants Their MTV!" *Marketing & Media Decisions* 20 (Spring 1985): 61–68.

———. "An Ad by Any Other Name Is Still an Add." *Marketing & Media Decisions* 20 (December 1985): 70–76, 126–27.

———. "Radio Daze." *Marketing & Media Decisions* 22 (April 1987): 71–72.

Passer, Harold C. *The Electrical Manufacturers, 1875–1900: A Study in Competition, Entrepreneurship, Technical Change, and Economic Growth*. Studies in Entrepreneurial History. Cambridge: Harvard University Press, 1953.

Perry, Dick. *Not Just a Sound: The Story of WLW* [Cincinnati]. Englewood Cliffs, NJ: Prentice-Hall, 1971.

Pusateri, C. Joseph. *Enterprise in Radio: WWL* [New Orleans] *and the Business of Broadcasting in America*. Washington, DC: University Press of America, 1980.

Radio Employee Compensation and Fringe Benefits Report. Washington, DC: National Association of Broadcasters, 1988– .

Radio Financial Report. Washington, DC: National Association of Broadcasters, 1982. Annual.

"Radio: The Static Is Coming from Its Own Ranks." *Ad Forum* 4 (December 1983): 16–17.

Radio Station Salaries. Washington, DC: National Association of Broadcasters, 1994– . Biennial.

Ramstad, Evan. "Disney Buys ABC Network for $19 Billion: Deal Creates World's Largest Purveyor of Entertainment." *Houston Chronicle*, August 1, 1995, 1.

Ratzlaff, John T., and Leland I. Anderson. *Dr. Nikola Tesla Bibliography*. Palo Alto, CA: Ragusan Press, 1979.

Reade, Leslie. *Marconi and the Discovery of Wireless*. London: Faber & Faber, 1963.

Reck, Franklin R. *Radio from Start to Finish*. New York: Thomas Y. Crowell, 1942.

Regulation. Washington, DC: Cato Institute, 1977– . Quarterly.

Reiter, Allan. "Short-Haul Transmission: Tune In, Turn On, Save Cash." *Network World 5* (June 1988): 47–48.

Reitman, Judith. "Financial Cable Nets Mean Business." *Marketing & Media Decisions* 20 (April 1985): 60–65, 156–58.

Rhymer, Paul. *The Small House Half-Way Up in the Next Block: Paul Rhymer's Vic and Sade* [radio program]. Edited by Mary Frances Rhymer. New York: McGraw-Hill, 1972.

Robinson, Thomas Porter. *Radio Networks and the Federal Government.* New York: Columbia University Press, 1943. Reprint. Dissertations in Broadcasting. New York: Arno Press, 1979.

Rolo, Charles J. *Radio Goes to War: The Fourth Front.* New York: G. P. Putnam's Sons, a "Current History" Book, 1942.

Rosenfeld, Judith. "Syndication and the Networks Battle." *Marketing Communications* 11, no. 8 (September 1986): 24–27.

Ross, Stephen R., and Barrett L. Brick. "The Cable Act of 1984—How Did We Get There and Where Are We Going?" *Federal Communications Law Journal* 39, nos. 1, 2 (May 1987): 27–52.

Routt, Edd. *The Business of Radio Broadcasting.* Blue Ridge Summit, PA: GL/Tab Books, 1972.

Sanger, Elliott M. *Rebel in Radio: The Story of WQXR.* New York: Hastings House, Communication Arts Books, 1973.

Sarnoff, David. *Principles and Practices of Network Radio Broadcasting: Testimony of David Sarnoff, President, Radio Corporation of America, Chairman of the Board, National Broadcasting Company, Inc., before the Federal Communications Commission, Washington, D.C., November 14, 1938 and May 17, 1939.* New York: RCA Institutes Technical Press, 1939.

———. *Looking Ahead: The Papers of David Sarnoff.* New York: McGraw-Hill, 1968.

Schaefer, George. *From Live to Tape to Film: Sixty Years of Inconspicuous Directing.* Directors Guild of America Oral History Series. Hollywood, CA: Directors Guild of America; Metuchen, NJ: Scarecrow Press, 1996.

Schariff, Edward E. "The Boom in Television Business Shows." *Institutional Investor* 18 (March 1984): 129–38.

Schechter, Abel Alan, and Edward Anthony. *I Live on Air.* New York: Frederick A. Stokes, 1941.

Schleier, Curt. "TV Syndication: First-Run Programming on Fast Track." *Advertising Age* 56 (January 1985): 16, 18.

Schmeckebier, Laurence F. *The Federal Radio Commission: Its History, Activities and Organization.* Service Monographs of the U.S. Government, no. 65. Washington, DC: Brookings Institution, 1932. Reprint. New York: AMS Press, 1974.

Schramm, Wilbur et al. *Television in the Lives of Our Children.* Stanford, CA: Stanford University Press, 1961.

Schubert, Paul. *The Electric Word: The Rise of Radio.* New York: Macmillan, 1928.

Security Management. Arlington, VA: American Society for Industrial Security, 1972– . Monthly.

Seifer, Marc J. *Wizard: The Life and Times of Nikola Tesla: Biography of a Genius.* Secaucus, NJ: Carol, a Birch Lane Press Book, 1996.

Seldes, Gilbert V. *The Great Audience.* New York: Viking Press, 1950. Reprint. Westport, CT: Greenwood Press, 1970.

———. *The Public Arts.* New York: Simon & Schuster, 1956. Reprint. Classics in Communication and Mass Culture Series. New Brunswick, NJ: Transaction, 1994.

Selman-Earnest, Cora. *Black Owned Radio and Television Stations in the United States from 1950–1982: A Descriptive Study.* Ph.D. diss., Wayne State University, 1985. Ann Arbor, MI: University Microfilms International, 1987.

Settel, Irving. *A Pictorial History of Radio.* Secaucus, NJ: Citadel Press, 1960; New York: Grosset & Dunlap, 1967.

———. *A Pictorial History of Television.* 2d ed., enl. New York: Frederick Ungar, 1983.

Sevareid, Eric. *Not So Wild a Dream.* New York: Knopf, 1946.

———. *In One Ear: 107 Snapshots of Men and Events Which Make a Far-Reaching Panorama of the American Situation at Mid-Century.* New York: Knopf, 1952.

———. *This Is Eric Sevareid.* New York: McGraw-Hill, 1964.

Shiers, George, assisted by May Shiers. *Bibliography of the History of Electronics.* Metuchen, NJ: Scarecrow Press, 1972.

Shiers, George, comp., assisted by May Shiers. *Early Television: A Bibliographic Guide to 1940.* Garland Reference Library of Social Science, vol. 582. New York: Garland, 1997.

"A Short Course in Cable, 1988." In *Broadcasting/Cablecasting Yearbook 1988,* D3, D363. Washington, DC: Lawrence B. Taishoff, 1988.

Shulman, Arthur, and Roger Youman. *The Golden Age of Television: How Sweet It Was.* New York: Bonanza Books, 1979.

Shurick, Edward P. J. *The First Quarter-Century of American Broadcasting.* Kansas City, MO: Midland, 1946.

Siepmann, Charles A. *Radio in Wartime.* New York: Oxford University Press, 1942.

———. *Radio's Second Chance.* Boston: Little, Brown, an Atlantic Monthly Press Book, 1946.

———. *Radio, Television, and Society.* New York: Oxford University Press, 1950.

———. *Television and Education in the United States.* Paris: UNESCO [United Nations Educational, Scientific, and Cultural Organization], 1952.

Sivowitch, Elliot N. "A Technological Survey of Broadcasting's 'Pre History,' 1876–1920." *Journal of Broadcasting* 15, no. 1 (winter 1970): 1–20.

———. "A Technological Survey of Broadcasting's Prehistory, 1876–1920." In *American Broadcasting: A Source Book on the History of Radio and Television,* edited by Lawrence W. Lichty and Malachi C. Topping, 18. New York: Hastings House, 1975.

Skornia, Harry J., and Jack William Kitson, eds. *Problems and Controversies in Television and Radio.* Palo Alto, CA: Pacific Books, 1968.

Slate, Sam J., and Joe Cook. *It Sounds Impossible.* New York: Macmillan, 1963.

Slutsker, Gary. "Computers/Communications: Good-Bye Cable TV, Hello Fiber Optics." *Forbes* 142 (September 19, 1988): 174–79.

Small, William J. *To Kill a Messenger: Television News and the Real World.* Studies in Public Communication. New York: Hastings House, Communication Arts Books, 1970.

Smead, Elmer E. *Freedom of Speech by Radio and Television.* Washington, DC: Public Affairs Press, 1959.

Sobel, Robert. *RCA.* New York: Stein & Day, 1986.

Spivak, John L. *Shrine of the Silver Dollar.* New York: Modern Age Books, 1940.

Stark, Phyllis. "On the Air." *Billboard* 106 (November 1, 1994): 120.

Stedman, Raymond William. *The Serials: Suspense and Drama by Installment.* 2d ed., rev. and enl. Norman: University of Oklahoma Press, 1971.

Sterling, Christopher H. *Second Service: A History of Commercial FM Broadcasting to 1969.* 3 vols. Ph.D. diss., University of Wisconsin, Madison, 1969. Ann Arbor, MI: University Microfilms, 1970.

Sterling, Christopher H., and John M. Kittross. *Stay Tuned: A Concise History of American Broadcasting.* Belmont, CA: Wadsworth, 1978.

Stern, Bill. *The Taste of Ashes: An Autobiography.* New York: Henry Holt, 1959.

Stoddard, Rob. "Decade of Deregulation: Three Experts Examine 10 Years of Regulation." *Satellite Communications* 9 (April 1987): 15–26.

Summers, Harrison B., comp. *Radio Censorship.* The Reference Shelf, vol. 12, no. 10. Bronx, NY: H. W. Wilson, 1939.

Summers, Harrison B., ed. *A Thirty-Year History of Programs Carried on National Radio Networks in the United States, 1926–1956.* Columbus: Ohio State University, 1958. Reprint. History of Broadcasting: Radio to Television. New York: Arno Press, 1971.

Summers, Robert E. *America's Weapons of Psychological Warfare.* The Reference Shelf, vol. 23, no. 4. Bronx, NY: H. W. Wilson, 1951.

Summers, Robert E., comp. *Wartime Censorship of Press and Radio.* The Reference Shelf, vol. 15, no. 8. Bronx, NY: H. W. Wilson, 1942.

Summers, Robert E., and Harrison B. Summers. *Broadcasting and the Public.* Belmont, CA: Wadsworth, 1966.

Susskind, Charles. *Popov and the Beginnings of Radiotelegraphy.* San Francisco: San Francisco Press, 1962.

Swing, Raymond. *Good Evening! A Professional Memoir.* Harcourt, Brace, & World, 1964.

Technology Review. Cambridge: Alumni Association, Massachusetts Institute of Technology, 1899– . Frequency varies.

Tell, Lawrence J. "Station Break: Independent TV Operators Headed for a Shakeout." *Barron's* 66 (January 1986): 13, 34–35.

Tesla, Nikola, with Ben Johnston. *My Inventions: The Autobiography of Nikola Tesla.* Williston, VT: Hart Brothers, 1982. (First published in *Electrical Experimenter Magazine,* 1919.)

Thayer, Frank. *Legal Control of the Press.* 1st–4th eds. Westbury, NY: Foundation Press, 1944–1962.

Thomas, Bob. *Winchell.* Garden City, NY: Doubleday, 1971.

Thomas, Lowell. *History As You Heard It.* Garden City, NY: Doubleday, 1957.

Thomson, Charles A. H. *Television and Presidential Politics: The Experience in 1952 and the Problems Ahead.* Washington, DC: Brookings Institution, 1956.

Tinker, Grant, and Bud Rukeyser. *Tinker in Television: From General Sarnoff to General Electric.* New York: Simon & Schuster, 1994.

"TV News: The Rapid Rise of Home Rule." *Newsweek,* October 17, 1988, 94.

Tyler, Kingdon S. *Modern Radio.* San Diego: Harcourt, Brace, 1947.

Udell, Gillman G., comp. *Radio Laws of the United States: 1978 Edition.* Washington, DC: U.S. Government Printing Office, 1978.

Ulloth, Dana Royal, Peter L. Klinge, and Sandra Eells. *Mass Media, Past, Present, Future.* St. Paul, MN: West, 1983.

U.S. Congress. House. Committee on Energy and Commerce. Subcommittee on Telecommunications, Consumer Protection, and Finance. *Satellite Communications/Direct Broadcast Satellites.* Hearings. 97th Cong., 1st sess., December 15, 1981. Serial no. 97–81. Washington, DC: U.S. Government Printing Office, 1982.

———. House. Committee on Interstate and Foreign Commerce. *Regulation of Broadcasting: Half a Century of Government Regulation of Broadcasting and the Need for Further Legislative Action.* 85th Cong., 2d sess., 1958.

———. House. Committee on the Judiciary. Subcommittee No. 5. Subcommittee on Antitrust. *Monopoly Problems in Regulated Industries. Part 2. Volume 1. Television.* Hearings. 84th Cong., 2d sess., June 27, 28, July 11–13, 1956. Committee Serial 22 [includes FCC Order No. 37, docket No. 5060 "Report on Chain Broadcasting," May 1941, pp. 3533–3690]. Westport, CT: Greenwood Press, 1973. Microfiche.

———. House. Committee on Merchant Marine and Fisheries. *Government Control of Radio Communication: Hearings before the Committee on Merchant Marine and Fisheries.* 65th Cong., 3d sess., December 12–19, 1918. Washington, DC: U.S. Government Printing Office, 1919.

U.S. Congress. Senate. Committee on Commerce. *Fairness Doctrine.* Washington, DC: U.S. Government Printing Office, 1968.

———. Senate. Committee on Commerce. Subcommittee on Communications. *Satellite Communications.* Hearings. 88th Cong., 1st sess., February 18, 19, 27, 1983. Committee Serial 3.

U.S. Statutes. Vol. 48. Public Law 73–416. *Communications Act of 1934 with Amendments and Index Thereto.* Washington, DC: U.S. Government Printing Office, June 19, 1934.

Vallee, Rudy. *My Time Is Your Time.* New York: Obolensky, 1962.

Van Trees, Harry L. *Satellite Communications.* IEEE Press Selected Reprint Series. New York: IEEE Press, 1979; distributed by Wiley.

Vaughn, Robert, with Introduction by George McGovern. *Only Victims: A Study of Show Business Blacklisting.* New York: Limelight Editions, 1996. (Originally published New York: Putnam, 1972.)

Velia, Ann M. *KOB, Goddard's Magic Mast: Fifty Years of Pioneer Broadcasting.* Las Cruces: New Mexico State University, 1972.

Wagner, Paul H. *Radio Journalism.* Minneapolis: Burgess, 1940.

Waller, Judith C. *Radio: The Fifth Estate.* 2d ed. Boston: Houghton Mifflin, 1950.

Walley, Wayne. "Network TV Pressure Point." *Advertising Age 59* (June 1988): 102.

Ward, Jack. *The Supporting Players of Television, 1959–1983.* Cleveland, OH: Lakeshore West, 1996.

Warren, Alan. *This Is a "Thriller": An Episode Guide, History, and Analysis of the Classic 1960s Television Series.* Jefferson, NC: McFarland, 1996.

Warren, Donald I. *Radio Priest: Charles Coughlin, the Father of Hate Radio.* New York: Free Press, 1996.

Watson, Mary Ann. *The Expanding Vista: American Television in the Kennedy Years.* Chapel Hill, NC: Duke University Press, 1994.

WBIL Tuskegee. Tuskegee, AL: WBIL Tuskegee, 1975.

Webster, James G., and Lawrence W. Lichty. *Ratings Analysis: Theory and Practice.* Communication Textbook Series. Broadcasting. Hillsdale, NJ: L. Erlbaum Associates, 1991.

Weinberg, Meyer. *TV in America: The Morality of Hard Cash.* New York: Ballantine, 1962.

Weisberg, Louis. "Networks Feel Breeze from Independents' Upswing." *Advertising Age* 55 (February 6, 1984): M14, M18.

Welter, Therese R. "Fiber Optics vs. Satellites." *Industry Weekly* 232 (February 23, 1987): 50, 55.

Wentz, Laurel. "U.S. TV News Invasion." *Advertising Age* 57 (November 1986): 69.

Wertheimer, Linda, ed. *Listening to America: Twenty-five Years in the Life of a Nation as Heard on National Public Radio.* Boston: Houghton Mifflin, 1995.

"Westinghouse Completes CBS Acquisition." *New York Times*, November 25, 1995, A47.

Whelan, Kenneth. *How the Golden Age of Television Turned My Hair to Silver.* New York: Walker, 1973.

White, David Manning, and Richard Averson. *Sight, Sound, and Society: Motion Pictures and Television in America.* Boston: Beacon Press, 1968.

White, Llewellyn. *The American Radio: A Report on the Broadcasting Industry in the United States from the Commission on Freedom of the Press.* Chicago: University of Chicago Press, 1947. Reprint. New York: Arno Press, 1971.

White, Paul Welrose. *News on the Air.* New York: Harcourt, 1947.

"Why TV News Has Been Losing Its Audience." *Business Week*, April 16, 1984, 137, 141.

Wilson, George. "When Memphis Made Radio History." *American Visions* 8 (August 1993): 22–25.

Wold, Robert N. "How New Is SNG?" *Satellite Communications* 12 (January 1988): 35–36.

Wolf, Frank. *Television Programming for News and Public Affairs: A Quantitative Analysis of Networks and Stations.* Praeger Special Studies in U.S. Economic, Social, and Political Issues. New York: Praeger, 1972.

Wolf, Mark. "Lucrative Formula Yields Supply of Success: Syndicators Take Different Roads but Reach Same Plateau." *Advertising Age* 55 (February 1984): M12–M13.

Wolf, Marvin J. "The Lion in Winter: Vision, Risk-Taking Defined Legendary Career of ABC's Chief Architect." *Variety* 357 (December 5, 1994): 49.

Wood, William A. *Electronic Journalism.* New York: Columbia University Press, 1967.

"World of Interest in Media Deals: Demand Abroad for U.S. Entertainment Fueling Mergers." *Chicago Tribune*, August 6, 1995, 1.

World Radio TV Handbook. Copenhagen, Denmark: O. Lund Johansen, 1961– . Annual. Imprint varies.

Wylie, Max. *Best Broadcasts of 1938–39*. New York: McGraw-Hill, 1939.

———. *Best Broadcasts of 1939–40*. New York: McGraw-Hill, 1940.

———. *Clear Channels: Television and the American People, a Report to Set Owners*. New York: Funk & Wagnalls, 1955.

Yang, Eleanor. "Delays Blur Local Debut of HDTV: Major Networks, including a Chicago Station, Are Having Trouble Meeting FCC-Imposed Deadlines on Digital Broadcasting." *Chicago Tribune*, August 19, 1998, 1.

Yellin, David G. *Special: Fred Freed and the Television Documentary*. New York: Macmillan, 1973.

Zacks, Richard. "Surprise! Cable Produces Some Bright Spots." *Madison Avenue* 26 (April 1984): 80–82.

Zeidenberg, Leonard. "Two Decades of Crisis between Nixon and the Media." *Broadcasting & Cable* 124 (May 2, 1994): 16.

Part III

Electric, Gas, and Sanitary Services
ESIC 49.0

ELECTRIC SERVICES, 49.1
‗‗‗‗‗‗‗‗‗‗‗‗‗‗‗‗‗‗‗‗‗‗‗‗‗‗ JOHN L. NEUFELD

A century of commercially provided electricity has had a profound effect on human life: so essential is electrical service to twentieth-century society that a power failure of a few hours can be a major, even life-threatening, disruption. The impact of electricity on manufacturing, communication, transportation, and architecture is rooted in many industries. The electric services industry, better known as electric utilities, deserves a central position in this "electric revolution." Today, the firms in this industry supply nearly all of the electricity used in the United States.

Many characteristics of the electric services industry make it particularly amenable to analysis by business historians. The industry's classification is sufficiently clear-cut as to have been unaffected by changes in the Standard Industrial Classification (SIC). Furthermore, the set of firms in the industry has been fairly stable for many years, and most firms in business today were formed from the consolidation of smaller firms. Compared to most industries, the electric services industry has been, for much of its history, subject to government regulation at both the state and federal levels. Much operating information, which would be unavailable in other industries, has been put in the public domain as a result of this regulation. In addition, the U.S. Bureau of the Census (1905a, 1905b, 1905c, 1974) has regularly collected and published data on the industry since 1902. Despite the large amount of primary source material available on the industry, relatively few comprehensive histories have been prepared. Material has been written, however, on various aspects of the industry.

THOMAS A. EDISON AND THE ORIGINS
OF THE INDUSTRY

The scientific and commercial underpinnings of the electric services industry were developed during the nineteenth century, although the initial development of batteries occurred in the late eighteenth century. Both incandescent lighting and arc lighting were first demonstrated in England by Sir Humphry Davy, the former in 1802 and the latter in 1808. Michael Faraday produced a primitive electric generator in the 1830s. Perhaps the first successful use of electricity was for communication: the telegraph. William F. Cooke and Sir Charles Wheatstone developed a telegraphy system that was used in Europe during the 1840s, although it eventually was replaced by the system developed by Samuel F. B. Morse. By the 1850s virtually every state east of the Mississippi was tied into a national telegraphy network. Within thirty to forty years, almost the entire industry was monopolized by the Western Union Telegraph Company. The telephone industry began in the late 1870s but did not replace telegraphy for long-distance communication until the twentieth century.

The development of electric lighting, rather than the use of electricity in communication, gave rise to the electric services industry in the latter part of the nineteenth century. The need for artificial lighting had spawned the development of the gas-lighting industry only a few decades earlier. The first electric lighting systems were based on the arc light, which provided illumination by means of an electric arc between two carbon rods. Arc lights were used in 1844 and lit the streets of Paris in 1877. The first American electric utility was the California Electric Light Company, organized by Charles F. Brush in 1879 to provide arc lighting in San Francisco. Within two years, Brush arc stations were located in New York City, Cleveland, Albany, Baltimore, Philadelphia, Boston, Cincinnati, and other cities. A competing arc lighting system developed by the Thomson-Houston Company had systems operating in several cities within a few years. Despite this apparent progress, arc lights were severely limited in their usefulness. Their carbon rods needed frequent replacement, they gave off unpleasant, dangerous fumes, and they were wired in series so that if one light failed, the entire circuit would stop functioning. Their most serious problem, however, was that arc lights tended to be very bright, and their brightness was difficult to control. For these reasons arc lighting was most frequently used for street lighting and did not provide a substantial challenge to gas for indoor lighting.

Incandescent lighting had been viewed by many as the answer to the problems of arc lights. Incandescent lighting occurs when a flow of electricity heats a conductive filament until it glows. Early attempts to produce incandescent lights were frustrated by the tendency of the filament to become quickly destroyed by the intense heat to which it was subjected. A number of Frenchmen, Russians, British, and Americans worked on the problem but were unable to devise a light bulb that was sufficiently durable to be of commercial value. A key reason for these failures was the difficulty of creating and maintaining sufficient vacuum within the bulb to prevent oxidation, and the development of the high-vacuum Crookes tube provided the needed technology. The question of whether credit for the invention of the practical incandescent lamp should go to Thomas A. Edison or the Englishman Sir Joseph Swan remains problematic. Edison's place as the father of the electric services industry is, however, unchallenged, and his honored place in our national mythology has been responsible for the publication of many biographies about him.

Edison's successful achievement was to develop an entire system, technological and commercial, for the marketing of electric illumination. His concern was always economic as well as technological. Edison's laboratory, the forerunner of a modern corporate research and development (R&D) department, based its new system for distribution and metering on the model presented by the gas industry. These efforts first bore fruit when Edison's Pearl Street Station began operation in New York as the first electric utility supplying incandescent light. The Edison Electric Illuminating Company, owner and operator of the Pearl Street Station, is regarded as the first successful electric utility. The modern Consolidated Edison Company is a direct successor of that company. A detailed account of the Pearl Street story can be found in Matthew Josephson's ([1959] 1992) biography of Edison. Despite its clear technological success, the first electric utility had to struggle for commercial success against gas lighting, which introduced important innovations of its own, notably the Welsbach mantle, which substantially improved the efficiency and quality of gaslights. Nevertheless, the new industry spread quite rapidly, and over 3,600 power stations were in operation in the United States in 1902, although arc lighting remained a significant source of revenue. Ironically, Edison fathered not only the electrical services industry but also its most bitter competitor, the isolated plant. Generator sizes were sufficiently small that users of large amounts of electricity could opt to provide their own electricity in an "isolated plant" in lieu of purchasing the output of a utility. These isolated plants were particularly attractive to users who were already generating steam for other purposes and who could generate electricity as a by-product of these other activities. Office buildings, public institutions, and even large residences joined with industrial electricity users in installing and running generating equipment. Over time, only large industrial users retained isolated plants, but these remained important until at least 1930. Industrial electricity usage was very important to electric utilities because it tended to occur during the day, when little use of electricity was being made by residential users. The more even load that resulted when both industrial and residential users were served led to the more efficient use of generators and transmission and distribution equipment. The desirability of industrial customers resulted in utilities' offering them discounts through a system of complex rate structures that continues today.

Edison's creative genius led him to considerable commercial success. He established a number of different companies involved in the manufacture of various products, the operation of utilities, and the licensing of technology. An excellent description of Edison's business empire is available in Passer (1953). Edison had a number of competitors, who were able to build their enterprises on the patents of others and by infringing on Edison's patents. No competitor figured more prominently in the history of the industry than George Westinghouse (Garbedian 1943).

Growth was necessary for the success of an electric utility. Only in this way could the advantages of scale offered by large generating equipment be realized. Growth also gave the companies the opportunity to serve customers whose peak loads occurred at different times, thereby gaining the advantages of fuller capital use. A growing service area incurred higher transmission costs. An important source of savings was high transmission voltages; higher voltages permitted thinner transmission lines, but lower voltage electricity was more desirable for consumer use.

Westinghouse realized the implication of developments in alternating current (AC) transformers for long-distance power transmission and based his system on alternating current technology in contrast to Edison's direct current (DC) system. Edison's response was to defend his system over that of his competitor. Understandable as an initial reaction, Edison's rejection of alternating current became an unreasonable passion in the face of pressure from eminent scientists and from his own sales agents. Edison clung to the position that alternating current was more dangerous than direct current, which he demonstrated through the macabre electrocution of dogs, cats, and even a horse. This line of effort ultimately led to the adoption of an alternating current system by the State of New York for the execution of criminals. Nevertheless, the economic advantages of alternating current over direct current became so clear that Edison's refusal to develop an AC system threatened the market position of his companies and forced his colleagues to reduce their dependence on him. By 1892, ten years after Pearl Street, Edison had lost all influence over the industry he had created.

GROWTH IN THE EARLY INDUSTRY

The early electric utilities were an exclusively urban phenomenon. Transmission costs, particularly for DC systems, limited a plant's service area to its immediate neighborhood. The need to run distribution lines over (or under) the public streets forced electric utilities to seek municipal franchises in order to operate. These franchises were typically not exclusive and were often granted for time periods shorter than the expected life of the utility's capital. Electric service companies faced competition both from other utilities and from substitutes for centrally generated electricity. A resurgence in the gas-lighting industry caused many users to switch back to gas lighting from electric lighting at the close of the century. Moreover, isolated plants, rather than utilities, were the likely source of electricity for a large consumer. Often, firms operating streetcars or manufacturing ice would sell their surplus electricity in competition with utilities. Interesting descriptions of the conditions under which the early electric services industry operated can be found in some of the corporate histories. Jack Riley's (1958) history of Carolina Power & Light Company is especially rich in its depiction of electricity use in turn-of-the-century Raleigh, North Carolina.

Despite these struggles, new firms brought electricity to an increasing number of cities. According to the commissioner of labor, there were 3,032 plants in operation in the United States in 1898. A census of central electric light and power stations (U.S. Bureau of the Census 1905c) counted 2,805 power companies in 1902; 3,462 in 1907; 3,659 in 1912; and 4,224 in 1917, after which the number declined. These were times of industrywide technological progress. Neil (1942) details much of this progress: in 1882, Edison used the equivalent of 10 pounds of coal to generate a kilowatt-hour (kwh) of electrical energy; by 1902, the average for all electric plants in the United States had fallen to 6.70 pounds per kwh, and by 1922, the national average had fallen to 2.50 pounds.

The activity and excitement within the industry did not bring particularly good business conditions. Hyman (1985) provides evidence that profitability for the entire industry was low, and a number of sources relate failures of individual utilities. Between 1902 and 1912 the price of electricity fell by 44 percent; during the same period, consumer prices rose 20 percent. Higher efficiency resulted in lower prices rather than higher profits. In addition, many municipalities built or acquired their own electric utilities, a process heavily encouraged by the political agenda of Progressive reformers. Census figures show that the number of municipally owned companies continued to grow until after 1922. Security and profitability for the industry were not assured until firms became organized on a much larger scale and until state regulation was established.

CONSOLIDATION AND CONTINUED GROWTH

A critical underpinning to the consolidation of electric utilities was the ability to transmit power economically over long distances. One important impetus to that development was hydroelectric power. Hydroelectricity must be generated at the falls; its value is enhanced if it can then be transmitted some distance to customers. One of the earliest and most notable attempts to tap hydroelectricity on a large scale was the Niagara Falls project, begun in 1895. Although the original promoters hoped that Buffalo would be their primary market (the project had been organized by businessmen and financiers rather than by engineers and entrepreneurs), new industrial operations were attracted to the area and became economically more important than distant markets until after the turn of the century. Niagara demonstrated, however, the commercial feasibility of long-distance power transmission.

Hydroelectricity was also important in the West and there led to the consolidation of utilities. Sacramento, for example, was supplied in 1895 by a plant located twenty-two miles away. Charles M. Coleman (1952) described the process of consolidation in northern California. In 1905 the California Gas and Electric Corporation was the leading hydro company in northern California, but it did not have access to the huge potential market in San Francisco. A merger between the company and San Francisco Gas and Electric Company formed the modern Pacific Gas and Electric Company. But southern California depended heavily on hydropower to provide electricity to the growing population of Los Angeles. Long-distance transmission there led to consolidation in southern California and the formation of Southern California Edison.

Still another region where hydroelectricity was important was the Southeast, where the Southern Power Company (forerunner of the Duke Power Company) was established to provide power for the textile industry. The first large-scale interconnected power grid, known as the Great Southern Grid, had reached significant proportions by 1914. This grid connected power systems in North Carolina, South Carolina, Georgia, and Tennessee and made possible the further separation of electricity production and consumption.

Although the process of consolidation was occurring in many places, credit for the first development of a giant electric utility is usually accorded to one man, Samuel Insull. Insull was an Englishman who emigrated to America originally to become Edison's personal secretary. Insull held a number of positions in association with Edison, including head of sales and manufacturing at Edison General Electric. When General Electric was formed, and Edison was effectively removed from control, Insull moved to Chicago and there became president of the Chicago Edison Company (Commonwealth Edison after 1907). When he took over Chicago Edison in 1892, it was one of over twenty utilities supplying Chicago with electricity for lighting. In two decades, he made Commonwealth Edison into a large monopolistic utility generally regarded as the most innovative and most efficient in the industry. His business, political, and technological acumen has been discussed both by his biographer Forrest McDonald (1962) and by Thomas Hughes, whose *Networks of Power* (1983) is partly a comparison of Insull's experience of developing the electric power industry in Chicago with contemporary developments in London and Berlin.

Insull recognized the important efficiencies that could be realized by building a network that spanned an entire metropolitan area and served the broad range of uses to which electricity was being put. Insull managed his load to an extent previously unknown within the industry. His understanding of the importance of off-peak consumption led him, for example, to actively court those whose use of electricity was for the operation of mass transit. Previously, this use of electricity had been served by isolated plants. An important tool he used to achieve this aim was price discrimination; Insull offered low prices to those whose business he considered especially attractive. He encouraged the greater use of electricity for purposes other than lighting and sold electrical appliances and machine tools. Insull took advantage of economies of scale by pushing the technology of his time. He ordered steam turbine generators bigger than any that had been tested before. The new technology was a resounding success. Insull installed huge generating stations and converted old central stations into substations. Many of the substations were equipped with converters, allowing his system to embrace the incompatible systems that he had inherited.

In addition to his technical and commercial skills, Insull was quite accomplished in his ability to function within the political structure of Chicago. When he began his work in Chicago, he had to deal with the system of municipal franchises under the control of corruptible politicians. Although his own dealings were skillful, even masterful, he was concerned over the system of municipal regulation and over the burgeoning importance of municipally owned utilities. In 1898 before the leading industry trade group, the National Electric Light Association, Insull advocated a system of state regulation of the rates and service offered by privately owned utilities. His position ultimately became the association's position, though not until almost a decade later.

The movement to institute state regulation began in earnest in 1907, and in the next decade most states established regulatory commissions with the power to grant monopoly franchises and set rates. The conventional view of regulation has held that it is necessary in cases of "natural monopolies," such as electric utilities, where scale economies permit a larger producer to always undercut the prices charged by a smaller producer. This process would lead to the exit of all producers from the market except one, the largest, which could then proceed to exploit its monopoly position to the detriment of consumers. In this view, state regulation operates in the public interest by permitting electric service companies the efficiencies of monopoly operation while requiring those efficiencies to be passed on to consumers in the form of lower prices. An alternative position, expressed particularly by Jarrell (1986) but mentioned also by Hyman (1985), holds that state regulation came at the behest of the utilities. In this view, regulation was implemented more to protect the monopoly status and profits of electric service companies than to prevent those profits from becoming excessive.

THE RISE AND FALL OF UTILITY HOLDING COMPANIES

The financial importance of the fixed capital required by a firm in the electric services industry, coupled with the industry's rapid growth during its first decades of existence, made financing a particular problem. It was not uncommon for firms in the industry to pay suppliers and engineering consultants with stock in the firm. In this way General Electric, for example, acquired considerable interest in electric service companies. This stock ultimately came under the control of S. Z. Mitchell and the Electric Bond and Share Company; similar processes elsewhere led to the rise of utility holding companies. By acquiring a number of operating companies in a geographic region, holding companies were able to accelerate the consolidation of the industry and thereby contribute to more efficient operations. Even without the consolidation of operating companies, the holding companies enabled the industry to take advantage of important economies of scale in financing and in the provision of engineering services. There was, however, a darker side to their participation in the electric services industry.

Under state regulation, operating companies were permitted to charge prices just sufficient to enable them to recover the costs of doing business plus earn a reasonable profit. Although ostensibly designed to prevent the operating companies from earning excessive profits, state regulation encouraged holding companies, which were unregulated, to charge operating companies excessive fees for financing and engineering services. The operating companies, with the blessing of price regulation, could then pass these "expenses" on to their customers through higher rates.

Holding companies offered another attractive feature to their promoters: tremendous financial leverage. This financial leverage was achieved, in part, by having the voting common stock of a company represent only a portion of the company's total capitalization. Holding companies were then pyramided, an organization under which several operating companies were controlled (but not wholly capitalized) by lower-tier holding companies. A number of lower-tier holding companies would then be controlled (but not wholly capitalized) by an upper-tier holding company. Numerous tiers of such holding companies would be established with a single top-tier holding company above all. This top-tier holding company would have effective control over the entire structure, including all of the operating companies, even though its share of the total capitalization of the operating companies would be quite small. Hyman (1985) provides an excellent explanation of a hypothetical holding company, showing both the structure such companies typically assumed and the way both profits and losses flowed between the various tiers.

Although it was not the largest, the holding company structure created by Samuel Insull is the best known. Insull's empire operated in over 5,000 communities in thirty-two states stretching from Maine to Texas. At one time he was the chair of sixty-five different companies. Insull controlled at least $500 million with an investment of about $27 million, and one could argue that he controlled the lowest-level operating companies with an investment equal to 0.01 percent of the securities issued by those companies (Hyman 1985).

The holding company structure was so profitable to its promoters that it came to dominate the industry, and in the 1920s two-thirds of the privately owned electric service companies were owned by holding companies. The demand by holding companies sometimes led them to pay inflated prices for operating companies, a situation that aggravated the vulnerability of holding companies when the economic climate changed. In addition, these high prices induced many municipally owned operating companies to sell out to holding companies, inhibiting in the 1920s the movement for municipal ownership of electric utilities. This process led to a tremendous concentration of ownership in the industry. In 1932 the eight largest holding companies controlled 73 percent of private electric service companies in the United States.

The very success of the utility holding companies held the seeds of their disaster. As discussed later, the consolidation of the industry and concentration of ownership alarmed many; the holding company structure and such alternatives as government ownership became matters of intense political debate. The financial leverage that made the holding company structure so attractive to promoters also made it vulnerable during economic downturns. A reduction in the income of an operating company led to a disproportionate reduction in the dividends paid to a first-tier holding company. This effect was magnified at each level until at some level all payment would cease entirely, leaving higher-level holding companies unable to pay even their most senior bonds—all because of what, at the lowest level, may have been only a moderate drop in income. The stock market crash and the Great Depression created a tremendous strain on the holding company organization.

The 1932 crash of Insull's empire, in large part for reasons more complex than those outlined here, cost investors $1 billion. Insull, who had played such a pivotal role in the development of his industry, became the target of attack but refuted criminal charges that he had used the mails to defraud his investors. The experience caused many to lose their faith in private enterprise and became an important object lesson for the New Deal.

Although some holding companies doubtless could have survived the depression, they could not survive the punitive political climate. In 1935, despite intense lobbying from the industry and from investment bankers, Congress passed the Public Utility Holding Company Act. The new law required any company owning 10 percent or more of the stock of an electric utility to register with the Securities and Exchange Commission (SEC) and to conform to certain rules. In addition, it contained, at President Franklin D. Roosevelt's insistence, a "death sentence," which, although softened somewhat from the original, still forced the breakup of noncontiguous holding company systems and prohibited the pyramiding of holding companies. Over the following decades hundreds of operating companies were separated from holding company systems, and the number of holding companies declined substantially.

PUBLIC POWER, RURAL ELECTRIFICATION, AND TVA

Throughout the history of the electric services industry, there were always vocal advocates for public, rather than private, ownership of electric utilities, and the municipally owned sector of the industry was always important. In fact, the consolidation of private systems in the 1920s led to the disappearance through merger of 1,000 private companies, leaving the nation with more municipally owned systems in 1927 than privately owned ones. The municipal systems tended to be small, however, and accounted for less than 6 percent of the industry's total generating capacity. The excesses of the holding company structure, of course, provided fuel for the fires of public power advocates, whose influence led to a lengthy and detailed investigation of the electric power industry by the Federal Trade Commission starting in 1928. The benefits from consolidation and interconnection within the industry were not lost on the advocates of public power, and their advocacy shifted away from municipal ownership of local utilities to participation by higher levels of government in large utility systems. An important component of their position was a feeling that state utility regulation had failed to protect the public interest whenever it had come into conflict with the narrow self-interest of private utilities.

The new public power position may have originated in Pennsylvania through the actions of Morris L. Cooke and Governor Gifford Pinchot. In 1923 Pinchot appointed Cooke director of a specially created Giant Power Board, charged with producing a blueprint for the development of the electric services industry in the state. After considerable study, including an investigation of the costs of rural electrification, the board issued its proposal in 1925. Although privately owned utilities would have continued to produce and distribute electricity, they would have come under the considerable control of government agencies, particularly a new Giant Power Board that would have been responsible for overall industry planning and could have compelled the cooperation of private companies. Interconnection would have been mandatory; new power plants were to be constructed near coal mines and would have transmitted their power over board-determined transmission lines. Private utilities would have been compelled to serve the rural areas they had long neglected. Utility company valuation and rate setting would have been substantially altered. The plan was opposed by privately owned utilities and others fearful of the erosion of private property rights.

The industry united behind its own plan for utility interconnection, which originated during World War I, when a government engineer, William S. Murray, coined the term "Superpower" for his proposal to encourage utility interconnection. There was, in fact, considerable similarity between Giant Power and Superpower, but the latter omitted the controlling government planning apparatus and the compulsion to provide service in rural areas. The Giant Power proposal ultimately failed in the Pennsylvania legislature, but the debate focused attention on the role of government in the electrical services industry and involved many "power progressives," who would later play a role. The study that had preceded the Giant Power proposal also provided considerable factual material for the future debate.

Another controversy, contemporaneous with the Giant Power debate, led even more directly to federal intervention in the electrical services industry. The production of munitions during World War I required large quantities of nitrates, which were chiefly supplied from Chile. The desire to establish a domestic source of synthetic nitrates resulted in a project to construct nitrate plants and attendant hydroelectric generating facilities at Muscle Shoals, Alabama, on the Tennessee River. The war ended without the project's completion, and a debate arose over how to dispose of the facilities. Nitrates are a primary constituent of fertilizer, and the plants thus had potential value in peacetime. In addition, the as yet uncompleted Wilson Dam would have provided power above that needed for fertilizer production and would have improved navigation on the Tennessee River. The government was unsuccessful in its attempts to sell the facilities to private interests, including electrical services companies operating in the region.

The Muscle Shoals debate took over a decade to resolve; the events surrounding the issue are told in Hubbard's book on the subject. One of the most intriguing aspects of the issue occurred early in 1921, when Henry Ford bid for control of the Muscle Shoals complex. Ford, accompanied by Thomas Edison, took a dramatic nonstop trip from Dearborn to Muscle Shoals in his private railway car. Ford's professed goal was not profit but "industrial philanthropy." He spoke of building a new and larger Detroit in northern Alabama and of a lower price for fertilizer benefiting southern agriculture. His proclaimed goal was the elimination of wars, which, he said, were caused by the gold standard and an international conspiracy of Jewish financiers. Not surprisingly, the Ford proposal sparked an intense controversy. Opposition to the Ford plan came from the Power Progressives, led by Senator George W. Norris of Nebraska, but there was also opposition from the Alabama Power Company and from nearby industry concerned about being put at a competitive disadvantage by the Ford proposal. In 1924, after three years of intensive debate, Ford withdrew his offer.

The issue of Muscle Shoals continued to simmer, and Congress considered a number of proposals for private operation of the facilities. The passage of time made the nitrate production technology increasingly obsolete and strengthened the view of Muscle Shoals as a power project. Several factors strengthened the position of those advocating public ownership and control. A congressional investigation revealed apparent unethical behavior by lobbyists and officials of organizations backing private bids. Revelations from the continuing Federal Trade Commission (FTC) investigations of the privately owned electric utility industry cast it in an unfavorable light. Finally, the Depression contributed to a general decline in the public's esteem for private enterprise. In addition, the scope of the Muscle Shoals project was considerably broadened. A preliminary report of the Corps of Engineers issued in 1928 showed the feasibility of developing two hydroelectric sites other than Muscle Shoals with a combined capacity of 1 million horsepower, and Norris came to advocate a plan for the systematic development of the Tennessee River. On two occasions, Norris-sponsored bills providing for the public operation of Muscle Shoals passed Congress only to be vetoed by Presidents Calvin Coolidge and Herbert Hoover.

The Muscle Shoals controversy was finally resolved after the overwhelming victory of Franklin D. Roosevelt and the Democratic Party in the election of 1932. Roosevelt's campaign had taken the position that the development of utilities should generally remain a function of the private sector, with two exceptions. If private utilities were not rendering satisfactory service, the public sector should have the right to establish its own system; such a possibility would function as a "birch rod" forcing private companies to render efficient service at reasonable rates. In addition, Roosevelt maintained that all hydroelectric sites belonging to the government should be developed and operated by a public agency. In 1933 Congress enacted Roosevelt's bill establishing the Tennessee Valley Authority (TVA) with responsibility not only for Muscle Shoals but for the comprehensive development of the entire Tennessee River Valley. Norris' position became law, and the first dam constructed by the new TVA was named after him.

By most accounts, the Tennessee Valley Authority was a political, economic, and technical success. TVA provided support and encouragement to municipalities and cooperatives to acquire or build publicly owned distribution systems. Eventually, the entire TVA area was served almost exclusively by municipal, county, or cooperative distribution systems providing TVA-generated power. Either TVA or the publicly owned distribution systems bought out essentially all of the private power companies in the area. TVA had notable successes in the areas of navigation, flood control, the provision of cheap electricity, and regional development. The Tennessee Valley changed from being one of the least electrified regions in the nation to one of the most electrified. TVA power was the cheapest electricity in the nation, and TVA maintained such rates partly by encouraging massive increases in consumption levels through such activities as financing marketing campaigns to increase the usage of electrical appliances. Such electricity-intensive industries as the production of aluminum and fissionable uranium also kept the demand for TVA's power high and growing. The increased demand for electricity these policies encouraged eventually outstripped TVA's production capacity from hydroelectric sources and caused the agency to construct steam generating plants. In 1939 hydroelectricity accounted for virtually all of TVA's generation, but by 1956, 70 percent came from coal-burning steam plants.

TVA did not achieve all of the goals hoped for by its proponents. The second director of the agency, David E. Lilienthal, had hoped TVA would promote "grassroots democracy," which emphasized decentralized administration of the agency's centralized authority. The policy of distributing power through cooperatives and local government agencies was developed, in large part, to further this goal. Victor Hobday's (1969) study of the relationship between TVA and these public distribution agencies indicates that real grassroots participation seldom occurred. Some had hoped that TVA would be only the first of a nationwide network of similar agencies; TVA, in a real sense, embodied the ideals of Giant Power. The New Deal Public Works Administration funded several important dams, and the Bonneville Power Administration was created in 1937 to have authority over power development in the Pacific Northwest and to market power produced by the government dams built there. Nevertheless, TVA did not signal the beginning of a public power revolution restructuring the entire industry, although by 1970 it had become the largest electric utility in the United States. TVA eventually proved unable to avoid many of the problems that later plagued the private electric services industry.

Perhaps one of TVA's most important demonstrations was that the demand for electricity was elastic; lower prices for electricity would be accompanied by substantial increases in the quantity of electricity consumed. Although the basis of TVA's low rates remains an issue of enduring controversy, there is no question that TVA established the practicality of enormous extensions of electricity service. In particular, TVA demonstrated the feasibility of rural electrification.

Although electricity usage had spread far by the 1930s, it was still almost entirely an urban phenomenon. In 1930 less than 10 percent of American farms were on central station service, and about half again as many had home generating plants. This situation contrasted quite sharply with that in many European countries. Germany claimed 60 percent rural electrification in 1927; France, 50 percent by 1930; and Sweden, 50 percent by 1936. Finland, Denmark, Czechoslovakia, and New Zealand were far ahead of the United States as well. In some cases, these rates of electrification had been achieved only with heavy government subsidies. In the United States, power companies were reluctant to extend lines to thinly populated areas and often required huge deposits from farmers in order to be induced to do so. The rates charged rural areas usually contained a surcharge, sometimes resulting in rural electricity rates being a multiple of urban rates (Brown 1980).

In 1935 the Rural Electrification Administration (REA) was created as a temporary agency, and Roosevelt appointed Morris L. Cooke as its first director. The story of the REA has been told by D. Clayton Brown (1980), whose book also briefly discusses Cooke's earlier involvement with Giant Power. Cooke and many others regarded the provision of electricity as having enormous potential impact on the quality of life and productivity of farmers, and they argued that increased consumption would make the provision of electricity economic at lower rates. The REA's funds would be available as loans to encourage rural electrification. Cooke approached both private and municipal utilities to encourage their participation but found their response disappointing. Funding battles within the administration led Cooke to seek a statutory basis for REA with independent congressional funding, a goal that was achieved in 1936 under the sponsorship of Senator Norris. The REA's primary activity would be to extend loans to farmer cooperatives for the creation of electricity distribution networks and to individuals for wiring and the purchase of electrical appliances.

Under the directorship of John M. Carmody, the REA moved rapidly despite several instances of interference by private power companies. REA's success in establishing solvent rural cooperatives, both in the TVA service area and throughout the country, clearly demonstrated the feasibility of providing rural areas electricity at reasonable cost. Encouraged, perhaps, by this example, private power companies stepped up their own programs to provide electricity to rural areas. By 1939, 25 percent of farms had electric service. Progress on rural electrification continued during the next few years despite intense bureaucratic infighting and the occasional opposition of private utilities, but the pace slowed considerably during World War II, when materials were diverted in support of the war effort. In 1944 Congress directed the REA to loan funds at a subsidized 2 percent rate of interest. By 1953 virtually all farms had access to centrally generated electricity. The electrification of America was complete.

PEACE, PROSPERITY, AND GROWTH, 1945–1965

The postwar period was positive for the electric services industry. The struggle between public and private power advocates abated during the period; despite criticism of TVA as "creeping socialism," it managed to consolidate its support through the Dixon-Yates controversy during Dwight D. Eisenhower's administration. Most of the period's growth occurred in the private sector, although publicly owned units tended to stay that way, and TVA continued its substantial rate of growth. Electricity consumption grew at a faster rate than did the general economy, reflecting, in part, increased consumption per customer. Residential consumption grew at an especially rapid rate, and residential consumers were using four times as much electricity per customer in 1965 as in 1945. Increased uses were found for electricity in the electronics revolution and in space conditioning, particularly air-conditioning. Except for 1945–1946, the average price for electricity in the United States declined each year. For all users of electricity, the decline was 9 percent; for residential users it was 34 percent. During the same period the Consumer Price Index (CPI) increased 75 percent, and the gross national product (GNP) deflator increased 90 percent. The period was kind to utility investors as well, and the average stock price for electric utilities increased by 345 percent.

During the postwar period, the tendency of the industry to move toward greater centralization increased. Although the structure of the industry remained fragmented, interconnection increased, and "power pools," accounting for 50 percent of national capacity in 1970, were formed. The power pools were sometimes formed with federal support and encouragement and increased the efficiency with which electricity was delivered to consumers. These pools permitted the use of larger, more efficient generating plants, and the average size of generating plants in 1965 was more than five times what it had been twenty years earlier. Transmission costs declined through the period as higher voltages were used to transmit power. Distribution costs increased, but this impact was mitigated by the higher amounts of energy per customer the system was called upon to deliver.

Besides increased electricity use, other substantial changes occurred in the nation's and the industry's fuel use. Although the use of hydroelectricity continued to increase, the natural limit on the availability of appropriate sites resulted in a reduction of its relative importance. The use of coal in the United States declined substantially for all applications except the generation of electricity. Electricity generation came to account for a majority of all coal consumed in the United States, increasing the industry's vulnerability to environmental problems. By the mid-1960s other fuels began to replace coal. Natural gas became particularly attractive; it was clean and easier to handle and permitted the construction of simpler power plants. Its use was especially popular in the south-central region, and in 1969 natural gas supplied over a fifth of the power used to generate electricity. Fuel oil also grew in popularity, particularly along the East Coast, owing, in large part, to the declining cost of Middle East petroleum and the ease of off-loading that oil from supertankers.

The industry's positive experience during the two decades from 1945 to 1965 did not end suddenly. There was certainly little reason during that period to expect that the direction the industry had taken would not lead it to continued prosperity for the indefinite future. One sign of trouble occurred on November 9, 1965, when a relay switch in Ontario failed, resulting in a blackout affecting 30 million people over 80,000 square miles. The incident was testament to the problems that large-scale inter-connection could create. An investigation by the Federal Power Commission led to new reporting requirements for blackouts, and the resultant statistics revealed that blackouts resulting from equipment failure were more common than many had realized. Fortunately, the 1965 blackout did not occur in the dead of winter. If it had, serious disruption, even death, might well have resulted. As it was, a carnival atmosphere ensued, producing an increase in births in the area nine months later.

SEQUENCE OF CRISES, 1965–1985

The value of stock in private electric service corporations was at an all-time high in 1965. Although that value, along with the values of most stocks, declined somewhat between 1965 and 1970, the industry still seemed healthy. Electricity prices continued to decline. In 1970 the electric services industry had the largest value of capital assets and was the largest issuer of securities of any industry in the United States. Despite generating more than half the electricity in the world, these electric service corporations faced serious problems.

During the latter half of the 1960s and during the entire decade of the 1970s, the electric services industry encountered a series of unprecedented crises. In many cases the industry's reactions to those crises aggravated its situation. The energy and environmental crises had considerable effect on the entire American society, but the electric services industry was particularly vulnerable to their effects. During this period the industry grappled with a nuclear power crisis partly of its own making. All of these contributed to a situation of considerable financial difficulty for the industry. Although the threat this posed was not as severe as the threats the industry experienced early in its life, it created a sharp contrast with the good times enjoyed before 1965.

The energy crisis is often dated from the 1973 petroleum embargo of the United States by Arab members of the Organization of Petroleum Exporting Countries (OPEC) until at least 1980. Although electricity was not the energy source most directly affected, the energy crisis had a significant impact on the industry. It created strong pressures on electric service companies to shift their use of boiler fuels away from petroleum and natural gas. Oil-using utilities saw their fuel costs skyrocket. Utilities using natural gas faced increasing difficulty obtaining that fuel as a result of federal and state regulations. Legal requirements pressured utilities to convert boilers burning natural gas or petroleum to coal and forbade the construction of new petroleum or natural gas generating plants.

The electric service industry's environmental difficulties originally resulted from its position as the nation's largest consumer of coal. Environmental problems are created both by the extraction (strip mining) and by the burning of coal. Federal response to these problems, the Federal Strip Mining Control Act of 1977 and the Clean Air Acts, was resisted by utilities and increased the costs of electricity production. Although other federal policies were designed to encourage the use of coal, environmental regulations made the cost of new coal-burning power plants much more expensive and more capital-intensive. These factors contributed to the apparent attractiveness of an increasingly important alternative: nuclear energy.

During the 1950s considerable effort by the U.S. government was devoted to the commercialization of nuclear power for the generation of electricity. The world's first electricity-producing reactor was a small, government-sponsored breeder plant built in 1951. There was initially great hesitation on the part of private companies to become involved with the new technology, and the U.S. government responded by spending hundreds of millions of dollars on the Power Reactor Demonstration Program, which subsidized the construction of prototype reactors by large corporations. Considerable government propaganda was devoted to the task of convincing utilities and utility suppliers that nuclear power was soon destined to be the most economic means of producing electricity. Utilities were encouraged to become involved in nuclear power, in part, by the veiled threat that their failure to do so might put the government in the position of creating new "TVAs" to compensate for the failure of private enterprise. In 1963 Jersey Central Power & Light Company ordered the first privately owned power reactor from General Electric under a fixed price turnkey contract. A series of similar contracts seemed to establish the commercial viability of nuclear power.

In an atmosphere of euphoric salesmanship, described by Bupp and Derian (1978), utilities ordered fifty-one nuclear power plants during 1966 and 1967. These plants were sold under "cost-plus" contracts that shifted the risk of cost overruns to the utilities. It was a gamble the utilities lost. Mississippi Power and Light Company's Grand Gulf 1 plant, as described by Flavin (1983), was typical. When construction began in 1972, the plant's estimated cost was $300 million. At completion in 1983, the plant was several years behind schedule and $2.5 billion over budget. Nuclear power plants commonly cost five to ten times their original estimated costs. The willingness of the electric services industry to commit to this unproved technology is, in retrospect, astounding. From 1971 to 1974 U.S. utilities ordered enough nuclear power plants to increase U.S. generating capacity by

50 percent. The largest nuclear power program was that of TVA. Not only were enormous numbers of plants ordered, but the size of plants ordered continued increasing. By the late 1960s nuclear plants under construction were six times bigger than any in operation. The capacity of plants ordered in the United States increased nearly fourfold from 1962 to 1972. The attitude prevailing in the industry was perhaps the same as the one that had served Samuel Insull so well: push the technology to larger and larger scale. Unfortunately for the industry, it was unable to successfully push this technology.

Much of the problem for the industry arose from an erroneous belief that the traditionally rapid rate of growth of electricity consumption would continue indefinitely. During the two decades prior to the 1970s, consumption of electricity had increased every year at an average rate of around 7 percent.

The period, however, was one of falling prices for electricity. Electricity prices began to increase in the early 1970s, but in 1974, in the midst of the energy crisis and a recession, the sales of electricity fell for the first time since 1946. Since then, the year-to-year rate of growth has been below 3 percent. The fall in the rate of growth of sales reduced revenues below what had been expected, but there was a lag before utilities reacted by cutting their construction programs. Caught in a financial squeeze, utilities needed to raise prices even further to cover increasing costs. In retrospect, this period turned out to be a particularly unfortunate time for the electric services industry to be involved in a massive nuclear construction program. Compared to other generating technologies, nuclear power has very high construction costs and low operating costs. Furthermore, nuclear power plants take longer to construct than do other power plants. The heavy construction costs make the total cost of a nuclear power plant very sensitive to construction delays and to interest rate changes. Yet the reduction in the rate of growth of demand eventually raised questions about whether nuclear plants under construction would, in fact, be needed. Eventually, this led to a slowing or suspension of construction, which reduced current outlays on construction but retained the need to continue paying interest to finance the construction that had already occurred. The problem was further aggravated when interest rates in the United States rose to unprecedented levels in the late 1970s and early 1980s.

The difficulties that the electric services industry was undergoing made their securities less attractive to private investors. Those with heavy nuclear construction programs were looked on with particular disfavor, and they were the companies with the largest financing needs. In order to induce investors to purchase their bonds, electric service companies had to offer higher interest rates relative to the interest rates paid by other bonds. These higher interests further reduced profits, which depressed the price of their stocks. The need to raise capital forced electric service companies to sell additional stock as well as bonds, but by the mid-1970s the price of the stock of virtually all electric service companies had fallen below the companies' book value, diluting the ownership interests of current stockholders. This further reduced the attractiveness of utility stock and contributed to an average fall in the price of the stock of companies in the electric services industry of 50 percent during the decade from 1965 to 1975.

Nuclear power caused other problems for the financial services industry. Concerns over the safety of nuclear power produced an effective antinuclear movement in the United States, which pressed its position in public and before regulatory bodies. Much of the increased construction costs of nuclear plants went for safety enhancements and for increased record-keeping requirements in the interests of safety. The actions of nuclear critics before regulatory bodies may have contributed to the slowdown in plant construction, thereby increasing the financing costs associated with nuclear plant construction. The industry generally responded to this challenge by tenaciously defending the safety of nuclear generation, a position that seemed less plausible to the public following the accident at the Three Mile Island nuclear plant in Pennsylvania in 1979 and at the Chernobyl nuclear plant in the Soviet Union in 1986.

Recent years have brought what Flavin characterizes as "financial meltdown" to the nuclear power industry. Every nuclear reactor ordered since 1974 has been subsequently canceled: 108 nuclear reactor orders have been canceled; the capacity of these canceled plants exceeds the capacity of all U.S. plants in operation and under construction. In many cases, plants were canceled after hundreds of millions, even billions, of dollars had already been spent. These events have affected publicly owned utilities at least as much as their privately owned counterparts. TVA canceled at least a dozen plants and had numerous safety problems with its nuclear program. Perhaps the greatest financial crisis occurred at the Washington Public Power Supply System (WPPSS), a consortium of municipally owned electric utilities in Washington State formed in the late 1950s to finance and construct nuclear power plants. After issuing over $8 billion in bonds and canceling two nuclear plants on which over $2 billion had been spent, WPPSS defaulted on its bonds—the largest bond default in U.S. history. Although repercussions from the nuclear power imbroglio may continue, it appears the industry has already put most of the costs behind it. The lower rate of growth in consumption should protect it from similar problems in the near future.

The electric service industry in the 1990s is characterized by deregulation, privatization, merger, and antitrust. Economies of scale in production and distribution of electric power encourage the merger of firms into giant organizations. Combinations of utilities through holding companies like the Southern Company were accompanied by little public concern because the constituent firms were regulated. The end of the twentieth century, however, has brought an increasing press for deregulation of industry, so mergers of utilities are accompanied with increasing concern for the welfare of consumers.

Utilities not deregulated are gaining freedom of action within regulation. Public monopolies like Georgia Power Company are experimenting with purchasing agreements with separate firms for the production of peak-hour electricity. Because the producing firms sell power only to established and regulated companies, they are themselves unregulated—electricity is manufactured by a private firm beyond the control of the utility. As market forces gain a greater hold on the electric services industry, and those forces encourage merger, privatization of production facilities, and concentration of ownership and distribution, the alternative to a return to regulation is antitrust action. The opening decades of the twenty-first century promise to be a time of change in electric services in the United States as consumers, investors, and politicians struggle to find the most efficient way for a market society to generate and distribute electricity.

BIBLIOGRAPHIC ESSAY

The bibliography of electrical services divides into biographies, company histories, chronicles of government programs to supply electrical services, nuclear power, environmental problems, merger, regulation, and antitrust. Two biographies of Thomas Edison stand out (and are most frequently cited) from the scores of accounts of the great inventor's life and work: Robert Conot's *A Streak of Luck* (1979) and Matthew Josephson's *Edison: A Biography* ([1959] 1992). Other relevant biographies include H. Gordon Garbedian's *George Westinghouse: Fabulous Inventor* (1943), Forrest McDonald's *Insull* (1962), Wilson Whitman's *David Lilienthal: Public Servant in a Power Age* (1948), and Norman L. Zucker's *George W. Norris: Gentle Knight of American Democracy* (1966). An important life history is *Fighting Liberal: The Autobiography of George W. Norris* (1945).

The company histories in the Newcomen Society series are succinct statements, each published under the name of someone closely afilliated with the firm. The following Newcomen titles support the study of electric services: *Indiana and the Electric Age: The Story of Public Service Indiana* (Blanchar 1969); *Alabama Power Company and the Southern Company* (Branch 1967); *Power—From Horses to Atoms: The Story of the Toledo Edison Company* (Davis 1964); *The Missouri Public Service Company: A Saga of Free Enterprise* (Green 1967); *The Kansas Power and Light Company: Through Fifty Years to the Electric Economy* (Jeffrey 1975); *Pioneers in Public Service: The Story of Oklahoma Gas and Electric Company* (Kennedy 1972); *Detroit Edison Generates More than Electricity* (McCarthy 1983); *The History of Southwestern Public Service Company* (Nichols 1961); *Arizona Public Service Company* (Reilly 1970); *Nebraska Public*

Power District (Schaufelberger 1984); *A Cycle of Service: The Story of Public Service Electric and Gas Company* (Smith 1980); *Electric Power and People Power: The Story of the Mississippi Power Company* (Watson 1969); *American Electric Power: 75 Years of Meeting the Challenge* (White 1982).

Other company histories of the electrical services industry include *P. G. and E. of California: The Centennial Story of Pacific Gas and Electric Company, 1852–1952* (Coleman 1952); *Duke Power: The First Seventy-Five Years* (Maynor 1980); *The Force of Energy: A Business History of the Detroit Edison Company* (Miller 1971); *Carolina Power & Light Company, 1908–1958* (Riley 1958); and *History of the Philadelphia Electric Company, 1861–1961* (Wainwright 1961).

Electric services cannot be discussed without reference to the federal programs under the broad titles of Tennessee Valley Authority (TVA) and Rural Electrification Administration (REA). The following titles are starting points for research into the creation and operation of TVA and REA: *Electricity for Rural America: The Fight for the REA* (Brown 1980), *TVA: Fifty Years of Grass-Roots Bureaucracy* (Hargrove and Conkin 1983), *Sparks at the Grassroots: Municipal Distribution of TVA Electricity in Tennessee* (Hobday 1969), *Origins of the TVA: The Muscle Shoals Controversy, 1920–1932* (Hubbard, 1961). John Kyle's illustrated *Building of TVA* (1958) is a history not so much of legislation and policy as of the design and construction of the TVA dams. *The Making of the TVA* (Morgan 1974) and *TVA: Democracy on the March* (Lilienthal 1944) chronicle the tenure of the TVA's first two directors, Arthur E. Morgan and David E. Lilienthal. *George W. Norris: The Persistence of a Progressive, 1913–1933* (1971) is the second of Richard Lowitt's three volumes on Senator Norris, a leading proponent of continued government ownership of the hydroelectric facilities built at Muscle Shoals, Alabama, during World War I. Marguerite Owen's *Tennessee Valley Authority* (1973) is a title in Praeger's Library of U.S. Government Departments and Agencies.

Several studies provide a gateway to nuclear power generating and the environmental problems associated with nuclear plants and power production in general: D. Victor Anderson, *Illusions of Power: A History of the Washington Public Power Supply System* (WPPSS) (1985), focuses on facilities in Washington State, whereas Irvin C. Bupp and Jean-Claude Derian, *Light Water: How the Nuclear Dream Dissolved* (1978), describe the selling of American reactor technology throughout the world, documenting the problems produced by the proliferation of nuclear generating facilities. Bupp and Derian provide useful information on the electric services industry. Two books by Christopher Flavin, *Nuclear Power: The Market Test* (1983) and *Reassessing Nuclear Power: The Fallout from Chernobyl* (1987), offer insights into the economic problems associated with nuclear power generation. Allan R. Talbot's *Power along the Hudson: The Storm*

King Case and the Birth of Environmentalism (1972) reviews the first confrontation between environmentalists and a power company—Consolidated Edison. In *TVA and the Tellico Dam, 1936–1979*, William Bruce Wheeler and Michael J. McDonald (1986) link the conflict between TVA and environmentalists to the government's postwar goals and values.

Other volumes examine the industry more broadly. In *Networks of Power: Electrification in Western Society, 1880–1930*, Thomas P. Hughes (1983) compares the developing electric services industry in Chicago, Berlin, and London; Hughes provides additional information on the inventions of Edison and his contemporaries. *America's Electric Utilities: Past, Present, and Future* (Hyman 1985) offers the perspective of a stock analyst on financing, holding companies, and nuclear power but neglects public policy. Martin V. Melosi's *Coping with Abundance: Energy and Environment in Industrial America* (1985) is an economic history of energy use in the United States between 1920 and 1980. Melosi skillfully delineates the relationship between the industry and public policy. Harold C. Passer, *The Electrical Manufacturers, 1875–1900; A Study in Competition, Entrepreneurship, Technical Change, and Economic Growth* (1953), concentrates more on the electrical supply industry than on the electrical services industry, and M. L. Ramsay's *Pyramids of Power: The Story of Roosevelt, Insull, and the Utility Wars* (1937) lacks historical context.

Electric Utility Mergers: Principles of Antitrust Analysis (Frankena and Owen 1994) and *Antitrust Aspects of Electricity Deregulation* (U.S. Congress, House 1997d) set out the major issues facing electric service providers and their customers in the 1990s, whereas *Beyond Competition: The Economics of Mergers and Monopoly Power* (Karier 1993) addresses the broader issues surrounding mergers and market power.

BIBLIOGRAPHY

Abel, Jaison R. *An Economic Analysis of Marketing Affiliates in a Deregulated Electric Power Industry.* NRRI 98–07. Occasional Paper no. 22. Columbus, OH: National Regulatory Research Institute, 1998.

Anderson, D. Victor. *Illusions of Power: A History of the Washington Public Power Supply System (WPPSS).* New York: Praeger, 1985.

Barron, Lee. *Westinghouse Centennial, 1886–1986: Baltimore Divisions & Contracts Management: A History.* Baltimore: Barron's, 1985.

Blanchar, Carroll H. *Indiana and the Electric Age: The Story of Public Service Indiana.* New York: Newcomen Society in North America, 1969.

Bourne, Marlene Avis. *The Changing Electric/Natural Gas Business.* Business Opportunity Report E-087. Norwalk, CT: Business Communications, 1997.

Branch, Harllee, Jr. *Alabama Power Company and the Southern Company.* New York: Newcomen Society in North America, 1967.

Brown, D. Clayton. *Electricity for Rural America: The Fight for the REA.* Contributions in Economics and Economic History, no. 29. Westport, CT: Greenwood Press, 1980.

Bupp, Irvin C., and Jean-Claude Derian. *Light Water: How the Nuclear Dream Dissolved*. New York: Basic Books, 1978.

Chao, Hung-po, and Hillard G. Huntington. *Designing Competitive Electricity Markets*. International Series in Operations Research & Management Science, 13. Boston: Kluwer, 1998.

Coleman, Charles M. *P. G. and E. of California: The Centennial Story of Pacific Gas and Electric Company, 1852–1952*. New York: McGraw-Hill, 1952.

Conot, Robert. *A Streak of Luck*. New York: Sandview Books, 1979.

Czamanski, Daniel Z. *Privatization and Restructuring of Electricity Provision*. Privatizing Government, 1087–5603. Westport, CT: Praeger, 1999.

Davis, John K. *Power—From Horses to Atoms: The Story of the Toledo Edison Company*. New York: Newcomen Society in North America, 1964.

Duin, Spencer. *Case Studies of Just-in-Time Implementation at Westinghouse and IBM*. Library of American Production. Falls Church, VA: American Production and Inventory Control Society, 1986.

Flavin, Christopher. *Nuclear Power: The Market Test*. Washington, DC: Worldwatch Institute, 1983.

———. *Reassessing Nuclear Power: The Fallout from Chernobyl*. Washington, DC: Worldwatch Institute, 1987.

Frankena, Mark W., and Bruce M. Owen, with John R. Morris and Robert D. Stoner. *Electric Utility Mergers: Principles of Antitrust Analysis*. Westport, CT: Praeger, 1994.

Garbedian, H. Gordon. *George Westinghouse: Fabulous Inventor*. New York: Dodd, Mead, 1943.

Green, Richard C. *The Missouri Public Service Company: A Saga of Free Enterprise*. New York: Newcomen Society in North America, 1967.

Hargrove, Erwin C., and Paul K. Conkin, eds. *TVA: Fifty Years of Grass-Roots Bureaucracy*. Urbana: University of Illinois Press, 1983.

Hobday, Victor C. *Sparks at the Grassroots: Municipal Distribution of TVA Electricity in Tennessee*. Knoxville: University of Tennessee Press, 1969.

Hubbard, Preston J. *Origins of the TVA: The Muscle Shoals Controversy, 1920–1932*. Nashville, TN: Vanderbilt University Press, 1961.

Hughes, Thomas P. *Networks of Power: Electrification in Western Society, 1880–1930*. Baltimore: Johns Hopkins University Press, 1983.

Hyman, Leonard S. *America's Electric Utilities: Past, Present, and Future*. Arlington, VA: Public Utilities Report, 1985.

Jarrell, Gregg A. "The Demand for Electric Utility Regulation." In *Electric Power: Deregulation and the Public Interest*, edited by John C. Moorhouse. San Francisco: Pacific Research Institute for Public Policy, 1986.

Jeffrey, Balfour S. *The Kansas Power and Light Company: Through Fifty Years to the Electric Economy*. New York: Newcomen Society in North America, 1975.

Josephson, Matthew. *Edison: A Biography*. New York: McGraw-Hill, 1959. Reprint. New York: J. Wiley, 1992.

Karier, Thomas. *Beyond Competition: The Economics of Mergers and Monopoly Power*. Armonk, NY: M. E. Sharpe, 1993.

Kennedy, Donald S. *Pioneers in Public Service: The Story of Oklahoma Gas and Electric Company*. New York: Newcomen Society in North America, 1972.

Kyle, John H. *The Building of TVA*. Baton Rouge: Louisiana State University Press, 1958.

Lilienthal, David E. *TVA: Democracy on the March*. New York: Harper & Brothers, 1944.

Lowitt, Richard. *George W. Norris: The Persistence of a Progressive, 1913–1933*. Urbana: University of Illinois Press, 1971.

———. "The Federal Power Commission." In *Government Agencies*, edited by Donald Whitnah. Vol. 7, *Greenwood Encyclopedia of American Institutions*. Westport, CT: Greenwood Press, 1983.

Maynor, Joe. *Duke Power: The First Seventy-Five Years*. Albany, NY: Delmar, 1980.

McCarthy, Walter J., Jr. *Detroit Edison Generates More than Electricity*. New York: Newcomen Society in North America, 1983.

McDonald, Forrest. *Insull*. Chicago: University of Chicago Press, 1962.

Melosi, Martin V. *Coping with Abundance: Energy and Environment in Industrial America*. New York: Alfred A. Knopf, 1985.

Miller, Raymond C. *The Force of Energy: A Business History of the Detroit Edison Company*. East Lansing: Michigan State University Press, 1971.

Morgan, Arthur E. *The Making of the TVA*. Buffalo, NY: Prometheus Books, 1974.

Neil, Charles E. *Entering the Seventh Decade of Electric Power*. Washington, DC: Edison Electric Institute, 1942.

Nichols, H. L. *The History of Southwestern Public Service Company*. New York: Newcomen Society in North America, 1961.

Norris, George William. *Fighting Liberal: The Autobiography of George W. Norris*. New York: Macmillan, 1945.

Owen, Marguerite. *The Tennessee Valley Authority*. Praeger Library of U.S. Government Departments and Agencies, no. 35. New York: Praeger, 1973.

Passer, Harold C. *The Electrical Manufacturers, 1875–1900; A Study in Competition, Entrepreneurship, Technical Change, and Economic Growth*. Cambridge: Harvard University Press, 1953.

Philipson, Lorrin, and H. Lee Willis. *Understanding Electric Utilities and Deregulation*. Power Engineering, 6. New York: M. Dekker, 1998.

Public Utilities Reports, Inc. *Restructuring for the Twenty-First Century*. New York: Public Utilities Reports; Management Exchange, 1993.

———. *Utility of the Future: Proceedings & Papers*. New York: EXNET, 1995.

Ramsay, M. L. *Pyramids of Power: The Story of Roosevelt, Insull, and the Utility Wars*. New York: Bobbs-Merrill, 1937

Reed Consulting Group. *On the Brink of Competition: RCG's Guide to the Northeast Power Market*. Burlington, MA: Reed Consulting Group, 1997.

Reilly, William P. *Arizona Public Service Company*. New York: Newcomen Society in North America, 1970.

Riley, Jack. *Carolina Power & Light Company, 1908–1958*. Raleigh, NC: Carolina Power & Light Company, 1958.

Schatz, Ronald W. *The Electrical Workers: A History of Labor at General Electric and Westinghouse, 1923–1960*. The Working Class in American History. Urbana: University of Illionis Press, 1983.

Schaufelberger, Donald E. *Nebraska Public Power District.* New York: Newcomen Society in North America, 1984.

Schurr, Sam H., Calvin C. Burwell, Warren D. Devine, Jr., and Sidney Sonenblum. *Electricity in the American Economy: Agent of Technological Progress.* New York: Greenwood Press, 1990.

Simpson, John W. *Nuclear Power from Underseas to Outer Space.* La Grange Park, IL: American Nuclear Society, 1995.

Smith, Robert I. *A Cycle of Service: The Story of Public Service Electric and Gas Company.* New York: Newcomen Society in North America, 1980.

Stoler, Peter. *Decline and Fall: The Ailing Nuclear Power Industry.* New York: Dodd, Mead, 1985.

Talbot, Allan R. *Power along the Hudson: The Storm King Case and the Birth of Environmentalism.* New York: E. P. Dutton, 1972.

U.S. Bureau of the Census. *Census of Manufactures.* Washington, DC: U.S. Government Printing Office, 1905a– .

———. *Census of Electrical Industries: 1902.* Washington, DC: U.S. Government Printing Office, 1905b– . Quinquennial.

———. *Central Electric Light and Power Stations, 1902.* Washington, DC: U.S. Government Printing Office, 1905c.

———. *Annual Survey of Manufactures.* Washington, DC: U.S. Government Printing Office, 1974– .

U.S. Congress. House. Committee on Commerce. Subcommittee on Energy and Power. *Electricity: Public Power, TVA* [Tennessee Valley Authority], *BPA* [Bonneville Power Authority], *and Competition.* Hearings. 105th Cong., 1st sess., July 9, 1997. Washington, DC: U.S. Government Printing Office, 1997a. Serial no. 105–37.

———. House. Committee on Commerce. Subcommittee on Energy and Power. *Electricity Competition: Necessary Federal and State Roles.* Hearings. 105th Cong., 1st sess., September 24, 1997. Washington, DC: U.S. Government Printing Office, 1997b. Serial no. 105–49.

———. House. Committee on Commerce. Subcommittee on Energy and Power. *Electric Utility Industry Restructuring: Why Shouldn't All Consumers Have a Choice?* Hearings. 105th Cong., 1st sess. Washington, DC: U.S. Government Printing Office, 1997c. Serial no. 105–40.

———. House. Committee on the Judiciary. *Antitrust Aspects of Electricity Deregulation.* 105th Cong., 1st sess. Washington, DC: U.S. Government Printing Office, 1997d. Serial no. 19.

U.S. Congress. Senate. Committee on Energy and Natural Resources. *Competitive Change in the Electric Power Industry.* 105th Cong., 1st sess. Washington, DC: U.S. Government Printing Office, 1997. S. Prt. 105–25.

Wainwright, Nicholas B. *History of the Philadelphia Electric Company, 1861–1961.* Philadelphia: Philadelphia Electric, 1961.

Watson, A. J., Jr. *Electric Power and People Power: The Story of the Mississippi Power Company.* New York: Newcomen Society in North America, 1969.

Wheeler, William Bruce, and Michael J. McDonald. *TVA and the Tellico Dam, 1936–1979.* Knoxville: University of Tennessee Press, 1986.

White, W. S., Jr. *American Electric Power: 75 Years of Meeting the Challenge.* New York: Newcomen Society in North America, 1982.

Wilson, Robert B. *Nonlinear Pricing.* New York: Oxford University Press, 1993.

Whitman, Wilson. *David Lilienthal: Public Servant in a Power Age.* New York: H. Holt, 1948.

Zucker, Norman L. *George W. Norris: Gentle Knight of American Democracy.* Urbana: University of Illinois Press, 1966.

CHAPTER 5

GAS PRODUCTION AND DISTRIBUTION, 49.2

ELEANOR T. VON ENDE AND
KLAUS G. BECKER

Natural gas helps fuel the U.S. economy: in 1985 it supplied 48 percent of the energy burned by residences, 43 percent by commercial establishments, and 35 percent used in industry. Natural gas generates about 12 percent of all energy consumed for electric generation (American Gas Association [AGA] *Gas Facts* 1985). Over 226,000 producing wells, 150 natural gas pipeline companies, and more than 1,200 gas distribution companies deliver gas to over 166 million customers (Rosan 1987).

In contrast to the vertically integrated oil industry, gas companies sell natural gas at or near the wellhead, own pipelines (intrastate and interstate firms acquire natural gas from the producers and transport it), or sell gas locally (buy natural gas from the pipelines and sell it to consumers). With few exceptions, companies that dominate one market have little influence in the other two (Tussing and Barlow 1984). Regulation is largely responsible for the disintegration of the gas industry.

HISTORICAL DEVELOPMENT AND STRUCTURE

The Belgian physician Jan Baptista van Helmont is credited with the invention of manufactured gas. In 1577 he observed that certain fuels emanate a "wild spirit" or *geist* (Thompson and Smith 1941). Pioneers in the commercial adaptation of manufactured gas were William Murdock, a Scottish engineer and employee of James Watt, and the German inventor Frederick Albert Winsor. Murdock built an apparatus to manufacture gas from coke, wood, and other flammable substances; in 1792 "successfully transported gas through some seventy feet of iron and copper tubes"; and in 1798 "equipped the Boulton Watt Company at Soho in London with gas lighting" (Dorner 1987a). Winsor, who in 1804 was granted the first English patent for manufacturing gas, founded in 1812 the first English gas company, the London and Westminster Gas Light and Coke Company (Thompson and Smith 1941).

The commercialization of manufactured gas in the United States paralleled English beginnings. In the early 1800s demonstrations of gas lighting were popular: in 1807 David Melville of Newport, Rhode Island, lighted his home and in 1812 the town's bathhouse with gas produced by a process he patented in 1813. By 1817 he had made several installations for gas lighting in cotton mills in Massachusetts and Rhode Island (Dorner 1987a).

The first American gas company was established in Baltimore in 1816, when Rembrandt Peale, a portrait painter, contracted Benjamin Kugler to illuminate Peale's museum with gas. The project's success encouraged Peale and four other prominent citizens to form the Gas Light Company (GLC) of Baltimore that year. In February 1817 GLC supplied the city with its first operating gas street lamp (Norman 1922). By 1850 gas plants had been organized in Albany, Boston, Brooklyn, Chicago, Cincinnati, Louisville, New Orleans, New York City, Philadelphia, Pittsburgh, and Washington, D.C. From 1860 to 1899 the number of gas companies increased from 297 to 999, the capital invested grew from $43 million to $400 million, and the population served increased from 5 million to 25 million (Dorner 1987a).

The primary use of gas in the nineteenth century was illumination. Gas illumination held its own in competition with kerosene and improved kerosene lamps, but when electricity became a viable option for home illumination, promoters of gas began seeking new markets (Thompson and Smith 1941; Tussing and Barlow 1984). In 1883 the Estate Gas Stove Company of Hamilton, Ohio, built the first commercial gas range. In 1884 T.S.C. Lowe, who in the early 1870s had invented a new method of manufacturing gas with higher heat content, patented a hot-air house heating furnace. In 1885 the first residential gas range was patented, and in 1889 the first automatic gas water heater was introduced. By the end of 1897 the first gas steam radiator was invented and patented (Dorner 1987a).

Such inventions fueled a rise in sales of manufactured gas to 500 billion cubic feet by 1928 (Thompson and Smith 1941). Despite the growth in the use of manufactured gas during the late nineteenth and early twentieth centuries, by 1930 natural gas accounted for about 80 percent of all distributor sales in the United States. Natural gas offered some distinct advantages over the manufactured variety, most notable of which was that it generated twice as much energy per unit volume—1,000 BTU per metered cubic foot (mcf) as compared to 300–500 BTU per mcf for manufactured gas.

Although natural gas had been discovered in the early part of the nineteenth century (the first domestic well was drilled near Fredonia, New

York, in 1821) the industry remained localized until the mid-1920s. The confinement of its use to small towns near production areas was owing to a lag in pipeline technology. The first natural gas pipeline was built in 1872. A hollow log line stretching twenty-five miles was laid from a field near West Bloomfield, New York, to Rochester. Approximately $1.5 million was spent on the failed enterprise—the line did not work (AGA, *Gas Rate Fundamentals* 1987; AGA, *Regulation of the Gas Industry* 1987).

Several long-distance, high-pressure gas pipelines were built around 1900. The Indiana Natural Gas and Oil Company built two parallel, 120-mile-long lines from Greenstown, Indiana, to Chicago. In the Midwest, the first important gas transportation company, the Kansas Natural Gas Company, was formed to serve the Kansas City market in 1904. Gas produced in the Petrolia field in Texas was moved through a 100-mile line to Dallas in 1910. But such systems were the exception rather than the rule. Since pipelines rarely exceeded 150 miles in length, willing buyers and sellers of natural gas remained apart until the late 1920s, when technical advances in pipe manufacturing finally gave the pipeline and transmission industry a sound economic footing—large-diameter welded or seamless steel pipe could withstand high pressures (500 psi and more).

Technical advances, combined with the discovery and development of the Panhandle-Hugoton field (the biggest single accumulation of gas ever developed), the Monroe fields in Louisiana, and California's San Joaquin Valley, led to the pipeline boom of the late 1920s and early 1930s. The Natural Pipeline Company of America built a twenty-four-inch line over 1,000 miles from the Texas Panhandle to Chicago. In 1936 Panhandle Eastern Pipeline Company completed another 1,000-mile line to Detroit. Between 1925 and 1935 twenty-one transmission lines totaling 19,000 miles of pipe were built—Northern Natural Gas Company, Panhandle Eastern Pipe Line Company, Cities Services Gas Company (now Northwest Central Gas Company), Colorado Interstate Gas Company, Southern Natural Gas Company, Pacific Gas and Electric Company, and El Paso Natural Gas Company (Tussing and Barlow 1984).

The linking of natural gas production and distribution via interstate and intrastate pipelines encouraged integration. The holding company was the fundamental structure of the gas industry prior to the Great Depression because it offered advantages in financing and allowed gas companies to increase system efficiency and market power through vertical and horizontal integration. In 1930 the City Service Company controlled more than sixty-five gas transmission and distribution companies in twenty states (Tussing and Barlow 1984). Since interstate gas transmission companies were not yet regulated, state utility commissions, which were regulating the local distribution companies, found it especially difficult to protect consumers from monopoly pricing by holding companies that had successfully put transmission and distribution under the same management. State commissions were among the most vocal proponents of the Public Utility Holding Company Act, which in 1935 placed limitations on vertical and horizontal integration.

During the Great Depression and World War II, construction of long-distance pipelines came to a standstill. Throughout the depression years pipelines operated at less than 50 percent capacity. Most had been built on the basis of expected industrial sales, which, because of the sharp downturn in economic activity, did not materialize. Wartime spending stimulated energy consumption, particularly in the industrial centers of the East. But because of a steel shortage and other wartime difficulties gas pipeline construction remained at a minimum level. A notable exception was the Tennessee Gas Transmission system. Built in 1944, this system linked the large gas reserves found in south Texas with distribution companies in West Virginia. This 1,265-mile pipeline, the longest at the time, was built with the latest pipeline construction methods. Its success encouraged the building of similar high-pressure systems in the postwar years (AGA, *Gas Rate Fundamentals* 1987; AGA, *Regulation of the Gas Industry* 1987).

The postwar era saw a pipeline boom that lasted through the late 1960s. From 1945 to 1970 the miles of transmission pipeline increased 224 percent, from 82,200 miles to 266,700 miles. Distribution mains expanded from 201,500 miles to 594,800 miles, a 295 percent increase. Natural gas consumption rose from 2,195 billion cubic feet in 1946 to 16,044 billion cubic feet in 1970, a 730 percent increase. Even though total energy consumption increased by only 150 percent over this same period, the share of the total for natural gas increased from 4.2 percent to 33 percent. By the end of 1970, 81 percent of all U.S. households were heated with natural gas (Phillips 1984).

Market expansion can be traced to the discovery of new proven reserves, decreases in the price of gas compared with competitive fuels, and the creation of new markets. From 1942 to 1960 the price of natural gas increased only 40 percent; the price of oil increased by 120 percent, and coal by 140 percent (Rosan 1987). During the 1950s new gas markets were opened when pipeline companies extended their lines into New England, New York, the Pacific Northwest, and Florida. Proven gas reserves increased from 148 trillion cubic feet in 1945 to 292.9 trillion cubic feet in 1967 (Phillips 1984).

By 1970 proven reserves had decreased to 269.9 trillion cubic feet and continued to decline steadily at an average rate of 8,635 billion cubic feet over the next ten years. The decline in the gas reserves combined with rapid changes in the cost of production brought the postwar growth of the natural gas industry to an abrupt halt. The industry was suddenly faced with an acute gas shortage.

Before 1970 no natural gas shortages were observed. There had been some localized shortages during the twenty-five years after World War II, but these shortages were attributable to limitations on pipeline capacity. The amount of gas produced nationally was more than sufficient to meet the contractual demands for shipment by pipelines.

In a 1954 decision, the Supreme Court ruled that wellhead prices for natural gas were to be regulated by the Federal Power Commission (FPC), so the FPC imposed price ceilings on natural gas sold through interstate commerce. Ceiling prices were based on historical, rather than current, costs, so as producers were faced with higher production costs, the inevitable shortage appeared. The delay—from the early 1960s to the early 1970s—of the shortage was largely owing to a surplus of gas reserves attributable to oil exploration and development (Tussing and Barlow 1984).

In November 1970 three large pipeline companies, unable to meet their contractual obligations, were forced to curtail service to their customers—a full-scale crisis was on the way. During the 1970s the supply of interstate market gas began to fall short of contractual demands by greater amounts each year. For the period from September 1976 to August 1977 curtailments of contracted interstate gas shipments amounted to 3.77 trillion cubic feet, a significant amount since the reduction represented nearly 20 percent of the total supply of natural gas for that period (Braeutigam and Hubbard 1986). With the end of the postwar construction boom and little hope of maintaining adequate gas supplies, the interstate transmission businesses faced an unpromising future. Diversification, construction of offshore gathering systems, and supplementary gas ventures became important investment strategies for pipeline companies.

In November 1978, with still no end in sight to the natural gas shortage, Congress passed the Natural Gas Policy Act (NGPA) and the Public Utility Regulatory Policies Act (PURPA). The NGPA provided for a partial and phased-in deregulation of wellhead prices for natural gas. PURPA established federal standards for the termination of natural gas service and urged distribution companies to initiate innovative pricing schemes such as incremental pricing and seasonal price differentials. The NGPA and PURPA meant competition for an industry long regulated.

REGULATION

Government regulation of the gas industry can be traced to the earliest days of gas use, although until 1938 regulation was primarily a local and state matter. Significant federal regulation was introduced with the implementation of the Public Utility Holding Company Act of 1935 and the Natural Gas Act of 1938. In the early days of gas lighting, regulation was a government response to demands of gas plant companies. Manufactured gas companies petitioned municipalities and state legislatures for authority to cross private property and to lay distribution mains under city streets.

Furthermore, because of the scale and the fixed nature of gas plant investments, these companies also asked for protection from competition (Tussing and Barlow 1984). Municipalities and state legislatures, anxious to
provide their residents and constituents with the convenience of gas lighting, granted exclusive franchises to gas companies.

In 1816 the Gas Light Company of Baltimore was the first gas company
to receive an exclusive franchise. It was followed by the Gas Light Company of Boston in 1822 (Dorner 1987b). Numerous other gas companies
received exclusive franchises shortly thereafter. Municipalities and states
that limited competition also instituted safeguards to protect the public.
Local regulations covered service obligations, safety requirements, quality
standards, and, in some municipalities, price restrictions. As the industry
matured, its profitability became evident, and consequently, capital for investments was easier to attract, and exclusive franchises were less readily
granted. By the end of the last quarter of the nineteenth century, nonex-
clusive franchises had completely replaced the exclusive franchises.

As the number of gas companies increased, competition, particularly in
larger cities, was relied upon to protect the public interest. However, the
result of having more than one supplier of gas was often wasteful competition. In many cities, duplicate facilities and interminable price wars were
the result (Dorner 1987b). Both the industry and government attempted to
end wasteful competition. The industry's approach was to merge and consolidate companies; the government's alternative, especially where regulation proved ineffective, was municipal operation and ownership of gas
plants (Dorner 1987b). Today, about one-third of the 1,600 distribution
companies in the United States are government-owned.

As the gas industry developed and natural gas from outside the city limits
began to replace the locally manufactured gas, municipal governments were
no longer able to control gas prices and state regulation increased in importance. In 1907 the National Civic Federation, consisting of business,
labor, and civic leaders, issued a report recommending that private companies operating public utilities should be subject to regulation. The report
became the basis for instituting state public utility commissions and public
service commissions (AGA, *Gas Rate Fundamentals* 1987; AGA, *Regulation of the Gas Industry* 1987).

Led by New York and Wisconsin, by 1910 every state except Delaware
had a utility regulatory commission that regulated electric, water, telephone, and gas companies in the "public interest." State utility commissions determined the value of utility property, monitored construction,
determined depreciation rates, and approved rates, services, and general
policies of intrastate pipelines and local distribution companies.

Long-distance, high-pressure pipelines brought a need for federal regulation. Between 1911 and 1928 Oklahoma, West Virginia, and Missouri
asserted jurisdiction over interstate gas transactions (Tussing and Barlow

1984), but the Supreme Court ruled that state commissions did not have the authority to regulate either the shipments of, or the rates charged by, interstate pipeline companies at the city gate (Phillips 1984). Congress specifically excluded the transportation of natural gas from the jurisdiction of the Interstate Commerce Commission, which it established in 1887, so until 1938, the year the Natural Gas Act was passed, much of the natural gas industry was unregulated.

Regulation was compromised when holding companies that had been organized to own and manage large interstate pipelines integrated production, transmission, and distribution operations. State regulatory commissions could not prevent excessive gas cost charges when the distributing firm was controlled by a holding company. Moreover, regulated subsidiaries wrote service and supply commitments to overwhelm state commissions' power to protect consumers from monopoly pricing (Tussing and Barlow 1984).

A 1935 Federal Trade Commission report recommended adding to the regulation of rates for interstate pipelines limitations on holding companies and the implementation of a common carrier obligation. Congress acted immediately and passed the Public Utility Holding Company Act of 1935. Regulation of interstate pipelines was begun in 1938 by the NGPA that gave the Federal Power Commission authority to issue certificates of public convenience and to set rates for sales in interstate gas transactions between pipelines and distribution companies. The new law was not clear about regulation of wellhead prices. Despite sixteen years of contrary interpretation by the Federal Power Commission, the Supreme Court in its *Phillips* decision (*Phillips Petroleum Co. v. Wisconsin*, 347 U.S. 672) ruled that the Natural Gas Act did require federal oversight of wellhead prices.

Economic growth in the years following World War II brought expansion of the gas industry and more regulation by the Federal Power Commission under the auspices of sections 4, 5, and 7 of the Natural Gas Act. Pipelines could no longer be constructed or abandoned without commission approval, and all rates for gas transported and sold required approval by the commission (Cheatham 1987).

Regulation took a new turn with the natural gas shortage of the 1970s. Federal involvement in pipeline curtailment schedules began as early as 1971, when general guidelines were issued by the Federal Power Commission. In 1972 the commission approved the first curtailment plan, which was filed by El Paso Natural Gas Company (Tussing and Barlow 1984). In 1973 the commission issued a generic plan that favored residential and small commercial customers and assigned the lowest priority to large industrial customers. The lowest priority levels had to be cut off completely before reductions could be applied to the next level (Merriman and Bowman 1987). Later, in hearings for specific pipelines, the commission altered the priority steps to fit individual circumstances.

Distribution companies appealed to their state commissions for help and gained the right to refuse service to new customers and to deny requests of existing customers to upgrade their service from interruptible to firm loads. The Ohio Commission required distribution companies under its jurisdiction to submit detailed plans for new or increased peak-sharing and storage facilities. In addition, gas distributors were ordered to stop all marketing activities designed to attract new or increased loads. Other state commissions imposed strict limitations on the use of natural gas (Merriman and Bowman 1987).

In 1977 the Emergency Natural Gas Act gave the president of the United States the authority to circumvent the Natural Gas Act and order emergency deliveries to high-priority users and permit short-term purchases from intrastate pipelines, distribution companies, or any other person, with the provision that these suppliers would not become subject to federal regulation. In 1977 President Jimmy Carter issued his "National Energy Plan," and later that year Congress passed the Department of Energy Reorganization Act, which abolished the Federal Power Commission and established in its place the Federal Energy Regulatory Commission (FERC) to assume most of the FPC functions.

In 1978 Congress passed the National Energy Acts: the National Energy Conservation Policy Act, the Public Utility Regulatory Policy Act, the Power Plant and Industrial Fuel Use Act, the NGPA, and the Energy Tax Act. Within the gas industry, the most important was the NGPA, embodying the compromises resulting from an extended debate on the pros and cons of the regulation of natural gas prices at the wellhead. Even though the NGPA did not deal specifically with the regulation of interstate pipelines or local distribution companies, it changed them.

DEVELOPMENTS DURING THE 1980s

From 1972 to 1985 gas sales fell by 26 percent, and the industry faced a surplus of nearly 4 trillion cubic feet. The change from shortage to surplus can be traced to the NGPA's freezing wellhead prices of "old" gas—gas already flowing in April 1977. Prices for "new" gas, through phased deregulation, were supposed to reach market clearing levels by the beginning of 1985. For the transition period from 1978 to 1985 the NGPA specified a set of target prices that were linked to an expected price for crude oil of about fifteen dollars per barrel (Tussing and Barlow 1984). But by 1981 crude oil was selling for about forty dollars (thirty-four dollars in 1978 dollars), more than twice the expected level. Industry participants believed that oil prices and, consequently, the prices for new gas would continue to increase without limit (Carpenter, Jacoby, and Wright 1987). Since the price ceilings of the NGPA were still below the market clearing levels, pipelines were eager for long-term contracts that would ensure firm gas deliveries. Producers were able to include price-escalator clauses assuring them the highest possible price along with high take-or-pay obligations that reduced their volume risk by 80 to 90 percent. The previous shortage, coupled with the incentives of the NGPA and the pipelines' service obligations, led pipelines to bargain away contract flexibility in return for firm reserves. These inflexible contract provisions proved ill suited to the market conditions that developed in the early 1980s.

Instead of rising, crude prices fell, and the 1981–1983 recession reduced the demand for natural gas. In an unregulated market gas prices would have fallen as economic activity slowed and the lower prices of alternative fuels attracted users, but contract commitments and the gas industry's system of pricing and allocation were rigid, so gas prices rose. Higher wellhead prices and the effects of high take-or-pay obligations led to sharp increases in the price of gas at the burner tip, and users adjusted their purchases accordingly. Residential consumers, most of whom use gas primarily for space heating, reduced consumption by 2.9 percent from 1981 to 1985; commercial consumption decreased by 3.5 percent (EIA, *Natural Gas Monthly* 1986). The most price-sensitive customers, the large industrials, especially those with fuel-switching capabilities, reduced their gas consumption by 18 percent. It remained for pipeline and distribution companies to maintain loads and to allocate demand-side risks. Regulatory authorities restructured the industry to allow pipeline companies and local distributors to respond to price competition and the new demand-side constraints.

Soon after the enactment of the NGPA in 1978, the FERC gave blanket certificates for transportation of gas to interstate pipelines that allowed their customers—intrastate pipelines and local distribution companies—to acquire gas directly from producers and receive it from the interstate pipelines. Pipeline companies began to release contractually dedicated gas for direct sale by producers to other customers who would receive it via pipeline. These special marketing programs (SMPs) benefited producers by expanding their markets. SMPs benefited pipelines by relieving them of take-or-pay obligations. Local distributors gained a contribution to fixed costs from customers who stayed with gas because of the SMPs. By 1985 the FERC had approved more than thirty SMPs, and others were pending.

In May 1985 the U.S. District Court of Appeals for the Washington, D.C., circuit vacated the blanket certificate transportation program and overthrew Columbia Gas Transmission Corporation's SMP. The court reasoned that both the blanket certificate transportation program and the SMPs denied due consideration to "captive" customers, who were not permitted to directly participate. Both programs were ruled discriminatory. In response the FERC issued Order No. 436 in October 1985 to provide open and nondiscriminatory access to transportation by interstate pipelines. The order was supposed to address liabilities under take-or-pay contracts and block rates for purchased gas supplies, but the FEC delayed those rulings.

Order No. 436, designed to give consumers greater access to competitively priced natural gas, specified that pipelines electing to seek a blanket certificate for transportation must agree to provide open access to transportation on a first-come, first-served basis. Furthermore, it required pipelines to offer their customers, mainly local distribution companies, the right to reduce their contract demand obligations over a five-year period or to convert such contract demand entitlements to equivalent volumes of firm transportation rights. The order also required an unbundling of gathering, transportation, storage, and sales services and the establishment of separate prices for each of these services. The traditional merchant function of pipelines was not eliminated in the order.

The regulatory changes at the federal level also had a strong impact on the local distribution companies and their state commissions. In many cases local distribution companies have become transporters of gas as well as merchants. At least thirty-eight state commissions have considered the transportation issue. Some states have imposed mandatory transportation programs; others have provided for voluntary transportation by their local distribution companies. In addition, state commissions now closely monitor the distribution companies' gas purchasing practices to ensure that end users benefit from the more competitive natural gas field market and the advantages of the transportation rights conferred by Order No. 436.

BIBLIOGRAPHIC ESSAY

Reference Books

There are three comprehensive reference works on the gas industry. The Federal Trade Commission's *Final Report* (1936) is the result of a study of the entire structure of the gas industry, which was ordered by Congress in 1928. *Natural Gas Survey* (1975) was released by the Federal Power Commission. Its five volumes contain the Federal Power Commission's recommendations regarding the restructuring of the gas industry and the reports of the supply, transmission, and distribution task forces.

Regulation of the Gas Industry (1987), edited by the American Gas Association (AGA), comprises four volumes and supplements. Volume 1 is a collection of papers analyzing the evolution of the industry from its early days to the present and detailed descriptions of the development of state and federal regulation of the industry. Volume 2 deals exclusively with technical issues of the regulated pipeline and distribution companies as well as allowable costs, rate base, rate of return, and rate making. The glossary of gas terms in volume 3 may be helpful to researchers who are not familiar with industry jargon. The remaining sections in volume 3 and all of volume 4 are reprints of major statutes and regulations such as the Natural Gas Act, Natural Gas Policy Act, Public Utility Regulatory Act, Department of Energy Organization Act, and the National Energy Conservation Policy Act of 1978.

Detailed statistical information for the gas industry—current data on the industry's revenues, income, capital stock, production, proven reserves, imports, and consumption—is available from the American Gas Association annual *Gas Facts*. Other information can be found in Energy Information Administration publications like *Natural Gas Monthly* and *Monthly Energy Review* as well as in annual reports from the U.S Department of Energy. Projections of future supply and demand conditions are printed in the AGA's *Gas Energy Supply Outlook* and *The Gas Energy Demand Outlook 1984–2000* (Energy Information Administration 1985). The Energy Information Administration publishes the *Annual Energy Outlook*, and the U.S. Department of Energy publishes the *Energy Projections to the Year 2010* (1985).

Information on specific pipeline or distribution companies is available in the files of the state and federal regulatory commissions. Pipelines and distribution companies are required to file annual reports, cost of service studies, and rate schedules, which become public records.

Industry History

Edward J. Neuner's (1960) study of the structure, conduct, and performance of the natural gas field market is comprehensive. Morris A. Adelman (1962) addresses the field pricing of natural gas. Shorter treatments of the production sector are to be found in Braeutigam and Hubbard (1986) as well as in Breyer and MacAvoy (1973). Ronald R. Braeutigam and Glenn R. Hubbard examine the efficiency and income redistribution effects of wellhead price regulation and deregulation and offer an economic analysis of producer-pipeline contracts. Stephen Breyer and Paul W. MacAvoy address the natural gas shortage of the 1970s. A useful supplementary piece on this subject is MacAvoy's 1971 article, in which he identifies the gas shortage as one that was induced by regulation of the wellhead prices.

Among the book-length presentations on all three sectors of the industry—production, transmission, and distribution—are Malcolm W. H. Peebles' (1980) study of the evolution of the gas industry and Arlon R. Tussing and Connie C. Barlow's (1984) work on the industry's structural development. Tussing and Barlow's treatment of the pipeline boom is particularly interesting. Additional information on the history of the industry is provided in Clark (1963) and Phillips (1984) and in Chapter 1 of *Gas Rate Fundamentals* (AGA 1987). Stephen J. Dorner's (1987a) account of the beginnings of the gas industry deserves special attention. Dorner, manager of library services at the American Gas Association, offers an excellent description of the early days of manufactured gas and gas lighting. Louis Stotz and Alexander Jamison (1938) have written a history of the gas industry up to the 1930s. Their account includes the transition period from manufactured to natural gas. Among other vintage contributions dealing with the earlier days of the industry, Oscar E. Norman's (1922) describes the romance of the gas industry; this book and C. Woody Thompson and Wendell R. Smith's (1941) analysis are both worth reading. Thompson and Smith include some interesting statistical data on manufactured as well as natural gas consumption during the transition period. The post–World War II growth of the transmission and distribution segments of the industry is the subject of Richard A. Rosan's (1987) study of factors that contributed to industry growth: improved pipeline technology, the favorable relative price of gas, and the opening of new markets.

The gas shortage of the 1970s has been the subject of many studies. Richard M. Merriman and Peyton G. Bowman (1987) discuss the national emergency and the attempts to deal with it, such as curtailments, conservation, and the addition of supplementary gas supplies. John T. Wenders (1972) analyzes the causes of the shortage. One of the main concerns during the 1970s was the future of U.S. gas supplies. J. Daniel Khazzom's (1971) subject is the econometric model that was used by the Federal Power Commission to determine gas supplies.

Regulation has always played an important part in the development of the gas industry. Dorner (1987b) provides an account of the initial phases of regulation from the days of the gas franchises to the Natural Gas Act of 1938. Probably the most comprehensive list of regulatory acts affecting the gas industry is to be found in a publication by the Energy Information Administration entitled *A Chronology of Major Oil and Gas Regulations* (1982). James W. McKie (1957) presents an appraisal of the impact that state and federal regulation had on the industry from its beginnings to World War II. A complete treatment of the regulation of natural gas, its policies and politics spanning the time period from 1938 to 1978, is provided by Elizabeth M. Sanders (1981). Alfred E. Kahn's chapter on natural gas regulation in his book (1971, vol. 2) includes a noteworthy discussion of the natural monopoly characteristics of the transmission and distribution segments of the industry.

The era of the holding companies and the Public Utility Holding Company Act of 1935 are analyzed in Bonbright and Means (1932) and Ritchie (1955). John H. Cheatham (1987) offers an account of the increased regulatory activities of the Federal Power Commission during the post–World War II years, and Breyer and MacAvoy (1974), in a Brookings study, also analyze the workings of the Federal Power Commission.

Several authors address the regulatory responses to the natural gas shortage of the 1970s. The results of the Natural Gas Policy Act of 1978 are discussed in Merriman and Bowman (1987). Paul R. Carpenter, Henry D. Jacoby, and Arthur W. Wright (1987) present an economic analysis of the interactions of regulation and industry conditions.

David Muchow (1987a, 1987b) summarizes developments in the 1970s and 1980s. His exposition of FERC Order No. 436 illuminates the issues surrounding the gas industry in the 1990s. The deregulation of wellhead prices and the Federal Regulatory Commission Order No. 436 and its successor, Order No. 500, brought structural changes in the gas industry. Tussing and Barlow (1985) put the regulation and deregulation debate in a historical context. Harry G. Broadman (1986) discusses the need for reforms of the deregulation initiative. Loury (1983), as well as the already cited study by Braeutigam and Hubbard, analyzes the efficiency and equity impacts of wellhead deregulation.

Producer-pipeline contracts and take-or-pay obligations are discussed in Canes and Norman (1986). R. Glenn Hubbard and Robert J. Weiner (1986) also address the long-term contracting practices in the natural gas industry. John W. Griggs (1986) analyzes Order No. 436 and the resulting dual merchant-transporter status of the pipelines and distribution companies. Deborah Cohn and Robert Means (1983) have made what they call a preliminary analysis of common carriage of natural gas.

A Harvard study (1987) on the future of natural gas, edited by Joseph P. Kalt and Frank C. Schuller, is a collection of papers addressing current issues such as the redesign of regulatory policy and the design of competitive strategies for pipelines and distribution companies. Marlene Avis Bourne (1997) offers an analysis of the natural gas industry at the end of the 1990s.

BIBLIOGRAPHY

Adelman, Morris A. *The Supply and Price of Natural Gas.* Oxford, UK: Basil Blackwell, 1962.

American Gas Association (AGA). *Gas Facts.* Arlington, VA: American Gas Association, Department of Statistics, 1967– . Annual.

———. *The Gas Energy Supply Outlook.* Arlington, VA: American Gas Association, Policy Evaluation and Analysis Group, 1980– . Biennial.

———. *Gas Rate Fundamentals.* 4th ed. Arlington, VA: American Gas Association, 1987.

———. *Gas Stats: Monthly Gas Utility Statistical Report.* Arlington, VA: American Gas Association, Department of Statistics, 1987– . Quarterly.

———. *Industrial Sector Energy Analysis: Overview of Trends in Consumption and Factors Affecting Energy Demand.* Energy Analysis 1988–1. Arlington, VA: American Gas Association, Planning and Analysis Group, 1988.

———. *The Outlook for Gas Energy Demand, 1990–2010: A Report of the A.G.A. Gas Demand Committee.* Arlington, VA: American Gas Association, Planning & Analysis Group, Gas Demand Analysis Division, 1990.

————, ed. *Regulation of the Gas Industry*. 4 vols. New York: Matthew Bender, 1987.

American Gas Journal. New York: American Gas Light Journal, 1921– . Monthly.

Atlas, Pipelines of the United States Gulf Coast: Natural Gas, Crude Oil, Products. Tulsa, OK: PennWell, 1993.

Barcella, Mary L., and Melvin A. Conant. *Risk and Opportunity: The U.S. Gas Market, 1990–2010: Economics, Politics, and Regulation*. Washington, DC: Conant & Associates, 1990.

Blaydon, Colin C. "State Policies under Pressure." In *Drawing the Line on Natural Gas Regulation: The Harvard Study on the Future of Natural Gas*, edited by Joseph P. Kalt and Frank C. Schuller, 157–69. New York: Quorum Books, 1987.

Bonbright, James C., and C. Gardiner Means. *The Holding Company*. New York: McGraw-Hill, 1932.

Bourne, Marlene Avis. *The Changing Electric/Natural Gas Business*. Norwalk, CT: Business Communications, 1997.

Bradley, Robert L., Jr. *Oil, Gas, & Government: The U.S. Experience*. 2 vols. Lanham, MD: Rowan & Littlefield, 1996.

Braeutigam, Ronald R., and R. Glenn Hubbard. "Natural Gas: The Regulatory Transition." In *Regulatory Reform: What Actually Happened*, edited by Leonard W. Weiss and Michael W. Klass. Boston: Little, Brown, 1986.

Breyer, Stephen, and Paul W. MacAvoy. "The Natural Gas Shortage and the Regulation of Natural Gas Producers." *Harvard Law Review* 86 (April 1973): 941–87.

————. *Energy Regulation by the Power Commission*. Washington, DC: Brookings Institution, 1974.

Broadman, Harry G. "Natural Gas Deregulation: The Need for Further Reform." *Journal of Policy Analysis and Management* 5 (Summer 1986): 17–31.

————. "Deregulating Entry and Access to Pipelines." In *Drawing the Line on Natural Gas Regulation: The Harvard Study on the Future of Natural Gas*, edited by Joseph P. Kalt and Frank C. Schuller, 125–52. New York: Quorum Books, 1987.

Brown, Robert M. *Journey into Risk Country: The First Thirty Years of Apache Corporation*. Minneapolis: Apache, 1985.

Bufkin, I. David. *Texas Eastern Corporation, "a Pioneering Spirit."* New York: Newcomen Society in North America, 1983.

Butrica, Andrew J., with Deborah G. Douglas. *Out of Thin Air: A History of Air Products and Chemicals, Inc., 1940–1990*. New York: Praeger, 1990.

Canes, Michael E., and Donald A. Norman. *Analytics of Take-or-Pay Provisions in Natural Gas Contracts*. Washington, DC: American Petroleum Institute, 1986.

Carpenter, Paul R., Henry D. Jacoby, and Arthur W. Wright. "Adapting to Change in Natural Gas Markets." In *Energy—Markets and Regulation: Essays in Honor of M. A. Adelman*, edited by Richard L. Gordon, Henry D. Jacoby, and Martin B. Zimmerman, 1–29. Cambridge: MIT Press, 1987.

Castaneda, Christopher James. *Regulated Enterprise: Natural Gas Pipelines and*

Northeastern Markets, 1938–1954. Historical Perspectives on Business Enterprise. Columbus: Ohio State University Press, 1993.

Castaneda, Christopher James, and Joseph A. Pratt. *From Texas to the East: A Strategic History of Texas Eastern Corporation*. College Station: Texas A&M University Press, 1993.

Castaneda, Christopher James, and Clarance M. Smith. *Gas Pipelines and the Emergence of America's Regulatory State: A History of Panhandle Eastern Corporation, 1928–1993*. Studies in Economic History and Policy. New York: Cambridge University Press, 1996.

Chambers, Ann. *Natural Gas and Electric Power in Nontechnical Language*. Tulsa, OK: PennWell, 1999.

Cheatham, John H. "Regulation in the Post–World War II Period." In *Regulation of the Gas Industry*, edited by the American Gas Association, vol. 1, 3.3–3.29. New York: Matthew Bender, 1987.

Chilton's Energy. Radnor, PA: Chilton, 1976– . Monthly.

Chilton's Energy Pipelines and Systems. Houston, TX: Chilton, 1974.

Chilton's Oil & Gas Energy. Radnor, PA: Chilton, 1975.

Clark, James A. *A Chronological History of the Petroleum and Natural Gas Industries*. Houston, TX: Clark Book, 1963.

Cohn, Deborah, and Robert Means. *Common Carriage of Natural Gas: A Preliminary Analysis of the Issues*. Washington, DC: Federal Energy Regulatory Commission, 1983.

Coleman, Charles M. *P. G. and E. of California: The Centennial Story of Pacific Gas and Electric Company, 1852–1952*. New York: McGraw-Hill, 1952.

Dorner, Stephen J. "Beginnings of the Gas Industry." In *Regulation of the Gas Industry*, edited by the American Gas Association, vol. 1, 2.2–2.14. New York: Matthew Bender, 1987a.

———. "Initial Phases of Regulation of the Gas Industry." In *Regulation of the Gas Industry*, edited by the American Gas Association, vol. 1, 2.3.–2.14. New York: Matthew Bender, 1987b.

Duann, Daniel J. *Restructuring Local Distribution Services: Possibilities and Limitations*. NRRI 94–13. Columbus, OH: National Regulatory Research Institute, 1994.

Duncan, Susan J., ed. *The Public Utilities Reports 1982 Analysis of Investor-Owned Electric and Gas Utilities*. Arlington, VA: Public Utilities Reports, 1982.

Ellig, Jerome, and Joseph P. Kalt. *New Horizons in Natural Gas Deregulation*. Westport, CT: Praeger, 1996.

Energy Information Administration (EIA). *Monthly Energy Review*. Washington, DC: U.S. Department of Energy, Energy Information Administration, Office of Energy Data Operations, 1977– . Monthly.

———. *U.S. Imports and Exports of Natural Gas*. Washington, DC: U.S. Department of Energy, Energy Information Administration, Office of Oil and Gas Statistics, 1978–1981. Annual. See also *Natural Gas Monthly*.

———. *Natural Gas Annual*. Washington, DC: U.S. Department of Energy, Energy Information Administration, Office of Oil and Gas, 1980– . Annual.

———. *Annual Energy Outlook*. Washington, DC: U.S. Department of Energy, 1982– . Annual.

———. *A Chronology of Major Oil and Gas Regulations.* Washington, DC: U.S. Department of Energy, Energy Information Administration, Office of Oil and Gas Statistics, 1982.

———. *Natural Gas Monthly.* Washington, DC: U.S. Department of Energy, Energy Information Administration, Office of Oil and Gas Statistics, 1982– . Monthly.

———. *The Gas Energy Demand Outlook 1984–2000.* Washington, DC: U.S. Department of Energy, 1985.

———. *Capacity and Service on the Interstate Natural Gas Pipeline System 1990: Regional Profiles and Analysis.* Washington, DC: Energy Information Administration, 1992.

———. *Annual Energy Outlook 1997 . . . with Projections to 2015 . . .* Washington, DC: U.S. Department of Energy, Energy Information Administration, 1997.

———. *Deliverability on the Interstate Natural Gas Pipeline System.* Washington, DC: U.S. Department of Energy, Energy Information Administration, Office of Oil and Gas Statistics, 1998.

Esser, Robert. *After the Collapse: The Future of U.S. Natural Gas Supply.* Cambridge, MA: Cambridge Energy Research Associates, 1992.

Federal Power Commission. *Natural Gas Survey.* Washington, DC: U.S. Government Printing Office, 1975.

Federal Trade Commission. *Final Report.* Docket No. 92. 70th Cong. 1st sess., 1936.

Ffooks, Roger. *Natural Gas by Sea: The Development of a New Technology.* New York: Nichols, 1979.

Gallick, Edward C. *Competition in the Natural Gas Pipeline Industry: An Economic Analysis.* Westport, CT: Praeger, 1993.

Gas Industry. Natural Gas ed. Buffalo, NY: Periodicals Publishing; Natural Gas Association of America, 1907–1927.

Gemmel, William A. *From Small Beginnings: A History of South Jersey Industries, Inc. and South Jersey Gas Company, 1910–1985.* Folsom, NJ: W. A. Gemmel, 1987.

Griggs, John W. "Reconstructuring the Natural Gas Industry: Order No. 436 and Other Regulatory Initiatives." *Energy Law Journal* 7 (1986): 71–99.

Harunuzzaman, Mohammad, and Akim Mahbubur Rahman. *Pipeline Capacity Turnback: Problems and Options.* NRRI 97–22. Columbus: Ohio State University, National Regulatory Research Institute, 1997.

Hatcher, David B., and Arlon R. Tussing. *State Regulatory Challenges for the Natural Gas Industry in the 1990s and Beyond.* NRRI 92–10. Occasional Paper 15. Columbus: Ohio State University, National Regulatory Research Institute, 1992.

Herbert, John H. *Clean Cheap Heat: The Development of Residential Markets for Natural Gas in the United States.* New York: Praeger, 1992.

Hogan, William W. "The Boundaries between Regulation and Competition." In *Drawing the Line on Natural Gas Regulation: The Harvard Study on the Future of Natural Gas,* edited by Joseph P. Kalt and Frank C. Schuller, 69–86. New York: Quorum Books, 1987.

Hubbard, R. Glenn, and Robert J. Weiner. "Regulation and Long-Term Contracting in U.S. Natural Gas Markets." *Journal of Industrial Economics* 35 (September 1986): 71–79.

Juris, Andrej. *Development of Natural Gas and Pipeline Capacity Markets in the United States.* Policy Research Working Papers, 1897. Washington, DC: World Bank, Private Sector Development Department, Private Participation in Infrastructure Group, 1998.

Kahn, Alfred E. *The Economics of Regulation: Principles and Institutions.* 2 vols. New York: John Wiley & Sons, 1971.

Kalt, Joseph P. "Market for Power and the Possibilities for Competition." In *Drawing the Line on Natural Gas Regulation: The Harvard Study on the Future of Natural Gas,* edited by Joseph P. Kalt and Frank C. Schuller, 89–121. New York: Quorum Books, 1987.

———. *The Redesign of Rate Structures and Capacity Auctioning in the Natural Gas Pipeline Industry.* Cambridge: Harvard University, Energy and Environmental Policy Center, John F. Kennedy School of Government, 1988.

Kalt, Joseph P., and Frank C. Schuller. "Introduction: Natural Gas Policy in Turmoil." In *Drawing the Line on Natural Gas Regulation: The Harvard Study on the Future of Natural Gas,* edited by Joseph P. Kalt and Frank C. Schuller, 1–11. New York: Quorum Books, 1987.

Kelly, Edward M. *Trading Pipe: Transmission Capacity as a New Commodity.* Cambridge, MA: Cambridge Energy Research Associates, 1995.

Kelly, Edward M., and Thomas Robinson. *Beyond Order 636: Competition in the New Era of Gas Regulation.* Cambridge, MA: Cambridge Energy Research Associates, 1993.

Kennedy, John L. *Oil and Gas Pipeline Fundamentals.* 2d ed. Tulsa, OK: PennWell Books, 1993.

Khazzom, J. Daniel. "The FPC Staff's Econometric Model of Natural Gas Supply in the United States." *Bell Journal of Economics* 2 (Spring 1971): 51–93.

Knowles, Ruth Sheldon. *The First Pictorial History of the American Oil and Gas Industry, 1859–1983.* Athens: Ohio University Press, 1983.

Leib-Keyston & Company. *Pacific Gas and Electric and the Men Who Made It . . .* San Francisco: Leib-Keyston, 1926.

Loury, Glenn C. "Efficiency and Equity Impacts of Natural Gas Deregulation." In *Public Expenditure and Policy Analysis,* edited by Robert Haverman and Julius Margolis, 301–23. Boston: Houghton Mifflin, 1983.

MacAvoy, Paul W. "The Regulation-Induced Shortage of Natural Gas." *Journal of Law and Economics* 14 (April 1971): 167–99.

McKie, James W. *The Regulation of Natural Gas.* Washington, DC: American Enterprise Association, 1957.

Merriman, Richard M., and Peyton G. Bowman III. "The 1970s—A Period of Momentous Change." In *Regulation of the Gas Industry,* edited by the American Gas Association, vol. 1, 5.5–5.73. New York: Matthew Bender, 1987.

Muchow, David. "The Early 1980s—The Promises and Disappointments of NGPA." In *Regulation of the Gas Industry,* edited by the American Gas Association, vol. 1, 5A.3–5A.36. New York: Matthew Bender, 1987a.

———. "The Gas Industry—1985–2010—Major Problems and Suggested Solutions." In *Regulation of the Gas Industry*, edited by the American Gas Association, vol. 1, 6.6–6.93. New York: Matthew Bender, 1987b.

Natural Gas Atlas of the United States & Canada. 2d ed. Durango, CO: MAP-Search Services, 1992.

Natural Gas in the 1990's: Trends in Supply, Demand, and Transportation. Washington, DC: Natural Gas Intelligence, 1990.

Natural Gas Magazine. Cincinnati, OH: Natural Gas, 1920–36.

Natural Gas Requirements for Electric Generation through 2000: Can the Natural Gas Industry Meet Them? A Report to Edison Electric Institute and Electric Power Research Institute. EPRI P-6821. Boston: Jensen Associates, 1990.

Natural Gas Systems Handbook: Pipeline & Facilities Reference, United States & Canada. Durango, CO: MAPSearch Services, 1995.

Neuner, Edward J. *The Natural Gas Industry: Monopoly and Competition.* Norman: University of Oklahoma Press, 1960.

Newcomb, James, and Thomas Robinson, eds. *Natural Gas & Electric Power: Partners for the 1990s?* Cambridge Energy Forum. Cambridge, MA: Cambridge Energy Research Associates, 1989.

Norman, Oscar E. *The Romance of the Gas Industry.* Chicago: A. C. McClurg, 1922.

Parent, Leonard V., and H. deForest Ralph, Jr. *Business and Facility Profiles of 25 Selected Major Natural Gas Pipelines: Overview.* En Strategists, 1995.

Peebles, Malcolm W. H. *Evolution of the Gas Industry.* New York: New York University Press, 1980.

Phillips, Charles F. *The Regulation of Public Utilities: Theory and Practice.* Arlington, VA: Public Utilities Reports, 1984.

Pierce, Richard J. "Reconsidering the Roles of Regulation and Competition in the Natural Gas Industry." *Harvard Law Review* 97 (December 1983): 345–85.

Ritchie, Robert F. *Integration of Public Utility Holding Companies.* Ann Arbor: University of Michigan, 1955.

Riva, Joseph P., John J. Schanz, Jr., and John G. Ellis. *U.S. Conventional Oil and Gas Production: Prospects to the Year 2000.* Westview Special Studies in Natural Resources and Energy Management. Boulder, CO: Westview Press, 1985.

Rosan, Richard A. "Post–World War II Growth of the Gas Industry." In *Regulation of the Gas Industry*, edited by the American Gas Association, vol. 1, 3.3–3.29. New York: Matthew Bender, 1987.

Sanders, Elizabeth M. *The Regulation of Natural Gas, Policy and Politics, 1938–1978.* Philadelphia: Temple University Press, 1981.

Schuller, Frank C. "The Roles of Differentiation and Regulation." In *Drawing the Line on Natural Gas Regulation: The Harvard Study on the Future of Natural Gas*, edited by Joseph P. Kalt and Frank C. Schuller, 179–200. New York: Quorum Books, 1987.

Stotz, Louis, and Alexander Jamison. *History of the Gas Industry.* New York: Stettiner Brothers, 1938.

Tate, James H. *Keeper of the Flame: The Story of Atlanta Gas Light Company, 1856–1985.* Atlanta, GA: Atlanta Gas Light, 1985.

Thompson, C. Woody, and Wendell R. Smith. *Public Utility Economics.* New York: McGraw-Hill, 1941.

Tussing, Arlon R., and Connie C. Barlow. *The Natural Gas Industry: Evolution, Structure, and Economics.* Cambridge, MA: Ballinger, 1984.

————. "The Rise and Fall of Regulation in the Natural Gas Industry." *Public Utilities Fortnightly* 109 (May 1985): 15–23.

Tussing, Arlon R., and Bob Tippee, eds. *The Natural Gas Industry: Evolution, Structure, and Economics.* 2d ed. Tulsa, OK: PennWell Books, 1995.

U.S. Congress. Senate. Committee on Energy and Natural Resources. *State Regulation of Natural Gas Production.* Hearings. 102d Cong., 2d sess., June 18, 1992. S. Hrg. 102–814. Washington, DC: U.S. Government Printing Office, 1992.

————. Senate. Committee on Energy and Natural Resources. *Natural Gas Pipeline and Current Policies regarding Right-of-Way.* Hearings. 103d Cong., 2d sess., April 19, 1994. S. Hrg. 103–635. Washington, DC: U.S. Government Printing Office, 1994.

————. Senate. Committee on Energy and Natural Resources. *Natural Gas Issues.* Hearings. 105th Cong., 1st sess., July 23, 1997. S. Hrg. 105–226. Washington, DC: U.S. Government Printing Office, 1997.

U.S. Department of Energy. *Energy Projections to the Year 2010.* Washington, DC: U.S. Department of Energy, 1985.

Waters, L. L. *Energy to Move: Texas Gas Transmission Corporation.* Owensboro, KY: Texas Gas Transmission, 1985.

Wenders, John T. "Our National Gas Shortage: Causes and Cures." *Arizona Law Review* 21 (November 1972): 1–7.

World Trade in Natural Gas and LNG, 1985–2010: Trades and Prices, Pipelines, Ships, Terminals. New York: Poten & Partners, 1993.

Part IV

Wholesale Trade—Durable Goods
ESIC 50.0

CHAPTER 6 _____

LUMBER AND OTHER
CONSTRUCTION MATERIALS
WHOLESALING, 50.3
_____ K. Peter Harder

Aside from land itself, no economic resource but lumber has played as crucial and prolonged a role in the development of the American economy. This versatile, ubiquitous, seemingly limitless input provided the means with which to quickly and inexpensively activate the economic potential of the continent and to build an early infrastructure. Lumber continues to play a key role in farm, residential, and commercial construction.

In the nineteenth century, lumber fueled the high American standard of living with products ranging from toys and tools, to houses, fences, and barns, to major components in transportation and communication (plank roads, boardwalks, poles, railroad ties, trestles, bridges, warehouses, boats, and naval stores). Americans built towns, cities, and far-flung infrastructural enterprises with a generous supply of cheap, readily available lumber. From colonial times to the early nineteenth century, the resources needed for local and regional economic development were obtained directly and simply from the omnipresent forests. But with the growth of a national economy and dramatic improvements in transportation came the rapid exploitation of primary lumber regions for a larger market and the evolution of a complex system of distribution—the lumber wholesaling industry. Wholesale lumbering is a vital part of the U.S. economy in the twentieth century even as construction expands into other materials to satisfy contemporary architectural specifications, building styles, and commercial and industrial evolution. New materials notwithstanding, wholesaling is still dominated by lumber, plywood, millwork, and paneling products, though a significant segment of the industry supplies brick, stone, roofing, insulation, and other construction materials.

HISTORY AND FUNCTIONAL EVOLUTION
OF THE INDUSTRY

Lumber production and distribution began with the settlers' arrival in North America and soon blossomed into a major commercial activity. The first colonial sawmill producing lumber for market was established at Berwick, Maine, in 1631, and for the next two centuries American lumber production was predominant in New England and concentrated in Maine. By 1850 leadership in lumber production and distribution had moved west to the states of New York and Pennsylvania. Lumbering in the Great Lakes and central regions developed rapidly after 1870, first in Michigan, then in Wisconsin and Minnesota. In the period 1870–1900, the Great Lakes and central regions produced half the U.S. lumber output, but their lead was rapidly eclipsed by the South; in the decade before World War I, the South produced 35 to 40 percent of the nation's lumber. Stimulated by insatiable wartime demands and the Roaring Twenties, lumber production began in the last great untapped region, the Pacific Coast. Lumbering on the Pacific Coast reached its apex at about 50 percent of U.S. output during the period 1950–1970.

U.S. lumber production reached a high of 44.5 billion board feet in 1909—a staggering output that was not surpassed until the 1980s. Consumption peaked around 500 board feet per capita in the first decade of the twentieth century, a sum nearly double per capita consumption rates at century's end. Adjusted for minor cyclical fluctuations, lumber production data between 1940 and 1970 show an amazingly flat trend of about 35 billion board feet. However, more recent data (lumber production in cubic feet) reveal an increase in domestic lumber production (excluding plywood) of 33 percent and per capita consumption of about 15 percent in the years 1970–1988. Historically, lumber accounted for over half the U.S. processed wood resources, but in the 1980s it constituted slightly less than half (46 percent in 1988); the remainder was pulp, paper, plywood, and veneer production (U.S. Bureau of the Census, 1975, 1996b).

During the first 200 years of settlement in North America, the marketing and distribution of lumber were uncomplicated for all but a few specialized products like naval lumber. Forests were everywhere, and small sawmills served local markets. Lumber sold itself; there was no need for wholesale and retail infrastructure. By 1850 conditions had changed, and lumber wholesalers were distributing a product brought into local markets from afar.

Settlement of the western frontier, the dwindling of the New England white pine stocks, and the growing availability of cheaper lumber from other regions channeled the flow of capital into lumber mills and retail outlets. The geographic separation of lumber mills from their markets stimulated the wholesale lumber business. Wholesalers graded, dried, finished, and stored lumber, extending credit backward to millers and forward to retailers and coordinating transportation from mills to markets. Key lumber wholesale and distribution centers in the early to mid-1800s were Bangor, Maine; Albany and Tonawanda, New York; Williamsport, Pennsylvania; Burlington, Vermont; Baltimore, Maryland; Norfolk, Virginia; and Cleveland, Ohio (Kohlmeyer 1983; Horn 1951).

The shift of lumber production to the Great Lakes region, coupled with rapid settlement and urbanization of the central heartland, raised Chicago to preeminence as a lumber distribution and wholesaling center in the 1870s and 1880s. Its dominance was eclipsed at the turn of the century by the South and the West. At the same time, lumber production was coming under the control of giants, like Weyerhaeuser's conglomerate, that took over the finishing, transportation, and marketing functions typically coordinated by nineteenth-century wholesalers (Hidy, Hill, and Nevins 1963). As the twentieth century began, the immensity of these companies combined with the superior railroad transportation services they commanded at preferential high-volume rates to make it profitable for them to integrate vertically to the retail level. Giant size, however, was an exception to the rule. The greater part of the industry, especially the small mills, continued to rely on independent wholesalers. Industry spokesman Joseph E. Davies observed in the 1920s that "the wholesalers of the country [created] a vast and highly efficient agency of distribution" (Horn 1951). Estimates of the volume of lumber sold through wholesalers in the United States in the twentieth century fall between 50 and 80 percent of total lumber production, but two-thirds is a fairly typical figure. Greater concentration and vertical integration in softwood production meant that wholesalers handled a greater percentage of hardwoods than softwoods. Nonetheless, firms manufacturing lumber and wood products (SIC 24) have always been the least concentrated among all U.S. industry groups in the twentieth century (U.S. Bureau of the Census 1975).

Wholesaling in the lumber and construction materials industry is complex and not always straightforward. The largest, most important group has always been the merchant wholesalers. Some operated distribution yards at strategic transportation hubs or in major cities; others collected the output of the tens of thousands of small, scattered mills, especially in the South. Merchant wholesalers took title to shipments in return for coordinating transportation and preparing products for market. Office wholesalers maintain no yards: sales agents, brokers, and commission merchants distribute lumber without taking title to it. Manufacturing sales branches represent the sales operations of the larger, vertically integrated corporations that have encroached on the independent merchant wholesalers not so much in number of establishments as in percentage of sales. During the twentieth century, lumber lost its leading role in construction to other materials. The end of the century witnessed the rising importance of lumber exports and imports through wholesalers—in the 1990s about 25 percent of the lumber used in the United States was imported, 98 percent of it from Canada (U.S. Bureau of the Census 1996b).

The large lumber manufacturing firms that formed at the turn of the twentieth century began integrating forward into wholesaling and retailing in the 1920s but not at the expense of independent merchant wholesalers, who continued to dominate industry sales. Some of the big firms re-trenched: West Coast timber and paper giant Simpson, for example, estab-lished a lumber and wholesale division in the 1950s but dismantled it in the 1980s to placate its independent distributors (Spector 1990). Indepen-dent wholesalers remain at risk of myriad technological, cultural, and in-frastructural change; but increasingly fast, efficient national transportation and telecommunication networks have reduced the importance of the wholesaler as a market coordinator. Regional and national chains of lum-ber and building supply retail outlets and department and discount stores, together with the purchasing clout of large corporate housing construction giants, have taken business away from traditional distribution channels. Manufacturers—Weyerhaeuser is an example—are creating lumber-dealer franchising programs to tie retail dealers and home builders directly to the manufacturer and in the process are internalizing the work of the whole-saler. These and related changes have reduced the number of wholesalers and trimmed the historic 8 percent wholesale discount offered by manu-facturers.

The lumber and building materials industry was shaped by trade asso-ciations, antitrust, wars, and the Great Depression. Local dealer associa-tions appeared in key lumber wholesale cities in the 1860s and 1870s: the Cleveland Board of Lumber Dealers (1866), Lumbermen's Association of Chicago (1869), and the Lumber Exchange of Baltimore (1875). The trend spread to cities across the nation. The National Wholesale Lumber Deal-ers Association, founded in New York in 1893, rationalized wholesaler–retailer relations and resource management policies to guarantee an ade-quate supply of lumber (Harder 1997).

Industrial concentration ratios remained small in lumber manufacturing and wholesale; nonetheless, in the decade before World War I, the Justice Department repeatedly investigated accusations of concentration or of col-lusion and concerted selling practices. Though the industry escaped serious punishment, the antitrust division's concerns demonstrated a need for uni-fied action and response. The need for industry-wide measures was again emphasized when the War Industries Board sought to eliminate wholesalers from a streamlined wartime procurement system. The industry responded in 1920 by creating the American Wholesale Lumber Association, which would later join with the National Wholesale Lumber Dealers Association to form the National-American (later, North American) Wholesale Lumber Association. Membership was limited to wholesale establishments that did

Table 1
Number of Merchant Wholesale Establishments: U.S. Lumber and Construction
Materials, 1932–1954

1929	3,774
1933	2,636
1935	2,817
1939	3,303
1948*	5,890
1954	10,314

*Minor break in data comparability.

Source: U.S. Bureau of the Census, Historical Statistics of the United States, Colonial Times
    to 1970. Washington, DC: U.S. Government Printing Office, 1975. Series 274–371.

at least 60 percent of their business in lumber. Other major national trade
alliances include the Hardwood Distributors Association, National Forest
Products Association, and National Building Material Distributors Association.

The Great Depression and World War II tested the American lumber
industry's adaptability. Housing construction peaked in the mid-1920s,
then plunged 68 percent by 1932: from 1926 to 1932 domestic lumber
production fell 67 percent; wholesale lumber prices fell 41 percent; and
construction materials prices (including lumber) fell 28 percent. The number of merchant wholesalers in lumber and construction materials dropped
by 30 percent during the industry downturn between 1929 and 1933, but
by the end of the 1930s, their numbers had all but recovered (U.S. Bureau
of the Census 1975). The exigencies of streamlining wartime procurement
of lumber and construction materials once again stimulated government
efforts to bypass wholesalers: the Central Procurement Agency placed
three-quarters of its orders directly with producers; nevertheless, the number of merchant wholesalers increased 212 percent from 1939 to 1954 (see
Table 1).

STATISTICAL APPRAISAL OF THE INDUSTRY
IN THE 1990s

The wholesale lumber and construction materials industry has weathered
antitrust investigations, war, and depression. Industry sales compare well
with overall wholesaling in the United States, and the number of establishments and paid employees has grown faster than in other wholesaling sectors (Tables 2 and 3). In 1992 sales of $89.8 billion were reported for the
19,546 establishments wholesaling lumber and construction materials: 85

Table 2
All U.S. Wholesale Establishments, Select Dates 1929–1992: Number, Sales, Employees

Year	Number	Sales billions (current dollars)	Employees thousands
1929	163,830	65	1,550
1939	190,379	54	1,553
1958	285,996	285	2,791
1967	311,464	460	3,519
1992	495,500	3,238	5,791

Source: U.S. Bureau of the Census, *Historical Statistics of the United States, Colonial Times to 1970*. Washington, DC: U.S. Government Printing Office, 1975; U.S. Bureau of the Census, *Statistical Abstract of the United States*. Washington, DC: U.S. Government Printing Office, 1996.

Table 3
U.S. Merchant Wholesale Establishments: Lumber and Construction Materials, Select Dates 1929–1992: Number, Sales, Employees

Year	Number	Sales billions (current dollars)	Employees thousands
1929	3,774	$1.2	—NA—
1939	3,303	0.8	38.9
1958	9,463	6.27	102.7
1967	10,877	9.07	123.6
1992	16,355	63.76	180.8

Source: U.S. Bureau of the Census, *Historical Statistics of the United States, Colonial Times to 1970*. Washington, DC: U.S. Government Printing Office, 1975; U.S. Bureau of the Census, *1992 Census of Wholesale Trade. Establishment and Firm Size*. Washington, DC: U.S. Government Printing Office, 1995.

percent of those establishments were merchant wholesalers; the remainder were manufacturers' sales offices and branches, agents, brokers, and commission merchants. Merchant wholesalers account for 71 percent of total sales in the industry (Tables 4 and 5). The four largest firms posted 10.9 percent of national sales; the eight largest, 16.2 percent; and the fifty largest, 32.9 percent. One-third of all wholesale establishments employed fewer than five workers, and 14 percent employed more than twenty (U.S. Bureau

Table 4
Lumber and Other Construction Materials, Establishments, and Sales, 1992

Products	Establishments	Sales billions (current dollars)
Lumber, Plywood, Millwork, Wood Panels	8,364	56.0
Brick, Stone, and Related Construction Materials	4,285	10.1
Roofing, Siding and Insulation Materials	2,848	14.4
Flat Glass and Other Construction Materials	4,049	9.2
TOTAL	19,546	89.8

Source: U.S. Bureau of the Census, *1992 Census of Wholesale Trade. Geographic Area Series.* Washington, DC: U.S. Government Printing Office, 1995.

Table 5
Lumber and Other Construction Materials Wholesalers, 1992

Nature of Establishment	Number	Sales billions (current dollars)
Merchant Wholesalers	16,355	63.8
Manufacturers, Sales Branches, and Offices	2,020	21.3
Agents, Brokers, and Commission Merchants	1,171	4.7
TOTAL	19,546	89.8

Source: U.S. Bureau of the Census, *1992 Census of Wholesale Trade. Miscellaneous Subjects.* Washington, DC: U.S. Government Printing Office, 1995.

of the Census 1995a, WC92-S-1, Tables 3 and 5). In 1992 the top five states in number of wholesale establishments were California, Florida, Texas, New York, and Pennsylvania; in total sales, California, Texas, Oregon, Florida, and Washington. The top five city regions by number of wholesale establishments were New York, Los Angeles, Chicago, Seattle, and Philadelphia (U.S. Bureau of the Census 1995c, WC92-A-52 RV, Tables 4 and 5). Lumber, plywood, millwork, and wood panels accounted for 62 percent of sales industry-wide; brick, stone, roofing, insulation, and other construction materials made up the remainder (Table 4).

BIBLIOGRAPHIC ESSAY

Bibliographic materials for the lumber and construction materials wholesaling industry are part of the literature on forestry and forest products.

Among general reference works on forestry that cover wholesaling is the *Encyclopedia of American Forest and Conservation History* (1983), edited by Richard C. Davis. The two-volume encyclopedia includes "Lumber Distribution and Marketing" by Fred W. Kohlmeyer as well as essays on the regional development of the American lumber industry and the historiography of forestry and related industries. Ronald J. Fahl's *North American Forest and Conservation History: A Bibliography* (1977), a massive undertaking by the Forest History Society, lists titles related to lumber marketing and distribution. Among textbooks, Bryant (1922) contains a chapter on lumber distribution—"Lumber Trade Associations"—that reviews early antitrust policy. Stanley F. Horn (1951) and Nelson Courtlandt Brown (1958) discuss marketing and distribution. Brown emphasizes technique; Horn, description and history. The most useful text is Rich (1970), which provides descriptive and functional detail on the evolution of lumber marketing and the names of companies active in lumber wholesaling (e.g., Fir-Land Lumber Company, Samson Wholesale Lumber Company, and Ponderosa Pine Company).

Marketing information is published by national industrial organizations and trade associations like the North American Wholesale Lumber Association, National Forest Products Association, Hardwood Distributors Association, and National Building Material Distributors Association. Forestry industry journals offer data on lumbering and construction materials. In 1917 the Society of American Foresters merged *The Forestry Quarterly* with the *Proceedings of the Society of American Foresters* to produce the *Journal of Forestry*; the society publishes a technical journal as well, *Forest Science*. Also of interest are the *Journal of Forest History*, *American Lumberman*, and *Forest Industries*. Proceedings from conferences often include historiographical materials, as do regional lumber and history journals.

Industry case studies are useful. Hidy, Hill, and Nevins' classic, peerless study of the Weyerhaeuser Corporation (1963) is the richest of the type, but there are others, namely, Spector (1990), Bartelle (1925), and Smith (1972).

Regional studies of forestry and lumber trace developments in distribution. Mead (1966) makes an interesting case for an oligopsony in the Douglas fir market of the Pacific Northwest and West Coast, and Etcheson (1960) provides data and functional analysis on lumber distribution in this most important region in the twentieth century. Some other studies of interest on the Pacific Northwest and West Coast are Becker and Bellows (1914), Montgomery (1942), Tutt (1967), and Cox (1974). For studies on the South, see Reynolds and Pierson (1939b); for the Southwest, Brisbin (1967); for the Northeast, Allison (1960) and Brock (1963); and for the Midwest and the Great Lakes region, see Butler (1917), Crowe (1953), Dunbar (1955), Mason (1956), and Reynolds and Pierson (1939a).

Systematic data on the lumber and construction materials industries are readily available from standard federal government sources. For lumber production and consumption data as well as import, export, and wholesale trends in this industry, see the key U.S. Bureau of the Census publication *Historical Statistics of the United States, Colonial Times to 1970* (1975) and the annual *Statistical Abstract of the United States* (1996b). Also crucial for production and consumption data and for long-range forecasts are the periodic government reports furnished by the U.S. Forest Service (1990). For highly detailed data on the current lumber and construction materials industry, the *1992 Census of Wholesale Trade* compiled by the U.S. Bureau of the Census (1995a, 1995b, 1995c, 1995d, 1996a) is indispensable.

BIBLIOGRAPHY

Allison, R. C. "Marketing of Lumber Produced by Sawmills in Pennsylvania." Master's thesis, Pennsylvania State University, 1960.

American Lumberman. Chicago: *American Lumberman.* Formed by union of *Northwestern Lumberman* and *Timberman.* Weekly from 1899 to March 5, 1932; biweekly from March 19, 1932, until publication ceased with no. 3342, August 31, 1946. Continued by *American Lumberman & Building Products Merchandiser.*

American Lumberman & Building Products Merchandiser. Chicago: *American Lumberman,* 1946–1955. Continued by *American Lumberman and Building Products Merchandiser.*

American Lumberman & Building Products Merchandiser. Chicago: Vance, 1955– 1960. Biweekly. Continued by *Building Materials Merchandiser.*

Andrews, Ralph W. *Glory Days of Logging.* Seattle: Superior, 1956.

Bartelle, J. P. *Forty Years on the Road; or the Reminiscences of a Lumber Salesman.* Cedar Rapids, IA: Torch Press, 1925.

Becker, F. D., and S. B. Bellows, eds. *History of the Pacific Coast Shipper's Association and Organization of Wholesalers and Manufacturers of Pacific Coast Forest Products.* Seattle: Pacific Coast Shipper's Association, 1914.

Berton, John Louis. "An Evaluation of the Marketing Program of Arkansas Lumber Manufacturers in Selling to the Residential Construction Industry." Ph.D. diss., University of Arkansas, 1965.

Binns, Archie. *The Roaring Land.* New York: Robert M. McBride, 1942.

Brier, Howard Maxwell. *Sawdust Empire: The Pacific Northwest.* New York: Alfred A. Knopf, 1958.

Brisbin, Bryce James. "Marketing Problems of the Arizona Lumber Industry." D.B.A. diss., University of Southern California, 1967.

Brock, Samuel M. *Marketing Maine Lumber to the Northeastern Building Construction Industry.* Orono: University of Maine, 1963.

Brown, Nelson Courtlandt. *The American Lumber Industry, Embracing the Principal Features of the Resources, Production, Distribution, and Utilization of Lumber in the United States.* New York: John Wiley & Sons, 1923.

———. "Recent Developments in Lumber Distribution." *Journal of Forestry* 22 (January 1924).

———. *Lumber.* New York: John Wiley & Sons, 1958.

Bryant, Ralph Clement. *Lumber, Its Manufacture and Distribution.* New York: John Wiley & Sons, 1922.

Business Executives Research Committee. *The Forest Products Industry of Oregon: A Report.* Portland, OR: Business Executives Research Committee, 1954.

Butler, Ovid M. *The Distribution of Softwood Lumber in the Middle West: Wholesale Distribution.* U.S. Department of Agriculture Report no. 115. Washington, DC: U.S. Government Printing Office, 1917.

Casamajor, Paul, Dennis Teeguarden, and John A. Zivnuska. *Timber Marketing and Land Ownership in Mendocino County.* Agriculture Experiment Station Bulletin no. 772. Berkeley: University of California, 1960.

Chmelik, John T., David J. Brooks, and Richard W. Haynes. *United States Trade in Forest Products, 1978–1987.* PNW 240. Portland, OR: U.S. Department of Agriculture, Forest Service, Pacific Northwest Research Station, 1989.

Clawson, Marion. *Public Log Markets as a Tool in Forest Management.* Washington, DC: Resources for the Future, 1978.

Clepper, Henry. "The Literature of Forestry." *Journal of Forestry* 29 (1931): 469–73.

Cowlin, Robert W. "The Wholesale Middleman in the Lumber Industry." Master's thesis, University of California, Berkeley, 1928.

Cox, Reavis, Charles S. Goodman, and Franklin R. Root. *Adaptation to Markets in the Distribution of Building Materials.* Washington, DC: Producers' Council, 1963.

Cox, Thomas R. *Mills and Markets: A History of the Pacific Coast Lumber Industry to 1900.* Seattle: University of Washington Press, 1974.

———. *This Well-Wooded Land: Americans and Their Forests from Colonial Times to the Present.* Lincoln: University of Nebraska Press, 1985.

Crowe, W. S. "Historical Notes on Michigan's Lumber Industry." *Timber Producers' Bulletin* 119 (February 1953).

Dana, Samuel T., and Sally K. Fairfax, with Mark Rey and Barbara T. Andrews. *Forest and Range Policy, Its Development in the United States.* 2d ed. McGraw-Hill Series in Forest Resources. New York: McGraw-Hill, 1980.

Davis, Richard C., ed. *Encyclopedia of American Forest and Conservation History.* 2 vols. New York: Collier Macmillan, 1983.

Defebaugh, James E. *History of the Lumber Industry of America.* 2 vols. Chicago: American Lumberman, 1906–1907.

Duerr, William A. *Fundamentals of Forestry Economics.* American Forestry Series. New York: McGraw-Hill, 1960.

Dunbar, Willis F. *Michigan through the Centuries.* 4 vols. New York: Lewis Historical Publishing, 1955.

"The Dynamics of Distribution." *Proceedings of the Fifth Annual Forest Industries Marketing Conference,* edited by Stuart U. Rich. Eugene: University of Oregon, College of Business Administration, Forest Industries Management Center, 1968.

Egleston, Nathaniel H. *Report of Forestry.* Vol. 4. Washington, DC: U.S. Government Printing Office, 1884.

Ellefson, Paul V., and Robert N. Stone. *U.S. Wood-Based Industry: Industrial Organization and Performance.* New York: Praeger, 1984.

Etcheson, Warren W. *A Study of Pacific Northwest Lumber Wholesaling*. Portland, OR: Western Lumber Marketing Association, 1960.

Executive Office of the President. *Lumber Prices and the Lumber Products Industry. Interim Report*. Washington, DC: Council on Wage and Price Stability, 1977.

Fahl, Ronald J. *North American Forest and Conservation History: A Bibliography*. Santa Barbara, CA: ABC-Clio Press, 1977.

Fernow, Bernhard E. "American Lumber." In *One Hundred Years of American Commerce, 1795–1895*, edited by Chauncey M. Depew. New York: D. O. Haynes, 1895.

Ficken, Robert E. *The Forested Land: A History of Lumbering in Western Washington*. Seattle: University of Washington Press, 1987.

Fowler, R. M. "The Merchandising of Idaho White Pine." Master's thesis, State University of New York, College of Forestry, 1937.

Gamble, Thomas. *Naval Stores: History Production, Distribution, and Consumption*. Savannah, GA: Review Publishing & Printing, 1921.

Graham, Frank. "Sawmill Evolution: Mixed Cars." *Timberman* 29 (January 1928).

Harder, K. Peter. "Forestry." In *Extractives, Manufacturing, and Services: A Historiographical and Bibliographical Guide*, vol. 2 of *Handbook of American Business History*, edited by David O. Whitten and Bessie E. Whitten, 39–65. Westport, CT: Greenwood Press, 1997.

Hartman, George B. "The Iowa Sawmill Industry." *Iowa Journal of History and Politics* 40 (January 1942).

Hidy, Ralph, Frank E. Hill, and Allan Nevins. *Timber and Men: The Weyerhaeuser Story*. New York: Macmillan, 1963.

Holland, Israel I., G. I. Rolfe, and David A. Anderson. *Forests and Forestry*. 4th ed., rev. Danville, IL: Interstate Publishers, 1990.

Holtzclaw, Henry F. "The Lumber Industry and Trade." Ph.D. diss., Johns Hopkins University, 1917.

———. "Historical Survey of the Lumber Industry." *Southern Lumberman* 89 (August 3, 1918).

Horn, Stanley F. *This Fascinating Lumber Business*. 2d ed. Indianapolis: Bobbs-Merrill, 1951.

Hotchkiss, George W. *History of the Lumber and Forest Industry of the Northwest*. Chicago: G. W. Hotchkiss, 1898.

Irland, Lloyd C. *Is Timber Scarce? The Economics of a Renewable Resource*. School of Forestry and Environmental Studies Bulletin no. 83. New Haven, CT: Yale University, 1974.

———. "Do Giants Control Timber-Based Industries in North America?" *Forest Industries* 103 (June 1976): 40–41.

———. *Wilderness Economics and Policy*. Lexington, MA: Lexington Books, 1979.

———. *Wildlands and Woodlots: The Story of New England's Forests*. Forests of New England. Hanover, NH: University Press of New England, 1982.

———, ed. *Ethics in Forestry*. Portland, OR: Timber Press, 1994.

Isherwood, H. R., ed. *A Report on the Profitable Management of a Retail Lumber Business . . . Based on an Investigation of 491 Retail Lumber Yards in 38 States and Canada*. 5 vols. New York: A. W. Shaw, 1918.

Joy, A. C. "History of Lumbering in California." *Timberman* 30 (November 1929).

Kohlmeyer, Fred W. "Lumber Distribution and Marketing." In *Encyclopedia of American Forest and Conservation History*, edited by Richard C. Davis, · 365–70. New York: Collier Macmillan, 1983.

Latham, Bryan. "The Development of the American Timber Trade." *Wood* (September 1956–January 1957).

———. *Timber, Its Development and Distribution. A Historical Survey.* London: George G. Harrap, 1957.

———. *Wood: From Forest to Man.* London: George G. Harrap, 1964.

Lavender, David S. *Land of Giants: The Drive to the Pacific Northwest, 1750–1950.* Garden City, NY: Doubleday, 1958.

Leigh, Jack H. *The Timber Trade: An Introduction to Commercial Aspects.* New York: Pergamon Press, 1971.

The Lumberman. Portland, OR: Miller Freeman, 1949–1961. Continued by *Lumberman and Wood Industries*.

Lumberman and Wood Industries. Portland, OR: Miller Freeman, 1961–1962. Merged with *Timberman* to form *Forest Industries*.

"Marketing in the Changing World of the 1970s." *Proceedings of the Sixth Annual Forest Industries Marketing Conference*, edited by Stuart U. Rich. Eugene: University of Oregon, College of Business Administration, Forest Industries Management Center, 1969.

Mason, Philip P. *Lumbering Era in Michigan History (1860–1900).* Lansing: Michigan Historical Commission, 1956.

Mead, Walter J. *Competition and Oligopsony in the Douglas Fir Lumber Industry.* Berkeley: University of California Press, 1966.

Melton, William Ray. *The Lumber Industry of Washington and the Pacific Northwest.* Tacoma: National Youth Administration of Washington, 1938.

Merrick, Gordon D. *Trends in Lumber Distribution, 1922–1943.* Washington, DC: U.S. Forest Service, Division of Forest Economics Research, 1948.

———. "Trends in Distribution of Lumber, 1922–1943." *Southern Lumberman* 177 (September 1, 1948).

Montgomery, W. F. "Pioneer Lumber Dealers in Los Angeles." *Historical Society of Southern California Quarterly* 24 (June 1942).

Moore, Andrew G. T. "Traffic and Transportation in Lumber Merchandising." *Southern Lumberman* 177 (December 15, 1948).

Namorato, Michael V. "Lumber and Wood Products." In *Manufacturing: A Historiographical and Bibliographical Guide*, vol. 1 of *Handbook of American Business History*, edited by David O. Whitten and Bessie E. Whitten, 117–33. Westport, CT: Greenwood Press, 1990.

National Lumber Manufacturers Association. *Proceedings of the Golden Anniversary Meeting of the National Lumber Manufacturers Association at St. Louis, Missouri, May 8–10, 1952.* Washington, DC: National Lumber Manufacturers Association, 1952.

"New Marketing Insights for Forest Products Companies." In *Proceedings of the First Annual Forest Industries Marketing Conference*, edited by Stuart U. Rich. Eugene: University of Oregon, College of Business Administration, Forest Industries Management Center, 1964.

Potter, Neal, and Francis T. Christy, Jr. *Trends in Natural Resource Commodities: Statistics of Prices, Output, Consumption, Foreign Trade, and Employment in the United States, 1870–1957.* Baltimore: Johns Hopkins University Press, Resources for the Future, 1962.

Pulpwood Production. Montgomery, AL: Hatton, Brown, 1953–1956. Monthly. Continued by *Pulpwood Production and Sawmill Logging.*

Pulpwood Production and Sawmill Logging. Montgomery, AL: Hatton, Brown, 1956–1974. Monthly. Continued by *Pulpwood Production & Timber Harvesting.*

Pulpwood Production & Timber Harvesting. Montgomery, AL: Hatton, Brown, 1974–1977. Continued by *Timber Harvesting.*

Recknagel, Arthur B. *The Forests of New York State.* New York: Macmillan, 1923.

Reynolds, Robert V., and Albert H. Pierson. *Lumber Cut of the United States, 1870–1920: Declining Production and High Prices as Related to Forest Exhaustion.* U.S. Department of Agriculture Bulletin no. 1119. Washington, DC: U.S. Government Printing Office, 1923.

———. "Tracking the Sawmill Westward: The Story of the Lumber Industry in the U.S. as Unfolded by Its Trail across the Continent." *American Forests* 31 (November 1925).

———. "The Aggregate Cut of American Lumber, 1801–1935." *Journal of Forestry* 35 (December 1937).

———. *Forest Products Statistics of the Pacific Coast States.* U.S. Department of Agriculture Statistical Bulletin no. 65. Washington, DC: U.S. Government Printing Office, 1938.

———. *Statistics of Forest Products in the Rocky Mountain States.* U.S. Department of Agriculture Statistical Bulletin no. 64. Washington, DC: U.S. Government Printing Office, 1938.

———. *Forest Products Statistics of the Lake States.* U.S. Department of Agriculture Statistical Bulletin no. 68. Washington, DC: U.S. Government Printing Office, 1939a.

———. *Forest Products Statistics of the Southern States.* U.S. Department of Agriculture Statistical Bulletin no. 69. Washington, DC: U.S. Government Printing Office, 1939b.

———. *Forest Products Statistics of Central and Prairie States.* U.S. Department of Agriculture Statistical Bulletin no. 73. Washington, DC: U.S. Government Printing Office, 1941.

Rich, Stuart U. *Marketing of Forest Products: Text and Cases.* New York: McGraw-Hill, 1970.

Ritter, William M. *The Lumber Business: Organization, Production, Distribution, Observations and Comments on Efficiency and Service.* Nashville: *Southern Lumberman*, 1920.

Robinson, Gordon. *The Forest and the Trees: A Guide to Excellent Forestry.* Washington, DC: Island Press, 1988.

"Seattle as a Lumber Center." *American Lumberman* (December 2, 1911).

Sedjo, Roger A., and Samuel J. Radcliffe. *Postwar Trends in U.S. Forest Products Trade: A Global, National, and Regional View.* R 22. Washington, DC: Resources for the Future, 1981; distributed by Johns Hopkins University Press.

Sherman, Dorothy M. "A Brief History of the Lumber Industry in the Fir Belt of Oregon." Master's thesis, University of Oregon, 1934.

Smith, David C. *A History of Lumbering in Maine, 1861–1960.* University of Maine Studies, no. 93. Orono: University of Maine Press, 1972.

Spector, Robert. *Family Trees: Simpson's Centennial Story.* Bellevue, WA: Documentary Book, 1990.

Steer, Henry B. *Lumber Production in the United States, 1799–1946.* Miscellaneous Publication no. 669. Washington, DC: U.S. Department of Agriculture, 1948.

"Striking Changes in the Geography of the Lumber Traffic." *American Lumberman* (December 22, 1906).

Timber Harvesting. Montgomery, AL: Hatton, Brown, 1977– . Monthly.

The Timberman. Portland, OR: Miller Freeman, 1899–1962. Monthly. Merged with *Lumberman and Wood Industries* to form *Forest Industries.*

Tutt, George T. "Lumber Wholesaling in the Pacific Northwest." Master's thesis, University of Montana, 1967.

Twining, Charles E. *Phil Weyerhaeuser, Lumberman.* Seattle: University of Washington Press, 1985.

———. *F. K. Weyerhaeuser: A Biography.* St. Paul: Minnesota Historical Society Press, 1997.

U.S. Bureau of Corporations. *The Lumber Industry. Part IV. Conditions in Production and Wholesale Distribution including Wholesale Prices.* Washington, DC: U.S. Government Printing Office, 1914.

U.S. Bureau of the Census. *Historical Statistics of the United States, Colonial Times to 1970.* 2 vols. Washington, DC: U.S. Government Printing Office, 1975.

———. *1992 Census of Wholesale Trade. Commodity Line Sales.* Washington, DC: U.S. Government Printing Office, 1995a.

———. *1992 Census of Wholesale Trade. Establishment and Firm Size.* Washington, DC: U.S. Government Printing Office, 1995b.

———. *1992 Census of Wholesale Trade. Geographic Area Series.* Washington, DC: U.S. Government Printing Office, 1995c.

———. *1992 Census of Wholesale Trade. Miscellaneous Subjects.* Washington, DC: U.S. Government Printing Office, 1995d.

———. *1992 Census of Wholesale Trade. Measures of Value Produced, Capital Expenditures, Depreciable Assets, and Operating Expenses.* Washington, DC: U.S. Government Printing Office, November 1996a.

———. *Statistical Abstract of the United States.* Washington, DC: U.S. Government Printing Office, 1996b.

U.S. Forest Service. *Timber Depletion, Lumber Prices, Lumber Exports, and Concentration of Timber Ownership. Report on Senate Resolution 311, June 1, 1920.* Prepared by Assistant Forester Earle H. Clapp. Ann Arbor, MI: Xerox University Microfilms, 1975.

———. *An Analysis of the Timber Situation in the United States: 1989–2040.* Washington, DC: U.S. Government Printing Office, 1990.

Vinnedge, Robert W. *The Pacific Northwest Lumber Industry and Its Development.* Lumber Industry Series, no. 4. New Haven, CT: Yale University, School of Forestry, 1923.

———. "The Genesis of the Pacific Northwest Lumber Industry and Its Development." *Timberman* 35 (December 1933).

Vogel, John N. *Great Lakes Lumber on the Great Plains: The Laird, Norton Lumber Company in South Dakota.* Iowa City: University of Iowa Press, 1992.

Volkober, John Anton, Jr. "Factors Affecting the Competitive Position of the Pacific Northwest and British Columbia in United States Lumber Markets: Regional Advantage." Master's thesis, Reed College, Portland, OR, 1967.

Wand, Ben. "Fifty Years of Wholesaling Lumber." *Southern Lumber Journal* 42 (January 1938).

Weyerhaeuser, George Hunt. *"Forests for the Future": The Weyerhaeuser Story.* Newcomen Publication no. 1141. New York: Newcomen Society in North America, 1981.

Whiting, Perry. *Autobiography of Perry Whiting, Pioneer Building Material Merchant of Los Angeles.* Los Angeles: Smith-Barnes, 1930.

Wood, Richard G. *A History of Lumbering in Maine, 1820–1861.* Maine Bulletin, vol. 43, no. 15. Orono: University of Maine Press, 1935. Reprint. University of Maine Studies, 2d ser., no. 33. Orono: University of Maine Press, 1961.

Wood Technology. San Francisco: Miller Freeman, 1992– . Bimonthly.

World Wood. Portland, OR: Miller Freeman, 1960–1994. Monthly. Absorbed by *Wood Technology.*

Part V

Apparel and Accessory Stores
ESIC 56.0

CHAPTER 7

SHOE STORES, 56.6

JAMES L. WILES

The *Census of Retail Trade* (U.S. Bureau of the Census) identifies shoe stores as establishments primarily engaged in the retail sale of any one line, or a combination of the lines, of men's, women's, and children's footwear. Although shoe stores are the focus of this chapter, over the years a number of other outlets have also sold shoes. Recent census figures show, for example, that department, clothing, and miscellaneous retail stores account for 40 to 45 percent of shoe sales in the United States. The current structure of shoe retailing reflects changes in the channels through which finished products reach the American consumer.

The colonial and national periods, 1600 to 1865, can be termed the age of the merchant. Manufacturers played but a small part in the distribution of their products (Porter and Livesay [1971] 1989). "They were too busy trying to keep abreast of demand. Their main—one might even say only— problem was one of production" (Haring 1929). Leading commerce were the all-purpose merchants, who gave way as the nineteenth century wore on, to specialized wholesalers (Porter and Livesay [1971] 1989). Manufacturers sold their products to middlemen in major eastern cities, who in turn sold to retailers who visited the trading centers once or twice a year to replenish their stocks (Nystrom 1930).

In the post–Civil War years manufacturers pursued economies in the distribution of their products. Makers of complex equipment, like sewing machines and harvesters, established their own sales outlets because wholesalers could not provide instruction or maintenance for technologically advanced machinery (Porter and Livesay [1971] 1989). The first comprehensive survey of the distribution of complex products, the *Census of Busi-*

ness (U.S. Bureau of the Census), showed that in 1929 two-thirds of the shoes produced had been marketed by the manufacturers.

Changes at the retail level helped shape the structure of shoe sales. Some observers attribute these changes to the "wheel of retailing," a process in which new retail forms supplant or vigorously compete with the old (McNair 1958). New retailers appear on the scene as "low-status, low-margin, low-price operators" (Hollander 1960). Gradually, as these operations become more elaborate and more expensive, they become vulnerable to the challenge of new ventures. Eventually, these "new types" develop characteristics that expose them to still newer forms of competition (Hollander 1960). Thus, in urbanized sections of the United States, the general store gave way during the nineteenth century to the specialty store. The small-scale specialty store was challenged later in the century by the larger department store, which, by mid-twentieth century, would itself face the formidable competition of the postwar discount house. In the 1990s a revival of catalog shopping as well as the promise of electronic shopping may indicate that the wheel has turned again. Although its explanatory power is sometimes questioned, the wheel model retains a prominent place in retailing literature (Hollander 1960; Brown 1990).

The Massachusetts boot and shoe industry was among the first in the United States to produce goods for sale beyond the producers' immediate geographic area (Hoover 1937; Hazard [1921] 1969). Beginning in the 1760s, shoe shipments reached Boston for distribution to general stores and itinerant peddlers in less populated sections of the West and South. Shoe retailing had become more specialized in the major cities by 1800. Clothing stores sold shoes, and a few shoe stores operated in Boston, New York, and Philadelphia. In the late 1850s specialized shoe stores were the usual retail outlet in large cities; for the United States as a whole, however, general stores and clothing stores accounted for the greater portion of retail shoe sales (Jones 1936). All outlets were supplied by independent wholesalers.

At midcentury the shoe industry was one of the few in America with a national market (Atack 1985). Retailers offered a standardized, ordinary-grade shoe; after the Civil War, however, consumers in American cities were more interested in style than durability. Manufacturers responded to this change in taste by using different grades of leather to produce shoes of varying design and color (Hoover 1937).

Product differentiation forced shoe manufacturers into close contact with retailers since frequent style changes required rapid factory-to-store delivery to capitalize on shifting consumer demand. Manufacturers could deal with one jobber, sell directly to retailers, or set up outlets (Hoover 1937). Many who had begun selling to independent retailers in the early 1880s were by the end of the decade selling to chain-store retailers (Nystrom 1930). The Melville shoe store chain began operating in 1892. The G. R. Kinney chain opened in 1894, and that same year the W. L. Douglas Co. of Brockton, Massachusetts, became the first shoe manufacturer to open its own chain of retail outlets; by 1900, fifty-five Douglas Shoe Stores had been established. Advertising and brand names were closely associated with these developments (Lebhar 1963; Chatfield 1950).

It is difficult to assess nineteenth-century shoe retailing. Writing in 1923, Lawrence B. Mann declared: "No important field of business statistics has been so neglected by both governmental and private investigators as that of retail and wholesale merchandising." About thirty years later, Harold Barger (1955) commented on "the sharp contrast between the wealth of information available today and the sparsity of material prior to World War II." U.S. Bureau of the Census coverage of retail trade began in 1930 with the initial *Census of Business*. The bureau's coverage of this sector of the economy continues as the *Census of Retail Trade*.

Although the statistical picture of nineteenth-century shoe retailing is unclear, there is some information for the period 1869–1929. Barger (1955) estimates the scale of shoe store activity in the years up to 1929. Between 1869 and 1919 shoe store sales accounted for 2–2.5 percent of total retail sales in the United States; by 1919 that share had dropped to about 1.7 percent. Since World War II, the figure has hovered around 1 percent.

Looking more closely at shoe retailing itself, Barger finds that, in 1869, 70 percent of the value of shoes manufactured was sold to independent wholesalers for distribution to retail outlets. The balance was sold directly to retailers or reached retail stores by way of the manufacturer's own wholesaler. This 70:30 wholesaler-direct sale ratio persisted into the first decade of the twentieth century before declining to 51:49 in 1929 (Barger 1955). Barger's data reveal restructuring within shoe retailing. In 1869 general stores absorbed 22 percent of shoe output, dry goods and apparel stores 40 percent, and shoe stores 38 percent. By 1899 department stores took 4 percent of shoe output, and general stores 19 percent. The share for dry goods and apparel stores dropped to 26 percent; shoe stores handled 50 percent of shoe output, but only 5 percent of the shoes they sold were retailed through chain shoe store outlets. By 1929 department stores, with 18.5 percent of output, and shoe stores, with 52.7 percent, dominated shoe retailing; chains took almost 40 percent of the manufactured product distributed through shoe stores.

The 1930 census shows the structure of shoe retailing at the onset of the Great Depression. In 1929, 66 percent of retail shoe sales originated in shoe stores, 17 percent in department stores, and the balance in clothing and general stores (Hoover 1937). Some 24,000 shoe stores were operating in 1929, 21 percent of them affiliated with chains. The chains accounted for 38 percent of sales that year. In retailing as a whole, about 11 percent of the establishments were associated with chains (Lebow 1957).

As the depression deepened, the number of establishments fell by some

5,000 to a total of 19,000 in 1935. Most of the failed firms had been independent outlets; the number of chain-related stores remained about the same, at 5,000, but their share of the market increased to over 50 percent. Except for a small drop in 1939, the multiunits percentage of overall shoe store sales has increased steadily over the past sixty years. In 1992 chains operated 78 percent of all shoe stores and accounted for 83 percent of shoe store sales.

Dollar sales fell from $807 million in 1929 to $511 million by 1935, a 37 percent drop. Adjusted for price changes with an index of clothing and shoe prices, the decline is a less striking 19 percent. Employment in retail shoe stores fell from 83,400 in 1929 to about 69,000 in 1935, a 17 percent drop. As incomes shrank, consumers bought fewer and less expensive shoes (Mack 1954).

At the end of the 1930s signs of recovery were evident, although all measures remained below 1929 levels. The number of stores operating was up by some 1,500 over the 1935 figure; independents accounted for about 60 percent of that gain. Average annual employment in shoe stores increased by about 12 percent from 1935 to 1939. The chains and independents showed roughly comparable improvements.

Legislation had some effect on independent establishments in the late 1930s. The depression made the low prices offered by chain stores especially attractive and fueled their rapid growth. Independent merchants, unable to match the chains in the marketplace, sought relief from the federal government and their state governments. In Washington, the Robinson-Patman Act of 1936 "was the product of organized political efforts to preserve the traditional marketing system of independent merchants against the encroachment of mass distributors and chains" (Rowe 1962). The act sought "to make prices charged distributors accord with differences in cost" (Werne 1938), thus reducing the advantages in prices enjoyed by large buyers (Edwards 1959).

Resale price maintenance, or fair trade laws, emerged in the 1930s. After the Supreme Court upheld the right of a manufacturer to set minimum resale prices, legislation "aimed primarily at price-cutting retailers" proliferated: between 1935 and 1938, forty-two states enacted fair-trade laws, and in 1937 the federal fair-trade law, the Miller-Tydings Act, passed. Independent stores benefited, for chains could no longer sell below the manufacturer's price (Beckman and Nolen [1938] 1976).

Some states enacted "anti-chain store" tax laws. Although the last such tax was levied in 1941, at one time or another twenty-eight states passed statutes designed to curtail the number of stores operated by large chains; and from 1929 to 1939 the total number of chain units in the United States did decline, but the drop was associated primarily with filling-station and grocery chains (Lebhar 1963). The Census Bureau argued that "these totals show no indication that tax restrictions reduced the growth of other chains, in units or in sales volume" (U.S. Bureau of the Census, *Sixteenth Census of the United States: 1940. Census of Business*, Vol. 1, *Retail Trade: 1939*, Part 1). After World War II, *Census of Business* shoe store classifications changed. The independent versus chain dichotomy employed in the 1930s was dropped in favor of a single versus multiunit classification. While all chains were multiunits, not all multiunits were chains.

During the 1920s and 1930s and, indeed, up to the postwar "retail revolution," shoe stores retained a well-defined niche in American merchandising, even though chains were increasingly prominent in the trade. In 1948 independents made up about two-thirds of all shoe retailers; the stores were small and located in downtown business districts. Buying patterns were seasonal: boots for the winter months, Easter shoes, and summer items. Customer shopping habits were predictable: most sales were made on Friday evenings and Saturdays, and customers dressed to shop—men wore jackets and ties, and women sported hats and gloves.

The 1950s shattered a seemingly pleasant picture. "Immediately following World War II, the United States had an archaic pre-war marketing distribution system that was not geared to meet the needs of a dynamic postwar economy" (Lowrey 1969). Consumers were better educated, had higher incomes, and were more mobile. The "wheel of retailing" was turning. Consumers used their knowledge, money, and mobility to locate good-quality merchandise at a discount price (Bluestone et al. 1981). By the end of the 1950s discount stores were an established part of the retail scene (Lowrey 1969).

In shoe retailing, change took two major forms: discount shoe stores and shoe departments leased in the self-service apparel stores appeared in large numbers during the late 1950s (Tallman and Blomstrom 1960). Morse Shoe pioneered leasing departments in apparel discount chains in New England, the Midwest, and the far West. By the mid-1960s, Morse Shoe had nearly 400 leased self-service shoe departments. Its sales increased from $9 million in 1957 to $80 million by 1965 (Morse 1966).

Discount house innovations made it difficult for the small, independent retailer to survive. Cuts in service and in nonservice personnel, feasible in larger discount stores, permitted high sales volume per foot of floor space and per salesman (Oxenfeldt 1960). With the decline of "fair trade," small stores faced stiff price competition from the discounters (Lebow 1957). One observer argues that all levels of retailing, not just the small independents, were "too slow to spot the threat and were undersold" (Oxenfeldt 1960). Interestingly, a prewar study had pinpointed selling costs as a major determinant of total costs in the operation of chain shoe stores (Dean and Warren 1942).

Independent shoe stores declined in the aftermath of the retailing revolution. Despite general prosperity, 4,000 fewer independents were doing business in 1967 than in 1958. Beyond the competition from price-cutting chain discount stores, changing spatial location of retail trade hurt down-town retailers. Walk-in trade dwindled in areas where parking was scarce, for many shoppers preferred the more easily accessed malls. Small-business proprietors found mall rents prohibitive and the rising opportunity cost of being their own bosses more than they could afford. Clothing, hardware, grocery, drug, and shoe stores locked their doors and abandoned down-town business districts from Opelika, Alabama, to Philadelphia, Pennsyl-vania. Small-town America was down, if not out (Markin 1967).

The 1960s brought changes in living styles and consumer tastes. The move to casual and fad clothing shaped shoe retailing: the Frye boot and earth shoe of the 1960s, sneakers in the 1970s, "high-tech" walking shoes of the late 1970s and 1980s. The Nike athletic shoe started a boom in the mid-1970s; the 1992 census included athletic shoe stores as a distinct foot-wear outlet. Specialty stores proliferated, and by the 1980s athletic walking shoes—increasingly manufactured abroad—made up 30 to 50 percent of retail shoe sales.

Table 1 shows the changes in the number of retail shoe establishments since 1929, highlighting the growing importance of multiunit stores and the increase in sales volume since 1929. Adjusted for price changes, sales in 1982 stood at 3.8 times the 1929 figure. Since World War II, per capita shoe sales have more than doubled.

Shoe stores have retained a fairly constant share of U.S. retail activity. In 1929 shoe stores accounted for 1.7 percent of total retail sales. Although at century's end they account for 1.0 percent of sales, in 1982 they made up 1.9 percent of all retail establishments and accounted for 1.3 percent of employment in the retail sector.

Table 1 shows that (price-adjusted) sales per store have about doubled since 1948, while the number of employees per store has increased by about 75 percent. These figures indicate the trend toward larger stores and per-haps the reduced customer service associated with self-service discount op-erations.

Census data focus on shoe retailing. In 1982 shoe stores regained the approximately two-thirds share of the shoe retail market they had held in 1930. That share had fallen below 50 percent in the 1970s, but the end-of-the-century increase in the number of shoe stores reduced the department store's role in shoe retailing: between 1977 and 1982 shoe sales by de-partment stores fell absolutely as well as relatively. The family, or full-time, store has not regained the ground lost during the Depression. Its share of shoe store sales fell from 76 percent in 1929 to 62 percent by World War II and stood at 65 percent in 1982. Women's shoe stores have consistently accounted for about one-quarter of the shoe store sales since 1929, whereas men's shoe store sales have fluctuated moderately about the 10 percent mark.

The increase in store size and the growing significance of multiunits have

Table 1
Selected Measures of Retail Shoe Store Activity, 1929–1992

Establishments (000)	1929	1948	1972	1992
Total (%)	24.3 (100)	19.6 (100)	26.8 (100)	37.2 (100)
Single Units (%)	19.2 (79)	12.5 (64)	13.9 (52)	8.1 (22)
Multi-Units (%)	5.1 (21)	7.1 (36)	12.9 (48)	29.1 (78)
Sales ($000,000)				
Total (%)	807 (100)	1,467 (100)	3,982 (100)	16,590 (100)
Single Units (%)	501 (62)	621 (42)	1,434 (36)	2,820 (17)
Multi-Units (%)	306 (38)	846 (58)	2,548 (64)	13,770 (83)
Sales ($000,000 1948 = 100)	—	1,467	1,940	6,386
Sales per capita ($000,000 1948 = 100)	—	10.10	8.61	25.19
Sales per Store ($000,000 1948 = 100)	—	74,847	72,388	171,667
Employees per Store	2.9	3.9	4.8	4.9

Source: Compiled from the *Census of Business* and the *Census of Retail Trade*.

had some effect on concentration in the shoe store sector. In 1972 the four largest firms (based on sales) operated 12 percent of the shoe stores in the United States; by 1992 the four-firm figure had risen to 35 percent. As a percentage of shoe store sales, the four largest firms accounted for 20 percent of the total in 1972 and 39 percent in 1992.

The *Brown Shoe* case is pertinent to market concentration. Brown Shoe Company acquired G. R. Kinney Company in 1956. Both firms produced and sold shoes. In 1962 the U.S. Supreme Court declared the merger illegal, finding that it reduced competition at both the manufacturing and the retail level. "The prohibition of the Brown-Kinney merger is a means of forestalling a large number of other potential mergers in the shoe industry" (Martin 1963). The message was clear: the Court was discouraging increases in concentration. Nevertheless, by 1967 sixteen firms operated 101 or more retail shoe establishments, a total of 5,781 stores. Nineteen firms held 101 or more units in 1977, totaling 8,396 stores. In 1967, 1977, and 1982 these large multiunit operations accounted for an increasing percentage of retail shoe sales.

Retail trade margins widened for shoe stores in the post–World War II period. The margin is the difference between total sales and the cost of goods sold. Expressed as a percentage of sales, the figures for 1947 show that shoe store margins approximated those for retail trade as a whole: 31.5 percent for shoe stores and 29.7 percent overall. In the mid-1980s overall retail margins remained at 31 percent, while the shoe store figure had increased to about 45 percent. The changes reflect the lower operating costs of discount and multiunit operations as well as the profound changes in consumer tastes.

While the shoe store's place has remained the same in retailing as a whole, the shoe store itself has been altered almost beyond recognition. The growing importance of discount outlets and mall-based chain stores, the emphasis on store design and layout to enhance a marketing concept, the advent of scientific shopping analysis, and the proliferation of athletic footwear stores are a few indicators of the transformation.

Retailing will continue to change. From-home catalog shopping is an established and growing retail phenomenon: purchases by mail, telephone, and computer accounted for 2.3 percent of shoe sales in 1992. The importance of fit may limit the expansion of out-of-store sales of footwear. Consumer dissatisfaction with the impersonal and indifferent service available at shoe outlets may drive the "extended specialty store" that features out-of-store as well as in-store sales and emphasizes marketing. Shoe stores are well suited to this latest turn of the wheel of retailing (Sheth 1983; May 1989; Bates 1989).

BIBLIOGRAPHIC ESSAY

General Studies

Victor S. Clark's *History of Manufactures in the United States* (1929) and Malcolm Keir's *Manufacturing* (1928) afford useful background material on the distribution of manufactured goods up to the Great Depression. Chester E. Haring's *The Manufacturer and His Outlets* (1929) is more directly tied to distribution. A more recent contribution is *Merchants and Manufacturers: Studies in the Changing Structure of Nineteenth-Century Marketing* ([1971] 1989), a good exposition by Glenn Porter and Harold C. Livesay of changing patterns in the American system of marketing.

For the study of distribution, a valuable source of statistical data for the pre-*Business Census* years is Barger's *Distribution's Place in the American Economy since 1869* (1955). His work adds a quantitative dimension to shoe retailing of that period. Paul H. Nystrom surveys retail history in general in *Economics of Retailing* (1930), with some attention to the development of specialized shoe outlets. Thomas D. Clark's *Pills, Petticoats, and Plows: The Southern Country Store* (1944) studies the southern country store, an important shoe outlet in the last century. Works that supply context by portraying broader changes in the distribution and marketing system include Alfred D. Chandler, Jr.'s *Visible Hand: The Managerial Revolution in American Business* (1977), Fred Mitchell Jones's *Middlemen in the Domestic Trade of the United States 1800–1860* (1937), Theodore N. Beckman and Nathanael H. Engle's revised edition of *Wholesaling: Principles and Practice* (1949), and David O. Whitten's *Emergence of Giant Enterprise, 1860–1914: American Commercial Enterprise and Extractive Industries* (1983).

Several useful journal articles focus on retailing history and practice and include information on shoe retailing. J. M. Cassels' "The Marketing Machinery of the United States" (1936), Ralph M. Hower's "Urban Retailing 100 Years Ago" (1938), and Jones' "Retail Stores in the United States, 1800–1860" (1936) are examples. In "The Importance of Retail Trade in the United States" (1923), Mann attempts to assess the status of that sector in the absence of adequate statistical material. The sixty-fifth anniversary number of the *Journal of Retailing* (Fall 1989) was a forum for authoritative essays on retailing.

Specific Issues in Retailing

Strategies for small retailers are reviewed in Joseph D. Phillips' *Some Industrial and Community Conditions for Small Retail Survival* (1964). Many works deal indirectly with shoe stores. Chain stores are addressed in Wadsworth H. Mullen's "Some Aspects of Chain-Store Development" (1924), Boyce F. Martin's "The Independent et al., versus the Chains" (1930), Harry R. Tosdal's "Some Recent Changes in the Marketing of Consumer Goods" (1933), and Paul T. Cherington's "Small Retailer: An Appraisal" (1939). Theodore N. Beckman and Herman C. Nolen take a more detailed look at the phenomenon in *The Chain Store Problem: A Critical Analysis* ([1938] 1976). A later work, written by a strong advocate of the chains, is Godfrey M. Lebhar's *Chain Stores in America, 1859–1962* (1963).

Stanley C. Hollander and Glenn S. Omura argue that an assessment of the mall-based chain stores should include their impact on the socialization of American consumers. "Chain department stores anchored the malls while specialty chains filled much of the remaining area and paid most of the rent." Shoe stores are prominent examples of the latter in this new type of social center (1989).

The post–World War II revolution in retailing is explored by Malcolm P. McNair in his "Significant Trends and Developments in the Postwar

Period" (1958). James R. Lowrey reviews these developments in *The Retailing Revolution Revisited* (1969), while Gerald B. Tallman and Bruce Blomstrom examine discounting in their "Soft Goods Join the Retail Revolution" (1960). In *The Retail Revolution: Market Transformation, Investment, and Labor in the Modern Department Store* (1981), Barry Bluestone, Patricia Hanna, Sara Kuhn, and Laura Moore describe how department stores adjust to changing times.

Among the many works that gauge the impact of legislation and litigation on retailing are Corwin D. Edwards' *Price Discrimination Law* (1959) and Frederick M. Rowe's *Price Discrimination under the Robinson-Patman Act* (1962). The *Brown Shoe* merger case is examined in David D. Martin's "*Brown Shoe* Case and the New Antimerger Policy" (1963) and John Peterman's "*Brown Shoe* Case" (1975).

Shoe Stores

This final category lists works that deal explicitly with shoe retailing or with the merchandising of shoe manufacturing. Two substantial works are Blanche Evans Hazard's *Organization of the Boot and Shoe Industry in Massachusetts before 1875* ([1921] 1969) and Edgar M. Hoover, Jr.'s *Location Theory and the Shoe Leather Industries* (1937). Although they deal primarily with shoe production, Hazard and Hoover provide authoritative information on shoe marketing as well. Ross Thomson's *Path to Mechanized Shoe Production in the United States* (1989) devotes a brief section to the evolution of shoe markets. An earlier view, by a respected shoe manufacturer, also addresses shoe retailing: William B. Rice, "The Boot and Shoe Trade" (1895). In "The Long-Run Behavior of Costs in a Chain of Shoe Stores" (1942), Joel Dean and James R. Warren employ economic theory and statistical methods in studying shoe retailing during the interwar period.

Several company histories address shoe manufacturers' methods of production and distribution. *The Story of the George E. Keith Company* (n.d.) and "A Brief History of the W. L. Douglas Company" (Chatfield 1950) chronicle the two major manufacturers-retailers. *The Endicott Johnson Corporation* (Smith 1956) deserves mention here as well.

A number of trade journals publish information on shoe retailing activities. Occasional articles on shoe retailing appear in such general publications as *Business Week, Forbes,* and *Fortune.* Other sources of trade news are *Stores, Advertising Age,* and *Chain Store Age.* Each August edition of *Chain Store Age* includes rankings by dollar sales of the top chains and specialty chains. Directories such as the *Market Share Reporter, American Big Businesses Directory,* and *Dun's Business Rankings* also present shoe store figures. Many of these sources are available on the Internet or CD Rom. *Footwear News,* published weekly in New York, contains trade news and feature articles. For intercensus years, the American Footwear Industries Association's annual publication *Footwear Manual* is helpful as a statistical source.

The principal source of quantitative data on shoe stores is, of course, the U.S. Census Bureau's *Census of Business* and the *Census of Retail Trade*. In addition to these quinquennial volumes, the Census Bureau publishes the *Monthly Retail Trade Report* and the annual *Current Business Reports*. The latter contains information on sales and inventories and, occasionally, on gross margins. The two publications cover the post–World War II period.

BIBLIOGRAPHY

Advertising Age. Chicago: Crain Communications, 1930– . Weekly.

American Big Businesses Directory. Omaha, NE: American Business Directories, 1993– . Annual.

Atack, Jeremy. *Estimation of Economies of Scale in Nineteenth Century United States Manufacturing*. New York: Garland, 1985.

Barger, Harold. *Distribution's Place in the American Economy since 1869*. Princeton, NJ: Princeton University Press, 1955.

Bates, Albert D. "The Extended Specialty Store." *Journal of Retailing* 65 (Fall 1989): 379–88.

Beckman, Theodore N., and Nathanael H. Engle. *Wholesaling: Principles and Practice*. Rev. ed. New York: Ronald Press, 1949.

Beckman, Theodore N., and Herman C. Nolen. *The Chain Store Problem: A Critical Analysis*. New York: McGraw-Hill, 1938. Reprint. Getting and Spending. New York: Arno Press, 1976.

Bluestone, Barry, Patricia Hanna, Sara Kuhn, and Laura Moore. *The Retail Revolution: Market Transformation, Investment, and Labor in the Modern Department Store*. Boston: Auburn House, 1981.

Brown, Stephen. "The Wheel of Retailing: Past and Future." *Journal of Retailing* 66 (Summer 1990): 143–49.

Business Week. New York: McGraw-Hill, 1929– . Weekly.

Cassels, J. M. "The Marketing Machinery of the United States." *Quarterly Journal of Economics* 50 (August 1936): 658–79.

Chain Store Age. New York: Lebhar-Friedman, 1995– . Monthly.

Chandler, Alfred D., Jr. *The Visible Hand: The Managerial Revolution in American Business*. Cambridge: Harvard University Press, 1977.

Chatfield, Charles W. "A Brief History of the W. L. Douglas Company." *Bulletin of the Business Historical Society* 24 (December 1950): 159–83.

Cherington, Paul T. "The Small Retailer: An Appraisal." *Harvard Business Review* 17 (Spring 1939): 326–30.

Clark, Thomas D. *Pills, Petticoats, and Plows: The Southern Country Store*. Indianapolis: Bobbs-Merrill, 1944.

Clark, Victor S. *History of Manufactures in the United States*. 3 vols. New York: Peter Smith, 1929.

Copeland, Melvin T. "Some Present-Day Problems in Distribution." *Harvard Business Review* 9 (April 1931): 299–310.

Dean, Joel, and James R. Warren. "The Long-Run Behavior of Costs in a Chain of Shoe Stores." *Journal of Business* 15 (April 1942): 1–54.

D & B Business Rankings. Bethlehem, PA: Dun & Bradstreet, 1997– . Annual.

Dun's Business Rankings. Parsippany, NJ: Dun's Marketing Services, 1982–1996. Annual.

Edwards, Corwin D. *The Price Discrimination Law.* Washington, DC: Brookings Institution, 1959.

Footwear Focus. New York: National Shoe Retailers Association, 1984–1986. Bimonthly. See also *NSRA News.*

Footwear Manual. Arlington, VA: American Footwear Industries Association, 1974–1993. Annual.

Footwear News. New York: Fairchild, 1945– . Weekly.

Forbes. New York: Forbes, 1918– . Biweekly.

Fortune. Chicago: Time, 1930– . Monthly.

Frimpter, D., and Dennis Macchio. *The U.S. Footwear Industry: An Economic, Marketing, and Financial Investigation.* Merrick, NY: Morton Research, 1977.

Haring, Chester E. *The Manufacturer and His Outlets.* New York: Harper & Brothers, 1929.

Hazard, Blanche Evans. *The Organization of the Boot and Shoe Industry in Massachusetts before 1875.* Harvard Economic Studies, vol. 23. Cambridge: Harvard University Press, 1921. Reprint. Library of Early American Business and Industry, 18. Reprints of Economic Classics. A. M. Kelley, 1969.

Hollander, Stanley C. "The Wheel of Retailing." *Journal of Marketing* 25 (July 1960): 37–42.

Hollander, Stanley C., and Glenn S. Omura. "Chain Store Developments and Their Political, Strategic, and Social Interdependencies." *Journal of Retailing* 65 (fall 1989): 299–325.

Holloway, Edward. *Kinney Shoes: The First Sixty Years, 1894 to 1955.* G. R. Kinney, 1955.

Hoover, Edgar M., Jr. *Location Theory and the Shoe Leather Industries.* Harvard Economic Studies, vol. 55. Cambridge: Harvard University Press, 1937.

Hower, Ralph M. "Urban Retailing 100 Years Ago." *Bulletin of the Business Historical Society* 12 (December 1938): 91–101.

Jones, Fred Mitchell. "Retail Stores in the United States, 1800–1860." *Journal of Marketing* 1 (October 1936): 134–42.

———. *Middlemen in the Domestic Trade of the United States, 1800–1860.* Illinois Studies in the Social Sciences, vol. 21, no. 3. Urbana: University of Illinois, 1937. Reprint. History of American Economy. New York: Johnson Reprint, 1968.

Journal of Retailing. New York: New York University, Institute of Retail Management, 1925– . Quarterly.

Keir, Malcolm. *Manufacturing.* Industries of America. New York: Ronald Press, 1928.

Konopa, Leonard J. "An Analysis of Some Changes in Retailing Productivity between 1948 and 1963." *Journal of Retailing* 44 (Fall 1968): 57–67.

Lebhar, Godfrey M. *Chain Stores in America, 1859–1962.* 3d ed. New York: Chain Store Publishing, 1963; "Statistical Supplement." 3d ed. New York: Chain Store Age Books, 1967.

Lebow, Victor. "The Crisis in Retailing." *Journal of Retailing* 33 (Spring 1957): 17–26.

Lowrey, James R. *The Retailing Revolution Revisited.* Muncie, IN: Ball State University Press, 1969.

Mack, Ruth P. *Factors Influencing Consumption: An Experimental Analysis of Shoe Buying.* New York: National Bureau of Economic Research, 1954.

Mann, Lawrence B. "The Importance of Retail Trade in the United States." *American Economic Review* 13 (December 1923): 609–17.

Market Share Reporter. Detroit: Gale Research, 1991– . Annual.

Markin, R. J. "The Demise of the Marginal Retail Establishment." *Journal of Retailing* 43 (Summer 1967): 28–37.

Martin, Boyce F. "The Independent et al. versus the Chains." *Harvard Business Review* 9 (October 1930): 47–56.

Martin, David D. "The *Brown Shoe* Case and the New Antimerger Policy." *American Economic Review* 53, no. 3 (June 1963): 340–58.

May, Eleanor G. "A Retail Odyssey." *Journal of Retailing* 65 (Fall 1989): 356–67.

McNair, Malcolm P. "Significant Trends and Developments in the Postwar Period." In *Competitive Distribution in a Free High-Level Economy and Its Implications for the University,* edited by Albert B. Smith. Pittsburgh: University of Pittsburgh Press, 1958.

Morse, Alfred L. "Faces behind the Figures." *Forbes,* July 15, 1966, 30.

Mullen, Wadsworth H. "Some Aspects of Chain-Store Development." *Harvard Business Review* 3 (October 1924): 69–80.

NSRA News. New York: National Shoe Retailers Association, 1986– . Bimonthly.

Nystrom, Paul H. *Economics of Retailing.* New York: Ronald, 1930.

Oxenfeldt, Alfred R. "The Retailing Revolution: Why and Wither?" *Journal of Retailing* 36 (fall 1960): 157–62.

Peterman, John. "The *Brown Shoe* Case." *Journal of Law and Economics* 18 (April 1975): 81–146.

Phillips, Joseph D. *Some Industrial and Community Conditions for Small Retail Survival.* Urbana: University of Illinois, Small Business Management Research Reports, 1964.

Porter, Glenn, and Harold C. Livesay. *Merchants and Manufacturers: Studies in the Changing Structure of Nineteenth-Century Marketing.* Baltimore: Johns Hopkins Press, 1971. Reprint. Chicago: Elephant Paperbacks, 1989.

Rice, William B. "The Boot and Shoe Trade." In *One Hundred Years of American Commerce,* edited by Chauncey M. Depew, 566–74. New York: D. O. Haynes, 1895.

Rowe, Frederick M. *Price Discrimination under the Robinson-Patman Act.* Boston: Little, Brown, 1962.

Savitt, Ronald. "Looking Back to See Ahead: Writing the History of American Retailing." *Journal of Retailing* 65 (Fall 1989): 326–55.

Shaw, A. W. "Some Problems in Market Distribution." *Quarterly Journal of Economics* 26 (August 1912): 703–65.

Sheth, Jagdish N. "Emerging Trends for the Retailing Industry." *Journal of Retailing* 59 (Fall 1983): 6–18.

Smith, G. Ralph. *The Endicott Johnson Corporation.* New Orleans: Loyola University, College of Business Administration, 1956.

Spalding, Lewis A. "Strategies for Shoes." *Stores* 61 (December 1979): 36–37.

Stores. New York: National Retail Merchants Association, 1947– . Monthly.

The Story of the George E. Keith Company. Brockton, MA: George E. Keith Co., n.d.

Tallman, Gerald B., and Bruce Blomstrom. "Soft Goods Join the Retail Revolution." *Harvard Business Review* 38 (September–October 1960): 133–43.

Thomson, Ross. *The Path to Mechanized Shoe Production in the United States.* Chapel Hill: University of North Carolina Press, 1989.

Tosdal, Harry R. "Some Recent Changes in the Marketing of Consumer Goods." *Harvard Business Review* 11 (January 1933): 156–64.

U.S. Bureau of the Census. *Census of Business.* Washington, DC: U.S. Government Printing Office, 1929, 1933, 1935, 1939, 1948, 1954, 1958, 1963, 1967.

———. *Monthly Retail Trade Report.* Washington, DC: U.S. Government Printing Office, 1946–1963.

———. *Census of Retail Trade.* Washington, DC: U.S. Government Printing Office, 1972, 1977, 1982, 1987, 1992.

———. *Current Business Reports.* Washington, DC: U.S. Government Printing Office, 1972–1992. Annual.

Weld, L.D.H. "Marketing Agencies between Manufacturer and Jobber." *Quarterly Journal of Economics* 31 (August 1917): 571–99.

Werne, Benjamin, ed. *Business and the Robinson-Patman Law: A Symposium.* New York: Oxford University Press, 1938.

Whitten, David O. *The Emergence of Giant Enterprise, 1860–1914: American Commercial Enterprise and Extractive Industries.* Contributions in Economics and Economic History, no. 54. Westport, CT: Greenwood Press, 1983.

Wooster, Harvey A. "A Forgotten Factor in American Industrial History." *American Economic Review* 16 (March 1926): 14–27.

Part VI

Depository Institutions
ESIC 60.0

CHAPTER 8

FEDERAL RESERVE BANKS, 60.1
H. BRUCE THROCKMORTON

The Federal Reserve Act, written primarily by Representative Carter Glass of Virginia (with the assistance of H. Parker Williams, economist and associate editor of the New York *Journal of Commerce*) and signed into law by President Woodrow Wilson on December 23, 1913, gave the nation its first central banking system—whether the first (1791–1811) and second (1816–1836) Banks of the United States were precursors is a topic of debate. The House of Representatives had passed the bill by a vote of 287 to 85 on September 18, 1913; the Senate, by a vote of 54 to 34 on December 19. The act designated a Reserve Bank Organization Committee to determine not fewer than eight or more than twelve municipalities to be Federal Reserve cities and to divide the nation into districts. The committee was composed of the secretary of the treasury (William G. McAdoo), the secretary of agriculture (David F. Houston), and the comptroller of the currency (John Skelton Williams). Since Williams' appointment had not yet been confirmed by the Senate, most of the work was done by the other two committee members.

Each Federal Reserve Bank was to have a nine-member board of directors: three Class A directors chosen by the member banks to represent them; three Class B directors chosen by member banks to represent commerce, agriculture, or industry within the district—not bank-connected; three Class C directors appointed by the Federal Reserve Board. One Class C director was to be designated as chairman and another, as vice chairman. The Federal Reserve Board was to have seven members: the secretary of the Treasury and comptroller of the currency were ex officio members. The other five were to be appointed by the president and confirmed by the Senate for ten-year terms. The first board included Charles S. Hamlin as governor, Fredric A. Delano as vice-governor, Paul M. Warburg, Adolph C. Miller, and William P. G. Harding. Williams and McAdoo were the ex officio members. The Board was sworn into office on August 10, 1914, and continued the work started by the Reserve Bank Organization Committee.

National banks are required to join the Federal Reserve, and qualified state banks are free to enlist. Member banks subscribe to Fed stock in the amount of 6 percent of their capital and surplus—one-half is paid in, and the other half is subject to call. The Fed opened for business in twelve cities (Boston, New York, Philadelphia, Cleveland, Richmond, Atlanta, Chicago, St. Louis, Minneapolis, Kansas City, Dallas, and San Francisco) on November 16, 1914.

The Federal Reserve System was intended "to give the country an elastic currency, provide facilities for discounting commercial credits, and improve the supervision of the banking system" (Board of Governors of the Federal Reserve System 1994). All U.S. paper money is provided by the Fed in the form of Federal Reserve notes. Since there are no limitations on the amount of currency to be issued, it is perfectly elastic.

The Fed, through the discount window, is lender of last resort to the finance industry. Although the original law extended discounting, then called rediscounting, to member banks only, over the course of the twentieth century changes in legislation have opened the discount window to most U.S. financial institutions as it has also extended Fed control to most of the financial community.

The Fed shares federal supervisory authority with the Office of the Comptroller of the Currency (OCC) and the Federal Deposit Insurance Corporation (FDIC). Nonbank depository institutions are regulated by the Federal Home Loan Bank Board (FHLBB) for savings and loan associations and the National Credit Union Administration (NCUA) for credit unions. The Federal Savings and Loan Insurance Corporation (FSLIC) insures deposits in savings and loan associations much as the FDIC insures deposits at commercial banks. The Federal Financial Institutions Examination Council was established in 1978 to prescribe uniform standards and to promote cooperation among the federal supervisory agencies. The council comprises the chairmen of the FHLBB, the NCUA, and the FDIC as well as the comptroller of the currency and a Federal Reserve Board governor appointed by the chairman of the board.

Although many of the functions of the Fed remain as stated in the Federal Reserve Act, legislation has altered operations. Key amendments to the Federal Reserve Act include the Banking Act of 1935, the 1970 amendments to the Bank Holding Company Act, the International Banking Act of 1978, the Full Employment and Balanced Growth Act of 1978, the Depository Institutions Deregulation and Monetary Control Act of 1980, the Financial Institutions Reform, Recovery, and Enforcement Act of 1989, and the Federal Deposit Insurance Corporation Improvement Act of 1991. Operations of the Federal Reserve System have also been affected by the Securities Exchange Act of 1984 as well as several consumer laws such as the Truth in Lending Act, the Fair Credit Billing Act, the Equal Credit Opportunity Act, the Fair Credit Reporting Act, the Consumer Leasing Act, the Real Estate Settlement Procedures Act, the Electronic Fund Transfer Act, and the Federal Trade Commission Improvement Act (Board of Governors 1994).

Although the Fed was created as an independent agency, it was housed in the Treasury building until 1935, the year the secretary of the Treasury and the comptroller of the currency were removed from the Federal Reserve Board. The Fed is independent in that it is not supported by public money. Indeed, the Federal Reserve System contributes about 95 percent of its net earnings to the Treasury. The Federal Reserve Act designates that Federal Reserve Banks are not-for-profit corporations required to pay a 6 percent dividend to their stockholders and to hold enough to maintain each bank's surplus equal to its paid-in capital stock (Board of Governors 1994).

CREDIT CONTROLS

Open Market Activities

The Federal Reserve System earns interest on U.S. Treasury bonds and bills and other U.S. government agency obligations that it buys and sells on the open market (open market operations) to change the level of reserves in the banking system. The Banking Act of 1933 created the Federal Open Market Committee (FOMC) to set policy, and the Banking Act of 1935 provided for twelve voting members: the Board of Governors and five Federal Reserve Bank presidents.

Because open market operations influence interest rates, and the secretary of the treasury was a member of the Board of Governors during World War I, the Fed maintained bond rates in the best interest of the Treasury. The Fed was released by the accord of March 3, 1951: the Treasury agreed to exchange the marketable 1.5 percent bonds for nonmarketable 2.75 percent bonds with a twenty-nine-year maturity; the Fed agreed to maintain an orderly market during the transition to new conditions, and to keep the discount rate at 1.75 percent (and not change it without consulting the Treasury); and the Fed and the Treasury agreed to consult in setting a strategy for financing the debt (Kettl 1986).

The FOMC meets at least eight times a year to determine monetary policy. After each meeting, the committee issues a directive to the Federal Reserve Bank of New York to guide open market operations until the next meeting. The Federal Reserve Bank of New York acts as the committee's agent in the buying and selling of securities. The manager of the System

Open Market Account is president of the Federal Reserve Bank of New York (a permanent member of the FOMC). From 1936 until the early 1960s, the Fed kept the committee's minutes secret. In 1965 information for all meetings prior to 1960 was made public, and the Fed planned to release minutes after a five-year waiting period. From 1967 to 1975 minutes were released after the passage of ninety days, and in 1975 this was changed to forty-five days. In the 1990s minutes of a committee meeting were released after the following meeting.

Discounting

The Federal Reserve Act requires the Fed to discount commercial paper— make loans to member banks against collateral. Higher discount (loan) rates discourage borrowing, and lower rates encourage borrowing. Initially (1914 and 1915), discount rates ranged from 6 to 6.5 percent, but they fell to 4 percent and stayed there until the United States entered World War I. During the postwar recession the rate rose to 7 percent, fell to 3 percent in 1924, then peaked at 6 percent during the stock market crisis of 1929. For most of the depression the rate stayed around 1 to 1.5 percent and fell as low as .5 percent during the prosperous World War II years as part of the agreement between the Fed and Treasury to maintain an orderly market for government securities (Beckhart 1972; Prochnow 1960; Weissman 1936).

Reserve Requirements

Fed member banks are required to hold a designated percentage of their deposits on reserve at Federal Reserve Banks. Title I of the Monetary Control Act of 1980 imposed universal reserve requirements on all depository institutions: member banks, nonmember banks, mutual savings banks, savings banks, savings and loan associations, and credit unions. From 1917 until 1959 all reserves were held as deposits in Federal Reserve Banks. From December 1959 to November 1960 banks could count part of their vault cash as reserves. Since that time, all vault cash can be used to meet reserve requirements. Although there have been several changes in the structure of reserve requirements since 1936, the use of reserve requirement changes as a monetary policy device has been infrequent since 1959.

Fiscal Agency

National banks and subtreasuries performed federal fiscal functions until 1916, when Federal Reserve Banks became fiscal agent, custodian, and depository for the Treasury. The Treasury maintains interest-earning deposits at about 15,000 financial institutions in the United States where tax receipts are deposited, and disbursements are made by transfer of funds to a Federal Reserve Bank, which issues a check. Although some governmental agencies (particularly Social Security) make direct deposits into financial institutions by means of the Automated Clearing House (ACH) device, most disbursements are still made by the Federal Reserve Banks.

Federal Reserve Banks sell Treasury securities and issue, service, and redeem U.S. savings bonds but no longer float loans for the Treasury as they did during World War I. The Federal Reserve Banks are reimbursed by the Treasury and other federal agencies for much of the expense incurred in the fiscal agency functions (Clark 1935; Board of Governors 1994). The Fed, particularly, the Federal Reserve Bank of New York, acts as fiscal agent for foreign central banks and international organizations—the International Monetary Fund, for example. The most important of such transactions are the daily receipt and payment of funds in dollars (for a service charge).

Currency Supply

Since 1963 the only paper money issued in the United States has been Federal Reserve notes—before 1963 Federal Reserve notes were issued along with U.S. notes (the fabled greenback first issued as nonredeemable fiat money during the Civil War) and silver certificates that dated from the 1890s. The minimum denomination of Federal Reserve notes was five dollars; one- and two-dollar bills were silver certificates. Silver certificates were called in by the Treasury in 1967, and holders were offered a premium for their currency based on the market price for silver. This incentive forced most silver certificates out of circulation (Bach 1950).

Prior to 1945 there was a 40 percent gold certificate requirement as collateral for Federal Reserve notes. Gold certificates, which represented gold owned by the Treasury, were issued by the Treasury to the Federal Reserve Banks. In 1945 the gold certificate requirement for Federal Reserve notes was lowered from 40 to 25 percent. It remained at that level until 1968. This last link between gold and the domestic money supply was eliminated in 1968.

Although Federal Reserve notes are obligations of the Federal Reserve Banks, they are produced by the U.S. Bureau of Printing and Engraving in Washington, D.C. Federal Reserve notes are secured by legally authorized collateral, for the most part U.S. government and federal agency securities owned by the Federal Reserve Banks. At one time, Federal Reserve notes were considered obligations of the U.S. government. Federal Reserve notes are legal tender for all debts, public and private. In the 1920s they were not considered legal tender in the United States but were accepted as such in Cuba (Goldenweiser 1925).

Check Collection

Checks may be cleared by direct local exchange or through correspondent banks, local clearinghouses, or the Federal Reserve System—in 1993 the Fed cleared 19 billion checks with a value of over $4 trillion (Board of Governors 1994). Originally, checks were cleared through the Gold Settlement Fund, later called the Interdistrict Settlement Fund. Each Federal Reserve Bank contributed gold certificates to this fund through which interdistrict checks were cleared. In the 1970s electronic funds transfer and automated clearinghouses replaced the fund system.

Selective Controls

Congress has extended Fed authority beyond the national monetary system.

Margin Requirements

The Securities Exchange Act of 1934 and its amendments authorize the Board of Governors to regulate the use of credit for the purchase or carrying of securities—a response to the stock market crash of 1929. The margin requirement is the minimum amount (expressed as a percentage) the buyer must put up (rather than borrow). The Fed limits securities credit by use of Regulation T (brokers and dealers), Regulation U (banks), and Regulation G (other lenders). Regulation G and special margin requirements for bonds convertible into stocks were adopted March 11, 1968. Regulation X addresses the use of credit attained abroad for stock purchases in the United States (Board of Governors 1994; Eastburn 1965).

From late 1937 until early 1945 margin requirements were 40 percent. In the World War II years of the early 1940s, the stock market was steadily rising and using larger amounts of credit. Margin requirements increased to 50, 75, and finally 100 percent in early 1946. They remained at this restrictive level for a little more than one year. Since that time, the highest level reached was 90 percent from October 1958 until July 1960. The lowest requirement in the postwar years, 50 percent, was in effect from March 1949 to January 1951, February 1953 to January 1955, January 1958 to August 1958, July 1962 to November 1963, and since January 1974 (Bach 1950).

Consumer Credit

President Franklin Roosevelt's Executive Order 8843 of August 9, 1941, directed the board of Governors to subject consumer credit to selective controls. Pursuant to this order, the Board issued Regulation W effective September 1, 1941. The intent of the order was to reduce inflationary pressures, reduce the volume of consumer credit, and channel scarce materials toward war production. The subsequent fall in consumer credit may have been more a reflection of the scarcity of durable goods than a result of the credit controls (Bach 1950; Beckhart 1972; McNeill 1980).

Controls on minimum down payments and maximum maturities on consumer durable goods were in effect from September 1, 1941, until November 1, 1947, again from September 20, 1948, until June 30, 1949, and finally from September 18, 1950, until May 7, 1952. Common down payments were one-third of the price with common maturity schedules of twelve, fifteen, or eighteen months during the war years. Maturity schedules were increased to twenty-one and twenty-four months in 1949. During the Korean War years, down payments ranged from 10 percent to one-third, and maturities were usually fifteen or eighteen months (Prochnow 1960).

Congress terminated consumer credit controls as of November 1, 1947, but reinstated them from August 16, 1948, to June 30, 1949. Title VI of the Defense Production Act of 1950 allowed Regulation W to be reinstated during the Korean War. Regulation W was suspended May 7, 1952 (Prochnow 1960).

Real Estate Credit

The Fed regulated real estate credit briefly, issuing Regulation X on October 12, 1950, and suspending it September 16, 1952. Under the Defense Production Act of 1950 the president was granted temporary authority to regulate credit for new construction; he delegated his authority to the Board of Governors of the Federal Reserve System—the regulation applied only to new construction, not to the sale of existing houses (Eastburn 1965).

Regulation X established maximum loan values, maximum maturities, and minimum amortization terms for the construction or purchase of one- and two-family homes on which construction started after August 3, 1950. This was the only U.S. attempt to regulate real estate lending by means of a selective credit control. The statutory authority terminated in June 1958 (Prochnow 1960).

Interest on Time Deposits

The Banking Act of 1933 prohibited the payment of interest on demand deposits, so the Fed, with Regulation Q, began restricting the interest payable on member-bank time and savings deposits on November 1, 1933. The control was eventually extended to all insured banks and savings and loan associations.

From November 1, 1933, until January 31, 1935, the maximum rate of interest payable on savings accounts and on postal savings was 3 percent. The rate was lowered to 2.5 percent on February 1, 1935, and stayed at that level until the end of 1956, when it was set at 3 percent for five years

(1961), 4 percent until mid-1973, and 5 percent until mid-1979. The restriction was eliminated by legislation in 1980. The postal savings system was closed March 28, 1966.

Moral Suasion

Moral suasion is the public relations of monetary control. Sometimes referred to as "jawboning" or "open-mouth" policy, it includes oral or written statements, appeals, or warnings, often accomplished by press releases, speeches, and congressional testimony. Moral suasion is a call for voluntary restraint on the part of the banking system. It often takes the form of exhortations of the Federal Reserve Banks toward the commercial banks. Since the effectiveness of moral suasion cannot easily be measured, its results are suspect (Bach 1950; Beckhart 1972; Eastburn 1965). In the 1990s the impact of statements by the chairman of the Federal Reserve (Greenspan) were reflected in the Dow-Jones industrial average as jawboning became more important to the stock market than to the banking system.

Truth in Lending

Although the Federal Reserve System no longer regulates consumer credit by establishing minimum down payment and maximum maturity strictures, it is partly responsible for the enforcement of consumer credit legislation. The key portion of the Consumer Credit Protection Act of 1968 is truth in lending. In response to the act the Board of Governors formulated Regulation Z, which provides for disclosure of finance charges and the annual percentage rate (APR) charged for credit. Although the Fed has sole responsibility for preparing truth-in-lending regulations, it can enforce such regulations only in respect to member banks. It shares enforcement with eight other federal agencies, with the Federal Trade Commission having the greatest portion of the enforcement task. The Fed also enforces the Fair Credit Billing Act and the Equal Credit Opportunity Act (Board of Governors 1994).

LEGISLATION

Banking Act of 1933

The Banking Act of 1933 was signed into law by President Franklin Roosevelt on June 16, 1933. Although commonly referred to as the Glass-Steagall Act, Glass-Steagall was signed into law by President Herbert Hoover on February 27, 1932 (*U.S. Code*, vol. 47). The Banking Act prescribes twelve-year terms for the six appointed governors of the Federal Reserve System. One of the appointees was to be appointed governor and another vice-governor. The secretary of the Treasury was to remain the presiding officer.

Perhaps the most important provision of the Banking Act of 1933 is the creation of the Federal Deposit Insurance Corporation. The FDIC was to begin operation on July 1, 1934, with all Federal Reserve member banks subject to its regulations. It was financed by a $150 million appropriation from the Treasury plus the sale of stock to member banks and to Federal Reserve Banks. Class A stock was to be sold to banks equal to .5 percent of their total deposits. Class B stock was to be sold to Federal Reserve Banks. Dividends would be paid on Class A, but not on Class B, stock. Nonmember banks would be able to join the FDIC as of July 1, 1936.

The Banking Act separated commercial and investment banking and set new rules for national banks. After one year from the date of passage of the act, commercial banks could no longer engage in the sale of stocks and bonds, nor could they act as underwriters. (In 1998, during a raging bull market, congressmen began discussing the repeal of the prohibition of bank investment in the stock market.) No new national bank could be organized with less than $100,000 in capital or less than $200,000 in places of more than 50,000 population. National banks were allowed to establish branches in accordance with state law. The act also amended the Clayton Act of 1914 to outlaw interlocking directorates on the part of bank directors (*U.S. Code*, vol. 40).

Banking Act of 1935

The Banking Act of 1935, signed into law by President Roosevelt on August 23, 1935, had three major provisions: Title I, Federal Deposit Insurance Corporation; Title II, amendments to the Federal Reserve Act; and Title III, technical amendments—clarification of the Banking Act of 1933. Title I details the activities of the FDIC and supersedes the Banking Act of 1933. Title II made two important changes in the structure of the Federal Reserve System: the Board of Governors was to have seven appointed members, each serving a fourteen-year term. The secretary of the Treasury and the comptroller were no longer a part of the Fed's ruling body. One member of the board was designated chairman, and another as vice-chairman, both for four years. The act created a twelve-member Federal Open Market Committee (FOMC) to include the Board of Governors and five representatives of Federal Reserve districts. The districts were to alternate membership on the FOMC (*U.S. Code*, vol. 49).

Bank Holding Company Act of 1956

The Bank Holding Company Act of 1956 was signed into law by President Dwight Eisenhower on May 9, 1956. The act defined a bank holding company as an organization that owned 25 percent or more of the voting shares of two or more banks or that controlled the election of a majority of the directors of two or more banks. Existing bank holding companies were required to register with the Board of Governors; new ones must be approved by that body.

International Banking Act of 1978

Until 1978 there was no federal regulatory framework for agencies and branches of foreign banks doing business in the United States. The International Banking Act of 1978 created a federal regulatory structure to promote competitive equity between domestic and foreign banking institutions in the United States. The act limited interstate domestic deposit-taking activities of foreign banks, provided the option of federal licensing for agencies and branches of foreign banks, authorized the Federal Reserve Board to impose reserve requirements on agencies and branches of foreign banks, required federal deposit insurance for branches of foreign banks engaged in retail deposit-taking, gave Edge corporations broader powers and permitted foreign banks to own Edge corporations, and subjected foreign banks that operate agencies and branches in the United States to the non-banking prohibitions of the Bank Holding Company Act (Key 1979).

Edge corporations—authorized by a 1919 amendment to the Federal Reserve Act—are chartered by the Board of Governors to engage in international banking. They may not carry on business in the United States unless it is incidental to their international business (Prochnow 1960).

Full Employment and Balanced Growth Act of 1978

The Full Employment and Balanced Growth Act of 1978 (Humphrey-Hawkins Act) amends the Employment Act of 1946 and requires the Federal Reserve System to show how monetary goals fit the president's economy policy. The Fed must submit its monetary policy goals to Congress along with an explanation of how they relate to the short-term objectives of the president's *Economic Report* within thirty days after the president has transmitted that report to Congress. In semiannual reports the Fed is required to describe the Federal Open Market Committee's projections of gross national product, inflation, and unemployment for the coming year (Kettl 1986).

Depository Institutions Deregulation and Monetary Control Act of 1980

The Depository Institutions Deregulation and Monetary Control Act (DIDMCA) was signed into law by President Jimmy Carter on March 31, 1980. The legislation is divided into nine titles.

Title I, the Monetary Control Act of 1980, imposes universal reserve requirements for all depository institutions and directs the Board of Governors to establish a fee schedule for currency and coin services of a nongovernmental nature, check-clearing and collection, wire transfer, automated clearinghouse, settlement, securities safekeeping, Federal Reserve float, and any new service that the Federal Reserve System offers.

Title II, the Depository Institutions Deregulation Act of 1980, calls for an orderly phaseout of maximum rates of interest payable on time and savings deposits (Regulation Q).

Title III, the Consumer Checking Account Equity Act of 1980, authorizes the continuation of automatic transfer services from savings to checking accounts. It also extends nationwide the authority of depository institutions to offer NOW (negotiable order of withdrawal) accounts and increases the insurance of federally insured institutions from $40,000 to $100,000 per account.

Title IV, Powers of Thrift Institutions and Miscellaneous Provisions, authorizes savings and loan associations to invest up to 20 percent of their assets in consumer loans, commercial paper, and corporate debt securities. Federally chartered savings and loans are authorized to offer credit card services. State stock savings and loans are authorized to convert to federal stock charters. Federal mutual savings banks are authorized to make commercial, corporate, and business loans not to exceed 5 percent of a bank's assets. Such loans must be within the state in which the bank is located or within seventy-five miles of its home office. Federal mutual savings banks are authorized to accept demand deposits in connection with a commercial, corporate, or business loan relationship.

Title V preempted state mortgage usury laws unless the state overruled the preemption.

Title VI, Truth in Lending Simplification and Reform Act, reduces the number of disclosures required of lending institutions and directs the use of simple English descriptive phrases such as annual percentage rate and finance charge.

Title VII, Amendments to the National Banking Laws, authorizes the comptroller of the currency to assign examiners to examine foreign operations of state member banks when requested by the Federal Reserve. The Bank Holding Company Act amendments that prohibit the acquisition of a bank outside the holding company's home state are extended to include trust companies.

Title VIII, the Financial Regulation Simplification Act of 1980, states that regulations should be simply and clearly written and should not impose unnecessary costs and paperwork burdens (McNeill 1980).

Title IX is Foreign Control of U.S. Financial Institutions. Until July 1, 1980, the Fed, OCC, FDIC, and FHLBB were prohibited from approving any application for the takeover of a domestic financial institution by a foreign person. Takeover is defined as the acquisition of 5 percent or more of an institution's stock or assets (McNeill 1980).

Garn-St. Germain Depository Institutions Act of 1982

The Garn-St. Germain Depository Institutions Act of 1982 exempts the first $2.1 million in deposits from reserve requirements. By 1987 that exemption had been increased to $2.9 million. Perhaps the most important feature of this legislation is the creation of the Money Market Deposit Account (MMDA), which allows competition with money market mutual funds. Depository institutions can issue MMDAs with no regulatory interest rate if a minimum balance of $2,500 is maintained. Up to six automatic or preauthorized withdrawals can be made per month with no withdrawal restrictions if made in person, by messenger, or by mail (Sinkey 1986, 168).

The Garn-St. Germain Act authorizes governmental units to place deposits in NOW accounts and federally chartered savings and loans to accept demand deposits. Thrifts were also allowed to make charter changes. They can convert from state to federal and from federal to state, and they may switch between mutual and stock form and between savings and loan and savings bank charters (Sinkey 1986).

FEDERAL RESERVE LEADERSHIP SINCE 1935

The Banking Act of 1935 gives the chairman of the Fed considerable influence over monetary policy. Seven men have held that position since its creation. Marriner S. Eccles served from 1935 to 1948, and Thomas B. McCabe, to 1951. William McChesney Martin, Jr., served the longest tenure of any chairman, from 1951 until 1970, when he was succeeded by Arthur F. Burns, who held office for eight years (1970–1978). G. William Miller was chairman for one year before being appointed secretary of the Treasury. Paul A. Volcker, who was chairman from 1979 until 1987, was succeeded by Alan Greenspan.

Marriner S. Eccles

Marriner S. Eccles, appointed to the Federal Reserve Board and designated governor on November 15, 1934, became chairman of the Board of Governors after passage of the Banking Act of 1935. Eccles came to Washington from Utah in early 1934 to serve as an assistant to the secretary of the Treasury. He had headed a group of banks in Utah and served as an officer or director of several corporations. Eccles worked closely with the president and the Treasury during the New Deal and World War II, but after the war he sought a Fed free from Treasury influence. His efforts bore fruit in the administration of his successor when the Federal Reserve-Treasury Accord was reached in 1951 (Weissman 1936; Kettl 1986; Bach 1950).

Thomas Bayard McCabe

In 1948 President Truman appointed Thomas B. McCabe of Pennsylvania to the board and designated him chairman. McCabe, who had been president of Scott Paper Company since 1927, was appointed a director of the Philadelphia Federal Reserve Bank in 1937 and became its chairman in 1939 (*Federal Reserve Bulletin* 1948). McCabe inherited the peg controversy—the peg was the interest rate dictated by the Treasury. The Fed called for an end to the peg, but President Truman was committed to maintaining it. The president called the entire FOMC to meet in his office on January 31, 1951, the only such meeting in the history of the Federal Reserve System. McCabe resigned and returned to the private sector on March 31, 1951 (Kettl 1986).

William McChesney Martin, Jr.

President Truman appointed William McChesney Martin, Jr., of New York to replace McCabe. Martin, who assumed his duties as chairman on April 2, 1951, had been a bank examiner for the Federal Reserve Bank of St. Louis and president of the New York Stock Exchange. Although drafted into the army during World War II, he rose to the rank of colonel. He became assistant secretary of the Treasury in 1949 and was serving in that capacity when asked to chair the Federal Reserve Board. His nineteen-year chairmanship coincided with the presidencies of Truman, Eisenhower, Kennedy, Johnson, and Nixon (*Federal Reserve Bulletin* 1951).

Although Martin usually accommodated presidential policy, there was confrontation in 1965–1966 over federal financing of the Vietnam War. Nevertheless, in the early 1960s the Federal Reserve's Operation Twist reduced long-term interest rates in support of the Kennedy administration. "From a weak and dispirited organization playing a supporting role in 1951, the Fed by the end of the 1960s was a powerful organization recognized as an economic policy maker in its own right" (Kettl 1986, 110).

Arthur F. Burns

Arthur F. Burns assumed chairmanship of the Fed on January 31, 1970. Burns, a New York resident of Austrian birth, was educated at Columbia University (Ph.D. in economics), where he taught before joining the National Bureau of Economic Research: president (1959), chairman (1967). He chaired the president's Council of Economic Advisors from 1953 to

1956 and was an adviser to President Nixon until January 1969, when he assumed the chair of the Federal Reserve Board (*Federal Reserve Bulletin* 1970).

Burns, who viewed price stability as the primary goal of the Fed, faced a new problem: stagflation—inflation, slow growth, and high unemployment. Burns resigned the board on March 31, 1970, when President Carter declined to reappoint him as chairman (Kettl 1986).

G. William Miller

Attorney G. William Miller of California, President Jimmy Carter's choice for chairmanship of the Federal Reserve Board, took office on March 8, 1978. Miller, when appointed, was chairman of the Board of Textron Corporation and director of the Federal Reserve Bank of Boston (*Federal Reserve Bulletin* 1978). Inflation was out of control, so, when Miller voted against an increase in the discount rate, the board majority opposed him. After losing the vote and the confidence of his colleagues at the Fed and the presidential administration, Miller resigned effective August 6, 1979, to become secretary of the Treasury (Kettl 1986).

Paul A. Volcker

President Carter chose Paul A. Volcker to succeed Miller as Federal Reserve chairman. Volcker received a bachelor of arts degree from Princeton in 1949 and a master of arts in political economy and government from Harvard in 1951. He served in various positions with the Treasury Department, Chase Manhattan Bank, and the Federal Reserve Bank of New York before becoming undersecretary of the Treasury for monetary affairs from 1969 until 1974. He was named president and chief executive officer of the Federal Reserve Bank of New York in 1975 (*Federal Reserve Bulletin* 1979).

Volcker, who inherited the inflation Miller ignored, fought the rising price level while accommodating presidential policy. In 1979 the Fed adopted an experiment in monetarism. The Federal Reserve had been attempting to regulate the money supply by pegging the rate of interest on federal funds, those reserves available for interbank lending on a very short-term (overnight) basis. On October 6, 1979, Volcker convinced the FOMC to "shift to a more automatic process that involved directly targeting the level of reserves available to the banking system—nonborrowed reserves— rather than pegging the federal funds rate" (Berry 1987, H4). This experiment in monetarism lasted for approximately three years (Kettl 1986).

Volcker's anti-inflation stance has been criticized by those convinced that restrictive monetary policies caused the severe economic decline of 1981–1982. However, the rate of inflation did fall substantially during his tenure.

Several changes in banking took place in the early 1980s. Volcker "generally fought to require that commercial banks stick to their traditional knitting of taking deposits and making sound loans to credit worthy borrowers" (Berry 1987, H3).

Volcker's status as an inflation fighter pleased President Ronald Reagan, who reappointed him as chairman in 1983. Volcker declined reappointment in 1987.

Alan Greenspan

President Reagan appointed Alan Greenspan to succeed Volcker as Federal Reserve chairman in August 1987. Greenspan had been considered for the position in 1983, when the president chose Volcker. At the time of his appointment, Greenspan headed the New York consulting firm of Townsend-Greenspan and Company. He had served as chairman of the Council of Economic Advisors under President Ford. Greenspan has been characterized as a "stern foe of inflation" and "an outspoken backer of Mr. Volcker" (Blustein 1987, 17).

Greenspan's tenure as chairman of the Federal Reserve System coincides with the great bull market of the 1990s and the longest economic expansion since World War II. Originally appointed by Republican president Ronald Reagan, Greenspan was reappointed by Democrat William J. Clinton. The chairman is not seen as accommodating the president or anyone else. He has used his growing prestige as head of the most powerful financial institution in the world to separate himself from politics. Price stability has been his goal. In 1998 inflation was reduced to near zero as a financial crisis in Asia threatened the world with the first major deflation since the 1930s. Nevertheless, the United States enjoyed full employment and the first federal budget surplus in three decades.

Greenspan is probably the most public of the seven chairmen of the Fed. He takes advantage of his popular image to scold stock market speculators and warn the world that good times are not guaranteed but must be pursued carefully ("Wall Street Rides High Again on Words of Alan Greenspan" 1998). His own wealth is invested in Treasury bonds.

In 1999 Greenspan was regarded as a successful leader watching over one of the most prosperous U.S. economies in history. The final evaluation of his tenure at the Fed will be determined by the course of events in the last years of the twentieth century. The financial collapse of Russia—the Soviet Union when Greenspan took office—the Asian crisis, a roller-coaster stock market, a president mired in scandal, and a U.S.-led North Atlantic Treaty Organization (NATO) war in Europe are likely to produce an economic crisis in the final years of Greenspan's Clinton-appointed term of office. How Greenspan manages the complex times he is certain to face will determine his place in the history of the Fed and the nation.

BIBLIOGRAPHIC ESSAY

The Federal Reserve System is the best source of information on its creation and operation. Perhaps the most informative single publication is *The Federal Reserve System: Purposes & Functions*, published by the Board of Governors of the Federal Reserve System (1994) and available free from Publications Services, Division of Support Services, Board of Governors of the Federal Reserve System, Washington, DC 20551.

In addition to the monthly *Federal Reserve Bulletin* published by the Fed, each of the twelve Federal Reserve Banks issues a panoply of periodicals and studies that embody the work of its economics division. District banks' research publications address regional, national, and international economic issues and are available free or at minimum cost. See, for example, "Time Well Spent: The Declining *Real* Cost of Living in America," the 1997 Annual Report of the Federal Reserve Bank of Dallas. The Federal Reserve Bank of Philadelphia's semiannual *Fed in Print. Economics and Banking Topics* is a guide to publications by and about the Federal Reserve System and Federal Reserve Banks.

The gateway to Federal Reserve publications is the World Wide Web, and the address is http://www.bog.frb.fed.us. The site provides access to thousands of Federal Reserve bulletins, pamphlets, articles, and books. From the Board of Governors home page the web sites maintained by the twelve district banks can be accessed, so much of what the Federal Reserve System publishes is indexed, abstracted, and reproduced electronically.

The Fed is also the topic of other government authorities. The U.S. General Accounting Office's *Federal Reserve System* (1996) is an example.

Accounts of the activities of the Fed are available in every newspaper in America and many abroad. Newsmagazines rarely publish without some mention of the Fed and the chairman of the board.

Although the Federal Reserve System is not likely to fall victim to its political and professional enemies in the fashion of the two Banks of the United States, it is the target of fear and loathing and the subject of academic and professional analysis. Silvano A. Wueschner's *Charting Twentieth-Century Monetary Policy: Herbert Hoover and Benjamin Strong, 1917–1927* (1999) traces the early political battles over U.S. monetary policy and gives form to the shadowy origins of Federal Reserve operations. J. Lawrence Broz views the Fed from a global perspective in *The International Origins of the Federal Reserve System* (1997). Other recent studies of the U.S. central bank include Donald F. Kettl, *Leadership at the Fed* (1986); G. G. Garcia, *The Federal Reserve* (1988); William Greider, *Secrets of the Temple* (1989); Gary Taylor, *The Federal Reserve System* (1989); David C. Wheelock, *The Strategy and Consistency of Federal Reserve Monetary Policy* (1991); Claire Helene Young, *An Evaluation of*

Federal Reserve Policy, 1924–1930 (1992); Cheney L. Clifford, *The Shell Game at the Fed* (1994); G. Edward Griffin, *The Creature from Jekyll Island* (1995); Mark Toma, *Competition and Monopoly in the Federal Reserve System* (1997); J. Kevin Corder, *Central Bank Autonomy: The Federal Reserve System in American Politics* (1998); and Thomas Mayer, *Monetary Policy and the Great Inflation in the United States: The Federal Reserve and the Failure of Macroeconomic Policy, 1965–1979* (1998).

BIBLIOGRAPHY

Bach, G. L. *Federal Reserve Policy-Making.* New York: Alfred A. Knopf, 1950.

"Bank Holding Company Act of 1956." *Federal Reserve Bulletin* (May 1956): 444–53.

"Bank Holding Company Act Amendments of 1970." *Federal Reserve Bulletin* (January 1971): 29–33.

Beckhart, Benjamin Haggott. *Federal Reserve System.* New York: American Bankers Association, 1972.

Berry, John M. "The Volcker Era." *Washington Post,* June 7, 1987, H1, H3–H5.

Blustein, Paul. "Nominee Greenspan Shares Volcker's Goals but Not Yet His Clout." *Wall Street Journal,* June 3, 1987, 1, 17.

Board of Governors of the Federal Reserve System. *The Federal Reserve System: Purposes & Functions.* Washington, DC: Federal Reserve System, 1994.

Broz, J. Lawrence. *The International Origins of the Federal Reserve System.* Ithaca, NY: Cornell University Press, 1997.

Burgess, Warren Randolph. *The Reserve Banks and the Money Market.* Rev. ed. New York: Harper, 1946. Reprint. New York: Garland, 1983.

Carnes, W. Stansbury, and Stephen D. Slifer. *The Atlas of Economic Indicators: A Visual Guide to Market Forces and the Federal Reserve.* New York: HarperBusiness, 1991.

Chandler, Lester Vernon. *Benjamin Strong, Central Banker.* Washington, DC: Brookings Institution, 1958. Reprint. New York: Arno Press, 1979.

Clark, Lawrence E. *Central Banking under the Federal Reserve System.* New York: Macmillan, 1935.

Clifford, Cheney L. *The Shell Game at the Fed.* Hobbs, NM: MEC, 1994.

"Consumer Advisory Council: Meetings." *Federal Reserve Bulletin* (November 1976): 974–77.

Corder, J. Kevin. *Central Bank Autonomy: The Federal Reserve System in American Politics.* Financial Sector of the American Economy. New York: Garland, 1998.

D'Arista, Jane W. *The Evolution of U.S. Finance.* Vol. 1, *Federal Reserve Monetary Policy, 1915–1935.* Vol. 2, *Restructuring Institutions and Markets.* Columbia University Seminar Series. Armonk, NY: M. E. Sharpe, 1994.

Eastburn, David P. *The Federal Reserve on Record.* Philadelphia: Federal Reserve Bank of Philadelphia, 1965.

Federal Reserve Bank of Philadelphia. *Fed in Print. Economics and Banking Topics.* Philadelphia, 1990– . Semiannual.

Federal Reserve Board: Laws and Regulations [compiled from *CCH Federal Banking Law Reporter*, May 1994]. Chicago: CCH, 1994.

Federal Reserve Bulletin. Washington, DC, May 1915– . Monthly.

Fisher, Irving. *Stabilizing the Dollar.* Brookfield, VT: Pickering & Chatto, 1996.

Garcia, G. G. *The Federal Reserve.* Cambridge, MA: Ballinger, 1988.

Goldenweiser, Emanuel Alexandrovich. *Federal Reserve System in Operation.* McGraw-Hill, 1925.

———. *American Monetary Policy.* New York: McGraw Hill, 1951. Reprint. New York: Garland, 1983.

Greider, William. *Secrets of the Temple.* New York: Simon & Schuster, 1989.

Griffin, G. Edward. *The Creature from Jekyll Island.* Westlake Village, CA: American Media, 1995.

Harding, W.P.G. "The Banking System of the United States." In *The Science of Modern Business Administration.* Book 8. New York: P. F. Collier & Son, 1923.

Havrilesky, Thomas M. *The Pressures on American Monetary Policy.* 2d ed. Boston: Kluwer Academic, 1995.

Hyman, Sidney. *Marriner S. Eccles, Private Entrepreneur and Public Servant.* Stanford, CA: Stanford University, Graduate School of Business, 1976.

Jones, David M. *The Politics of Money: The Fed under Greenspan.* New York: New York Institute of Finance, 1991.

Katz, Bernard S., ed. *Biographical Dictionary of the Board of Governors of the Federal Reserve.* Westport, CT: Greenwood Press, 1992.

Kettl, Donald F. *Leadership at the Fed.* New Haven, CT: Yale University Press, 1986.

Key, Sydney J. "Implementation of the International Banking Act." *Federal Reserve Bulletin* (October 1979): 785–96.

Khademian, Anne M. *Checking on Banks: Autonomy and Accountability in Three Federal Agencies.* Washington, DC: Brookings Institution Press, 1996.

Klebaner, Benjamin J. *Commercial Banking in the United States: A History.* Hinsdale, IL: Dryden Press, 1973

Knipe, James L. *The Federal Reserve and the American Dollar: Problems and Policies, 1946–1964.* Chapel Hill: University of North Carolina Press, 1965.

Livingston, James. *Origins of the Federal Reserve System: Money, Class, and Corporate Capitalism, 1890–1913.* Ithaca, NY: Cornell University Press, 1986.

Marquis, Milton H. *Monetary Theory and Policy.* Minneapolis/St. Paul, MN: West, 1996.

Mayer, Thomas. *Monetarism and Macroeconomic Policy.* Economists of the Twentieth Century. Aldershot, Hants, UK, and Brookfield, VT: Edward Elgar, 1990.

———. *The Political Economy of American Monetary Policy.* New York: Cambridge University Press, 1990.

———. *Monetary Policy and the Great Inflation in the United States: The Federal Reserve and the Failure of Macroeconomic Policy, 1965–1979.* Cheltenham, Glostershire, UK, and Northampton, MA: Edward Elgar, 1998.

McCulley, Richard T. *Banks and Politics during the Progressive Era: The Origins of the Federal Reserve System, 1897–1913.* Financial Sector of the American Economy. New York: Garland, 1992.

McMahon, Marshall E. *Federal Reserve Behavior, 1923–1931.* Financial Sector of the American Economy. New York: Garland, 1993.

McNeill, Charles R. "The Depository Institutions Deregulation and Monetary Control Act of 1980." *Federal Reserve Bulletin* (June 1980): 444–53.

Moore, Carl H. *The Federal Reserve System: A History of the First 75 Years.* Jefferson, NC: McFarland, 1990.

Neikirk, William. *Volcker: Portrait of the Money Man.* New York: Congdon & Weed, 1987.

Patrick, Sue Carol. *Reform of the Federal Reserve System in the Early 1930s: The Politics of Money and Banking.* Financial Sector of the American Economy. New York: Garland, 1993.

Prochnow, Herbert V., ed. *The Federal Reserve System.* New York: Harper & Brothers, 1960.

"Regulation Y." *Federal Reserve Bulletin* (August 1956): 835–40.

Santow, Leonard Jay. *Helping the Federal Reserve Work Smarter.* Armonk, NY: M. E. Sharpe, 1994.

Sinkey, Joseph F., Jr. *Commercial Bank Financial Management.* 2d ed. New York: Macmillan, 1986.

Solow, Robert M., and John B. Taylor. *Inflation, Unemployment, and Monetary Policy.* Edited by Benjamin M. Friedman. First Alvin Hansen Symposium on Public Policy, Harvard University, April 24, 1995. Cambridge: MIT Press, 1998.

Taylor, Gary. *The Federal Reserve System.* New York: Chelsea House, 1989.

"Time Well Spent: The Declining *Real* Cost of Living in America." Annual Report of the Federal Reserve Bank of Dallas, 1997.

Toma, Mark. *Competition and Monopoly in the Federal Reserve System.* New York: Cambridge University Press, 1997.

"Truth in Lending." *Federal Reserve Bulletin* (February 1969): 98–103.

Tuch, Hans N., ed. *Arthur Burns and the Successor Generation: Selected Writings of and about Arthur Burns.* Lanham, MD: University Press of America, 1988.

Turnbull, Laura Shearer. *The Benjamin Strong Collection of International Finance in the Princeton University Library, 1925–1951: An Informal History.* Princeton, NJ: Princeton University Library, 1952.

United States Code Congressional and Administrative News. St. Paul, MN: West, 1953– . Annual.

U.S. Code. Washington, DC: U.S. Government Publishing Office, 1926– .

U.S. Congress. House. Committee on Banking, Finance, and Urban Affairs. *Federal Reserve Act Amendments.* Washington, DC: U.S. Government Printing Office, 1984.

———. House Committee on Banking, Finance, and Urban Affairs. *The Federal Reserve Accountability Act of 1993.* Washington, DC: U.S. Government Printing Office, 1994.

———. House Committee on Banking, Finance, and Urban Affairs. Subcommittee on Domestic Monetary Policy. *The Politicization of Monetary Policy.* Hearings. 102d Cong., 2d sess., July 8, 1992. Serial no. 102–135.

U.S. Congress. Senate. Joint Economic Committee. *The Humphrey-Hawkins Act and the Role of the Federal Reserve.* Hearings. 104th Cong., 1st sess., March 16, 1995. S. Hrg. 104–324.

U.S. General Accounting Office (U.S. GAO). *Federal Reserve System.* Washington, DC: U.S. GAO, 1996.

"Wall Street Rides High Again on Words of Alan Greenspan." *Columbus (Georgia) Ledger-Enquirer,* September 9, 1998, C4.

Weissman, Rudolph L. *The New Federal Reserve System.* New York: Harper & Brothers, 1936.

Wells, Wyatt C. *Economist in an Uncertain World: Arthur Burns and the Federal Reserve, 1970–78.* Columbia Studies in Contemporary American History. New York: Columbia University Press, 1994.

Weyforth, William O. *The Federal Reserve Board: A Study of Federal Reserve Structure and Credit Control.* Johns Hopkins University Studies in Historical and Political Science, n.s. no. 19. Baltimore: Johns Hopkins Press, 1933. Reprint. New York: AMS Press, 1983.

Wheelock, David C. *The Strategy and Consistency of Federal Reserve Monetary Policy.* New York: Cambridge University Press, 1991.

Woolley, John T. *Monetary Politics: The Federal Reserve and the Politics of Monetary Policy.* New York: Cambridge University Press, 1984.

Wueschner, Silvano A. *Charting Twentieth-Century Monetary Policy: Herbert Hoover and Benjamin Strong, 1917–1927.* Contributions in Economics and Economic History, no. 210. Westport, CT: Greenwood Press, 1999.

Young, Claire Helene. *An Evaluation of Federal Reserve Policy, 1924–1930.* New York: Garland, 1992.

Youngman, Anna Prichitt. *The Federal Reserve System in Wartime.* New York: National Bureau of Economic Research, Financial Research Program, 1945.

CHAPTER 9

MUTUAL SAVINGS BANKS, 60.3

RICHARD C. SCHIMING

PRE–CIVIL WAR

The concept of the mutual savings bank originated in Scotland and England. The Reverend Henry Duncan (1774–1846) is traditionally credited with inaugurating the prototype of the modern mutual savings bank in Ruthwell, Scotland, in 1810. This financial innovation quickly spread to the other side of the Atlantic. The first two mutual savings banks in the United States were the Provident Institution for Savings in the Town of Boston and the Philadelphia Savings Fund Society, both of which were chartered in 1816. These financial intermediaries issued no stock but were owned by their depositors, who received the investment income of the bank as dividends on their savings. The management of the mutual savings bank was a self-perpetuating board of trustees who operated the bank but received no payment for their services.

The unique motivation behind the founding of mutual savings banks was to help the less fortunate members of society by encouraging them to save. The dominant financial intermediary of the time, the commercial bank, generally did not accept small deposits from households and was not interested in making loans to households. Noblesse oblige compelled the trustees of mutual savings banks to encourage thrift among the working poor. Depositors could earn a modest rate of return on their savings, a secure investment given the conservative fiscal strategy pursued by the trustees.

By 1840 the nature of both the mutual savings bank and its management had changed. Part-time management by philanthropists was replaced by professional management by men who viewed the banks as a career and not a hobby. This change in management personnel led to a corresponding change in management philosophy. The portfolio of assets that had provided a small, but safe, rate of return was now diversified into a wider range of investments with greater earning potential—corporate stocks and bonds, business loans, mortgages.

These new managers often sought to maximize the growth of their mutual saving banks as a confirmation of their expertise. Since the mutual structure did not permit traditional profits, managers stressed expansion of the institution by seeking deposits from anyone wishing a safe investment.

A characteristic of mutual savings banks that continues to the present is their limited geographic range: New England and the eastern seaboard states. The western states lacked a cadre of philanthropists willing to sponsor these institutions, and outside the northeastern United States there were fewer poor wage earners who would deposit in mutual savings banks. Spurred by the success of the innovative competitors, commercial banks had begun to accept small deposits and were fast capturing the major market of the mutuals.

1860 TO WORLD WAR I

By 1860 mutual savings banks were well established within their limited geographic area. They had been successful in pioneering the savings function among the working poor. Several mutual savings banks were ranked in the listing of the ten largest businesses in 1860.

Many key indicators point to the vigor of the mutuals even during the turbulent economic conditions after the Civil War. A total deposit base of $150 million in 1860 had increased to nearly $4 billion by 1915 (Welfling 1968). In the New England and New York markets, mutual savings banks were often the dominant financial intermediary. The dramatic increase in the number of new mutuals chartered peaked in the 1870s.

The apparent vitality of the mutuals obscured their deteriorating condition vis-à-vis other financial intermediaries. The share of total savings held by mutual savings banks was 61 percent in 1880, but that share had fallen to only 30 percent by 1915 (Welfling 1968). After the Panic of 1873 decimated the financial system, the managers of mutual savings banks had adopted a more conservative investment strategy. State regulators established a list of permissible investments that further restricted the mutuals' opportunities to innovate. The combination of geographic confinement and increased competition from other financial intermediaries in services previously dominated by mutual savings banks led to their relative decline.

WORLD WAR I TO WORLD WAR II

The Roaring Twenties and the Great Depression shaped mutual savings banking in the United States. A booming economy in the 1920s fueled both an inflow of deposits and an increased reliance on residential mortgages as the primary earning asset in the portfolio of mutual savings banks. The Great Depression was easier on the mutuals than on other financial intermediaries. Unlike their major competitors, the savings and loans and commercial banks, mutual savings banks had an admirable record of protecting their depositors' funds. Management's innate caution and conservative investment strategies meant that only a handful of mutual savings banks failed even during the worst days of the Great Depression. While commercial banks and especially savings and loans suffered heavy losses, the share of savings held by mutual savings banks rose for the first time in many decades.

Observers of the mutuals' performance after the worst of the Great Depression argue that these financial intermediaries squandered what had been strong competitive advantages in public image and depositors' confidence. Positioned to reclaim their former dominance, mutual savings banks let slip the golden opportunity. Their increased reliance on mortgage lending throughout the 1920s, followed by waves of foreclosures in the 1930s, had seriously reduced the mutuals' enthusiasm for that particular earning asset in their portfolios. The mutuals faltered, opening the door for savings and loans, which now had both deposit insurance and a more aggressive management that was willing to reenter the mortgage markets. On the eve of World War II, the savings and loans had again outdistanced their closest rivals in the residential mortgage markets.

POST–WORLD WAR II

Between 1945 and 1960 mutual savings banks expanded within their limited geographical area. Whereas the number of mutual savings banks with branches more than doubled, the actual number of branches more then tripled (National Association of Mutual Savings Banks 1962). Operating income grew as deposit growth accelerated, and mortgage lending again became the major earning asset. By 1980 mortgages accounted for about 60 percent of the assets held by mutual savings banks; corporate and other bonds constituted the second largest block of assets held.

But this absolute growth in assets, savings, and numbers was offset by a relative decline in the importance of mutual savings banks: the mutuals were growing, but other financial intermediaries were growing faster. The 1960s and 1970s brought calls for change from the financial community: mutual savings banks should be permitted to break out of the regulatory and geographic straitjacket that limited their performance, to offer a wider variety of financial services, to hold a more diverse set of assets, to compete more directly with other financial intermediaries. Specialization had proved a hindrance.

Legislation and regulatory decisions since 1976 have changed mutual savings banking. In that year, depository institutions in New England began offering NOW (negotiable orders of withdrawal) accounts. Pioneered by mutual savings banks in Massachusetts, these interest-bearing checking accounts represented a major change in the competitive environment. From their inception, mutual savings banks had been chartered only by the states in which they operated. The Financial Institutions Regulation and Interest Rate Control Act of 1978 permitted existing mutual savings banks to opt for federal chartering, allowing them to choose for themselves the more advantageous type of charter, state or federal.

The 1980s generated economic challenges as well as opportunities. Rapidly rising interest rates were creating the worst possible economic environment for mutual savings banks. Because their assets were primarily long-term mortgages and bonds and their liabilities overwhelmingly short-term deposits, these banks were paying higher interest rates to depositors while holding low interest rate assets. The result was heavy losses for the mutuals and mergers that reduced their numbers.

Important changes came in the form of landmark legislation: the Depository Institutions Deregulation and Monetary Control Act of 1980 and the Garn-St. Germain Act of 1982. The first dramatically changed the regulatory environment and removed restrictions that had limited competition among financial intermediaries. The 1980 legislation brought all of them under essentially the same set of regulations and regulators so that one form of financial intermediary would not be treated more leniently than another.

But the Garn-St. Germain Act had the greater influence on mutual savings banks. This legislation permitted the mutuals to diversify their portfolios with shorter-term assets like commercial and consumer loans. Garn-St. Germain also increased the chartering options for mutual savings banks by permitting new banks to obtain either state or federal charters. The latter proved especially popular, for federally chartered mutual savings banks can be organized as either stock (owned by stockholders) or mutual (owned by depositors) forms. Mutual savings banks and savings and loans now have broad freedom to convert from one form of depository institution to the other.

As a result of these legislative changes, mutual savings banks are an important part of a larger process evident since 1980, namely, the blurring of distinctions among financial intermediaries. All offer essentially the same financial services; hence, the demarcation between mutual saving banks and other financial intermediaries is now less clear. Indeed, the distinction between mutual savings banks and savings and loans is disappearing so quickly that they are often lumped together as "savings institutions" for statistical compilations and are represented by one industry association, the United States League of Savings Institutions.

The nomenclature has become confused. The thrift institutions earlier divided into savings and loans (which were either federally chartered or state chartered), credit unions (which could also be federally or state chartered), and mutual savings banks (which were state chartered). All three types of thrift institutions employed the mutual form of ownership. Then, during the 1980s, savings and loans began to abandon their discredited legacy to become "savings banks." Mutual savings banks could obtain a federal charter and also convert to a stock form of ownership. Consequently, much of the literature now refers to "thrift institutions" or "savings banks," and little effort is made to differentiate the traditional mutual savings banks. Despite this blurring in terminology, mutual savings banks retain distinctive operational features, hold a more diverse portfolio of assets than other thrifts, and remain geographically concentrated.

During the 1980s the difficulties faced by mutual savings banks fell closer to the smaller set of problems experienced by commercial banks than to the catastrophic problems of the savings and loans. Mutual savings banks held a more diversified group of assets with shorter maturities, maintained a generally stronger balance sheet with more net worth, and were less tempted by the new portfolio possibilities that so damaged the savings and loans. Indeed, mutual savings banks are insured by the Bank Insurance Fund of the FDIC rather than by the Savings Association Insurance Fund, which covers savings and loans. Clearly, the regulators found the mutual savings banks and the commercial banks healthier than the savings and loans.

In 1990 commercial banks held 32 percent of the total assets in U.S. financial intermediaries; life insurance companies held 13 percent; private pension funds, 12 percent; savings and loans, 11 percent; mutual savings banks, 3 percent; and credit unions, 2 percent. The share of intermediary assets held by mutual savings banks has steadily waned over the past forty years: 8 percent in 1950, 7 percent in 1960, 6 percent in 1970, 4 percent in 1980, 3 percent in 1990. Mutual savings banks held 15 percent of the residential mortgages in 1960; by 1990, their share had fallen to 5 percent, well behind the 31 percent held by mortgage pools, 27 percent by savings and loans, and 16 percent by commercial banks (Kaufman 1993).

In 1982 the Puget Sound Mutual Savings Bank converted from a mutual to the stock form of ownership, inaugurating a trend that has become the most important issue involving mutual savings banks. The essence of the mutual savings bank is that its depositors own the bank, and its board of trustees operates it. Garn-St. Germain permits conversion to stock form. Proponents argue that converting from the mutual form to the stock form injects essential new capital into the institution, improves the quality of management, and leads to a more efficiently run financial intermediary. Opponents stress the new owners' capture of windfall profits at the expense of depositor-owners, the vulnerability of the stock form to mergers and takeovers that jeopardize the bank's independence and lead to increased concentration of banking power in the community, and the loss of the distinction that depositors enjoy as owners (Ornstein 1985).

When a mutual savings bank converts to the stock form of organization, depositors have the right to buy stock at a discounted price. Few exercise the purchase option, thus making stock available to shrewd speculators who make minimum deposits to gain access to discounted stock that may yield windfall capital gains. Moreover, the managers engineering the conversion are likely to receive generous compensation for their efforts.

The attraction of probable windfall gains from converting a mutual savings bank to a stock company has encouraged regulators to formulate rules to govern conversions and speculators to seek loopholes in those rules. The procedure for conversion has mutated into variations like merger-conversion and liquidation-purchase. The future is likely to find regulators continuing their efforts to protect depositors and speculators attempting with equal vigor to surmount that protection.

BIBLIOGRAPHIC ESSAY

Books

The first sources are early classics, studies of individual mutual savings banks, anniversary celebrations of specific institutions, and surveys of mutual savings banks in general. These are usually more descriptive than analytical and are often based on official correspondence and records. Many of the works have been annotated in other collections of historical bibliographies. Examples of classics are Bennett (1924), Keyes (1876–1878), Knowles (1936), Robinson (1917), Sherman (1934), Thon ([1935] 1983), and Willcox (1916).

The more recent volumes are clustered around 1966, the 150th anniversary of mutual savings banks in the United States. The first of these major surveys was *Mutual Savings Banking: Basic Characteristics and Role in the National Economy* by the National Association of Mutual Savings Banks (1962). This trade association monograph is part of a major overview of the U.S. financial system that was conducted in the early 1960s by the Commission on Money and Credit. The well-documented comparative study focuses on major trends, especially those since World War II.

Another important anniversary volume is Weldon Welfling's *Mutual Savings Banks: The Evolution of a Financial Intermediary* (1968). Welfling examines the historical development of mutual savings banks in the United States over 150 years and investigates the industry's quest for new geographic territory, investment opportunities, and chartering alternatives, especially federal chartering. Welfling is a rich source of factual and bibliographic information, numerous tables and charts, and an extensive bibliography.

The final volume in this triad of works is Alan Teck's *Mutual Savings Banks and Savings and Loan Associations: Aspects of Growth* (1968). Like the others, Teck presents a historical overview of the growth of the savings industry, documented by a wide variety of tables, charts, and appendixes and approximately 150 bibliographic entries. After his examination of the past, Teck, too, concludes that mutual savings banks should be given greater opportunities for chartering, permitted a wider range of investment assets for their portfolios, and encouraged to expand geographically beyond the narrow confines of New England and the eastern seaboard.

The unanimity in diagnoses of, and solutions to, the problems of mutual savings banks is interesting. Even more striking is the degree to which the recommendations of the trade association and academic authors have been incorporated into legislative and regulatory changes since the mid-1970s.

In *Management and Control in the Mutual Savings and Loan Association*, Alfred Nicols (1972) anticipates major issues and arguments surrounding the conversion of thrifts to stock form. *Savings Banking: An Industry in Change* is Franklin H. Ornstein's (1985) review of many of those same issues in the early 1980s.

Articles

One category of articles is historical studies of individual mutual savings banks in particular locations. These reviews by economic historians trace the early evolution of mutual savings banks from primitive charitable depositories into the forerunners of today's sophisticated financial intermediaries. They consider the investment strategies followed by the trustees of the early mutual savings banks, specifically, the rationality of their decisions (Olmstead 1972, 1974; Davis and Payne 1958). Were the banks' investments made in the interest of the depositors, the trustees, or the government? Were those investments socially beneficial or wasteful?

A second series of articles published from 1972 to 1982 describes the chartering and organizational options available to mutual savings banks. The authors offer insights into the relationship of mutual savings banks to other financial intermediaries and the somewhat limiting structure of the typical mutual form of organization (Eisenbeis and McCall 1972; Allen 1976; Lucarelli and Teague 1979; Dunham, 1982).

A third series of articles comprises a technical discussion of operational behavior and decision making in mutual savings banks. These are for readers with a strong interest in the theoretical underpinnings of the mutuals, for the writers draw on sophisticated statistical or analytical evidence (Black and Schweitzer 1981; Macbeth and Downey 1973; McCall and Murphy 1971; Murphy and Weintraub 1970; Thalheimer and Ali 1979).

Later articles detail the costs and benefits of conversion from a mutual to a stock form. Relative efficiency (Simons 1992; Masulis 1987; Cebenoyan et al. 1993), expense preference (Mester 1989; Krinsky and Thomas 1995), the risk behavior of management in both forms (Carter and Stover 1990), and relative profitability (Barth, Brumbaugh, and Kleiden 1994; Simons 1992) have all been addressed in recent years.

The disposition of windfall profits generated during the conversion process has been a common topic in the business and popular press. Numerous articles provide insight into the regulatory issues surrounding conversion (Macey 1993; Schifrin 1993; Bradsher 1994; Meredith 1994; Hansell 1994; Karr 1994; Fox 1995a, 1995b).

Those seeking a more theoretical analysis of the events of the 1980s can turn to an article that attempts to assess the behavior of thrifts—specifically, federal savings and loans and federal savings banks—during those turbulent years. Sylvia Hudgins and George Morgan (1993) focus on how thrifts in general responded to the changing regulatory and economic environment. The lessons learned apply to mutual savings banks as well.

One article demands special mention. George J. Benston's nearly 100-page "Savings Banking and the Public Interest" (1972) is crucial to an understanding of recent legislative and regulatory treatment of mutual savings banking. Benston argues that less overall regulation of savings banking, greater powers of investment and portfolio diversification, and geographic expansion would better serve the public interest. His conclusions are buttressed by eighteen figures and eight tables as well as an interesting discussion of European mutual savings banks.

The literature on mutual savings banks is sparse in comparison to the volumes on other financial intermediaries. The works cited in this chapter treat the mutuals as a separate institution with a unique history and organizational structure. However, given the convergence in form and function among American financial intermediaries, much of the pertinent literature since 1980 could be applicable to mutual savings banks.

BIBLIOGRAPHY

Allen, Charles E. "Stock Conversions—Where We Are Now." *Federal Home Loan Bank Board Journal* 9 (March 1976): 2–8.
Ballaine, Wesley Charles. "Development and Economic Aspects of the Laws Regulating Investments of Mutual Savings Banks." Ph.D. diss., University of Chicago, 1940.
Barth, J. R., R. D. Brumbaugh, Jr., and A. W. Kleiden. " 'Windfall' Gains in Mutual-to-Stock Conversion of Thrift Institutions." *Challenge* 37 (July–August 1994): 43–49.
Bennett, Frank P., Jr. *The Story of Mutual Savings Banks*. Boston: Frank P. Bennett, 1924.
Benston, George J. "Savings Banking and the Public Interest." *Journal of Money, Credit, and Banking* 4 (February 1972): 133–226.
Black, Harold A., and Robert L. Schweitzer. "An Analysis of Market Segmentation

in Mortgage Lending between a Commercial Bank and a Mutual Savings Bank." *American Real Estate and Urban Economic Association Journal* 9 (fall 1981): 234–40.

Bradsher, Keith. "New Curbs on Sale of Mutual Banks." *New York Times*, April 22, 1994, D2.

Carter, R. B., and R. D. Stover. "The Effects of Mutual to Stock Conversions of Thrift Institutions on Managerial Behavior." *Journal of Financial Services Research* 4 (July 1990): 127–44.

Cebenoyan, A. S. et al. "The Relative Efficiency of Stock versus Mutual S&Ls: A Stochastic Cost Frontier Approach." *Journal of Financial Services Research* 7 (June 1993): 151–70.

Cook, Laurence, and Leslie E. Arndt. *Mutual Savings and Loan Association, F.A.: 100 Years of Thrift and Homeownership, 1887–1987*. Bay City, MI: Mutual Savings and Loan Association, F.A., 1988.

Davis, Lance E., and Peter L. Payne. "From Benevolence to Business: The Story of Two Savings Banks." *Business History Review* 32 (winter 1958): 386–406.

Directory of American Savings and Loan Associations. Baltimore: T. K. Sanderson, 1955–1991.

Directory of the Mutual Savings Banks of the United States. New York: National Association of Mutual Savings Banks, annual.

Directory/National Council of Savings Institutions. Washington, DC: National Council of Savings Institutions, annual.

Directory of the Savings Banks of the United States and Membership of NAMSB. New York: National Association of Mutual Savings Banks, annual.

"Does Mutuality Offer Longevity?" *US Banker* 106, no. 1 (January 1996): 10.

Dunham, Constance. "Mutual Savings Banks: Are They Now or Will They Ever Be Commercial Banks?" *New England Economic Review*, May–June 1982, 51–72.

Eisenbeis, Robert A., and Alan S. McCall. "Some Effects of Affiliations among Mutual Savings and Commercial Banks." *Journal of Finance* 27 (September 1972): 865–77.

Fact Book of Savings Institutions. Washington, DC: National Council of Savings Institutions, 1988.

Finney, Katherine. *History of Mutual Savings Banks in Northampton, Massachusetts*. Ph.D. diss., Columbia University, 1944. New York: King's Crown Press, 1945.

Fox, Justin. "Mutual Conversion Taking New Route—Via Liquidation Sale." *American Banker* 160, no. 3 (June 22, 1995a): 119.

———. "OTS Warns against Liquidating Mutuals." *American Banker* 160, no. 3 (June 29, 1995b): 124.

Hansell, Saul. "Who Owns Savings Bank Riches?" *New York Times*, January 28, 1994, D1.

Hudgins, Sylvia, and George Emir Morgan. "Regulatory Changes and Federal Mutual Thrift Behavior: Evidence from the 1980s." *Journal of Money, Credit, and Banking* 25 (November 1993): 828–53.

Johnson, Eugene. "CUs: The Last of the Mutuals." *Credit Union Magazine* 63, no. 10 (October 1997): 64–72.

Jones, Robert J., Thomas R. Dwyer, and Robert S. Mintz. "IRS Clarifies Conversions of Financial Institutions from Mutual to Stock Form." *Journal of Bank Taxation* 6, no. 1 (fall 1992): 9.

Karr, Albert. "FDIC Proposes Rules for Banks' Conversions." *Wall Street Journal*, January 25, 1994, A5.

Kaufman, George. "The Incredible Shrinking S&L Industry." In *Readings on Financial Institutions and Markets*, edited by Peter S. Rose, 5th ed., 137–39. Homewood, IL: Irwin, 1993.

Keyes, Emerson W. *A History of Savings Banks in the United States from Their Inception in 1816 Down to 1874*. 2 vols. New York: Bradford Rhodes, 1876–1878.

Knowles, Charles E. *History of the Bank for Savings in the City of New York, 1819–1929*. 2d ed. New York: Bank for Savings, 1936.

Krinsky, I., and H. A. Thomas. "Savings and Loan Ownership Structure and Expense-Preference." *Journal of Banking and Finance* 14 (April 1995): 165–70.

Lintner, John Virgil. *Mutual Savings Banks in the Savings and Mortgage Markets*. Boston: Harvard University, Graduate School of Business Administration, Division of Research, 1948.

Lucarelli, Alphonse S., and Robert F. Teague, Jr. "Converting into a Stock Company, Yes or No?" *Federal Home Loan Bank Board Journal* 22 (September 1979): 3–9.

Macbeth, Thomas G., and Gerald F. Downey. "The Monetary Consequences of Demand Deposit Creation by Mutual Savings Banks—The Commonwealth of Massachusetts Case." *Marquette Business Review* 17 (spring 1973): 1–8.

Macey, Jonathan R. "Mutual Banks Take Your Money and Run." *Wall Street Journal*, December 29, 1993, A8.

Masulis, Ronald W. "Changes in Ownership Structure: Conversions of Mutual Savings and Loans to Stock Charter." *Journal of Financial Economics* 27, no. 1 (March 1987): 29–59.

McCall, Alan S., and Neil B. Murphy. "A Note on Evaluating Liquidity under Conditions of Uncertainty in Mutual Savings Banks." *Journal of Financial and Quantitative Analysis* 6 (September 1971): 1165–69.

Meredith, Robyn. "FDIC Sets New Rules for Mutual Thrifts Converting to Stock." *American Banker* 159, no. 27 (February 9, 1994): 3.

Mester, Loretta J. "Testing for Expense Preference Behavior: Mutual versus Stock Savings and Loans." *Rand Journal of Economics* 20 (Winter 1989): 483–98.

Morris, Kathleen, with Seanna Browder. "Energizer Banker: Washington Mutual's CEO Is Dealing as Fast as He Can." *Business Week* no. 3535, Industrial/Technology Edition (July 14, 1997): 54.

Murphy, Neil B., and Harry Weintraub. "Evaluating Liquidity under Conditions of Uncertainty in Mutual Savings Banks." *Journal of Financial and Quantitative Analysis* 4 (January 1970): 559–68.

Mutual Savings Banking: Facts & Figures. New York: National Association of Mutual Savings Banks, 1964–1970. Annual.

Mutual Savings Banks. Austin, TX: Sheshunoff, annual. See also *Savings Banks of America*.

National Association of Mutual Savings Banks. *Analysis of the Investment Laws* of Eleven of the States in Which Mutual Savings Banks Are Located (Revised to Include 1932 Legislative Changes). New York: National Association of Mutual Savings Banks, 1932.

———. Mutual Savings Banking: Basic Characteristics and Role in the National Economy. A Monograph Prepared for the Commission on Money and Credit. Trade Association Monographs. Englewood Cliffs, NJ: Prentice-Hall, 1962.

National Fact Book of Mutual Savings Banking. New York: National Association of Mutual Savings Banks, 1970–1981. Annual.

National Fact Book of Savings Banking. New York: National Association of Mutual Savings Banks, 1982–1983. Annual.

National Fact Book of Savings Institutions. Washington, DC: National Council of Savings Institutions, 1984–1987. Annual. See also Fact Book of Savings Institutions.

Nicols, Alfred. Management and Control in the Mutual Savings and Loan Association. Lexington, MA: Lexington Books, 1972.

Olmstead, Alan L. "Investment Constraints and New York City Mutual Savings Bank Financing of Antebellum Development." Journal of Economic History 32 (December 1972): 811–40.

———. "New York City Mutual Savings Bank Portfolio Management and Trustee Objectives." Journal of Economic History 34 (December 1974): 815–34.

Ornstein, Franklin H. Savings Banking: An Industry in Change. Reston, VA: Reston, 1985.

Payne, Peter L., and Lance E. Davis. The Savings Bank of Baltimore, 1818–1866: A Historical and Analytical Study. Johns Hopkins University Studies in Historical and Political Science, ser. 72, no. 2. Baltimore: Johns Hopkins Press, 1956. Reprint. Companies and Men. New York: Arno Press, 1976.

Robinson, Edward L. 1816–1916: One Hundred Years of Savings Banking. New York: American Bankers Association, 1917.

Savings Bank Journal. New York: National Association of Mutual Savings Banks of the United States, 1921–1983. Monthly.

Savings Banks of America. Austin, TX: Sheshunoff, 1989–   . Annual.

Savings Institutions. Chicago: United States League of Savings Institutions, 1983–1992. Monthly.

Savings Institutions Sourcebook. Chicago: United States League of Savings Institutions, 1984–1989. Annual.

Schifrin, Matthew. "The Merger-Conversion Game." Forbes 151, no. 13 (June 21, 1993): 43.

Sherman, Franklin J. Modern Story of Mutual Savings Banks. New York: J. J. Little & Ives, 1934.

Simons, Katerina. "Mutual-to-Stock Conversions by New England Savings Banks: Where Has All the Money Gone?" New England Economic Review, March–April 1992, 45–53.

Teck, Alan. Mutual Savings Banks and Savings and Loan Associations: Aspects of Growth. New York: Columbia University Press, 1968.

Thalheimer, Richard, and Mukhtar M. Ali. "Time Series Analysis and Portfolio Selection: An Application to Mutual Savings Banks." Southern Economic Journal 45 (January 1979): 821–37.

Thon, Robert W., Jr. *Mutual Savings Banks in Baltimore*. Johns Hopkins University Studies in Historical and Political Science, ser. 53, no. 3. Baltimore: Johns Hopkins Press, 1935. Reprint. New York: AMS Press, 1983.

U.S. Congress. House. Committee on Banking and Currency. *Federal Charter Legislation for Mutual Savings Banks*. Washington, DC: U.S. Government Printing Office, 1963.

———. House. Committee on Banking and Currency. Subcommittee on Bank Supervision and Insurance. *Federal Charter Legislation for Mutual Savings Banks, 1966*. Hearings on H.R. 11508. 89th Cong., 2d sess. Washington, DC: U.S. Government Printing Office, 1966.

———. House. Committee on Banking and Currency. Subcommittee on Bank Supervision and Insurance. *Federal Charter Legislation for Mutual Savings Banks, 1967*. Hearings on H.R. 15, H.R. 10745, and H.R. 11139. 90th Cong., 1st sess., July 13–20, 1967. Washington, DC: U.S. Government Printing Office, 1967.

U.S. National Recovery Administration. *Code of Fair Competition for Mutual Savings Banks as Approved on October 9, 1933 by President Roosevelt . . .* Washington, DC: U.S. Government Printing Office, 1933.

———. *Code of Fair Competition for Mutual Savings Banks as Approved on October 9, 1933 by President Roosevelt . . .* Washington, DC: U.S. Government Printing Office, 1934.

Welfling, Weldon. *Mutual Savings Banks: The Evolution of a Financial Intermediary*. Cleveland: Case Western Reserve University Press, 1968.

Willcox, James M. *A History of the Philadelphia Savings Fund Society, 1816–1916*. Philadelphia: J. B. Lippincott, 1916.

Wilson, Michael L. "Well-Run Mutuals Deserve the Needed Latitude to Succeed." *America's Community Banker* 112, no. 5 (May 1991): 14–16.

Zinski, Christopher J., and Michael S. Melbinger. "Mutual-to-Stock Conversions Create Valuable Opportunities for Using Employee Stock Plans." *Journal of Bank Taxation* 7, no. 4 (Summer 1994): 164.

CLEARINGHOUSE ASSOCIATIONS, 60.5

_____ HUGH T. ROCKOFF

Clearinghouses facilitate interbank exchanges by providing a convenient place for canceling offsetting debts. How a bank clearinghouse works can be illustrated with a simple numerical example. Suppose there are three banks in a city, and as a result of the flow of transactions, their accounts at the end of the day stand as shown in Table 1.

Bank A has received checks drawn on B for $100, and B has received checks drawn on A for $105. Bank A records a credit in its account with B of $100 and a debit of $105. Bank B's accounts show the reverse: a credit with A of $105 and a debit of $100. Bank A will know that it has checks drawn on B for $100 and on C for $100, but without some communication with the other banks, A cannot know the amount of claims on it held by other banks. If banks were left to settle individually between themselves, a wild scramble would result. Bank B, suspecting that it had a positive balance with A, would send an agent to A to settle accounts; Bank C, suspecting that it had positive balances, might send its agent to A and B. As the number of banks increased, the number of bank agents running about town would also increase.

Now consider what would happen if agents of all the banks met in one place and drew up a combined account similar to the one shown in Table 1. Accounts could be settled much more efficiently: Bank A would pay $15 into the clearinghouse, Bank B would pay in $5, and Bank C would take out $20. A large volume of transactions, here $595, could be settled with a minimum transfer of $20 in cash. If the banks expect that surpluses and deficits will even out over time, the use of cash can be further reduced. Bank C might simply keep the $20 as a credit in its clearinghouse account

Table 1
Sample Interbank Accounts

	In Account with Bank	Credit $	Debit $	$ Net Difference
Bank A	B	100	105	-5
	C	100	110	-10
	total	200	215	-15
Bank B	A	105	100	+5
	C	85	95	-10
	total	190	195	-5
Bank C	A	110	100	+10
	B	95	85	+10
	total	205	185	+20
Total		595	595	0

to be used later when it runs a deficit. No cash need change hands in clearing this large volume of transactions.

In the Table 1 example, the advantage of using a clearinghouse is small. Only three separate transactions would be needed in any case for the banks to settle: one between A and B, one between B and C, and one between A and C. But as the number of banks grows, the number of separate transactions increases. Between twenty-five banks, 300 separate transactions—the formula is $(\frac{1}{2})(n)(n-1)$ where n is the number of banks—would be needed for all of the banks to settle independently. The reduction of 300 separate transactions to twenty-five payments to, or withdrawals from, the clearinghouse is a major gain.

The early history of the clearinghouse system is murky, but the first clearinghouse is reputed to have been established in London about 1773. Distinguished British economist William Stanley Jevons described his visit to the London Clearing House c. 1875, where "the settlement of the reciprocal claims of the twenty-six principal city banks . . . representing as it does the completion of the business of no small part of the world" took place "in a room of moderate dimensions, entered from a narrow passage running from the post-office in King William Street across to Lombard Street" (1878, 263).

The room did not seem to me large enough for the convenient and wholesome transaction of such vast and increasing work. Although some banks employ as many as six clerks, the pressure is very great at times. The facility which these clerks acquire by practice in making and adding up entries is very great, but the intense head work performed against time, in an atmosphere far from pure, and in the midst of bustle and noise arising from the corrections shouted from one clerk to another across the room, must be exceedingly trying. Brain disease is occasionally the consequence. (1878, 268)

Before the New York Clearing House Association was established, the situation in New York was much like the Table 1 example. Porters carrying bags of gold or checks roamed from bank to bank settling accounts. They would meet on the steps of one of the Wall Street banks to sort out the confusion, yet an observer could be pardoned for describing the result as chaos rather than order. As early as 1831 Albert Gallatin, a former secretary of the U.S. Treasury and president of the National Bank of New York, had written about the advantages of establishing a clearinghouse in New York, but not until the economic expansion of the 1850s (produced by the discovery of gold in California, eastern Australia, and elsewhere) did the need for a clearinghouse become acute. Between 1849 and 1853 the number of banks in New York increased from twenty-four to fifty-seven, raising the number of potential interbank settlements from 276 to 1,596.

Bank bookkeeper George D. Lyman's suggestion led directly to the formation of the New York Clearing House Association on October 4, 1853. Its utility was quickly apparent, and clearinghouses were soon established in other major cities. In their early years the clearinghouses performed many of the regulatory functions later assumed by federal agencies. A check on a bank is really a "double claim." The person who accepts a check has a claim on both the individual who wrote it and the bank on which the check is drawn; hence, it is almost impossible to set up a secondary market in bank checks. Organized markets require a degree of uniformity in the product being traded. Even two checks drawn on the same bank may have different credit characteristics, so people who accept checks cannot get information on the soundness of the bank on which the check is drawn from prices in a secondary market. Individual banks have an incentive to reduce their reserve holdings and to take other risk-increasing actions, since the riskiness of the bank will not be reflected in the price of deposits and may not lead to a loss of deposits (Gorton 1985).

Clearinghouses provide a solution to this information problem. They impose standards on banks—capital requirements, reserve requirements, interest rate ceilings, reporting standards—and deny entry or suspend or expel members that violate those standards. In some cases clearinghouses investigate rumors of mismanagement in individual banks. However, not all of their actions maximize the safety of the banking system or provide the public with information unobtainable through more familiar market mechanisms. A clearinghouse can, for example, act as the manager of a cartel and enforce rules designed to create monopoly profits for the banks.

THE CENTRAL BANKING ROLE OF CLEARINGHOUSES, 1857–1913

Much of the scholarly interest in clearinghouses centers on their role as substitutes for central banks before the establishment of the Federal Reserve System. Before World War II, the nation's banking system was subject to severe panics. The United States had a fractional reserve banking system with few guarantees to depositors or noteholders (holders of bank-issued paper money) that their money was safe beyond the assets of the bank that had issued their claims. When rumors circulated about the solvency or liquidity of a bank, holders of claims on that bank demanded payment of their claims—a run on the bank—even if the bank did not have specie (gold and silver) enough to redeem all of its outstanding notes (most notes were secured with commercial paper, the loans that bring banks an interest income). Once the bank had exhausted its specie reserves, it was forced to close. Fears about individual banks would sometimes escalate into an economy-wide panic that closed all banks, the sound with the weak.

The failure of a single large firm, perhaps in conjunction with other bad economic news, could create a widespread crisis of confidence in the banking system and precipitate a general restriction on the conversion of bank money into cash (gold and silver or in some periods greenbacks or Federal Reserve notes). When banks reduced loans (call loans could be recalled immediately, but others were reduced by the bank's refusal to renew at expiration of the loan period) to conserve and rebuild their reserves, they contracted money and credit, causing many business failures and sometimes economic depression. Severe financial crises occurred in 1857, 1873, 1893, 1907, and 1930–1933 and lesser ones in other years.

For most of the first 150 years of U.S. history there was no government agency to act as lender of last resort, to aid failing banks, or to frustrate the disintegration of the financial system after a panic. Clearinghouses, particularly the New York Clearing House Association, were the only stabilizing influence during financial downturns. Few businessmen, regulators, or academics had any confidence in the clearinghouses' capacity for stabilizing American financial institutions, but some scholars suggest that they showed a potential for dealing with the financial instabilities inherent in a fractional reserve banking system.

The pattern of response was set during the Panic of 1857. The origin of that crisis appears to have been the failure of the Ohio Life Insurance and Trust Company in August 1857. The collapse of this supposedly conservative institution fueled a rapid withdrawal of balances from New York and a stock market panic. Banks in many parts of the country, as well as those in New York, soon suspended conversion of banknotes and deposits into specie.

During panics, banks contract their loans to build up reserves, a reasonable policy for a single bank but a disaster for the banking system. The newly created New York Clearing House responded to the panic by creating a loan committee whose members all agreed to increase their loans by the same proportion. Increasing loans relieved the pressure on the money market; increasing loans by the same proportion ensured that no one bank suffered severe adverse clearing balances.

The New York Clearing House also issued clearinghouse loan certificates against the notes of country banks (which were not then redeeming in specie) owned by members of the Clearing House. By allowing the banks to settle their balances with these certificates, the Clearing House reduced the pressure on weaker banks, making it easier for them to resume specie payments. Albeit the loan certificates were a small, temporary step, the Clearing House had moved toward issuing a nonredeemable, private fiat currency and was operating in some measure as a lender of last resort.

The practices employed in 1857 were used in subsequent panics along with notable innovations. In the Panic of 1860 (spawned by the threat of civil war) clearinghouse loan certificates were issued against New York State bonds, U.S. bonds, and other bank assets, further weakening the link between the loan certificates and specie. In the 1860 crisis the committee equalized losses on collateral for certificates and equalized specie reserves among banks to stabilize Clearing House members that might otherwise close and undermine the credibility of the system. Opposed by banks, the innovation did not become part of the institutionalized response to panics.

The Panic of 1873 brought a new twist. Banks were allowed to issue certified checks marked "payable through the clearinghouse" that circulated as currency. The checks, not redeemable for specie, were acceptable because bank A could use bank B's checks in making payments to a clearinghouse and because they were the liability of the clearinghouse, not a bank. The clearinghouses had moved another step closer to issuing a private fiat currency. In 1873 many clearinghouses outside New York issued loan certificates in imitation of the successful New York precedent.

Clearinghouse certificates were issued in the minor panics of 1884 and 1890 and in the major panic of 1893. There were signs that by 1893 the issue of loan certificates had become a well-established drill. The New York Clearing House began issuing certificates before any banks had restricted or suspended specie payment. In some areas clearinghouses issued loan certificates in denominations as low as $0.25. Offering clearinghouse loan certificates and subsequently restricting cash payments eased the position of the banks and reduced the pressure to contract loans but did not prevent or cure the crisis. Gold went to a premium in terms of cash: as the public regained confidence in the soundness of the banking system, the premium gradually disappeared, and banks resumed specie payments.

The evolution of institutionalized policy toward panics was not a continuous, upward path marked by growing success. The New York Clearing

House's response to the Panic of 1907, the last panic before federal legislation designed to mitigate crises, revealed the natural limits of clearinghouses as a substitute for a publicly owned lender of last resort. The classic analysis is by Oliver M. W. Sprague in his *History of Crises under the National Banking System* ([1910] 1977), a volume written for the prestigious National Monetary Commission, which was set up in the wake of the crisis. The commission's work led to the establishment of the Federal Reserve System.

Sprague, who viewed the Panic of 1907 as unnecessary, criticizes the New York Clearing House banks: before the crisis, these banks had failed to maintain reserves commensurate with their preeminent position in the money market (in particular, they had not held adequate reserves against the deposits of the trust companies, which themselves had kept inadequate reserves); they had ignored the signs of an approaching stringency in the money market that called for strengthening reserves; the banks had made a fetish of required reserve ratios, failing to go below the required minimum when it would have been wise to do so, even if certain penalties might have been imposed; they had waited too long to issue clearinghouse loan certificates and had not equalized reserves among member banks.

Sprague may be right in his censure of the New York Clearing House banks; to this day, no one has made a closer study of the history of the panics under the National Banking Act. The system was far from secure, for it depended on finely timed corrective measures (the accumulation of reserves, for instance) that appeared contrary to the direct pecuniary interests of the banks. Moreover, the expectations set up by earlier crises made the necessary quality of judgment even higher in 1907 than in the past. "The committee knew that the issuance of clearing-house certificates would immediately bring about a restriction of cash payments throughout the country, causing widespread business inconvenience and embarrassment. Hoping that the panicky condition might subside, the committee postponed from day to day the issuance of clearing-house certificates" (Sprague [1910] 1977, 257).

Experience had created a connection in the public mind, or so the committee believed, between the issuance of loan certificates and suspension of specie payments. (Sprague claims that this misapprehension sprang from events in 1893, but the committee had to deal with the public perception, right or wrong.) Issuing securities could exacerbate, rather than allay, fear. In normal times loan certificates were a deterrent to panic, but when tensions mounted, their use was complicated by the possibility of their having a reverse effect.

The clearinghouses had some tools for dealing with small problems. Rumors that an individual bank was taking undue risks, for example, could be investigated; if the rumors proved true, the offending bank could be disciplined with the threat of expulsion from the clearinghouse. But, unlike a central bank, the clearinghouses did not continually supply liquidity to the market and could not discretely increase liquidity to eliminate the threat of a panic. The contrast between the clearinghouses' inability to consistently influence events and the Bank of England's greater success in deterring panics makes this point: in the second half of the nineteenth century, the United States experienced several major panics; Great Britain, none.

In reaction to the Panic of 1907, Congress passed the Aldrich-Vreeland Act of 1908. The act provided for an emergency currency that could be issued by groups of banks during financial crises. Intended as a stopgap until the Federal Reserve System was established and operating, the emergency currency was issued on only one occasion, the outbreak of World War I. The currency seemed to work well, preventing the fear and uncertainty produced by the outbreak of war from degenerating into a full-blown financial crisis. The Aldrich-Vreeland currency, coupled with the establishment of the Federal Reserve in 1913, eliminated the need (or so it appeared) for the New York Clearing House to act as lender of last resort. The advent of deposit insurance in 1934 further reduced the need for the clearinghouses to play a serious regulatory role.

CLEARINGHOUSES AND COMPETITION

"People of the same trade [wrote Adam Smith] seldom meet together, even for merriment and diversion, but the conversation ends in a conspiracy against the public, or in some contrivance to raise prices" (*Wealth of Nations* 1776, bk. 1, Chapter 10, pt. 2). It is altogether natural that bankers would use clearinghouses as a vehicle for limiting interest rates paid on deposits or for other competitive practices. Banks that were too aggressive in pursuing customers could be penalized by exclusion from the clearinghouse. Throughout much of the nineteenth and twentieth centuries, banking regulators encouraged clearinghouses to impose on member banks standards that have worked against consumers in the short run but have contributed in the long run to the safety and soundness of the banking system. Deposit interest rates are the clearest example.

Limiting the interest paid on deposits works against consumers and in favor of banks, particularly when entry into banking is restricted. From the Civil War to the Great Depression, clearinghouses set limits on interest paid on deposits, particularly interbank deposits, to prevent competition and discourage banks from investing in risky securities. Depositors monitored the assets of the banks with an eye to keeping their money in low-risk, low-interest institutions. But since clearinghouses could not influence nonmember banks, their power to control interest on deposits was limited. The trust companies in New York prospered by paying high interest rates on deposits because they maintained small reserves and made high-risk loans. After financial difficulties at several trusts sparked the Panic of 1907, state banking officials encouraged clearinghouses to set interest rate limits on deposits. By the end of the 1920s clearinghouse rules limited interest on deposits. In 1929 the American Bankers Association surveyed banks in 160 clearinghouse cities. Bank officers were asked how they set interest rates on deposits: 58 percent of the respondents relied on clearinghouse rules; 14 percent, on agreement among the banks; 14 percent, on custom; and 14 percent, on individual action (Fischer 1968). Federal legislation in the 1930s eliminated interest on deposits until deregulation of the financial sector began in the 1970s.

Clearinghouses and banks were considered exempt from antitrust laws until the mid-1960s, when in a series of cases launched in Minnesota (*United States v. Duluth Clearinghouse Association* is one case), banks were charged with having violated the Sherman Antitrust Act by establishing maximum interest rates and setting various service charges. Criminal as well as civil charges were brought. The banks pleaded no contest to the criminal proceedings, and penalties were levied. Civil proceedings were terminated by a consent judgment that prohibited many contested practices, including the setting of maximum interest rates on deposits (Fischer 1968).

THE MODERN CLEARINGHOUSE

An immediate effect of the Federal Reserve System was to reduce the need for clearing checks through private clearinghouses. Together, the Fed and the Federal Deposit Insurance Corporation (the FDIC was established in 1934) mitigate the banks' reliance on clearinghouses as lenders of last resort. Nevertheless, clearinghouses continue to play a role in the American banking system, most recently by adapting computers to automate the check clearing process and offering other new services to customers. Legislation that requires the Federal Reserve to charge full cost for the clearing services it provides has promoted competition between private-sector clearinghouses and the Fed.

By 1968 banks in California were using automated clearing, although the district Federal Reserve Bank provided the basic computer services. The New York Automated Clearing House (NYACH), a private system established in 1975 by the New York Clearing House Association, handles clearing for a large number of banks and financial intermediaries, but the final settlements are made on the books of the Federal Reserve. Innovations like "cash concentration" and the automatic deposit of paychecks are possible through automated clearing. Cash concentration permits a business firm with diverse operations in different parts of the country to collect cash balances overnight into a central account. Automatic deposit of paychecks eliminates the risk, time, and "shoe leather" costs of depositing paychecks by hand. The U.S. Treasury quickly adopted automatic deposit for distributing all Social Security payments directly to banks, but in 1998 federal courts guaranteed Social Security recipients their choice of check or automatic deposit.

In 1970 the New York Clearing House Association established CHIPS (Clearinghouse Interbank Payment System), a computerized network of foreign and domestic banks specializing in the international transfer of funds. By the mid-1980s CHIPS was clearing over 90 percent of the dollar payments moving between countries—a volume of transactions that represents much of the world's business since the dollar is the basic unit of account in international transactions. The dollar volume handled by CHIPS was then some $400 billion per day.

Clearinghouses in the twenty-first century may prove even more important than their twentieth-century counterparts. As the checkless society evolves, the Federal Reserve and the private-sector clearinghouses will likely work together, for the Fed can offer safety and the clearinghouses the capacity to quickly adopt new technologies. Instead of working through cumbersome open market operations or discount rate changes, the Board of Governors of the Federal Reserve may influence the economy by instantly increasing or decreasing the net balances of all economic agents. Whatever the merits of such speculations, there is little doubt that modern finance is moving toward a fully electronic payments mechanism in which the clearinghouses will play a major role.

BIBLIOGRAPHIC ESSAY

Although several important works address clearinghouses and clearinghouse associations, discussions of bank clearing and clearinghouses are usually embedded in examinations of banking. Specific books and articles include *The Banks of New York, Their Dealers, the Clearinghouse, and the Panic of 1857* (Gibbons 1859), "Clearinghouses and the Origin of Central Banking in the U.S." (Gorton 1985), "The Joint Production of Confidence: Endogenous Regulation and 19th Century Commercial Bank Clearinghouses" (Gorton and Mullineaux 1987), and "The Central Banking Role of Clearinghouse Associations" (Timberlake 1984). Publications are also available from the New York Clearing House Association.

History of Crises under the National Banking System (Sprague [1910] 1977) and *The Regulation and Reform of the American Banking System, 1900–1929* (White 1983) are examples of a more general coverage of banking that includes discussions of clearing.

BIBLIOGRAPHY

American Bankers Association. *The Clearing House; Facts Covering the Origin, Developments, Functions, and Operations of the Clearing House, and Explaining the Systems, Plans, and Methods Promulgated by the Clearing*

House Section of the American Bankers Association, by Jerome Thralls. New York: American Bankers Association, Clearing House Section, 1916.

————. *Clearinghouse Association Report. Results of the American Bankers Association Clearinghouse Survey—Suggested Guidelines for Establishing New Clearinghouse Associations.* Washington, DC: American Bankers Association, Operations and Automation Division, 1981.

Andrew, A. Piatt. "Substitutes for Cash in the Panic of 1907."*Quarterly Journal of Economics* 22 (August 1908): 497–516.

Cannon, James Graham. *Clearing-houses: Their History, Methods, and Administration.* New York: D. Appleton, 1908. Reprint. The Rise of Commercial Banking. New York: Arno Press, 1980.

"Clearing House Association of the Southwest." *Texas Banking* 86, no. 5 (May 1997): 14–15+ .

Coy, Peter. "A Way to Beat the Bank: Check Processing Goes Self-Service." *Business Week,* no. 3572, Industrial/Technology Edition (April 6, 1998): 30.

Davis, Henry A. *Electronic Data Interchange and Corporate Trade Payments.* Morristown, NJ: Globecon Group, Financial Executives Research Foundation, 1988.

Federal Reserve Bank of New York. *Payment Systems Studies.* Compiled and edited by Adam Starchild. Princeton, NJ: University Press of New Jersey, 1991.

Fischer, Gerald C. *American Banking Structure.* New York: Columbia University Press, 1968.

Fry, Maxwell J. et al. *Payment Systems in Global Perspective.* Routledge International Studies in Money and Banking, 5. New York: Routledge, 1999.

Garvy, George. *Debits and Clearings Statistics and Their Use.* Rev. ed. Washington, DC: Board of Governors of the Federal Reserve System, 1959. Reprint. Westport, CT: Greenwood Press, 1982.

Gibbons, James S. *The Banks of New York, Their Dealers, the Clearinghouse, and the Panic of 1857.* New York: D. Appleton, 1859.

Gilpin, William J., and Henry E. Wallace. *Clearing House of New York City.* New York: M. King, 1904.

Gorton, Gary. "Clearinghouses and the Origin of Central Banking in the U.S." *Journal of Economic History* 45, no. 2 (June 1985): 277–83.

Gorton, Gary, and D. J. Mullineaux. "The Joint Production of Confidence: Endogenous Regulation and 19th Century Commercial Bank Clearinghouses." *Journal of Money, Credit and Banking* 19 (November 1987): 457–68.

Hallatt, Harry H. *Our Dual Economy: A Capital Idea.* N.p., 1966.

Humphrey, David B. *Payment Systems: Principles, Practice, and Improvements.* World Bank Technical Paper, no. 260. Washington, DC: World Bank, 1995.

————, ed. *The U.S. Payment System: Efficiency, Risk, and the Role of the Federal Reserve: Proceedings of a Symposium on the U.S. Payment System.* Sponsored by the Federal Reserve Bank of Richmond, May 25–26, 1988, Williamsburg, VA. Boston: Kluwer Academic, 1990.

Jevons, William Stanley. *Money and the Mechanism of Exchange.* New York: D. Appleton, 1878.

Kelley, Edward W., Jr. "Payments Risk Management in the Private Sector." *World of Banking* 16, no. 1 (Spring 1997): 8–11.

Klinkerman, Steve. "Checks at a Crossroads." *Banking Strategies* 73, no. 3 (May–June 1997): 32–38.

Lacker, Jeffrey M. "The Check Float Puzzle." *Economic Quarterly—Federal Reserve Bank of Richmond* 83, no. 3 (Summer 1997): 1–25.

Littlefield, Neil O. "Payments: Articles 3, 4, and 4A." *Business Lawyer* 52, no. 4 (August 1997): 1527–45.

Magee, Harvey White. *A Treatise on the Law of National and State Banks, including the Clearing House and Trust Companies, with an Appendix Containing the National Bank Act as Amended, and Instructions Relative to the Organization of National Banks.* 2d ed., rev. and enl., containing the Federal Reserve Act of 1913–1914. Albany, NY: M. Bender, 1914.

Marlin, Steven. "ECP [Electronic Check Presentment] Footholds: New York, Michigan, Texas." *Bank Systems & Technology* 34, no. 12 (December 1997): 32.

———. "The Fed Upholds Its Processing Role." *Bank Systems & Technology* 35, no. 3 (March 1998): 10.

———. "Banks Test CAs [Certifications Authority software] in NACHA [National Automated Clearing House Association] Pilot." *Bank Systems & Technology* 35, no. 4 (April 1998): 14.

———. "NACHA Kicks Off Bank CA Pilot." *Bank Systems & Technology* 35, no. 7 (July 1998): 21.

———. "NACHA to Hold Lockbox Pilot." *Bank Systems & Technology* 36, no. 3 (March 1999): 18.

Marshall, Jeffrey. "Codifying Change." *USBanker* 107, no. 12 (December 1997): 22.

Monterey, Fernando. "Handling Major Headaches: ACH [Automated Clearing House] Meets OFAC [Office of Foreign Asset Control]." *ABA Banking Journal* 89, no. 12 (December 1997): 34.

Murphy, Patricia A. "Electronic Check 'Re-presentment' Aids Retailers in Fight against Bad Check Losses." *Stores* 81, no. 4 (April 1999): 80–84.

National Automated Clearing House Association. *Regulation E, ACH: Impact and Compliance.* Washington, DC: National Automated Clearing House Association, 1980.

———. *ACH Receivers Handbook.* Washington, DC: National Automated Clearing House Association, 1986.

———. *Introduction to ACH Corporate Payments*, by Patricia A. Murphy. Washington, DC: National Automated Clearing House Association, 1986.

———. *ACH Marketing Handbook.* Washington, DC: National Automated Clearing House Association, 1987.

———. *Guide to ACH Processor Selection & Evaluation: Result of NACHA's Private Sector Alternatives Project.* Washington, DC: National Automated Clearing House Association, 1987.

———. *Resources on ACH Risk: A Compendium of Papers.* Herndon, VA: National Automated Clearing House Association, 1991.

———. *Uniform Commercial Code Article 4A and the Automated Clearing House System*, by Paul E. Homrighausen, Robert G. Ballen, and Natalie H. Diana. Herndon, VA: National Automated Clearing House Association, 1991.

———. *ACH Compliance Manual: How to Comply with ACH-Related Rules &*

Regulations. Herndon, VA: National Automated Clearing House Association, 1992.

————. *ACH Origination Handbook*. Herndon, VA: National Automated Clearing House Association, 1992.

————. *The Accredited ACH Professional Handbook: ACH—An Overview*, by William Woehrle. Herndon, VA: National Automated Clearing House Association, 1993.

————. *Revised ACH Origination Handbook*. Herndon, VA: National Automated Clearing House Association, 1995.

————. *Revised Uniform Commercial Code Article 4A and the Automated Clearing House Network*, by Jane E. Larimer. Herndon, VA: National Automated Clearing House Association, 1997.

————. *The RDFI Handbook: Everything You Need to Know about Receiving ACH Transactions*. Herndon, VA: National Automated Clearing House Association, 1998.

"NACHA Adopts Rule Requiring EDI Capability." *ABA Bank Compliance* 19, no. 1, Regulatory & Legislative Advisory Issue (January 1998): 5.

"NACHA Test Shows Bank CA Model." *Bank Systems & Technology* 35, no. 11 (November 1998): 13.

New York Clearing House Association. *The New York Clearing House*. New York: New York Clearing House Association, 1912.

————. *The Federal Reserve Re-examined*. New York: New York Clearing House Association, 1953.

————. "Clearing House Interbank Payments System." New York: New York Clearing House Association, n.d.

————. "New York Automated Clearing House." New York: New York Clearing House Association, n.d.

————. "New York Clearing House Association." New York: New York Clearing House Association, n.d.

Ritter, Lawrence S., and William L. Silber. *Principles of Money, Banking, and Financial Markets*. 5th ed. New York: Basic Books, 1985.

Rivlin, Alice M., and Laurence H. Meyer. "Statement to the Congress." *Federal Reserve Bulletin* 83, no. 11 (November 1997): 878–87.

Rolnick, Arthur J., Bruce D. Smith, Warren E. Weber, and Randall S. Kroszner. "Lessons from a Laissez-Faire Payments System: The Suffolk Banking System (1825–58)/Commentary." *Federal Reserve Bank of St. Louis* 80, no. 3 (May–June 1998): 105–20.

Rossi, Marco. *Payment Systems in the Financial Markets: Real-Time Gross Settlement Systems and the Provision of Intraday Liquidity*. Ph.D. diss., Universite Catholique de Louvain, 1965. Rev. ed. New York: St. Martin's Press, 1998.

Simonson, George M. *The Clearing House of New York City*. Edited by Moses King. New York: M. King, 1898.

Sprague, Oliver M. W. *History of Crises under the National Banking System*. 1910. Reprint. Fairfield, NJ: Augustus M. Kelley, 1977. See also U.S. National Monetary Commission.

Stavins, Joanna. "A Comparison of Social Costs and Benefits of Paper Check Presentment and ECP [Electronic Check Presentment] with Truncation." *New England Economic Review*, July–August, 1997, 27–44.

Steeples, Douglas W., and David O. Whitten. *Democracy in Desperation: The Depression of 1893*. Contributions in Economics and Economic History, no. 199. Westport, CT: Greenwood Press, 1998.

Summers, Bruce J., ed. *The Payment System: Design, Management, and Supervision*. Washington, DC: International Monetary Fund, 1994.

Timberlake, Richard, Jr. "The Central Banking Role of Clearinghouse Associations." *Journal of Money, Credit and Banking* 16 (February 1984): 1–15.

Turner, Paul S. *Law of Payment Systems and EFT*. Gaithersburg, MD: Aspen Law & Business, 1999.

U.S. Congress. House. Committee on Banking, Finance, and Urban Affairs. Subcommittee on Domestic Monetary Policy. *The Role and Activities of the Federal Reserve System in the Nation's Check Clearing and Payments System*. 98th Cong., 2d sess., November 1984. Committee Print 98–17.

———. House. Committee on Agriculture. *Financial Institutions Safety and Consumer Choice Act of 1991*. Hearings on H.R. 6. 102d Cong., 1st sess., September 11, 1991. Serial no. 102–30.

U.S. Congress. Senate. *Clearing Houses*. Prepared for the National Monetary Commission by James Graham Cannon. 61st Cong., 2d sess., 1910. Senate Doc. 491. Washington, DC: U.S. Government Printing Office, 1910. See also U.S. National Monetary Commission, 1911.

U.S. General Accounting Office. *An Examination of Concerns Expressed about the Federal Reserve's Pricing of Check Clearing Activities: Report to the Chairman, Committee on Banking, Housing, and Urban Affairs, United States Senate, by the Comptroller General of the United States*. Washington, DC: U.S. General Accounting Office, 1985.

U.S. National Monetary Commission. *Clearing Houses*, by James Graham Cannon. Vol. 6, no. 1. Washington, DC: National Monetary Commission, 1911.

———. *History of Crises under the National Banking System*, by Oliver M. W. Sprague. Vol. 5, no. 3. Washington, DC: National Monetary Commission, 1911.

White, Eugene Nelson. *The Regulation and Reform of the American Banking System, 1900–1929*. Princeton, NJ: Princeton University Press, 1983.

Wholesale Automation Banking. New York: Frost & Sullivan, 1980.

Willoughby, Jack. "Checks and Balances." *Institutional Investor* 31, no. 5 (May 1997): 23.

Part VII

Nondepository Credit
Institutions
ESIC 61.0

CHAPTER 11

MORTGAGE BANKERS AND BROKERS, 61.6

DONALD R. STABILE

Mortgage bankers and brokers are financial intermediaries who bring together borrowers and investors in the market for loans that are secured by real estate. The mortgage banker writes loans for borrowers, packages loans or groups of loans for purchase by investors, and services loans for investors for a fee. Before the 1980s the typical mortgage company was a small firm with little publicly held stock and a minimum of government regulation (Whiteside 1983; Klaman 1959). Historically, mortgage banking has been influenced by events in the real estate market (which determined the type of borrower), by changes in the financial markets (which made for different types of investors and altered their needs), and by increasing governmental intervention in the housing markets and in the regulation of financial markets. Over the last sixty years, the federal government's activities have been a dominant force in the evolution of the industry from its initial concentration in farm loans to its present focus on residential and commercial housing. The majority of mortgage banks operating at the end of the twentieth century were formed after World War II.

LAND BANKS

In the years after the American Revolution, settlers moved westward into present-day Ohio, Kentucky, Illinois, and Indiana. Land banks were formed to help finance the expansion by making loans in local areas in the West, primarily by borrowing in Europe. Much of that early westward expansion was fueled by speculation in land, and when the advances in land prices did not materialize, the land banks failed, entered bankruptcy, and disappeared as a source of finance (Dennis n.d.).

In the nineteenth century the purchase of farmland was seldom financed with bank mortgages. Most western farmland was settled by homesteading a parcel of free government land. These parcels were usually passed on to family members, but land transfers that entered the market were likely to be seller-financed. At the turn of the twentieth century, the funds loaned out by individuals financing real estate purchases amounted to more than the mortgages issued by financial institutions (Whiteside 1983). Even so, mortgage banking was increasingly important in real estate finance.

After the Civil War, farm mortgage companies sprang up in the Midwest and the newly developing Plains states. Land was free under the Homestead Act, but farmers still needed a source of funds for improving the land and making it productive. Wood for homes and barns and barbed wire for fences were expensive investments, so farmers financed the purchase of these materials. Although some individuals made mortgage loans, mortgage banking companies wrote many of the loans to farmers (Bogue 1955).

Early mortgage companies financed their lending by selling bonds. As the industrial East expanded, money accumulated in banks, insurance companies, and the accounts of wealthy individuals; mortgage bankers channeled these surplus funds into the Midwest and the Plains states where there were credit shortages (Dennis n.d.; Whiteside 1983).

The J. B. Watkins Land Mortgage Company of Lawrence, Kansas, typical of nineteenth-century mortgage companies, was organized in 1878 as a proprietorship. Watkins first acted as a direct mortgage broker and later, to gather funds, developed mortgage-backed bonds for sale to investors. His loans to farmers throughout Kansas and Nebraska ranged from $300 to $1,000 but averaged about $500. In 1874 interest rates on loans in Kansas were 12 percent, but rates declined over the next decade. Watkins agents operating on commission made the initial contact with borrowers and ensured that the provisions of the mortgage were carried out (Bogue 1955).

Once mortgages were issued, Watkins Land Mortgage sought investors to purchase them. To sell its mortgages and bonds quickly, the company maintained sales offices in London and New York City and agents in eleven cities in the Northeast, even placing advertisements in local and church newspapers. Nearly all sales of mortgages and bonds were to individual rather than institutional investors. To improve the marketability of his mortgages or mortgage-backed bonds, Watkins advertised that he would guarantee payment of interest and principal, but when investors doubted his ability to make good on the guarantee, he reduced it to cover just interest payments. During the first half of 1883 the company showed a profit of $42,000. Watkins expanded the company into Colorado and began purchasing land on his own. He diluted his capital, and the company went bankrupt during the agricultural depression of the early 1890s (Bogue 1955).

Drought conditions in the Plains states in the late nineteenth century led to many mortgage defaults, and the concentration of mortgage banking companies in the region accounted for many bankruptcies among companies lacking the financial strength to hold on to the foreclosed land or to meet payments to investors. Over half of the 167 mortgage banking companies operating in 1891 were located in Kansas, Nebraska, and Missouri, and the bulk of the remainder were in Colorado, Iowa, North Dakota, South Dakota, and Minnesota. Some of these early companies survive today; one, the Utah Mortgage Company, has been in business since 1892 (Davis 1965; Klaman 1959; Hyman 1982).

The mortgage banker's stock-in-trade was knowledge of local real estate conditions and long-term contacts with eastern investors. The mortgage banker–investor relationship was formalized by sale of a commitment from the investor to the mortgage banker. The commitment was a contract wherein the investor agreed to purchase mortgages from the banker as long as they met certain specifications such as interest rate, type and use of property, credit worthiness of the borrower, and length of the loan term. Given the commitment, the mortgage banker would originate mortgages locally and deliver them to the investor. The mortgage banker also earned a fee for collecting payments, ensuring that the borrower maintained the property value, and handling refinance or foreclosure if the borrower could not make the payments (Whiteside 1983).

Between the time mortgage loans were made and were transferred to the investor, the mortgage banker kept them in an inventory that was financed through short-term lines of credit with commercial banks. The typical farm loan was made for three to five years and secured with a 50 percent down payment. Interest payments were collected during the term of the loan, either semiannually or at harvest time. The face amount came due at the end of the term, but another loan could be negotiated then. By 1900 about $4 billion in loans, nearly all to farmers, had been made by 200 mortgage banking companies. In 1914 forty-five mortgage bankers met in New York to form the Farm Mortgage Bankers Association. By the end of the first year, membership had reached 200 (Whiteside 1983; Dennis n.d.; Geltner 1988).

The Federal Farm Loan Act of 1916 established federally sponsored land banks as another source of loans for farmers and ranchers. Borrowers were required to subscribe to stock in the local Land Bank Association. Local associations transferred mortgages to regional Federal Land Banks but retained servicing responsibilities. In the early years, the Land Bank System expanded farm credit during emergencies. By the 1930s the Land Bank System had become part of the Farm Credit Administration; and from the end of World War II until the 1960s, Land Bank loans increased from about $30 million a year just before the war to $650 million a year in 1961, when total mortgages held by the system reached $2.8 billion. To some extent this growth came at the expense of mortgage bankers, for the Land Bank share of total mortgages ranged from 2 percent in 1920, to a high of 40 percent during 1934, then back down to 7 percent in 1937. By 1961, however, its share had reached nearly 20 percent despite the absence of an emergency (Colean and Sauner n.d.). During this same period, the mortgage banking industry was beginning to finance residential housing.

RESIDENTIAL MORTGAGES IN THE 1920s AND 1930s

About 1900, loans on single-family homes in urban areas were available from a few mortgage bankers or from mutual savings banks or savings and loan associations. Although the Federal Reserve Act of 1913 allowed national banks to make real estate loans, home mortgages remained a small fraction of mortgage lending. Until the end of the 1930s, the typical home mortgage loan retained the features of a farm loan: it was a short-term loan with interest due semiannually and payment of principal due at the end of the loan. Refinancing imposed heavy costs on borrowers (Dennis 1989; Whiteside 1983).

After World War I residential mortgages became more common. In 1923 the Farm Mortgage Bankers Association changed its name to the Mortgage Bankers Association (MBA). In 1927 the MBA began admitting as members mortgage bankers making urban loans. The 1920s were years of extensive land speculation, and the value of real estate escalated. The 1920s boom fueled another mortgage banking development (Dennis n.d.; Hoffman 1956).

When a borrower defaulted, the mortgage banker usually compensated the investor with either a new loan in exchange for the one defaulted or a buyback of the defaulted paper. Compensation was more an industry custom than a legal obligation. As the 1920s boom continued and mortgage bankers grew confident of success, many guaranteed payment of both principal and interest. Known as mortgage guarantee companies, these bankers wrote loans for sale as mortgages to institutional investors or as mortgage-backed bonds to individual investors; these mortgages were held by a trustee. When real estate values crashed, mortgage guarantee companies were unable to meet their obligations, and nearly all disappeared into receivership (Dennis n.d.).

The Great Depression marks the end of the 1920s real estate boom despite earlier evidence of decline. Widespread unemployment and the difficulties in the banking system led to loan defaults. The unemployed failed to meet their semiannual interest payments; even those lucky enough to remain employed and make their interest payments found it impossible to refinance the principal amount of their short-term loans (Whiteside 1983). Moreover, because payments were made semiannually, a mortgage could go into default months before bankers were alerted by nonpayment.

Nevertheless, few first mortgages were foreclosed. In the Midwest farm belt especially, states legislated moratoriums against mortgage foreclosures if there was any chance the loan could be repaid. In urban areas, mortgage bankers often volunteered to accept a moratorium on foreclosures. Most foreclosures during the 1930s came from second and third mortgage holders who had to move for foreclosure to avoid losing their security (Dennis n.d.).

To reduce mortgage defaults, the federal government established the Home Owners' Loan Corporation (HOLC) in 1933, and authorized the HOLC to exchange its bonds for mortgages in default; the mortgages acquired by HOLC were then set up under a revised payment schedule. Throughout the 1930s, government intervention was evident in the home mortgage industry. The National Housing Act of 1934 created the Federal Housing Administration (FHA) to provide government insurance on mortgages used for construction loans and long-term mortgages for home buyers. The National Association of Real Estate Boards had lobbied for many of the government programs that benefited the real estate industry (Dennis n.d.; Whiteside 1983; Davies 1958).

The FHA mortgage insurance was not immediately popular in the financial community, whose members had been hurt by the earlier mortgage guarantee companies, but it proved to be of great benefit to the mortgage banking industry. If a borrower met the credit and down payment standards set by the FHA, a twenty-year mortgage could be arranged that called for monthly payments of both interest and principal. Because the mortgages were insured, the mortgage banker could easily place them with an investor, and a national mortgage market was established through the existing correspondence system whereby mortgage bankers originated loans and transferred them to insurance companies. Surplus mortgage funds could then be moved to areas of the country where they were in short supply (Dennis n.d.).

The federally guaranteed system was supplemented in 1938 with the formation of the Federal National Mortgage Association ("Fannie Mae"), which would purchase mortgages but leave the servicing to mortgage bankers. When market conditions improved, Fannie Mae would resell the mortgages to private investors (Dennis 1989).

THE POSTWAR HOUSING BOOM

At the end of World War II, servicemen returning from the war married and began families, generating an especially high demand for residential housing. The national housing stock had barely changed in the fifteen years of depression and war. Now the federal government took two important steps to spur the supply of housing: the Servicemen's Readjustment Act of 1944 established a program to guarantee any mortgage loan made to a veteran who qualified for credit (these Veterans Administration (VA) mortgages often required no down payment), and Fannie Mae purchased large numbers of VA mortgages to increase the acceptability of mortgages with low down payments, long terms of life, and monthly payments of interest and principal (Whiteside 1983).

By the 1950s the mortgage market boasted the largest concentration of long-term credit in the United States. Mortgage bankers were beneficiaries of market growth: from 1946 to 1960 the typical mortgage firm had evolved from a small family-owned business into a large corporation (Dennis n.d.). Moreover, many new firms had entered the industry. Of 854 companies approved in 1954 for origination of FHA mortgages, 194 (23 percent) had been incorporated between 1950 and 1954, and 251 (29 percent) between 1945 and 1949. Nearly 90 percent of these new firms held assets of less than $2 million. The total assets of FHA-approved mortgage companies rose from $160 million in 1945 to $1.8 billion in 1954, whereas the average of firm assets rose from $347,000 to $2.1 million. The industry showed a slightly higher concentration of assets: firms with assets above $5 million (8 percent industrywide) held 22 percent of the assets in 1945; firms above that threshold in 1954 (6 percent industrywide) held 36 percent of the assets (Klaman 1959).

The growth in assets size does not give a complete picture of development in the industry because few mortgage banks hold on to mortgages as a long-term asset. The mortgages serviced also show how the industry was growing, and here the gains were impressive. The volume of mortgages being serviced by mortgage bankers rose from $6 billion in 1951 to $20 billion by the end of 1955. The industry's share of total mortgage debt for one- to four-family residences thereby increased from a little over 10 percent to nearly 25 percent (Klaman 1959).

The growth of the mortgage banking industry created a period of above-normal profits that may account for the widespread entrance of new firms at midcentury. As the geographic distribution of the industry shifted slightly, the Pacific Coast and the Southwest, primarily California and Texas, gained at the expense of the historically heavy concentrations in the Midwest and the Plains states. Mortgage bankers became slightly more active in financing new homes and construction loans; the bulk of loans in the industry (83 percent in 1955) were either VA-backed (58 percent) or FHA-backed (25 percent) (Klaman 1959).

As mortgage banking expanded in the 1950s, bankers were forced to find new sources of investment funds. For the large sums they needed, mortgage bankers turned less to individual investors and more to institutional investors, primarily insurance companies. Sales to individual investors were only 5 percent of the total market in 1955. As the industry advanced, however, the type of commitment available from investors changed. By the 1950s, a period of credit shortage, regular commitments for a fixed amount of mortgage loans were not readily obtainable from institutional investors; instead, commitments for a stated period of time, usually two years, became the rule. With mortgage origination less certain, mortgage companies maintained more mortgages in their inventories and relied more heavily on short-term credit from commercial banks (Klaman 1959).

THE SHIFT TO INCOME PROPERTY

By the late 1950s the postwar boom in residential housing was over; but demographic shifts had created a higher demand for apartments, and out-migration from the central city increased the demand for suburban shopping centers and office buildings. Mortgage companies adjusted to these changes by supplying more funds for the construction and purchase of income-producing properties. Mortgage bankers had made these kinds of loans in the past, and by 1963, 114 of the 880 members of the MBA reported that their main business was in loans for income property. As growth continued, construction loans increased and loans for multifamily units rose from 9.5 percent of all loans originated in 1963 to 16.7 percent in 1972; for the same years, nonfarm, nonresidential loans rose from 16 percent to 20 percent (Kidd 1977).

Institutional investors, especially insurance companies, led mortgage companies into new markets in the second half of the century. Demand for income-producing properties was pushing up yields at the same time that returns on residential property were declining. In 1955 insurance companies put 75 percent of their mortgage portfolios into single-family housing; by 1960 that figure had dropped to 50 percent. By the early 1970s almost all mortgage funds provided by insurance companies were for income properties (Dennis n.d.).

As the loan structure diversified, life insurance companies began loosening their correspondent relationships with individual mortgage bankers. Previously, mortgage bankers had held exclusive territories within which they originated and serviced loans for insurance companies; by the 1960s, life insurance companies not only encouraged any mortgage companies in an area to offer them mortgages but also originated and serviced their own mortgages for developers. Even when mortgage bankers had originated the loans, the insurance companies often serviced them after purchase (Kidd 1977).

The migration of insurance companies out of single-family housing was accompanied by other changes in real estate finance. As interest rates rose in the late 1960s and early 1970s, depositors shifted funds away from banks or savings and loans to money market mutual funds. Banks and savings and loans were forced to reduce their mortgage accounts; mortgages originated by savings and loans had been 51 percent of the residential market in 1960 but were only 31 percent in 1982 (Whiteside 1983).

In 1968 the federal government established the Government National Mortgage Association ("Ginnie Mae") to make residential mortgage pools more acceptable to investors by insuring the payment of interest and principal. Lenders pool FHA and VA mortgages, use them to back securities they issue, then pay a fee to Ginnie Mae to guarantee the securities; the fees pay for operating costs and losses as well as provide a profit for Ginnie Mae. The lenders, usually mortgage bankers, sell the securities and use the proceeds to replenish their stocks of loanable funds (Whiteside 1983).

The formation of Ginnie Mae spurred the issuance of securities backed by conventional mortgages and a second-mortgage market that, in turn, furthered the development of a national mortgage market. The act that had created Ginnie Mae, the Housing and Urban Development Act of 1968, also placed Fannie Mae in private hands. The Emergency Home Finance Act of 1970 established the Federal Home Loan Mortgage Corporation ("Freddie Mac") to bolster the secondary market for conventional mortgages that savings and loans originate (Whiteside 1983; Dennis 1989).

Changes in the real estate market have altered the function and operation of mortgage banking but not its growth. In 1974 mortgage bankers originated 20 percent of the residential mortgages, including 78 percent of the FHA mortgages. By 1982 they were originating 29 percent of the residential mortgages, including 86 percent of the FHA mortgages and 81 percent of the VA mortgages. Their share of conventional mortgages rose from 2 percent in 1970, to 7 percent in 1980, to 16 percent in 1982 (Dennis n.d.; Whiteside 1983).

GOVERNMENT REGULATION

Unlike commercial banking or the savings and loan industry, mortgage banking does not come under the direct regulation and supervision of government agencies. Mortgage bankers that are approved as lenders by the FHA or that provide servicing for Fannie Mae and Ginnie Mae are subject to audit by those agencies, however; and the industry must adhere to the legal controls on the personal finance industry. The truth-in-lending provision of the Consumer Protection Act of 1968 (Federal Reserve Regulation Z) requires lenders to disclose to borrowers in writing all terms of a loan as well as the annual percentage rate charged. The Real Estate Settlement Procedures Act of 1974 (as amended in 1976) requires mortgage lenders to inform borrowers in advance of loan settlement costs and limits real estate and escrow requirements imposed by lenders. The Home Mortgage Disclosure Act of 1975 sought to end the practice of "redlining" by requiring lenders to report where loans were distributed geographically in their area of service (Dennis 1989).

RECENT DEVELOPMENTS

The Depository Institutions Deregulation and Monetary Control Act of 1980 initiated an era of rapid change and innovation in the financial services industry, and competition intensified. Under the act, mortgage lenders were, for example, able to offer adjustable rate mortgages (ARMs), allowing them to match mortgage rates with the cost of securing funds from investors (Dennis 1989).

On the investor side of the market, there was a revival of interest in residential mortgages among life insurance companies, reversing a decline dating to the 1960s. In addition, the development of conventional mortgage-backed securities promised to be a new source of funds for mortgages. In the early 1980s Freddie Mac had increased the impact of its operations when it ceased charging a fee to lenders that did not belong to the Federal Home Loan Bank System and opened its operations to mortgage bankers (Harter and Schell 1981; Whiteside 1983).

Competition has increased for the mortgage banker's traditional functions of originating and servicing mortgages. The growth of bank holding companies and their legal entrance into mortgage banking under Regulation Y added one important element to the market, and in the early 1980s, savings and loans began changing their activities in the secondary mortgage market, selling more mortgages and purchasing fewer whole mortgages. Likewise, savings and loans and commercial banks are evolving into a hybrid system wherein they assume functions traditionally provided by mortgage bankers (Allen 1982; Harter and Schell 1981).

The problems that evolved in the savings and loan crisis of the late 1980s signalled changes for mortgage bankers. Other financial institutions moved more directly into mortgages. Large banks like Citicorp and Chase, insurance companies like Prudential and Travelers, and consumer credit companies as diverse as Sears, General Motors, and Ford have established mortgage banking subsidiaries (Feldstein 1989). As other firms enter the market, traditional mortgage bankers are squeezed in all three areas of operations. More firms translate into greater competition to originate mortgages. Moreover, because investors originate mortgages for their own portfolios, mortgage bankers find it more difficult to secure commitments from them. The direct origination of mortgages by former investors also reduces the service contracts and fees that mortgage bankers had come to rely on as a steady source of income. Adjustable rate mortgages have made the mortgage banking industry more capital intensive: adjustable rate mortgages are harder to market to investors; hence mortgage banking companies are forced to hold these in their portfolios longer than they hold fixed rate paper (Reiss and Duncan 1989).

Some of the pressures of change in the mortgage market are offset by the government-sponsored Ginnie Mae, Fannie Mae, and Freddie Mac. Nevertheless, many mortgage banking companies will either be edged out of the industry or forced to merge with other companies. Mergers of mortgage banks burgeoned from twelve in 1986, to twenty-five in 1987, to twenty-eight in 1988. In 1987, fifteen companies originated nearly 20 percent of the $449.1 billion market for new mortgage loans (Reiss and Duncan 1989).

Changes in the institutional structure of mortgage banking that began in the 1960s snowballed for three decades. The 1990s were distinguished by a move to privatize the federal mortgage support agencies and efforts to end lending institutions' discriminatory practices in granting mortgages. Redlining, for example, enables lenders to deny loans to applicants who live or work within carefully delineated geographic locales. These no-loan areas on local maps are traditionally outlined in red. Lending institutions defend the practice on the grounds of high losses experienced or expected in the redlined regions. In an era of federally mandated equal opportunity, discrimination against a loan applicant because of place of residence or work, or of race, color, or gender is intolerable and increasingly illegal.

American business has historically demanded government operation of enterprises that offer social and especially business benefits but not profits. If an enterprise displays any profit potential, business groups insist on wresting the profitable segments of the operation away from government, leaving the unprofitable business to the public institutions. The Republican-dominated Congress of the mid-1990s investigated the possibilities for privatizing Fannie Mae and Freddie Mac. If Republicans remain in power long enough, the profitable portions of these and other mortgage-related government activities may well be given over to the private sector. The unprofitable, yet socially desirable, responsibilities will be left in the public sector.

The reverse mortgage may be the distinguishing feature of the real estate landscape of the future. Private housing has become so expensive that buyers are increasingly treating mortgages as commitments that will never be paid off. Home buyers purchase the largest structure they can afford the monthly mortgage payments on, intending to make payments until they can sell the house and refinance a larger one. The optimal house will be paid for until the buyers have enough invested to permit them to withdraw their money from the mortgage rather than continue making payments.

BIBLIOGRAPHIC ESSAY

"The history of the mortgage company has yet to be written" (Davis 1965), and the same may be said of the industry. As long as the industry remains monopolistic and competitive, company histories will be little more than anecdotal reminiscences (Hyman 1982). A survey of the industry can be found in Baker, Kellogg & Co., *The Development of the Mortgage Bank* (1926), Phillip E. Kidd, *Mortgage Banking 1963 to 1972* (1977), and John M. Boyle, *A Survey of the Mortgage Banking Industry* (1983).

Although mortgage banking is discussed in articles across a range of financial periodic and scholarly literature, information is concentrated in *Mortgage Banking* (formerly *Mortgage Banker*), the journal of the MBA and perhaps the best starting point for any study of mortgage banking—it includes an annual index cataloged by author and topic. Other sources of articles include *Commercial Investment Real Estate Journal, Federal Reserve Bulletin, Forbes, Housing Economics, Institutional Investor, Mortgage Banking, National Real Estate Investor, National Underwriter,* and *Real Estate Finance.*

Federal government publications are perhaps the best source of information on mortgage banking. Federal legislation has shaped the modern industry and is rarely passed without extensive debate, hearings, and criticism: the press prints thousands of pages of opinion for every sentence of law. Moreover, the federal government publishes most of the debate on bills, and those publications are unequaled sources of information. *Federal Farm Loan Act* (Walsh 1916), *Authorize Payment of Farm-Loan Mortgages with Bonds Issued by the Mortgage Banks* (U.S. Congress 1932), and *FNMA and FHLMC Rates of Return* (U.S. General Accounting Office 1996b) represent eighty years of government publications on the mortgage industry. Late–twentieth-century issues like discrimination in mortgage lending and privatization of federal mortgage lending functions are set out in detail in government publications, the first stop for any researcher interested in timely topics: *Guaranteed Farm Operating Loans for Socially Disadvantaged Persons* (U.S. Department of Agriculture 1993), *H.O.W. Homeownership Opportunities for Women: National Partners in Homeownership* (U.S. Department of Housing and Urban Development 1996a), and *Privatization of Fannie Mae and Freddie Mac: Desirability and Feasibility* (U.S. Department of Housing and Urban Development 1996b).

Andrew Caplin et al.'s *Housing Partnerships: A New Approach to a Market at a Crossroads* (1998) is a good starting point for studying the reverse-mortgage phenomenon. In addition to a lively discussion of the alternatives facing home buyers at the end of the twentieth century, Caplin et al. provide an extensive bibliography to promote further research of the topic.

BIBLIOGRAPHY

Allen, Melissa L. "Bank Holding Companies: Continuing Evolution." *Mortgage Banking* 42, Special Issue (1982): 20–25.

ABA Bank Compliance. Washington, DC: American Bankers Association, 1994– . Eight no. per year.

ABA Banking Journal. New York: Simmons-Boardman for American Bankers Association, 1979– . Monthly.

American Bankers Association. *New Opportunities in the Mortgage Market: Interim Financing of F.H.A. and V.A. Mortgages and the Nationwide Mortgage Market.* New York: American Bankers Association, Economic Policy Commission, Savings and Mortgage Division, 1959.

America's Community Banker. Washington, DC: America's Community Bankers, 1995. Monthly.

Baker, Kellogg & Co. *The Development of the Mortgage Bank.* New York: Baker, Kellogg, 1926.

Bielski, Lauren. "Home Equity Loans on the Web." *ABA Banking Journal* 91, no. 3 (March 1999): 42–44.

Bogue, Allan G. *Money at Interest: The Farm Mortgage on the Middle Border.* Ithaca, NY: Cornell University Press, 1955.

Boyle, John M. *A Survey of the Mortgage Banking Industry.* Prepared for the Subcommittee on Economic Goals and Intergovernmental Policy of the Joint Economic Committee. 98th Cong., 1st sess., 1983. S. Prt. 98–29. Washington, DC: U.S. Government Printing Office, 1983.

Brueggeman, William B., and Jeffrey D. Fisher. *Real Estate Finance and Investments.* Irwin Series in Finance. Homewood, IL: Irwin, 1993.

Caplin, Andrew, Sewin Chan, Charles Freeman, and Joseph Tracy. *Housing Partnerships: A New Approach to a Market at a Crossroads.* Cambridge: MIT Press, 1998.

Clayton, Michelle. "Wall Street Sells Mortgages on the Cheap." *America's Community Banker* 8, no. 3 (March 1999): 42.

———. "Would You Get a Mortgage or Credit Card Over the Internet?" *America's Community Banker* 8, no. 3 (March 1999): 42.

Cohen, Joseph Louis, with Alice Ring. *The Mortgage Bank: A Study in Investment Banking.* London: Sir I. Pitman & Sons, 1931.

Colean, Miles L. *Mortgage Companies: Their Place in the Financial Structure.* Trade Associations Monographs. Englewood Cliffs, NJ: Prentice-Hall, 1962.

Colean, Miles L., and Raymond J. Sauner. *The Federal Land Bank System.* Washington, DC: Mortgage Bankers Association of America, n.d.

Dandord, David P. "Online Mortgage Business Puts Consumers in Driver's Seat." *Secondary Mortgage Markets* 16, no. 1 (April 1999): 2–8.

Davies, Janet Pearl. *Real Estate in American History.* Washington, DC: Public Affairs Press, 1958.

Davis, Lance E. "The Investment Market, 1870–1914: The Evolution of a National Market." *Journal of Economic History* 25 (1965): 255–99.

DeHuszar, William Ivan. *Handbook of Mortgage Loan Servicing Practices.* Chicago: Mortgage Bankers Association of America, 1949.

————. *Mortgage Loan Administration*. New York: McGraw-Hill, 1972.

Dennis, Marshall W. *Evolution of an Industry: Development of Mortgage Banking*. Washington, DC: Mortgage Bankers Association of America, n.d.

————. *Residential Mortgage Lending*. 2d ed. Englewood Cliffs, NJ: Prentice Hall, 1989.

Derivatives Quarterly. New York: Institutional Investor, 1994– . Quarterly.

Dunham, Constance R. *The Unknown Lenders: The Role of Mortgage Banks in the Chicago Metropolitan Area* [Part I]. Chicago: Woodstock Institute, 1991. See also Ernestine L. Jackson and Constance R. Dunham, 1993.

Fabozzi, Frank J., ed. *The Handbook of Mortgage Backed Securities*. 4th ed. Chicago: Probus, 1995.

"Fannie Mae Launches Exchange Offer for up to $15bn to Boost Benchmark Note Liquidity." *Euroweek* no. 593 (March 12, 1999): 4

"Fannie Mae Sets Super-Benchmark." *Euroweek* no. 595 (March 26, 1999): 1–3.

"Fannie Mae Rings Callable Changes with Benchmark Note Programme." *Euroweek* no. 597 (April 9, 1999): 3.

"Fear of Fannie and Freddie; Their Expansion Plans Are Enraging Some Heavy Hitters." *Business Week*, no. 3624, Industrial/Technology Edition (April 12, 1999): 110.

Federal Reserve Bulletin. Washington, DC: U.S. Government Printing Office, May 1915– . Monthly. Washington, DC: Board of Governors of the Federal Reserve System, January 1979– . Monthly.

Feldman, Judy. "New Online Options for Home Loans." *Money* 28, no. 4 (April 1999): 182.

Feldstein, Stuart A. "The Changing of the Guard." *Mortgage Banking* 49 (September 1989): 10–16.

Flannagan, W. W. *The Federal Farm Loan Act, Approved July 17, 1916 . . . with Marginal Notes and Index*. Prepared for the Joint Committee on Rural Credits. 64th Cong., 1st sess., 1916. Senate Doc. 500. Washington, DC: U.S. Government Printing Office, 1916.

Forbes. New York: Forbes, 1917– . Biweekly.

Geltner, Sharon. "1914." *Mortgage Banking* 49 (October 1988): 51–55.

Glenn, David W. "Future Trends in Housing Finance." *Mortgage Banking* 59, no. 7 (April 1999): 36–40.

Harter, Thomas R., and Schuyler E. Schell. "Competition and Evolution in the Residential Mortgage Market." *Mortgage Banker* 41 (January 1981): 23–27.

Healy, Tom. "Forecasting a Default Risk in Mortgage Portfolios." *America's Community Banker* 8, no. 4 (April 1999): 6.

Hoffman, G. J., Jr. *The Mortgage Banker of Yesterday and Today*. Pamphlet. Library of Mortgage Bankers Association of America. Jacksonville, FL: Stockton, Whately, Davin, privately published, 1956.

Holt, W. Stull. *The Federal Farm Loan Bureau, Its History, Activities, and Organization*. Service Monographs of the United States Government, no. 34. Baltimore, MD: Johns Hopkins Press, 1924. Reprint. New York: AMS Press, 1974.

Housing Economics. Washington, DC: National Association of Home Builders of the United States, 1987– . Monthly.

"HUD: Mortgage Broker Fees Not Illegal Per Se." *ABA Bank Compliance* 20, no. 4, Regulatory & Legislative Advisory Edition (April 1999): 6.

Hyman, Sidney. "Evolution of a Mortgage Banker." *Mortgage Banking* 43 (December 1982): 18–24.

Institutional Investor. New York: Institutional Investor, 1976– . Monthly.

Investment Dealers' Digest. New York: IDD, 1934/35– .

Jackson, Ernestine L., and Constance R. Dunham. *The Unknown Lenders, Part II: Mortgage Company Lending Patterns in Lansing and Grand Rapids, Michigan.* Chicago: Woodstock Institute, 1993.

Journal of Housing Economics. Duluth, MN: Academic Press, 1991– . Quarterly.

Kidd, Phillip E. *Mortgage Banking 1963 to 1972: A Financial Intermediary in Transition.* Credit Research Center Monograph, no. 5. West Lafayette, IN: Purdue University, Krannert Graduate School of Management, 1977.

Kinney, James M., and Richard T. Garrigan. *The Handbook of Mortgage Banking: A Guide to the Secondary Mortgage Market.* Homewood, IL: Dow Jones-Irwin, 1985.

Klaman, Saul B. *The Postwar Rise of Mortgage Companies.* Washington, DC: National Bureau of Economic Research, 1959.

LaMalfa, Tom. "A Varied Breed: Mortgage Brokers." *Mortgage Banking* 59, no. 7 (April 1999): 92–102.

Lederman, Jess, ed. *The Handbook of Mortgage Banking: Trends, Opportunities, and Strategies.* Rev. ed. Chicago: Probus, 1993.

Madden, John Thomas, and Marcus Nadler. *Foreign Securities: Public and Mortgage Bank Bonds—An Analysis of the Financial, Legal, and Political Factors.* New York: Ronald Press, 1929.

Mazzagetti, Dominick A. *Structuring Mortgage Banking Transactions.* Boston: Warren, Gorham, & Lamont, 1996.

McDonough, J. E. "The Federal Home Loan Bank System." *American Economic Review* 24, no. 4 (December 1934): 668–85.

McTague, Jim. "Fannie's Foes." *Barron's,* April 26, 1999.

Money. Chicago: Time, 1972– . Monthly.

"MortgageAuction.com Launches Online Home Financing Auction." *Mortgage Banking* 59, no. 7 (April 1999): 112.

Mortgage Banker. Washington, DC: Mortgage Bankers Association of America, 1939–1981. Monthly.

Mortgage Bankers Associated with Savings Institutions: A Directory of Subsidiary Operations. Chicago: United States League of Savings Institutions, 1990.

Mortgage Banking. Washington, DC: Mortgage Bankers Association of America, 1981– . Monthly.

National Real Estate Investor. Atlanta: Communication Channels, 1959– .

National Underwriter. Chicago: National Underwriter, 1917– . Weekly.

O'Leary, Christopher. "Fannie Mae Buying Spree, Street Hire Signal New Push." *Investment Dealers' Digest,* March 15, 1999, 9–10.

Persons, Charles E. "Credit Expansion, 1920–1929, and Its Lessons." *Quarterly Journal of Economics* 45, no. 1 (November 1930): 94–130.

Peterson, James R. "Commercial Mortgage Conduits Bounce Back." *ABA Banking Journal* 91, no. 4 (April 1999): 55–56.

Pope, Jesse E. "Agricultural Credit in the United States." *Quarterly Journal of Economics* 28, no. 4 (August 1914): 701–46.

Real Estate Finance. Boston: Federal Research Press, 1984– . Quarterly.

Real Estate Finance Journal. Boston: Warren, Gorham, & Lamont, 1985– . Quarterly.

Redstone, Allan J. "Mortgage Shopping in the Future." *Mortgage Banking* 59, no. 7 (April 1999): 86–90.

Reiss, Dale Ann, and Joseph Duncan. "The Consolidation Trend." *Mortgage Banking* 49, no. 5 (February 1989): 62–66.

Robinson, Louis N. "The Morris Plan." *American Economic Review* 21, no. 2 (June 1931): 222–35.

"Secondary Market Support Is Key." *Mortgage Banking* 59, no. 7 (April 1999): 62–63.

Secondary Mortgage Markets. Washington, DC: Federal Home Loan Mortgage Corp., Economic Research Department, 1984– . Quarterly.

"Servicers on Their Hedging Strategies." *Mortgage Banking* 59, no. 7 (April 1999): 28.

Stock, James H. "Real Estate Mortgages, Foreclosures, and Midwestern Agrarian Unrest, 1865–1920." *Journal of Economic History* 44, no. 1 (March 1984): 89–105.

Townsend, Anthony M., and Anthony Hendrickson. "The Internet and Mortgage Brokerage: New Challenges, New Opportunities." *Real Estate Finance Journal* 14, no. 4 (Spring 1999): 11–14.

U.S. Congress. Conference Committees. *The Federal Farm Loan Act.* Washington, DC: U.S. Government Printing Office, 1916.

U.S. Congress. Congressional Budget Office. *The Federal Home Loan Banks in the Housing Finance System.* Washington, DC: Congress of the United States, Congressional Budget Office, 1993.

U.S. Congress. House. Committee on Agriculture. *Cooperative Land-Mortgage Banks.* Washington, DC: U.S. Government Printing Office, 1912.

———. House. Committee on Banking, Finance, and Urban Affairs. Subcommittee on Consumer Affairs and Coinage. *H.R. 5170, the Mortgage Refinancing Reform Act of 1992.* Hearings. 102 Cong., 2d sess., May 27, 1992. Serial no. 102–126.

———. House. Committee on Banking, Finance, and Urban Affairs. Subcommittee on Housing and Community Development. *The Federal Home Loan Bank System.* Hearings. 102d Cong., 2d sess., June 9, 10, and 11, 1992. Serial no. 102–129.

———. House. Committee on Banking, Finance, and Urban Affairs. Subcommittee on Consumer Credit and Insurance. *Community Investment Practices of Mortgage Banks.* Hearings. 103d Cong., 2d sess., September 28, 1994. Serial no. 103–167.

———. House. Committee on Banking and Financial Services. Subcommittee on Capital Markets, Securities, and Government Sponsored Enterprises. *Oversight Hearing on Federal Home Loan Bank System.* Hearings. 104th Cong., 1st sess., September 27, 28, 1995. Serial no. 104–33.

———. House. Committee on Banking and Financial Services. Subcommittee on Capital Markets, Securities, and Government Sponsored Enterprises. *Over-*

sight of the Federal National Mortgage Association (Fannie Mae) and the Federal Home Loan Mortgage Corporation (Freddie Mac). Hearings. 104th Cong., 2d sess., April 17, June 12, July 24, 31, August 1, 1996. Serial no. 104–55.

———. House. Committee on Rules. *Authorize Payment of Farm-Loan Mortgages with Bonds Issued by the Mortgagee Banks*. Washington, DC: U.S. Government Printing Office, 1932.

U.S. Congress. Senate. Committee on Banking, Housing, and Urban Affairs. Subcommittee on Housing and Urban Affairs. *Housing Institutions Modernization Act of 1971*. Hearings on S. 1617. 92d Cong., 1st sess., October 13–15, 1971.

———. Senate. Committee on Banking, Housing, and Urban Affairs. Subcommittee on Housing and Urban Affairs. *FNMA-FHLMC Underwriting*. Hearings. 95th Cong., 2d sess., December 19, 1978.

U.S. Department of Agriculture. *Guaranteed Farm Operating Loans for Socially Disadvantaged Persons*. Program Aid no. 1511. Washington, DC: U.S. Department of Agriculture, Farmers Home Administration, 1993.

———. *Increase Volume & Expand into Untapped Rural Markets with the Guaranteed Rural Housing Loan Program*. Program Aid no. 1555. Washington, DC: U.S. Department of Agriculture, 1995.

U.S. Department of Housing and Urban Development. *H.O.W. Homeownership Opportunities for Women: National Partners in Homeownership*. Washington, DC: U.S. Department of Housing and Urban Development, 1996a.

———. *Privatization of Fannie Mae and Freddie Mac: Desirability and Feasibility*. Washington, DC: U.S. Department of Housing and Urban Development, Office of Policy Development and Research, 1996b.

U.S. General Accounting Office. *FNMA and FHLMC Benefits Derived from Federal Ties*. GAO/GGD-96–98R. Washington, DC: General Accounting Office, General Government Division, 1996a.

———. *FNMA and FHLMC Rates of Return*. GAO/GGD-96–157R. Washington, DC: General Accounting Office, General Government Division, 1996b.

U.S. Laws, Statutes, etc. *Laws Pertaining to Agricultural Short Term and Intermediate Credit Unions*. Washington, DC: U.S. Government Printing Office, 1936.

Walsh, Thomas James. *Federal Farm Loan Act*. Washington, DC: U.S. Government Printing Office, 1916.

Whiteside, Deborah. *The Evolution of Mortgage Banking*. Washington, DC: Mortgage Bankers Association of America, 1983.

Wiprud, Arne Clarence. *The Federal Farm Loan System*. St. Paul, MN: Virtue Printing, 1919.

———. *The Federal Farm-Loan System in Operation*. New York: Harper & Brothers, 1921.

Part VIII

Insurance Carriers
ESIC 63.0

CHAPTER 12

MEDICAL SERVICE AND HEALTH INSURANCE, 63.2

Marvin N. Fischbaum

From modest beginnings health expenditures in the United States have increased to more than $500 billion, or over 11 percent of national income. The nation's spending on healthcare, whether measured on a per capita basis or as a percentage of national income, is the highest in the world. The magnitude and variability of these expenses have made the issue of financing healthcare a primary public concern. In most industrialized countries healthcare finance has evolved from reliance on direct payment, to some use of voluntary insurance, to a broader pattern of subsidized insurance, and then to comprehensive compulsory insurance. In the United Kingdom healthcare finance evolved one step further to government administration through the National Health Service (Starr 1982a).

In the United States no single system of paying for healthcare predominates. Government both finances and provides health services directly through military hospitals, veterans hospitals, the National Institutes of Health, state hospitals for the chronically ill, and municipally owned acute care or general hospitals. Medicaid combines government finance with the private provision of healthcare. Medicare Part A is an example of compulsory health insurance; Medicare Part B is subsidized voluntary insurance. Blue Cross and Blue Shield offer voluntary health insurance through not-for-profit entities. Commercial insurers include both stock and mutual companies. A variety of health maintenance organizations provide healthcare on a prepayment basis. Others involved in the financing of healthcare include fraternal societies, mutual benefit societies, unions, and employers. Direct payment and charity are still important elements in the healthcare payment picture. This hodgepodge reflects not only a complex history, for older methods of finance coexist with recent innovations, but also a national ambivalence toward market mechanisms for financing healthcare.

THE EARLY PERIOD—SICKNESS INSURANCE

While health insurance in its modern form is conventionally dated to 1929 (Califano 1986), the earliest U.S. experiments with prepaying, or insuring against, the costs of sickness date to the middle of the nineteenth century. In calling the coverage sickness insurance, Americans followed the practice of the literal Germans rather than that of the fastidious English. Coverage from commercial insurers, fraternal organizations, and establishment funds began at that time.

Commercial health insurance dates to the chartering of the Massachusetts Health Insurance Company of Boston in 1847. That company, as well as a number of imitators, soon failed. Much more successful was the Travelers Insurance Company, chartered in 1863. Initially, Travelers adopted the British practice of providing trip insurance for railroad passengers. The policy evolved quickly, and soon an annual premium covered accident hazards fairly inclusively (Faulkner 1960).

In 1890 a mutual casualty company, the Saint Lawrence Life Association, added a health insurance rider to its accident policy. The Federal Life and Casualty Company of Detroit entered the market in 1891, followed by the more general entrance of casualty companies between 1897 and 1899. Policies insured primarily against loss of income, typically for a period of up to six months, but limited coverage to specified diseases and could be canceled at any time. Early commercial insurers in the United States set rates based on the underwriting experience of the British friendly societies (Faulkner 1960). Policies covering most diseases were introduced in 1903; a noncancelable policy became available in 1907, and lifetime disability coverage dates to 1910 (Osler 1952). About 1913 large life insurance companies, including Metropolitan Life and Connecticut General, expanded their group industrial life insurance to provide group coverage for accident and sickness policies (Follmann 1963). From then until 1930 policy coverage changed only slightly (Faulkner 1960).

Businessmen and professionals constituted the primary market for commercial accident and health insurance. Policies paid a weekly indemnity in instances of disabling sickness or accident. Medical benefits were usually included in the policy but approximated only 10 percent of benefits paid, or between 5 and 6 percent of premiums earned. Most policies paid an indemnity for hospitalization equal to 25 to 100 percent of the weekly indemnity and paid surgical benefits according to a schedule. As benefits emphasized loss of income rather than medical expenses, policies were not ordinarily offered to those under eighteen or over sixty-five or to women. Occupations were rated, and all blue-collar occupations entailed at least an element of hazard. The broadest coverage was available only to the highest-rated categories, and premiums increased with perceived risk. With few exceptions health insurance was available only in conjunction with accident insurance. In 1930 total premiums written on accident and health insurance totaled slightly over $150 million (Williams 1932).

Fraternal societies, the providers of the second type of sickness insurance, evolved from European antecedents, especially British. When Britain adopted compulsory national health insurance in 1911, it utilized the existing network of friendly societies. These social associations of ordinary workers afforded both fellowship and help to members in need, and their insurance or self-help features were noted approvingly by Daniel Defoe in 1697. Initially, friendly societies offering sickness insurance were undercapitalized and often failed until underwriting experience, government regulation, and nationwide networks of societies like the Odd Fellows, Druids, and Foresters shored them up in the nineteenth century (Levy 1944). In the 1840s the Odd Fellows introduced sickness benefits in the United States. The initial benefits schedule had to be scaled back because of unexpectedly high expenses, but the concept survived (Cassedy 1986). By the first decade of the twentieth century, an estimated 25 to 30 percent of American workers were members of fraternal societies (Starr 1982a). While American lodges universally followed the British practice of furnishing life insurance, provisions for dealing with a sickness were spotty. In 1914 only 3 of 179 societies provided sickness insurance to a national membership (Schwartz 1965).

More often benefits were provided by local chapters of fraternal orders and by immigrant benefit societies (Starr 1982a). In San Francisco *La Société Francaise de Bienfaisance Mutuelle* operated a hospital for its members as early as 1851; three years later, the German Benevolent Society established its hospital. Cigar makers in Tampa and Jewish immigrants in New York held membership in lodges that paid doctors about a dollar a year per covered individual. More generally, lodges paid modest weekly benefits to partially compensate for lost earnings. At their peak early in the twentieth century, fraternal organizations may have covered the largest proportion of those with sickness benefits. In New York, of the 170,000 covered by sickness insurance, over 100,000 received benefits during 1914 from fraternal organizations (Schwartz 1965).

The third source of sickness insurance was associated with employment. Coverage and control varied considerably. Benefits were provided by unions or by funds organized within an establishment by workers, or by management, or jointly. Establishment-based plans were concentrated in dangerous industries and in remote locations.

Before 1930 only a small, generally skilled minority of workers belonged to unions. A survey in 1907 found that of 125 national unions, only 19 provided sickness benefits. These unions represented 375,000 workers and paid $830,000 in benefits. Of 530 local unions surveyed, 346 provided sickness benefits, but these locals employed only 100,000 workers, and benefits totaled just $200,000 (Rubinow 1913).

Company-controlled funds were more significant than union funds. In 1907 company funds covered over 600,000 workers and provided over $3,200,000 in benefits (Rubinow 1913). By 1930, 540,000 workers in the mining and lumber industries and an additional 530,000 workers employed by railways, along with southern textile workers and a scattering elsewhere in manufacturing, had some sort of company-controlled coverage. Increasingly, especially in remote areas, companies provided service benefits in addition to, or instead of, a fixed indemnity per week of disability. To the chagrin of organized medicine, companies often ran their own clinics or hospitals or contracted with healthcare providers (Williams 1932).

Mutual benefit associations grew out of the tradition of passing the hat for workers in need. Dues and benefits were modest, but workers and the companies funded the associations and to varying degrees shared organizational control. A 1928 survey put membership within responding firms at 758,000—76 percent of the employees in those firms (Williams 1932).

A wide miscellany of approaches to healthcare financing are of interest, but more for novelty than for impact. Some evolved from employment-based healthcare arrangements. Six manufacturing establishments in Roanoke Rapids, North Carolina, a town of 10,000 population, joined together in 1914 to bring adequate healthcare facilities to the community. By 1930 employees of those firms, along with schoolteachers, could receive medical and hospital service for a fixed monthly charge (Williams 1932). In Washington State and Oregon, lumber and railway companies contracted with physician groups for medical services. County medical societies in those two states responded by offering service contracts (Goldmann 1948).

By 1930 millions of Americans were eligible for compensation in the event of disabling illness, but in most cases the benefits fell far short of the costs. A survey of Chicago workers for the twelve months beginning July 1917 found that although 23.7 percent had some sort of sickness insurance, benefits paid only 5.9 percent of lost wages (Morgan 1922). In a 1919 report to the Ohio Insurance Commission, John R. Commons estimated that about 35 percent of workers had some insurance, but it covered no more than 10 to 15 percent of risk (Commons and Altmeyer 1919). In 1929 an estimated $177.9 million for accident and health insurance premiums and $51 million for mutual benefit association premiums totaled less than 10 percent of the $2.4 billion cost of medical care (Avnet 1944). By 1930 the major European states had already adopted compulsory national health insurance. Why, then, was there so little coverage in the United States, and why were the vehicles of coverage so heterogeneous?

ECONOMIC THEORY AND THE QUESTION OF HEALTH INSURANCE

Health insurance in the United States before 1929 was rare; benefits were small, and deductibles typically excluded the first week of disability. In an *American Economic Review* article in 1963, Kenneth Arrow demonstrates that if actuarially fair insurance could be provided, risk-averse individuals would demand complete insurance. Administrative costs would lead to deductibles, and the insurance company's aversion to risk, combined with insufficient scale to eliminate risks, would encourage coinsurance. Arrow (1963) speculates that many redistributive government programs simply provide social insurance that markets neglect. Much of the socially desirable health insurance is not available because moral hazard makes coverage unattractive to commercial providers. He suggests that increasing the scope of health insurance, possibly through government programs, would improve social well-being.

To insurance companies, moral hazard describes the loss experience of a population covered by insurance that is worse than the loss experience of the general population. In a response to Arrow, Mark V. Pauly (1968) shows that insurance experience will reflect moral hazard whenever the demand for healthcare services obeys the law of demand—when a greater quantity is purchased at lower prices. Furthermore, this source of moral hazard can offset, in part or in its entirety, any gain in utility from risk reduction. Suppose that all individuals are alike and that for a given operation they value the eighth day in the hospital at $600, the ninth day at $300, and the tenth day at $100. If the hospital charges $400 per day, private pay patients will stay in the hospital eight days, whereas those with complete insurance would choose to stay ten days. Insurance policies would have to reflect the $800 cost of the two extra days, even though the gain to social value would be only $400. Coinsurance, and to a degree, deductibles, makes policyholders more responsive to price and thereby reduces moral hazard. Pauly (1968) argues that free markets provide the socially optimal level of insurance.

In "The Market for 'Lemons' " George A. Akerlof (1984) demonstrates that adverse selection can lead to seriously malfunctioning markets. In a broad sense adverse selection is a form of moral hazard. If the population covered by health insurance suffers from a higher rate of morbidity than the population at large, the cost of complete health insurance must be higher than the average expenses of the noninsured. Adverse selection may result from an asymmetrical distribution of knowledge. People who purchase health insurance know more about the status of their own health than do the companies that sell insurance. If everyone purchases health insurance, those sicker than average will find health insurance a good buy.

But if only those anticipating higher than average health expenses purchase health insurance, then only those sicker than the average of those who purchase health insurance will clearly find it a good buy. This process can continue until only the worst risks purchase insurance because the rates are so high, and the rates are so high because only the worst risks purchase insurance. If risks are continuously distributed, without a class of worst risks there may be no market at all (Akerlof 1984). Since the mid-1980s, economic literature on the operation of health insurance markets has shifted focus. Medicare and Medicaid have reduced the concern over gaps in health insurance coverage, allowing economists to refocus on healthcare cost inflation, moral hazard, and second-best optimality (Pauly 1986).

THE BEGINNINGS OF MODERN HEALTH INSURANCE

American mythology ascribes health insurance to the Blue Cross movement, a plan devised by Justin H. Kimball in 1929. While the truth may be more complex, the myth is a useful point of departure. Kimball, executive vice president of Baylor University, was responsible for the university's medical center. Earlier, he had been superintendent of the Dallas public schools and a lawyer with insurance companies. Reviewing the sick benefits records of schoolteachers and the records of the Baylor University Hospital, Kimball estimated the teachers' hospital expenses at fifteen cents per month. Under Kimball's Baylor plan, teachers were offered coverage for specified hospital services for fifty cents per month; three-fourths of them signed up. Schoolteachers made an ideal group because they had job security and earned too much to be eligible for charity care but not enough to be safe from catastrophic hospital costs. The Baylor plan was quickly extended, first to employees of the *Dallas News*, then to other groups. Other Dallas hospitals soon implemented competing prepayment arrangements (Anderson 1975).

Pierce Williams (1932) could find little difference between the Baylor University plan and the plans offered at Roanoke Rapids, North Carolina, since 1917 and at Grinnell, Iowa, since 1918. All three plans provided a limited schedule of hospital service benefits for a fixed periodic payment, but Baylor and Roanoke Rapids limited enrollees to members of specified employee groups. In Dallas, however, group enrollment afforded an essential mechanism for avoiding adverse selection, whereas the isolated location of Grinnell and Roanoke Rapids inherently limited the problem. After 1929 rapidly declining revenues increased hospital administrators' receptivity toward experimentation. The Baylor plan was discussed at the 1931 meetings of the American Hospital Association (Anderson 1975).

Service benefit plans provided by a single hospital gave way to multi-hospital plans organized on a community basis. In 1932 Frank Van Dyke started the first large-scale community plan in Newark, New Jersey; a year later, E. A. van Steenwyk organized a community plan in St. Paul, Minnesota. Rufus Rorem took the lead in advising communities on how to establish community hospital insurance. Initially, Rorem had worked out of the Julius Rosenwald Foundation but later received a grant from the foundation to the American Hospital Association. Rorem would serve as executive director of the Blue Cross Association from its inception in 1936 until 1946 (Anderson 1975, 1985).

The American Hospital Association (AHA) and local hospital councils considered single hospital plans competitive. To promote the advantages of the community plans to the public, the AHA and the local councils emphasized that subscribers were permitted free choice of hospital and physician. The AHA lobbied successfully for legislation that exempted hospital service corporations from state regulation of insurance providers. By 1937 subscribers to community-wide plans outnumbered those in single-hospital plans by 800,000 to 125,000; by 1938 enrollment in Blue Cross plans had reached 1.4 million (Law 1974; Starr 1982a).

The Baylor plan was similar to modern health maintenance organizations (HMOs) as well as to Blue Cross; subscribers were limited to benefits from a single provider. In 1929 the Ross-Loos Clinic began providing comprehensive, prepaid medical and hospital care, initially to members of the Los Angeles Department of Water and Power. Ross-Loos has evolved into a substantial HMO but initially was no dramatic departure from contract medicine in the Pacific Northwest. Perhaps the biggest stir of 1929 was created by physician Michael Shadid. With financial help from the Oklahoma Farmers' Union, Shadid organized a cooperative Hospital Association in Elk City, Oklahoma, where he drew the ire of local physicians and the AMA in a conflict that attracted national attention. Another physician, Sidney Garfield, provided prepaid healthcare as early as 1933 and beginning in 1938 treated the employees of Henry J. Kaiser. His efforts evolved into the Kaiser-Permanente Foundations (Starr 1982a).

In the 1930s the leadership of the American Medical Association (AMA) was concerned that voluntary insurance could be a way station to compulsory insurance and that insurance covering physician fees could intrude into the doctor–patient relationship. Service benefits, in particular, interfered with physicians' adjusting fees according to a patient's ability to pay (Clark 1962). Medical insurance sponsored by county medical societies in Washington State and Oregon was tolerated only because it was a response to the growth of contract medical practices for employed groups (Anderson 1985; Goldmann 1948). As late as 1938 the AMA opposed any plan that paid service benefits instead of indemnities; but the following year the California Medical Association, responding to the threat of compulsory insurance in the state, sponsored a plan that provided service benefits to families with annual incomes under $3,000 and indemnity benefits for those above that income level. Other medical societies followed suit, generally keeping to the split service-indemnity approach. In 1942 the AMA tacitly approved service benefits but only in plans sponsored by state medical societies; within a year the AMA had created a commission similar to Blue Cross to coordinate the societies' plans. Thus, the AMA found itself the sponsor, albeit reluctant, of Blue Shield (Starr 1982a).

The Great Depression and competition from Blue Cross spurred a metamorphosis in commercial insurance. As group sales of sickness insurance declined, the ratio of benefits to premiums rose on individual policies. Commercial hospitalization insurance was first offered in 1934. At first covering only the employee and not the family, this insurance paid a fixed indemnity set at three dollars per day. Underwriters gradually liberalized policies by reducing the minimum group size, including dependents, providing flexible benefits, and offering the option of surgical coverage. Most firms supplying hospital insurance were small, and many were specialized. In 1940 commercial hospital insurance covered 2.5 million people; Blue Cross, over 6 million (Clark 1962).

THE GROWTH DECADES

Between 1940 and 1960 the number of Americans with hospital insurance increased from 12 million to 122.5 million, and those with surgical coverage rose from 4.9 million to over 111.5 million (Health Insurance Association of America 1983). Employers' group policies protected wage earners and their families, but the self-employed and casually employed, the unemployed and unemployable—as well as their dependents—and the elderly were without insurance (Somers and Somers 1961).

Government policies contributed to the rapid growth in the medical services industry. During World War II, a wage freeze made it almost impossible for businesses to recruit in the tight labor market, so in 1942 the National War Labor Board's approving wage increases in the form of nonwage benefits opened the floodgates to fringe benefits, especially health insurance (Anderson 1975; Fein 1986). Tax policies that allowed employer contributions to health insurance to be deducted as a cost without taxing employees on those contributions encouraged companies to expand their benefits. But the clearest immediate stimulus came from a ruling by the Supreme Court. In the *Inland Steel* case, settled in 1948, the Court established the right of unions under the Taft-Hartley Act to bargain collectively for welfare benefits and to strike if agreement could not be reached. The settlement in an ensuing strike established a nationwide pattern of health insurance in the steel industry; a similar pattern of coverage was quickly adopted in the automobile industry (Munts 1967; Clark 1962; Follmann 1963).

Commercial insurers proved aggressively competitive, and the large life insurance firms soon dominated sales. By 1957 commercial insurers had overtaken the Blue plans, at least in numbers covered (Clark 1962). Those gains had required their overcoming advantages held by the Blues. In addition to their early start, the Blues were exempt from federal income taxes and were not only tax-exempt in most states but also the beneficiaries of special legislation exempting them from insurance regulation and financial reserve requirements (Sindelar 1988). Moreover, in the industrial Northeast, hospitals and physicians granted substantial discounts to Blue Cross and Blue Shield (Frech 1988).

Critics argue that the Blues spent their advantages on administrative slack and the wrong kinds of insurance. H. E. Frech and Paul B. Ginsburg (1978) found a positive correlation between the administrative costs of a Blue Cross plan and its tax advantage over commercial rivals. The Blues, organized and controlled by providers, structured insurance benefits in the interests of hospitals and doctors. Specifically, first dollar coverage or low deductibles combined with little or no coinsurance stimulated high expenditures on healthcare and facilitated higher prices (Frech 1988). In *Blue Cross: What Went Wrong?* Sylvia A. Law (1974) emphasizes that Blue plans did not use their market power to constrain costs or regulate the providers.

Defenders disputed the critics' claim that the Blues were soft or inefficient, pointing out that they returned a larger percentage of premiums as benefits than the commercials did; their more complete coverage, they asserted, reflected consumer preferences (Berman 1978). The Blues lost market share partly because of the lack of geographical coordination—each of the plans was autonomous. Insured patients requiring out-of-district healthcare encountered difficulties that were lessened but not removed by the interplan service bank developed in 1946 and implemented in 1949. Providing uniform benefits to a firm's employees across the country proved a more serious problem, one resolved by establishing a syndicate for each contract, an approach that enabled Blue Cross to win the first collectively bargained health insurance agreements in the steel industry (Anderson 1975).

Their reliance on community rating was the heart of the Blues' competitive disadvantage: whatever the composition of a group, old or young, sick or healthy, rich or poor, blue-collar or professional, the rate per insured was the same. Information was not used to discriminate among risks. Community rating stemmed from a conscious desire to subsidize high risks on the assumption that such subsidies serve the public interest. Commercial insurers preferred experience rating. Groups with more favorable composition were attracted by the commercials' lower rates, leaving Blue Cross and Blue Shield with an increasingly adverse pool of risk (Fein 1986). Pressed by the competition, Blue Cross adopted a more flexible underwriting policy and stabilized market share.

CAMPAIGNS FOR COMPULSORY HEALTH INSURANCE

After two decades of rapid growth in voluntary insurance furnished through employment groups, most Americans enjoyed substantial protection against the financial hazards of illness. The success of the system emphasized the remaining pockets of uninsured. John F. Kennedy's election to the presidency in November 1960 revived a long-standing drive for compulsory insurance.

That drive had begun near the end of the Progressive Era, after the adoption of compulsory health insurance in Britain in 1911. The American Association for Labor Legislation (AALL) led the fight for comprehensive social insurance comprising workmen's compensation, sickness insurance, old age pensions, and unemployment insurance. Membership in the AALL was broadly based, but social scientists, especially economists, eventually dominated the leadership. Reflecting the European experience, the AALL sought a natural progression in social legislation, and after securing workmen's compensation, the association concentrated its energy on the next stage, sickness insurance. The AALL formulated model legislation, then sought its adoption state by state (Lubove 1968; Fox 1986).

Initially, reformers were optimistic. The leadership of the American Medical Association was sympathetic. Spokesmen for the National Association of Manufacturers and the National Civic Federation appeared dubious but were not implacably opposed to comprehensive social insurance. Samuel Gompers, president of the American Federation of Labor, came out against the model legislation, but the concept itself found favor among other labor leaders. Lobbyists for insurance companies predictably opposed legislation that would close out markets.

Optimism waned when it became clear that practicing physicians feared compulsory insurance, viewing it as an opening gambit that could lead to further state control. State medical societies led the attack on the proposed legislation. The AMA leadership backed off from its initial support, and that leadership was replaced by a group unalterably opposed to any move in the direction of state financing of medicine. A number of legislatures in large industrial states debated the AALL's model bills, but in the end not a single state adopted compulsory health insurance (Starr 1982a).

Ready to try again by 1926, reformers organized the Committee on the Costs of Medical Care (CCMC). Investigations funded by eight philanthropic foundations enabled the CCMC to provide the first clear picture of the size and composition of the healthcare sector. In 1932 the CCMC published its reports. The majority report did not clearly support compulsory health insurance but favored expansion of voluntary health insurance and government subsidies for individuals with low incomes. Eight of the physicians on the panel submitted a minority report opposing any form of insurance except that controlled by the medical profession. The AMA quickly endorsed the minority report (Starr 1982a).

The prospects for compulsory insurance revived with the coming of the New Deal. When President Franklin D. Roosevelt established the cabinet-level Committee for Economic Security, health insurance was on its agenda. The president and his top advisers decided, however, that passage of Social Security and unemployment insurance should not be imperiled by the attachment of a controversial health insurance proposal. Roosevelt eventually set up the Interdepartmental Committee to Coordinate Health and Welfare Activities and under it a Technical Committee on Medical Care. The Technical Committee listed among its objectives the development of a scheme to finance healthcare. It focused on a barely controversial proposal to provide federal funding for hospital construction (Starr 1982a).

In 1939 Senator Robert Wagner sponsored a comprehensive health bill that contained a provision for financial support to states willing either to pay for healthcare for the indigent or to develop a more general program of health insurance. Roosevelt backed away from the measure. The Wagner-Murray-Dingall bill of 1943 provided for comprehensive national health insurance. Wagner knew the bill had no chance of passage but expected it to pave the way for future legislation (Poen 1979).

Harry S Truman was the first president to come out strongly in favor of national health insurance, and he made the issue a cornerstone of his bid for election in 1948. Successive Wagner-Murray-Dingall bills were introduced during his terms in office. In opposition, the AMA launched the most expensive lobbying effort to that date and successfully associated national health insurance with socialism and anti-American activities (Starr 1982a). All of the Truman-era bills died in committee (Anderson 1985).

There was little action on healthcare issues during the presidency of Dwight D. Eisenhower until Representative Aimee Forand introduced a bill in 1957 to provide hospital insurance for the aged under Social Security. Compulsory health insurance again became a major national issue. The administration responded in 1960 with a plan to provide financial support to those states willing to underwrite health insurance for the aged indigent. The voluntary insurance would contain a deductible in excess of 10 percent of income together with coinsurance. The ensuing debate led to passage of the Kerr-Mills Act, under which federal funding was granted to states that purchased medical assistance for the aged poor (Fein 1986).

President John F. Kennedy actively supported the concept of hospital insurance for the elderly funded through Social Security, now called the King-Anderson bill, but made little headway with Congress. President Lyndon B. Johnson had somewhat greater success in 1964, steering the program, by then known as Medicare, through the Senate but not through a House-Senate conference.

With the Democratic landslide in the 1964 election, passage of Medicare seemed assured. Opponents waged a last-ditch effort, offering substitute proposals that focused on gaps in Medicare coverage. Eldercare, the program of the AMA, was limited to the poor but included physician fees as well as hospital costs. The Republican alternative, sponsored by Congressman James Byrnes, proposed voluntary participation by the elderly in a program that would also include out-of-hospital expenses. These efforts yielded a quite different result from that intended. Rather than substitute a more limited insurance scheme, Congress grafted onto Medicare elements from rival legislation. The King-Anderson proposal, expanded in terms of days covered, became Medicare Part A—mandatory hospital coverage for the elderly funded through Social Security. The Republican proposal inspired Medicare Part B—voluntary insurance for physician fees subsidized by revenues from the general fund. Medicare used ideas from Eldercare, a quantum leap from Kerr-Mills. The law enacted was larger, more comprehensive, more expensive than any sponsor had thought possible (Fein 1986).

Even before the passage of Medicare many Americans had supported greater U.S. spending on healthcare. After 1965 medical costs exploded. The issue of national health insurance did not suddenly go away, but increasingly the debate was couched in terms of expected effect on total healthcare spending. Opponents argued that the country could ill afford national health insurance; proponents contended that countries with national health insurance spent a smaller proportion of national income on healthcare than the United States did. When Senator Edward Kennedy proposed a Health Security Act in 1969, he included incentives for prepaid group practice as a way to constrain costs. Between 1969 and 1974 momentum for national health insurance seemed to grow, and many—proponents and opponents alike—thought its eventual adoption inevitable. Other major proposals by 1974 included one authored by Abraham Ribicoff providing catastrophic coverage only and one supported by the Richard M. Nixon administration mandating that employers provide insurance meeting specified minimum standards. A compromise Kennedy-Mills bill never made it out of committee, and the issue of national health insurance faded (Fein 1986).

As healthcare costs escalated in the last quarter of the twentieth century, legislators shifted their priorities from providing adequate insurance coverage to constraining expenditures. Facilitated by new legislation, mechanisms for third-party payment have evolved with increasing rapidity. These changes threaten the existence of the health insurance industry.

A 1972 act establishing Professional Service Review Organizations, whereby outside physicians would monitor Medicare claims, was symbolically important, for it signaled that Congress was willing to question even the authority of physicians in its effort to rein in costs. The law had little tangible impact, however (Anderson 1985).

The HMO legislation of 1973 was more significant. The act superseded state laws, established standards, and provided financial start-up assistance. Furthermore, it required employers with group health insurance to offer employees the option, when available, of subscribing to a qualified HMO. In 1973 prepaid group practices (like Kaiser-Permanente and Ross-Loos) and independent practice associations (like the San Joaquin County Foundation for Medical Care) enrolled a stable population of about 3.6 million. HMO enrollment increased slowly at first but accelerated in the 1980s, reaching 16.7 million in 1985 (Fein 1986; Frech and Ginsburg 1988). Between 1981 and 1987 HMO membership grew from 4 percent of the workers covered by group health plans to 16 percent (Gabel et al. 1988). Large life insurance companies have entered the HMO business and in the process have become healthcare providers.

In exempting self-insured health plans from state regulation, the Employment Retirement Income and Security Act (ERISA), passed in 1974, conferred on self-insured plans the advantages that Blue Cross once had over commercial carriers. Beyond the avoidance of taxes and burdensome reserve requirements, self-insured plans are also exempt from meeting mandated specifications of minimum coverage or from supporting assigned risk pools. In one survey, the percentage of firms self-insuring rose from 21 to 42 between 1981 and 1985; half of that increase came in 1984 (Jensen and Gabel 1988). Another study showed 52 percent of employers self-insuring in 1987 (Gabel et al. 1988). Insurance companies still administer the financing of healthcare, but with the growth of self-insurance and HMOs, their insurance responsibilities are diminishing.

The administration of healthcare finance is not passive. Increasingly, third-party payers manage healthcare. While Medicare initially followed the lead of Blue Cross in paying retrospectively on the basis of usual, customary, and reasonable charges, it switched in 1983 to prospective payment based on expected cost within diagnostic related groups. A set price replaced cost plus. Prospective payment is increasingly popular with the states in administering Medicaid and with commercial insurers as well. Preferred provider organizations (PPOs) constitute a second level of managed care midway between a closed panel HMO and complete freedom of choice. Enrollees in PPOs are encouraged through differential rates of coinsurance to select those "preferred providers" willing to limit charges to the insurer. By 1987, 11 percent of the employees in firms with group health plans were covered by PPOs (Gabel et al. 1988).

The adoption of managed care concepts, even in conventional insurance, has been swift. Preadmission certification was required of no more than 5 percent of the employees in conventional plans in 1984. The number rose to 20 percent in 1986 and to 42 percent in 1987. Mandatory second opinions have expanded at a similar pace (Gabel et al. 1988).

When William J. Clinton assumed the presidency of the United States in 1993, he immediately addressed national healthcare. Assuming his election was a mandate for universal healthcare, the president commissioned studies to lay the framework for legislation (Reams, 1996). The issue was more volatile than expected, and the negative response may have been responsible for Clinton's loss of the Democratic control of Congress to the Republicans in the first off-year elections of his tenure in office. A reduction in the rate of healthcare cost increases was perhaps a more positive response to the national fear that federal intrusion into healthcare would disrupt the medical care delivery system.

In the last decade of the twentieth century, medical care cost inflation slowed before reaccelerating in 1998. Mechanisms for financing medical care and indeed the very nature of the healthcare delivery system continue in a state of flux.

BIBLIOGRAPHIC ESSAY

The Social Transformation of American Medicine is an excellent starting point for a study of the history of healthcare in the United States since Paul Starr (1982a) places special emphasis on the role of healthcare financing. The unpublished and dated (1962) dissertation by David Henry Clark is still useful. Odin W. Anderson (1985) and Rashi Fein (1986) focus on public policy issues as well as historical perspectives.

Because there is no compendium of the early development of health and sickness insurance, researchers must depend on contemporary accounts. Particularly impressive are the studies associated with the American Association for Labor Legislation (AALL), especially Isaac M. Rubinow's *Social Insurance* (1913) and the work commissioned by the Committee on the Costs of Medical Care (CCMC), most particularly Williams' *Purchase of Medical Care through Fixed Periodic Payment* (1932). A chapter in Follmann (1963) may still be the best concise statement of the history of commercial health insurance.

The familiarity of the Blue Cross story may stem from the sympathetic, yet scholarly, historical account by Anderson (1975). Law (1974) provides a more critical evaluation from a consumerist perspective, while in a variety of articles Frech criticizes Blue Cross from the very different perspective of an advocate of free markets.

The economics of health insurance has attracted scholars who have produced a complex body of work. The review article by Pauly (1986) is the logical point of entry into this literature.

The continuing debate over publicly mandated health insurance has been well chronicled. Roy Lubove (1968) documents the story of the AALL and its attempts to pass legislation state by state. Ronald L. Numbers (1978) relates how initial sympathy to that legislation within the medical elite turned to strident opposition when rank-and-file physicians found their voice. The story of the efforts within the bureaucracy of the New Deal to put the issue of compulsory health insurance on the national agenda is told by Daniel S. Hirshfield (1970). Monte M. Poen (1979) takes up where Hirshfield leaves off and relates the virulent debate over national health insurance during the Truman years. The final push that led to Medicare and Medicaid has been documented repeatedly, but Theodore R. Marmor's 1973 study is most often referred to. In *American Health Care Blues*, Irwin Miller (1996) relates how the Blue Cross and Blue Shield Association sponsored HMOs as an option for its subscribers.

Jack E. Fincham and Albert I. Wertheimer's *Pharmacy and the U.S. Health Care System* (1998) comprises eighteen essays in which healthcare professionals address a wide range of issues facing the American medical system at the end of the twentieth century. John R. Wolfe (1993) looks to the future of American healthcare for the aged in *The Coming Health Crisis: Who Will Pay for Care for the Aged in the 21st Century?*, and Eli Ginzberg, in *Tomorrow's Hospital: A Look to the Twenty-first Century* (1996), evaluates the current status and the future of America's more than 5,000 hospitals as he anticipates the effect of social and economic change on rural, suburban, and academic medical centers.

Periodicals yield the most current information on recent developments. The following are useful: *Health Affairs; Health Care Financing Review; Inquiry; Journal of Health Politics, Policy and Law; Milbank Quarterly*. Moreover, guides to the literature are helpful in directing research. A recent one is Barbara A. Haley and Brian Deevey's *American Health Care in Transition: A Guide to the Literature* (1997).

BIBLIOGRAPHY

Aaron, Henry J. *Serious and Unstable Condition: Financing America's Health Care.* Washington, DC: Brookings Institution, 1991.

Ackroyd, Ted J. *Health and Medical Economics: A Guide to Information Sources.* Detroit: Gale Research, 1977.

Akerlof, George A. "The Market for 'Lemons': Quality Uncertainty and the Market Mechanism." In *An Economic Theorist's Book of Tales: Essays That Entertain the Consequences of New Assumptions in Economic Theory*, 7–22. New York: Cambridge University Press, 1984.

Altman, Stuart H., Uwe E. Reinhardt, and David Shactman, eds. *Regulating Managed Care: Theory, Practice, and Future Options.* San Francisco: Jossey-Bass, 1999.

American Association of Health Plans (AAHP). *The Regulation of Health Plans: A*

Report from the American Association of Health Plans. Washington, DC: AAHP, 1998.

Anderson, Odin W. *Blue Cross since 1929: Accountability and the Public Trust.* Cambridge, MA: Ballinger, 1975.

———. *Health Services in the United States: A Growth Enterprise since 1875.* Ann Arbor, MI: Health Administration Press, 1985.

Andrews, Theodora. *A Bibliography of the Socioeconomic Aspects of Medicine.* Littleton, CO: Libraries Unlimited, 1975.

Arrow, Kenneth J. "Uncertainty and the Welfare Economics of Medical Care." *American Economic Review* 53 (December 1963): 941–73.

Avnet, Helen Hershfield. *Voluntary Medical Insurance in the United States: Major Trends and Current Problems.* New York: Medical Administration Service, 1944.

Ayres, Stephen M. *Health Care in the United States: The Facts and the Choices.* The Last Quarter Century, no. 4. Chicago: American Library Association, 1996.

Ball, Robert M. *Reflections on Implementing Medicare: Implementation Aspects of National Health Care Reform.* Washington, DC: National Academy of Social Insurance, 1993.

Berman, Howard. Comment on the paper "Competition among Health Insurers." In *Competition in the Health Care Sector: Past, Present, and Future,* edited by Warren Greenberg, 238–61. Proceedings of a conference sponsored by the Bureau of Economics, Federal Trade Commission. Washington, DC: Federal Trade Commission, 1978.

Blades, C. A. et al. *The International Bibliography of Health Economics: A Comprehensive Annotated Guide to English Language Sources since 1914.* New York: Macmillan, 1986.

Boase, Joan Price. *Health Care Reform or Health Care Rationing: A Comparative Study.* Canadian-American Public Policy, no. 26. Orono: University of Maine, Canadian-American Center, 1996.

Brookings Institution. *Bibliography on Health Economics and Related Material.* Chicago: American Medical Association, Council on Medical Service, 1956.

Califano, Joseph A., Jr. *American Health Care Revolution: Who Lives? Who Dies? Who Pays?* New York: Random House, 1986.

Callahan, Michael R., Andrew J. Demetriou, and Thomas E. Dutton. *Combinations and Alliances in the Health Care Industry.* Englewood Cliffs, NJ: Prentice-Hall Law & Business, 1994.

Cassedy, James H. *Medicine and American Growth, 1800–1860.* Madison: University of Wisconsin Press, 1986.

Clark, David Henry. *An Analytical View of the History of Health Insurance, 1910–1959.* Ph.D. diss., University of Wisconsin, 1962. Ann Arbor, MI: University Microfilms, 1975.

Commons, John R., and A. J. Altmeyer. "The Health Insurance Movement in the United States." In *Health, Health Insurance, Old Age Pensions: Report, Recommendations, Dissenting Opinions.* Columbus: Ohio Insurance Commission, 1919.

Culyer, Anthony J., Jack Wiseman, and Arthur Walker. *An Annotated Bibliography of Health Economics: English Language Sources.* New York: St. Martin's Press, 1977.

Drake, David F. *Reforming the Health Care Market: An Interpretive Economic History.* Washington, DC: Georgetown University Press, 1994.

Elmer, J. C. Herbert. "Risky Business? Non-Actuarial Pricing Practices and the Fundamental Viability of Fraternal Sickness Insurers." *Explorations in Economic History* 33 (April 1966): 195–226.

Epstein, Richard A. *Mortal Peril: Our Inalienable Right to Health Care?* Reading, MA: Addison-Wesley, 1997.

Falk, Isidore Sydney. *Security against Sickness: A Study of Health Insurance.* New York: Da Capo Press, 1972.

Faulkner, Edwin J. *Health Insurance.* New York: McGraw-Hill, 1960.

Feigenbaum, Susan. "Risk Bearing in Health Care Finance." In *Health Care and Its Costs: Can the U.S. Afford Adequate Health Care?*, edited by Carl J. Schramm, 105–44. New York: W. W. Norton, 1987.

Fein, Rashi. *Medical Care, Medical Costs: The Search for a Health Insurance Policy.* Cambridge: Harvard University Press, 1986.

Fincham, Jack E., and Albert I. Wertheimer, eds. *Pharmacy and the U.S. Health Care System.* 2d ed. Binghamton, NY: Haworth Press, Pharmaceutical Products Press, 1998.

Follmann, J. F., Jr. *Medical Care and Health Insurance: A Study in Social Progress.* Homewood, IL: Richard D. Irwin, 1963.

Fox, Daniel M. *Health Policies, Health Politics: The British and American Experience, 1911–1965.* Princeton, NJ: Princeton University Press, 1986.

Frech, H. E. III. "Monopoly in Health Insurance: The Economics of *Kartell v. Blue Shield of Massachusetts.*" In *Health Care in America, the Political Economy of Hospitals and Health Insurance*, edited by H. E. Frech III, 353–72. San Francisco: Pacific Research Institute for Public Policy, 1988.

Frech, H. E. III, and Paul B. Ginsburg. "Competition and Health Insurance." In *Competition in the Health Care Sector: Past, Present, and Future*, edited by Warren Greenberg, 210–37. Proceedings of a conference sponsored by the Bureau of Economics, Federal Trade Commission. Washington, DC: Federal Trade Commission, 1978.

———. "Competition among Health Insurers Revisited." *Journal of Health Politics, Policy and Law* 13 (Summer 1988): 279–91.

Fuchs, Victor R. *The Future of Health Policy.* Cambridge: Harvard University Press, 1993.

———, ed. *Individual and Social Responsibility: Child Care, Education, Medical Care, and Long-Term Care in America.* Chicago: University of Chicago Press, 1996.

———. *Who Shall Live? Health, Economics, and Social Choice.* Expanded ed. Economic Ideas Leading to the 21st Century, vol. 3. River Edge, NJ: World Scientific, 1998.

Gabel, Jon R. et al. "The Changing World of Health Insurance." *Health Affairs* 7 (Summer 1988): 48–65.

Garbarino, Joseph W. *Health Plans and Collective Bargaining.* Berkeley: University of California Press, 1960.

Ginzberg, Eli. *Tomorrow's Hospital: A Look to the Twenty-first Century.* New Haven, CT: Yale University Press, 1996.

Ginzberg, Eli, Howard Berliner, and Miriam Ostow. *Improving Health Care of the Poor: The New York City Experience.* New Brunswick, NJ: Transaction Publishers, 1997.

Goldmann, Franz. *Voluntary Medical Care Insurance in the United States.* New York: Columbia University Press, 1948.

Grey, Michael R. "The Medical Care Programs of the Farm Security Administration 1932–1947: A Rehearsal for National Health Insurance." *American Journal of Public Health* 84 (October 1994): 1678–87.

Haley, Barbara A., and Brian Deevey. *American Health Care in Transition: A Guide to the Literature.* Westport, CT: Greenwood Press, 1997.

Havighurst, Clark C. *Health Care Choices: Private Contracts as Instruments of Health Reform.* Washington, DC: AEI Press for the American Enterprise Institute, 1995.

Health Affairs. Millwood, VA: Project Hope, 1981– . Quarterly.

Health Affairs. Philadelphia: University of Pennsylvania, 1972–1985. Quarterly.

Health Affairs Information Guide Series. Gale Information Guide Library. Detroit: Gale Research, 1978– .

Health Care Financing Review. Washington, DC: U.S. Department of Health, Education, and Welfare; Health Care Financing Administration; Office of Research, Demonstrations, and Statistics, 1979– . Quarterly.

Health Insurance Association of America. *Sourcebook of Health Insurance Data, 1982–83.* Washington, DC: The Association, 1983.

Heirich, Max. *Rethinking Health Care: Innovation and Change in America.* Boulder, CO: Westview Press, 1998.

Hirshfield, Daniel S. *The Lost Reform: The Campaign for Compulsory Health Insurance in the United States from 1932 to 1943.* Cambridge: Harvard University Press, 1970.

Hollingsworth, Helen, and Margaret Coyne Klem. *Selected Bibliography on Medical Economics, including Sections on Health Status, Expenditures for Medical Care, Medical Facilities, Public Health, Industrial Medical Care, Medical Care for Recipients of Public Assistance, Health Insurance and Prepayment Hospital and Medical Care in the United States, Health Insurance in Foreign Countries.* Social Security Board, Bureau of Research and Statistics, Bureau Memorandum no. 60. Washington, DC: U.S. Government Printing Office, 1945.

Hollingsworth, J. Rogers. *A Political Economy of Medicine: Great Britain and the United States.* Baltimore: Johns Hopkins University Press, 1986.

Inquiry. Chicago: Blue Cross Association, 1963– . Quarterly.

Jensen, Cathy A., and Jon R. Gabel. "The Erosion of Purchased Health Insurance." *Inquiry* 25 (Fall 1988): 328–42.

Journal of Health Politics, Policy and Law. Durham, NC: Duke University Press, 1976– . Quarterly.

Law, Sylvia A. *Blue Cross: What Went Wrong?* New Haven, CT: Yale University Press, 1974.

Leavitt, Judith Walzer, and Ronald L. Numbers. *Sickness and Health in America:*

Readings in the History of Medicine and Public Health. 3d ed. Madison: University of Wisconsin Press, 1997.

Lee, Philip R., Carroll L. Estes, and Liz Close, eds. *The Nation's Health.* 5th ed. Jones & Bartlett Series in Health Sciences. Boston: Jones & Bartlett, 1997.

Levit, Katharine R. et al. "National Health Expenditures, 1994." *Health Care Financing Review* 17, no. 3 (Spring 1996): 205–42.

Levy, Hermann. "The Economic History of Sickness and Medical Benefits since the Puritan Revolution." *Economic History Review* 14 (1944): 135–60.

Lubove, Roy. *The Struggle for Social Security, 1900–1935.* Cambridge, MA: Harvard University Press, 1968.

Mamorsky, Jeffrey D. *Health Care Benefits Handbook.* New York: Aspen, 1997.

Marmor, Theodore R. *The Politics of Medicare.* Chicago: Aldine, 1973.

Mason, Kent A., and William L. Sollee. *Retiree Health Benefits: Funding, Accounting and Cost Containment Issues.* Englewood Cliffs, NJ: Prentice-Hall Law & Business, 1992.

McAdams, Robert W., Mary L. Gallagher, and Charles D. Weller. *Managed Care Contracts Manual.* Gaithersburg, MD: Aspen, 1996.

Medical Affairs. Philadelphia: University of Pennsylvania, 1959–1972. Quarterly.

Milbank Memorial Fund Quarterly. Health and Society. New York: Cambridge University Press for Milbank Memorial Fund, 1973–1985.

Milbank Quarterly. New York: Cambridge University Press for Milbank Memorial Fund, 1986– .

Miller, Irwin. *American Health Care Blues: Blue Cross, HMOs, and Pragmatic Reform since 1960.* New Brunswick, NJ: Transaction Publishers, 1996.

Milligan, Maureen A. *Essential Community Provider Issues in Medicaid Managed Care.* Master's thesis, University of Texas at Austin, 1995. Special Project Report Series. Austin: University of Texas at Austin, Lyndon B. Johnson School of Public Affairs, 1996.

Morgan, Gerald. *Public Relief of Sickness.* New York: Macmillan, 1922.

Munts, Raymond. *Bargaining for Health: Labor Unions, Health Insurance, and Medical Care.* Madison: University of Wisconsin Press, 1967.

Newman, Barry, Virginia Peabody, and Pamela Sande. *The COBRA Guide: Practical Solutions to Administration and Management.* Chicago: Irwin Professional, 1996.

Numbers, Ronald L. *Almost Persuaded: American Physicians and Compulsory Health Insurance, 1912–1920.* Henry E. Sigerist Supplements to the Bulletin of the History of Medicine, n.s. 1. Baltimore: Johns Hopkins University Press, 1978.

———. "The Third Party: Health Insurance in America." In *The Therapeutic Revolution: Essays in the Social History of American Medicine,* edited by Morris J. Vogel and Charles E. Rosenberg, 177–200. Philadelphia: University of Pennsylvania Press, 1979.

———, ed. *Compulsory Health Insurance: The Continuing American Debate.* Contributions in Medical History, no. 11. Westport, CT: Greenwood Press, 1982.

O'Brien, Lawrence J. *Bad Medicine: How the American Medical Establishment Is Ruining Our Healthcare System.* Amherst, NY: Prometheus Books, 1999.

Offner, Paul. *Medicaid and the States: A Century Foundation Report.* The Devolution Revolution, 2. New York: Century Foundation Press, 1998.

Osler, Robert W. *Guide to Accident and Sickness Insurance.* Indianapolis: Rough Notes, 1952.

Pauly, Mark V. "The Economics of Moral Hazard: Comment." *American Economic Review* 58 (June 1968): 531–37.

———. "Taxation, Health Insurance, and Market Failure in the Medical Economy." *Journal of Economic Literature* 24 (June 1986): 629–75.

Perritt, Henry H., Jr. *Health Care Legislation Update and Analysis.* Employee Benefits Library. New York: Wiley Law, 1995.

Poen, Monte M. *Harry S Truman versus the Medical Lobby: The Genesis of Medicare.* Columbia: University of Missouri Press, 1979.

Procuniar, Corey. *The COBRA Administrator Handbook.* A Word & Brown Employee Benefits Publication. Orange, CA: Word & Brown Insurance Administrators, 1992.

Reams, Bernard D., Jr., comp. *Health Care Reform, 1993–1994: The American Experience: Clinton and Congress—Law, Policy, and Economics: A Legislative History of the Health Security Act of 1993 with Related Materials.* 31 vols. Buffalo, NY: William S. Hein, 1996.

Reverby, Susan, and David Rosner. *Health Care in America: Essays in Social History.* Philadelphia: Temple University Press, 1979.

Rosenbloom, Deborah. *Employee Benefits: A Guide for Health Care Professionals.* Aspen Health Law Center Current Issues. Gaithersburg, MD: Aspen, 1998.

Rubinow, Isaac M. *Social Insurance.* New York: Henry Holt, 1913.

Schwartz, Jerome L. "Early History of Prepaid Medical Care Plans." *Bulletin of the History of Medicine* 39 (September–October 1965): 450–75.

Shepard's Contemporary Health Care Issues Journal. Colorado Springs, CO: Shepard's/McGraw-Hill, 1994– .

Sindelar, Jody L. "The Declining Price of Health Insurance." In *Health Care in America, the Political Economy of Hospitals and Health Insurance,* edited by H. E. Frech III, 259–91. San Francisco: Pacific Research Institute for Public Policy, 1988.

Somers, Herman Miles, and Anne Ramsay Somers. *Doctors, Patients, and Health Insurance: The Organization and Financing of Medical Care.* Washington, DC: Brookings Institution, 1961.

Starr, Paul. *The Social Transformation of American Medicine.* New York: Basic Books, 1982a.

———. "Transformation in Defeat: The Changing Objectives of National Health Insurance 1915–1980." In *Compulsory Health Insurance: The Continuing American Debate,* edited by Ronald L. Numbers, 119–35. Westport, CT: Greenwood Press, 1982b.

Steele, Charles J., and Scott J. Morris, eds. *ERISA* [Employment Retirement Income and Security Act of 1974] *and Managed Care: Decisions Shaping the Industry.* Alexandria, VA: Capitol, 1993.

Strosnider, J. Steve, and John D. Grad. *Third Party Payments.* ACA Legal Series, vol. 9. Alexandria, VA: American Counseling Association, 1993.

Thomasson, Melissa A. "From Sickness to Health: The Twentieth-Century Development of the Demand for Health Insurance." Ph.D. diss., University of Arizona, 1998.

Twentieth Century Fund. *Medicaid Reform: A Twentieth Century Fund Guide to the Issues.* Basics. New York: Twentieth Century Fund Press, 1995.

———. *Medicare Reform: A Twentieth Century Fund Guide to the Issues.* New York: Twentieth Century Fund Press, 1995.

U.S. Congress. House. Committee on Ways and Means. Subcommittee on Health. *Private Health Insurance Reform Legislation.* Hearings on H.R. 2121, H.R. 1565, and H.R. 3626. 102d Cong., 2d sess., March 12, 1992. Serial 102–88.

———. House. Committee on Ways and Means. Subcommittee on Social Security. *Examining Health Care Coverage for Americans with Disabilities.* Hearings. 103d Cong., 2d sess., February 23, 1994. Serial 103–67.

———. House. Committee on Economic and Educational Opportunities. Subcommittee on Employer-Employee Relations. *Hearings on H.R. 995, the ERISA Targeted Health Insurance Reform Act.* 104th Cong., 1st sess., March 10 and 28, 1995. Serial no. 104–26.

———. House. Committee on Education and the Workforce. Subcommittee on Employer-Employee Relations. *Hearing on H.R. 1515, the Expanded Portability and Health Insurance Coverage Act (EPHIC).* 105 Cong., 1st sess., May 8, 1997. Serial no. 105–29.

———. House. Committee on Education and the Workforce. Subcommittee on Employer-Employee Relations. *Hearing on H.R. 1415, the Patient Access to Responsible Care Act (PARCA).* 105 Cong., 1st sess., October 23, 1997. Serial no. 105–61.

U.S. Congress. Senate. Committee on Finance. Subcommittee on Health for Families and the Uninsured. *Health Care in America: A System in Crisis.* Hearings on S. 1227. 102d Cong., 2d sess., October 22, 1992. S. Hrg. 102–1070.

———. Senate. Committee on Labor and Human Resources. *HealthAmerica Legislation. Hearings on S. 1227 Examining Reform of the Nation's Health Care System to Assure Access to Affordable Health Care for All Americans, Focusing on Health and Economic Implications.* 102d Cong., 1st sess., June 11–12, 1991—Pt. 1, July 24 and 31, 1991—Pt. 2. S. Hrg. 102–322.

———. Senate. Committee on Labor and Human Resources. *Long-Term Care Insurance Improvement and Accountability Act. Hearings on S. 2141, to Amend the Public Health Service Act to Improve the Quality of Long-Term Care Insurance through the Establishment of Federal Standards.* 102 Cong., 2d sess., April 29, 1992.

———. Senate. Committee on Labor and Human Resources. *Health Insurance Purchasing Cooperative Act . . . to Promote the Use of State-Coordinated Health Insurance Buying Programs and Assist States in Establishing Health Insurance Purchasing Cooperatives, through Which Small Employers May Purchase Health Insurance.* Hearings. 102 Cong., 2d sess., May 7, 1992. S. Hrg. 102–630.

———. Senate. Committee on Labor and Human Resources. *Health Insurance Reform Act of 1995: Hearing . . . on S 1028, to Provide Increased Access to Health Care Benefits, to Provide Increased Portability of Health Care Benefits, to Provide Increased Security of Health Care Benefits, and to Increase the Purchasing Power of Individuals and Small Employers.* 104th Cong., 1st sess., July 18, 1995. S. Hrg. 104–138.

————. Senate. Committee on Labor and Human Resources. *Employer Group Purchasing Reform Act of 1995: Hearing . . . on S. 1062, to Amend the Employee Retirement Income Security Act of 1974.* 104 Cong., 1st sess., July 25, 1995. S. Hrg. 104–146.

————. Senate. Committee on Labor and Human Resources. *Health Insurance and Domestic Violence: Hearing . . . on Examining Proposals to Prohibit Insurers from Denying Health Insurance Coverage, Benefits, or Varying Premiums Based on the Status of an Individual as a Victim of Domestic Violence, including Related Provisions of S. 524, S. 1028, and H.R. 1201.* 104th Cong., 1st sess., July 28, 1995. S. Hrg. 104–199.

————. Senate. Committee on Labor and Human Resources. *Improving the Health Status of Children . . . on Examining Proposals . . . including S. 435 and S. 525, Focusing on Pediatric Care, Public Health, Mental Health, and Substance Abuse Issues.* Hearings. 105 Cong., 1st sess., April 18, 1997. S. Hrg. 105–39.

————. Senate. Committee on Labor and Human Resources. *Health Insurance Portability and Accountability Act of 1996, First-Year Implementation Concerns.* Hearing. 105 Cong., 2d sess., March 19, 1998. S. Hrg. 105–490.

————. Senate. Committee on Labor and Human Resources. *Federal Legislation Relating to Health Care Quality.* Hearings. 105th Cong., 2d sess., March 24, 1998. S. Hrg. 105–510.

U.S. General Accounting Office. *Access to Health Care: States Respond to Growing Crisis: Report to Congressional Requesters.* GAO/HRD-92–70. Washington, DC: General Accounting Office, 1992.

————. *Health Insurance: How Health Care Reform May Affect State Regulation: Statement of Leslie G. Aronovitz, Associate Director, Health Financing Issues, Human Resources Division, before the Subcommittee on Health. Committee on Ways and Means, House of Representatives.* Testimony, GAO/T-HRD-94–55. Washington, DC: General Accounting Office, 1993.

————. *Employer-Based Health Plans: Issues, Trends, and Challenges Posed by ERISA: Report to Congressional Requestors.* GAO/HEHS-95–167. Washington, DC: General Accounting Office, 1995.

U.S. National Library of Medicine. *Bibliography of the History of Medicine.* Department of Health, Education, and Welfare publication. Bethesda, MD: National Library of Medicine, 1965–   .

Wekesser, Carol. *Health Care in America: Opposing Viewpoints.* Opposing Viewpoints Series. San Diego: Greenhaven Press, 1994.

Williams, Pierce. *The Purchase of Medical Care through Fixed Periodic Payment.* New York: National Bureau of Economic Research, 1932.

Williamson, Stan, Robert E. Stevens, David L. Loudon, and R. Henry Migliore. *Fundamentals of Strategic Planning for Healthcare Organizations.* Haworth Marketing Resources. Innovations in Practice & Professional Services, edited by William J. Winston. Binghamton, NY: Haworth Press, 1997.

Wolfe, John R. *The Coming Health Crisis: Who Will Pay for Care for the Aged in the 21st Century?* Chicago: University of Chicago Press, 1993.

Part IX

Hotels and Other Lodging Places
ESIC 70.0

CHAPTER 13

HOTELS AND OTHER LODGING PLACES, 70.0

SPIRO G. PATTON

The lodging or hospitality industry is as ancient as travel. Historically, lodging establishments first served the needs of merchants and government officials, the only people who traveled to any extent. Inns and taverns were small proprietary operations located at strategic rest stops or in central towns and villages. As the means of travel relied on human, animal, and water power for centuries, these businesses remained the nucleus of the industry until the nineteenth century.

The British country inn was reproduced in America at ports of entry, key stagecoach stops, and frontier posts to provide lodging and meals to merchants, public officials, westbound settlers, and the wealthy few who traveled for pleasure. Like their British and ancient antecedents, these inns were small proprietary operations serving a local market. In the late twentieth century a restoration movement has put many historic inns back in business (Lathrop 1926).

Rapidly growing U.S. cities had little housing for immigrants. While many new arrivals found employment in domestic service or as apprentices, situations that included housing, those bound for the frontier or industrial employment required accommodations. Urban concentration created a profitable opportunity for hotels: the first hotel in the United States, City Hotel of New York City, boasted seventy-three rooms in 1794 but functioned as little more than an extended inn. Boardinghouses and commercial dormitories offered shelter to many. Boardinghouses were usually private homes with extra rooms, although some proprietary operations were run by church or ethnic organizations. Dormitories were larger and were run by factory owners to house and monitor employees, especially women (Kalt 1971).

The opening of Tremont House in Boston in 1829 was a watershed in American lodging. Perhaps the first true hotel in the United States, the Tremont featured private rooms with washbasins, soap, and towels; an intercom from the front desk to each room—in the years before wire communications, hotel personnel and patrons spoke into tubes much like those used on boats and ships—and bellboys, who provided food and other services directly to the patrons. Designed by Isaiah Rogers, the Tremont set the standard for luxury and elegance in urban hotels (Rosenthal 1967).

As entrepreneurs duplicated the Tremont House ambience in other cities, their hotels became symbols of status and featured attractions in commercial propaganda. Developers sought the best architects and engineers to create grandiose structures, and operators vied in offering innovative services. City hotels prided themselves on elegantly furnished restaurants that served the finest European cuisine. Local hotels in small towns became centers for private and public entertainment and business. A satisfied patron might be tomorrow's successful businessman who promotes the town to others (D. King 1957).

In the latter half of the nineteenth century hotels like the Tremont House symbolized opulence and catered to the most affluent guests, while less prosperous visitors found accommodations at inns or boardinghouses. Dormitory arrangements became the norm on industrial campuses and in the emerging system of colleges and universities. The country inn, bypassed by railroads, faded into obscurity until the restoration movement of the late twentieth century (Kalt 1971).

In the early decades of the twentieth century hotels adopted corporate management techniques to cope with larger facilities, taking advantage of the managerial revolution in the nineteenth century that had created a pool of trained managers and new classes of traveling salesmen and executives (Chandler 1977; Whitten 1983). Top executives could afford luxury accommodations, but salesmen and middle managers represented a market for clean, comfortable accommodations priced between sumptuous hotels and rustic country inns or boardinghouses. Ellsworth Milton Statler was the first entrepreneur to exploit the new market: his Buffalo (New York) Statler, opened in 1908, offered midrange accommodations of private rooms with full baths, electric lighting fixtures, fire and security protection, and food and room services—amenities without the trappings of luxury appealed to ordinary travelers. Building on his success in Buffalo, Statler opened similar hotels in other cities; his was the first U.S. hotel chain, and its operation set an example for others (Fetherling 1982).

The American lodging industry grew with the nation in the first three decades of the twentieth century. As the population expanded westward, many rural Americans left the country for the city. Automobiles replaced horse-drawn vehicles, and travelers increasingly chose their private cars over trains, making the motor inn, or motel, the fastest growing lodging unit (Kalt 1971). The Great Depression hurt the lodging business, but World War II generated an economic boom fed by rising incomes, geographical mobility, more leisure time, and increased interest in travel. The burgeoning population, a splendid highway system, and cheap, dependable automobiles and inexpensive fuel combined with fast, comfortable airliners operated by competitive companies offering safe air travel at bargain prices stimulated the lodging industry and continued the wartime boom into the final years of the twentieth century (Belasco [1979] 1997).

The most notable lodging development since 1950 has been the evolution of motels, or motor inns, characterized by on-site parking and limited service (albeit in recent years several motel chains have upgraded their properties to the status of hotels). In the 1990s many hotels are reallocating space for long-term residency or for offices. But the fastest growing segments of the industry are recreational and entertainment facilities, including resorts, casinos, and convention center complexes (Patton 1986).

The lodging industry exhibits increasing concentration of market power in franchise chains, some of which are part of diversified hospitality conglomerates like the Marriott Corporation. Even foreign-based corporations from Europe, Canada, and Japan have entered U.S. markets. Industry competition runs along functional and geographic lines (Wyckoff and Sasser 1981).

Disposable income is the driving force behind the lucrative lodging business. The United States continues to ride a long wave of prosperity as the twentieth century turns into the twenty-first. American prosperity, combined with growing international affluence and a global economy, promises a bright future for the hotel industry.

BIBLIOGRAPHIC ESSAY

Literature on the lodging industry can be broken into three categories: histories of segments of the industry, biographical material on hoteliers and lodging entrepreneurs, and histories of establishments or locales (resorts). The industry and its entrepreneurs are increasingly the subject of scholarly work, and trade journals are a good source of statistics and trends.

A vintage work is Elsie Lathrop's (1926) history of early American inns and taverns, a study that set the standard for subsequent research. Kalt (1971) is a brief textbook history, but Wyckoff and Sasser (1981) is a solid economic study—a survey with in-depth case histories indicative of their Harvard Business School affiliation. Warren James Belasco ([1979] 1997) has researched the early decades of the motel industry and its antecedents, the autocamps and tourist courts, and Lawrence R. Borne (1983) has written the "complete" history of dude ranches in the American West. Supplementing these books are articles on industry segments. Leon Rosenthal (1967) focuses on the earliest years of the hotel industry, paying special attention to the Tremont House of Boston. Doris King's (1957) article on lodging facilities in the 1820s and 1840s is unique in both topic and approach. Using a class analysis, King contrasts the luxurious accommodations in the cities with the meager facilities for the transient working class. Dianne Newell (1974) writes about the railroad station-hotel, a type of establishment that flourished in the mid-to-late nineteenth century. Richard Van Orman (1966, 1968) describes the state of lodging facilities in the Old West during the mid-nineteenth century; Jerome Rodnitzky's (1968) article on dude ranching is an antecedent of Borne's definitive work; Paul Lancaster (1982) and Phil Patton (1986) offer contemporary views on the motel industry; and Martha Saxton (1978) explores an interesting segment of the resort industry—the honeymoon resort, particularly the elaborate facilities developed in the Pocono Mountains of Pennsylvania.

Sketches of entrepreneurs can be found in local histories, but standard biographies are available as well. J. Willard Marriott's story is a popular account of one of the most famous contemporary lodging entrepreneurs (O'Brien 1977), Peter Bulkley (1975) traces the career of Horace Fabyan, founder of a nineteenth-century resort in New Hampshire, and another nineteenth-century New Hampshire hotelier, Abel Hutchins, is the subject of an article by Bryant Tolles (1972). Especially interesting is Evelyn Banning's (1981) sketch of Ulysses S. Grant, Jr., who built a hotel in San Diego in 1910. Three studies yield a composite view of E. M. Statler, the nation's first chain entrepreneur: *A Bed for the Night: The Story of the Wheeling Bellboy, E. M. Statler, and His Remarkable Hotels* (Jarman 1952); *Statler, America's Extraordinary Hotelman* (Miller 1968); "The McClure House and E. M. Statler" (Fetherling 1982). James Vining (1982) relates the story of Slater Burgesser, a spa operator in Illinois, and Elmer Barber (1978) writes about Willis Evans, an early resort operator in Washington State. Isabell Howell's (1983) monograph on John Armfield, a nineteenth-century spa operator in Tennessee, is notable if only for its length. Cheryl Romo (1985) ravels a mystery at the Bar-W dude ranch in California during the 1920s. Perhaps the most newsworthy of all hotel moguls are the Helmsleys. Their story can be traced through hundreds of newspaper articles stretched over many years or reviewed in Richard Hammer's *The Helmsleys: The Rise and Fall of Harry and Leona* (1990).

The greatest concentration of literature on individual establishments spotlights the northeast quarter of the United States. Edward Hungerford's (1925) history of the Waldorf-Astoria includes details of the construction and management of the fabled hotel as well as a biographical sketch of the hotel's original proprietor, George C. Boldt. Although a popularized account, Hungerford's work remains a standard. Harold K. Hochschild's (1962) study of the Blue Mountain Lake Resort in the Adirondacks of New York State (1870–1900) is remarkable for its extensive use of company records and correspondence. A brief article by Phyllis Kihn (1965) on the

American Hotel of Hartford during the period 1845–1848 provides insight into the operations of an early urban hotel. Wayne Temple's (1968) description of a century of operations at the St. Nicholas Hotel of Springfield, Illinois, includes an account of Abraham Lincoln's visits to the hotel. As part of his ongoing research on the history of Rochester, New York, Blake McKelvey (1969) provides a survey of the lodging industry in that city from 1877 to 1960. H. Ray Woerner (1969) surveys lodgings in Lancaster, Pennsylvania, from colonial times until 1920.

Four articles concentrate on early accommodations in New York State, from urban hotels to spas to state parks: Ivan Steen (1979) reviews British travelers' commentaries on the quality of service in New York City hotels throughout the 1850s; Nancy Evans (1970) focuses on the Sans Souci, a fashionable resort between 1803 and 1887; Carl Starace (1970), on the Fire Island Surf Hotel, the precursor of Fire Island Sate Park; and William Hills (1974), on the Hotel Woodruff in Watertown. Louise B. Roomet (1976) surveys the resort facilities of Vermont from 1820 to 1875. Lilly Setterdahl and Hiram Wilson (1978) provide an interesting account of Bishop Hill, a Swedish religious colony in Illinois that operated its own hotel during the mid-nineteenth century. Maury Klein (1978) has written the story of the Narragansett Pier Resort in Rhode Island.

Blanche Linden (1981) surveys the lodging industry of Cincinnati. Stephen Davis (1982) presents a revisionist interpretation of the Tremont House in Chicago, an intent clearly spelled out in the article's title. Using the methodology of the new social history, Bulkley (1980) analyzes the socioeconomic characteristics of White Mountain, New Hampshire, tourists in the 1850s. Bob Boelio (1981) surveys Michigan's lodging industry during the nineteenth century. David Francis (1980) describes the activity at Johnson's Island, Ohio, during the resort era. Charles Parker (1984) has written a history of Ocean Grove, New Jersey, a fashionable Methodist resort camp operating between 1869 and 1910, and Laura Mumma (1986) offers a sketch of Eagles Mere, a resort in northeastern Pennsylvania during the early twentieth century.

In the literature on the lodging industry of the South and Southwest, an early reference is Anna Durham's (1969) history of Tyree Springs, a spa resort north of Nashville that flourished before 1940; Neil Pond's (1978) article is a follow-up to Durham's account. Royster Lyle (1971) relates the history of hotels in Rockbridge County, Virginia, a boom area at the end of the nineteenth century. Amine Kellam (1974) describes Cobb's Island, a popular hunting and fishing resort off the Virginia coast during the nineteenth century, and Catharine Bishir (1977) discusses accommodations on the North Carolina coast at Old Nags Head, a popular antebellum resort that retained its clientele after the Civil War. James Livingood (1981) sketches the Crutchfield House, a noted rooming house of antebellum Chattanooga, Tennessee, frequented by military officers on both sides during

the war. William Hair (1984) surveys inns along stagecoach routes in antebellum Georgia, and Harvey K. Newman (1999) delineates the role of
tourism in the growth of Atlanta, Georgia, from the Civil War era to the
late twentieth century.

Several studies emphasize the diversity of the lodging industry across the
United States. Charles Roundy (1973) offers an area-specific contribution
to the dude ranching literature, focusing on the early years in Wyoming,
1890–1930. Donovan Hofsommer (1975), well noted in transportation history, relates transportation modes to the development of resorts in Iowa's
Spirit Lake County from 1880 to 1940. An interesting study is presented
by Lynn Weiner (1979), who examines the Young Women's Christian Association (YWCA) of Minneapolis and its boarding homes for working
women at the turn of the century. Lee Whittlesey (1980) describes Marshall's Hotel in Yellowstone Park, which flourished at the turn of the nineteenth century. Peter Ognibene (1984) explores the early history (1935–
1953) of Sun Valley, Idaho, billed as the nation's first "ski spa." Suzanne
Julin (1982) analyzes the early history of Hot Springs, South Dakota; Marilyn McMillan (1985) relates the early decades of White Sulphur Springs,
Montana, 1866–1904; and Claum-M. Naske (1985) describes the brief life
of Chena Hot Springs, Arizona, a retreat for prospectors from 1905 to
1920. Douglas Steeples (1999) delineates three eras in Calico, California—
silver mining town, borax-producing center, tourist ghost town.

Bill Grimstad (1966) recounts the early history of the Hotel del Coronado on San Diego Bay. Grimstad's piece was followed by Monroe Buckley's (1975) monograph marking the hotel's centennial. In the same locale,
John Packard (1968) surveys San Diego's hotels in the 1880s. Dorothy
Holland (1972) discusses the Planter's House of St. Louis, Missouri, in the
late nineteenth century. Joe Frantz's (1973) monograph covers the first century at the Driskill Hotel in Austin, Texas. Ronald Rayman (1977) sketches
the history of the Yo Semite House of Stockton, California, which flourished between 1869 and 1923. Other sources include Wallace Stegner's
(1981) follow-up to John Gadd's (1968) history of Saltair, a resort on the
Great Salt Lake in Utah; Ellen Shipley's (1978) history of the short-lived
(1917–1929) resort of Bella Vista, Arkansas; and Sylvia Loughlin's (1981)
on Iron Springs, Arizona. The most famous springs, Hot Springs, Arkansas,
is the subject of a monograph by Dee Brown (1982). The twentieth-century
resort at Mammoth Lakes, California, is discussed in a monograph by
Adele Reed (1982), and Barbi Wetzel (1985) surveys the history of the
Pioneer Hotel, Elko, Nevada, during the past century. Evalena Berry (1985)
covers yet another Arkansas watering place, Sugar Loaf Springs. Bruce Ashcroft (1986) describes the Montezuma Hotel in Las Vegas, Nevada, between 1881 and 1903.

Works of more recent vintage exhibit new areas of interest and outlets
for research ranging from government, to university presses, to trade journals. In a study published by the U.S. Department of Transportation, Rich-

ard Carillo, Daniel Jepson, and Sarah Pearce (1995) combine archaeology and history in exploring the site of the Tremont House Hotel in downtown Denver, Colorado. Jeronima Echeverria (1999) adds *Home Away from Home: A History of Basque Boardinghouses* to the University of Nevada's Basque Series. Dude ranching remains a popular topic: *Old-Time Dude Ranches Out West* (Flood 1995) and *Sharing Your Home on the Range* (Bryan, Hitchcock, and Spitz 1991). Back East, Tony Scherman (1998), writing for *American Legacy*, highlights the Hotel Theresa, once the pre-eminent hotel in Harlem.

Trade journals, a familiar source of historical trends and statistics, range from the *Rooming House Hotel News* (1924) to the contemporary *American Hotel Journal, Trends in the Hotel Industry*, and *National Trend of Business, Lodging Industry*. Supplementing the journals is a wide range of handbooks, guidebooks, and directories: *A Guide to Monastic Guest Houses* (Regalbuto 1998); *At Home in Hostel Territory* (Thomas 1994); *The Laws of Innkeepers: For Hotels, Motels, Restaurants, and Clubs* (Sherry 1993); *The Equal Opportunity Handbook for Hotels, Restaurants, and Institutions* (Stokes 1979); *Who's Who among Innkeepers: A Biographical Reference Work about Hotel, Motel, and Resort Managers and Owners in America* (1974).

BIBLIOGRAPHY

American Hotel & Motel Association. *AH & MA Reports*. Washington, DC: American Hotel & Motel Association, 1989– .

American Hotel Journal. Pontiac, IL: American Hotel Journal, 1951– . Monthly.

Ashcroft, Bruce. "The Montezuma Hotel: Playground of Kings and Cowboys." *Palacio* 91 (1986): 8–15.

Ayres, Harry V. *Hotel du Pont Story: Wilmington, Delaware, 1911–1981*. Wilmington, DE: Serendipity Press, 1981.

Baeder, John. *Gas, Food, and Lodging*. New York: Abbeville Press, 1982.

Baldwin, Grace Rosen, with Mary-Alice Wightman. *Come Live with Me* [Women benefactors, lodging houses in Richmond, VA]. Lively, VA: Brandylane, 1994.

Banning, Evelyn I. "U.S. Grant, Jr., a Builder of San Diego." *Journal of San Diego History* 27 (1981): 1–16.

Barber, Elmer F. "Palouse County Resort Pioneer." *Pacific Northwesterner* 22 (1978): 40–46.

Bauchum, Rosalind G., and James W. A. Bauchum. *New Concepts in Hotel and Convention Center Designs: Selected Sources of Information*. Architecture Series—Bibliography, 0194-1356; A-729. Monticello, IL: Vance Bibliographies, 1982.

Belasco, Warren James. *Americans on the Road: From Autocamp to Motel 1910–1945*. Cambridge: MIT Press, 1979. Reprint. Baltimore: Johns Hopkins University Press, 1997.

Bernstein, Joel H. *Families That Take in Friends: An Informal History of Dude Ranching*. Stevensville, MT: Stoneydale Press, 1982.

Berry, Evalena. *Sugar Loaf Springs: Heber's Elegant Watering Place*. Conway, AR: River Road Press, 1985.

Bibliographic Research Library. *Hotel Architecture and the Work of Morris Lapidus: A Selected Bibliography*. Architecture Series—Bibliography, 0194–1356; A 1402. Monticello, IL: Vance Bibliographies, 1985.

Birch, Eugenie Ladner, ed. *The Unsheltered Woman: Women and Housing in the 80s*. New Brunswick, NJ: Rutgers University, Center for Urban Policy Research, 1985.

Bishir, Catharine W. "The 'Unpainted Aristocracy': The Beach Cottages of Old Nags Head." *North Carolina Historical Review* 54 (1977): 367–92.

Black, Naomi. *Dude Ranches of the American West*. Lexington, MA: S. Greene Press, 1988.

Boelio, Bob. "Inns and Taverns." *Chronicle* 17 (1981): 27–33.

Bolton, Whitney. *The Silver Spade: The Conrad Hilton Story*. New York: Farrar, Straus, & Young, 1954.

Borne, Lawrence R. *Welcome to My West: I. H. Larom, Dude Rancher, Conservationist, Collector*. Cody, WY: Buffalo Bill Historical Center, 1982.

———. *Dude Ranching: A Complete History*. Albuquerque: University of New Mexico Press, 1983.

Borsenik, Frank D. *Literature of the Lodging Market: An Annotated Bibliography*. Occasional Paper. East Lansing: Michigan State University, Graduate School of Business Administration, Division of Research, Bureau of Business and Economic Research, 1966.

Bouet, Thierry, and Pino Cacucci. *Hotel People*. Washington, DC: Smithsonian Institution Press, 1999.

Boynton, Mia. *A Gift of Native Knowledge: The History of Russell's Motor Camps in Rangely, Maine*. Northeast Folklore, vol. 28. Orono, ME: Northeast Folklore Society, 1991.

Brown, Dee Alexander. *The American Spa: Hot Springs, Arkansas*. Little Rock, AR: Rose, 1982.

Bryan, William L., Julie Davies Hitchcock, and Elin Spitz. *Sharing Your Home on the Range: A Handbook for Farm/Ranch Hospitality Providers*. New York: Underhill & Wild Wing Foundations, 1991.

Buckley, Monroe. *The Crown City's Brightest Gem: A History of the Hotel del Coronado*. San Diego: Hotel del Coronado, 1975.

Bulkley, Peter B. "Horace Fabyan, Founder of the White Mountain Grand Hotel." *Historic New Hampshire* 30 (1975): 53–77.

———. "Identifying the White Mountain Tourist, 1853–54: Origin, Occupation, and Wealth as a Definition of the Early Hotel Trade." *Historic New Hampshire* 35 (1980): 107–62.

Burt, Nathaniel. *Jackson Hole Journal*. Norman: University of Oklahoma Press, 1983.

Carillo, Richard F., Daniel A. Jepson, and Sarah J. Pearce. *Exploring the Colorado Frontier: A Study in Historical Archaeology at the Tremont House Hotel, Lower Downtown Denver*. Washington, DC: U.S. Department of Transportation, Federal Highway Administration; Denver: Colorado Department of Transportation, Archaeological Unit, 1995.

Case, Frank. *Tales of a Wayward Inn* [Algonquin Hotel]. Garden City, NY, 1940.
———. *Do Not Disturb* [Algonquin Hotel]. Garden City, NY, 1943.
Casper, Dale E. *The Architecture of American Hotels: Projects and Designs, 1983–
    1987*. Architecture Series—Bibliography, 0194–1356; A-1971. Monticello,
    IL: Vance Bibliographies, 1988.
Chandler, Alfred D., Jr. *The Visible Hand: The Managerial Revolution in American
    Business*. Cambridge: Harvard University Press, 1977.
Chervenak, Keane, & Company. *The State of Information Processing and Related
    Technology in the Hotel/Motel Industry*. New York: American Hotel & Mo-
    tel Association, 1976.
Comfort, Mildred Houghton. *Conrad N. Hilton, Hotelier: A Biography*. Men of
    Achievement Series. Minneapolis: T. S. Denison, 1964.
Community Service Society of New York. *Life in One Room: A Study of the Room-
    ing House Problem in the Borough of Manhattan*. New York: Community
    Service Society of New York, Committee on Housing, 1940.
Conner, Nancy. *The Unknown Motel: A Guide to Bargain Motels Off the Beaten
    Track*. Walnut Creek, CA: Nancy Conner, 1994.
Coplin, Maxine. *A National Guide to Guest Homes*. Mill Valley, CA: Home on
    Arrange, 1981.
Crockett, Albert Stevens. *Peacocks on Parade: A Narrative of a Unique Period in
    American Social History and Its Most Colorful Figures* [Peacock Alley,
    Waldorf-Astoria Hotel, 1890–1914]. New York: Sears, 1931. Reprint. The
    Leisure Class in America. New York: Arno Press, 1975.
Crowninshield, Frank, ed. *The Unofficial Palace of New York: A Tribute to the
    Waldorf-Astoria*. New York: Privately printed, 1939.
Dabney, Thomas Ewing. *The Man Who Bought the Waldorf: The Life of Conrad
    N. Hilton*. New York: Duell, Sloan, & Pearce, 1950.
Dane, Suzanne G. *The National Trust Guide to Historic Bed & Breakfasts, Inns,
    and Small Hotels*. 5th ed. New York: Wiley, 1999.
Davies, Thomas D., and Kim A. Beasley. *Accessible Design for Hospitality: ADA
    Guidelines for Planning Accessible Hotels, Motels, and Other Recreational
    Facilities*. 2d ed. New York: McGraw-Hill, 1994.
Davis, Stephen M. "Of the 'Class Dominated Princely': The Tremont House Hotel."
    Chicago History 11 (1982): 26–36.
Dearing, Albin Pasteur. *The Elegant Inn: The Waldorf-Astoria Hotel, 1893–1929*.
    Secaucus, NJ: Stuart, 1986.
Dees, Jesse Walter. *Flophouse: An Authentic Undercover Study of Flophouses, Cage
    Hotels, including Missions, Shelters and Institutions Serving Unattached
    (Homeless) Men. A Sociological Study That Includes English Origins of
    Mass Relief, Samples of American Mass Relief and a Modern Investigation
    of Public and Private Policies in Chicago*. Francestown, NH: M. Jones, 1948.
Donzel, Catherine, Alexis Gregory, and Marc Walter. *Grand American Hotels*.
    New York: Vendome, 1989.
Duke, Donald. *Fred Harvey, Civilizer of the American Southwest*. Arcadia, CA:
    Pregel Press, 1995.
Dunning, Glenna. *Resort Hotels in the Eastern United States: An Annotated Bib-

liography. Architecture Series—Bibliography, 0194–1356; A 1937. Monticello, IL: Vance Bibliographies, 1987.

Durham, Anna T. "Tyree Springs." *Tennessee Historical Quarterly* 28 (1969): 156–65.

Echeverria, Jeronima. *Home Away from Home: A History of Basque Boarding-houses*. Basque Series. Reno: University of Nevada Press, 1999.

Elliot, William Harvard. *A Description of Tremont House*. Boston: Gray & Bowen, 1830.

Evans, Nancy Goyne. "The Sans Souci, a Fashionable Resort Hotel in Ballston Spa." *Winterthur Portfolio* 6 (1970): 111–26.

Fetherling, Doug. "The McClure House and E. M. Statler." *Upper Ohio Valley Historical Review* 12 (1982): 12–17.

Fitt-Peaster, Hilton, and Jenny Fitt-Peaster. *Colorado Cabins, Lodges & Country B&Bs*. 3d ed. Boulder, CO: Rocky Mountain Vacation Publishing, 1997.

Flood, Elizabeth Clair. *Old-Time Dude Ranches Out West*. Salt Lake City: Gibbs-Smith, 1995.

Foster, George H., and Peter C. Weiglin. *The Harvey House Cookbook: Memories of Dining along the Santa Fe Railroad*. Atlanta, GA: Longstreet Press, 1992.

Francis, David W. "Johnson's Island: A History of the Resort Era." *Inland Seas* 36 (1980): 257–63.

Frantz, Joe B. *The Driskill Hotel*. Austin, TX: Encino, 1973.

Fretz, Franking Kline. "The Furnished Room Problem in Philadelphia." Ph.D. diss., University of Pennsylvania, 1911.

Gadd, John D. C. "Saltair, Great Salt Lake's Most Famous Resort." *Utah Historical Quarterly* 36 (1968): 198–221.

Gardner, Roberta Homan, and Peter Andrews. *The Southwest, a Guide to the Inns of Arizona, New Mexico, and Texas*. Country Inns of America. New York: Holt, Rinehart, & Winston, an Owl Book, 1982.

Graham, Roberta. *Alaska's Backcountry Hideaways: Southcentral*. Seattle: Pacific Search Press, 1986.

Graham, Thomas. "Flagler's Magnificent Hotel Ponce de Leon." *Florida Historical Quarterly* 54 (1975): 1–17.

Grimstad, Bill. "Sand Fleas and Salad Days." *American West* 3 (1966): 36–47.

Haber, Mel. *Bedtime Stories of the Ingleside Inn*. Northridge, CA: Lord John Press, 1996.

Hair, William I. "Stagecoaches and Public Accommodations in Antebellum Georgia." *Georgia Historical Quarterly* 68 (1984): 323–33.

Halper, Evan, and Paul Karr. *Hostels, U.S.A.: The Only Comprehensive, Unofficial, Opinionated Guide*. 2d ed. Old Saybrook, CT: Globe Pequot Press, 1999.

Hammer, Richard. *The Helmsleys: The Rise and Fall of Harry and Leona*. New York: New American Library, 1990.

Harriman, Margaret Case. *Blessed Are the Debonair* [Algonquin Hotel]. New York: Rinehart, 1956.

Havemeyer, Harry W. *Along the Great South Bay; From Oakdale to Babylon, the Story of a Summer Spa, 1840–1940*. Mattituck, NY: Ameron House, 1996.

Hayner, Norman Sylvester. *The Hotel: The Sociology of Hotel Life*. N.p., 1923.

Headley, Madge. *A Study of Housing Conditions Made for the New York State Department of Health. Investigation of Summer Boarding Houses in Vicinity of New York City, in Sullivan and Ulster Counties.* Albany: New York State Department of Health, Division of Public Health Education, 1916.

Helberg, Kristin. *The Belvedere and the Man Who Saved It.* Baltimore: Pumpkin, 1986.

Henry, David Ford. *Hotel Henry.* Pittsburgh: David Ford Henry, 1904.

Hills, William P. "Watertown's Hotel Woodruff." *York State Tradition* 28 (1974): 15–20, 25.

Hines, Duncan. *Lodging for a Night.* 4th ed. Bowling Green, KY: Adventures in Good Eating, 1941.

Hochschild, Harold K. *Adirondack Resort in the Nineteenth Century: Blue Mountain Lake 1870–1900, Stagecoaches and Luxury Hotels.* Syracuse, NY: Syracuse University Press, 1962.

Hoffman, Abraham. "Mountain Resorts and Trail Camps in Southern California's Great Hiking Era, 1884–1938." *Southern California Quarterly* 58 (1976): 381–406.

Hofsommer, Donovan L. *Prairie Oasis: The Railroads, Steamboats and Resorts of Iowa's Spirit Lake County.* Des Moines, IA: Waukon & Mississippi, 1975.

Holland, Dorothy. "The Planter's House." *Bulletin of the Missouri Historical Society* 28 (1972): 109–17.

Hotel and Travel Index. U.S. Hotel Guest Study. Secaucus, NJ: Reed Travel Group, 1990– .

Hotel Review Pictorial. Chicago: Ahrens, 1907– . Monthly.

Howell, Isabel. *John Armfield of Beersheba Springs.* Beersheba Springs, TN: Beersheba Springs Historical Society, 1983.

Hungerford, Edward. *The Story of the Waldorf-Astoria.* New York: G. P. Putnam's Sons, 1925.

Hyde, Floy Salls. *Water over the Dam at Mountain View in the Adirondacks: Early Resort Days in the Great North Woods.* Mountain View, NY, 1970.

Information Bureau on Women's Work. *Rooms, Inquire Within.* Toledo, OH: Information Bureau on Women's Work, 1927.

Ingram, Paul L. *The Rise of Hotel Chains in the United States, 1896–1980.* Garland Studies in Entrepreneurship. New York: Garland, 1996.

Inn Review [small hotels & country inns]. Lafayette, IN: H. R. Associates, 1982– . Monthly (except August and December).

Jaffe, Miles, Julie Robinson, Robert Hults, and Maria Ricke. *Great Ski Inns and Hotels of America.* New York: Ski the Best; Andover, MA: Brick House, 1988.

Jakle, John A., Keith A. Sculle, and Jefferson S. Rogers. *The Motel in America.* The Road and American Culture. Baltimore: Johns Hopkins University Press, 1996.

James, George Wharton. *The H.M.M.B.A.* [Hotel Men's Mutual Benefit Association] *in California.* Pasadena, CA: G. W. James, 1896.

———. *The 1910 Trip of the H.M.M.B.A.* [Hotel Men's Mutual Benefit Association] *to California and the Pacific Coast.* San Francisco: Press of Bolte & Braden, 1911.

Jarman, Rufus. *A Bed for the Night: The Story of the Wheeling Bellboy, E. M. Statler, and His Remarkable Hotels.* New York: Harper, 1952.

Johnson, Wallace E., with Eldon Roark. *Together We Build: The Life and Faith of*

Wallace E. Johnson. Originally published in 1978 as *Work Is My Play.* New York: Hawthorn Books, 1978.

Jones, James B., Jr. *The Development of Motor Tourism in Tennessee's Southern Corridor, circa 1910–1945: A Case Study Exploring Options for the Recognition and Preservation of Cultural Resources Associated with One Aspect of the More Recent Past.* Study Unit no. 11. Nashville: State Historical Preservation Office, Tennessee Historical Commission, Comprehensive Cultural Resource Management Planning Section, 1991.

Juhola, Helen Adams. *Life in a Rooming House.* Helena, MT: Falcon Press, 1986.

Julin, Suzanne. "South Dakota Spa: A History of the Hot Springs Health Resort, 1882–1915." *South Dakota Historical Collections* 41 (1982): 193–272.

Kalt, Nathan. *Introduction to the Hospitality Industry.* Indianapolis: Bobbs-Merrill, 1971.

Kellam, Amine Cosby. "The Cobb's Island Story." *Virginia Cavalcade* 23 (1974): 18–27.

Kihn, Phyllis. "The American Hotel, 1845–48." *Connecticut Historical Society Bulletin* 30 (1965): 26–32.

Kilgore, Gene. *Gene Kilgore's Ranch Vacations: The Complete Guide to Guest and Resort, Fly-Fishing, and Cross-Country Skiing Ranches in the United States.* 5th ed. Santa Fe, NM: John Muir Publications, 1998.

King, Bucky. *The Dude Connection.* Laramie, WY: Jelm Mountain Press, 1983.

King, Doris Elizabeth. "The First-Class Hotel and the Age of the Common Man." *Journal of Southern History* 23 (1957): 173–88.

Kishikawa, Hiro, and Shinjiro Kirishiki. *Urban Hotel in U.S.A.* Shohan edition. Great Hotels of the World, vol. 3. Tokyo: Kawade Shobo Shinsha, 1991.

Klein, Maury. "Summering at the Pier." *American History Illustrated* 13 (1978): 32–43.

Kleinfield, Sonny. *The Hotel: A Week in the Life of the Plaza* [Westin Plaza Hotel]. New York: Simon & Schuster, 1989.

Koziara, Edward Clifford, and Karen Shallcross Koziara. *The Negro in the Hotel Industry.* Racial Policies of American Industry, Report no. 4. Philadelphia: University of Pennsylvania, Wharton School of Finance and Commerce, Industrial Research Unit, 1968; distributed by University of Pennsylvania Press.

Kramer, Jack, and Matthew Barr. *The Last of the Grand Hotels.* New York: Van Nostrand Reinhold, 1978.

Lancaster, Paul. "The Great American Motel." *American Heritage* 33 (1982): 100–108.

Lanier, Pamela. *Elegant Small Hotels: A Connoisseur's Guide.* A Lanier Guide. Berkeley, CA: Lanier Publishing International, 1995.

Lathrop, Elsie. *Early American Inns and Taverns.* New York: McBride, 1926.

Lent, Henry Bolles. *The Waldorf-Astoria: A Brief Chronicle of a Unique Institution Now Entering Its Fifth Decade.* New York: Privately printed for Hotel Waldorf-Astoria Corporation, 1934.

Linden, Blanche M. G. "Inns to Hotels in Cincinnati." *Cincinnati Historical Society Bulletin* 39 (1981): 127–52.

Livingood, James W. "Chattanooga's Crutchfields and the Famous Crutchfield House." *Civil War Times Illustrated* 20 (1981): 20–25.

Long Island Railroad Company. *Long Island and Real Life*. New York: Long Island Railroad Company, Passenger Department, 1916.

Loughlin, Sylvia. "Iron Springs, Arizona: Timeless Summer Resort." *Journal of Arizona History* 22 (1981): 235–54.

Lyle, Royster, Jr. "Rockbridge County's Boom Hotels." *Virginia Cavalcade* 20 (1971): 5–13.

Lynn, Sandra. *Windows on the Past: Historic Lodgings of New Mexico*. Albuquerque: University of New Mexico Press, 1999.

Macgregor, William Laird. *Hotels and Hotel Life, at San Francisco, California, in 1876*. San Francisco: S. F. News, 1877.

Margolies, John. *Home Away from Home: Motels in America*. Boston: Little, Brown, a Bulfinch Press Book, 1995.

McCarthy, James Remington, and John Rutherford. *Peacock Alley: The Romance of the Waldorf-Astoria*. New York and London: Harper & Brothers, 1931.

McGinty, Brian. *The Palace Inns: A Connoisseur's Guide to Historic American Hotels*. Harrisburg, PA: Stackpole Books, 1978.

McKelvey, Blake. "From Stagecoach Taverns to Airline Motels." *Rochester History* 31 (1969): 1–24.

McMillan, Marilyn. "An El Dorado of Ease and Elegance: Taking the Waters at White Sulphur Springs, 1866–1904." *Montana* 35 (1985): 36–49.

McMillon, Bill. *The Old Lodges & Hotels of Our National Parks*. South Bend, IN: Icarus Press, 1983.

Miller, Floyd. *Statler, America's Extraordinary Hotelman*. New York: Statler Foundation, 1968.

Morehouse, Ward. *The Waldorf-Astoria: America's Gilded Dream*. New York: M. Evans, 1991.

Morey, Kathy. *Hot Showers, Soft Beds, and Dayhikes in the Sierra: Walks and Strolls near Lodgings*. Berkeley, CA: Wilderness Press, 1996.

Morsman, Edgar Martin. *The Postmistress of Saddlestring, Wyoming*. Deephaven, MN: E. M. Morsman, 1998.

Mrozowski, Stephen A., Grace H. Ziesing, and Mary C. Beaudry. *Living on the Boott: Historical Archaeology at the Boott Mills Boardinghouses*. Amherst: University of Massachusetts Press, 1996.

Mumma, Laura Sickel. "Eagles Mere: Of Cottages and Kings." *Pennsylvania Heritage* 12 (1986): 18–25.

Naske, Claum-M. "Curing Crippled Prospectors: The Wonderful Waters of Chena Hot Springs." *Alaska Journal* 15 (1985): 16–22.

National Opinion Research Center. *The Homeless Man on Skid Row: A Research Report on Housing and Home Finance Agency Demonstration Project Number III.D-1*. Chicago: U.S. Housing and Home Finance Agency, 1959.

National Trend of Business, Economy Lodging Industry. Philadelphia: Laventhol & Horwath, 1983– . Monthly.

National Trend of Business Economy/Limited-Service Lodging Industry. Philadelphia: Laventhol & Horwath, 1986– . Monthly.

National Trend of Business, Lodging Industry. Philadelphia: Laventhol & Horwath, 1982– . Monthly.

Newell, Dianne. "The Short-Lived Phenomenon of Railroad Station-Hotels." *Historic Preservation* 26 (1974): 31–36.

Newman, Harvey K. *Southern Hospitality: Tourism and the Growth of Atlanta.* Tuscaloosa: University of Alabama Press, 1999.

O'Brien, Robert. *Marriott: The J. Willard Marriott Story.* Salt Lake City: Deseret Book, 1977.

Ognibene, Peter J. "At the First Ski Spa, Stars Outshone the Sun and Snow." *Smithsonian* 15 (1984): 108–19.

Outlook, U.S. Lodging Industry. Philadelphia: Laventhol & Horwath, Leisure Time Industries Department, 1986– .

Packard, John C. "San Diego's Early Hotels." *Southern California Quarterly* 59 (1968): 267–78.

Parker, Charles A. "Ocean Grove, New Jersey: Queen of the Victorian Methodist Camp Meeting Resorts." *Nineteenth Century* 9 (1984): 19–25.

Patton, Phil. "America's Home Away from Home Is Still a Good Motel." *Smithsonian* 16 (1986): 126–37.

Photographs, Hotel Sinton. Cincinnati, OH: Schultz Printing Works, 1907.

Piedmont, Donlan. *Peanut Soup and Spoonbread: An Informal History of Hotel Roanoke.* Blacksburg, VA: Virginia Tech Real Estate Foundation, 1994.

Pond, Neil. "Tennessee's Tyree Springs: The Most Celebrated Watering Place in the State." *Kentucky Folklore Record* 24 (1978): 64–73.

Potomac Appalachian Trail Club. *The Potomac Appalachian Trail Club's Cabins.* Washington, DC: The Club, 1988.

Rayman, Ronald. "Deluxe Combinations: Stockton's Yo Semite House, 1869–1923." *California Historical Quarterly* 56 (1977): 164–69.

Reed, Adele. *Old Mammoth.* Edited by Genny Smith. Palo Alto, CA: N.p., 1982.

Regalbuto, Robert J. *A Guide to Monastic Guest Houses.* 3d ed. Harrisburg, PA: Morehouse, 1998.

Reinecke, John E. *A History of Local 5, Hotel and Restaurant Employees and Bartenders International Union (AFL-CIO), Honolulu, Hawaii.* Edited by Edward D. Beechert. Honolulu: University of Hawaii, Labor-Management Education Program, 1970.

Rodnitzky, Jerome L. "Recapturing the West: The Dude Ranch in American Life." *Arizona and the West* 10 (1968): 111–26.

Romo, Cheryl. "The Mystery of Hans Wiesel and the Bar-W: Brave Struggle against Great Odds." *American West* 22 (1985): 66–71.

Roomet, Louise B. "Vermont as a Resort Area in the Nineteenth Century." *Vermont History* 44 (1976): 1–13.

Rooming House Hotel News. Chicago: Chicago Rooming House Association, 1924.

Rosen, Shirley. *Truman of St. Helens: The Man and His Mountain.* Seattle: Madrona; Longview, WA: Longview, 1981.

Rosenthal, Leon S. "Hotels: Pioneers in Progress." *American History Illustrated* 1 (1967): 42–53.

Roundy, Charles G. "The Origins and Early Development of Dude Ranching in Wyoming." *Annals of Wyoming* 45 (1973): 5–26.

Rubin, Jay, and Michael J. Obermeier. *Growth of a Union: The Life and Times of Edward Flore* [Hotel and Restaurant Employees' International Alliance and Bartenders' International League of America]. New York: Historical Union Association, 1943.

Saunders, Neil. *Great Hotels and Motels at Half Price across America*. Lanham, MD: Madison Books, 1995; distributed by National Book Network.

Saxton, Martha. "The Bliss Business: Institutionalizing the American Honeymoon." *American Heritage* 29 (1978): 80–87.

Schaeffer, John. *A Place in the Sun: The Evolution of the Real Goods Solar Living Center*. White River Junction, VT: Chelsea Green, 1997.

Scherman, Tony. "The Theresa." *American Legacy* 3, no. 4 (Winter 1998): 12–20.

Schmidt, Arno. *Notes from the Chef's Desk* [Waldorf-Astoria Hotel]. Edited by Jule Wilkinson. Boston: Cahners Books International, 1977.

Schriftgiesser, Karl. *Oscar* [Tschirky] *of the Waldorf*. New York: E. P. Dutton, 1943.

Scott, David Logan, and Kay Woelfel Scott. *The Complete Guide to National Park Lodges*. Old Saybrook, CT: Globe Pequot Press, 1998.

Setterdahl, Lilly, and J. Hiram Wilson. "Hotel Accommodations in the Bishop Hill Colony." *Swedish Pioneer Historical Quarterly* 29 (1978): 180–97.

Sherry, John E. H. *The Laws of Innkeepers: For Hotels, Motels, Restaurants, and Clubs*. 3d ed. Ithaca, NY: Cornell University Press, 1993.

Shipley, Ellen Lampton. "The Pleasures of Prosperity: Bella Vista, Arkansas, 1917–29." *Arkansas Historical Quarterly* 37 (1978): 99–129.

Shipp, P. Royal, and Robert Moore Fisher. *The Postwar Boom in Hotels and Motels*. Staff Economic Studies, no. 6. Washington, DC: Board of Governors of the Federal Reserve System, 1965.

Siefkin, David. *Meet Me at the St. Francis: The First Seventy-five Years of a Great San Francisco Hotel*. San Francisco: St. Francis Hotel, 1979.

Smith, Horace Herbert. *Crooks of the Waldorf, Being the Story of Joe Smith, Master Detective*. New York: Macaulay, 1929.

Smith, Michael E. *Alaska's Historic Roadhouses*. Prepared by Department of Natural Resources, Alaska Division of Parks, Office of Statewide Cultural Programs. Miscellaneous Publications, History and Archaeology Series, no. 6. Boulder, CO: Western Interstate Commission for Higher Education, 1974.

Starace, Carl A. "Fire Island Surf Hotel." *Long Island Forum* 33 (August 1970): 56–59; (September 1970): 188–94.

Starr, Raymond Leo. *Marion* [W. Isbell]. New York: Vantage Press, 1987.

Steen, Ivan D. "Palaces for Travelers: New York City's Hotels in the 1850s as Viewed by British Visitors." *New York History* 51 (1979): 269–86.

Steeples, Douglas. *Treasure from the Painted Hills: A History of Calico, California, 1882–1907*. Contributions in Economics and Economic History, no. 205. Westport, CT: Greenwood Press, 1999.

Stegner, Wallace. "Xanadu by the Salt Flats." *American Heritage* 32 (1981): 81–87.

Steinback, Elsa Kny. *Sweet Peas and a White Bridge on Lake George When Steam Was King*. Burlington, VT: G. Little Press, 1974.

Stokes, Arch Y. *The Equal Opportunity Handbook for Hotels, Restaurants, and Institutions*. Stokes Employee Relations Series. Boston: CBI, 1979.

Stokes, Harry. *Hotel Gettysburg: A Landmark in Our Nation's History*. Edited by Elise Scharf Fox. Gettysburg, PA: Downtown Gettysburg, 1988.

Strasma, Norman, and Janice Strasma. *Norm Strasma's Inn Marketing* [small ho-

tels and country inns]. Kankakee, IL: Norman & Janice Strasma, 1994– .
Monthly (except August and December).

Sutton, Horace. *Confessions of a Grand Hotel: The Waldorf-Astoria.* New York:
Holt, 1953.

Temple, Wayne C. "Abraham Lincoln and Others at the Saint Nicholas." *Lincoln
Herald* 70 (1968): 79–124.

Thomas, Janet. *At Home in Hostel Territory: A Guide to Friendly Lodgings from
Seward to Santa Cruz.* Anchorage: Alaska Northwest Book, 1994.

Thompson, Tom, and Marthea Thompson. *Cabins, Cottages & Resorts of
Northern California.* Meadow Vista, CA: Rustic Getaways, 1994.

Tolles, Bryant F., Jr. "Abel Hutchins and the Building Contract for the Phoenix
Hotel, Concord, New Hampshire." *Historic New Hampshire* 29 (1972):
224–34.

Trends in the Hotel Industry. United States. New York: Pannell, Kerr, Forster,
1981– . Quarterly.

U.S. Congress. Senate. Committee on Public Buildings and Grounds. Various Bills
and Resolutions. Hearings. 78th Cong., 2d sess., January 20, 1944.

U.S. Laws, Statutes, etc. *Federal Hotel & Motel Laws.* Canoga Park, CA: Hotel
Law Pub. Service, 1977.

U.S. Office for Emergency Management. *Guide to the Organization and Operation
of Homes Registration Offices.* Washington, DC: Executive Office of the
President, Office for Emergency Management, Division of Defense Housing
Coordination, 1941.

Van Orman, Richard A. *A Room for the Night: Hotels of the Old West.* Bloomington: Indiana University Press, 1966.

———. "Hotels of the Old West." *American History Illustrated* 3 (1968): 38–44.

Vining, James W. "Slater Burgesser and His Famous Spring." *Western Illinois Regional Studies* 5 (1982): 184–95.

Wakefield, Manville B. *To the Mountains by Rail: People, Events and Tragedies
. . . The New York, Ontario and Western Railway and the Famous Sullivan
County Resorts.* Grahamsville, NY: Wakefair Press, 1970.

The Waldorf-Astoria Manuals. Vol. 1, *Manual of Procedure for the Front Office
Tower Apartments, Floor Clerk's Service, Patrons' History, Outgoing Mail
Division, Foreign Department, Latin-American Department, Travel Repre-
sentative.* Stamford, CT: Dahl, 1947.

Watkin, David et al. *Grand Hotel: The Golden Age of Palace Hotels: An Architectural and Social History.* Translated from the French by Daniel K.
Wheeler, Martine Meade, and Murray Syllie. New York: Vendome Press,
1984; distributed in the United States by Viking Press.

Weiner, Lynn. "Our Sister's Keepers: The Minneapolis Women's Christian Association and Housing for Working Women." *Minnesota History* 46 (1979):
189–200.

Welfare Council of New York City. *Homeless Men in New York City, Report.*
New York: Welfare Council of New York City, Project Committee on
Homeless Men, 1949.

Wetzel, Barbi. "Pioneer Hotel." *Northeastern Nevada Historical Society Quarterly*
2 (1985): 35–45.

Whitten, David O. *The Emergence of Giant Enterprise: 1860–1914: American*

Commercial Enterprise and Extractive Industries. Contributions in Economics and Economic History, no. 54. Westport, CT: Greenwood Press, 1983.

Whittlesey, Lee H. "Marshall's Hotel in the National Park." *Montana* 30 (1980): 42–51.

Who's Who among Innkeepers: A Biographical Reference Work about Hotel, Motel, and Resort Managers and Owners in America. New York: Rating, 1974.

Williamson, Jefferson. *The American Hotel.* New York: Knopf, 1930. Reprint. The Leisure Class in America. New York: Arno Press, 1975.

Wilson, Kemmons, with Robert Kerr. *Half Luck and Half Brains: The Kemmons Wilson, Holiday Inn Story.* Nashville, TN: Hambleton-Hill, 1996.

Wilson, Richard Guy, ed. *Victorian Resorts and Hotels: Essays from a Victorian Society Autumn Symposium.* Nineteenth Century (Victorian Society in America), vol. 8, nos. 1–2. Philadelphia: Victorian Society in America, 1982.

Wittemann, Ad, ed. *Hotel Housekeeping Runner.* Las Vegas: Camelot Consultants, 1989.

Woerner, H. Ray. "The Taverns of Early Lancaster and the Later Day Hotels." *Journal of the Lancaster County Historical Society* 73 (1969): 37–95.

Wolfe, Albert Benedict. *The Lodging House Problem in Boston.* Harvard Economic Studies, vol. 2. Boston: Houghton Mifflin, 1906.

Women's Rest Tour Association. *American Lodging List Issued by the Women's Rest Tour Association.* Boston: WRTA, 1931.

Wyckoff, D. Daryl, and W. Earl Sasser. *The U.S. Lodging Industry.* Lexington, MA: Lexington Books, 1981.

Zimmermann, George. *Travel Writers Recommend America's Best Resorts.* New York: Dutton, 1989.

Part X

Personal Services
ESIC 72.0

CHAPTER 14

FUNERAL SERVICE AND CREMATORIES, 72.6

MARGARET S. BOND

When Jessica Mitford's *American Way of Death* appeared in 1963, fifteen years after novelist Evelyn Waugh's *The Loved One*, the traditional mode of body disposal was an expensive celebration that would have brought a smile to the face of Thorstein Veblen, 1857–1929 (economist and author of *Theory of the Leisure Class*, 1899, and originator of the term "conspicuous consumption"). Waugh's fiction and Mitford's facts exposed the speciousness of ceremonies for the dead that impoverish survivors. When Mitford's updated *American Way of Death Revisited* was published in 1998, the author had herself been dead since 1996 (details of how her remains were handled have not been made public), and the traditional American funeral was in decline: more and more Americans were choosing inexpensive burial or cremation for family members or themselves, and the burial industry was in flux as mortuary managers struggled to cut variable costs and spread fixed costs over a larger market share through consolidation. In the late twentieth century, the funeral industry was finally incorporating operational changes institutionalized a century before in the nation's smokestack industries (Alger 1996; "Barbarians at the Pearly Gates" 1996; "Death's Future" 1998; Gill 1996; Heinz 1999; Howarth 1996; Mitford 1998; Roberts 1997; Smith 1996).

ORIGINS AND DEVELOPMENT OF CARE FOR THE DEAD

An anthropological investigation in Iraq revealed funeral practices of Neanderthal man that date ceremonial disposal of the dead to at least 60,000 years ago (Sullivan 1968). In ancient Egypt human remains were embalmed in the belief that souls would return to them. Ancient Greeks masked the odor of putrefying flesh with perfumes and spices; later Greeks, however, practiced cremation. The Romans practiced both burial and cremation, but preceding either, the body lay in state for viewing. To the Hebrews, cremation was an indignity to the body, and burial was required on the evening of the day of death. Early Christian burials were unpretentious until customs changed, and embalming gained popularity—Leonardo da Vinci devised venous injections to preserve corpses long enough for him to immortalize them on anatomical plates (Habenstein and Lamers 1955).

Colonial American funerals were simple ceremonies: mourners accompanied the coffin to the grave, lowered it into the earth, then refilled the grave. During the nineteenth century, the American undertaker became a specialist at laying out the dead and rose to prominence partly because of the church's unwillingness to maintain authority over the burial process. The Civil War created a market for embalming soldiers who had died far from home, and the assassination of President Abraham Lincoln stimulated public awareness of embalming—the funeral procession with his body on display traveled from Washington, DC, to Springfield, Illinois. At the end of the nineteenth century, states began to pass licensing legislation to regulate the practice of embalming: boards of health issued burial and cremation permits and made death certificates a legal part of the management of the dead.

During the nineteenth century, funeral services once conducted in private homes—parlors in well-to-do homes included a coffin door, a coffin-sized opening to ease the delivery and removal of a casket—moved to professional preparation and display facilities. In small towns undertakers prepared bodies in the home, sold caskets (often built to specification in a local cabinet shop and decorated by a local seamstress in her home), delivered the body to the cemetery, and opened and closed the grave. If the deceased had no family or friend with a parlor for viewing, the undertaker might employ his back room as a home parlor and himself and his staff as surrogate family to greet visitors. This practice gave the undertaker's establishment the epithet of funeral parlor and began the evolution of large parlor, laboratory, and chapel into the twentieth-century funeral home (Bowman [1959] 1990).

ORGANIZATION OF THE FUNERAL ESTABLISHMENT

Some 22,500 funeral establishments and 9,600 cemeteries were operating in the United States in 1997. In the last years of the 1990s, the funeral industry reports its profit before taxes at 7.9 percent ("Funeral Services" 1997).

About 2 million people a year die in the United States, so on average each funeral home conducts eighty funerals. The average is, of course, meaningless, for it cloaks the diverse pattern of funerals and their markets.

The typical community mortuary is a family operation located in a town of about 20,000, less than 100 miles from a major metropolitan area. The facility occupies a building in the geographical center of the business district. The bereaved family and the funeral director arrange for the burial and associated ceremony in the same office where purchase records, bills, and receipts are prepared. Beyond the office are two main rooms, one where folding chairs are placed in rows for funeral services and one a preparation room equipped to carry out embalming, cosmetizing, dressing, and casketing of the dead—the preparation room resembles an operating room in a modern hospital. There is also a casket selection room. Most funerals are for people from the immediate community. Because funerals are not spaced at planned intervals, however, personnel have more to do sometimes than at others; although activities are routinized, personnel do not follow a specified schedule.

The cosmopolitan mortuary is located in a city of over 1 million people, usually near a metropolitan hospital. The complexity of the firm's organization increases. The firm rents limousines, hearses, flower cars, service cars, as the need arises. The drivers of these vehicles are union employees whose only function is to drive. The building occupies most of one city block. The business and accounting office handles and houses all statistical records, family histories, billings, purchases, sales, and so on. It is staffed by accountants, statisticians, and typists whose jobs are confined to papers and books. The dispatch office is the nerve center where calls from bereaved families are received. As the director talks with the family on the phone, he completes three forms, one used in the internal operation of the funeral home until the funeral, one for filing the death certificate with the board of health, and one for the bookkeeping office. A large selection room displays about forty caskets and other funeral merchandise. A preparation room equipped with embalming tables and dressing tables is locked and never open to the public.

The typical cosmopolitan funeral home conducts about 400 funerals a year. At the top of the service organization is the owner, seldom glimpsed by the public. Next in line are family-controlled managerial positions, often occupied by figureheads, for in the next level are the actual managers. There is only one licensed manager, and although he is a licensed funeral director, his responsibilities are limited to occasionally counseling the bereaved in the planning of the funeral service. These counselors are inextricably caught up in the process of sales. Next in line are the supervisors in charge of personnel logistics, followed by the licensed funeral directors who conduct and direct funerals and attend bereaved families. Under the funeral directors are the "removal men" whose responsibility is to go to the place of death with the appropriate equipment and remove the body. They pick up burial permits and death certificates and deliver them to offices of vital statistics, help with embalming, and accompany hearse drivers to cemeteries

(Salomone 1967). A chief embalmer is assisted by the removal men not otherwise occupied. Many people carry out the task of embalming, and often one person begins and another finishes a job. The apprentices occupy the lowest level in the organizational hierarchy. Apprentices are registered with the state's department of health as certified trainees in the field and may assist at embalming. Usually, however, they run errands, clean up, put up flowers, or perform any other job that is not the direct responsibility of someone else. The dispatcher handles personnel and equipment for funeral arrangements and communicates with cemeteries and churches.

For the American funeral director the educational requirements are scant. Some states specify educational requirements only for embalmers, but generally funeral directors or embalmers must have completed one or two years of college plus one year of mortuary science courses followed by one or two years as an apprentice or trainee. The funeral director, like the physician, has access to the human body. When a body is entrusted to him, the bereaved family believes the funeral director's competence to be such that he will not damage the body and that he will do no more than is necessary to carry out his occupational duties.

Whether community or metropolitan, the funeral home is usually long established, family-owned, and successful. The financial profit is related to the sale of funerary merchandise, especially caskets. As Americans became more conscious of the status value of the casket, funeral directors saw an opportunity to operate more profitably by stocking more expensive merchandise.

FUNERAL AND BURIAL COSTS

In the United States funeral expenditures are divided among the funeral director, crematory or cemetery, clergyman, and florist. The largest portion goes to the director, whose charges include the casket, his professional services, use of the necessary equipment and facilities, and motor equipment. Since bereaved people often have no experience of death and funerals, it is the director's job to familiarize them with funeral practices.

Undertakers view their role as indispensable since they provide a service that few people want to perform themselves. They are called upon to render service for which there is no price tag: preparing for burial the mutilated bodies of suicides, accident and disaster victims, and those who have died from disfiguring illnesses. Undertakers also point out that they provide funerals for welfare and charity cases and for the indigent, often at a financial loss (Raether 1971; Ellenberg 1997).

Critics of the funeral industry argue that overhead costs are exaggerated. Some funeral home conglomerates draw on a pool of services in cities where they own more than one funeral home. Teams of embalmers, undertakers, chauffeurs, and salespeople are sent where they are needed, and a fleet of funeral coaches supplies transportation. Pooling allows the organizations to serve, say, six funeral homes with only twice the number of cars they would need for one firm. A central dispatcher handles calls at night.

The price of a typical adult funeral is based on five major components: coffin, embalming, extras, vault, and cemetery. Although federal law requires mortuaries to itemize charges, funerals are built around the choice of coffin. If the family chooses an expensive casket, the funeral home staff will press for more extras than might be expected of those who select the bottom of the line. Even though strict product and service bundling has been outlawed since the 1970s, funerals are still constructed around the coffin; and coffin sales changed drastically in the last quarter of the twentieth century.

Coffin

Basing the price of a funeral on the cost of the coffin originated at the end of the nineteenth century, when undertakers were called the "Dismal Traders." Coffin makers advised furniture dealers to mark up the wholesale cost of the casket three times to cover out-of-pocket costs, fixed costs or overhead, and profit. As undertaking developed into a full-time business, the markup increased to four or five to one.

The bereaved family is tempted with solid copper caskets and 18-gauge lead-coated steel boxes for long-lasting protection. To anesthetize sales resistance, funeral personnel emphasize the casket's comfort, durability, beauty, and craftsmanship. Sixty color-matched shades (even silver) are available for the lining of the casket. Some caskets are equipped with foam rubber and innerspring mattresses; some offer a "Perfect Posture" bed.

There are many types and styles of coffins. In the "full couch" the entire body can be viewed. The "half-couch" shows the body from the waist up; the "hinge cap" is similar to the half-couch. On the "lift-lid" the upper half lifts off the case. The most expensive woods used are oak, birch, maple, cherry, mahogany; the less expensive woods—pine, chestnut, cypress, red cedar—are covered with cloth. Most adult caskets are made of steel. Linings range from muslin to velvet. Pressured to sell costly merchandise and services, funeral personnel may coerce consumers into purchasing the more expensive coffins by pitching protective features, hoping to instill guilt in survivors who, by not purchasing a costly coffin, would expose the deceased to the elements. Deprecatory terms like "orange crates," "rowboats," "stovepipes" are used to describe the cheap coffins. In many funeral homes the cheapest coffins are shown not in the selection room but in a dimly lighted space under the stairs, in the basement, behind curtains. Funeral directors and casket manufacturers vulgarize cheap caskets by using tawdry or garish linings and poor finishing. Customers are urged to protect the body by choosing expensive coffins sealed with rubber gaskets.

The coffin market is a window on the interment revolution of the late twentieth century. When Mitford published *American Way of Death* in 1963, caskets were, despite their daily use throughout the United States, neither advertised nor mentioned in polite conversation. Nor was there competition or a visible market. Potential buyers gave no thought to a coffin until suddenly (in most cases) a death created an immediate need. Funeral arrangements were purchased in a whirl that included a visit to a warehouse where the coffin became a ubiquitous fixture in a welter of decision making.

Viewing the selection at the warehouse did little to lift the cloak of mystery surrounding the coffin, for the buyer was left with no more information after the purchase than before. An expensive purchase was made without the buyer's knowing what was bought, what was delivered, or how much had been paid for it. The coffin chosen from the display was not necessarily the one used for the burial; after all, had distraught survivors the presence of mind to examine the item at point of purchase, then again at the viewing or funeral? Moreover, if the coffin was bundled into a funeral package, its price was indiscernible.

The 1998 *American Way of Death Revisited* was released into a world vastly changed since 1963, and many of the changes in the mortuary industry can be traced to reactions to Mitford's original volume. Caskets are no longer restricted to funeral home warehouses but can be examined, compared, and bargained for like most products in the U.S. market. Coffin superstores display hundreds of models all clearly priced. Competition for buyers encourages coffin sellers to advertise and to employ marketing tactics established in other durable goods markets. Courts have ruled that mortuaries cannot restrict their services to customers who buy coffins from them. Morticians in the 1990s practice the old ways when possible—some buyers prefer the cloaked-marketing system because it requires few decisions—even so, the nontraditional funeral buyer is not a marginal apparition but a trailblazer into the future (Alger 1996; "Casket Catalog Alive and Kicking" 1997; "Casket Stores Offer Bargains to Die For" 1997; Cavanaugh 1996; "Low-Cost Options Attract Consumers in Competitive $16 Billion Funeral Industry" 1998; "Milwaukee Area Firm Wants to Franchise Low-Cost Funeral Services" 1997; "Traditional Funeral Services Are Facing a Serious Illness" 1999; "A True Lifetime Value" 1997).

Embalming

An open-coffin funeral demands embalming and the extra costs of producing a viewable body. Most funeral directors include it in the cost whether or not it is really done. When survivors ask that embalming not be done, a charge for "preservation" (i.e., refrigeration) will be added that can cost as much as embalming. Undertakers maintain that embalming protects public health, yet nowhere in the United States is embalming required by law. The practice has been misrepresented by undertakers, and many funeral buyers assume it is a legal requirement. Without embalming, the undertaker's services could shrink to a few simple tasks. Since Federal Trade Commission regulations forbid the misleading of funeral buyers about embalming, morticians have turned to lobbying, advertising, public relations, and educational materials to promote funerals "with the body present."

Extras

Although items and services considered extras vary among funeral homes, burial clothes, newspaper death notices, copies of death certificates, and out-of-town transportation of the body are always so designated. Morticians pay for these on behalf of the funeral buyers and are reimbursed later.

Autopsy

Autopsy by a medical examiner and sometimes by a coroner is required by law when death occurs without an attending physician or under questionable circumstances. In some states every prison inmate, upon death, automatically becomes a coroner's case, necessitating an autopsy. In rare instances, autopsies are performed, usually after arterial, but not cavity, embalming is completed.

The general purpose of autopsy is to determine the cause of death as well as to provide detailed information about anatomic abnormalities. Many people are uncomfortable at the thought of a postmortem examination. Their uneasiness may be based on the belief that the body is mutilated during the process or that their religion forbids autopsy because it prevents a proper burial with the body intact.

Vault

The container enclosing the coffin when it is placed in the ground is a costly component of twentieth-century American burials. There is no evidence that it offers permanent or prolonged protection for a body, as vault manufacturers imply; instead, a sealed, airtight vault may hasten decomposition. A vault is not required by law but can be required by cemetery operators, who claim that a container keeps the ground from collapsing as the coffin disintegrates. Some cemeteries sell concrete grave liners for less than the steel or fiberglass vaults sold by funeral homes. Because of extensive promotion by vault companies and undertakers as well as cemetery requirements, three-fourths of all burials include a coffin enclosure. Extensive flooding in the 1980s and 1990s swept some cemeteries clean, sending coffins floating down swollen rivers. Newspaper photographs of distraught relatives wearing protective masks while searching among recovered coffins probably did more to promote the sale of vaults than any advertising could.

Cemetery

Funeral buyers are often surprised to learn there are cemetery costs in addition to the price of the funeral: the purchase price of the plot, opening and closing the grave, installing a marker or monument, care of the grave site, and recording fees. Just as a grave liner is manufactured for a fraction of what buyers pay for it, a grave opened or closed with a backhoe in just twenty minutes costs on average $900. Owners of private cemeteries are sometimes accused of deceptive or exploitative practices, including bundling monuments with the sale of grave plots, misinforming consumers about legal requirements for vaults, and failing to maintain graves as agreed under perpetual care contracts.

In many locales the city or county government, local churches, or community service organizations minimize costs to residents by owning, operating, and maintaining nonprofit public burial grounds. Towns with public cemeteries rarely prevent private firms from establishing competitive facilities for those who would pay extra for burial in a special place not open to the general public.

Despite a strong American market for earth burials, some cemeteries cannot attract sales, while others cannot meet the demand for space. The best-known grave site in the United States is the national cemetery at Arlington, Virginia, where the few remaining burial spaces are dispensed under the supervision of top federal authorities. It is an unusual year if the newspapers fail to report a scandal over an Arlington interment with a supplementary story about other federal cemeteries that attract few new burials. The National Association of Cemeteries estimates that the unfilled capacity of burial grounds of all types can provide for ground burial in the United States for less than a century. Fifty-five national cemeteries in twenty-seven states have space available, but sites are running out in urban and suburban areas. Some cities, like San Francisco, forbid burial within their limits, creating demand for burial space in the suburbs and the development of "cities of the dead," towns where the dead vastly outnumber the living because the leading local industry is burial and grave maintenance. In New York City's Calvary Cemetery, more than 2 million bodies are buried in 500 acres (Mitford 1963). In Nashville, Tennessee, a twenty-story skyscraper containing 258,000 crypts is the nation's tallest community mausoleum. Built in the shape of a cross, the building is known as the "Death Hilton."

Cremation

Cremation is an inexpensive alternative to a conventional burial—most crematories charge only a few hundred dollars to incinerate a body. Some crematories require the body to be delivered in a coffin, but fiberboard or plain wood is all that is legally required. Ashes can be buried, scattered, pulverized, or placed in a cemetery's columbarium. For direct cremation the undertaker transports the body in a simple container to the crematorium (Mitford 1985). In the mid-1990s about 22 percent of the American dead were cremated; by the year 2010, the industry anticipates a 40 percent cremation rate.

Cremation is the second C in the trio of coffins, cremation, and consolidation that signifies the interment revolution of the late twentieth century. Because cremation costs at most about half as much as ground burial, the growth of that alternative is likely to continue until more bodies are incinerated than buried. The best hope for the mortuary operators is advertising to promote the notion of a moral obligation in choosing burial over cremation. The second best alternative for maintaining profits is burial insurance and creative marketing to push the earnings from a cremation upward with expensive containers for the body and the ashes, extravagant services, and elaborate storage facilities for the ashes or complicated scatterings in outer space, midocean, and so on (Alger 1996; "Cremation Rates" 1999; Kubasak 1990; Lankford 1996; "Low-Cost Options" 1998; "Neighbors Will Burn With Envy" 1994; "Philadelphia Firm Offers Unusual Ash Scattering Service" 1996).

HEALTH AND FUTURE OF THE FUNERAL INDUSTRY

The funeral industry, like other American businesses at the end of the twentieth century, faces a changing market. People are eschewing the traditional funeral for inexpensive burials or cremation. The industry, dominated by a large number of small mortuary firms, is in the grips of a consolidation movement likely to run well into the twenty-first century. Equity Corporation International of Houston, Texas, for example, owns 250 funeral homes and seventy-five cemeteries. As late as 1997 the publicly traded mortuary and cemetery companies represented less than 25 percent of the revenue for the industry but, at the present rate of change, may account for more than 50 percent in the early decades of the twenty-first century ("Agreement Is Made to Sell Cemeteries, Funeral Homes" 1999; "Consolidation Continues in 'Death-Care' Industry" 1996; "Consolidation

Seen Alive, Well in Death-Care Industry" 1997; "Equity Corp.'s Tough Deals Standards" 1998).

BIBLIOGRAPHIC ESSAY

Mitford's books reveal the burial industry over thirty-five years of the interment revolution: the original *American Way of Death* (1963) may be the salvo that opened the battle; *The American Way of Death Revisited* (1998) describes the U.S. funeral market three decades into the revolution. Mitford's views can be compared with those of other industry observers: Alger (1996), "Barbarians at the Pearly Gates" (1996), Canine (1999), Cronin (1996), Ellenberg (1997), "Funeral Services—The U.S. Funeral Services Industry" (1998), Gill (1996), Heinz (1999), Howarth (1996), Roberts (1997), Smith (1996), *U.S. Funeral Services Industry* (1997).

The literature on the consolidation movement in the funeral service industry is too recent for monographic studies. Articles in business journals and newspapers offer an outline of the early developments and expectations for the future: "Agreement to Sell Cemeteries" (1999), "Consolidation Continues" (1996), "Consolidation Alive" (1997), "Deadly Competition" (1998), "Death's Future" (1998), "Funeral Prospects" (1995), "Funeral Services" (1998), Smith (1996).

An inquiry into industry trends as seen by insiders demands a study of mortuary trade journals: *American Cemetery; American Funeral Director; Cemetery Management; The Director* (National Funeral Directors Association); *Funeral Monitor: For All Concerned with the Service of Funerals; Funeral Service; Funeral Service Insider Newsletter; International Cemetery & Funeral Management: Official Publication of the International Cemetery & Funeral Association; Markers: The Annual Journal of the Association for Gravestone Studies; Medical & Healthcare Marketplace Guide; Mortuary Management; National Funeral Director and Embalmer; National Funeral Service Journal; Professional Embalmer; U.S. Funeral Services Industry: A Marketing, Competitive, and Operational Analysis.*

BIBLIOGRAPHY

"Agreement Is Made to Sell Cemeteries, Funeral Homes." *Wall Street Journal*, March 2, 1999, B9.
Alger, Alexandra. "The New (and More Convenient) American Way of Death." *Forbes* 158, no. 10 (October 21, 1996): 324.
American Cemetery. Chicago: Prettyman, monthly.
American Funeral Director. Canton, OH: Kates-Boylston, monthly.
"Barbarians at the Pearly Gates." *The Economist* 340, no. 7985 (September 28, 1996): 79.
Bowman, LeRoy. *The American Funeral: A Study in Guilt, Extravagance, and Sub-

limity. Washington, DC: Public Affairs Press, 1959. Reprint. Detroit: Omnigraphics, 1990.

Canine, John. *What Am I Going to Do with Myself When I Die?* Stamford, CT: Appleton & Lange, 1999.

"Casket Catalog Alive and Kicking." *Catalog Age* 14, no. 12 (November 1997): 18.

"Casket Stores Offer Bargains to Die For." *Wall Street Journal*, February 19, 1997, B.

Cavanaugh, Tim. "Bargain Pine Boxes." *American Demographics* 18, no. 9 (September 1996): 21.

Cemetery Management. Falls Church, VA: American Cemetery Association, monthly.

Cemeteries of the U.S.: A Guide to Contact Information for U.S. Cemeteries and Their Records. Detroit: Gale Research, 1994– . Every three years.

"Coffin Company Acquired." *New York Times*, June 25, 1997, C6.

"Consolidation Continues in 'Death-Care' Industry." *Bank Loan Report* 11, no. 32 (August 5, 1996): 4.

"Consolidation Seen Alive, Well in Death-Care Industry." *Going Public: The IPO Reporter* 21, no. 47 (November 24, 1997): 8.

Consumer Reports. *Funerals: Consumers' Last Rights.* New York: Norton, 1977.

"Cremation Rates." *USA Today*, January 12, 1999, 1A.

Cronin, Xavier A. *Grave Exodus: Tending to Our Dead in the Twenty-First Century.* New York: Barricade Books, 1996.

"Dancing on Graves." *Forbes* 153, no. 5 (February 28, 1994): 64.

"Deadly Competition: Diocese Efforts to Bolster Funeral Business Grave Concern to Industry." *Crain's Cleveland Business*, July 27, 1998, 1.

"Death Be Not (So) Profitable." *Business Week*, October 5, 1998, 100.

"Death's Future." *Marketing News* 32, no. 2 (January 19, 1998): 15.

"Death Watch? Black Funeral Homes Fear a Gloomy Future as Big Chains Move In." *Wall Street Journal*, July 18, 1997, A1.

The Director. Milwaukee: National Funeral Directors Association, monthly.

Ellenberg, William. *Death: Through the Eyes of a Funeral Director.* Douglasville, GA: Anneewakee River Press, 1997.

"Equity Corp.'s Tough Deals Standards." *Mergers & Acquisitions* 32, no. 4 (January 1998): 43.

Frederick, Edwin C., Sr. *The Last Laugh: Fifty Years of Unusual Undertakings.* Brentwood, NH: Wicked Good Books, 1997.

Funeral Monitor: For All Concerned with the Service of Funerals. Monterey, CA: Abbott & Hast, 48 issues a year.

"Funeral Prospects." *Forbes* 156, no. 6 (September 11, 1995): 45.

Funeral Service. Chicago: Trade Periodical, monthly.

Funeral Service Insider Newsletter. New York: ATCOM, weekly.

"Funeral Services." *Medical & Healthcare Marketplace Guide*, January 1997.

"Funeral Services—The U.S. Funeral Services Industry." *Medical & Healthcare Marketplace Guide*, January 1998, 1:I-665+ .

Gill, Richard T. "Whatever Happened to the American Way of Death?" *Public Interest* 123 (Spring 1996): 105.

Habenstein, Robert W., and William W. Lamers. *The History of American Funeral Directing*. Milwaukee: Bulfin Printers, 1955.

Harrah, Barbara K., and David F. Harrah. *Funeral Service: A Bibliography of Literature on Its Past, Present, and Future, the Various Means of Disposition, and Memorialization*. Metuchen, NJ: Scarecrow Press, 1976.

Heinz, Donald. *The Last Passage: Recovering a Death of Our Own*. New York: Oxford University Press, 1999.

Holt, Dean W. *American Military Cemeteries: A Comprehensive Illustrated Guide to the Hallowed Grounds of the United States, including Cemeteries Overseas*. Jefferson, NC: McFarland, 1992.

Howarth, Glennys. *Last Rites: The Work of the Modern Funeral Director*. Amityville, NY: Baywood, 1996.

Hughes Wright, Roberta, and Wilbur B. Hughes III. *Lay Down Body: Living History in African American Cemeteries*. Edited by Gina Renee Misiroglu. Detroit: Visible Ink Press, 1996.

International Cemetery & Funeral Management: Official Publication of the International Cemetery & Funeral Association. Reston, VA: International Cemetery & Funeral Association, monthly.

"Is There a Layaway Plan?" *Marketing News* 33, no. 6 (March 15, 1999): 13.

"Justice Department Backs Independent Funeral Homes' Request." *Hackensack (New Jersey) Record*, January 19, 1999.

Kubasak, Michael W. *Cremation and the Funeral Director: Successfully Meeting the Challenge*. Malibu, CA: Avalon Press, 1990.

Lankford, Kimberly. "Funeral Insurance Is Alive and Well." *Life Association News* 91, no. 1 (January 1996): 33.

Levine, Joshua, and Seth Lubove. "Cash and Bury." *Forbes* 149, no. 10 (May 11, 1992): 162.

"Loewen Acquisitions." *Globe & Mail*, November 21, 1996, B2.

"Low-Cost Options Attract Consumers in Competitive $16 Billion Funeral Industry." *About Women & Marketing* 11, no. 5 (May 1998): 10.

Lycar, Elizabeth, and Lorrie Guymer Hutton. *Quite an Undertaking: The Story of Violet Guymer, Canada's First Female Licensed Funeral Director*. Kelowna, British Columbia: Nip & Tuck, 1996.

Markers: The Annual Journal of the Association for Gravestone Studies. Worcester, MA: Association for Gravestone Studies, annual.

Medical & Healthcare Marketplace Guide. Philadelphia: IDD Enterprises, 1975. Annual.

"Milwaukee Area Firm Wants to Franchise Low-Cost Funeral Services." *Milwaukee Journal Sentinel*, April 7, 1997.

Mitford, Jessica. *The American Way of Death*. New York: Simon & Schuster, 1963.

———. "Til Death Do Ye Part." *Consumer Digest*, March/April 1985, 82–83.

———. *The American Way of Death Revisited*. Rev. ed. New York: Alfred A. Knopf, 1998.

Mortuary Management. Los Angeles: Berg, 1914– . Eleven issues annually.

"Mourning a Dying Institution." *Chicago Tribune*, April 18, 1998, 2:11.

National Funeral Director and Embalmer. Chicago: National Funeral Directors & Morticians Association.

National Funeral Service Journal. Chicago: Trade Periodical, 1959–1966. Monthly. Continued by *Funeral Service.*

"Neighbors Will Burn with Envy." *Business Week,* September 26, 1994, 8.

Palmeri, Christopher. "Funereal Prospects." *Forbes* 156, no. 6 (September 11, 1995): 45–46.

"Patents: Coffins." *New York Times,* February 26, 1996, C2.

"Philadelphia Firm Offers Unusual Ash Scattering Service." *Philadelphia Inquirer,* April 1, 1996.

Pine, Vanderlyn, R. *Caretaker of the Dead: The American Funeral Director.* New York: Irvington, 1975; distributed by Halsted Press.

———. *A Statistical Abstract of Funeral Service Facts and Figures of the United States: The Findings of a Survey of 1981 Funeral Service Income and Expense Data.* Milwaukee: National Funeral Directors Association of the United States, 1982.

Pine, Vanderlyn R., and Derek L. Phillips. "The Cost of Dying: Sociological Analysis of Funeral Expenditure." *Social Problems,* Winter 1970, 405–17.

Poe, Randall. "The Selling of Mortality." *Across the Board,* March 1986, 34–39.

Professional Embalmer. Chicago: Undertakers Supply.

Raether, Howard C. *Successful Funeral Service Practice.* Englewood Cliffs, NJ: Prentice-Hall, 1971.

"Reports by Funeral Giants Suggest Loewen's Woes Unique." *Globe & Mail,* October 26, 1998, B7.

Roberts, Darryl J. *Profits of Death: An Insider Exposes the Death Care Industries.* Chandler, AZ: Five Star Publications, 1997.

Ruhl, Jack M. "Providing Advisory Services to Funeral Directors." *The CPA Journal* 63, no. 3 (March 1993): 36.

Salomone, Jerome J. "The Status of Funerals and Funeral Directors." *American Funeral Director* 90 (October 1967): 69–74.

Schwartz, Martin L., Marvin A. Jolson, and Ronald H. Lee. "The Marketing of Funeral Services: Past, Present, and Future." *Business Horizons* 29, no. 2 (March/April 1986): 40–46.

Showalter, Paul. "The Business of Death." *Venture* 9, no. 1 (January 1987): 30–33.

Smith, Ronald G. E. *The Death Care Industries in the United States.* Jefferson, NC: McFarland, 1996.

Statistical Abstract of Funeral Service Facts and Figures of the United States. Milwaukee: National Funeral Directors Association of the United States, annual.

Sullivan, Walter, "The Neanderthal Man Liked Flowers." *New York Times,* June 13, 1968, 1–43.

"Traditional Funeral Services Are Facing a Serious Illness." *Wall Street Journal,* March 22, 1999, B4.

"A True Lifetime Value." *Direct* 9, no. 12 (September 15, 1997): 18.

"Turning Cold Data into Hot Leads." *Business Marketing* 82, no. 2 (February 1998): 14.

U.S. Federal Trade Commission. "Funeral Industry Practices—Trade Regulation Rule." *Federal Register* 2 (September 24, 1982).

U.S. Funeral Services Industry: A Marketing, Competitive, and Operational Analysis. Tampa, FL: Marketdata Enterprises, 1997.

"VA Buys Medina Land for Cemetery." *Cleveland Plain Dealer*, September 6, 1995, 1B.

Van Beck, Todd W. *Winning Ways: The Funeral Profession's Guide to Human Relations*. Stamford, CT: Appleton & Lange, 1998.

Yost, Lance. *The Path to Funeral Consultancy*. Chandler, AZ: Five Star Publication, 1998.

Zipser, Andy. "Grave Error." *Barron*'s 75, no. 34 (August 21, 1995): 15–16.

Part XI

Business Services
ESIC 73.0

CHAPTER 15

ADVERTISING AGENCIES, 73.1

R. D. PETERSON

Advertising agencies are service establishments primarily engaged in contracting on commission for space in magazines, newspapers, and periodicals; for time on radio or television; or for other advertising media. Agencies create and place nearly all national magazine advertising and approximately half the newspaper advertising. They buy most of the radio and television time used for advertising but are less likely to contract for local newspaper, point-of-purchase, and direct mail advertising.

As enterprises that plan, prepare, and place advertising for clients, agencies provide various marketing services, such as pricing, product development, market research, and sales training, as well as management activities. The advertising agency industry includes firms that perform advertising and collateral services offered to a common group of buyers. In the four-digit census industry SIC 7311, (1) only advertising agencies are considered; (2) media, advertisers, and management consultant firms are not included; but (3) no firms are excluded that perform advertising and collateral services. Advertising agencies seldom diversify into areas not associated with advertising and related marketing services. Although all buyers of advertising are not common customers to all agencies, SIC 7311 delimits this study of advertising agencies (*Standard Industrial Classification Manual 1987*, 360).

Agencies (independent contractors, not agents) encompass an advertiser, an agency, and a medium. The agency supplies advertising and other services for a client—a firm wishing to advertise—by creating copy and placing it in newspapers and magazines or on television and radio. Agencies are paid with media commissions and special fees or charges for advertising and related marketing tasks. The development of the advertising agency began in colonial America.

INCEPTION: 1704 TO 1840

Some scholars of advertising argue that there were no advertising agencies in Europe or in America before 1800 (Hower 1949), but historical accounts suggest an earlier beginning. In its April 24, 1704, edition the *Boston News-Letter*, the first American newspaper, announced its willingness to sell space in the paper for messages. The first paid advertisement appeared there in May 1704 (Presbrey [1929] 1968). Colonial postmasters, newsdealers, and solicitors functioned as early "advertising agencies."

Postmasters

Colonial publishers supplemented their income from activities other than printing. Some sold medicine, Bibles, even slaves; many were postmasters or employees of the postal department and could, for a low fee, hire local postriders to carry newspapers. Advertising copy for colonial newspapers could be left at the post office: a postmaster might accept messages for publication in a number of different papers in return for a commission (Lee 1916; Hower 1949).

Newsdealers

American newspaper publishers in the early nineteenth century, like their French counterparts, disregarded the meager income available from advertisements (Presbrey [1929] 1968). Newspaper subscribers resented the presence of advertising, and publishers were embarrassed to seek it (Mott 1947). Advertising was accepted but not solicited. This passive attitude toward selling space placed most of the burden on the advertiser, who sought a convenient method of getting advertising messages to publishers. Stationers, booksellers, and other news agents forwarded advertisements and subscriptions to newspaper publishers.

Solicitors

Competition heated up as advertisers expanded beyond local markets. Publishers discovered that advertising revenue was essential to the survival of their newspapers when publication expenses could not be met with the income received from subscriptions alone. Many instructed their employees to solicit advertising from merchants and manufacturers. Early advertising solicitors soon found they could represent several papers at once.

Tasks Performed

Most eighteenth-century advertisements were similar to classified ads in present-day newspapers: simple, informative copy occasionally enhanced by art or illustrations. Advertisers dealt directly with the publishers, except when postmasters or newsdealers became intermediaries; these middlemen conveyed printing instructions to publishers, negotiated rates, checked for proper insertion and content, and sent money for payment.

NEWSPAPER AGENTS: 1841 TO 1855

As markets expanded in the first half of the nineteenth century, businesses began to broaden their sales efforts. Poor communication and transportation facilities hindered direct contact between advertisers and publishers. In 1841 Volney B. Palmer—an advertising solicitor for the Pottsville, Pennsylvania, *Miner's Journal*—established himself as an independent selling agent by claiming to represent, on a full-time basis, several newspapers instead of one. Between 1841 and about 1855 other newspaper agents worked the Northeast.

By 1842 there were more than 1,400 newspapers in the United States, but having little direct knowledge of these, newspaper agents spent a great deal of time compiling lists of newspapers from information obtained in other papers and from postmasters, newsdealers, and ink and paper dealers. An agent's list was a valuable proprietor right (Presbrey [1929] 1968).

Some publishers printed a schedule of rates, but most did not. Apparently, they failed to realize the value of advertising, for there was much confusion concerning rates. Agents engaged in clever bargaining that sometimes left nearly half the proceeds of a space sale as their commission. Newspaper agents were not risk-takers; they only represented the newspaper and incurred no loss if space remained unsold. During this period many publishers allowed agents a discount varying from 10 to 50 percent (Rowell 1926) but generally 25 percent (Hower 1949).

Newspaper agents called on business owners, bargained and established the rate for space, and helped advertisers select newspapers by showing copies of the publications they represented. Some offered to write advertisements, suggested illustrations, even gave advice on when to advertise. After finalizing an agreement, the agents forwarded instructions to publishers along with payment for the space (less a commission). The beginnings of modern agency practices appeared in media selection, creation of copy and art, campaign planning, and the commission method of agency compensation.

SPACE JOBBER: 1856–1864

The number of newspaper agents increased after 1841 along with competition, discounting, and innovative services. Around 1856 some agents in Boston, New York, and Philadelphia gave up commission work to operate as independent jobbers, selling the advertising space available to them from publishers (Hower 1949). The authority of middlemen to establish rates sparked competition that forced some agents to sell space at prices below publishers' rates. Publishers who accepted rate reductions usually regarded revenue from advertising as a windfall gain (Hower 1949); others repudiated rates made by their agents and demanded full payment. Agents became dealers in space, representing neither publishers nor advertisers but bargaining with both. The split between agents and publishers made agents representatives of advertisers. Space jobbers performed the same advertising tasks as newspaper agents: selecting media, bargaining on rates, collecting payment, and advising on copy, illustration, and strategy.

SPACE WHOLESALER: 1865–1874

In 1865 George P. Rowell began buying space from publishers in large quantities and selling it to advertisers in smaller lots, sometimes at rates lower than those other agents offered. Rowell, an advertising solicitor for the *Boston Post*, had discovered that publishers would sell an entire column of space cheaply for a year in advance because of the uncertainty in selling it daily or weekly. Rowell not only made money selling this space but reduced his costs further by persuading publishers to give him a 3 percent discount if he paid cash for space thirty days in advance (Rowell 1926). A few advertising agents began to contract early with publishers they represented at a fixed dollar amount, agreeing to assume risk and to manage all the advertising space in a publication. Advertising agents followed these schemes until space jobbers, who had been independent merchant middlemen purchasing to order, became space wholesalers, independent merchant middlemen purchasing to inventory. The space wholesaler, as a merchant middleman, bore the risk he assumed from publishers.

Space wholesalers continued to enhance services they offered advertisers. Some attempted to determine whether circulation rates were accurate. In 1869 Rowell made available to agents and advertisers *Rowell's American Newspaper Directory*, a compilation of 5,411 newspapers published in the United States and 367 from Canada (Presbrey [1929] 1968). The wholesalers continued to research the media during this period, helped generate copy, and arranged typesetting and electrotyping for only the cost of contracting this work to outside firms. Most of the arrangements for rate making, collecting payments, and advising carried over from the space jobbers to the space wholesalers. These forerunners of the modern advertising agency specialized by medium (Presbrey [1929] 1968) and represented the advertiser rather than the medium.

SEMISERVICE: 1875–1889

The agent's role in providing more than space to advertisers was rapidly evolving. The period between 1875 and 1889 was one of experimentation, a time during which entrants into the nascent industry attempted to compete with established firms by offering additional services to customers. N. W. Ayer and Son of Philadelphia installed a printing department in 1875 and billed advertisers at published rates. In 1878 J. Walter Thompson countered Ayer's innovation by offering space for sale in thirty magazines; later, Ayer and others announced they, too, could handle magazine as well as newspaper advertising (Hower 1949). Media selection was emphasized during the period of semiservice as publishers began to establish their own departments for selling space: agents turned from selling space for publishers to buying it for advertisers. Space wholesalers continued to give advice about copy and even wrote copy if pressured by advertisers, but by 1880 advertising agents regularly offered this service (Sandage and Fryburger 1958). Toward the end of the period of semiservice, five activities essential to planning, preparing, and placing advertising were accepted by advertisers, agents, and media as part of routine agency work: background work for the advertisement, writing copy, creating artwork, mechanically reproducing copy, and selecting media. Agents continued to bargain for rates and began collecting payment from advertisers.

BASIC SERVICE: 1890–1925

At the turn of the twentieth century, an expanded advertising industry waited to guide Americans to a cornucopia of goods and services for sale. The telegraph was well established; the telephone was an accepted means of local communication; wireless broadcasting was poised to change the American way of life. The Gilded Age had spawned a myriad of magazines and newspapers thriving on the revenue generated by announcements of products—familiar, improved, or new—and an endless stream of services. Billboards and car cards, popular advertising ephemera in the period of semiservice, enjoyed renewed utility in the brief epoch of electric trolleys and interurban trains and helped launch the American motorcar phenomenon. Between 1890 and 1925 the five tasks routinized during the semiservice period were the modus operandi of advertising agencies.

About 1890 agencies began to employ clever copywriters and artists; one agency in the 1890s boasted that it paid its copywriter $28,000 annually (Burt 1940). Innovations in advertising reproduction emphasized the quality of illustrations: a three-color process supplemented lithography, and silhouetting became common; soon continuity of copy and illustration, called serial advertising, was introduced (*Printers' Ink* 1939). Agencies began to employ art directors around 1900.

In 1901 the Curtis Publishing Company announced a published set card rate, a commission system, and an agency recognition policy (Kleppner 1966). From now on agencies would be forced to charge their regular published rates instead of cutting prices. But these policies affected advertisers as well, for they could no longer receive the agencies' commission if they placed advertisements directly with publishers (Kleppner 1950).

In 1910 agencies established research departments to reinforce clients' advertising plans (Presbrey [1929] 1968). Layout construction, artwork, and supervised engraving became regular agency services. By 1917 more than 100 advertising agencies had formed a trade association; the American Association of Advertising Agencies eventually endorsed a list of service standards still relevant today: study the product, analyze the market, examine company sales methods, study media, formulate a definite plan, create advertising copy, order space and time, check and verify insertions, audit and bill for service, and cooperate with sales efforts (American Association of Advertising Agencies 1958).

EXPANDED SERVICES AFTER 1926

Before 1926 planning and preparing advertising for publication constituted 90 percent of an agency's activities (Erbes 1939). After standardizing basic advertising services, agencies turned to marketing and management. In the 1930s extra services required little effort from the agency; but during the 1940s and 1950s extra services expanded to include new product development, market testing, and motivation research. These complex, detailed tasks required more personnel time, greater effort, and more skillful scientific application than in earlier periods. Although their basic jobs were buying space, writing copy, and preparing art, agency personnel increasingly found themselves counseling clients on the complexities of market surveys, package design, and pricing. Clients were urged to take advantage of new techniques in advertising media—outdoor advertising, direct mail, and radio advertising.

A 1939 survey of 153 representative advertisers disclosed that 134 of them sought "agency participation in at least one or more of the broader phases of marketing activity," including sales training, product design, and channels planning (Erbes 1939). A survey of 111 national advertisers revealed that many business executives considered the ability of some agencies to render extra services limited, and the other "outside specialists [were] better able to perform certain functions than the advertising agency" (*Printers' Ink* 1941).

World War II did little to restrict the expansion of agency services, and by 1946 "keener competition [had] forced both old and new agencies to depart from the old conception . . . and accept new duties all completely out of line with their genuine responsibilities" (Sollish 1946). Some of these duties were developing merchandising ideas, conducting research for new products, and personal selling (Dever 1947).

The notion that advertising agencies should provide additional services had been institutionalized in much of the marketing and advertising literature produced between 1950 and 1960. By 1972 most agencies had adopted a total marketing view and offered a full range of promotional efforts: merchandising, point-of-purchase displays, contests, public relations, sales forecasting, new product planning, and package development. In the 1980s some agencies assumed general management activities.

Business and the advertising agencies that illuminate it changed in the closing decades of the twentieth century. Legal limits on tobacco advertising cut billions of dollars from agencies already faced with a declining market for their services: in industries seeking to curb costs through combination and consolidation, a prime target for company cost-cutters is the advertising budget—when BP took over Gulf Oil, a brand name disappeared along with the advertising account.

The merger mania of the 1980s and 1990s forced advertising agencies to reduce their own costs through mergers and consolidations. Internationalization has transfigured advertising much as it has the rest of the business world. Saatchi and Saatchi, founded as recently as 1970 in London, was by 1987 the largest advertising agency in the world; yet the internal politics of expansion by takeover that fueled the firm's meteoric rise drove out founders Maurice and Charles Saatchi. The running battle for accounts and artists waged by the original firm (renamed Cordiant) and M&C Saatchi (the brothers' new firm) typifies the advertising agency industry at the turn of the millennium (Fallon 1989; Kleinman 1989; Fendley 1996; Goldman 1997).

Changes within advertising are exacerbated by technological developments. The drawing board of the 1970s has been permanently displaced by the computer monitor. Just as many facets of life have been altered by computers, the opportunities for better living and better advertising have expanded. Digital television and interactive programing promise a new world for agencies to wrangle over. The World Wide Web, unknown in 1980, is a fertile market for advertising in the 1990s. Agencies mired in the past, unable to vie for a place in the new world immediately before them, must settle for a place in history: the future belongs to the innovators (Mason 1999).

INDUSTRY STRUCTURE

The history of the advertising industry can be understood in light of certain structural conditions that have developed to allow established firms and entrants to compete. Two elements of industrial structure are entry conditions and differentiation. Entry conditions are crucial structural elements in the advertising agency business.

Conditions of Entry

Entry barriers permit established sellers (but not entrants) to receive a price above their average cost. Entry is forestalled if hopeful firms cannot cover long-run total costs. Among advertising agencies, effective entry is a difficult process because certain advantages favor existing companies.

Establishing a new agency appears easy, and on the surface there is freedom of entry. With little more than a computer, essential software, and prospective clients, an advertising agency can be organized; no legal restrictions like patents, copyrights, or licenses block entry. Since no extensive production process is involved, the scarcity of strategic raw materials does not inhibit entry. Nor is an agency a capital-intensive operation requiring expensive machinery and facilities.

There are several sources of human capital for agency entry. An account executive in an established agency may leave it to establish his own enterprise but continue to represent advertisers previously served, or a number of specialists—artists, copywriters, and production people—may leave their present employer and open an agency by taking accounts with them. Often, a manager in a large-budget advertiser resigns to set up a separate firm. Agencies are also opened by persons who have worked for a medium in some phase of advertising, perhaps as time and space salespersons, commercial artists, or copywriters. But entry into advertising is restrained by two trade practices: prepayment to media (financial requirements) and media commissions (cost advantages).

Financial Requirements

Advertising agencies ordinarily prepay media costs and service charges from printers, artists, and other specialists, then bill their clients for payment at a later date. Because agencies contract for time or space weeks before an advertisement appears, they are legally liable to media before advertisers are committed. Since large agencies prepay media costs, other agencies, including entrants, are likewise expected to prepay. Agencies need working capital to purchase these inventories of services and media time and space. Insufficient working capital is a barrier to effective entry into the advertising agency industry.

Cost Advantages

Among agencies, a percentage effect acts as a deterrent to entry because the standard media commission system of remuneration is available to established firms but may not be granted to entrants. The traditional method of payment in the advertising business involves a brokerage relationship among the advertiser, the medium, and the agency: the medium bills the agency, rather than the advertiser, for time, space, and other services. The agency then bills and collects from the advertiser the full amount billed by the medium but remits this amount, less a commission, to the medium. A cash discount may be allowed the advertiser if it pays promptly. An agency is not granted the commission for placing advertising unless it is recognized by the medium that is to broadcast or publish the message. Recognition is defined as an "agreement by a medium owner to consider an agency entitled to a commission for the purchase of its facilities in behalf of clients on the basis of fulfillment of various requirements set up by the medium" (Graham 1952).

Differentiation

A firm can distinguish its output from that of rivals if the product or service is differentiable in the minds of buyers. Design, quality, location, and terms of trade are prevalent forms of product differentiation, but the greater the number of variables important to buyers, the greater the opportunity for differentiation.

In advertising, motives and appeal as well as illustration, copy, and media can be shown in any number of combinations; hence, in the market for advertising services, buyers (advertisers) and sellers (agencies) are not paired at random, as they would be if services were homogeneous, but according to preferences that are based on perceived differences. Many advertisers stress, for example, personalized working arrangements and imaginative copy (Young 1963). The frequency of account turnovers suggests advertising services vary among agencies (Selegman 1956).

Advertising agencies must establish a means of distinguishing their output from that of other agencies, convince prospective clients of these differences, and persuade them to purchase the differentiated services. Documenting high exposure or readership per dollar spent on advertising is one way of differentiating media selection, or an agency may stress close contact with clients by assigning an account executive to the advertiser's headquarters. Adept consumer and market research enables agencies to identify buyers' motives and product appeal, information that can be incorporated into an advertising campaign that boosts sales or profits for their clients.

Agencies promote their own services through house advertising, house organs, and speculative presentations (Graham 1952). Established agencies offering a range of services may easily woo clients away from entrants that are thinly capitalized or unable to demonstrate acceptable exposure ratings. Service differentiation then becomes a barrier to entry. The failure rate among entrants is attributed to lack of originality and success in managing advertising campaigns ("Is There a Place for the Small Agency?" 1954). Too often entrants are unable to provide the extent of service and ideas that established agencies can (Orth 1965).

The American advertising agency evolved slowly over a period of nearly 300 years from an informal, passive concession into a formal, active institution. It is no longer an agent, in the legal sense of the concept, but an independent contractor; instead of aligning itself with the medium, the agency represents the advertiser. It no longer confines output to planning, preparing, and placing advertisements for others but directs complete marketing and management programs. Once a small local service enterprise, a modern agency may employ hundreds in a multiunit organization immersed in the technology that drives communications. As an institution, the advertising agency adapts readily to a changing economic, social, and technical environment. In a free society that values and fosters open communication, advertising agencies will continue to bring prospective customers into contact with willing sellers.

BIBLIOGRAPHIC ESSAY

The respected trade journal *Printers' Ink* chronicles advertising from 1888 to 1967, when *Printers' Ink* was absorbed by *Marketing/Communications; Potentials in Marketing* continued *Marketing Communications* until 1998, when the succession was assumed by *Potentials*. In one incarnation or another the *Printers' Ink* line is likely to continue into the new millennium. The trade literature reflects the advertising and the advertising agency industry. New journals appear often enough—*Consumer Advertising* began publishing in 1964—but lasting power is rare: *Consumer Advertising* was absorbed by *Marketing/Communications* in 1967. *Advertising Age* and *Modern Publicity*, established in 1930, have demonstrated staying power, and *Adweek*, which appeared during the hard times of the 1970s, when advertising budgets were feeling the squeeze from lost tobacco accounts, has survived by matching the times. The various editions of *Adweek* are available to differing markets: the eastern edition in New York, the southeastern in Atlanta, and the midwestern in Chicago are published by A/S/M Communications; the western edition in Los Angeles is published by BPI Communications, and the southwestern edition in Dallas, by Southwest Advertising.

Both fiction and nonfiction writers find advertising and advertising agencies compelling topics with reader appeal. Truth, or nonfiction, is no less fascinating than tales from the imagination. Sloan Wilson's fictional *Man in the Gray Flannel Suit* epitomized the 1950s popular conception of advertising agencies and the men who ran them—Hollywood turned the tale into a film starring Gregory Peck. Between 1970 and 1987 Maurice and Charles Saatchi transformed their agency into the world's largest, only to lose control to an insider-revolution. The true story of the Saatchi brothers and the firm they founded is the subject of at least four books: Ivan Fallon, *The Brothers: The Saatchi & Saatchi Story* (1989); Alison Fendley, *Saatchi & Saatchi: The Inside Story* (1996); Kevin Goldman, *Conflicting Accounts: The Creation and Crash of the Saatchi & Saatchi Advertising Empire*

(1997); and Philip Kleinman, *Saatchi & Saatchi: The Inside Story* (1989). Can a motion picture be far behind?

Fiction writers continue to build plots around advertising and advertising agencies. Douglas Lockhart's *The Paradise Complex: An Exploration of the Forbidden* (1997) stirs religion and advertising into a genre thriller. London police may have closed the account on the death of an advertising agent, but Bernie Lee's freelance advertising writer Tony Pratt and his wife, Pat, conclude that *Murder Takes Two* (1992). In *Executive Jungle: A Novel* (1998), David Levy uses fiction to expose the advertising world much as Frederic Wakeman did in *The Hucksters* (1946) fifty years earlier. Levy draws on his experience as an ad man.

Fictional stories of advertising men and women stand apart from the reality of the Madison Avenue life because they have beginnings and endings with a complete story filling the gap between. Life, while not so tidy, offers boundless options. Andy Law's *Creative Company: How St. Luke's Became "The Ad Agency to End All Ad Agencies"* (1999) is a series of case studies from the files of St. Luke's—interesting tales from the real world without the neatly tied ends of a novel. Other nonfictional descriptions of advertising and advertising agencies include Stewart Alter, *Truth Well Told: McCann-Erickson and the Pioneering of Global Advertising* (1994); Jonathan Bond and Richard Kirshenbaum, *Under the Radar: Talking to Today's Cynical Consumer* (1998); Bart Cummings, *The Benevolent Dictators: Interviews with Advertising Greats* (1984); William J. Hampton, *The First 80 Years: An Informal History of the Campbell-Ewald Company* (1991); Paul Harper, *Working the Territory: 60 Years of Advertising from the People of Needham Harper Worldwide* (1985); Nancy Millman, *Emperors of Adland: Inside the Advertising Revolution* (1988); Randy Scotland, *The Creative Edge: Inside the Ad Wars* (1994), the story of Vickers and Benson, Ltd.; Karen Stabiner, *Inventing Desire: Inside Chiat/Day: The Hottest Shop, the Coolest Players, the Big Business of Advertising* (1993); Jon Steel, *Truth, Lies, and Advertising: The Art of Account Planning* (1998).

BIBLIOGRAPHY

Ad. New York: Praeger, 1966– . Annual.

A-D [art directors, production managers, and their associates]. New York: A-D, 1940–1942. Bimonthly.

Advertiser & Agency Red Books. New Providence, NJ: National Register, quarterly.

Advertising Age. Chicago: Advertising, 1930–1969; Crain Communications, 1969– . Weekly.

Advertising Agency. Entrepreneur Business Guide, no. 1223. Irvine, CA: Entrepreneur Magazine Group, 1993.

Advertising Age's Creativity. New York: Crain Communications, 1993– . Monthly.

Advertising Growth Trends. Lincolnshire, IL: Schonfeld & Associates, annual.

Advertising Research Directory/ARF. New York: Advertising Research Foundation, 1985– . Annual.

Advertising World. Evanston, IL: Directories International, 1974–1985. Bimonthly. Continued by *International Advertiser.*

Adweek. Atlanta, GA: A/S/M Communications, weekly.

Adweek. Boston: AdEast Enterprises, 1987– . Weekly.

Adweek. Chicago: A/S/M Communications, 1981– . Weekly.

Adweek. Dallas: Southwest Advertising, weekly.

Adweek. Los Angeles: BPI Communications, weekly.

Adweek. New York: A/S/M Communications, 1979– . Weekly.

Adweek Agency Directory. National edition. New York: Adweek, 1983– . Annual.

Adweek Client/Brand Directory. National edition. New York: A/S/M Communications, 1989–1998. Annual.

Adweek's Ad Day. New York: Adweek, 1984– . Daily (with exceptions).

Agency: A Publication of the American Association of Advertising Agencies. New York: Act III, 1990– . Quarterly.

"Agency Competition Often Results in Giving Too Much Service." *Printers' Ink,* May 2, 1941, 11, 83.

Agency List of the Standard Advertising Register. New York: National Register, 1917–1964. Annual.

Alter, Stewart. *Truth Well Told: McCann-Erickson and the Pioneering of Global Advertising.* McCann-Erickson Worldwide, 1994.

American Advertising: The American Advertising Federation Magazine. Washington, DC: The Federation, quarterly.

American Association of Advertising Agencies. *Outline of Activities.* New York: American Association of Advertising Agencies, 1958.

ANA Advertising Management Policy Committee. *Evaluating Agency Performance.* New York: Association of National Advertisers, 1979.

ARF Annual Conference Directory. New York: Advertising Research Foundation, 1997– . Annual.

Arlen, Michael J. *Thirty Seconds.* New York: Farrar, Straus & Giroux, 1980. Reprint. New York: Penguin, 1984.

Ayer: 125 Years of Building Brands. Philadelphia: Ayer Press, 1990.

Barker, David. "Ad Agencies Alone Can Offer a True Brand Understanding." *Campaign,* December 13, 1996, 29.

Blue Book of Creative Services Buyers. New York: A. F. Lewis, 1997– . Annual.

Bond, Jonathan, and Richard Kirshenbaum. *Under the Radar: Talking to Today's Cynical Consumer.* New York: Wiley, 1998.

Brandweek. New York: Adweek L.P., 1992– . Forty-seven a year.

The Brandweek Directory. New York: ASM Communications, 1998– . Annual. Continues *Adweek Client/Brand Directory.*

Burandt, Gary, and Nancy Giges. *Moscow Meets Madison Avenue: The Adventures of the First American Adman in the U.S.S.R.* New York: HarperBusiness, 1992.

Burt, F. Allen. *American Advertising Agencies.* New York: Harper & Brothers, 1940.

Buxton, Edward, and Susan Fulton. *New Business for Ad Agencies: The Complete Book of Tactics and Strategies for Winning New Clients as Told to the Authors by Successful Ad Agencies and the Companies Who Selected Them.* New York: Executive Communications, 1987.

Centre on Transnational Corporations. *Transnational Corporations in Advertising: Technical Paper.* New York: United Nations, 1979.

Consumer Advertising. New York: Decker Communications, 1964–1967. Monthly. Absorbed by *Marketing/Communications.*

Credits. New York: Carnegie/Hawkins, 1982– . Monthly.

Cowan, D. S., and R. W. Jones. *Advertising in the 21st Century: A Model of Advertising Agency Development during the Next Fifty Years.* London: Hutchinson, 1968.

Cummings, Bart. *The Benevolent Dictators: Interviews with Advertising Greats.* Chicago: Crain Books, 1984.

Current Advertiser Practices in Compensating Their Advertising Agencies. New York: Association of National Advertisers, 1983.

Dalby, Simon. "Tangible Results Guarantee True Advertising Happiness." *Campaign,* December 6, 1996, 31.

Day, Ralph L. "Linear Programming in Media Selection." *Journal of Advertising Research,* June 1962.

Dever, Edward J., Jr. "Services That Advertisers Expect from Agencies." *Printers' Ink,* January 10, 1947, 45–56.

Directory of Advertising & Marketing Services. New York: Executive Communications, 1994– . Annual.

Dorn, Edward G. II. *How to Buy and Price Advertising Services.* Palatine, IL: CEL Publications, 1998.

———. *How to Build an Agency New Business SWAT Team.* Palatine, IL: CEL Publications, 1999.

Dru, Jean-Marie. *Disruption: Overturning Conventions and Shaking Up the Marketplace.* New York: John Wiley & Sons, an Adweek Book, 1996.

Erbes, P. H., Jr. "How Agencies Organize to Handle Today's Range of Service Duties." *Printers' Ink,* April 27, 1939, 33.

Fallon, Ivan. *The Brothers: The Saatchi & Saatchi Story.* Chicago: Contemporary Books, 1989.

Fearon, Robert. *Advertising That Works: How to Create a Winning Advertising Program for Your Company.* The Entrepreneur's Guide Series. Chicago: Probus, 1991.

Fendley, Alison. *Saatchi & Saatchi: The Inside Story.* New York: Arcade, 1996; distributed by Little, Brown.

Gamble, Frederick R. *What Advertising Agencies Are, What They Do, and How They Do It.* New York: American Association of Advertising Agencies, 1962.

Geo. P. Rowell & Company Newspaper Advertising Bureau. *An Advertising Agency: A Statement Intended to Make Plain the Nature and Methods of the Business, and the Changes Necesitated [sic] by the Lapse of Time and*

Other Circumstances. New York: Geo. P. Rowell & Co.'s Newspaper Advertising Bureau, 1878.

Goldman, Kevin. *Conflicting Accounts: The Creation and Crash of the Saatchi & Saatchi Advertising Empire.* New York: Simon & Schuster, 1997.

Graham, Irvin. *Advertising Agency Practice.* New York: Harper & Brothers, 1952.

Haase, Albert E. *The Advertising Appropriation.* New York: Harper, 1931. Reprint. History of Advertising. New York: Garland, 1985.

Hall, Emma. "Is Advertising as Effective as Planners Believe?" *Campaign*, November 29, 1996, 12.

Hameroff, Eugene J., and Herbert S. Gardner. *The Advertising Agency Business: The Complete Manual for Management & Operation.* 3d ed. Lincolnwood, IL: NTC Business Books, 1998.

Hampton, William J. *The First 80 Years: An Informal History of the Campbell-Ewald Company.* Warren, MI: Lintas: Campbell-Ewald, 1991.

Harper, Paul. *Working the Territory: 60 Years of Advertising from the People of Needham Harper Worldwide.* Englewood Cliffs, NJ: Prentice-Hall, 1985.

Hower, Ralph M. *The History of an Advertising Agency.* Cambridge: Harvard University Press, 1949.

IAA World News. New York: International Advertising Association, 1995– . Bimonthly.

Inside PR. New York: Editorial Media Marketing International, 1990–1994. Monthly.

Inside PR's Magazine of Reputation Management. New York: Editorial Media Marketing International, 1995– . Six times a year.

International Advertiser. New York: Directories International, 1985–1988; New York: International Advertising Association, 1988–1994. Quarterly. Continued by *IAA World News.*

"Is There a Place for the Small Agency?" *Western Advertising*, November 1954, 21.

Journal of Advertising. Athens, GA: Board of Directors, American Academy of Advertising, 1972– . Quarterly.

Journal of Advertising. Provo, UT: Board of Directors, Journal of Advertising, 1972– . Quarterly.

Journal of Current Issues and Research in Advertising. Clemson, SC: CtC Press, 1992– . Semiannual.

Kagan's Advertising Forecast. Carmel, CA: Paul Kagan Associates, 1998– .

Keeler, Floyd Y., and Albert E. Haase. *The Advertising Agency.* New York: Harper & Brothers, 1927. Reprint. History of Advertising. New York: Garland, 1985.

Kent, Felix H., and Elhanan C. Stone. *Legal and Business Aspects of the Advertising Industry, 1984.* Patent, Copyright, Trademark, and Literary Property Course Handbook Series, no. 179. Practising Law Institute, 1984.

Kleinman, Philip. *Saatchi & Saatchi: The Inside Story.* Lincolnwood, IL: NTC Business Books, 1989.

Kleppner, Otto. *Advertising Procedure.* 4th ed. New York: Prentice-Hall, 1950.

———. *Advertising Procedure.* 5th ed. Englewood Cliffs, NJ: Prentice-Hall, 1966.

Kreiff, Allan. *How to Start and Run Your Own Advertising Agency.* New York: McGraw-Hill, 1993.

Law, Andy. *Creative Company: How St. Luke's Became "The Ad Agency to End All Ad Agencies."* New York: Wiley, 1999.

Lee, Bernie. *Murder Takes Two.* New York: D. I. Fine, 1992.

Lee, James M. *History of American Journalism.* Boston: Houghton Mifflin, 1916.

Levy, David. *Executive Jungle: A Novel.* Amherst, NY: Prometheus Books, 1998.

Lockhart, Douglas. *The Paradise Complex: An Exploration of the Forbidden.* Shaftesbury, Dorset, UK, and Rockport, MA: Element, 1997.

Marin, Allan, ed. and comp. *50 Years of Advertising as Seen through the Eyes of Advertising Age, 1930–1980.* Chicago: Crain Communications, 1980.

Marketing Communications. New York: United Business Publications, 1970–1989. Monthly. Continued by *Potentials in Marketing.*

Marketing/Communications. New York: Decker Communications, 1967–1972. Monthly.

Marketer's Guide to Media. New York: Adweek, 1992– . Annual.

Mason, Bruce. "Agencies in the Millennium." *Advertising Age* 70, no. 13, Midwest region edition (March 29, 1999): 28.

McNamara, Jay. *Advertising Agency Management.* Homewood, IL: Dow Jones-Irwin, 1990.

Millman, Nancy. *Emperors of Adland: Inside the Advertising Revolution.* New York: Warner Books, 1988.

Modern Publicity. New York: Studio, 1930– . Annual.

Mott, Frank L. *American Journalism.* New York: Macmillan, 1947.

Myers, Jack. *ADbashing: Surviving the Attacks on Advertising: Why the Future of Advertising and Media Depend upon the Changes We Make and the Risks We Take Today.* Parsippany, NJ: American Media Council Worldwide Marketing Leadership Panel, 1993.

Nevett, Terence R., ed. *Cases in Advertising Management.* Lincolnwood, IL: NTC Business Books, 1992.

Ogilvy, David. *Confessions of an Advertising Man.* Rev. ed. New York: Atheneum, 1988.

Orth, Penelope. "Can Agencies Stop Account Piracy?" *Printers' Ink*, June 10, 1965.

Papers of the American Association of Advertising Agencies, 1927. New York: Ronald Press, 1927. Reprint. History of Advertising. New York: Garland, 1985.

PM [production managers, art directors, and their associates]. New York: PM, 1934–1940. Bimonthly. Continued by *A-D*.

Potentials. Minneapolis: Lakewood, 1998– . Monthly.

Potentials in Marketing. Minneapolis: Lakewood, 1983–1998. Monthly. Continued by *Potentials.*

Presbrey, Frank Spencer. *The History and Development of Advertising.* New York: Doubleday, 1929. Reprint. New York: Greenwood Press, 1968.

Printers' Ink. New York: Printers' Ink, 1888–1967. Semimonthly. Continued by *Marketing/Communications.*

Printers' Ink Monthly. New York: Romer, 1919–1941. Monthly. Absorbed by *Printers' Ink.*

Profiles/Center for Advertising History. Washington, DC: National Museum of American History, Smithsonian Institution, 1991– .

PROMO. Danbury, CT: Smith Communications, 1987– . Monthly.

PROMO. Sourcebook. Danbury, CT: Smith Communications, 1994– . Annual.

Reid, Alasdair. "Are Full-Service Agencies Making a Comeback?" *Campaign,* October 11, 1996, 20.

Retail Ad Week. New York: Retail Reporting Bureau, 1971– . Weekly.

Retail Ad World. New York: Milton B. Conhaim, 1998– . Monthly.

Ring, Jim. *Advertising on Trial: Managing Your Agency for Effective Results.* London: Pitman, 1993.

Rothenberg, Randall. *Where the Suckers Moon: An Advertising Story.* New York: Knopf, 1994; distributed by Random House.

Roster and Organization. New York: American Association of Advertising Agencies, 1975– . Annual.

Rowell, George P. *Forty Years an Advertising Agent.* New York: Franklin, 1926.

Russell, Thomas, and W. Ronald Lane. *Kleppner's Advertising Procedure.* 14th ed. Upper Saddle River, NJ: Prentice-Hall, 1999.

Salz, Nancy L. *How to Get the Best Advertising from Your Agency: The Guide to Quickly Building a Productive Team.* 3d ed. Burr Ridge, IL: Irwin Professional, 1994.

Sandage, Charles E., and E. Fryburger. *Advertising Theory and Practice.* Homewood, IL: Irwin, 1958.

Scotland, Randy. *The Creative Edge: Inside the Ad Wars* [Vickers & Benson Ltd]. New York: Viking, 1994.

Selegman, Daniel. "The Amazing Advertising Business." *Fortune,* September 1956, 106–8.

Sigel, Efrem, and editors of *Communications Trends. Classified Advertising Markets, 1987–90.* CTI Reports. Larchmont, NY: Communications Trends, 1987.

Simon, Milton. *How to Own and Operate a One-Person Advertising Agency.* Hillside, IL: Castanea Press, 1988.

Snapshots. New York: Media Market Resources, 1996– . Annual.

Sollish, Joseph. "Just What Is an Advertising Agency?" *Printers' Ink,* November 15, 1946, 194.

Space & Time. New York: David A. Munro.

SRDS Business Publication Advertising Source. Des Plaines, IL: Standard Rate & Data Service, 1995– . Monthly.

SRDS Manufacturing Publication Advertising Source. Des Plaines, IL: Chilton, 1995– . Annual.

SRDS Newspaper Advertising Source. Des Plaines, IL: Standard Rate & Data Service, 1995– . Monthly.

Stabiner, Karen. *Inventing Desire: Inside Chiat/Day: The Hottest Shop, the Coolest Players, the Big Business of Advertising.* New York: Simon & Schuster, 1993.

Standard Directory of Advertising Agencies. Skokie, IL: National Register, 1964– . Semiannual. Included in *Advertiser & Agency Red Books.*

Standard Industrial Classification Manual 1987. Washington, DC: Office of Management and Budget, Executive Office of the President, 1987; distributed by U.S. Government Printing Office.

Steel, Jon. *Truth, Lies, and Advertising: The Art of Account Planning.* New York: Wiley, 1988.

Tylee, John. "Report Tells Agencies to Be Wary of Mergers." *Campaign*, December 6, 1996, 8.

USadreview. New York: Retail Reporting, 1991– . Quarterly.

Vardar, Nukhet. *Global Advertising: Rhyme or Reason*. London: P. Chapman, 1992.

Wakeman, Frederic. *The Hucksters*. New York: Rinehart, 1946.

Weilbacher, William M. *Choosing an Advertising Agency*. Chicago: Crain Books, 1983.

Wilson, Sloan. *The Man in the Gray Flannel Suit*. New York: Simon & Schuster, 1955.

Young, J. O. "Agency Selection: A New Approach." *Printers' Ink*, March 22, 1963, 23–29.

Young, Murray, and Charles Steilen. "Strategy-Based Advertising Agency Selection: An Alternative to 'Spec' Presentations." *Business Horizons* 39, no. 6 (November/December 1996): 77–80.

Part XII

Health Services
ESIC 80.0

CHAPTER 16 _____

NURSING AND PERSONAL CARE FACILITIES, 80.5

_____ JOSEPH A. GIACALONE

The history of nursing homes in the United States is brief, originating in federal income maintenance and health policy legislation beginning with the Social Security Act of 1935 and its amendments that helped finance proprietary, not-for-profit, and public nursing homes and their services (Vladeck 1980; Waldman 1983; Silverman 1991; Bonn 1999). Although most nursing homes are privately owned, the bulk of their income comes from public sources: the 1985 National Nursing Home Survey reported that of the 19,100 certified nursing homes, 75 percent were under proprietary control, 20 percent operated as nonprofit institutions, and about 5 percent were public institutions—ownership distribution of beds closely paralleled that of facilities (American Health Care Association 1988; Hing, Sekscenski, and Strahan 1989). For the same year, $16.5 billion of the $35 billion spent on nursing home care came from government sources; other public programs, such as Social Security Retirement benefits, provide some of the funds used for private payments.

In America physicians and hospitals control health services, including nursing home care. Fiscal responsibility for Medicaid, the principal funding source for nursing home care, is shared by the states and the federal government. Within broad guidelines, each state exercises discretion in determining eligibility requirements and the services covered. This decentralization accounts for the substantial interstate variation in the quantity, quality, and cost of nursing home care (Estes and Lee 1985).

ORIGINS OF THE NURSING HOME INDUSTRY

The origins of the nursing home industry lie in five types of facilities—county poorhouses, state mental hospitals, homes for the aged run by religious organizations, proprietary boardinghouses, and hospital-affiliated nursing homes (Waldman 1983). Most of the residents in these facilities were poor or disabled elderly. Unable to pay for proprietary care and without the protection of a voluntary agency or group, the elderly were forced onto a public dole shaped by the philosophy of the Elizabethan poor laws. County poorhouses provided a minimal existence under conditions that were often disgraceful. Too frequently, sick or disabled residents of the poorhouses were relegated to the state mental hospitals, often their only long-term care alternative. Except for a few hospital-based nursing homes, no facilities provided medical or nursing services for the poor. In 1935 only 200,000 of the nearly 7 million Americans over age sixty-five were institutionalized, but many of the others endured a minimal standard of living with limited healthcare alternatives (Vladeck 1980).

FROM SOCIAL SECURITY TO MEDICARE

The Social Security Act of 1935, critical to the nursing home industry, became the centerpiece of American social welfare policy and subsequently of healthcare policy. Nursing homes were not addressed in the statute, but the income maintenance programs it created provided purchasing power for payment of nursing home care; amendments targeted healthcare services and their financing.

The old age assistance (OAA) program was a system of noncontributory, means-tested old age pensions funded by matching grants-in-aid to the states. This federal–state relationship set the pattern for future public funding. Important to the development of proprietary nursing homes was the statutory exclusion of OAA benefits to residents of public institutions. Homes under voluntary control also benefited by the OAA payments. As the healthcare needs of the elderly increased, all segments of the nursing home industry added health services to the mainstay of personal and domiciliary care. By the beginning of World War II, the future of the industry was visible (Vladeck 1980).

The income maintenance features of the Social Security Act increased demand for nursing home care, and legislation in the 1940s and 1950s increased supply. The Hospital Survey and Construction Act, commonly known as Hill-Burton, was enacted in 1946. The extensive financial support for hospital construction established the hospital as the hub of the U.S. healthcare delivery system. Although nursing homes were not included in the original Hill-Burton Act, the 1954 amendments provided financial support for constructing and renovating government and nonprofit nursing facilities. Hill-Burton financial support was extended only to institutions that affiliated with hospitals and that met established standards for staffing and quality of care as well as for construction and design. Proprietary nursing homes, not included in Hill-Burton financing, sought and received aid from other sources: in 1956, proprietary nursing homes became eligible under the general loan authority of the Small Business Administration, but Section 232 of the Housing Act of 1959 offered more flexible mortgage insurance for the proprietary sector.

Amendments to the Social Security Act in 1950 not only removed the restriction on OAA payments to residents of public medical facilities but permitted direct payments as well to the vendors of medical care and mandated state-established licensing requirements for nursing homes. Although the states established minimal requirements, these were rarely enforced, and the federal licensing provision foreshadowed regulatory initiatives such as the Hill-Burton restrictions mentioned earlier.

A final legislative development predating Medicare was the Medical Assistance for the Aged (MAA) program, an expansion of the vendor payment program but with two important exceptions. First, states were permitted to define medical indigence separately from need for OAA income assistance. Second, there was no ceiling on federal matching funds—an important provision that became part of the Medicare/Medicaid systems and helped escalate the costs of healthcare. By 1965 some 300,000 persons were receiving nursing home care financed under MAA. Between 1960 and 1965 vendor payments for nursing home care rose tenfold (Vladeck 1980; Waldman 1983).

The earliest data for nursing home care estimated national expenditures as $33 million in 1940. These expenditures rose to $187 million in 1950, $526 million in 1960, and $1.3 billion by 1965. Per capita expenditures increased from $0.25 in 1940, to $6.22 in 1965. By 1965 the industry employed over 350,000 workers, of whom about 27,000 were registered nurses and about 37,000 were licensed practical nurses. The facilities inventory mandated by the 1954 Hill-Burton amendments had identified 9,000 facilities with a total of 260,000 beds in skilled nursing homes and personal care homes with skilled nursing. Estimates in 1960 counted over 10,000 facilities with almost 400,000 residents.

THE MEDICARE/MEDICAID ERA

The 1965 amendments to the Social Security Act were and continue to be the cornerstone of U.S. healthcare policy. Although falling short of national health insurance, the Medicare and Medicaid programs represented a pivotal breakthrough in the public financing of healthcare. Since 1965 consumer expenditures for healthcare and the cost of delivering that care have accelerated rapidly. National health expenditures, which were just over $40 billion in 1965, doubled by 1972 then more than tripled from the 1972 level to reach $286.9 billion by 1982. The comparable figures for nursing home care were about $1.3 billion in 1965, $6.5 billion in 1972, and $27.3 billion in 1982. Although all segments of healthcare expenditures rose significantly, nursing home care registered the largest percentage increase over that period (Gibson, Waldo, and Levit 1983; Estes and Lee 1985). Like the cost of other healthcare services, expenditures on nursing home care continued to escalate during the 1980s, reaching $50.9 billion by 1990 and $72.3 billion by 1994 (Levit et al. 1996).

Nursing home care had not been a major objective in earlier legislation, nor was it in the 1965 Social Security Act amendments. Medicare, which financed acute, physician-directed, hospital-based care, was the target of the changes; however, Medicaid turned out to be the key program for the nursing home industry. The 1967 Moss amendments provided the authority for nursing home participation in Medicaid. The conditions for participation under Medicaid established standards in many areas, the most important of which was staffing. Participating homes were required to provide twenty-four-hour nursing services, the services of a registered nurse, and a charge nurse on each shift. These requirements—coupled with others covering medical supervision, pharmacy, fire safety, dietary standards, and sanitation—were aimed at improving the quality of care but obviously raised the industry's cost structure substantially. The services eligible for reimbursement and the manner of reimbursement became and continue to be major issues for the industry and the government (Newcomer and Bogaert-Tillis 1985; Swan and Harrington 1985). Quality improvement and cost containment ultimately became conflicting objectives (Porell et al. 1998).

Cost containment was difficult under Medicaid's open-ended policy. Unlike Medicare, an insurance program, Medicaid is a welfare program. The federal–state financial responsibility was shared, but the states defined medical indigence and determined covered services. This unlimited financial commitment plus the high cost of services ultimately forced reconsideration of long-term care arrangements and their financing (Vogel and Palmer 1983, 1985; Harrington et al. 1985; Rivlin and Wiener 1988).

Providing residents with *skilled* nursing care was essential for a nursing home's participation in Medicare and Medicaid. However, large numbers of nursing home residents required health-related institutional care without skilled nursing. Passage of the Miller Amendment in 1967 established financial support for the eligible residents of intermediate care facilities (ICF) under the cash assistance titles of the Social Security Act. The ICF benefit program was transferred to Medicaid in 1971 and has had a significant impact on the industry. In 1982 Medicaid disbursed $4.98 billion to ICFs, exceeding the $4.43 billion disbursed to skilled nursing facilities (SNFs): the ICF reimbursement rate was limited to no more than 90 percent of a state's average SNF rate (Waldman 1983).

The ICF program introduced the level-of-care concept and its myriad consequences. Initially, it led to a reclassification of many residents and facilities from SNF to ICF to take advantage of the new funding eligibility. Subsequently, the program created the issue of proper level-of-care placement on admission and the potential problem of reclassifying residents as their physical conditions changed.

Public Law 92-603, enacted in October 1972, implemented comprehensive changes in the Social Security Act. A new system of Supplemental Security Income (SSI) was created. Eligibility for SSI automatically assured eligibility for Medicaid. A monitoring system, Professional Standards Review Organization (PSRO), was devised to oversee quality of care under the Medicare and Medicaid programs. For the nursing homes industry, the category of skilled nursing facility was created out of the combination of skilled nursing home and extended-care facility. Section 249 of the law required the states to reimburse nursing home care under Medicaid on a reasonable cost-related basis, as under Medicare (Vladeck 1980; Waldman 1983).

The SNF/ICF standards put a premium on recordkeeping to establish a facility's eligibility for reimbursement of its costs from public funds. The recordkeeping process itself generated costs that did little to enhance the quality of care. Prior to the regulatory fervor that swept the industry following the scandals of the 1970s, fraudulent records were often the basis for unethical profits; yet, recordkeeping persists as the surrogate for quality care. Moreover, assessing compliance with technological standards, like the standards of the Life Safety Code for fire protection, is much easier than assessing overall quality of care (Vladeck 1980).

The quality of care issue came to the forefront in the nursing home scandals of the early 1970s. Legislative investigations, most notably in New York, revealed patient abuse, mistreatment, inadequate services performed by underqualified personnel, theft of residents' funds, and manipulation of the reimbursement system for personal profit. Not surprisingly, these revelations unleashed a wave of regulations designed to improve the situation. The regulatory process included standards, inspection, and sanctions. Federal standards for Medicare and Medicaid participation establish the minimal level of care, which states may exceed but rarely do. Enforcing higher standards raises costs, creating a dilemma for states that find the additional financing burdensome. In any case, existing standards are enforced unevenly by state and municipal jurisdictions. The main sanction, closing a facility, is rarely used because of the transfer trauma for residents and administrators' fear of eliminating needed beds. Less disruptive alternatives, such as fines and civil receivership, show greater potential for generating improvements, but the evidence for the effectiveness of particular sanctions is not definitive (Vladeck 1980).

COST CONTAINMENT: THE ISSUE OF THE 1980s

As the American population aged, the demand for nursing home care increased. The cost of providing that care, like all other medical care costs, rose significantly. Neither private nor public ability to pay kept pace. Increasing life expectancy considerably limited how long private funds could last. Total expenditures on nursing home care rose from $8.7 billion in 1980 to over $72 billion in 1994. Average annual expenditure per nursing home resident rose from $5,100 in 1970, to $23,300 in 1985, to almost $30,000 by 1990. After exhausting their private funds, many residents were categorized as medically indigent. Meanwhile, federal and state fiscal problems put severe constraints on public funding—pressure for cost control was intense.

If nursing care were a proprietary industry, market forces would keep costs in check. About 60 percent of nursing facilities and beds are under proprietary control, but market forces are mitigated since 55 percent of the industry's revenues, as late as 1994, derive from public sources (Levit et al. 1996). Covered services and method of reimbursement have a critical effect on costs.

Although decentralized fiscal and political responsibility allows each state considerable discretion in reimbursement, the fundamental principle has been to cover all reasonable medically related costs. Since nursing homes must perform many other nonmedical functions, they face severe resource constraints. The public interest in keeping total expenditures down requires some objective standard, which "medically necessary" seems to provide. The "physician as gatekeeper" is well established in American health policy (Estes and Lee 1985).

Cost-related reimbursement for nursing homes was first mandated by the 1965 Medicare statute and extended to Medicaid in the 1972 amendments. This method replaced flat rate systems that were largely per capita estimates of what a state could budget for nursing home care. Originally, cost-related reimbursement was retrospective, that is, based on the expenditures incurred after the services had been provided. Since no prior limits were set, retrospective systems were inherently inflationary. In an effort to hold down costs, most states had, by 1983, switched to prospective reimbursement systems in which the rates are set prior to the delivery of services. Prepricing of individual services is based on a formula derived from historical costs and trends (Swan and Harrington 1985).

In another approach to cost containment the number of new nursing home beds has been limited by certificates of need (CON). The 1974 National Health Planning and Resources Development Act was passed to encourage rational, controlled planning of health services. Before new facilities can be funded or constructed, need must be demonstrated. Empirical research has not established the effectiveness of CON programs in controlling costs.

In the late 1980s, cost containment and the financing of long-term care were complicated by two pieces of legislation: the Omnibus Budget Reconciliation Act (OBRA) of 1987 mandated nursing home reform—survey inspection procedure and nurse's aide training raised the cost structure of long-term care facilities; the 1988 Medicare Catastrophic Coverage Act (MCCA) liberalized the eligibility requirements for Medicare and increased benefit periods. In addition to increasing costs, MCCA shifted more of the financial responsibility from state Medicaid programs to federal Medicare. The funding by premium increases and tax surcharges for Medicare enrollees sparked considerable controversy. Though MCCA operated for only one full year, 1989, the legislation's liberal Medicare nursing home benefits led to an immediate and substantial escalation of federal expenditures. Before the repeal of MCCA, some 1,300 new Medicare-certified skilled nursing facilities had entered the market, and many other SNFs had shifted beds from noncertified to certified status, resulting in a 67 percent increase in admissions. Although previous Medicare eligibility requirements were reinstated for January 1990, Medicare SNF expenditures remained high since facilities that had made large investments for certification were reluctant to cut back. Medicare nursing home admissions and payments remained perversely higher than they would otherwise have been (Manton, Stallard, and Woodbury 1994).

TRENDS IN THE 1990s AND BEYOND

By 1991 the number of nursing and related care institutions had grown to 33,006 facilities with 1,921,000 beds and 1,729,000 residents. Of these, 9,674 were skilled nursing facilities with 567,000 beds. Population projections for the year 2000 indicate there will be 10 million more persons over the age of sixty-five than there were in 1980. About one-third of the persons eighty-five and older are highly dependent on others for personal care needs, but only 3 percent of persons sixty-five to seventy-four are dependent. The institutionalization rate rises from about 1 percent for the sixty-five to seventy-four cohort, to 22 percent for those eighty-five and over (Weissert 1985). The Social Security Administration estimates that by the year 2030 the number of persons aged sixty-five and over and those seventy-five and over will have doubled from the 1990 levels. In a 1991 study of lifetime use of nursing home care, Peter Kemper and Christopher Murtaugh concluded that the risk of entering a nursing home and spending a considerable amount of time there is substantial: of all persons twenty-five or older who died in 1986, 29 percent had spent some time in a nursing home, and almost half had spent at least one year in such a facility. Among the elderly who died between the ages of sixty-five and seventy-four, the probability of nursing home use was 17 percent; for those between the ages of seventy-five and eighty-four, the probability was 36 percent; and for those between eighty-five and ninety-four, 60 percent. Kemper and Murtaugh project that 43 percent of the persons turning sixty-five in 1990 will use a nursing home. Clearly, these demographic trends are driving the future of the long-term care industry.

Despite a slowing in the rate of growth in national health expenditures (Burner and Waldo 1995), the concern over the cost of U.S. healthcare intensified in the first half of the 1990s. High on the political agenda was balancing the federal budget, and a prime target was government spending on Medicare and Medicaid. By mid-decade both political parties were committed to slowing the rate of growth or reducing outright this element of government expenditure. Although President William J. Clinton's wholesale reform of the U.S. healthcare system was not adopted, the need to make changes that would reduce the system's cost to the government was clearly recognized. Any change in Medicare and Medicaid funding arrangements and levels will have an impact on the long-term care industry. The move to managed care in the general healthcare delivery system has resulted in some cost savings, although there is considerable controversy about its impact on quality of care. Managed care has had no significant impact on the nursing home industry thus far, but the "continuum of care" concept will tighten the links between the acute care environment and long-term care.

Corporate nursing home chains, an innovation of the 1980s, continue to influence industry structure. By 1986 ten publicly held chains owned or leased almost 170,000 beds and managed another 13,000 beds. By 1996 the number of chains had grown considerably, and the ten largest accounted for over 290,961 beds in 2,471 facilities. Over this period, Beverly Enterprises was the largest entity: in 1996 it owned or managed 637 facilities, more than twice the number held by its closest competitor. Seven corporate chains were expected to have 1996 total operating revenues in excess of $1 billion (Fisher 1997).

Investor-owned nursing home chains are estimated to control about 20 percent of overall facility capacity. Although the chains are largely composed of skilled nursing and health-related facilities, many have diversified into newer segments of the long-term care industry, including subacute care, assisted-living, respiratory and rehabilitation therapies, and home care. The early 1990s were marked by considerable merger activity. Before corporatization, the industry had been characterized by small, individual ownership with thin capitalization, even in the proprietary sector. The corporate chains have brought more sophisticated management to the industry as well as the latest in computerized information systems. Economies of scale, especially in purchasing, provide cost control advantages not attainable by small, independent units.

Long-term care insurance is an initiative in the private payment mechanism but one that has had little impact. Payments for nursing home care by private insurance rose from $0.2 billion in 1980 to $2.2 billion in 1994; yet this amount covered only 3 percent of the 1994 expenditures on nursing home care. The Health Insurance Association of America (HIAA) reported that 3.8 million long-term care insurance policies were sold between 1987 and 1994. Increasingly, employers are offering coverage as an employee benefit (Hosay 1993). According to the HIAA, the cumulative employer-sponsored policies sold grew from 20,000 in 1988, to 440,000 in 1994. The insurance industry sees good market potential for such policies, and Congress passed legislation in 1996 allowing some deductibility for premiums; notwithstanding, long-term care insurance is unlikely to become a significant payment mechanism in the near future.

Developing alternatives to institutionalized care would, proponents argue, be less expensive and better for the well-being of the elderly. The expansion of home care, assisted-living housing arrangements, social/health maintenance organizations, and day care are among the more widely discussed alternatives (Rivlin and Wiener 1988). Expenditures on home care delivered by home health agencies have grown tremendously in the 1990s. This trend works against institutionalization in a nursing home; nonetheless, the nursing home industry has diversified by delivering a variety of subacute care services previously provided by hospitals. Moreover, many nursing home firms have entered the assisted-living market, which combines housing for the elderly with certain long-term care services that may culminate in care at a skilled nursing facility. Day care is also provided by many nursing homes. The nursing home industry is adapting to the continuum of care environment and redefining itself as it approaches the third millennium and the accompanying expansion in the elderly population (Packer-Tutsman 1995; Grimaldi 1999).

BIBLIOGRAPHIC ESSAY

The nursing home industry's growth dates from the 1965 passage of the Medicare/Medicaid legislation. Its cottage industry origins, small-scale pluralistic ownership pattern, and dependence on government legislation and financing all contributed to the scarcity of intense scholarship on the production of nursing home services. The scandals of the 1970s combined with the surge in publicly financed nursing home expenditures to open the industry to serious study. Still, much of what has been written was frequently subsidiary to public policy issues in healthcare or welfare programs. There remains an opportunity for objective economic treatment of the industry from a historical perspective.

Bruce C. Vladeck's 1980 *Unloving Care: The Nursing Home Tragedy*, commissioned by the Twentieth Century Fund, is the standard, if normative, work on the industry. Vladeck addresses noneconomic and public policy issues but includes economic topics and their evolution. Legislative history, demographics, financing, development of the industry's capacity, and regulation are set out in historical perspective. *Unloving Care*, accompanied by an excellent bibliographical note, is the starting point for any study of the industry. Vladeck became the head of the Health Care Financing Administration under President Clinton.

Caring for the Disabled Elderly (1988) is Alice M. Rivlin and Joshua M. Wiener's comprehensive analysis of the industry complete with a model for projecting changes in the financing of long-term care and their evaluation of alternative delivery and financing mechanisms.

Legislative History and Public Policy

In addition to Vladeck's review of the legislative history that was so critical to the evolution of the nursing home industry, there are several other studies of value. Vladeck relied heavily on Markus (1972), which provided the earliest comprehensive presentation. Saul Waldman (1983) presents most of the subsequent legislation. Important to the development of public policy for the nursing home industry were seven reports issued by the U.S. Senate, Special Committee on Aging, Subcommittee on Long-Term Care (1974–1976). Of interest also is *Too Old, Too Sick, Too Bad: Nursing Homes in America* (1977), in which Frank Moss and Val J. Halamandaris have abstracted the subcommittee's reports. Senator Moss, who was responsible for the 1967 legislation establishing the standards for nursing home participation in Medicaid, was chairman of the subcommittee, and Halamandaris was the committee's chief investigator. A key player in the development and administration of Medicare was Joseph A. Califano, secretary of health, education, and welfare. Califano ([1986] 1989) describes the "revolution" in American healthcare. Although long-term care receives only brief attention, the work provides a perspective on the total healthcare delivery system, of which the nursing home industry is a vital part. The historical roots of the biomedical acute-care model, the welfare approach, and decentralization are described by Carroll L. Estes and Philip R. Lee (1985). Useful insights on the industry's early history can be found in two state studies: Ethel McClure's 1968 volume on Minnesota poor farms traces the origins of homes for the aged; William C. Thomas, Jr. (*Nursing Homes and Public Policy* 1969) documents the New York State experience.

Additional perspectives on the evolution of the nursing home industry can be gleaned from two other sources. Robert Burmeister and Susan J. Warner (1984) briefly chronicle the history of the American College of Health Care Administrators (ACHCA), originally organized as the American College of Nursing Home Administrators. Essentially, their article describes the changes in administrator credentialing that paralleled the industry's rapid growth. In honor of its twenty-fifth anniversary, the American Association of Homes for the Aging (AAHA) published a detailed history of its organization in the September 1986 issue of the association's journal, *Contemporary Long-Term Care*.

The ACHCA has its roots in the American Nursing Home Association, now known as the American Health Care Association, which represents the industry's proprietary sector. The AAHA is the organization representing the not-for-profit segment of the industry. The development of both organizations reveals the impact of legislation on the nursing home segment of the U.S. healthcare system.

Demand and Supply Studies

After 1975 systematic economic analysis of the nursing home industry became increasingly common. Spurred by the tremendous rise in public expenditures for nursing home services and the public outcry over scandals in the industry, researchers began to study the industry as an autonomous sector of the U.S. healthcare system. Statistical data available in the post-Medicare period have been the basis for analysis of crucial economic relationships.

A good summary of several demand studies is provided by Charlene Harrington and James H. Swan (1987). The work of Barry R. Chiswick (1976), B. D. Dunlop (1976), and William J. Scanlon (1980) receives special attention. Chiswick found that nursing home demand is positively related to age, the female labor force participation rate, the percentage of the state's population living in urban areas, and the percentage of the state's elderly population with low income. Dunlop, too, found that age, urban population, and income are significant positive demand factors. He established that the percentage of a state's population that is married affects nursing home utilization negatively. This finding, coupled with Chiswick's on female labor force participation rates, suggests that care of aging parents by married female children is a major alternative to institutionalization. Scanlon confirmed these earlier findings on age, especially the state's population over eighty-five; urbanization; and marital status. To these factors, he adds climate, showing that warmer states have a lower utilization rate. Contrary to Chiswick and Dunlop, Scanlon found that the state's percentage of low-income elderly is negatively related to nursing home utilization, a development he attributes to wealthier states' supporting larger nursing home populations.

Harrington and Swan's 1987 article also reviews other studies and additional factors relating to utilization of nursing home service, including the impact of disability levels, changes in Medicaid eligibility, effect of co-payments, and the availability of alternatives to institutionalization. Another worthwhile contribution is "Factors Determining the Demand for Nursing Home Services" (1986), an excellent summary of the demand estimation literature in which C. E. Lamberton, W. D. Ellingson, and K. R. Spear use economic and need (health-based) variables to develop separate regression models for private-pay and Medicaid demand. A later study is James D. Reschovsky's "The Roles of Medicaid and Economic Factors in the Demand for Nursing Home Care" (1998).

Research on industry supply is not as extensive as that on demand. Worth consideration is Spitz and Silvers (1981), an excellent historical overview of capital formation and funding. Bernard Friedman (1982), using data from Rhode Island, provides insights into the rationing of nursing home beds. An empirical approach to estimating an undersupply of nursing home beds is developed by Swan and Harrington (1986).

Ronald J. Vogel (1983) examines the industrial organization of the nursing home sector, encompassing its market structure, conditions of entry, product differentiation, and the government's role as a buyer of nursing home services. An interesting contribution of the article is an investment model for firms in the industry. Hans C. Palmer and Vogel (1983) formulate a simple heuristic model of the nursing home as a tool for understanding the behavior of the providers. Models of the for-profit and not-for-profit sectors are constructed on private, Medicare, and Medicaid demand and the subsidy effects systematically examined.

Costs and Their Reimbursement

The rising secular trend in U.S. healthcare costs has been well documented both in absolute terms and as a percentage of gross national product in annual expenditures reports published in the *Health Care Financing Review*. Such close scrutiny of costs is characteristic of an industry substantially funded with public moneys. The cost of nursing home care has been one of the fastest growing segments of healthcare in the last decade (Doty, Liu, and Wiener 1985). In a period when budgetary stringency at all levels of government is a major political issue, systematic analysis of nursing home costs and their reimbursement and containment has been extensive. Most of these studies are statistical, and many of the researchers employ regression analysis, using historical data from one or more states. Two overviews of nursing home cost studies are Bishop (1980) and Palmer (1983). R. E. Schlenker (1985) on patient-level costs is another example. Swan and Harrington (1985) track emerging reimbursement trends for retrospective and prospective methods, both facility-specific and class-based. Alternatives for reimbursing capital expenditures are examined in Spitz (1982). Robert J. Newcomer and Marjorie P. Bogaert-Tillis (1985) introduce cost containment efforts, including certificates of need, professional standards review organization, rate setting, and diagnostic related groups (DRGs). The impact of several cost containment devices on utilization and expenditures is evaluated in Harrington and Swan (1987). Specific aspects of both Medicare and Medicaid as they pertain to nursing homes are now subject to regular analysis. Silverman (1991), an article on Medicare-covered SNF services, and Swan et al. (1993), an examination of Medicaid trends, are illustrative. The cost implications of home health agencies as an alternative to skilled nursing facilities in the delivery of long-term care are of increasing interest (Manton, Stallard, and Woodbury 1994). Inevitably, cost containment sparks controversy about its effect on the quality of care. Studies like Jarrett (1981–1982), Nyman (1985), Cohen and Spector (1996), and Grimaldi (1999) offer a look at this issue.

Data Sources

The Standard Industrial Classification number for Nursing and Personal Care Facilities is 80.5; for skilled Nursing Facilities, 80.51; for health-related (personal care) facilities, 80.52. The primary source of data for the industry is the federal government. Income maintenance and healthcare fall under the jurisdiction of the Department of Health and Human Services, formerly the Department of Health, Education, and Welfare. The Social Security Administration, the Health Care Financing Administration (HCFA), and the National Center for Health Statistics are especially fruitful sources of historical statistics. HCFA publishes the quarterly *Health Care Financing Review*, which annually publishes an article entitled "National Health Expenditures"; authorship varies but see, for example, Gibson, Waldo, and Levit (1983), Levit et al. (1985), Waldo, Levit, and Lazenby (1986), and Levit et al. (1996). The periodic *National Master Facility Inventory*, *National Long-Term Care Survey*, and the *National Nursing Home Survey* merit close attention. In the private sector, the American Health Care Association represents proprietary ownership and publishes the *Long-Term Care Data Book*. The American Association of Homes for the Aging represents voluntary ownership and provides selected data on the nonprofit sector. Information on the corporate sector of the industry is best obtained from research reports of securities firms, but some useful industry data can be found in the monthly issues of *Provider* magazine, published by the American Health Care Association. The biggest problem with data is comparability. The various data sources use different definitions of the industry, ranging from the narrow skilled nursing facility to the broadest measures of long-term care.

BIBLIOGRAPHY

American Association of Homes for the Aging. "History of the AAHA." *Contemporary Long-Term Care*, September 1986, 36–69+.

American Health Care Association. *Long-Term Care Data Book*. Washington, DC: American Health Care Association, 1988.

Bishop, C. E. "Nursing Home Cost Studies and Reimbursement Issues." *Health Care Financing Review* 1, no. 3 (Spring 1980): 46–64.

Bonn, Karen L. "Nursing Old and New." *Nursing Homes* 48, no. 3 (March 1999): 72–74.

Breger, William N., and William R. Pomeranz. *Nursing Home Development: A Guide to Planning, Financing, and Constructing Long-Term Care Facilities*. New York: Van Nostrand Reinhold, 1985.

Bua, Robert N. *The Inside Guide to America's Nursing Homes: Rankings and*

Ratings for Every Nursing Home in the United States. New York: Warner Books, 1997.

Burmeister, Robert, and Susan J. Warner. "Long Term Care Administration: Past, Present and Future." *American Health Care Association Journal*, May 1984, 14–20.

Burner, Sally T., and Daniel R. Waldo. "National Health Expenditure Projections, 1994–2005." *Health Care Financing Review* 16, no. 4 (Summer 1995): 221–42.

Califano, Joseph A. *America's Health Care Revolution: Who Lives? Who Dies? Who Pays?* New York: Random House, 1986; New York: Simon & Schuster, a Touchstone Book, 1989.

Chiswick, Barry R. "The Demand for Nursing Home Care: An Analysis of the Substitution between Institutional and Noninstitutional Care." *Journal of Human Resources* 11 (1976): 295–316.

———. "The Demand for Nursing Home Care: A Comment." *Journal of Human Resources* 15 (1980): 287–92.

Cohen, J. W., and W. D. Spector. "The Effect of Medicaid Reimbursement on Quality of Care in Nursing Homes." *Journal of Health Economics* 15, no. 1 (February 1996): 23–48.

Cooney, Cyprian Jerome. *The Awakening of the Nursing Home Industry.* Springfield, IL: Thomas, 1986.

Doty, Pamela, Korbin Liu, and Joshua Wiener. "An Overview of Long-Term Care." *Health Care Financing Review* 6, no. 3 (Spring 1985): 69–78.

Dunlop, B. D. "Determinants of Long Term Care Facility Utilization by the Elderly: An Empirical Analysis." Working paper. Washington, DC: Urban Institute, 1976.

———. *The Growth of Nursing Home Care.* Lexington, MA: D. C. Heath, 1979.

Estes, Carroll L., and Philip R. Lee. "Social, Political, and Economic Background of Long Term Care Policy." In *Long Term Care of the Elderly: Public Policy Issues*, edited by Charlene Harrington et al. Sage Library of Social Research, vol. 157. Beverly Hills, CA: Sage, 1985.

Fisher, Christy. "Top 1996 Nursing Facility Chains." *Provider*, January 1997, 35–42.

Friedman, Bernard. "Economic Aspects of the Rationing of Nursing Beds." *Journal of Human Resources* 17 (1982): 59–71.

Gibson, R. M., D. R. Waldo, and K. R. Levit. "National Health Expenditures, 1982." *Health Care Financing Review* 5, no. 1 (Fall 1983): 1–31.

Grachek, Marianna Kern. "JCAHO [Joint Commission on the Accreditation of Healthcare Organizations] Accreditation: The Importance of Outcomes." *Nursing Homes* 48, no. 3 (March 1999): 52–54.

Grimaldi, Paul L. "New Skilled Nursing Facility Payment Scheme Boosts Medicare Risk." *Journal of Health Care Finance* 25, no. 3 (Spring 1999): 1–9.

Harrington, Charlene, Robert J. Newcomer, Carroll L. Estes, and Associates, eds. *Long Term Care of the Elderly: Public Policy Issues.* Sage Library of Social Research, vol. 157. Beverly Hills, CA: Sage, 1985.

Harrington, Charlene, and James H. Swan. "The Impact of State Medicaid Nursing Home Policies on Utilization and Expenditures." *Inquiry* 24 (Summer 1987): 157–72.

Health Care Financing Review. Washington, DC: National Center for Health Care Statistics, 1979–1995; Baltimore: U.S. Department of Health and Human Services, Health Care Financing Administration, 1995– . Quarterly.

Helbing, Charles, and Elizabeth Cornelius. "Skilled Nursing Facilities." *Health Care Financing Review, 1992 Annual Supplement,* 97–123.

Hing, Esther, Edward Sekscenski, and Genevieve Strahan. *The National Nursing Home Survey: 1985 Summary for the United States.* DHHS Publication no. (PHS) 89–1758. Vital and Health Statistics. Series 13, Data from the National Health Survey, no. 97. Hyattsville, MD: U.S. Department of Health and Human Services, Public Health Service, Centers for Disease Control, National Center for Health Statistics, January 1989.

Hirth, Richard A. "Consumer Information and Competition between Nonprofit and For-Profit Nursing Homes." *Journal of Health Economics* 18, no. 2 (April 1999): 219–40.

Hosay, Cynthia. "New Issues in Long-Term Care." *Employee Benefits Journal* 18, no. 4 (December 1993): 5–8.

Inquiry. Chicago: Blue Cross Association, 1963– . Quarterly.

Jarrett, Jeffrey E. "The Relationship of Cost Variations, Prospective Rate Setting, and Quality of Care in Nursing: A Hedonic Examination." *Review of Business and Economic Research* 17 (Winter 1981–1982): 67–77.

Journal of Health Economics. Amsterdam, the Netherlands: North-Holland, 1982– . Quarterly.

Journal of Human Resources. Madison: University of Wisconsin Press, 1966– . Quarterly.

Kemper, Peter, and Christopher Murtaugh. "Lifetime Use of Nursing Home Care." *New England Journal of Medicine* 324 (February 1991): 595–600.

Koff, Theodore H., and Kristine M. Bursac, comps. *Long Term Care: An Annotated Bibliography.* Bibliographies and Indexes in Gerontology, no. 25. Westport, CT: Greenwood Press, 1995.

Lamberton, C. E., W. D. Ellingson, and K. R. Spear. "Factors Determining the Demand for Nursing Home Services." *Quarterly Review of Economics and Business* 26 (Winter 1986): 74–90.

Levit, Katherine R., Helen Lazenby, Daniel R. Waldo, and Lawrence M. Davidoff. "National Health Expenditures, 1984." *Health Care Financing Review* 7, no. 1 (Fall 1985): 1–35.

Levit, Katherine R. et al. "National Health Expenditures, 1994." *Health Care Financing Review* 17, no. 3 (Spring 1996): 205–42.

Manton, Kenneth, Eric Stallard, and Max Woodbury. "Home Health and Skilled Nursing Facility Use, 1982–90." *Health Care Financing Review* 16, no. 1 (Fall 1994): 155–78.

Markus, Glenn R. *Nursing Homes and the Congress: A Brief History of Developments and Issues.* Washington, DC: Library of Congress, 1972.

McClure, Ethel. *More than a Roof: The Development of Minnesota Poor Farms and Homes for the Aged.* St. Paul: Minnesota Historical Society, 1968.

Morrow, Gloria. *The Social and Economic Impact of Nursing Homes.* Washington, DC: National Foundation for Long Term Health Care, 1978.

Moss, Frank, and Val J. Halamandaris. *Too Old, Too Sick, Too Bad: Nursing*

Homes in America. Germantown, MD: Aspen Systems, 1977. See also U.S. Congress, 1974–1976.

National Master Facility Inventory. Hyattsville, MD: U.S. Department of Health and Human Services; Public Health Service; Office of Health Research, Statistics, and Technology; National Center for Health Statistics. Irregular.

National Nursing Home Survey. Data from the National Health Survey. Hyattsville, MD: U.S. Department of Health, Education, and Welfare; Public Health Service; Office of the Assistant Secretary for Health; National Center for Health Statistics. Irregular.

Newcomer, Robert J., and Marjorie P. Bogaert-Tillis. "Medicaid Cost Containment Trials and Innovations." In *Long Term Care of the Elderly: Public Policy Issues,* edited by Charlene Harrington et al. Sage Library of Social Research, vol. 157. Beverly Hills, CA: Sage, 1985.

Nursing Home Market Report & Directory: Industry Characteristics, Trends, and Market Projections: Comparative Analysis. Chicago: SMG Marketing Group, 1995.

Nursing Homes: Long Term Care Management. Cleveland, OH: International, 1991– . Bimonthly.

Nursing Homes and Senior Citizen Care. Potomac, MD: Centaur, 1986–1991. Bimonthly. Continued by *Nursing Homes: Long Term Care Management.*

Nyman, John. "Prospective and 'Cost-Plus' Medicaid Reimbursement, Excess Medicaid Demand, and the Quality of Nursing Home Care." *Journal of Health Economics* 4 (1985): 237–59.

Packer-Tutsman, Judy. "The Future of Long Term Care." *Provider,* August 1995, 47–50.

Palmer, Hans C. "Studies of Nursing Home Costs." In *Long-Term Care: Perspectives from Research and Demonstrations,* edited by Ronald J. Vogel and Hans C. Palmer. Washington, DC: U.S. Department of Health and Human Services, Health Care Financing Administration, 1983.

Palmer, Hans C., and Ronald J. Vogel. "Models of the Nursing Home." In *Long-Term Care: Perspectives from Research and Demonstrations,* edited by Ronald J. Vogel and Hans C. Palmer. Washington, DC: U.S. Department of Health and Human Services, Health Care Financing Administration, 1983.

Patcher, Michael A., and Pallassana R. Balgopal. *Excellence in Nursing Homes: Care Planning, Quality Assurance, and Personnel Management.* New York: Springer, 1993.

Porell, Frank, Francis G. Caro, Ajith Silva, and Mark Monane. "A Longitudinal Analysis of Nursing Home Outcomes." *Health Services Research* 33, no. 4 (October 1998): 835–65.

Provider. Washington, DC: American Health Care Association, 1986– . Monthly.

Reschovsky, James D. "The Roles of Medicaid and Economic Factors in the Demand for Nursing Home Care." *Health Services Research* 33, no. 4 (October 1998): 787–813.

Rivlin, Alice M., and Joshua M. Wiener. *Caring for the Disabled Elderly: Who Will Pay?* Washington, DC: Brookings Institution, 1988.

Scanlon, William J. "A Theory of the Nursing Home Market." *Inquiry* 17 (Spring 1980): 25–41.

Schlenker, R. E. "Estimating Patient-Level Nursing Home Costs." *Health Services Research* (April 1985): 103–28.

Silverman, Herbert. "Medicare-Covered Skilled Nursing Facility Services, 1967–1988." *Health Care Financing Review* 12, no. 3 (Spring 1991): 103–8.

Spitz, Bruce. "States' Options for Reimbursing Nursing Home Capital." *Inquiry* 19 (Fall 1982): 246–56.

Spitz, Bruce, and J. B. Silvers. "The Nursing Home: Capital Formation and Funding." *Hospital Financial Management*, April 1981, 33–50.

Swan, James H., and Charlene Harrington. "Medicaid Nursing Home Reimbursement Policies." In *Long Term Care of the Elderly: Public Policy Issues*, edited by Charlene Harrington et al. Sage Library of Social Research, vol. 157. Beverly Hills, CA: Sage, 1985.

———. "Estimating Undersupply of Nursing Home Beds in States." *Health Services Research* 21 (April 1986): 59–78.

Swan, James H., Charlene Harrington, Leslie Grant, John Luehrs, and Steve Preston. "Trends in Medicaid Nursing Home Reimbursement, 1978–89." *Health Care Financing Review* 14, no. 4 (Summer 1993): 111–32.

Thomas, William C., Jr. *Nursing Homes and Public Policy: Drift and Decisions in New York State*. New York: Cornell University Press, 1969.

U.S. Congress Senate. Special Committee on Aging. *Federal Implementation of OBRA 1987 Nursing Home Reform Provisions*. Hearings. 101st Cong., 1st sess., May 18, 1989. S. Hrg. 101–698.

U.S. Congress. Senate. Special Committee on Aging. Subcommittee on Long-Term Care. *Nursing Home Care in the United States, Failure in Public Policy*. Introductory Report and Supporting Papers, Nos. 1–7. Washington, DC: Government Printing Office, 1974–1976.

Vladeck, Bruce C. *Unloving Care: The Nursing Home Tragedy*. A Twentieth Century Fund Study. New York: Basic Books, 1980.

Vogel, Ronald J. "The Industrial Organization of the Nursing Home Industry." In *Long-Term Care: Perspectives from Research and Demonstrations*, edited by Ronald J. Vogel and Hans C. Palmer. Washington, DC: U.S. Department of Health and Human Services, Health Care Financing Administration, 1983.

Vogel, Ronald J., and Hans C. Palmer, eds. *Long-Term Care: Perspectives from Research and Demonstrations*. Washington, DC: U.S. Department of Health and Human Services, Health Care Financing Administration, 1983.

———. *Long-Term Care: Perspectives from Research and Demonstrations*. Rockville, MD: Aspen Systems, 1985.

Waldman, Saul. "A Legislative History of Nursing Home Care." In *Long-Term Care: Perspectives from Research and Demonstrations*, edited by Ronald J. Vogel and Hans C. Palmer. Washington, DC: U.S. Department of Health and Human Services, Health Care Financing Administration, 1983.

Waldo, Daniel R., Katherine R. Levit, and Helen Lazenby. "National Health Expenditures, 1985." *Health Care Financing Review* 8, no. 1 (Fall 1986): 1–21.

Weissert, William G. "Estimating the Long-Term Care Population: Prevalence Rates and Selected Characteristics." *Health Care Financing Review* 6, no. 4 (Summer 1985): 83–88.

Young, M. Therese. *Surviving the Not So Golden Years: Vital Medical and Financial Strategies for Anyone Planning to Grow Old*. New York: Shapolsky, 1991.

CHAPTER 17

HEALTH MAINTENANCE
ORGANIZATIONS, 80.81
MARTIN A. STROSBERG

Health maintenance organizations (HMOs) are legal entities that supply comprehensive medical care services to voluntarily enrolled members at a prepaid, fixed price (e.g., a monthly premium). Prepaid group practices or independent practice associations (IPAs) render health services and control costs more efficiently than the traditional fee-for-service system because physicians assume some financial risk for the services they deliver. Several studies demonstrate how HMOs achieve their savings (Luft [1981] 1987; Luft and Trauner 1981).

PREPAID GROUP PRACTICES AND INDEPENDENT
PRACTICE ASSOCIATIONS (IPAs)

The acceptability and respectability of group medical practice were established by William and Charles Mayo in the 1890s in the form of the internationally renowned Mayo Clinic of Rochester, Minnesota (Clapesattle 1941). Inspired by the Mayo experience, other group practices were established across the country but were not as prevalent on the East Coast. Although groups represented an important departure from solo practice, they did not introduce the HMO feature of prepayment and posed no threat to organized medicine.

Industrial medicine, an early form of prepaid group practice, emerged in the late 1800s and early 1900s with the growth of the railroad, mining, and lumber industries. Organized clinical services were provided for those working under hazardous conditions in secluded locations where medical facilities and practitioners were unavailable (Havinghurst 1970).

Many of the modern HMOs were established in the economically depressed years between the two world wars, when the cooperative movement offered a pale shaft of hope for the desperate. Unstable employment conditions exacerbated the usual difficulties working families faced when medical care was needed: who would provide help when the family had no money, and how could accumulated bills be paid when employment was irregular? In that environment of insecurity the idea of monthly prepayment of all medical costs was appealing: a group of people might readily be persuaded to join in a prepayment pool for purposes of underwriting the availability of comprehensive medical services for everyone in the group. MacColl (1966) chronicles the development of consumer-sponsored prepaid group practices.

The Community Hospital of Elk City, Oklahoma, was the first medical cooperative. In 1929 Dr. Michael A. Shadid offered the farmers of the community the opportunity to buy shares in a new hospital and form a lay organization modeled after the consumer co-ops found throughout rural America. Later, Shadid provided medical, surgical, and laboratory services in exchange for annual membership dues in the cooperatives. The combination of prepayment and consumer participation through the cooperative arrangement constituted a radical departure from traditional fee-for-service practice and aroused bitter opposition from local physicians (Shadid 1939, 1947, [1956] 1992).

The first urban cooperative was formed in 1937 in Washington, D.C., by the employees of the federally sponsored Home Owners' Loan Corporation. Because the cost associated with illness was the most common cause of mortgage default, the employees established the Group Health Association, which was open to all federal employees (MacColl 1966).

Group Health Cooperative of Puget Sound, based in Seattle, is another example of an urban cooperative. Inspired by the writings and lectures of Shadid, the cooperative, formed in the early 1940s, had by 1945 acquired the clinics and hospital of a group practice that had been providing services on a contract basis to a number of industrial firms in the Seattle area. The physicians and their patients remained with the cooperative, forming the core of a network of services that extended beyond the metropolis to adjacent rural communities (MacColl 1966).

Whereas the cooperatives arose to provide medical care for the entire community, the Kaiser Foundation Health Plan grew out of a program established in 1933 by Dr. Sidney Garfield to provide medical care for workers employed on construction projects in southern California. From 1938 until the end of World War II, the Kaiser organization utilized Dr. Garfield and his prepaid group practice arrangement to serve workers and their families first on its Grand Coulee Dam project in Washington State, then in its shipbuilding and steelmaking plants on the West Coast. After the war, the program was opened to the general public, and the Kaiser Foundation Health Plan was established to enroll groups, collect dues, and provide membership services. In the 1960s the Kaiser-Permanente Health Plan (Permanente is the name of the medical group) was the largest HMO in the United States, serving 4.6 million members, most of them located on the West Coast (MacColl 1966).

Also in California and even earlier than Garfield, Drs. Donald Ross and H. Clifford Loos had, in 1929, contracted to provide comprehensive medical care to the workers and families of the Los Angeles Department of Water and Power. By 1935 the Ross-Loos Clinic enrolled more than 12,000 workers and 25,000 dependents (Starr 1982).

At the instigation of New York mayor Fiorello La Guardia, the Health Insurance Plan (HIP) of Greater New York was formed to serve municipal workers. Open to enrollment by 1947, HIP soon became one of the largest HMOs on the East Coast.

Several unions, including the United Mine Workers, United Auto Workers, and the Teamsters, have formed or sponsored HMOs. Regardless of sponsorship, these early prepaid group practices were invariably opposed by local physicians organized into county and state medical societies. Shadid and his colleagues had been denied membership in the county medical society, and physicians wishing to join Shadid were dissuaded by threats to revoke their licenses. The Elk City experiment could not have succeeded without the support of the powerful state Farmer's Union (Shadid 1939, 1947, [1956] 1992).

Group Health Association (GHA) of Washington, D.C., was the target of a campaign to deny GHA physicians admitting privileges in the city hospitals. MacColl (1966) summarizes the objections raised by organized medicine to GHA and other prepaid group practices: an inadequate funding base; corporate practice with no free choice of physicians; advertising and solicitation (unethical by definition); interference in the doctor–patient relationship; no incentive for doctors on salary to practice good medicine; exploitation of physicians' labor by nonphysicians; socialized medicine. In 1938, responding to the alleged suppression of the GHA, the Antitrust Division of the U.S. Department of Justice indicted the American Medical Association (AMA) and the local medical society for Sherman antitrust violations. The Supreme Court upheld the conviction of the AMA (*AMA v. United States*, 317 U.S. 519 [1943]). Despite the Court's decision, organized medicine continued to use its influence in state legislatures to impede the development of prepaid group practice. Thirty years later, opposition was effectually overcome by the passage of the federal HMO Act of 1973.

Prepaid group practices developed simultaneously with other innovations for financing hospital and medical care. In 1929 Baylor University Hospital agreed to provide twenty-one days of specified hospital care in return for six dollars per year from Dallas, Texas, schoolteachers enrolled in the Baylor Plan. The concept of providing a service benefit in return for prepayment grew into the Blue Cross plans that blanketed the nation and helped hospitals solve their cash flow problems by stabilizing revenue base and patient flows (Anderson 1975). In the 1930s and 1940s Blue Shield plans offered similar arrangements for financing physicians' services. Starr (1982) differentiates the "service benefit plans" of Blue Cross (BC) and Blue Shield (BS) from the "direct service" plans of prepaid group practice: in BC/BS plans, hospitals and physicians not only maintained monopoly control but escaped managerial (nonphysician) controls on medical practice.

Utilization review by a third party has always been repugnant to organized medicine. In the 1940s the Oregon State Medical Society initiated what was to become the Blue Shield Plan to squeeze out of business a private, profit-making "indemnity" insurance company that had been particularly aggressive in controlling physicians' fees through utilization review (Goldberg and Greenberg 1977b).

The response of organized medicine to prepaid group practice has not always been so reactionary. In an effort to protect professional autonomy of fee-for-service medicine and to prevent the Kaiser-Permanente plan from gaining a foothold in the San Joaquin Valley of California, the San Joaquin County Medical Society formed the Foundation for Medical Care (FMC) in 1954. The FMC established a prepaid health insurance program contracting with Blue Cross as the fiscal intermediary for a comprehensive benefit package. In return for fee-for-service payment, the participating physicians, practicing in their own offices, agreed to accept FMC fee schedules and FMC peer review of submitted claims to control utilization: if the prepayment fund were depleted, they risked reduced fees (Egdahl 1973). The San Joaquin experiment was successfully replicated in other parts of the country. Ultimately, the FMC model became known as the Independent Practice Association (IPA) and was included in the definition of health maintenance organization, even though IPA did not comprise group practice.

THE PROFESSION OF MEDICINE AND FEE-FOR-SERVICE MEDICINE

Organized medicine's antagonism to the concept of the HMO is rooted in the defining characteristics of the medical profession and its tradition of fee-for-service medicine. Eliot Freidson claims that the "only truly important and uniform criterion for distinguishing professions from other occupations is . . . autonomy—a position of legitimate control over work" (1974, 82). By allowing the medical profession control over state licensure, medical education, and the credentialing system, the state has granted it a monopoly over the therapeutic technologies. In *Professional Dominance*, Freidson (1970) describes the methods by which the profession achieved its self-regulatory status. Rosemary Stevens (*American Medicine and the*

Public Interest [1971] 1998) continues the analysis of professional control over the credentialing system.

At the core of the therapeutic process is the doctor–patient relationship. Organized medicine claims that fee-for-service reimbursement is essential to preserving the inviolability of this relationship and physicians' autonomy. Many of the HMO's attributes are perceived to threaten this relationship because they alter traditional fee-for-service medicine and may loosen physicians' control over working conditions and economic security. The defensive actions taken by the AMA and state and county medical societies are part of an overall struggle to keep the practice of medicine independent of both government control (socialized medicine) and corporate control. Until World War II, medicine had "escaped" the corporation and the hierarchical control of industrial capitalism (Starr 1982).

AMA policies and ethical standards prohibit the corporate practice of medicine: it is wrong for an investor to make a profit from physicians' labor; the full return on their labor must go to the physicians; that is, there must be no capital formation other than what the physicians accumulate. Supporters of this position claim that medicine departs significantly from the classical competitive market model because of the inherent uncertainty in the therapeutic process, patients' inability to comprehend medical contingencies, and patients' dependence on physicians for information; hence, nonmarket social institutions have arisen to protect patients (Arrow 1963).

PUBLIC POLICY AND HEALTH MAINTENANCE ORGANIZATIONS

Despite the opposition of organized medicine, public support has always been strong for prepaid group practice. In 1927 the now-famous Committee on the Costs of Medical Care was formed. The committee of medical and business community elite published twenty-five volumes on the economic aspects of medical care, including the final report, *Medical Care for the American People* ([1932] 1972). The committee came out squarely for prepaid group practice in recommending that "organized groups of consumers unite in paying into a common fund in weekly installments, and in arranging with organized groups of medical practitioners . . . to furnish them and their families with virtually complete medical services" (Committee on the Costs of Medical Care [1932, 121] 1972). The AMA quickly endorsed the minority report opposing prepaid group practice ("The Committee on the Costs of Medical Care" 1932).

Except for occasional setbacks in the courts, organized medicine was able to blunt the growth of HMOs for four more decades. However, in the early years of President Richard Nixon's administration, a fortuitous set of circumstances arose: escalating Medicare and Medicaid costs posed a national dilemma; the new Republican administration had no articulated healthcare policy with which to "scoop" the Democrats; a weakened AMA had ex-hausted itself in a successful fight over the appointment of the assistant secretary of health in the U.S. Department of Health, Education, and Welfare (DHEW).

Paul Elwood, executive director of the American Rehabilitation Foundation, a Minneapolis-based think tank on health policy issues, had access to the health policy leadership of the Nixon administration (mostly Californians). A "Kaiser-like" healthcare delivery organization could, he suggested, be the key to reorganizing the healthcare industry. Joseph L. Falkson (1980) analyzes the development of the health maintenance strategy in policy formation and implementation stages, from the late 1960s to the late 1970s. Falkson recounts Elwood's rationale for the term "health maintenance organization":

The use of "health" rather than "medical" was desirable since prevention, early diagnosis, and early treatment were to be emphasized. "Maintenance" focused on maintaining health rather than treating illness. And "organization" was a term possessing a neutrality unavailable in such terms as "corporation group practice or partnership." The term "health maintenance organization," however, was unique and not immediately assailable from either the left or the right. It was a politically nebulous and, therefore, desirable phrase. (Falkson 1980, 32)

The appeal to the Republican administration was that the HMO strategy would, according to Elwood (1977), represent a market reform; that is, the federal government's role in health affairs would contract to one of providing "investment capital" to stimulate the development of competing HMOs, which would have incentives to organize themselves so as to deliver healthcare efficiently. The previous Democratic administration had emphasized central planning and regulation and the expansion of federal categorical grants (Falkson 1980). Moreover, the idea of competition and marketplace incentives was a significant departure from the concept of community-oriented prepaid group practice endorsed by the Committee on the Costs of Medical Care. The HMO strategy was broad enough to include the FMC/IPA model.

Falkson (1980) and Brown (1983) analyze the legislative and bureaucratic politics that led to the Nixon administration's active endorsement of the HMO strategy as the cornerstone of its healthcare policy and to the eventual passage of the HMO Act of 1973. The act, in addition to eliminating most of the restrictive state statutes that had impeded HMO growth, provided project grants and start-up capital for developing HMOs.

THE EXPANSION OF THE HMO MOVEMENT

The HMO Act of 1973 (Title XIII of the Public Health Service Act) and subsequent amendments set up a federal program to provide technical and financial assistance for promoting the development and growth of new HMOs and for increasing the number of enrollees. The U.S. Department of Health and Human Services has given out $145 million in grants (for planning and development) and $219 million in loans (for initial operating expenses and construction). These funds helped start up 114 operational HMOs (Iglehart 1984). After the federal government withdrew its financial support in the early 1980s, investment by the private sector built up large, publicly traded, investor-owned HMOs.

The *Investor's Guide to Health Maintenance Organizations* (Touche Ross & Co. 1982) identifies four measures of HMO viability: average annual enrollment growth rate, return on sales (after-tax net income divided by premium revenue), operating margin (premium revenues minus benefits expenditures, divided by premium revenue), the ratio of general and administrative expenses to total expenses. By March 1987 there were 654 HMOs, with a total membership of 27.7 million (*InterStudy Edge* 1987). The 1990s merger mania created giant HMOs: enrollment had increased to 77.3 million by 1996 and, only a year later, to 83.7 million ("HMO Enrollment Grows 8.2 Percent in 1997" January 1997). Both government and business see the development of competitive, market-driven, for-profit and not-for-profit HMOs as a major strategy for healthcare delivery and cost containment.

The 1990s was the decade of managed health. High inflation rates in the 1980s were at least partially driven by the rapidly accelerating costs of medical care associated with advancing (and expensive) technology and an aging population. President William J. Clinton's initiative on comprehensive healthcare broached a maelstrom. Fearing rationing of medical care and no choice of physicians, the press, the public, and the medical community reacted strongly, squelching plans in the earliest stages. The president and the First Lady—Hillary Rodham Clinton was a strong voice for reform—suffered a stunning defeat in their efforts to revamp American healthcare. Clinton's second term was derailed by scandal, impeachment, and a U.S-led North Atlantic Treaty Organization (NATO) war in Europe: twentieth-century healthcare reform was shelved.

Business and the general public, aware that the rising cost of medical care invited federal intervention, cooperated to stem the rate of increase: enrollees shifted out of standard medical insurance plans into HMOs. The initial savings in medical costs gained by HMO rules and regulations helped bring U.S. inflation to bay: the official measure in 1998 was a consumer price index of about 0.8, but most observers concluded there was sufficient error in the market basket to discount the 0.8 to zero.

By 1999 the savings from HMO enrollments had been exhausted, and medical costs once again threatened the price level status quo. The end of the decade and the century found the strongest American economy since the beginning of macroeconomic accounting in 1929. The inflation of the

Johnson administration and the deficits of the Reagan administration had been reined in, and the U.S. Congress had a budget surplus to devote to medical reform (some economists argued there was no surplus, but most agreed that the deficit was gone, and the federal government had money to dispose of without increasing taxes). HMOs promise to remain important players in national healthcare, but innovations in organization, financing, and operation are essential to containing rising medical costs.

BIBLIOGRAPHIC ESSAY

Bloom and Kosco (1973), Pinel (1974), Cook (1979), Sharma (1979), Parker (1981), Bauchum (1984), and Snider (1987) are sources of bibliographic information on HMOs before the mid-1980s. Moreover, the work of Odin W. Anderson and his associates documents the creation and development of HMOs in the decades before the Clinton administration's proposed healthcare reform.

The healthcare industry is a large part of the American economy. Renowned theorist Kenneth Arrow has established the theoretical foundation for economic analysis of medicine and healthcare (Arrow 1951, 1963, 1973a; Arrow et al. 1996). Lawrence D. Brown's contributions are also an integral part of the health policy literature (1982, 1983, 1987, 1988, 1991).

The 1990s—years of HMO dominance—provides a vast literature on healthcare. In *Health against Wealth* (1997), George Anders examines the medical profession cum public enterprise as issues unfolded in the 1990s. Other works illuminating the changes in private and public approaches to healthcare in the 1990s are Warren Greenberg's studies (1991, 1998), Gordon A. Miller and Tom Mann's *Speak Now or Forever Rest in Peace* (1997), Irwin Miller's *American Health Care Blues* (1996), and Alan J. Steinberg's *Insider's Guide to HMOs* (1997).

The healthcare trade and periodic literature is as volatile as the industry itself. Many journals prominent in the 1980s disappeared before the 1990s. New titles and reorganized, merged, or absorbed chronicles continue to offer up-to-date information on HMOs and diverse forms of managed care systems. Statistical measures for HMOs and other healthcare organizations can be found in *Best's Aggregates & Averages, Best's Managed Care Reports HMO, Guide to HMOs & Health Insurers, Healthcare Blue Book,* and *HMO Risk Sharing & Capitation*. The American Association of Health Plans publishes *Healthplan* bimonthly; *Managed Healthcare News* is published monthly, and *Managed Health Care Overview* and *Medical Group Practice Digest* are annuals.

BIBLIOGRAPHY

Anders, George. *Health against Wealth: HMOs and the Breakdown of Medical Trust*. Thorndike, ME: G. K. Hall, 1997.

Andersen, Ronald, and Odin W. Anderson. *A Decade of Health Services: Social Survey Trends in Use and Expenditure.* Chicago: University of Chicago Press, 1967.

Andersen, Ronald, Joanna Lion, and Odin W. Anderson. *Two Decades of Health Services: Social Survey Trends in Use and Expenditure.* Cambridge, MA: Ballinger, 1976.

Anderson, Odin W. *Blue Cross since 1929: Accountability and the Public Trust.* Cambridge, MA: Ballinger, 1975.

———. *Health Services in the United States: A Growth Enterprise since 1875.* Ann Arbor, MI: Health Administration Press, 1985.

———. *HMO Development: Patterns & Prospects: A Comparative Analysis of HMOs.* Chicago: Pluribus Press; University of Chicago, Center for Health Administration Studies, 1985.

———. *The Health Services Continuum in Democratic States: An Inquiry into Solvable Problems.* Ann Arbor, MI: Health Administration Press, 1989.

———. *Health Services as a Growth Enterprise in the United States since 1875.* 2d ed. Ann Arbor, MI: Health Administration Press, 1990.

———. *The Evolution of Health Services Research: Personal Reflections on Applied Social Science.* Jossey-Bass Health Series. San Francisco: Jossey-Bass, 1991.

Anderson, Odin W., and Harold Alksne. *An Examination of the Concept of Medical Indigence.* New York: Health Information Formation, 1957.

Anderson, Odin W., and George Rosen. *An Examination of the Concept of Preventive Medicine.* New York: Health Information Foundation, 1960.

Appleby, Jean M. "Top 25 Areas with High HMO Penetration." *Managed Healthcare* 9, no. 3 (March 1999): 72.

Arrow, Kenneth. *Social Choice and Individual Values.* Yale University, Cowles Foundation for Research in Economics, monograph 12. New York: Wiley, 1951.

———. "Uncertainty and the Welfare Economics of Medical Care." *American Economic Review* 53 (December 1963): 941–69.

———. *Theoretical Issues in Health Insurance.* Noel Buxton Lecture. Colchester, UK: University of Essex, 1973a.

———. *Welfare Analysis of Changes in Health Coinsurance Rates.* Prepared for the U.S. Office of Economic Opportunity. Rand Report R-1281-OEO. Santa Monica, CA: Rand, 1973b.

Arrow, Kenneth, et al. *Benefit-Cost Analysis in Environmental Health and Safety Regulation: A Statement of Principles.* Washington, DC: American Enterprise Institute for Public Policy Research, 1996.

Bauchum, Rosalind G. *The Economics of Health Maintenance Organizations: A Bibliography.* Monticello, IL: Vance Bibliographies, 1984.

Berman, Avis, ed. *The Challenge of the Next Ten Years for Health Maintenance Organizations: A Symposium.* Claverack, NY: Cladwell B. Esselstyn Foundation, 1980.

Best's Aggregates & Averages. HMO United States. Oldwick, NJ: A. M. Best, 1998– . Annual.

Best's Managed Care Reports HMO. Oldwick, NJ: A. M. Best, 1993– . Annual.

Birnbaum, Roger W. *Health Maintenance Organizations: A Guide to Planning and Development.* New York: Spectrum; Halsted Press, 1976.

Bloom, Alan, and Paul Kosco. *Selected Annotated Bibliography on Health Maintenance Organizations (HMOs) and Organized Health Care Systems.* Washington, DC: U.S. Department of Health, Education, and Welfare; Health Services Administration; Bureau of Community Health Services; Office of Organization Development, 1973.

Brown, Lawrence D. *The Political Structure of the Federal Health Planning Program.* Washington, DC: Brookings Institution, 1982.

———. *Politics and Health Care Organization: HMOs as Federal Policy.* Washington, DC: Brookings Institution, 1983.

———, ed. *Health Policy in Transition: A Decade of Health Politics, Policy, and Law.* Durham, NC: Duke University Press, 1987. Originally published without Preface or Index as volume 11, number 4 of *Journal of Health Politics, Policy, and Law.*

———, ed. *Health Policy in the United States: Issues and Options.* Project on Social Welfare and the American Future, no. 4. New York: Ford Foundation, 1988.

———, ed. *Health Policy and the Disadvantaged.* Durham, NC: Duke University Press, 1991.

Buchanan, Joan, and Shan Cretin. *Fee-for-Service Health Care Expenditures: Evidence of Selection Effects among Subscribers Who Choose HMOs.* Santa Monica, CA: Rand, 1986.

"Business on the Critical List." *The Economist* 350, no. 8106 (February 13, 1999): 65–66.

Chisman, Forrest P., Lawrence D. Brown, and Pamela J. Larson, eds. *National Health Reform: What Should the State Role Be?* Washington, DC: National Academy of Social Insurance, 1994.

Clapesattle, Helen. *The Doctors Mayo.* Minneapolis: University of Minnesota Press, 1941.

Coile, Russell. *The Five Stages of Managed Care: Strategies for Providers, HMOs, & Suppliers.* Chicago: Health Administration Press, 1997.

Coleman, Sinclair B. *Health Maintenance Organizations as an Instrument for Cost Containment Policy.* Santa Monica, CA: Rand, 1979.

Committee on the Costs of Medical Care. *Medical Care for the American People: The Final Report of the Committee on the Costs of Medical Care, Adopted October 31, 1932.* Chicago: University of Chicago Press, 1932. Reprint. Medicine & Society in America. New York: Arno Press, 1972.

"The Committee on the Costs of Medical Care." *Journal of the American Medical Association* 99 (December 3, 1932): 1950–51.

Connolly, John J. *The ABCs of HMOs: How to Get the Best from Managed Care.* New York: Castle, Connolly Medical, 1997.

Cook, Joseph Lee, and Earleen H. Cook. *Health Maintenance Organizations and Prepaid Group Practices: A Bibliography.* Monticello, IL: Vance Bibliographies, 1979.

Curtis, Rick, Trisha Kurtz, and Larry S. Stepnick, eds. *Creating Consumer Choice in Healthcare: Measuring and Communicating Health Plan Performance Information.* Chicago: Health Administration Press, 1998.

"Don't Look Now. HMO's Are Hiking Rates." *U.S. News & World Report.* July 12, 1999, 44.

Egdahl, Richard H. "Foundations for Medical Care." *New England Journal of Medicine* 288 (March 8, 1973): 491.

Egdahl, Richard H., and Paul M. Gertman, eds. *Quality Assurance in Health Care.* Germantown, MD: Aspen Systems, 1976.

———. *Quality Health Care: The Role of Continuing Medical Education.* Germantown, MD: Aspen Systems, 1977.

———. *Technology and the Quality of Health Care.* Germantown, MD: Aspen Systems, 1978.

Egdahl, Richard H., and Diana Chapman Walsh, eds. *Health Services and Health Hazards: The Employee's Need to Know.* Springer Series on Industry and Health Care, no. 4. New York: Springer-Verlag, 1978.

———. *Industry and HMOs—A Natural Alliance.* Springer Series on Industry and Health Care, no. 5. New York: Springer-Verlag, 1978.

———. *Containing Health Benefit Costs: The Self-Insurance Option.* New York: Springer-Verlag, 1979.

Elwood, Paul M., Jr. et al. "The Health Maintenance Strategy." *Medical Care* 9 (June 1977): 291–98.

Espinoza, Galina. "Death of an HMO." *Money* 28, no. 5 (May 1999): 140–48.

"Expect a Boost in HMO Profits." *Trustee* 52, no. 3 (March 1999): 4.

Falkson, Joseph L. *HMOs and the Politics of Health System Reform.* AHA Catalog no. 1183. Chicago: American Hospital Association, 1980.

Fox, Peter D., and LuAnn Heinen, with Richard J. Steele. *Determinants of HMO Success.* Ann Arbor, MI: Health Administration Press Perspectives, 1987.

Freeborn, Donald K., and Clyde R. Pope. *Promise and Performance in Managed Care: The Prepaid Group Practice Model.* Baltimore: Johns Hopkins University Press, 1994.

Freidson, Eliot. *Professional Dominance: The Social Structure of Medical Care.* New York: Atherton Press, 1970.

———. *Profession of Medicine: A Study of the Sociology of Applied Knowledge.* New York: Dodd, Mead, 1974.

———. *Doctoring Together: A Study of Professional Social Control.* Chicago: University of Chicago Press, 1980.

Goldberg, Lawrence G., and Warren Greenberg. *Economic Report on the Health Maintenance Organization and Its Effects on Competition: Staff Report to the Federal Trade Commission.* Washington, DC: Federal Trade Commission, Bureau of Economics, 1977a.

———. "The Effect of Physician-Controlled Health Insurance." *Journal of Health Politics, Policy, and Law* 1, no. 2 (Spring 1977b): 48–78.

Greenberg, Warren. *Competition, Regulation, and Rationing in Health Care.* Ann Arbor, MI: Health Administration Press, 1991.

———. *The Health Care Marketplace.* New York: Springer, 1998.

———, ed. *Competition in the Health Care Sector: Ten Years Later.* Durham, NC: Duke University Press, 1988.

Greenlick, Merwyn R., Donald K. Freeborn, and Clyde R. Pope, eds. *Health Care Research in an HMO: Two Decades of Discovery.* Baltimore: Johns Hopkins University Press, 1988.

Greenwald, Judy. "Analysts Predict Improved HMO Stock Performance." *Business Insurance* 33, no. 12 (March 22, 1999): 7.

Gross, Martin L. *The Medical Racket: How Doctors, HMOs & Hospitals Are Failing the American Patient*. New York: Avon Books, 1998.

Guide to HMOs & Health Insurers: A Quarterly Compilation of Health Insurance Company Ratings & Analysis. Palm Beach Gardens, FL: Weiss Ratings, 1998.

Hann, Leslie Werstein. "Keeping Score." *Best's Review* 99, no. 7 (November 1998): 31–34.

Havinghurst, Clark. "Health Maintenance Organizations and the Market for Health Services." *Law and Contemporary Problems* 35 (Autumn 1970): 716–46.

Healthcare Blue Book. Atlanta, GA: Billian, 1995– . Annual.

Healthplan. Washington, DC: American Association of Health Plans, 1996– . Bimonthly.

Henderson, John A., and Susen N. Dunmire, eds. *Health Maintenance Organizations: Industry Characteristics, Trends, and Market Projections: Comparative Analysis*. Chicago: SMG Marketing Group, 1989.

Higgins, Michael. "Second Opinions on HMOs." *ABA Journal* 85 (April 1999): 60–65.

"HMO Enrollment Grows 8.2 Percent in 1997." *Healthcare Financial Management* 53, no. 1 (January 1997): 21–22.

HMO Risk Sharing & Capitation: A National Study. Santa Rosa, CA: Healthcare Data Bank, 1995.

Holmes, Dari et al. *National HMO Firms, 1985: A Report on Companies That Own or Operate HMOs in Two or More States*. Excelsior, MN: InterStudy, 1986.

Iglehart, J. K. "HMOs (For Profit and Not-for-Profit) on the Move." *New England Journal of Medicine* 310, no. 18 (May 3, 1984): 1203–8.

InterStudy Edge. Excelsior, MN: InterStudy, 1987.

Iversen, Laura Himes, and Cynthia Longseth Polich. *The Future of Medicare and HMOs*. Excelsior, MN: InterStudy, 1985.

Iversen, Laura Himes et al. *Improving Health and Long-Term Care for the Elderly: An Examination of Medicare, Capitation, and HMOs*. Excelsior, MN: InterStudy, Center for Aging and Long-Term Care, 1986.

Keating, Peter. "How Healthy Is Your HMO?" *Money* 28, no. 3 (March 1999): 30.

Kraus, Nancy. *Managed Care: A Decade in Review 1980–1990*. Excelsior, MN: InterStudy, 1991.

Kronick, Richard, and Joy de Beyer. *Medicare HMOs: Making Them Work for the Chronically Ill*. Chicago: Health Administration Press; Association for Health Services Research, 1999.

Lerner, Monroe, and Odin W. Anderson. *Health Progress in the United States, 1900–1960: A Report of Health Information Foundation*. Chicago: University of Chicago Press, 1963.

Luft, Harold S. *Health Maintenance Organizations: Dimensions of Performance*. New York: John Wiley & Sons, 1981. Reprint. New Brunswick, NJ: Transaction Books, 1987.

———, ed. *HMOs and the Elderly*. Washington, DC: Association for Health Services Research; Ann Arbor, MI: Health Administration Press, 1994.

Luft, Harold S., and Joan B. Trauner. *The Operations and Performance of Health Maintenance Organizations: A Synthesis of Findings from Health Service Research.* San Francisco: Institute for Health Policy Studies, 1981.

MacColl, William A. *Group Practice and Prepayment of Medical Care.* Washington, DC: Public Affairs Press, 1966.

Mackie, Dustin L., and Douglas K. Decker. *Group and IPA HMOs.* Rockville, MD: Aspen Systems, 1981.

Mader, Thomas W. *Health Maintenance Organizations: A Research Report.* SRI Long Range Planning Service Report 558. Menlo Park, CA: Stanford Research Institute, 1975.

Managed Healthcare News. Manhasset, NY: Health Week, 1991– . Monthly.

Managed Health Care Overview. Washington, DC: AMCRA Foundation, 1994– . Annual.

McKinlay, John B., ed. *Health Maintenance Organizations.* Cambridge: MIT Press, 1981.

Medical Group Practice Digest. Kansas City, MO: Hoechst Marion Roussel, 1994– . Annual.

Miller, Gordon A., and Tom Mann. *Speak Now or Forever Rest in Peace: The Very Real Dangers of HMOs and What You Can Do about Them.* Salem, OR: Gordon A. Miller, 1997.

Miller, Irwin. *American Health Care Blues: Blue Cross, HMOs, and Pragmatic Reform since 1960.* New Brunswick, NJ: Transaction Publishers, 1996.

The National Directory of Managed Care Organizations. 2d ed. Manasquan, NJ: Managed Care Information Center, 1998.

Nelson, Harry. *Nonprofit and For-Profit HMOs: Converging Practices but Different Goals?* New York: Milbank Memorial Fund, 1997.

"New Developments in Managed Health Care Industry May Bring about Significant Change." *Employee Benefit Plan Review* 53, no. 3 (September 1998): 10–12.

Parker, Deborah. *Health Maintenance Organizations: Empirical Evidence of Performance and Operation.* Monticello, IL: Vance Bibliographies, 1981.

Pinel, Patricia N. *Comprehensive Bibliography on Health Maintenance Organizations, 1970–1973.* Denver: Medical Group Management Association, 1974.

Prince, Michael. "Health Care Costs on the Rise Again." *Business Insurance* 32, no. 51 (December 21, 1998): 24.

Robinson, James C. "The Future of Managed Care Organizations." *Health Affairs* 18, no. 2 (March/April 1999): 18.

Shadid, Michael A. *A Doctor for the People: The Autobiography of the Founder of America's First Co-Operative Hospital.* New York: Vanguard Press, 1939.

———. *Doctors of Today and Tomorrow.* New York: Cooperative League of the U.S.A., 1947.

———. *Crusading Doctor: My Fight for Cooperative Medicine.* Boston: Meador, 1956. Reprint. Norman: University of Oklahoma Press, 1992.

Shapiro, Joseph P. "There When You Need It: *U.S. News* Ranks 271 of the Nation's HMOs and Looks at an Innovator That Stresses Preventive Medicine." *U.S. News & World Report,* October 5, 1998, 64–72.

Sharma, Prakash C. *A Selected Bibliographic Research Guide to Health Maintenance Organizations and Prepaid Group Practice. Monticello, IL: Vance Bibliographies, 1979.

Snider, Erica M. *Health Maintenance Organization: Subject Analysis with Reference Bibliography*. Washington, DC: ABBE Publishers Association, 1987.

Starr, Paul. *The Social Transformation of American Medicine*. New York: Basic Books, 1982.

―――. *The Logic of Health-Care Reform: Why and How the President's Plan Will Work*. New York: Whittle Books in association with Penguin Books, 1994.

Steinberg, Alan J. *The Insider's Guide to HMOs: How to Navigate the Managed-Care System and Get the Health Care You Deserve*. New York: Plume, 1997.

Stevens, Robert, and Rosemary Stevens. *Welfare Medicine in America: A Case Study of Medicare*. New York: Free Press, 1974.

Stevens, Rosemary. *American Medicine and the Public Interest*. New Haven, CT: Yale University Press, 1971. Reprint. Berkeley: University of California Press, 1998.

―――. *In Sickness and in Wealth: American Hospitals in the Twentieth Century*. New York: Basic Books, 1989. Reprint. Baltimore: Johns Hopkins University Press, 1999.

Touche Ross & Co. *Investor's Guide to Health Maintenance Organizations*. DHHS Publication no. (PHS) 82–50185. Rockville, MD: U.S. Department of Health and Human Services, Public Health Service, Office of the Assistant Secretary for Health, Office of Health Maintenance Organizations, Division of Program Promotion, 1982.

U.S. General Accounting Office. *Managed Health Care: Effect on Employers' Costs Difficult to Measure: Report to the Chairman, Subcommittee on Health, Committee on Ways and Means, House of Representatives*. Washington, DC: General Accounting Office, 1993.

Walsh, Diana Chapman, and Richard H. Egdahl. *Payer, Provider, Consumer: Industry Confronts Health Care Costs*. Springer Series on Industry and Health Care, no. 1. New York: Springer-Verlag, 1977.

Wechsler, Jill. "Medicare Retirees Happy with HMOs, Study Shows." *Managed Healthcare* 9, no. 4 (April 1999): 10.

Wojcik, Joanne. "Health Care Merger Activity Continues." *Business Insurance* 32, no. 51 (December 21, 1998): 28.

Part XIII

Educational Services
ESIC 82.0

CHAPTER 18 ⎯⎯⎯⎯⎯⎯⎯⎯⎯⎯⎯⎯⎯⎯⎯⎯⎯⎯⎯

EDUCATIONAL SERVICES, 82.0
⎯⎯⎯⎯⎯⎯⎯⎯⎯⎯⎯⎯⎯⎯⎯⎯ JOSEPH FINKELSTEIN

U.S. education developed in tandem with social, cultural, political, and economic institutions. In the first two centuries of national development Americans emphasized openness, heterogeneity, democracy, pragmatism, and functionalism yet sustained broad religious and ethical values derived from both the Judeo-Christian heritage and the classical-humanist elements of Western civilization (Butts and Cremin 1953; Boyer 1987). The admixture of goals generated divisive conflict that often left education adrift without leaders, direction, support, or resources—crises that forced society to redefine the role of educators and their institutions (Kerr 1972; Bowen [1977] 1997; Riesman 1980).

Although critical of their educational system, Americans keep it high on the list of national priorities, for they believe that education is the foundation of productivity and prosperity. To maintain that foundation, citizens must regularly reassess the educational system, redirecting it if necessary. Change is kept in check by those who oppose alterations in what they regard as a functioning mechanism that should not be tampered with. The push for change and the pull for status quo are what make American society work. Innovation, experimentation, the freedom to make mistakes, and a commitment to democratic education from three levels of government within a federal political system and a market-dominated economy combine to make the American education system unique.

THE COLONIAL PERIOD

Although colonial educational institutions and the philosophy that drove them came to the New World with the first immigrants, people in each of the thirteen colonies found their own way of teaching children. New England colonial governments dominated education and used the schools to inculcate religious values. In the course of the eighteenth century, citizens demanded separation of church and state: the control of education broadened, and towns assumed increasing responsibility for their schools and what was taught in them; nevertheless, the principle of central authority remained a permanent legal base for future educational developments.

In the South, education was supervised by the Church of England. The church's focus was indigent children, especially orphans, and apprentices, and their needs were overseen at the parish level. Although civil authority retained power over education, the wealthy educated their children privately without recourse to public authority. The sparseness and diffusion of population, the heterogeneity of backgrounds and religion, and institutionalized and legal slavery contributed to an educational system very different from its counterparts in New England and the Middle Colonies.

In New York, the Dutch favored private and church schools; in Pennsylvania, the Penns assumed public and state responsibility for education, and Pennsylvania in its state constitution (1776) reaffirmed this commitment:

A school or schools shall be established in every county by the legislature, for the convenient instruction of youth, with such salaries to the masters, paid by the public, as may enable them to instruct youth at low prices; and all useful learning shall be duly encouraged and promoted in one or more universities. (Butts and Cremin 1953, 108)

On the eve of the Revolution, the 4 million people in the English colonies in America were better educated than most Europeans. The American commitment to democratic education would become a model for Western Europe. Virginian Thomas Jefferson's "Bill for the More General Diffusion of Knowledge," proposed in 1779, was the philosophical foundation for the universal extension and expansion of education in the nineteenth century. The state did not adopt his scheme, but Jefferson's framework of a system of public schools—from primary, to secondary, to university, largely free and grounded in merit with a democratic curriculum that emphasized reason, science, languages, history, geography, and mathematics—broke the standard of religious and Bible-oriented instruction and would ultimately prevail. Jefferson knew that only a free and freely educated society could maintain the democracy of the country. If all schools were to come under the control of public officers and public financing, and all children were to be educated at public expense, political control had to be decentralized and placed in the hands of local officials (Butts and Cremin 1953; Bailyn 1960; Handlin and Handlin 1970).

FROM REVOLUTION TO CIVIL WAR

In the 100-odd years from 1763—the end of the Seven Years' War (French and Indian War in America) and the beginning of the American Revolution (not to be confused with the War of Independence, which began in 1776)—until the end of the Civil War in 1865, American education took on its distinctive patina. What emerged was an educational system different from European antecedents, a unique outgrowth of a new nationalism, a sense of strength brought on by eastern industrial growth and a vast western frontier. The century saw the radical solution to the two greatest questions since the revolt against the Crown: the end of separatism and the abolition of slavery. In education this was a century of creation.

By 1866 the common school was financed and directed at the local level and offered the elements of reading, writing, and arithmetic and perhaps history. Which children were admitted to the schools varied from community to community. Some prohibited children of color, especially in the South; most barred Native Americans; and in the Southwest, children of Spanish ancestry sought education in church schools or received none. Children from Catholic households were educated in the church by priests and nuns or went to the more liberal public schools and kept their religious preference quiet. Jewish children were rarely welcome in American public schools.

The American educational program embodied six precepts: moral and character development (the dominant aim of all education); mental discipline (the teaching of mathematics to strengthen logical reasoning); universal literacy and the dissemination of information; education for citizenship; vocational or practical competence; individual success (Butts and Cremin 1953). Few schools had the physical facilities or the resources to achieve these aims for even a small part of society, but the agenda captured the energy of local and state officials and set American and European education apart.

The common school system led to the high school, supported by public funds and offering a curriculum that left open to choice and merit the student's entry to a public university. A single system without fees, open to all social classes, was a national goal that Americans insisted they had attained. Another century would pass before the nation faced the harsh truth of institutionalized racial discrimination in public and private education. The Morrill Act of 1863 granted each state 30,000 acres of public land (or scrip) per each of its congressmen to be used to support state colleges of agricultural and mechanical arts; funds could be allocated to existing institutions or used to establish new ones. Land-grant colleges (e.g., Cornell University in New York State) reinforced the democratic concept of the open and attainable university education for select American males. Opposed by private institutions committed largely to classical and liberal education, the land-grant colleges developed as outstanding contributors to agriculture and the more pragmatic needs of society.

Because the Morrill Act was passed during the Civil War, special legislation was necessary after the war to provide land-grant moneys for the states of the defunct Confederacy. Schools like Clemson (South Carolina), the University of Georgia, the University of Florida, North Carolina State University, and Auburn University (Alabama) opened to white males, later extended enrollment to white women, and, in the 1960s, were forced by federal mandate to admit black citizens.

In the years before a majority of white Americans agreed that the equal rights policy established by the U.S. Constitution extended to black citizens, the second Morrill Act (passed in 1890) financed black agricultural and mechanical arts colleges in states that refused to admit their black citizens into the federally supported land-grant institutions. Schools like Florida Agricultural and Mechanical University, South Carolina State University, and Alabama State University helped black Americans gain the training and confidence to demand, pursue, and secure their constitutional rights in the 1960s (Christy and Williamson 1992).

As the twentieth century draws to a close, southern states, prodded by federal agencies and federal courts, have moved to integrate the black land-grant colleges into the state college and university systems previously comprising schools for whites only. Historically black colleges and universities must be given the financial support necessary to bring them up to national standards. Resistance to federally directed educational reform, the reluctance of many black Americans to lose their distinctive institutions, and the difficulties of rebuilding long-neglected facilities and faculties will push the equal education issue into the twenty-first century.

FROM THE CIVIL WAR TO WORLD WAR I

The half century between the end of the Civil War and the end of World War I witnessed a second industrial revolution. The structure and capital needs of agriculture and agriculturally derived industries—textiles, meat packing, dairying—differed radically from the structure and capital needs of industries producing automobiles, airplanes, electricity, oil, and industrial chemicals. (Later, those industries producing telephones, wireless, televisions, and, in the late twentieth century, computers would comprise a third industrial revolution, the information age.) New era firms were dominated by oligopolies, and entrepreneurs changed and expanded American education (Chandler 1959, 1962, 1977, 1990; Josephson 1934; Steeples and Whitten 1998; Whitten 1983).

Although many ideas competed for preeminence in this post-Darwinian period, two that towered over all and affected most fundamentally the movements in the educational system were the democratic ideal and the democratic way of life embodied in the framework for the curriculum. For fifty years the great force behind this thrust was John Dewey, whose model for defining, observing, formulating hypotheses, elaborating consequences, and active testing was American. Dewey's linked formulation of problem solving and "project method," as well as the social nature of learning and the universal application of scientific method, marked his genius. In every area of teaching and teacher training Dewey made an impact, but especially notable was his contribution to the rise of a scientific educational establishment (Wirth 1970, [1966] 1989).

In the nineteenth century Americans who wished to study science, especially the newest science of organic chemistry, repaired to German universities. Early in the twentieth century the advanced study of industrial chemistry and chemical engineering was established in the United States. Departments and schools were established or expanded. Institutions like Johns Hopkins University and the Massachusetts Institute of Technology (MIT) received new help. MIT accepted massive gifts from George Eastman, the mysterious Mr. X. Outside the established universities, industrial America created modern research laboratories. Graduates of MIT, Columbia, Purdue, Yale, Rensselaer Polytechnic Institute, the University of Rochester, and other prominent institutions went to work in the labs at Kodak, General Electric, American Telephone and Telegraph (Bell), and DuPont and in the new industries.

The dean of Columbia Teachers College wrote in 1908: "There is one educational principle that is peculiarly American. It is that every man, because he is a man and an American citizen, should be liberally educated as far as circumstances permit" (Butts and Cremin 1953, 364). Not everyone agreed with the dean's statement of educational principles. Extensions of federal influence in education were bitterly opposed. Catholic bishops spoke for many religious denominations and for millions of parents who feared the secular impact on their children: "We urge and enjoin Catholic parents to provide their beloved children . . . an education which is truly Christian and Catholic. Further, that they defend them throughout infancy and childhood from the perils of a purely secular education . . . that they therefore send them to parochial or other truly Catholic schools" (Butts and Cremin 1953, 364).

A proposal by the Republican congressman from Massachusetts for the establishment of a national system of education was never voted on. Five attempts by Senator Blair (R-NH) to extend federal support to education were defeated. Even the crushing problem of a devastated South, home to 4 million freed blacks at the end of the Civil War, could not move the barriers. Although a Federal Department of Education was established in 1867, significant legislation was not passed until World War I. In 1914 the Smith-Lever Act extended federal matching grants to the states for agriculture and home economic education, and in 1917 the Smith-Hughes Act broadened the program to pay the salaries of teachers of agricultural and industrial subjects and to help in their training. These contributions from the central government notwithstanding, the United States led the industrial world in opposition to federal financial support for education.

Industrialization stimulated urbanization, which, in turn, fostered massive school buildings and large student bodies. Larger schools spawned professional administrators versed in industrial management and teachers associations—the National Teachers Education Association and the American Federation of Teachers—much like the unions that protected factory workers. The professionalism that Chandler cites as a strategic feature of the Progressive Era/Gilded Age spilled over into public education (Chandler 1977). Professional education, influenced by the Flexner Report on the training of medical doctors, emphasized graduate training and certification as well as the expansion of accrediting bodies and state certification boards. Although professional education was to be a function of postcollege work, on lower levels the primary goal of college entrance still dominated. Within the lower systems linguistic, verbal, and book-centered education was the norm, although clerical, business, and industrial subjects grew in importance for the larger group of students who ended their formal study when they completed high school. How to manage the explosive expansion of knowledge remained a central concern of teachers at all levels of education. They could not know that the information revolution was in the making.

WORLD WAR I TO MID-TWENTIETH CENTURY

The United States emerged from the interwar period as the strongest industrial nation in a world in need of leadership that Americans were loath to render. U.S. global prestige evolved slowly, forged on the anvil of the Great Depression, the New Deal, and World War II. Education was not forgotten, but it did not hold center stage. The burning issue of equal educational opportunities for all was neglected in favor of debate over control of schools, funding, teacher qualifications, curriculum, and public versus private and parochial education. The American system was minimized by Western European intellectuals but admired by most of the world.

New Deal legislation provided for a wide variety of federal programs in agricultural education, vocational training, and rehabilitation for the handicapped. During the depression the federal government paid for milk and subsidized school lunches and sponsored programs like those administered by the National Youth Administration to help keep students in school. By 1935 the federal government was accelerating a broad-based educational program to train workers in defense-related industries: aviation, shipbuilding, radio communication, and so on. The armed services paid directly for reserve officer training programs in colleges and universities throughout the country. The New Deal marks the beginning of serious federal involvement in American education.

THE SECOND HALF OF THE TWENTIETH CENTURY

The second half of the twentieth century saw American education move closer to the democratic ideals voiced by the nation. History was made when Congress passed the Servicemen's Readjustment Act of 1944, known as the G.I. Bill of Rights. Veterans who wished to continue their education could apply for federal funds to pay tuition, buy books and supplies, and finance counseling and subsistence. By 1951 almost 8 million veterans had taken advantage of the G.I. Bill. Over 2 million went to college, another 3 million received school training, and more than 2 million benefited from subsidized on-the-job training. At the end of hostilities in Korea and later in Vietnam, similar benefits were granted. The G.I. Bill changed the course of life for millions of young Americans and altered the national educational philosophy. In economic terms of social welfare and national wealth, the country's net worth was advanced by billions of dollars.

The decades since the end of World War II have brought changes in the social, economic, and political fabric of the United States (D. Bell 1973). These changes have generated educational innovations and controversy. A third industrial revolution is gathering energy and momentum on a dozen technological fronts. The need for trained people adds a new urgency to educational reform and expansion to deal with the extraordinary increase in numbers of students.

To a degree unimagined in 1945, the postwar world has been, and will continue to be, one of change and uncertainty. Affluence and economic growth have changed the lifestyles and expectations of every American, especially those of younger citizens. The Economic Opportunity Act of 1964 provided the legal framework for hundreds of social programs: by 1967, 7 million deprived children had received educational benefits, and almost 1 million had gone on to college. Through programs such as Head Start youngsters are offered early training to help them compete successfully in the educational system. At the other end of the spectrum, over 1 million Americans received on-the-job training, educational improvement of a different order. Of course, by the end of the 1960s, the public's will to carry the War on Poverty had flagged, but the federal government's involvement in education continued.

Another permanent addition to the postwar system of education is the broad system of loans and grants to students under a variety of programs and terms (D. Bok 1982). Tens of billions of dollars have helped millions of students complete their educations. Other successful programs include Fulbright and Smith-Mundt exchange scholarships for students and faculty.

In addition to federal funding for education, private foundations—taking advantage of federal tax breaks allowed for philanthropic ventures—like Ford, Rockefeller, and Carnegie have put money into scholarships and educational institutions (Lynton 1984). The MacArthur Foundation gives grants to geniuses, and the Marshall Foundation funds exchanges with Germany.

Half as big as the public expenditures on education are the programs supported and paid for by big business. They range from employers' matching gifts to colleges; to contracts with university departments for specialized research, tuition refunds, or outright gifts of cash or equipment (IBM and Apple Computer); to in-house training and education programs like GE's Crotonville or McDonald's Hamburger College. Philanthropy in the United States has reinforced the American commitment to democracy through educational achievement.

BIBLIOGRAPHIC ESSAY

The history of education in classically descriptive terms from the foundation of the commonwealth to the middle of the twentieth century is R. Freeman Butts and Lawrence A. Cremin's *History of Education in American Culture* (1953). Although their treatment is chronological and descriptive, the volume is still important for its systematic integration of American culture and educational developments. Bernard Bailyn's brief essay *Education in the Forming of American Society* (1960) is a worthwhile and thoughtful piece on the colonial period; Thorstein Veblen's *Higher Learning in America* ([1918] 1954) is a searing criticism of American higher education early in this century. The federal study *A Nation at Risk* (U.S. Department of Education 1983) is more telling than Ernest L. Boyer's *College* (1987), which superficially surveys the scene in the mid-1980s. Although a work of wider context than education, Daniel Bell's *The Coming of Post-Industrial Society* (1973) should be included in any attempt to fathom our present concerns. A delightful book is Helen L. Horowitz's *Campus Life* (1987).

Four studies range broadly over a wide area. Two date from the 1970s, and two from the 1980s. An important book in its day, Clark Kerr's *The Uses of the University with a Postscript—1972* (1972) is still impressive. Howard Bowen's *Investment in Learning: The Individual and Social Value of American Higher Education* ([1977] 1997) reviews the economics of educational expenditures. The educational establishment is always in need of resources, so society must determine priorities. Derek Bok's *Higher Learning* (1986) merits examination. Perhaps the best of Boyer's writing on education is *High School: A Report on Secondary Education in America* (1983).

The multifaceted educational programs run or sponsored by businesses demand attention. This hidden program barely compares with the public systems of formal education, but it has no historian, no analyst, no champion. There are nevertheless three sources that approach the topic: Lewis M. Branscomb and Paul C. Gilmore's article in *Daedalus* (1975), Ernest A. Lynton's *The Missing Connection between Business and the Universities* (1984), and Seymour Lusterman's studies for the Conference Board, *Education in Industry* (1977) and *Trends in Corporate Education and Training* (1985).

Two best-sellers from the 1980s address contemporary concerns about American education: Allan Bloom's *The Closing of the American Mind* (1987) and Eric Hirsch's *Cultural Literacy: What Every American Needs to Know* (1987). Bloom asserts that America has slipped its cultural moorings to Plato and Rousseau, and Hirsch, that our students no longer have any historical data bank of information. Both books are flawed, but each reflects the public's broad concern about the problems facing teachers and the educational establishment.

BIBLIOGRAPHY

AAUW Journal. Washington, DC: American Association of University Women, 1962–1978. Quarterly. Continued by *Graduate Woman.*

Abernathy, W. J., Kim Clark, and Alan Kantrow. *Industrial Renaissance.* New York: Basic Books, 1983.

Adelman, Clifford, ed. *Assessment in American Higher Education: Issues and Contexts.* Washington, DC: U.S. Department of Education, Office of Educational Research and Improvement, 1986.

Adkins, Douglas L. "The American Educated Labor Force: An Empirical Look at Theories of Its Formation and Composition." In *Higher Education and the Labor Market,* edited by Margaret S. Gordon. New York: McGraw-Hill, 1974.

Alford, Harold, Jr., ed. *Power and Conflict in Continuing Education: Survival and Prosperity for All?* Wadsworth Series in Continuing Education, edited by Philip E. Frandson. Belmont, CA: Wadsworth, 1980.

Almanac of Higher Education. Reprinted from the *Chronicle of Higher Education Almanac.* Chicago: University of Chicago Press, 1990–1995. Annual.

Altback, Philip G., ed. *Adult Education and Training in Industrialized Countries.* New York: Praeger, 1982.

American Association for Higher Education. *Current Issues in Higher Education, no. 3: Partnerships with Business and the Professions.* Washington, DC: American Association for Higher Education, 1981.

American Association of School Administrators. *Business and Industry—Partners in Education.* Arlington, VA: American Association of School Administrators, 1984.

American Council on the Teaching of Foreign Languages. *Provisional Proficiency Guidelines.* Reprinted in *Foreign Language Proficiency in the Classroom and Beyond,* edited by Charles J. James. Lincolnwood, IL: National Textbook

Company for American Council on the Teaching of Foreign Languages, 1985.

American Society for Training and Development. *ASTD National Report.* Washington, DC: American Society for Training and Development, 1980.

Anderson, Richard E., and Elizabeth Swain Kasl. *Costs and Financing of Adult Education and Training.* Lexington, MA: Lexington Books, 1982.

Anderson, Richard E., and Elizabeth Swain Kasl, with Jonathan C. Derek et al. *The Costs and Financing of Adult Education and Training.* Lexington, MA: Lexington Books, 1982.

Anderson, Richard E., and Joel W. Meyerson. *Financing Higher Education in a Global Economy.* New York: American Council on Education, 1990; sponsored by National Center for Postsecondary Governance and Finance.

————, eds. *Productivity and Higher Education: Improving the Effectiveness of Faculty, Facilities, and Financial Resources.* Princeton, NJ: Peterson's Guides, 1992.

André, Rae, and Peter J. Frost, eds. *Researchers Hooked on Teaching: Noted Scholars Discuss the Synergies of Teaching and Research.* Thousand Oaks, CA: Sage, 1997.

Argyris, Chris. *On Organizational Learning.* Oxford, UK: Blackwell Business, 1992.

Argyris, Chris, and David A. Schon. *Theory in Practice: Increasing Professional Effectiveness.* San Francisco: Jossey-Bass, 1974.

Ashby, Eric. *Adapting Universities to a Technological Society.* San Francisco: Jossey-Bass, 1974.

Association of American Colleges. *Integrity in the College Curriculum: A Report to the Academic Community: The Findings and Recommendations of the Project on Redefining the Meaning and Purpose of Baccalaureate Degrees.* Washington, DC: Association of American Colleges, Project on Redefining the Meaning and Purpose of Baccalaureate Degrees, 1985.

————. *Liberal Learning and the Arts and Sciences Major.* 3 vols. Washington, DC: Association of American Colleges, Project on Liberal Learning, Study-in-Depth, and the Arts and Sciences Major, 1991–1992.

Bailyn, Bernard. *Education in the Forming of American Society: Needs and Opportunities for Study.* Chapel Hill: University of North Carolina Press, 1960.

Baker, Jeanette Sledge. "An Analysis of Degree Programs Offered by Selected Industrial Corporations." Ph.D. diss., University of Arizona, 1983. Ann Arbor, MI: University Microfilms International, 1983. Microfiche.

Barton, Paul E. *Worklife Transitions.* New York: McGraw-Hill, 1982.

Baytos, Lawrence M. "Nine Strategies for Productivity Improvement." *Personnel Journal* 58, no. 7 (July 1979): 449–56.

Becker, Gary S. *Human Capital: A Theoretical and Empirical Analysis, with Special Reference to Education.* 2d ed. Chicago: University of Chicago Press, 1974.

————. "Underinvestment in College Education." *American Economic Review* 5 (May 1980): 346–54.

Bell, Daniel. *The Reforming of General Education: The Columbia College Experience in Its National Setting.* New York: Columbia University Press, 1966.

————. *The Coming of Post-Industrial Society.* New York: Basic Books, 1973.

Bell, T. H. *U.S. Department of Education Annual Report, Fiscal Year 1984.* Washington, DC: U.S. Government Printing Office, 1984.

Berg, Ivar. *Education and Jobs: The Great Training Robbery.* New York: Praeger, 1970.

Birnbaum, Robert. *How Academic Leadership Works: Understanding Success and Failure in the College Presidency.* San Francisco: Jossey-Bass, 1992.

Blackmond, Donna G. "Graduate Education in Chemical Engineering: A Workshop." *Chemical Engineering Education* 20, no. 4 (Fall 1986): 174–77.

Blackwell, David, and Leon Henkins. *Mathematics Report of the Project 2061 Phase I Mathematics Panel.* Washington, DC: American Association for the Advancement of Science, 1989.

Blitz, Jan H., ed. *The American University: Problems, Prospects and Trends.* Buffalo, NY: Prometheus, 1985.

Bloom, Allan David. *The Closing of the American Mind.* New York: Simon & Schuster, 1987.

Boaz, David, ed. *Liberating Schools: Education in the Inner City.* Washington, DC: CATO Institute, 1991.

Bok, Derek. *Beyond the Ivory Tower: Social Responsibility of the Modern University.* Cambridge: Harvard University Press, 1982.

———. *Higher Learning.* Cambridge: Harvard University Press, 1986.

Bok, Sissela. *Alva Myrdal: A Daughter's Memoir.* Reading, MA: Addison-Wesley, 1991.

Botkin, James, Dan Dimancescu, and Ray Stata. *Global Stakes.* Cambridge, MA: Ballinger, 1982.

Bowen, Howard R. *Investment in Learning: The Individual and Social Value of American Higher Education.* Carnegie Council Series. San Francisco: Jossey-Bass, 1977. Reprint. Baltimore: Johns Hopkins University Press, Johns Hopkins Paperbacks, 1997.

Bowen, William G., and Derek Bok, with James L. Shulman et al. *The Shape of the River: Long-Term Consequences of Considering Race in College and University Admissions.* Princeton, NJ: Princeton University Press, 1998.

Bowles, Samuel, and Herbert Gintis. *Schooling in Capitalist America.* New York: Basic Books, 1976.

Boyer, Ernest L. *High School: A Report on Secondary Education in America.* New York: Harper & Row; Carnegie Foundation for the Advancement of Teaching, 1983.

———. *College: The Undergraduate Experience in America.* New York: Harper & Row; Carnegie Foundation for the Advancement of Teaching, 1987.

Boyer, Ernest L., and Fred M. Hechinger. *Higher Learning in the Nation's Service.* Washington, DC: Carnegie Foundation for the Advancement of Teaching, 1981.

Boyer, Ernest L., and Martin Kaplan. *Educating for Survival.* New Rochelle, NY: Change Magazine Press, 1977.

Branscomb, Lewis M., and Paul C. Gilmore. "Education in Private Industry." *Daedalus* (Winter 1975): 222–31.

Broadwell, Martin M. *The Supervisor and On-the-Job Training.* 3d ed. Reading, MA: Addison-Wesley, 1986.

Broyles, Susan G. *Full Enrollment in College and Universities 1983.* National Center for Education Statistics. Washington, DC: U.S. Government Printing Office, 1985.

Brubacher, John S. *On the Philosophy of Higher Education.* San Francisco: Jossey-Bass, 1971.

———. *The Courts and Higher Education.* San Francisco: Jossey-Bass, 1982.

Brubacher, John S., and Willis Rudy. *Higher Education in Transition: A History of American Colleges and Universities.* 4th ed. Foundations of Higher Education. New Brunswick, NJ: Transaction Publishers, 1997.

Bruner, Jerome. *The Culture of Education.* Cambridge: Harvard University Press, 1996.

Bruyn, Severyn T. *A Future for the American Economy: The Social Market.* Stanford, CA: Stanford University Press, 1991.

Burtless, Gary, ed. *Does Money Matter? The Effect of School Resources on Student Achievement and Adult Success.* Washington, DC: Brookings Institution Press, 1996.

Butts, R. Freeman, and Lawrence A. Cremin. *A History of Education in American Culture.* New York: Henry Holt, 1953.

Byrne, John A., and Cynthia Greene, with a team of *Business Week* editors. *Business Week's Guide to the Best Executive Education Programs: Guide to America's Top B-Schools for Management Training and Executive MBAs.* New York: McGraw-Hill, 1993.

Carnegie Commission on Higher Education. *The Fourth Revolution: Instructional Technology in Higher Education.* New York: McGraw-Hill, 1972.

———. *Purposes and the Performance of Higher Education in the United States Approaching the Year 2000.* New York: McGraw-Hill, 1973.

Carnegie Council on Policy Studies in Higher Education. *Three Thousand Futures: The Next Twenty Years for Higher Education: Final Report of the Carnegie Council on Policy Studies in Higher Education.* San Francisco: Jossey-Bass, 1980.

Carnevale, Anthony P. *Human Capital: A High Yield Corporate Investment.* Washington, DC: American Society for Training and Development, 1983.

———. *America and the New Economy.* Alexandria, VA: American Society for Training and Development; Washington, DC: U.S. Department of Labor, Employment, and Training Administration, 1991.

———. *America and the New Economy: How New Competitive Standards Are Radically Changing American Workplaces.* Jossey-Bass Management Series. San Francisco: Jossey-Bass, 1991.

Carnevale, Anthony P., Leila J. Gainer, and Ann S. Meltzer. *Workplace Basics: The Essential Skills Employers Want.* Jossey-Bass Management Series. ASTD Best Practices Series. San Francisco: Jossey-Bass, 1990.

———. *Workplace Basics Training Manual.* Jossey-Bass Management Series. ASTD Best Practices Series. San Francisco: Jossey-Bass, 1990.

Carnevale, Anthony P., Leila J. Gainer, and Eric R. Schulz. *Training the Technical Work Force.* Jossey-Bass Management Series. ASTD Best Practices Series. San Francisco: Jossey-Bass, 1990.

Carnevale, Anthony P., and Harold Goldstein. *Employee Training: Its Changing Role and an Analysis of New Data.* Washington, DC: American Society for Training and Development, 1983.

Carnevale, Anthony P., and S. Kanu Kogod. *Tools and Activities for a Diverse Work Force*. Prepared by American Society for Training and Development. Department of Labor Grant Number K-4031–3-00–80–60. New York: McGraw-Hill, 1995.

Carnevale, Anthony P., and Jeffrey D. Porro. *Quality Education: School Reform for the New American Economy: Executive Summary*. Prepared by American Society for Training and Development. Washington, DC: U.S. Department of Education, Office of Educational Research and Improvement, 1994.

Carnevale, Anthony P., and Susan Carol Stone. *The American Mosaic: An In-Depth Report on the Future of Diversity at Work*. New York: McGraw-Hill, 1995.

Carnoy, Martin, and Henry M. Levin. *Schooling and Work in the Democratic State*. Stanford, CA: Stanford University Press, 1985.

Carr, Harold. "What Makes a Curriculum Exemplary." *Vocational Education Journal* 61, no. 4 (May 1986): 22–25.

Casement, William. *The Great Canon Controversy: The Battle of the Books in Higher Education*. New Brunswick, NJ: Transaction Publishers, 1996.

Cavusgil, S. Tamer, and Nancy E. Horn, eds. *Internationalizing Doctoral Education in Business*. East Lansing: Michigan State University Press, 1997.

Chance, Jerry M., and Jerry G. Gaff. *General Education: Issues and Resources*. Washington, DC: Association of American Colleges, Society for Values in Higher Education, Project on General Education Models, 1980.

Chandler, Alfred D., Jr. "The Beginnings of 'Big Business' in American History." *Business History Review* 33 (Spring 1959): 1–31.

———. *Strategy and Structure: Chapters in the History of the Industrial Enterprise*. Cambridge: MIT Press, 1962.

———. *The Visible Hand: The Managerial Revolution in American Business*. Cambridge: Harvard University Press, 1977.

———. *Scale and Scope: The Dynamics of Industrial Capitalism*. Cambridge: Harvard University Press, 1990.

Change. San Diego: Centre for Leadership Development, 1992– . Bimonthly.

Change in Higher Education. Washington, DC: Heldref, 1970– . 6 times a year.

Charner, Ivan, and Catherine A. Rolzinski. "New Directions for Responding to a Changing Economy: Integrating Education and Work." *New Directions for Continuing Education* 33 (Spring 1987): 5–15.

Choate, Pat. "American Workers at the Rubicon." *Commentary* (Summer 1982): 3–10.

Christy, Ralph D., and Lionel Williamson, eds. *A Century of Service: Land-Grant Colleges and Universities*. New Brunswick, NJ: Transaction Publishers, 1992.

Chronicle of Higher Education. Washington, DC: Chronicle of Higher Education, 1966– . 48 times a year.

Chronicle of Higher Education Almanac. Washington, DC: The Chronicle, 1988– . Annual.

Chubb, John, and Terry Moe. *Politics, Markets, and America's Schools*. Washington, DC: Brookings Institution, 1990.

Clark, Donald M. "Connecting School–Business Partnerships with Educational Reform." *School Business Affairs* 53, no. 2 (February 1987): 24–25.

Clifford, Geraldine Jonçich, and James W. Guthrie. *Ed School: A Brief for Professional Education*. Chicago: University of Chicago Press, 1988.

Clotfelter, Charles T., ed. *Studies of Supply and Demand in Higher Education*. Chicago: University of Chicago Press for the National Bureau of Economic Research, 1993.

Clotfelter, Charles T., Ronald G. Ehrenberg, Malcolm Getz, and John J. Siegfried. *Economic Challenges in Higher Education*. Chicago: University of Chicago Press, 1991.

Conover, Donald K. "New Directions in Corporate Training." *Vocational Education Journal* 62, no. 3 (April 1987): 23–25.

Cookson, Peter W., Jr. *School Choice: The Struggle for the Soul of American Education*. New Haven, CT: Yale University Press, 1994.

Cooperative Education Record Center. *Undergraduate Programs of Cooperative Education in the U.S. and Canada*. Boston: Northeastern University, Cooperative Education Research Center, 1978.

Craig, Robert L. "Introduction to the Conference on the Nature and Extent of Employee Training and Development." *Proceedings of the ASTD National Issues Forum*. Washington, DC: American Society for Training and Development, 1983.

Craig, Robert L., and Christine J. Evers. "Employers and Educators: The Shadow Education System." In *Business and Higher Education: Toward New Alliances*, edited by Gerard G. Gold. San Francisco: Jossey-Bass, 1981.

Cremin, Lawrence A. *The American Common School: An Historic Conception*. New York: Columbia University, Teachers College, Bureau of Publications, 1951.

———. *The Transformation of the School: Progressivism in American Education 1876–1957*. New York: Knopf, 1961.

Crews, Kenneth D. *Copyright, Fair Use, and the Challenge for Universities: Promoting the Progress of Higher Education*. Chicago: University of Chicago Press, 1993.

Cross, K. Patricia. "New Frontiers for Higher Education: Business and Professions." In *Partnerships with Higher Education*. Washington, DC: American Association for Higher Education, 1981.

Cuthbert, Marion V. *Education and Marginality: A Study of the Negro Woman College Graduate*. Ph.D. diss., Columbia University, 1942. New York: Teachers College, 1942. Reprint. New York: Garland, 1987.

Davis, Josephine D., ed. *Coloring the Halls of Ivy: Leadership and Diversity in the Academy*. Bolton, MA: Anker, 1994.

Davis, Leroy. *A Clashing of the Soul: John Hope and the Dilemma of African American Leadership and Black Higher Education in the Early Twentieth Century*. Athens: University of Georgia Press, 1998.

Davis, Stan, and Jim Botkin. *The Monster under the Bed: How Business Is Mastering the Opportunity of Knowledge for Profit*. New York: Simon & Schuster, 1994.

Derber, Charles. "Worker Education for a Changing Economy: New Labor–Academic Partnerships." *New Directions for Continuing Education* 33 (Spring 1987): 49–57.

Digest of Education Statistics, 1997. ED411612. Washington, DC: U.S. Office of Educational Research and Improvement, 1998.

Drucker, Peter F. *The New Society: The Anatomy of Industrial Order.* New York: Harper, 1950. Reprint. New Brunswick, NJ: Transaction Publishers, 1993.

Education Almanac 1985–1986: Facts and Figures about Our Nation's System of Education. Reston, VA: National Association of Elementary School Principals, 1984.

Education Times. Washington, DC: Education Times, 1980– . 48 times a year.

Emmerij, Louis. "Paid Educational Leave: A Proposal Based on the Dutch Case." In *Financing Recurrent Education: Strategies for Increasing Employment, Job Opportunities, and Productivity,* edited by Henry M. Levin and Hans G. Schutze. Beverly Hills, CA: Sage, 1983.

Fact Book on Higher Education. New York: Macmillan, 1984– ; New York: American Council on Education, 1989–1990– ; Phoenix, AZ: Oryx Press, 1997– . Biennial.

Fantini, Mario D., and Robert L. Sinclair, eds. *Education in School and Nonschool Settings.* Yearbook of the National Society for the Study of Educators, 84, pt. 1. Chicago: National Society for the Study of Education, 1985; distributed by University of Chicago Press.

Fay, Jack R. *Accounting Certification, Educational, and Reciprocity Requirements: An International Guide.* Westport, CT: Quorum Books, 1992.

Finkin, Matthew W., ed. *The Case for Tenure.* Ithaca, NY: Cornell University Press, ILR Press, 1996.

Fischgrund, Tom, ed. *The Insider's Guide to the Top 10 Business Schools.* 5th ed. Boston: Little, Brown, 1993.

Fisher, Bernice M. *Industrial Education: American Ideals and Institutions.* Madison: University of Wisconsin Press, 1967.

Flexner, Abraham. *Medical Education in the United States and Canada.* New York: Carnegie Foundation for the Advancement of Teaching, 1910.

Freed, Jann E., and Marie R. Klugman. *Quality Principles and Practices in Higher Education: Different Questions for Different Times.* Oryx Press Series on Higher Education. Washington, DC: American Council on Education; Phoenix, AZ: Oryx Press, 1997.

Fuller, Bruce, and Richard Rubinson, eds. *The Political Construction of Education: The State, School Expansion, and Economic Change.* New York: Praeger, 1992.

Gaff, Jerry G. *General Education Today: A Critical Analysis of Controversies, Practices, and Reforms.* Jossey-Bass Series in Higher Education. San Francisco: Jossey-Bass, 1983.

Gardner, James E. *Training Interventions in Job-Skill Development.* Reading, MA: Addison-Wesley, 1981.

Garrison, Don. "War without Guns: Workplace Training and Retraining." *Community, Junior, and Technical College Journal* 57, no. 3 (December–January 1986/1987): 20–23.

Gerald, Debra E. *Projections of Education Statistics to 1992–93: Methodological Report with Detailed Projection Tables.* Washington, DC: National Center for Education Statistics, 1985.

Getman, Julius. *In the Company of Scholars: The Struggle for the Soul of Higher Education*. Austin: University of Texas Press, 1992.

Gibbons, J. F., W. R. Kincheloe, and K. S. Down. "Tutored Videotape Instruction: A New Use of Electronic Media in Education." *Science* 195 (1977): 1139.

Gold, Gerard G. "A Reform Strategy for Education: Employer-Sponsored Teaching Internships." *Phi Delta Kappa* 68, no. 15 (January 1987): 384–87.

Gold, Gerard G., ed. *Business and Higher Education: Toward New Alliances*. New Directions for Experiential Learning, no. 13. San Francisco: Jossey-Bass, 1981.

Gold, Gerard G., and Ivan Charner. "Employer-Paid Tuition Aid: Hidden Treasure." *Educational Record* 64, no. 2 (Spring 1983): 45–47.

Goldberg, Bruce. *Why Schools Fail*. Washington, DC: Cato Institute, 1996.

Goldstein, Harold. "Using Data on Employee Training from the Survey of Participation in Adult Education (C.P.S.)." *Proceedings of the ASTD National Issues Forum*. Washington, DC: American Society for Training and Development, 1983.

Goldstein, Irwin L. *Training in Organizations: Needs Assessment, Training, Communication*. Information Bulletin no. 89. New York: Conference Board, 1981.

Gordon, Margaret S., ed. *Higher Education and the Labor Market*. Carnegie Commission on Higher Education. New York: McGraw-Hill, 1974.

Gormley, William T., Jr. *Everybody's Children: Child Care as a Public Problem*. Washington, DC: Brookings Institution, 1995.

Graduate Woman. Washington, DC: American Association of University Women, 1978–1988. Bimonthly. Continued by *Outlook/American Association of University Women*.

Grant, W. Vance, and Thomas D. Snyder. *Digest of Education Statistics 1985–86*. Washington, DC: U.S. Government Printing Office, 1986.

Gray, Denis et al. "Industry-University Projects and Centers: An Empirical Comparison of Two Federally Funded Models of Cooperative Science." *Evaluation Review* 10, no. 6 (December 1986): 776–93.

Green, Madeleine F., ed. *Minorities on Campus: A Handbook for Enhancing Diversity*. Washington, DC: American Council on Education, 1989.

Gregory, Sheila T. *Black Women in the Academy: The Secrets to Success and Achievement*. Rev. and updated ed. Lanham, MD: University Press of America, 1999.

Guay, Diane, "The Ruling Metaphors in Education." *Thrust for Educational Leadership* 16, no. 4 (January 1987): 28–29.

Guyon, Janet. "Culture Class: G. E.'s Management School Aims to Foster Unified Corporate Goals." *Wall Street Journal*, August 10, 1987, 29.

Habbe, Stephen. *College Graduates Assess Their Company Training*. New York: Conference Board, 1963.

Halstead, Kent, ed. *Higher Education: Bibliographic Yearbook 1987*. Washington, DC: Research Associates of Washington, 1987.

Handlin, Oscar, and Mary F. Handlin. *The American College and American Culture: Socialization as a Function of Higher Education*. Carnegie Commission on Higher Education. New York: McGraw-Hill, 1970.

Hanson, Katharine H., and Joel W. Meyerson, eds. *Higher Education in a Changing*

Economy. Macmillan Series in Higher Education. New York: American Council on Education; New York: Maxwell Macmillan International, 1990.

Hanushek, Eric A., with Charles S. Benson et al. *Making Schools Work: Improving Performance and Controlling Costs.* Washington, DC: Brookings Institution, 1994.

Harvard Committee. *General Education in a Free Society.* Cambridge: Harvard University Press, 1945.

Harvey, William B., ed. *Grass Roots and Glass Ceilings: African American Administrators in Predominantly White Colleges and Universities.* Albany: State University of New York Press, 1999.

Hawthorne, Elizabeth M., Patricia A. Libby, and Nancy S. Nash. "The Emergence of Corporate Colleges." *Journal of Continuing Education* 31 (Fall 1983): 1–9.

Higher Education Amendments of 1986, Public Law 99-498. National Archives and Records Administration, Office of the Federal Register, 1986.

Higher Education Technical Amendments Act of 1987, Public Law 100-50. National Archives and Records Administration, Office of the Federal Register, 1987.

Hirsch, Eric Donald. *Cultural Literacy: What Every American Needs to Know.* Boston: Houghton Mifflin, 1987.

Hoffman, Charlene, Thomas D. Snyder, and Bill Sonnenberg. *Historically Black Colleges and Universities, 1976–1994.* Washington, DC: U.S. Department of Education, Office of Educational Research and Improvement, National Center for Education Statistics, 1996.

Hoffman, Emily P., ed. *Essays on the Economics of Education.* Kalamazoo, MI: Upjohn Institute, 1993.

Hofstadter, Richard. *Anti-Intellectualism in American Life.* New York: Knopf, 1963.

Hollenbeck, Kevin. *Classrooms in the Workplace.* Kalamazoo, MI: Upjohn Institute, 1993.

Holmes, Alexander B. *Ethics in Higher Education: Case Studies for Regents.* Norman: University of Oklahoma Press, 1996; sponsored by the Oklahoma State Regents for Higher Education, Regents Education Program.

Horowitz, Helen L. *Campus Life.* New York: Knopf, 1987.

Horton, Carrell. *The Black Doctorate.* Lanham, MD: University Press of America; Washington, DC: National Association for Equal Opportunity Research Institute, 1988.

Houle, Cyril. *Continuing Learning in the Professions.* San Francisco: Jossey-Bass, 1980.

Hoy, John C., and Melvin H. Bernstein, eds. *Business and Academia: Partners in New England's Economy.* Hanover, NH: University Press of New England, 1981.

———. *Financing Higher Education: The Public Investment.* Boston: Auburn House, 1982.

Hunt, Carle M., Kenneth W. Oosting, Robert Stevens, David Loudon, and R. Henry Migliore. *Strategic Planning for Private Higher Education.* Binghamton, NY: Haworth Press, 1997.

Information Technology in Postsecondary Education. Washington, DC: Higher Education Washington, 1998– . Biweekly.

Institute for Educational Leadership. *Technology and Education.* Proceedings of the National Conference on Technology and Education, January 26–28, 1981. Washington, DC: Institute for Educational Leadership, 1981.

Jencks, Christopher, and David Riesman. *The Academic Revolution.* Chicago: University of Chicago Press, 1968.

Johnson, Daniel M., and David A. Bell, eds. *Metropolitan Universities: An Emerging Model in American Higher Education.* Denton: University of North Texas Press, 1995.

Johnston, Joseph A., Norman C. Guplers, and Laura Lundeen Wright. "Business–Education Collaboratives for College Career Centers." *Journal of Career Development* 13, no. 1 (Fall 1986): 68–76.

Josephson, Matthew. *Robber Barons.* New York: Harcourt, Brace, & World, 1934.

Joynt, Pat. "Research-Based Projects as a Learning Strategy in Business Schools." *Human Relations* 36 (January 1983): 69–92.

Justiz, Manuel J., and Marilyn C. Kameen. "Business Offers a Hand to Education." *Phi Delta Kappa* 68, no. 5 (January 1987): 379–83.

Katchadourian, Herant, and John Boli. *Careerism and Intellectualism among College Students.* San Francisco: Jossey-Bass, 1985.

———. *Cream of the Crop: The Impact of Elite Education in the Decade after College.* New York: Basic Books, 1994.

Katz, Joseph. *A New Vitality in General Education: Planning, Teaching, and Supporting Effective Liberal Learning.* Washington, DC: Association of American Colleges, Task Group on General Education, 1988.

Kearsley, Greg. *Costs, Benefits, and Productivity in Training Systems.* Reading, MA: Addison-Wesley, 1982.

Kelly, Robert Lincoln. *American Colleges and the Social Order.* New York: Macmillan, 1940.

Kerr, Clark. *The Uses of the University with a Postscript—1972.* Cambridge: Harvard University Press, 1972.

Kimmons, Willie James. *Black Administrators in Public Community Colleges: Self-Perceived Role and Status.* New York: Carlton Press, a Hearthstone Book, 1977.

Knox, Kathleen. *Polaroid Corporation's Tuition Assistance Plan: A Case Study.* Washington, DC: National Management Institute, 1979.

Komarovsky, Mirra. *Women in College: Shaping New Feminine Identities.* New York: Basic Books, 1985.

Kreiger, James. "Pilot Plants Enhance Brazosport Lab Courses." *Chemical and Engineering News* 64, no. 43 (October 27, 1986): 26–27.

Labaree, David F. *How to Succeed in School without Really Learning: The Credentials Race in American Education.* New Haven, CT: Yale University Press, 1997.

Ladd, Everett Carll, Jr., and Seymour Martin Lipset. *The Divided Academy: Professors and Politics.* New York: McGraw-Hill, 1975.

Ladd, Helen F., ed. *Holding Schools Accountable: Performance-Based Reform in Education.* Washington, DC: Brookings Institution, 1996.

Laird, Duggan. *Approaches to Training and Development*. Reading, MA: Addison-Wesley, 1978.

Langer, Victor. "Developing a Computer-Integrated Manufacturing Education Center." *New Directions for Continuing Education* 33 (Spring 1987): 27–37.

Lemann, Nicholas, and Joshua Wolf Shenk. "The Wee Reform: Is Clinton's Education Plan a Big Waste of Money?" *U.S. News & World Report* 122, no. 19 (May 19, 1997): 22–25.

Levin, Henry, and Hans G. Schutze, eds. *Financing Recurrent Education: Strategies for Increasing Employment, Job Opportunities, and Productivity*. Beverly Hills, CA: Sage, 1983.

Lewis, Lionel S. *Marginal Worth: Teaching and the Academic Labor Market*. New Brunswick, NJ: Transaction Publishers, 1996.

Lineberry, William P., ed. *American Colleges: The Uncertain Future*. New York: H. W. Wilson, 1975.

Linkages between the Education and Employment and Training Systems. 2 vols. Youth Knowledge Development Report: Institutional Linkages 12.2, 12.3. Washington, DC: U.S. Department of Labor, Employment and Training Administration, 1980.

Lloyd, John H. "The Opportunity of Private Sector Training." *Vocational Education Journal* 62, no. 3 (April 1987): 20–22.

Lusterman, Seymour. *Education in Industry*. Report no. 719. New York: Conference Board, 1977.

———. *Trends in Corporate Education and Training*. New York: Conference Board, 1985.

Lusterman, Seymour, and Harriet Grolin. *Educating Students for Work: Some Business Roles*. New York: Conference Board, 1980.

Luxenburg, Stan. "Education at AT&T." *Change* (December–January 1978/1979): 26.

Lynton, Ernest A. "Colleges, Universities and Corporate Training." In *Business and Higher Education: Toward New Alliances*, edited by Gerard G. Gold. San Francisco: Jossey-Bass, 1981.

———. "A Role for Colleges in Corporate Training and Development." In *Current Issues in Higher Education, no. 3: Partnerships with Business and the Professions*. Washington, DC: American Association for Higher Education, 1981.

———. "A Curriculum for Tomorrow's World." In *In Opposition to Core Curriculums*, edited by James W. Hall and Barbara L. Kevles. Westport, CT: Greenwood Press, 1982.

———. "Improving Cooperation between Colleges and Corporations." *Educational Record* 63, no. 4 (Fall 1982): 20–25.

———. "Higher Education's Role in Fostering Employee Education." *Educational Record* 64, no. 4 (Fall 1983): 18–25.

———. "Occupational Maintenance: Recurrent Education to Maintain Occupational Effectiveness." *CAEL News* 7, no. 1 (September 1983): 6–8, 19; no. 2 (October 1983): 4–7, 15.

———. "Reexamining the Role of the University." *Change* 15, no. 7 (1983).

———. *The Missing Connection between Business and the Universities*. Boston:

University of Massachusetts, John W. McCormack Institute of Public Affairs; New York: American Council on Education/Macmillan, 1984.

Lynton, Ernest A., and Sandra E. Elman. *New Priorities for the University: Meeting Society's Needs for Applied Knowledge and Competent Individuals.* Jossey-Bass Higher Education Series. San Francisco: Jossey-Bass, 1987.

Maher, Frances A., and Mary Kay Thompson Tetreault. *The Feminist Classroom: An Inside Look at How Professors and Students Are Transforming Higher Education for a Diverse Society.* New York: Basic Books, 1994.

Mahoney, James R. *Community College Centers for Contracted Programs.* Washington, DC: American Association of Community and Junior Colleges, 1982.

Massy, William F., ed. *Resource Allocation in Higher Education.* The Economics of Education, edited by William F. Massy. Ann Arbor: University of Michigan Press, 1996.

May, William W., ed. *Ethics and Higher Education.* American Council on Education/Oryx Press Series on Higher Education. Phoenix, AZ: Oryx Press, 1998.

Mayhew, Lewis B. *The Quest for Quality: The Challenge for Undergraduate Education in the 1990s.* Jossey-Bass Series in Higher Education. San Francisco: Jossey-Bass, 1990.

McKinney, Kitzie. "Toward an International Partnership: Business Activities and the Foreign Language Curriculum." *ADFL Bulletin* [Association of Departments of Foreign Languages (U.S.)] 18, no. 2 (January 1987): 34–37.

Means, Barbara. *Technology and Education Reform: The Reality behind the Promise.* San Francisco: Jossey-Bass, 1994.

Mellon, Donald E. *The Role of Entrepreneur-Educator in Private Business Education in the U.S. from 1850–1915: A Study in Conditioned Entrepreneurship.* New York: Garland, 1986.

Mirenoff, William, and Lester Rindler. *The Comprehensive Employment and Training Act: Impact on People, Places, Programs; An Interim Report.* Washington, DC: National Academy of Sciences, 1976.

Molnar, Alex. *Giving Kids the Business: The Commercialization of America's Schools.* Boulder, CO: Westview Press, 1996.

Mullin, Mark H. *Educating for the 21st Century: The Challenge for Parents and Teachers.* Lanham, MD: Madison Books, 1991.

Mykleby, Charles. "How to Get a Little Help from Your Corporate Friends." *Principal* 66, no. 4 (March 1987): 36–37.

Oakes, Jeannie, and Martin Lipton. *Making the Best of Schools.* New Haven, CT: Yale University Press, 1990.

Orlans, Harold. *The Effects of Federal Programs on Higher Education: A Report to the U.S. Commissioner of Education.* Washington, DC: Brookings Institution, 1962.

O'Reilly, John F. "Create Professional Staff through Education and Trust." *Rough Notes* 123, no. 1 (January 1980): 25, 48, 50.

Outlook/American Association of University Women. Washington, DC: The Association, 1989– . Quarterly.

Pelikan, Jaroslav. *The Idea of the University: A Reexamination.* New Haven, CT: Yale University Press, 1992.

Peterson, Richard E. et al. *Adult Education and Training in Industrialized Countries.* New York: Praeger, 1982.

Pierce, Joseph A. *Negro Business and Business Education: Their Present and Prospective Development.* Plenum Studies in Work and Industry, edited by Ivar Berg and Arne L. Kalleberg. New York: Plenum, 1995.

Plisko, Valena White, and Joyce D. Stern, eds. *The Condition of Education: 1985.* Statistical Report. Washington, DC: National Center for Education Statistics, 1985.

Quade, Quentin L. *Financing Education: The Struggle between Governmental Monopoly and Parental Control.* New Brunswick, NJ: Transaction Publishers, 1996.

Ravitch, Diane. *The Great School Wars, New York City, 1805–1973: A History of the Public Schools as Battlefield of Social Change.* New York: Basic Books, 1974.

————. *The Revisionists Revised: A Critique of the Radical Attack on the Schools.* New York: Basic Books, 1978.

————. *The Troubled Crusade: American Education, 1945–1980.* New York: Basic Books, 1983.

————. *The Schools We Deserve: Reflections on the Educational Crises of Our Time.* New York: Basic Books, 1985.

————. *What Do Our 17-Year-Olds Know? A Report on the First National Assessment of History and Literature.* New York: Harper & Row, 1987.

————. *Debating the Future of American Education: Do We Need National Standards and Assessments?* Brookings Dialogues on Public Policy. Washington, DC: Brookings Institution, 1995.

————. *National Standards in American Education: A Citizen's Guide.* Washington, DC: Brookings Institution, 1995.

Reuben, Julie A. *The Making of the Modern University: Intellectual Transformation and the Marginalization of Morality.* Chicago: University of Chicago Press, 1996.

Riesman, David. *On Higher Education: The Academic Enterprise in an Era of Rising Student Consumerism.* San Francisco: Jossey-Bass, 1980.

Rolzinski, Catherine A., and Ivan Charner. "Improving Practice: Lessons for the Case Studies." *New Directions for Continuing Education* 33 (Spring 1987): 75–85.

Roueche, John E., George A. Baker, and Suanne D. Roueche. *College Responses to Low-Achieving Students: A National Study.* Orlando, FL: Harcourt Brace Jovanovich, HBJ Media Systems, 1984.

Roueche, John E., Laurence F. Johnson, Suanne D. Roueche, and Associates. *Embracing the Tiger: The Effectiveness Debate and the Community College.* Washington, DC: Community College Press, 1997.

Rudolph, Frederick. *Curriculum: A History of the American Undergraduate Course of Study since 1636.* Prepared for the Carnegie Council on Policy Studies in Higher Education. San Francisco: Jossey-Bass, 1977.

Rudolph, Frederick, with John R. Thelin. *The American College and University: A History.* New York: A. Knopf, 1962. Reprint. Athens: University of Georgia Press, 1990.

Sadker, Myra, and David Sadker. *Failing at Fairness: How America's Schools Cheat Girls.* New York: Charles Scribner's Sons, 1994.

Scott, Robert. "Proven Partners, Government and Education." *Community, Junior*

and Technical College Journal 57, no. 3 (December–January 1986–1987):
  16–19.

Sims, Serbrenia J. *Diversifying Historically Black Colleges and Universities: A New
  Higher Education Paradigm.* Contributions to the Study of Education, no.
  62. Westport, CT: Greenwood Press, 1994.

Skrentny, John D. *The Ironies of Affirmative Action: Politics, Culture, and Justice
  in America.* Chicago: University of Chicago Press, 1996.

Smith, Hayden W. "The Outlook for Corporate Financial Aid to Higher Education." *Proceedings of the Academy of Political Science* 35, no. 2 (1983):
  156–72.

Smith, Page. *Killing the Spirit: Higher Education in America.* New York: Viking,
  1990.

Smith, Robert M. *The American Business System and the Theory and Practice of
  Social Science: The Case of the Harvard Business School, 1925–1945.* New
  York: Garland, 1986.

Smith, Walter S., and Thomas Owen Erb. "Effects of Women Science Career Role
  Models on Early Adolescents' Attitudes toward Scientists and Women in
  Science." *Journal of Research in Science Teaching* 23, no. 8 (November
  1986): 667–76.

Snider, William D. *Light on the Hill: A History of the University of North Carolina
  at Chapel Hill.* Chapel Hill: University of North Carolina Press, 1992.

Snyder, Karolyn J., and Robert H. Anderson. "What Principals Can Learn from
  Corporate Management." *Principal* 66, no. 4 (March 1987): 22–26.

Snyder, Thomas D. *Digest of Education Statistics 1987.* Washington, DC: U.S.
  Government Printing Office, 1987.

———, ed. *120 Years of American Education: A Statistical Portrait.* Washington,
  DC: U.S. Department of Education, Office of Educational Research and Improvement, National Center for Education Statistics, 1993.

———. *Chartbook of Degrees Conferred, 1969–70 to 1993–94.* Washington, DC:
  U.S. Department of Education, Office of Educational Research and Improvement, 1997.

Snyder, Thomas D., and Charlene M. Hoffman. *State Comparisons of Educational
  Statistics, 1969–70 to 1996–97.* Washington, DC: U.S. Department of Education, Office of Educational Research and Improvement, National Center
  for Education Statistics, 1998.

Sperling, John, and Robert W. Tucker. *For-Profit Higher Education: Developing a
  World-Class Workforce.* New Brunswick, NJ: Transaction Publishers, 1997.

Starr, Harold, Harold Merz, and Gale Zahniser. *Using Labor Market Information
  in Vocational Planning.* Research and Development Series, 228. Columbus:
  Ohio State University, National Center for Research in Vocational Education, 1982.

Steeples, Douglas, ed. *Institutional Revival: Case Histories.* San Francisco: Jossey-
  Bass, 1986.

———. *Successful Strategic Planning: Case Studies.* San Francisco: Jossey-Bass,
  1988.

———. *Managing Change in Higher Education.* San Francisco: Jossey-Bass, 1990.

Steeples, Douglas, and David O. Whitten. *Democracy in Desperation: The Depres-*

sion of 1893. Contributions in Economics and Economic History, no. 199. Westport, CT: Greenwood Press, 1998.

Stenberg, Carl W. III, and William G. Colman. *America's Future Work Force: A Health and Education Policy Issues Handbook*. Westport, CT: Greenwood Press, 1994.

Stern, David, Neal Finkelstein, James R. Stone III, John Latting, and Carolyn Dornsife. *School to Work: Research on Programs in the United States*. Stanford Series on Education & Public Policy, edited by Henry M. Levin, no. 17. Washington, DC: Falmer Press for the National Center for Research in Vocational Education, 1995.

Sullivan, Eugene J. *Guide to Undergraduate External Degree Programs in the United States*. 2d ed. New York: Macmillan, 1983.

Sykes, Charles J. *Profscam: Professors and the Demise of Higher Education*. New York: Regnery Gateway, 1988.

Thomas, Carol H., and James L. Thomas, eds. *Directory of College Facilities and Services for the Disabled*. 2d ed. Phoenix, AZ: Oryx, 1986.

Thompson, Daniel C. *A Black Elite: A Profile of UNCF Colleges*. New York: Greenwood Press, 1986.

Traub, James. *City on a Hill: Testing the American Dream at City College*. Reading, MA: Addison Wesley, a William Patrick Book, 1994.

United Negro College Fund. *United Negro College Fund Archives: A Guide and Index*. Ann Arbor, MI: University Microfilms International, 1985.

U.S. Congress. Senate. Committee on Labor and Human Resources. *The Workplace and Higher Education: Perspective for the Coming Decade, 1979*. Hearings. 96th Cong., 2d sess., June 1979.

U.S. Department of Education. *Computers in Education: Realizing the Potential*. Report of a Research Conference. Washington, DC: Office of the Assistant Secretary for Educational Research and Improvement, 1983.

———. *A Nation at Risk: The Imperative for Educational Reform*. Washington, DC: Superintendent of Documents for the National Commission on Excellence in Education, 1983.

———. *Involvement in Learning: Realizing the Potential of American Higher Education: Final Report*. Washington, DC: National Institute of Education, Study Group on the Conditions of Excellence in American Higher Education, 1984.

———. *The Nation Responds: Recent Efforts to Improve Education*. Washington, DC: U.S. Government Printing Office, 1984.

———. *Cooperative Programs for Transition from School to Work*. Washington, DC: National Institute of Handicapped Research, Office of Special Education and Rehabilitative Services, 1985.

———. *Contractor Report: Private Schools and Private School Teachers. Final Report of the 1985–1986 Private School Study*. Washington, DC: Office of Educational Research and Improvement, Center for Education Statistics, 1987.

Valentine, P. F., ed. *The American College*. New York: Philosophical Library, 1949.

Van Slyck, Abigail A. *Free to All: Carnegie Libraries and American Culture, 1890–1920*. Chicago: University of Chicago Press, 1995.

Veblen, Thorstein. *The Higher Learning in America: A Memorandum on the Conduct of Universities by Business Men.* New York: B. W. Huebsch, 1918. Reprint. Stanford, CA: Academic Reprints, 1954.

Veysey, Laurence R. *The Emergence of the American University.* Chicago: University of Chicago Press, 1965.

Weingartner, Rudolph H. *Undergraduate Education: Goals and Means.* Phoenix, AZ: Oryx Press for American Council on Education, 1993.

Weistein, Laurence M. "Employers in the Private Sector." In *The Costs and Financing of Adult Education,* edited by Richard Anderson and Elizabeth Swain Kasl, with Jonathan C. Derek et al. Lexington, MA: Lexington Books, 1982.

Whitehead, Alfred North. *The Aims of Education and Other Essays.* New York: Free Press, 1957.

Whitten, David O. *The Emergence of Giant Enterprise, 1860–1914: American Commercial Enterprise and Extractive Industries.* Contributions in Economics and Economic History, Number 54. Westport, CT: Greenwood Press, 1983.

———. *A History of Economics and Business at Auburn University.* Montreux, Switzerland: Gordon & Breach, 1992.

Wilson, Logan, ed. *Emerging Patterns in American Higher Education.* Washington, DC: American Council on Education, 1965.

Wilson, Robin. "Proprietary Schools' Growing Share of Pell Grant Money Means Less for College Students, Campus Officials Warn." *Chronicle of Higher Education,* July 22, 1987, 1, 18.

Wirth, Arthur G. *The Vocational-Liberal Studies Controversy between John Dewey and Others, 1900–1917.* Saint Louis, MO: Washington University, Graduate Institute of Education; Washington, DC: U.S. Office of Education, Bureau of Research, 1970.

———. *Education in the Technological Society: The Vocational-Liberal Studies Controversy in the Early Twentieth Century.* Intext Series in Foundations of Education. Scranton, PA: Intext Educational Publishers, 1972. Reprint. Washington, DC: University Press of America, 1980.

———. *Productive Work in Industry and Schools: Becoming Persons Again.* Lanham, MD: University Press of America, 1983.

———. *John Dewey as Educator: His Design for Work in Education, 1894–1904.* New York: Wiley, 1966. Reprint. Lanham, MD: University Press of America, 1989.

———. *Education and Work for the Year 2000: Choices We Face.* Jossey-Bass Education Series. San Francisco: Jossey-Bass, 1992.

Witham, Larry. *Curran vs. Catholic University: A Study of Authority and Freedom in Conflict.* Riverdale, MD: Edington-Rand, 1991.

Wolfe, Joseph. "The Teaching Effectiveness of Games in Collegiate Business Courses: A 1973–1983 Update." *Simulation and Games* 16 (1985): 251–88.

Woodside, William S. "The Corporate Role in Public Education." *Social Policy* 15 (Fall 1984): 44–45.

Zaragoza, Federico, and Richard Huber. "Customized Training with CBO's." *Vocational Education Journal* 62, no. 3 (April 1987): 32–33.

Zigler, Edward, and Susan Muenchow. *Head Start: The Inside Story of America's Most Successful Educational Experiment.* New York: Basic Books, 1992.

Zweigenhaft, Richard L., and G. William Domhoff. *Blacks in the White Establishment: A Study of Race and Class in America.* New Haven, CT: Yale University Press, 1991.

Part XIV

Social Services
ESIC 83.0

CHAPTER 19 ————————————————————————

SOCIAL SERVICES, 83.0

————————————— JOSEPH FINKELSTEIN AND
NADIA EHRLICH FINKELSTEIN

THE LEGACY OF THE POOR LAW

For three centuries American society and especially its business communities have striven to reconcile the promise of a new land with the poverty of those unable to help themselves. The urban landscape has been transformed in a third industrial (information) revolution—the reconstruction of the economic, technological, political, and social underpinnings of America. Unfortunately, resources will not be evenly distributed, and social problems, intractable in the past, will be overwhelming in the future.

Although the American dilemma can be traced to the Judeo-Christian foundations of society, contemporary social service emerged in its modern forms and dimensions with the transformation of America into a powerful industrial nation at the end of the nineteenth century. Before this dramatic surge of industrialization, poverty, physical and mental illness, alcoholism, and marital and family issues were perceived as more manageable. Social problems were relieved by family, neighbors, church, and private voluntary programs, plus minimal public help. Now, at the turn of the twentieth century, social and geographic mobility, heightened expectations of personal gratification, the weakening of family and community ties, the rise in divorce and single parenthood, and the increase in longevity have belatedly pressured the federal government into weaving a social net not only for citizens in acute need but as a last resort for all citizens (Steeples and Whitten 1998).

The institutional forms of American social welfare are rooted in the English seventeenth-century poor laws. Parish poor relief differed from aid to the blind, aged, crippled, and orphaned. In ignorance of mental illness, society treated the deranged harshly. Help for victims of unemployment, alcoholism, or general poverty was intermittent, haphazard, and moralistic. The poor law reform of 1834 influenced the American philosophy of care. The new system of centralized reconnaissance was intended to improve on the poorly organized local efforts of aid throughout the previous era: the indigent were soon gathered into workshops, and outdoor relief (payments to people able to live on their own with help from others) was replaced with indoor relief (aid to the poor that required them to live under the roof and control of the supporting charity). The poor hated the workshops (workhouses), the regimen of middle-class, quasi-moralistic standards, and especially the separation of families. Despite its failings, indoor relief lasted in Britain until 1911. Victorian society believed that rising affluence would reduce the number of poor, which society preferred to believe was small. All twentieth-century industrial societies have been forced to accept and deal with the problems of social welfare, but England, and especially Germany, forged ahead of the United States in developing social programs (Hannon 1997).

The United States was prosperous enough throughout the frontier era to neglect social welfare legislation. Most Americans were farmers or somehow connected with the land, and underemployment, more than unemployment, is the rascal of extractive industries. Moreover, in the first century of constitutional government the market was a small part of the national economy. When the market faltered, the unemployed were absorbed into the nonmarket sector or aided through private charities sponsored by churches, social organizations, and local governments. The depression of 1893 was the first business collapse serious enough to force Americans to consider rigging a social safety net financed by the greater society. Nearly a half century would pass before the Great Depression made social welfare legislation an issue that could no longer be ignored.

In the American federal system, the power of local government, reinforced by the dictates of formal religion, worked against a unified social welfare policy. The Pierce Veto of 1871, which denied the federal government the right to intervene in social welfare issues, reflected attitudes deeply ingrained in social Darwinism. Individual states did better—New York, Massachusetts, Wisconsin—but most states did little or nothing to help their citizens. Some problems attracted more attention than others: Dorothea Dix promoted prison reform, and Jane Addams, the welfare of children; others advocated the humane treatment of the mentally ill. Private, voluntary, religious, and quasi-religious charities filled a void and may have delayed the time when governments had to shore up their people or witness the collapse of society (Cnaan 1999).

INDUSTRIALIZATION AND THE GENESIS OF SOCIAL SERVICES

The last quarter of the nineteenth century and the first quarter of the twentieth are marked by the beginnings of social concern in a modern sense, an outgrowth of the second industrial revolution and the Progressive movement. The era, which included the Gilded Age, brought a change in the petroleum industry: the market for illuminating oil diminished, but demand for petroleum-based fuel to operate automobiles and airplanes took its place. Electricity opened vistas for energizing new machinery for home and industrial use. Big business harnessed economies of scale by organizing as trusts—Standard Oil, American Tobacco, United States Steel—to monopolize markets; but the Sherman Antitrust Act of 1890 either brought monopolies under government regulation—American Telephone and Telegraph—or made them illegal and forced big business into schemes to maximize profits in oligopolies—a few large sellers like Ford, General Motors, and Chrysler in automotives and Armour, Hammond, Morris, Swift, and Wilson in meat packing (Chandler 1959, 1962, 1977, 1990; Steeples and Whitten 1998; Whitten 1983).

The transformation of the agricultural-rural ethos of the nineteenth century into the industrial-urban ethic of the twentieth was accompanied by protest from farmers and workers, who were destined to play a smaller role in America's future. The new era witnessed the worsening of social ills as the urban framework succumbed to the crises of an industrial order. Waves of immigrants made New York City the most densely populated municipality of the Western world. If the federal government was constitutionally restrained from acting to lessen human suffering in an age of tumult, no such barrier hindered state governments: notwithstanding, state help for the needy was minuscule, so private and voluntary organizations helped those in greatest need.

The Charity Organization Society (COS) of New York and similar associations rose to prominence during turn-of-the-century social and economic change. Most of the work done by the COS and its offshoots followed the traditional patterns of helping and care established in the nineteenth century. Although indoor versus outdoor relief still dominated public rhetoric, fundamental changes were taking place. Social support was becoming scientific, quantitative, and professional.

The origins of social work education in the United States can be traced to 1885 at Harvard University. In Dr. Francis Peabody's Philosophy II class, the course content included "The Questions of Charity, Divorce, the Indians, Labor, Prisons, Temperance etc." The academic foundation of American social work did not equip the practitioner with essential skills (Bruno 1957, 133).

In 1897 Mary Richmond called for the professionalization of social

work, until then in the hands of apprentices and volunteers. She aptly argued that practitioners "had a right to demand from the profession 'further
opportunities for education and development, and [to] earn a living' " (Berengarten 1987, 1). In 1898 the first summer school in philanthropic work
was established under the auspices of the Charity Organization Society of
New York. The formal session gave social work a professional identity and
was the forerunner of the Columbia University School of Social Work, the
oldest professional school in the discipline. The school celebrated its centennial and the centennial of the profession in 1998.

Schools of social work opened around the United States, some freestand-
ing, some affiliated with universities offering a diploma or a bachelor's
degree. Social work training integrated practice, knowledge, and skills from
psychiatry, psychology, and economics into a foundation in sociology. Social work is an established profession: schools of social work award bachelor's, master's, and doctoral degrees in courses of study accredited by the
Council of Social Work Education. Many states require licensing or certification for private practitioners and professionals employed by agencies.
State agencies are held to licensing standards and may be accredited by
nationally recognized bodies such as the Council on Accreditation of Services for Families and Children or the Joint Commission on Accreditation
of Health Care Organizations.

A dynamic psychosocial approach to human problems evolved with the
professionalization of social work. Procedures include social casework (influenced by Freudian psychology), social group work, and community organization. Instead of concentrating on the social policy issues that
determine the work and home environments of Americans, social workers
developed sophisticated techniques for addressing intrapsychic factors troubling their clients. It is not surprising, then, that much of social work practice is based on family therapy contributions by practitioner-teachers
including Nathan W. Ackerman (1994), Murray Bowen (1985), and Salvador Minuchin (1974). Beyond immediate familial matters are those of
society reflected by the community and the workplace.

THE NEW DEAL AND SOCIAL CRISIS

The stock market crash of 1929 and the Great Depression that followed
mark a great divide in the history of social welfare. Never before were so
many millions of Americans made destitute by the shutdown of the economic system; never before were so many millions in need of help. The
Hoover administration remained aloof. Almost half the states took bold, if
limited, action to alleviate distress. Franklin Delano Roosevelt was not con-
strained by legal arguments. The New Deal moved decisively into direct
relief, tried to aid recovery, and, in the Social Security Act of 1935, produced the first major federal social insurance program in the United States.

By far the most important facet of New Deal legislation was its framers' recognition of a federal responsibility for the welfare of a citizenry unable to help itself.

The Supreme Court declared federal welfare efforts constitutional, creating a serious obstacle for those who would refuse federal aid to needy Americans. Social Security was a compromise, an agreement to provide an omnibus program of minimum income maintenance. Some parts of the program were aimed at specific cohorts, the elderly, the unemployed, the blind, and children, for example; others were financed by selective contributions, federal-state or employer-employee, for example. Some issues were set aside as politically unattainable, the most important being health and disability insurance, which had been steadfastly opposed by the powerful American Medical Association and by many employers.

Modest in its benefits, the Social Security Act and its later amendments remain the keystone in the evolution of American social welfare policy. Major social areas were, and still are, covered by the legislation: unemployment insurance in the form of separate state programs, reimbursed by the federal government; old age benefit payments and old age maintenance, collected, invested, and dispersed by the federal government but paid for by employer-employee contributions; payments to care for needy dependent children (Aid to Dependent Children, ADC) and Survivors Insurance (SI), the cost to be largely borne by the federal government. Provisions in the original legislation were included to promote the health of mothers and children in areas suffering severe economic distress; to provide medical, surgical, and corrective services for crippled children; to aid homeless and neglected children; to vocationally rehabilitate the physically disabled; and to aid the needy blind. All these programs were to be financed by matching federal funds and state aid. Many of the original entitlements remain in place.

Very little was radical in any of these provisions of the law. But Roosevelt and his advisers were aware of the Townsend plan, a grassroots movement originating on the West Coast, which had proposed that the federal government give $200 a month to any American over sixty who had less than that income. Those who would frame the Social Security program knew the boundaries of the American political process: not until the Great Society Programs of the mid-1960s was the social net substantially enlarged or enhanced (Church 1998).

Along with the legal enactments of 1935, the New Deal and its direct welfare programs—beginning with the Federal Emergency Relief Administration (FERA) and followed by the Works Progress Administration (WPA), the Civilian Conservation Corps (CCC), the National Youth Administration (NYA), and many more—changed the nature of social welfare in the United States, changed who delivered the service, and changed how it was delivered. The numbers of client populations and professional staff needed to service them rose quickly, pushing aside some of the concerns that had remained from the 1920s. The old sensitivities about whether social work was a profession were shunted aside by the reality of millions in need of help and the difficulties of helping them. If the immediate problems of the 1930s had been rooted in the economic failure of the country and called for relief in material needs, World War II and the postwar world brought back the need for individual help and treatment. Neither social relief of poverty nor individual treatment of psychological and emotional needs could be neglected in American society. The postwar world recognized that modern life created too many strains, too heavy burdens for millions of people to handle without support (Rose 1994).

THE GREAT SOCIETY AND THE WAR ON POVERTY

If most Americans rejected the number and percentage of those in need portrayed in Michael Harrington's *The Other America* (1969), they were nonetheless shocked by the revelation of poverty in an affluent society. Harrington's small volume awakened middle-class America and the Kennedy administration to the needs of millions of Americans. On the return flight from Dallas after the tragic death of John F. Kennedy, Lyndon Johnson asked his aides to look into a program of what might be done for the poor. The Great Society and its War on Poverty were the outcome.

The Economic Opportunity Act of 1964 provided five avenues of escape from poverty. Underprivileged young Americans, workers, farmers, and volunteers, were to join in this concerted attack. The Office of Economic Opportunity was to be the national headquarters; the cost was set at under $1 billion, just 1 percent of the national budget. Fourteen task forces labored on the outlines of the antipoverty programs, and eventually some 400 government agencies were involved. By the fall of 1965, it was estimated that the cost of the Great Society programs would be $7 billion and would more than double ($19 billion) by the end of the decade. The medical program alone was to move from the estimated cost of $4.6 billion to $100 billion by the mid-1980s. But President Johnson could point to significant achievements as legal barriers to equality were struck down. Millions of children received educational benefits—in 1967 almost 1 million went to college. More than 3.5 million Americans had been treated under Medicare, and healthcare had been extended to older people who could not afford it. Nine million new workers received pay based on a higher minimum wage, and 1 million more were in new training programs. One thousand local communities had set up self-help programs to relieve poverty in poor neighborhoods; 1 million young Americans were given a chance to escape from the self-sustaining culture of poverty through neighborhood Youth Corps or Head Start programs.

The Johnson administration programs can be grouped under ten categories: (1) four basic programs of income support—AFDC (Aid to Families

with Dependent Children), SSI (Supplemental Security Income), unemployment compensation, and improved Social Security benefits; (2) healthcare—
Medicare and Medicaid; (3) low-income housing; (4) education—Head
Start and other compensative programs; (5) manpower services—Job Corps
and other work-related programs; (6) civil rights—legal services for minorities; (7) community action programs; (8) economic opportunity; (9) full
employment; (10) income redistribution.

However meaningful and desirable the goals of the Great Society, the
targets moved steadily ahead of the social planners. Nevertheless, the social
welfare efforts, long overdue, edged the United States toward a more just
and equitable society and provided reasonably efficient services. The efforts
of the Reagan administration to cut funding for social programs did not
save money but did reinstitute the judgmental attitude that has historically
characterized our approach to those in need of services (Murray 1984;
Hanson 1998).

Indictments and judgments against the Great Society programs are exaggerated and often simply incorrect. Critics charge that programs were
poorly planned and wastefully administered, with no attempt to estimate
the future and ongoing costs of entitlements. Conservatives insist that the
War on Poverty overextended government and pushed the nation too far,
too fast. These programs, they admonish, exacerbated racial tensions and
social conflicts; contributed to inflating the hopes of minority groups, ultimately alienating much of the black community; and created a "welfare
mess." The evidence does not support these crude generalizations used to
destroy newer initiatives; in fact, for millions of Americans a great deal of
permanent good was accomplished. America reduced the statistical levels
of poverty to new lows, and the Great Society programs mark the most
important social effort since World War II.

As the Great Society drew to a close, many individual programs were
shifted to other agencies or carried on through state efforts. Often bureaus
continued with limited funding. The federal government remains the primary provider of social services, in the form of either direct aid or grants
to states. Despite congressional wrangling over the amounts needed or the
distribution of resources to specific needs, the most important change in
the history of American social service is the public's accepting the perma-
nency of the federal government's support: private efforts play an important role but can no longer provide the resources that the problems
demand. Now, when issues of social service are of universal concern, the
responsibility for resolving them extends to every American and every level
of government.

HUMAN NEEDS AND THE WORKPLACE

Traditionally, the business community has played a large role in determining welfare policy (sometimes a positive role, sometimes negative, for

business associations and many businessmen opposed the New Deal's Social Security program for ideological or financial reasons). Closer to the province of business, however, are those concerns that affect operations in the marketplace. This broad area of work-related problems is one of the most rapidly growing concerns in the social service industry. The specific social services workers need reflect the breakdown of traditional family life; the large numbers of women entering the workforce and their need for child care; alcoholism; drug abuse; AIDS in the workplace; to wit, the broader human issues in American society today (Takahashi and Dear 1997).

No single problem predominates, for many individuals share the problems of poverty, single parenthood, insufficient education, and minority status; but a likely common denominator is social isolation. What is necessary to break the cycle of poverty and dependence? Attaining and keeping a job, even at minimum pay; avoiding the social isolation of a single parent raising a child alone; securing the equivalent of a high school education. Millions of people are unable to meet these three conditions; for those millions, achieving any one of these would be an enormous accomplishment. Despite the rhetoric of the Far Right, no one trapped in poverty wishes to languish there. The number of those caught in poverty in the United States is large compared to those in other industrial countries and has increased with the leveling off of federal programs in the 1980s. Nevertheless, low unemployment in the 1990s helped many, since multiple incomes within the family may be the most viable exit from poverty for people whose take-home pay is modest.

Single-parent households headed by women were probably the most imposing social problem facing America at end of the century. At least one in five children in the United States live in poverty, almost half of them are black, and more than a third are Hispanic. By 1993 over half of all poor families with children under age eighteen were headed by a single woman. Without intervention by the social service network and, indeed, the entire community, the children of these substandard households will cost society either indirectly, by producing far below their potential as adults, or directly, through welfare payments or in the criminal justice system (Rose 1995).

Impaired performance in the workplace is a growing concern in society, particularly in business. Inappropriate absenteeism, self-destructive work attitudes, poor social skills, alcoholism, and drug dependence are as much a problem for employers as for employees. As businesses, government agencies, and households come to understand the link between personal satisfaction and life on the job, social services will be increasingly regarded as a necessary and even desirable investment. The success of American enterprise lies not only in the new technologies born of the third industrial revolution but also in a competent, productive workforce.

CONCLUSION

The first major social concern of the twenty-first century will be the aging of the population. The growing number of people over fifty-five years old is setting the stage for a surge in the demand for social services. Millions of people and billions of dollars are involved. The problem is too large for any but the federal government. New Deal social programs enhanced by the Great Society, but trimmed by 1990s conservative legislation, will have to be upgraded to meet the challenge of the new millennium (Peterson 1999; Cooper 1999).

The passage of the Welfare and Medicaid Reform Act of 1996 speaks to the allocation of limited resources. This new act is hardly a panacea and will create as many problems as it solves (Grigsby 1998). Philosophically, the act replaces welfare with workfare and limits the amount of time re-cipients may receive public moneys as support (Koretz 1998). Limiting as-sistance to mothers of preschool children seriously jeopardizes the children, who are, after all, the workforce of the future. The act is based on the assumption that welfare recipients are made up primarily of able-bodied people capable of becoming productive human beings if given training and opportunities (Hagstrom 1998). The population, however, is diverse and complex. No one formula will answer, for their needs include education and training, transportation, adequate housing, healthcare, readily availa-ble child care beyond the normal nine-to-five day or for sick children whose parents work, and an aggressive effort to curtail the ready availability of drugs to slow down the national epidemic of drug addiction (Castro 1997).

By 1999 the impact of welfare reform was evident. Despite the strongest economy in history and the purging of welfare rolls across the United States—5 million families were on the dole in 1994, and that number was down to 2.7 million by the end of 1998—poverty continues to plague the nation. "Most American who have been swept from welfare rolls have jobs and earn more than they got from the government—but not enough to escape poverty or even, sometimes, to keep the phone connected." Accord-ing to the Associated Press, homelessness is rare, but most families taken off welfare are still struggling: "Substantial numbers say there was a time when they couldn't afford to buy food—43 percent in Florida and 32 per-cent in Wisconsin. Many get behind in paying utility bills—59 percent in Florida alone. In Wisconsin, 68 percent say they are 'just barely making it from day to day' " ("Leaving Welfare" 1999).

BIBLIOGRAPHIC ESSAY

The literature of social issues is as broad as the spectrum of published work and broadcast observations. The daily newspaper of any city or town in America includes stories of social problems and proposed solutions. Radio and television journalists depend on social problems to fill their time on the air. Works of fiction; entertainment on stage, radio, television, and videocassette; and daily conversation are laced with social issues, and it is the rare individual who has not formulated a solution to most social dilemmas. A starting point for social services research is the National Association of Social Workers journal *Social Work*, a bimonthly publication that began in 1956, when it continued the American Association of Social Workers quarterly *Social Work Journal* (1948–1955). *Social Work Journal* continued *The Compass*, which published six times a year from 1921 to 1948.

Nancy Ellen Rose's *Put to Work: Relief Programs of the Great Depression* (1994) is an introduction to the social programs of the New Deal and the vast body of literature devoted to them. Charles A. Murray's *Losing Ground: American Social Policy, 1950–1980* (1984) is a critical analysis of the Great Society programs often cited by antiwelfare activists in their arguments for privatizing or eliminating social programs at the expense of government support of social services for the needy.

In "Our Hidden Safety Net" (1999), Ram Cnaan examines the role of religion in American charitable giving. Part of the article is an analysis of a 1997 study of the community social services provided by 113 historic churches in six cities. Richard Cimino and Don Lattin, in *Shopping for Faith* (1998), anticipate conflict between church and state in the years ahead, and the fulcrum of battle will be social services. Although religious organizations are usually efficient at managing social problems, the separation of church and state raises the question of church workers introducing religious doctrine into functions sanctioned and paid for by the state ("Welfare May Spark Church–State Conflict" 1999).

Sandra Isaacson (1998) and Cynthia G. Wagner (1999) review Jonathan Crane's edited volume *Social Programs That Work* (1998), a Russell Sage Foundation study of successful aid campaigns. One program that works offers tutoring to help disadvantaged children improve their reading skills.

Privatizing is the preeminent buzzword of the 1990s. By decade's end, the social observers were able to estimate the impact of contracting social services to private firms in search of profits. Paul Seidenstat's *Contracting Out Government Services* (1999) is a starting point for the study of privatizing what has been a public responsibility. Seidenstat's bibliography is a guide to the resources on privatization.

With welfare reform looming in the mid-1990s, state and federal agencies and organizations began searching for options. Keon S. Chi's "Replacing Welfare: Options for the Future" (1997) presents the findings of the Council of State Governments' survey of state human services agencies in all fifty states as well as recommendations for welfare reform from the U.S. Department of Health and Human Services, American Public Welfare Association, and state-funded Temporary Aid to Needy Families agencies.

Stephen T. Moore examines the role of management science in late twentieth-century social work in "Social Welfare in a Managerial Society" (1998). Howard Karger and Joanne Levine (*The Internet and Technology for the Human Services* 1999) provide valuable information on network resources for social work.

Two studies represent opposite ends of the welfare reform spectrum at the close of the twentieth century: Virginia I. Postrel's *The Future and Its Enemies: The Growing Conflict over Creativity, Enterprise, and Progress* (1998) and Rebecca M. Blank's *It Takes a Nation: A New Agenda for Fighting Poverty* (1997). Postrel considers the free market the answer to America's social problems; if society is allowed sufficient freedom and flexibility, she argues, the private sector will solve the welfare dilemma. Blank, however, makes a strong case for a social welfare policy that would extend the Great Society concepts of the Johnson administration.

BIBLIOGRAPHY

Abbot, Edith. *Some American Pioneers in Social Welfare: Select Documents with Editorial Notes.* 1937. Reprint. New York: Russell & Russell, 1963.

Ackerman, Nathan W. *Treating the Troubled Family.* Master Work Series. Northvale, NJ: J. Aronson, 1994.

Agranoff, Robert, with Valerie Lindsay Rinkle. *Intergovernmental Management: Human Services Problem-Solving in Six Metropolitan Areas.* SUNY Series in Public Administration. Albany: State University of New York Press, 1986.

Anderson, Albert. *Ethics for Fundraisers.* Philanthropic Studies. Bloomington: Indiana University Press, 1996.

Anderson, Charlene, and Carolyn Stark. "Psychosocial Problems of Job Relocation: Preventive Roles in Industry." *Social Work* 33, no. 1 (January–February 1988): 38–41.

Andrews, Frank Emerson. *Corporate Giving.* New York: Russell Sage Foundation, 1952. Reprint. Philanthropy and Society. New Brunswick, NJ: Transaction Publishers, 1993.

Annotated Directory of Selected Family-Based Service Programs. 5th ed. Iowa City, IA: National Resource Center on Family Based Services, 1987.

Annunziata, Frank, Patrick D. Reagan, and Roy T. Wortman, eds. *For the General Welfare: Essays in Honor of Robert H. Bremner.* American University Studies, ser. 9, History, vol. 48. New York: P. Lang, 1989.

Axel, Helen, ed. *Corporate Strategies for Controlling Substance Abuse.* Conference Board Report no. 883. New York: Conference Board, 1986.

Axinn, June, and Herman Levin. *Social Welfare: A History of the American Response to Need.* 4th ed. White Plains, NY: Longman, 1997.

Axinn, June, and Mark J. Stern. *Dependency and Poverty: Old Problems in a New World.* Lexington, MA: Lexington Books, 1988.

Bailis, Lawrence Neil. *Bread or Justice: Grassroots Organizing in the Welfare Rights Movement.* Lexington, MA: Lexington Books, 1974.

———. *Job Training for the Homeless: Report on Demonstration's First Year.* Research and Evaluation Report Series, 91-F. Prepared by R.O.W. Sciences,

Rockville, MD. Washington, DC: U.S. Department of Labor, Employment and Training Administration, Office of Strategic Planning and Policy Administration, 1991.

Bakalinsky, Rosalie. "People vs. Profits: Social Work in Industry." *Social Work* 25, no. 6 (November–December 1980): 471–75.

Ballew, Julius R., and George Mink. *Case Management in Social Work: Developing the Professional Skills Needed for Work with Multiproblem Clients*. 2d ed. Springfield, IL: Thomas, 1996.

Bardwich, Judith M. "How Executives Can Help 'Plateaued' Employees." *Management Review* 76, no. 1 (January 1987): 40–46.

Beckett, Joyce O. "Plant Closings: How Older Workers Are Affected." *Social Work* 33, no. 1 (January–February 1988): 29–33.

Bennett, Tess, Barbara V. Lingerfelt, and Donna E. Nelson. *Developing Individualized Family Support Plans: A Training Manual*. Cambridge, MA: Brookline Books, 1990.

Berenbeim, Ronald E. *Company Programs to Ease the Impact of Shutdowns*. Conference Board Report no. 78. New York: Conference Board, 1986.

———. *Corporate Programs for Early Education Improvement*. Conference Board Report no. 1001. New York: Conference Board, 1992.

Berengarten, Sidney, ed. *The Columbia University School of Social Work: A History of Social Pioneering*. New York: Columbia University School of Social Work, 1987.

Beyer, Janice M., and Harrison Trice. *Implementing Change: Alcoholism Policies in Work Organizations*. New York: Free Press, 1978.

Blank, Rebecca M. *It Takes a Nation: A New Agenda for Fighting Poverty*. New York: Russell Sage Foundation; Princeton, NJ: Princeton University Press, 1997.

Bowen, Murray. *Family Therapy in Clinical Practice*. Northvale, NJ: J. Aronson, 1985; distributed by Scribner Book Companies.

Brandt, Lilian. *Growth and Development of AICP* [Association for Improving the Condition of the Poor] *and COS* [Charity Organization Society]: *A Preliminary Exploratory Review*. New York: Community Service Society of New York, Committee on the Institute of Welfare Research, 1942.

Breckinridge, Sophonisba Preston, comp. *Public Welfare Administration in the United States: Select Documents*. Chicago: University of Chicago Press, 1927. Reprint. University of Chicago Social Service Series. New York: Johnson Reprint, 1970.

Bremer, William W. *Depression Winters: New York Social Workers and the New Deal*. American Civilization. Philadelphia: Temple University Press, 1984.

Bremner, Robert Hamlett. *The Discovery of Poverty in the United States*. Philanthropy and Society. New Brunswick, NJ: Transaction Publishers, 1992. Originally published as *From the Depths*. New York: New York University Press, 1956.

———. *American Philanthropy*. Chicago History of American Civilization. Chicago: University of Chicago Press, 1960.

Brisolara, Ashton. *The Alcoholic Employee: A Handbook of Useful Guidelines*. Drug Abuse and Alcoholism Series. New York: Human Sciences Press, 1979.

Brock, William Ranulf. *Welfare, Democracy, and the New Deal*. New York: Cambridge University Press, 1988.

Bruno, Frank J. *Trends in Social Work 1874–1956: A History Based on the Proceedings of the National Conference of Social Work*. New York: Columbia University Press, 1957.

Bryan, Mary Lynn McCree, Nancy Slote, and Maree de Angury, eds. *The Jane Addams Papers: A Comprehensive Guide* [guide and indexes to the microfilm collection entitled the Jane Addams Papers, 1860–1960]. Bloomington: Indiana University Press, 1996.

Bullard, Peter D. *Preventing Employee Theft*. Portland, OR: Pro Seminar, 1983.

Burlingame, Dwight F., and Dennis R. Young, eds. *Corporate Philanthropy at the Crossroads*. Philanthropic Studies. Bloomington: Indiana University Press, 1996.

Butler, John. "GM's Approach to Substance Abuse Treatment." *Business & Health* 4, no. 3 (March 1987): 12–13.

Cantor, Nathaniel. *Employee Counseling: A New Viewpoint in Industrial Psychology*. McGraw-Hill Industrial Organization and Management Series, edited by L. C. Morrow. New York: McGraw-Hill, 1945.

Caputo, Richard K. *Welfare and Freedom American Style II: The Role of the Federal Government, 1941–1980*. Federal Responses to People in Need, vol. 2. Lanham, MD: University Press of America, 1994.

Carling, Paul J. *Return to Community: Building Support Systems for People with Psychiatric Disabilties*. New York: Guilford, 1995.

Carson, Emmett D. *A Hand Up: Black Philanthropy and Self-Help in America*. Washington, DC: Joint Center for Political and Economic Studies Press; Lanham, MD: University Press of America, 1993.

Castro, Katherine. "Welfare Reform: How the New Law Affects LHAs [Local Housing Agencies]." *Journal of Housing and Community Development* 54, no. 1 (January–February 1997): 42–45.

Chandler, Alfred D., Jr. "The Beginnings of 'Big Business' in American History." *Business History Review* 33 (Spring 1959): 1–31.

———. *Strategy and Structure: Chapters in the History of the Industrial Enterprise*. Cambridge: MIT Press, 1962.

———. *The Visible Hand: The Managerial Revolution in American Business*. Cambridge: Harvard University Press, 1977.

———. *Scale and Scope: The Dynamics of Industrial Capitalism*. Cambridge: Harvard University Press, 1990.

Chapman, Fern Schumer. "Executive Guilt: Who's Taking Care of the Children?" *Fortune* 115, no. 4 (February 16, 1987): 30–37.

The Charitable Impulse in Eighteenth Century America: Collected Papers. Poverty in America. New York: Arno Press, 1971.

Chi, Keon S. "Replacing Welfare: Options for the Future." *Spectrum* 70, no. 2 (Spring 1997): 17–21.

Chilman, Catherine S., Fred M. Cox, and Elam W. Nunnally, eds. *Employment and Economic Problems*. Families in Trouble series, vol. 1. Newbury Park, CA: Sage, 1988.

Church, George J. "Taking Care of Our Own." *Time* 151, no. 9 (March 9, 1998): 106.

Chusmir, Leonard H., and Douglas E. Durand. "Stress and the Working Woman." *Personnel Journal* 64, no. 5 (May 1987): 38–43.

Cimino, Richard P., and Don Lattin. *Shopping for Faith: American Religion in the New Millennium.* San Francisco: Jossey-Bass, 1998.

Clifton, Robert L., and Alan M. Dahms. *Grassroots Organizations: A Resource Book for Directors, Staff, and Volunteers of Small, Community-Based Non-profit Agencies.* 2d ed. Prospect Heights, IL: Waveland Press, 1993.

Cnaan, Ram. "Our Hidden Safety Net." *Brookings Review* 17, no. 2 (Spring 1999): 50–53.

The Compass. New York: American Association of Social Workers, 1921–1948. Six times a year. Continued by *Social Work Journal.*

Cook, Fay Lomax, and Edith J. Barrett. *Support for the American Welfare State: The Views of Congress and the Public.* New York: Columbia University Press, 1992.

Cooper, Cary L., and Roy Payne, eds. *Stress at Work.* New York: Wiley, 1978.

Cooper, Richard N. "Gray Dawn." Review of *Gray Dawn: How the Coming Age Wave Will Transform America—and the World,* by Peter G. Peterson. *Foreign Affairs* 78, no. 2 (March–April 1999): 142–43.

Cornuelle, Richard C. *Reclaiming the American Dream: The Role of Private Individuals and Voluntary Associations.* New York: Random House, 1965. Reprint. Philanthropy and Society. New Brunswick, NJ: Transaction Publishers, 1993.

Crane, Jonathan, ed. *Social Programs That Work.* New York: Russell Sage Foundation, 1998.

Crimando, William, and T. F. Riggar. *Handbook for In-Service Training in Human Services.* Carbondale: Southern Illinois University Press, 1988.

Denis, Martin K. "Privacy Rights and Drug Testing: Is There a Conflict?" Part 2. *Employment Relations Today* 13, no. 4 (Winter 1986–1987): 347–56.

Devine, Edward T. *Organized Charity and Industry: A Chapter from the History of the Charity Organization Society of the City of New York.* Studies in Social Work, no. 2. New York: New York School of Philanthropy, 1915.

———. *When Social Work Was Young.* New York: Macmillan, 1939.

Dickson, William J., and F. J. Roethlisberger. *Counseling in an Organization: A Sequel to the Hawthorne Researches.* Boston: Harvard University, Graduate School of Business Administration, Division of Research, 1966.

Doherty, Vincent P. "Keeping White Collars Clean." *Security Management* 31, no. 4 (April 1987): 53–55.

Donovan, Rebecca. "Stress in the Workplace: A Framework for Research and Practice." *Social Casework: The Journal of Contemporary Social Work* (May 1987): 259–66.

Dunnette, Marvin D., ed. *Handbook of Industrial and Organizational Psychology.* Chicago: Rand McNally, 1976.

Dziegielewski, Sophia F. *The Changing Face of Health Care Social Work: Professional Practice in the Era of Managed Care.* Springer Series on Social Work. New York: Springer, 1998.

Eckles, Robert W. "Stress: Making Friends with the Enemy." *Business Horizons* 30, no. 2 (March–April 1987): 74–78.

Egan, Gerard. *Change Agent Skills in Helping and Human Service Settings.* Monterey, CA: Brooks/Cole, 1985.

Ehrenreich, John H. *The Altruistic Imagination: A History of Social Work and Social Policy in the United States.* Ithaca, NY: Cornell University Press, 1985.

Eiselein, Gregory. *Literature and Humanitarian Reform in the Civil War Era.* Philanthropic Studies. Bloomington: Indiana University Press, 1996.

Engelken, Cort. "Employee Assistance: Fighting the Costs of Spouse Abuse." *Personnel Journal* 66, no. 3 (March 1987): 31–34.

Epstein, Laura. *Brief Treatment and a New Look at the Task-Centered Approach.* 3d ed. New York: Maxwell Macmillan International, 1992.

Family. New York: American Association for Organizing Family Social Work, 1920–1946. Monthly. Continued by *Journal of Social Casework.*

Families in Society: The Journal of Contemporary Human Services. Milwaukee, WI: Family Service America, 1990– . Bimonthly.

Feit, Marvin D., and Peter Li. *Financial Management in Human Services.* Haworth Health and Social Policy. New York: Haworth Press, 1998.

Fisher, Jacob. *The Response of Social Work to the Depression.* Boston: G. K. Hall, 1980.

Follmann, Joseph F., Jr. *Alcoholics and Business: Problems, Costs, Solutions.* New York: AMACOM, 1986.

Gettman, Dawn, and Devon G. Pena. "Women, Mental Health, and the Workplace in a Transnational Setting." *Social Work* 31, no. 1 (January–February 1986): 5–11.

Gibelman, Margaret, and Harold W. Demone, Jr., eds. *The Privatization of Human Services.* 2 vols. Springer Series on Social Work. New York: Springer, 1998.

Ginsberg, Leon, and Paul R. Keys, eds. *New Management in Human Services.* 2d ed. Washington, DC: NASW Press, National Association of Social Workers, 1995.

Ginzberg, Eli, ed. *Employing the Unemployed.* New York: Basic Books, 1980.

Googins, Bradley, and Dianne Burden. "Employees Look to the Work Place for Help with Job–Family Problems." *Business and Health* 4, no. 4 (February 1987): 58.

Gorlin, Harriet. *Personnel Practices I: Recruitment, Placement, Training, Communication.* Information Bulletin no. 89. New York: Conference Board, 1981.

Greider, William. *One World, Ready or Not: The Manic Logic of Global Capitalism.* New York: Simon & Schuster, 1997.

Grigsby, Eugene, III. "Welfare Reform Means Business as Usual." *Journal of the American Planning Association* 64, no. 1 (Winter 1998): 19–21.

Gronberg, Kristen A. *Mass Society and the Extension of Welfare, 1960–1970.* Chicago: University of Chicago Press, 1977.

Hagstrom, Jerry. "No American Should Go Hungry." *Government Executive* 30, no. 9 (September 1998): 42–49.

Halpern, Susan. *Drug Abuse and Your Company.* New York: American Management Association, 1972.

Hamilton, Dona C., and Charles V. Hamilton. *The Dual Agenda: Race and Social*

Welfare Policies of Civil Rights Organizations. Power, Conflict, and Democracy. New York: Columbia University Press, 1997.

Hammack, David C., ed. *Making the Nonprofit Sector in the United States: A Reader.* Philanthropic Studies. Bloomington: Indiana University Press, 1998.

Hannon, Joan Underhill. "Shutting Down Welfare: Two Cases from America's Past." *Quarterly Review of Economics and Finance* 37, no. 2 (Summer 1997): 419–38.

Hanson, Ardis. "*Return to Community.*" Review of *Return to Community: Building Support for People with Psychiatric Disabilities,* by Paul J. Carling. *Journal of Behavioral Health Services & Research* 25, no. 1 (February 1998): 117.

Harrington, Michael. *The Other America: Poverty in the United States.* New York: Penguin Books, 1969.

Hollinger, Richard C., and John P. Clark. *Theft by Employees.* Lexington, MA: Lexington Books, 1983.

Hopkins, June. *Harry Hopkins: Sudden Hero, Brash Reformer.* Franklin and Eleanor Roosevelt Institute Series on Diplomatic and Economic History. New York: St. Martin's Press, 1999.

Hore, Brian D., and Martin A. Plant, eds. *Alcohol Problems in Employment.* London: Croom Helm in association with the Alcohol Education Center, 1981.

Horton, Thomas R. "Drugs in the Workplace." *Management Review* 76, no. 2 (February 1987): 34–37.

Howarth, Christine. *The Way People Work: Job Satisfaction and the Challenge of Change.* New York: Oxford University Press, 1984.

Huth, Stephen A. "Employer Approaches to Employee Substances Abuse." *Employee Benefit Plan Review* 41, no. 7 (January 1987): 40–41.

Isaacson, Sandra. "Social Programs That Work." Review of *Social Programs That Work,* edited by Jonathan Crane. *Library Journal* 123, no. 9 (May 15, 1998): 102.

Journal of Social Casework. New York: Family Service Association of America, 1946–1949. Continued by *Social Casework.*

Journal of Social Work Process. Philadelphia: University of Pennsylvania School of Social Work, 1937–1969. Annual.

Kagan, Sharon Lynn, with Peter R. Neville. *Integrating Services for Children and Families: Understanding the Past to Shape the Future.* New Haven, CT: Yale University Press in cooperation with the National Center for Service Integration, 1993.

Kahn, Alfred J., and Sheila B. Kamerman. *Integrating Services Integration: An Overview of Initiatives, Issues, and Possibilities.* New York: Cross-National Studies Research Program, Columbia University School of Social Work for the National Center for Children in Poverty, Columbia University School of Public Health, 1992.

Kamerman, Shelia B., Alfred J. Kahn, and Paul Kingston. *Maternity Policies and Working Women.* New York: Columbia University Press, 1983.

Karger, Howard J., and Joanne Levine. *The Internet and Technology for the Human Services.* New York: Longman, 1999.

Katz, Michael B. *Poverty and Policy in American History.* Studies in Social Discontinuity. New York: Academic Press, 1983.

———. *The Undeserving Poor: From the War on Poverty to the War on Welfare.* New York: Pantheon Books, 1990.

———. *Improving Poor People: The Welfare State, the "Underclass," and Urban Schools as History.* Princeton, NJ: Princeton University Press, 1995.

———. *In the Shadow of the Poorhouse: A Social History of Welfare in America.* New York: Columbia University Press, 1983. 10th anniversary ed. rev. and updated. New York: Basic Books, 1996.

———. ed. *The "Underclass" Debate: Views from History.* Princeton, NJ: Princeton University Press, 1993; sponsored by the U.S. Social Science Research Council, Committee for Research on the Urban Underclass.

Katz, Michael B., and Christoph Sachsse, eds. *The Mixed Economy of Social Welfare: Public/Private Relations in England, Germany, and the United States, the 1870s to the 1930s.* 1. Aufl. Baden-Baden: Nomos, 1996.

Keele, Harold M., and Joseph C. Kiger, eds. *Foundations.* Greenwood Encyclopedia of American Institutions, 8. Westport, CT: Greenwood Press, 1984.

King, Brent. "Drugs in the Workplace: Industry Wakes Up to an Epidemic—The Drug Test Debate." *Industrial Management* 11, no. 2 (March 1987): 24–28.

Kleiner, Brian H., and Greg Francis. "Understanding Workaholism." *Business* 37, no. 1 (January–March 1987): 52–54.

Kondratas, Anna, Alan Weil, and Naomi Goldstein. "Assessing the New Federalism: An Introduction." *Health Affairs* 17, no. 3 (May–June 1998): 17–24.

Konrad, Kai A. "Local Public Goods and Central Charities." *Regional Science and Urban Economics* 28, no. 3 (May 1998): 345–62.

Koretz, Gene. "States Ante Up for Workfare: Service Funds Rise as Cash Aid Falls." *Business Week* no. 3585, Industrial/Technology Edition (July 6, 1998): 20.

Kronenwetter, Michael. *Welfare State America: Safety Net or Social Contract?* Impact Book. New York: Franklin Watts, 1993.

Kurzman, Paul A., and Sheila H. Akabas. "Industrial Social Work as an Arena for Practice." *Social Work* 26, no. 1 (January–February 1981): 52–60.

Lagemann, Ellen Condliffe. *Philanthropic Foundations: New Scholarship, New Possibilities.* Philanthropic Studies. Bloomington: Indiana University Press, 1999.

Landy, Frank J., and Don A. Trumbo. *Psychology of Work Behavior.* Dorsey Series in Psychology. Homewood, IL: Dorsey Press, 1976.

Lau, Barbara. "Fun Breaks: Increasing Productivity—and Your Enjoyment of Life." *Management Quarterly* 27, no. 4 (Winter 1986–1987): 18–22.

"Leaving Welfare No Guarantee of Escaping Poverty." *Columbus (Georgia) Ledger-Enquirer*, May 12, 1999, A3.

Lecht, Leonard A., ed. *Employment and Unemployment: Priorities for the Next Five Years.* New York: Conference Board, 1977.

Leiby, James. *A History of Social Welfare and Social Work in the United States.* New York: Columbia University Press, 1978.

Lenckus, Dave. "Self-Funding Gives Social Services More Security." *Business Insurance* 32, no. 17 (April 27, 1998): 102.

Lyons, Paul U. "EAP's: The Only Real Cure for Substance Abuse." *Management Review* 76, no. 3 (March 1987): 38–41.

Macarov, David. "Reevaluation of Unemployment." *Social Work* 33, no. 1 (January–February 1988): 23–29.

Margo, Robert A. "It Takes a Nation." Review of *It Takes a Nation: A New Agenda for Fighting Poverty*, by Rebecca M. Blank. *Southern Economic Journal* 64, no. 2 (October 1997): 594–97.

Martinez-Brawley, Emilia E., and Sybil M. Delevan, eds. *Transferring Technology in the Personal Social Services*. Washington, DC: NASW Press, National Association of Social Workers, 1993.

Marts, Arnaud C. *Philanthropy's Role in Civilization: Its Contribution to Human Freedom*. New York: Harper, 1953. Reprint. Philanthropy and Society. New Brunswick, NJ: Transaction Publishers, 1991.

Matthews, Merrill, Jr. "Downsizing the Federal Government: Department of Health and Human Services." *Vital Speeches of the Day* 64, no. 14 (May 1, 1998): 440–41.

Mental Health and Social Work Career Directory. Career Advisor Series. Detroit: Gale Research, 1993. Biennial.

Mink, Gwendolyn. *Welfare's End*. Ithaca, NY: Cornell University Press, 1998.

Minuchin, Salvador. *Families and Family Therapy*. Cambridge: Harvard University Press, 1974.

Montgomery, Winfield S. *Fifty Years of Good Works*. Washington, DC: Smith Brothers, 1914. Daniel Murray Collection. Library of Congress. [Includes *A Half-Century of Good Works, 1863–1914*, by W. S. Montgomery, and *The Fifty-First Annual Report of the National Association for the Relief of Destitute Colored Women and Children, for the Year 1913*.]

Moore, Stephen T. "Social Welfare in a Managerial Society." *Health Marketing Quarterly* 15, no. 4 (1998): 75–87.

Morris, Michael, and John B. Williamson. *Poverty and Public Policy: An Analysis of Federal Intervention Efforts*. Westport, CT: Greenwood Press, 1986.

Murray, Charles A. *Losing Ground: American Social Policy, 1950–1980*. New York: Basic Books, 1984.

National Directory of Children, Youth & Families Services. Longmont, CO: Marion L. Peterson, 1991– . Biennial.

Noland, Robert L., ed. *Industrial Mental Health and Employee Counseling*. New York: Behavioral Publications, 1973.

Nordhaus-Bike, Anne M. "Street-Smart Health Care." *Hospitals & Health Networks* 72, no. 10 (May 20, 1998): 26.

Nykodym, Nick, and Jack L. Simonetti. *Business and Organizational Communication: An Experiential Skill Building Approach*. Columbus, OH: Grid Publishing, 1978.

Oates, Mary J. *The Catholic Philanthropic Tradition in America*. Philanthropic Studies. Bloomington: Indiana University Press, 1995.

Olasky, Marvin N. *The Tragedy of American Compassion*. Washington, DC: Regnery Gateway, 1992; distributed by National Book Network, Lanham, MD.

Ozawa, Martha N. "Development of Social Services in Industry: Why and How?" *Social Work* 25, no. 6 (November–December 1980): 434–39.

Patterson, James T. *The Welfare State in America, 1930–1980*. BAAS Pamphlets in American Studies, 7. Durham: British Association for American Studies, 1981.

————. *America's Struggle against Poverty, 1900–1994*. Cambridge: Harvard University Press, 1994.

Perlmutter, Felice Davidson. *Changing Hats: From Social Work Practice to Administration*. Silver Spring, MD: NASW Press, National Association of Social Workers, 1990.

————, ed. *Human Services at Risk: Administrative Strategies for Survival*. Politics of Planning Series. Lexington, MA: Lexington Books, 1984.

————, ed. *Alternative Social Agencies: Administrative Strategies*. New York: Haworth Press, 1988.

Peterson, Peter G. *Gray Dawn: How the Coming Age Wave Will Transform America—and the World*. New York: Times Books, 1999.

Plant, Martin A. *Drinking Careers: Occupations, Drinking Habits, and Drinking Problems*. London: Tavistock, 1979.

Plant, Martin A., Eric Single, and Tim Stockwell, eds. *Alcohol: Minimizing the Harm: What Works?* New York: Free Association Books, 1997.

Poole, Dennis L. "Social Work and the Supported Work Services Model." *Social Work* 32, no. 5 (September–October 1987): 434–39.

Postrel, Virginia I. *The Future and Its Enemies: The Growing Conflict over Creativity, Enterprise, and Progress*. New York: Free Press, 1998.

Prien, Erich P., Mark A. Jones, Louise M. Miller, Robert Gulkin, and Margaret Sutherland. *Mental Health in Organizations: Personal Adjustment and Constructive Intervention*. Chicago: Nelson-Hall, 1979.

Pumphrey, Ralph E., and Muriel W. Pumphrey, eds. *The Heritage of American Social Work: Readings in Its Philosophical and Institution Development*. New York: Columbia University Press, 1961.

Rapp, Charles A., and John Poertner. *Social Administration: A Client-Centered Approach*. New York: Longman, 1992.

Rhine, Shirley H. *Older Workers and Retirement*. Report no. 738. New York: Conference Board, Division of Economic Research, 1978.

————. *Managing Older Workers: Company Policies and Attitudes*. Research Report no. 860. New York: Conference Board, 1984.

Riggar, T. F., and R. E. Matkin. *Handbook for Management of Human Service Agencies*. Carbondale: Southern Illinois University Press, 1986.

Rose, Nancy Ellen. *Put to Work: Relief Programs of the Great Depression*. New York: Monthly Review Press, 1994.

————. *Workfare or Fair Work: Women, Welfare, and Government Work Programs*. New Brunswick, NJ: Rutgers University Press, 1995.

Safety Net Reexamined Policy Research Project. *The Social Safety Net Reexamined—FDR to Reagan: A Report*. Lyndon B. Johnson School of Public Affairs Policy Research Project Report, no. 86. Austin: University of Texas at Austin, Lyndon B. Johnson School of Public Affairs, 1989.

Samson, Gloria G. *The American Fund for Public Service: Charles Garland and Radical Philanthropy, 1922–1941*. Contributions in Labor Studies, no. 46. Westport, CT: Greenwood Press, 1996.

Schneewind, Jerome B. *Giving: Western Ideas of Philanthropy*. Philanthropic Studies. Bloomington: Indiana University Press, 1996.

Schorr, Alvin. *Common Decency: Domestic Policies after Reagan*. New Haven, CT: Yale University Press, 1986.

Schram, Sanford F. *Words of Welfare: The Poverty of Social Science and the Social Science of Poverty*. Minneapolis: University of Minnesota Press, 1995.

Schramm, Carl J., Wallace Mandell, and Janet Archer. *Workers Who Drink: Their Treatment in an Industrial Setting*. Lexington, MA: Lexington Books, 1978.

Schwartz, John J. *Modern American Philanthropy: A Personal Account*. Nonprofit Law, Finance, and Management Series. New York: Wiley, 1994.

Seidenstat, Paul, ed. *Contracting Out Government Services*. Privatizing Government. Westport, CT: Praeger, 1999.

Sheridan, Perter J. "Operation Red Block Signals 'Stop' to Alcohol and Drug Abuse." *Occupational Hazards* 49, no. 4 (April 1987): 43–45.

———. "Workplace Stress Spurs Costly Claims." *Occupational Hazards* 48, no. 5 (May 1987): 81–84.

Skidmore, Rex Austin. *Social Work Administration: Dynamic Management and Human Relationships*. 3d ed. Boston: Allyn & Bacon, 1995.

Skocpol, Theda. *Protecting Soldiers and Mothers: The Political Origins of Social Policy in the United States*. Cambridge: Harvard University Press, Belknap Press, 1992.

Smith, Bradford et al. *Philanthropy in Communities of Color*. Philanthropic Studies. Bloomington: Indiana University Press, 1999.

Smith, David H. *Entrusted: The Moral Responsibilities of Trusteeship*. Bloomington: Indiana University Press, 1995.

Social Casework. New York: Family Service America, 1950–1989. Monthly. Continued by *Families in Society: The Journal of Contemporary Human Services*.

Social Work. Silver Spring, MD: National Association of Social Workers, 1956– . Bimonthly.

Social Work Journal. New York: American Association of Social Workers, 1948–1955. Quarterly. Continued by *Social Work*.

Social Work Research. Washington, DC: National Association of Social Workers, 1994– . Quarterly.

Social Work Research & Abstracts. New York: National Association of Social Workers, 1977–1993. Continued in part by *Social Work Research*.

Society for Hospital Social Work Directors of the American Hospital Association. *A Reporting System for Hospital Social Work*. Chicago: American Hospital, 1984.

Sosin, Michael. *Private Benefits: Material Assistance in the Private Sector*. Orlando, FL: Academic Press, 1986.

Springer Series on Social Work. New York: Springer, 1984– . Irregular.

Stanton, M. Duncan, Thomas C. Todd, and Associates. *The Family Therapy of Drug Abuse and Addiction*. Guilford Family Therapy Series, edited by Alan S. Gurman. New York: Guilford Press, 1982.

Steeples, Douglas, and David O. Whitten. *Democracy in Desperation: The Depression of 1893*. Contributions in Economics and Economic History, no. 199. Westport, CT: Greenwood Press, 1998.

Swartz, Katharine. "It Takes a Nation." *Inquiry—Blue Cross and Blue Shield Association* 34, no. 4 (Winter 1997/1998): 275–77.

Takahashi, Lois M., and Michael J. Dear. "The Changing Dynamics of Community Opposition to Human Service Facilities." *Journal of the American Planning Association* 63, no. 1 (Winter 1997): 79–93.

Technology and Structural Unemployment: Reemploying Displaced Adults. Washington, DC: Office of Technology Assessment, 1986.

Thaw, Jack, and Anthony J. Cuvo. *Developing Responsive Human Services: New Perspectives about Residential Treatment Organizations.* Hillsdale, NJ: Erlbaum Associates, 1986.

Tishler, Hace Sorel. *Self-Reliance and Social Security, 1870–1917.* Series in American Studies, no. 8. Port Washington, NY: Kennikat Press, 1971.

Trattner, Walter I. *From Poor Law to Welfare State: A History of Social Welfare in America.* New York: Free Press, 1974.

Trice, Harrison M., and Paul M. Roman. *Spirits and Demons at Work: Alcohol and Other Drugs on the Job.* 2d ed. Ithaca, NY: Cornell University, New York State School of Industrial and Labor Relations, 1978.

U.S. Congress. *The New American State Papers: Social Policy.* 5 vols. Wilmington, DE: Scholarly Resources, 1972.

U.S. Congress. Senate. Committee on Agriculture, Nutrition, and Forestry. *Papers Presented at the National Conference on Nonmetropolitan Community Services Research.* 95th Cong., 1st sess., July 12, 1977. Committee Print.

Veninga, Robert L., and James P. Spradley. *The Work/Stress Connection: How to Cope with Job Burnout.* Boston: Little, Brown, 1981.

Vourlekis, Betsy S., and Roberta R. Greene, eds. *Social Work Case Management.* Modern Applications of Social Work. New York: A. de Gruyter, 1992.

Wagner, Cynthia G. "Social Programs That Work." Review of *Social Programs That Work*, edited by Jonathan Crane. *Futurist* 33, no. 4 (April 1999): 18–19.

Wald, Lillian D. *The House on Henry Street.* New York: H. Holt, 1915. Reprint. Philanthropy and Society. New Brunswick, NJ: Transaction Publishers, 1991.

Watson, Frank D. *The Charity Organization Movement in the United States.* 1922. Reprint. Poverty U.S.A. New York: Arno Press, 1971.

Waugh, Joan. *Unsentimental Reformer: The Life of Josephine Shaw Lowell.* Cambridge: Harvard University Press, 1997.

Weinbach, Robert W. *The Social Worker as Manager: A Practical Guide to Success.* 3d ed. Boston: Allyn & Bacon, 1998.

Weiner, Hyman J., Sheila H. Akabas, and John J. Sommer. *Mental Health Care in the World of Work.* New York: Association Press, 1973.

Weiss, Richard M. *Dealing with Alcoholism in the Workplace.* New York: Conference Board, 1980.

"Welfare May Spark Church–State Conflict." Review of *Shopping for Faith: American Religion in the New Millennium*, by Richard Cimino and Don Lattin. *Futurist* 33, no. 4 (April 1999): 19.

Whitten, David O. *Emergence of Giant Enterprise, 1860–1914: American Commercial Enterprise and Extractive Industries.* Contributions in Economics and Economic History, no. 54. Westport, CT: Greenwood Press, 1983.

Wood, Katherine, and Ludwig L. Geismar. *Families at Risk: Treating the Multiproblem Family.* New York: Human Sciences Press, 1989.

Woods, Robert A., and Albert J. Kennedy. *The Settlement Horizon.* New York: Russell Sage Foundation, 1922. Reprint. Philanthropy and Society. New Brunswick, NJ: Transaction Publishers, 1990.

Wyers, Norman L. "Economic Insecurity: Notes for Social Workers." *Social Work* 33, no. 1 (January–February 1988): 18.

Wyers, Norman L., and Malina Kaulukukui. "Social Services in the Workplace: Rhetoric vs. Reality." *Social Work* 29, no. 2 (March–April 1984): 167–72.

Yamatani, Hide. "Client Assessment in an Industrial Setting: A Cross-Sectional Method." *Social Work* 33, no. 1 (January–February 1988): 34–37.

Part XV

Membership Organizations
ESIC 86.0

CHAPTER 20

BUSINESS AND PROFESSIONAL
ORGANIZATIONS, 86.71

 DONALD R. STABILE

In 1991 an authoritative listing of national associations recorded over 22,000 organizations (Burek 1991). Individuals form and join organizations for reasons ranging from social pursuits to economic gain. This chapter addresses organizations associated with economic gain (Boulding 1953)—3,918 in trade and business, 1,416 in science and engineering, 1,291 in education, and 2,226 in health and medicine (Burek 1991). These business and professional groups are part of the organizational society that has evolved in the United States since the beginning of the Industrial Revolution—there were few national associations in 1850. The growth of national associations has gone hand in hand with the emergence of large integrated corporations and the national economy.

OVERVIEW

Adam Smith said of professional associations: "People of the same trade seldom meet together, even for merriment and diversion, but the conversation ends in a conspiracy against the public, or in some contrivance to raise prices" (Smith [1776] 1976). Organizations usually pursue the special interests of their members. European professional associations have roots in medieval guilds, mutual obligations, and strict rules. Because Europeans who emigrated to America sought escape from restrictions, the guilds they formed were mere shadows of Old World models. Guilds limited membership, but modern associations actively recruit members and function as a group of autonomous individuals (Bradley 1965; Gilb 1966).

Organizations coordinate members of a trade or profession and isolate their membership from the rest of society—detachment and a single voice may lead to confrontation between the membership and the greater society. Men and women join business and professional organizations in search of a greater voice, enhanced status, improved economic well-being, and social influence. Moreover, professionals see in organizations an opportunity to improve the status of their occupation for its own sake as well as for the improved income that accrues to high-status professions.

The American spirit of individualism thwarts trade and professional organization. Strong individuals are not likely to see the need for joining with others, so the success of a group may depend on the skills of its founders. In the course of the twentieth century advances in organizing skills and transportation and communication technology have fostered professional organizations: modern national organizations depend on telephones, fax machines, and e-mail to communicate with their membership (Boulding 1953) and commercial airlines to bring members from around the nation and the globe to annual meetings.

All voluntary organizations have a free-rider problem. If nonmembers can gain the same or similar advantages of members, some people will refuse to share in the expenses of the institution (Olson 1982). Business and professional organizations discourage free riding with federation structures—members join local chapters that affiliate with the national association—that apply peer pressure of personal contact to encourage membership. Positive inducements to join a trade or professional group include services to members—information pertinent to the industry or profession—membership prestige, and specialized journals. The strongest organizations are those with government backing—membership is a state requirement for practicing the profession or trade (Olson 1982).

Business and professional associations pursue the special interests of their members by reducing competition (limiting the size of the group) and lobbying for favorable legislation. Many organizations pursue goals for the benefit of society as a whole: gun control, environmental protection, prevention of drunk driving, and medical research are examples. No matter how beneficial a goal, however, it can be financed only at the expense of some other goal, because society cannot fund all projects. Thus, even the most useful activities engaged in by a group encounter organized opposition from other groups. National organizations arise not only for their own sake but to counter other national organizations that already exist.

BUSINESS ORGANIZATIONS

U.S. business and trade associations serve their members and promote the profit-driven market system. They comprise public policy associations—National Association of Manufacturers (NAM), U.S. Chamber of Commerce—that influence public policy by lobbying governmental bodies and marshaling public opinion, employers' associations attuned to labor markets and unions, and trade or industry associations—American Petroleum Institute, Edison Electric Institution (Steigerwalt 1980).

Business organizations are governed by elites of industry executives or professional managers and lobbyists. Most have headquarters in Washington, DC (Steigerwalt 1980). They do not share the professional associations' power of licensing or control over education to impose membership on business, but they do offer an important advantage to members: a voice in industry policy formulation. Moreover, members are drawn by the need to cooperate within an industry and coordinate for conflicts against competing industries (Steigerwalt 1980).

Apart from lobbying, business associations provide members with information about prices, production levels, technology, costs, advertising, research and development, and product standardization. They also promote codes of ethics for fair competition. Although such activities can enhance or impede competition, historically, associations endeavored to reduce competition, albeit with indifferent results (Steigerwalt 1980).

In 1853 the first trade organization, the American Brass Association, was formed in Connecticut to fix prices and restrict output; it ceased operations in 1869 (Steigerwalt 1980). Most of the associations established over the next fifty years foundered on the individualism of businessmen reluctant to share trade secrets in a nation solidly committed to competition (Galambos 1966). As communications and transportation advances made it easier for industry members to get to know one another, and as competition spread nationally, the environment for association growth improved.

The New England Cotton Manufacturers Association (1865) assailed mutually destructive competition (Galambos 1966). In 1873 the president of American Iron and Steel Association (1855)—renamed the American Iron and Steel Institute in 1909—stated association aims: "By frequent meeting together, asperities would be softened, greater courtesy would prevail, and new processes and improved methods of operating works would become more generally known." The Gilded Age also saw formation of the National Association of Wool Manufacturers, the American Bankers Association, and the Wire-Nail Association (Foth 1930; Edgerton 1916).

The twentieth century brought increased growth of national trade associations. Early Supreme Court decisions on the Sherman Antitrust Act of 1890 probably hastened the trend. At first the Court, in *United States v. Eastern Retail Lumber Association*, appeared to limit the operations of trade associations, but in the Standard Oil and American Tobacco cases the Court set forth its rule of reason that outlawed only unreasonable restraints of trade. By making monopolies in restraint of trade illegal and threatening conspiracies for the same purpose but by softening these rulings with the rule of reason, the Court enabled trade associations to do tacitly

what could not be done explicitly. They became a key institution for industry cooperation in limiting competition, subject only to the intensity of
enforcement of the antitrust act (Steigerwalt 1980).

By the 1920s trade associations were setting prices and standards, a practice strengthened during World War I, when the War Industries Board,
operating through trade associations and led by business executives, controlled much of the economy. A 1921 Federal Trade Association study
found 626 associations sharing market information, 276 sharing internal
data, and 107 open price associations (Himmelberg 1976). Two Supreme
Court decisions in the 1920s, *Maple Flooring Manufacturers' Association
v. United States* and *Cement Manufacturers' Protective Association v.
United States*, appeared to approve this system (Steigerwalt 1980). In a
1969 case, *United States v. Container Corporation of America*, however,
the Court limited the legality of information flows in associations where
there are few competitors and standardized products (Lynn and McKeown
1988).

The flowering of trade associations in the 1920s owes much to the efforts
of Herbert Hoover as secretary of commerce (1921–1929) and as president
(1929–1933). Hoover championed voluntary associations under government sponsorship to moderate business cycles and promote economic stability. He backed government collection and publication of industry data,
except for price information, to encourage knowledgeable decision making
by industry planning groups (Steigerwalt 1980).

Hoover was opposed by Attorney General Harry Daugherty and head of
the antitrust division of the Justice Department, William Donovan. A political confederate of President Warren G. Harding, Daugherty used his
knowledge of negative public sentiment against anti-competitive actions of
trade associations to win cases against them. Hoover, however, maintained
that associations brought about "intelligent" competition and promoted
industrial efficiency. When the *Maple Flooring* case approved some industry
association practices, trade association leaders applauded Hoover (Himmelberg 1976; Wueschner 1999).

Industry groups contributed to a spirit of cooperation in the 1920s. Base-
point pricing schemes were instituted during this period. Despite Federal
Trade Commission orders against these schemes, they continued. Industry
associations such as the Cement Institute and the American Iron and Steel
Institute lobbied successfully against laws designed to limit the base-point
system and won legal cases aimed at thwarting them; it was not until 1948
that the Supreme Court outlawed base-point pricing (Steigerwalt 1980).

Franklin D. Roosevelt supported trade associations: a principal component of the New Deal was the National Industrial Recovery Act of 1933.
Under NIRA auspices business groups developed industry codes of production levels, prices, and wages (Brady 1943). Industries without associations were organized, and existing organizations were strengthened (75

percent of code authorities were drawn from trade association leaders) with legal sanctions and incentives to encourage free riders to join a trade association. NIRA was declared unconstitutional by the Supreme Court in 1935 (Steigerwalt 1980).

When the NIRA codes were eliminated, industry associations lobbied Congress to duplicate the code with statute law. In 1937–1938 there were 1,244 national and regional trade associations, 500 to 600 of which participated in governmental activities (Tedlow 1988). The Robinson-Patman Act of 1936 restricted price discrimination to help small retail grocers combat large chain stores, and retail druggists gained resale price maintenance through the Miller-Tydings Act of 1937. By the 1940s trade associations were an established part of the U.S. economy (Steigerwalt 1980).

National business organizations, vigilant to the best interest of their membership, use their influence to prevent or blunt legislation designed to benefit the commonweal at the expense of business profits. They doggedly resist and promote deregulation. Safety, health, environmental, and employment discrimination laws have been modified at their behest. After suffering defeat in the passage of the National Labor Relations Act of 1937 (NLRA), which finally established the right of workers to join or form unions of their own choosing, business regrouped in support of the Taft-Hartley Act (1947) and the Landrum-Griffin Act (1959) to reduce the power NLRA had given to labor; a coalition of associations also led to the failure of the Labor Reform Act (1975). In national affairs, business organizations have had an influence far exceeding their numbers and greater than that of any other group (Steigerwalt 1980).

Industrywide business organizations, like their national cohorts, have successfully manipulated the federal system to their benefit. They are effective surrogates for the market power usually established by oligopolies or cartels. Industry lobbyists captured the agencies established to regulate them. Their political action committees (PAC) influence governmental affairs, although their leverage is blunted because it is not uniformly applied. Industry groups do fight one another, and to the extent that they do, power has been diffused among a number of groups (Galambos 1988).

In his defense of the Constitution (*Federalist #10*) James Madison anticipated special interest groups when he warned against political faction. He expected society to reduce the impact of factional politics, however, by playing opposing groups against one another. Business organizations do neutralize each other on some issues, but on others, like the power of unions, they consolidate their strength.

The National Association of Manufacturers

The NAM is a "peak association" that promotes the general interests of business. It was established in Cincinnati, Ohio, in 1895 at an assembly of over 600 U.S. manufacturers. Its founders, in addition to seeing the need for a national organization for business, determined to advocate legislation that promoted manufacturing, including the expansion of foreign trade and protection of domestic markets by tariffs. Any government policy was to be judged by its good or bad impact on business. Thomas I. Dolan was chosen as president (Steigerwalt 1964; Steeples and Whitten 1998).

NAM's beginning was inauspicious because full membership was limited to manufacturers. Membership grew when individual memberships were introduced—there were more than a 1,000 NAM members by 1899, nearly 3,000 by 1904, and 3,389 in 1913. A key to NAM success was publicity: In 1896 NAM began publishing *Circulars of Information* to promote its goals, one of which was the creation of a cabinet department in the federal government to address business issues. After eight years of NAM lobbying, the Department of Commerce and Labor was established in 1903. The NAM was also instrumental in promoting the construction of the Panama Canal and in establishing uniform freight rates on U.S. railroads.

In 1902 the NAM mounted a crusade against labor unions. Although it had previously fought legislation aimed at helping unions, the election of David M. Parry as NAM president moved the association to higher levels of opposition. The individual manufacturer viewed unions as obstacles to profits to be avoided at all costs. Parry nurtured this view. For the next decade the NAM fought legislation to limit the length of the working day, limit the injunctive power of courts in labor disputes, and void the use of the Sherman Act against unions, and it usually won.

In its 1904 constitution the NAM dedicated itself as an organization for the "maintenance of individualism." The irony of this pledge was probably not appreciated by its members. Nor was it always adhered to in practice, as the NAM became vocal in its support of protective tariffs as part of its quest for "sympathetic, co-operative and elastic" government policies toward business (but not labor). It did support workmen's compensation laws, which were enacted during the early 1900s (Steigerwalt 1964). In 1916 it worked with other associations to form the National Industrial Conference Board to conduct studies on behalf of business. During the 1920s it began promotion of the "American Plan" with its central element of the open shop in labor markets (Steigerwalt 1980).

The NAM, unprepared for the Great Depression, was bewildered by the New Deal. Membership had dropped from a high of 5,350 in 1922 to under 1,500 in 1933. Forced to reconstitute NAM to defend business in an increasingly hostile atmosphere, its directors undertook a full-blown public relations campaign. Led by a group of industrialists known as the "Brass Hats," NAM mounted an assault against the New Deal, especially those parts of the National Industrial Relations Act of 1933 (NIRA) and its labor provisions—labor unions were the enemy. Marketing surveys were taken to determine what ideas would work, and paid advertising messages were used. The goal was to sell the idea that industrial executives were the real leaders of the country and that harmony among all groups, but especially between capital and labor, was essential for prosperity (Tedlow 1976; Rose 1994).

Because the National Labor Relations Act (1937) was taken almost intact from Section 7A of NIRA, and because NIRA had been declared unconstitutional, NAM directors expected NLRA to be likewise ruled unconstitutional. That expectation dashed, NAM denigrated members of the National Labor Relations Board and their decisions and argued for repeal of the act itself. By the late 1930s NAM strategies were ambivalent: it encouraged its members to adapt to the new rules of labor relations (Harris 1982), hesitantly applying its campaign for industry harmony to its members. Some NAM members, however, resisted unions and used illegal tactics against them, as investigations by congressional committees discovered (Tedlow 1976). A part of the message of harmony had been aimed at middle-class swing groups, and to the extent they were swayed, the NAM did perhaps promote an appreciation of the need for a system of peaceful industrial relations (Tedlow 1988).

Nevertheless, the NAM campaign against the NLRA continued until passage of the Taft-Hartley Act in 1947. NAM also worked against other elements of the New Deal antibusiness legacy, such as the extension of price controls after World War II. It played a part in toning down the Employment Act of 1946 from being a "Full Employment Act," generally opposing all aspects of Keynesian economics (Tedlow 1976). In the 1950s NAM began using approaches to get business executives involved with the electoral process. It formed the Business-Industry Political Action Committee in 1963 to make its political programs more effective (Steigerwalt 1980). In 1991 NAM operated from headquarters in Washington, D.C., having 13,500 members, a staff of 180, and an annual budget of $14 million (Burek 1991).

Chambers of Commerce

There are in the United States thousands of city, county, township, and state chambers of commerce, all supporting commerce and business: adjudication of business disputes, passage of laws that would improve business activity, and the promotion of civic improvement and public works projects. The earliest, the Chamber of Commerce of the State of New York (CCSNY), was founded on April 5, 1768, at a meeting of twenty merchants, making it the first business association not officially affiliated with a government body. The initial meeting was called in response to the founders' disapproval of British colonial policy. After the American War of Independence, on April 13, 1784, the New York legislature reconfirmed the CCSNY charter.

CCSNY embarked on a mission of improving business conditions in the city. On January 3, 1786, members proposed a canal to link the state capital at Albany with Buffalo on Lake Erie—the Erie Canal—and when Governor DeWitt Clinton began building the canal three decades later, the CCSNY gave him strong support. CCSNY pursued civic affairs in the decades after the Civil War. It fought the corruption of the Tweed Ring, proposed the consolidation of all five boroughs into Greater New York, and fostered plans for portions of a subway system. Its members and officers included prominent businessmen and civic leaders, whose personal influence made the chamber a force in city affairs. During the 1920s CCSNY became increasingly dependent on full-time, permanent staff members, and after World War II permanent staff assumed the importance previously assigned volunteers. By the 1960s the chamber's research staff was an authority on the city's economic conditions. In 1988 the chamber had nearly 1,500 member firms (Stabile 1995). In addition to the CCSNY there were about forty other chambers of commerce in 1870, a total that approached 3,000 by 1930 (Brady 1943).

Begun in 1912, the national organization, the U.S. Chamber of Commerce (USCC), was among the last formed. Officials in the Department of State and the Department of Commerce and Labor became a driving force behind the formation of the USCC. Both agencies wanted to encourage manufacturing and exports but desired a national organization of businesses with which they could work. Large manufacturing firms had access to the government; the intent of a new organization was to give similar access to government for all business in a unified manner.

In 1907 delegates met in Washington at the office of the secretary of commerce and labor, Oscar Straus, and formed the National Council of Commerce. Response to the invitation to join was weak in a business community leery of too close a relationship with the federal government. Moreover, many conservative businessmen thought the membership fee of $100 excessive. There was also opposition from the National Board of Trade, which had, since 1868, sought the same goals as the new organization. The National Council of Commerce struggled on in name only.

The idea of a national organization for business retained appeal, especially as the National Board of Trade remained weak. During 1909 the Boston Chamber of Commerce took the initiative to start a national group. It was soon joined in this effort by the Chicago Association of Commerce and the NAM. They used their influence to push for reorganization of the National Board of Trade, effectively removing it from opposition. Officials of the Department of Commerce and Labor kept a studied distance from these activities.

In April 1912, 700 delegates from all parts of the country and 392 business groups met in Washington and formed the U.S. Chamber of Commerce, naming Harry Wheeler of the Chicago association as its president.

The organization committee was chaired by John Fahey of the Boston Chamber of Commerce. The U.S. Chamber kept its early ties with government and sought a federal charter. When that charter failed in the Senate in 1913, after passing in the House, the U.S. Chamber was incorporated in the District of Columbia in 1915 (Werking 1978).

By the 1980s the U.S. Chamber had 180,000 member corporations and about 7,000 state and local chambers of commerce under its umbrella. Its president stated the U.S. Chamber's primary duty: "to influence the United States Congress" (Lynn and McKeown 1988).

Operating out of offices in Washington, the U.S. Chamber of Commerce in 1991 had a staff of 1,100 and an annual budget of $65 million. Its members are drawn from local chambers of commerce, corporations, and other business associations. It trains its members to lobby at the state and local level. To promote greater acceptance of the business point of view on national issues, USCC produces two television shows, *Nation's Business Today* and *It's Your Business*, and publishes a monthly journal, *Nation's Business* (Burek 1991).

The Cotton Textile Industry

Because the cotton textile industry is one of the oldest manufacturing sectors of the U.S. economy, it is not surprising that it saw some of the earliest business organizations. The New England Cotton Manufacturers Association was established in 1865 to help mill agents and superintendents keep abreast of technical advances. By 1875 it had 97 members from every state in New England, and at the turn of the century 491 members represented twenty states. A second organization, the Arkwright Club of Boston, started meetings in 1880 and aimed at broader targets such as promoting the general interests of the industry; it made several attempts to cut back production during hard times, but without success. Similar efforts in the South by the Southern and Western Manufacturers' Association were failures that took down the initiating association. The Southern Cotton Spinners' Association, organized in 1897, tried to unite individual mill operators and executives to control industry production. These associations assumed the pattern of "dinner clubs," with most meetings taking the form of a social event.

Early in the twentieth century, the Arkwright Club started a New England Cotton Freight Bureau, a Cotton Bureau, a Cotton Classification Committee, and a Board of Appeal. It employed a permanent staff member to perform the duties associated with these service operations. The New England Cotton Manufacturers Association followed suit, changing its name to the National Association of Cotton Manufacturers in 1906 and undergoing a reorganization ten years later that brought professional staff aboard. The Southern Cotton Spinners' Association changed its name in

1903 to the American Cotton Manufacturers Association and moved in the same direction as the two northern groups.

Early attempts to link northern and southern textile producers failed. In 1913 members of the three regional organizations, goaded by a common interest in tariff reform, instituted the National Council of American Cotton Manufacturers. It added several specialized bureaus and initiated discussion on the feasibility of operating as an "open-price" organization. The national effort worked better in theory than in practice, however.

During the 1920s, when industry associations were being encouraged by Herbert Hoover at the Commerce Department and when the Supreme Court seemed to be taking a lenient view toward some of their activities, the textile industry renewed its bid for a stronger national association. The Cotton-Textile Institute was created in 1926 for the purpose of acting under an open-price plan. It also encouraged uniform accounting methods to ensure that the statistics shared under the plan would be comparable from firm to firm. It expected to provide marketing and product development services to help meet new competition from outside the industry, especially from synthetic fabrics. By keeping a close consultation with Hoover, the institute avoided any difficulties with the government. Despite sound strategy, measures for production control initiated during the late 1920s did not work.

At the outset of the New Deal, the Cotton-Textile Institute took part in its planning and had an important influence on Title I of the National Industrial Recovery Act. The act gave the institute greater authority over the industry with the ability to compel reluctant firms to follow its lead. It quickly began drafting an industry code and benefited from being the main source of data concerning industry conditions. The National Recovery Administration took part in drafting codes, which kept the institute from being dictatorial, but did not have sufficient personnel and capability to keep it completely in check. Overall, the final code for the cotton industry promised to bring a cooperative equilibrium to its members.

The impact of the textile code was ambiguous. The institute did not push strongly enough to curtail production. In New England smaller firms were kept from going under by the codes, but throughout the industry many executives found the costs of dealing with the codes in excess of the benefits. When the NIRA was declared unconstitutional in 1935, the textile industry reverted to its weak open-price plan of the 1920s under the direction of the Cotton-Textile Institute. Even this modest form of cartelization met difficulty under the renewed antitrust vigor that marked government policy after 1937 (Galambos 1966).

In 1991 the cotton textile industry association was the American Textile Manufacturers, which had been formed in 1949 by a merger of several institutions, including the Cotton-Textile Institute. With headquarters in

Washington, it had a professional staff of forty and published several industry journals (Burek 1991).

The weak status of the major national association in cotton textiles highlights the problems of building an effective membership group. With a large number of members in an industry with low entry barriers, it remained difficult to retain control over the entire field. Not only could nonmembers gain by being free riders on gains won by the institute, but members could profit by cheating on the industrywide agreement. There were few sanctions the institute could impose on uncooperative firms, and even when, under the NIRA, it had some sanctions, they were not enough. With the exception of struggling for protective tariffs, the textile industry rarely reached agreement on any industrywide strategy and accordingly remained a fragile industry in terms of profits, wages, and technical innovation. This ineffectiveness puts it at one extreme of a spectrum of industry organizations, at the opposite end of a range that extends to associations that have evolved to speak strongly for their industry.

The Automobile Industry

Automobile manufacturers' associations have waxed and waned with advances and declines in the industry. The National Association of Automobile Manufacturers commenced operations in 1900, but by 1904 some members left it to form the Motor and Accessory Manufacturers' Association. Its life ended in 1913, when it merged with the Automobile Board of Trade to form the National Automobile Chamber of Commerce. This organization sought improved freight rates and better highways and planned automobile expositions. In 1934 it changed its name to the Automobile Manufacturers Association.

During the 1930s the Automobile Manufacturers Association tried to establish an industry code under the National Industrial Recovery Act but folded in the face of opposition from Henry Ford. Eventually, the big three auto firms—Chrysler, Ford, and General Motors—joined the association under the guidance of Henry Ford II. The Automobile Parts and Equipment Manufacturers Association, a previously active group, dissolved in 1955, as many of its members had been taken over by the big three firms. An industry that had started out with many firms and several associations evolved into one with three dominant firms and one association in its manufacturing sector. In 1991 this association, which had changed its name in 1972 to the Motor Vehicle Manufacturers Association of the United States, operated from headquarters in Detroit with seven members, a staff of 109, and an annual budget of $14 million (Burek 1991).

The National Automobile Dealers Association (NADA) represents the interests of the retail sector where new cars are sold. Formed in 1917,

NADA helped dealers secure franchise contracts with manufacturers that allow sellers more freedom of action. NADA has also lobbied Congress on its own behalf and for small business. Association success lends credence to the notion that business organizations may diffuse power as well as concentrate it (Steigerwalt 1980). In 1991 NADA operated from headquarters in McLean, Virginia, and had 19,600 members, a staff of 405, and an annual budget of $10 million. Used car dealers have a separate association, the National Independent Automobile Dealers Association, established in 1946. In 1991 it had offices in Arlington, Texas, 15,000 members, a staff of eleven, and an annual budget of $1.2 million (Burek 1991).

The Iron and Steel Industry

Iron and steel trade associations first appeared in 1855 (Bradley 1965). The American Iron and Steel Institute (AISI), established in 1908, was headed for the next two decades by Elbert Gary, president of U.S. Steel. AISI's principal objective was to avoid harmful competition within the domestic industry and to forestall foreign rivals. Although there are forty-six other associations in the industry, the institute remains the largest, with sixty-three member companies throughout North America.

Other Industry Groups

Other associations in manufacturing and industry (date formed/members in 1991) include American Bakers Association (1897/500), National Coal Association (1917/150), American Dairy Association (1940/210,000), American Gas Association (1918/4,758), American Petroleum Institute (1919/200), American Trucking Association (1933/3,594), Rubber Manufacturers Association (1900/210), Paper Industry Management Association (1919/4,000), Wood Machinery Manufacturers Association (1899/120), National Glass Association (1948/2,875), National Electrical Manufacturers Association (1926/600), American Electronics Association (1943/3,500), Soap and Detergent Association (1926/145), Association of Home Appliance Manufacturers (1966/152), Equipment Manufacturing Institute (1894/420).

Hardware Manufacturing and Distribution

A pattern of development of countervailing associations can be seen in the hardware industry. Beginning in the post–Civil War period, the growing number of manufacturers of hardware products in the United States supplanted English imports that had dominated the market. Domestic cutlery had taken about 50 percent of the market by 1885, and in the next decade the value of imports of hardware from Britain was halved. Domestic hardware manufacturers shifted distribution from commission agents to whole-salers who dealt in large volumes and took title to products instead of taking them on consignment.

As the industry grew, it was troubled by excess capacity and high levels of competition that often led to drastic price reductions. In some sectors of the industry, as happened in many areas of manufacturing, consolidation of firms into national corporations aimed to alleviate these unprofitable conditions. Where consolidation was not possible, hardware manufacturers turned to the other avenue of industry control, the trade association.

Starting in the 1870s and 1880s, trade associations were started in such areas of hardware manufacturing as door locks, knobs, sledgehammers, tacks, circular saws, shovels, and sinks, with over fifty operating during this time. The associations were not always successful, as efforts to set quotas on production among members were breached as often as they were honored, for the limits left too much idle capacity. Some manufacturers had established brand names among consumers and had no need to restrain their sales, while others were multiproduct manufacturers that could use cross-subsidization techniques to undersell the association. Despite a few successful associations, notably in copperware, price stability, the overall aim, was not achieved during the 1870–1900 era.

Wholesale dealers of hardware had looked favorably upon manufactur-ers associations' efforts to steady prices, because they often suffered from rapid price declines. They purchased their inventories and lost money when prices fell. There was contention between manufacturers and wholesalers as well. Manufacturers sold to wholesalers at a price that took a discount from the set retail price. As prices fell, the value of the wholesalers' markup declined when the discount was held constant, and manufacturers often tried to lower the discount. Manufacturers' associations might set retail prices at a high level and sell to wholesalers in line with that level, but there was no guarantee that the retail level would hold. Wholesalers might buy at a high price from manufacturers and find that retailers would not buy from them at a comparable figure. Finally, manufacturers might sell directly to retailers, further undercutting the wholesalers' profits.

To combat these difficulties, wholesaler hardware dealers began orga-nizing their own associations. These started at the local level, with the Wholesale Hardware Association of Buffalo, New York, in 1879. During the next decade, similar groups were set up in Hartford, New York, New Haven, Baltimore, and Philadelphia, and others were added in the 1890s. These associations tried to reach price agreements at the local level and to compel manufacturers or their associations to meet their needs. These early efforts failed, as retail dealers could buy from wholesalers in other cities, and manufacturers and their groups could use their national organizations to unite against the wholesalers in a particular city.

These failures led wholesalers to form state associations in Minnesota,

New York, Iowa, and Texas. The Mississippi and Missouri Valley Hardware Association, a regional group, was formed in 1883. It sought to hold the line on prices and had enough cohesiveness in the area to establish boycotts against uncooperative manufacturers. A similar Southern Hardware Jobbers' Association was formed in 1891, but efforts to establish a New England association misfired.

Finally, in 1895 the National Hardware Association (NHA) was established, and by 1897 nearly three-quarters of the wholesalers had joined. Following the example of the two successful regional associations, the NHA hired a permanent secretary-treasurer, who negotiated pricing deals with manufacturers. In these deals, the wholesalers were given greater discounts from the set retail price and in return promised not to buy from manufacturers who broke ranks on set prices. Grievance committees were formed to handle complaints from wholesalers and manufacturers. The NHA also made up a list of hardware wholesaler dealers to keep products from the hands of other competitors and to prevent direct sale to retailers. It was able to deal with manufacturers associations where they existed and directly with manufacturers where they did not.

Greater price stability in the distribution of hardware products was attained. In many manufacturing industries, the problems of price stability and product distribution in a mass-production era were solved by horizontal and vertical integration in the single dominant firm. Because of the diversity of product lines involved with hardware, this solution was not feasible. Trade associations at the manufacturing and wholesale levels afforded an alternative (Becker 1971).

Small Business Associations

In keeping with the strategies of the wholesale hardware dealers and automobile dealers, many other sectors of small business have organized national associations, presumably to gain a degree of countervailing power against the larger economic agents they face in the marketplace. There has been little research into the history of small business associations.

The umbrella organization of small business is the National Federation of Independent Business, founded in 1943. With offices in San Mateo, California, in 1991 it had 560,000 members, an office staff of 225, a field staff of 675, and an annual budget of $52 million. It lobbies governments at all levels in the interests of its members, with members being invited to express those interests through ballots on various issues. The 1980s saw the formation of several other national organizations concerned with small business—the National Association for the Self-Employed (1981), the National Business Association (1982), the National Association of Private Enterprise (1984), and National Small Business United (1986). These associations, however, represent a tiny portion of the many small businesses in the United States, because it is difficult to organize in the face of a horde of free riders (Burek 1991).

National organizations of small businesses in specific lines of trade (year of formation/membership in 1991) include the National Retail Merchants Association (1911/55,000), National Association of Realtors (1908/805,000), National Funeral Directors Association (1882/14,500), National Home Furnishings Association (1929/13,500), Society of American Florists (1884/10,000), National Grain and Feed Association (1896/1,250), National Cosmetology Association (1921/55,000), North American Equipment Dealers Association (1900/8,200), American Society of Travel Agents (1931/22,000), Independent Insurance Agents of America (1896/34,000).

Financial Services

As the U.S. economy became more complex, there developed a wide array of financial services available to both business and consumers. Paramount among these services was banking. The American Bankers Association was formed—1875, with 300 members—in response to difficulties banks had during the 1873 recession. Its formal constitution, approved in 1876, charged the association "to promote the general welfare and usefulness of banks and banking institutions." To achieve these ends, it acted as a professional association, raising the educational attainments of bank employees; a trade association, representing the interests of the banking community before Congress; and a service organization, performing many functions for its member banks; The *Journal of the American Bankers Association* began publication in 1908. The association's membership spurted to 1,000 within a year and gradually increased to 1,500 by 1895; aided by efforts to reform the monetary system, its membership soared to over 11,000 in 1910 and nearly 25,000 in 1929. As banking suffered reverses during the Great Depression and mergers in subsequent years, the membership declined, hitting 16,841 in 1954 (Schneider 1956). To improve educational standards in the industry, it runs the American Institute of Banking, which trains around 150,000 students per year (Hope 1980). In 1991 the American Bankers Association had 11,000 members, a staff of 400 at its headquarters in Washington, DC, and an annual budget of $62 million (Burek 1991).

In 1914 a group of mortgage bankers met to form the Farm Mortgage Bankers Association with 200 members, mostly small firms that specialized as brokers of mortgage funds between eastern money centers and western farmers. As urbanization progressed, these firms began dealing more heavily in residential mortgages, and the association name was changed to the Mortgage Bankers Association to reflect this shift (Stabile 2000). In 1991 it had 2,800 members and a staff of 160 at its Washington headquarters.

Other associations dealing with financial services include the Credit

Union National Association, formed in 1934, and the United States League of Savings Institutions, formed in 1892 and 3,400 strong by 1991.

PROFESSIONAL ASSOCIATIONS

Professionals undergo extensive training to acquire skills and learning about a specialized discipline; this knowledge is used by independent practitioners with high principles to serve the public. Practitioners are accorded power and prestige because of their knowledge and because they are thought to put the interests of their clients above their personal gain. The aura of science is often attached to professionals (Gilb 1966; Larson 1977). In some professions there is general agreement among the public that licensing or other standards of competency are necessary for admittance to the field (Bradley 1965).

Training, social status, and high income aside, professionals in the United States are hostages to the market. To protect themselves, they form associations to foster and control the market for their abilities (Stabile 1984). These associations have two overriding ambitions: social acceptance for the profession from the outside world and a consensus on rules, standards, and procedures for professional activity among members (Miranti 1990).

On the eve of the Industrial Revolution there were three recognized professions in the modern sense: religious orders, lawyers, and medical doctors. These older professions, partly in the United States but especially in England, had been distinguished by special training in college or university. As such, they were reserved for the wealthy and carried the deference accorded to a high-status elite. Professions under this early view were gentlemen's pursuits (Haber 1991).

Industrialization and urbanization created centers of population where a professional could find many clients, while the spread of business methods and factory life created a need for professional services, especially those of lawyers and doctors. In the United States, with its far-flung borders and democratic society, entrance into a profession was unobstructed by social mores, and from 1830 to 1850 professions lost much of their station; many professionals avoided higher learning and went directly to work, learning on the job as an apprentice. The state licensing requirements for law and medicine were eased (Haber 1991).

In an effort to reduce the number of professionals and to improve their quality, leaders in several specialties promoted the growth of professional associations in the second half of the nineteenth century. In the United States eleven major professional associations, mainly in medicine and law, were formed between 1840 and 1887 (Larson 1977). The spread of professional associations was abetted by the Supreme Court. In *Dent v. West Virginia* the Court held that no one could practice a profession unless qualified as judged by an expert authority, which often wound up being the professional association (Haber 1991). Growth was also aided by rapid change in telephone communication, as the number of telephones in operation increased from 3,000 in 1870 to 1.3 million by 1900 (Bledstein 1976).

The advance of professionalism correlated with changes in the system of higher education. The number of colleges and universities increased from 563 in 1870, to 977 in 1900, to 1,907 in 1930; student enrollments kept pace with 52,000 in 1870, 238,000 in 1900, and 1.1 million in 1930. Harvard instituted its first graduate programs in 1872, and the number of schools of medicine expanded by 119 from 1850 to 1900, with law schools rising by 74 in the same period. Other professional schools kept pace (Bledstein 1976).

The second industrial revolution, which began in the United States in 1890, brought mass production manufacturing and large, integrated national firms. To control and administer these firms and the modern technology they employed, their operators employed large numbers of professionals—the steel industry, for example, discovered the value of industrial chemists for manufacturing top-quality steel (Chandler 1959, 1962, 1977, 1990; Steeples and Whitten 1998; Whitten 1983). The number of professionals increased fourfold from 1880 to 1930, and the number employed directly by business tripled between 1910 and 1930. These trends accompanied a split between independent professionals who were self-employed and those who were employed in the private sector: private sector professionals must often put their standards and aspirations against the profit requirements of their employers (Stabile 1984). Professional association was viewed as a solution to the conflict.

Professionals looked to their associations to limit the numbers of practitioners and require quality standards that would be enforced by peer members of the association where possible or by the authority of the government through licensing where necessary. Educational standards were also introduced. Professional associations ensured that where government sanctioning was needed, their members served on the appropriate licensing board or educational governance body. In this way the professional association distinguished the profession from the rest of the working world and delineated the position of the professional in society. They also set what, with few exceptions, remains the golden rule of the self-employed professional: "Thou shalt not compete unduly with thy fellow professionals" (Gilb 1966).

Medical and Health Organizations

The principal medical organization in the United States, the American Medical Association (AMA), was formed in 1846—through the efforts of Nathan Smith Davis, the driving force for the organization for many years—and held its first meeting in Philadelphia in May 1847 (it was initially called the National Medical Association) (King 1984). Medical societies had existed in the United States since 1735, when the first one was formed in Boston, but they had remained organized as state or county societies (Seavoy 1982). The organizing meeting of the AMA, which had eighty delegates, set forth conditions typical of modern professional associations. It proposed that medical schools should adopt high and uniform standards for the M.D. degree and that medical students be required to have a broad education before entering medical school. It also proposed a uniform code of ethics for the entire medical profession. The Preamble to that code stated clearly, "By union alone can medical men hope to sustain the dignity and extend the usefulness of their profession" (King 1984). Founders of the AMA recognized from the start the importance of a strong organization to further the interests of its members. The organization was to be built from the local level; delegates to the AMA were required to be members of their local society (Fishbein 1947).

The formation of the AMA centered around two ongoing struggles: members of the AMA, who characterized themselves as practitioners of regular medicine, were engaged in a dispute with practitioners of homeopathic medicine; a variety of medical schools had been established, including many designed mainly for profit, and these were turning out a large number of practitioners. The AMA's Committee on Education determined that there was an oversupply of doctors, which led to quackery, and that higher educational standards were needed (Fishbein 1947).

Along with the expansion of the affluent middle class came increased demand for medical services. In England there was a medieval tradition that granted monopoly in medical training to the British Royal College of Physicians. In the United States there was no such legal monopoly. The regulation of physicians was left to the individual states. The New York license criteria in 1797, for example, required only certification from other physicians as to a candidate's education and qualifications. Medical training consisted of an apprenticeship with a physician, perhaps supplemented by a brief period of formal schooling; there were only three medical schools in the United States in 1797 (King 1984).

To meet the demand for physicians, for-profit medical schools of varying degrees of competence opened, many with minimal entrance requirements and a course of study so easy it could be completed in less than a year. State chartering of these schools was lax (King 1984). Many of these schools specialized in homeopathic medicine, which at the time had curative powers on par with the primitive methods of the regular physicians (Larson 1977). Homeopathy treated disease by using medicines that would create the symptoms of fever in a person who was ill, on the theory that the induced fever would cure just as a fever cured illnesses where it naturally occurred. Practitioners of this approach had formed their own association, the American Institute of Homeopathy, in 1844 (King 1984).

To combat lax medical schools, the AMA tried to get them to raise their standards. For most of the nineteenth century, a license to practice medicine in most states was granted on certification of any medical degree; during the 1840s in New York, licensing was available, but it had ceased to be a requirement for the practice of medicine (King 1984). In the 1870s local medical societies began pushing for examination standards for state licensing, and by 1900 all states had them (Haber 1991).

In its fight against homeopathy, the AMA informed the public about the duties of the medical profession and fostered confidence in regular physicians. It also defined the field of medicine as exclusive of homeopathic practice. Efforts to establish chairs of homeopathic medicine in state university medical schools were fought, and any local medical society that did not subscribe to the AMA's code of ethics was barred from membership. In 1878 the Michigan State Medical Society was held to be in breach of the code of ethics for electing as delegate to the AMA convention a physician who encouraged students to study homeopathy (Fishbein 1947). The fight against homeopathy would diminish after 1910, when its practitioners began a policy of compromise and accepted many points of the AMA view of medicine (Burrow 1977).

In its struggle with homeopathy and unregulated medical schools, the AMA forged a new weapon with the appearance of the *Journal of the American Medical Association* (JAMA). Conceived in 1870, the first issue of the JAMA appeared in 1883. While concerned with association matters first, it began producing articles of medical and scientific interest along with promotional items. In 1889, for example, the JAMA began pushing for better licensing policies for physicians in the United States. It also sought to regulate the medical profession by promoting a system of county medical examiners to replace the coroner system and seeking a Department of Health in the federal government (Fishbein 1947). The medical profession became increasingly important during the latter part of the nineteenth century. Membership in the AMA grew to 2,100 in 1880 (King 1984), and the number of hospitals grew from under 200 in 1873 to 4,359 in 1909 (Larson 1977).

Despite these efforts, the AMA was not successful prior to 1900 and could not speak for the entire medical profession. In that year, it had only 9,000 out of 100,000 doctors as members, and the JAMA had 15,000 subscribers. A reorganization of the association that made it more responsive to members by using local medical societies as the organizing unit was ordered and put in place under the dynamic leadership of Joseph N. McCormack. By 1910 membership was over 70,000, and the JAMA was a leading attraction for potential members (Burrow 1963). Another important feature in the transformation of the AMA was the rise to leadership of physicians who took a research-oriented approach to medicine; their apparent success in making their research findings available brought a flood of small-town, general practitioners to the AMA. In 1940 nearly 120,000 physicians belonged to the AMA, 67 percent of all physicians (Gilb 1966). Physician membership reached 209,931 in 1980, 254,336 in 1992, and 262,321 in 1994 (www.ama-assn.org).

As its membership strengthened, the AMA stepped up its campaign against unsatisfactory medical schools by instituting a rating system. Reform of medical training had begun at Harvard in 1870 (King 1984), and the commencement of professional medical training at Johns Hopkins University School of Medicine in 1893 had set a new model for instruction (Duffy 1976). It was not uniformly followed, however. In 1907 there were 160 medical schools, of which 82 were given a rating above 70, 46 were rated between 50 and 70, and 32 fell below 70. In 1910 a rating scheme that placed medical schools in categories of A, B, or C was published in the JAMA, and the Council on Medical Education of the AMA credited the ratings with reducing the number of medical schools to 129 in 1911. A report by Abraham Flexner sponsored by the Carnegie Foundation that revealed the low quality of medical schools added to public concerns over medical education. The report reflected a bias toward the programs of the AMA Council on Medical Education (King 1984). Not all medical schools disappeared quietly. In 1923 Middlesex College of Medicine and Surgery refused entrance to AMA examiners and threatened suit if it was rated; this school continued in operation until 1945 (Fishbein 1947).

In 1910 the AMA began a system of accreditation for medical schools that gave the association a powerful weapon in its fight against unsatisfactory schools, and by 1962 only 88 medical schools (out of 444 established in total) remained in operation. By the 1930s pressure was being put on medical schools to limit their enrollments. The increase in stature of the AMA in 1910 also led to a burst of activity in forming state licensing boards between 1911 and 1915 (Gilb 1966). To overcome problems caused by the diversity of state licensing laws, in 1915 the AMA introduced its own National Board of Medical Examiners to examine and certify medical practitioners (Duffy 1976).

At the start of the twentieth century, the income of medical doctors was not exceptionally high and had not even kept pace with inflation during the preceding decades. Cries of overcrowding in the profession were made, based, in part, on over 25,000 students entering the many medical schools, which were producing about 5,000 graduates a year (Burrow 1977). The AMA's efforts to cut down on the number of graduates was successful; they declined from a peak of 5,747 in 1904 to 2,529 in 1922, and that peak was not surpassed until 1947 (Campion 1984). In addition, its leaders started drafting fee schedule guides to help physicians establish a uniform pricing scale (Burrow 1977).

While its efforts to enlist more members were successful, the AMA did not recruit all physicians. At its 1870 convention, the AMA voted 115 to 90 not to admit Afro-American physicians associated with Howard University Medical College and the Freedman's Hospital on the grounds that their National Medical Society admitted unlicensed physicians as members. The next year's convention saw an attack by the AMA president on allowing women to practice medicine. In 1876 Sarah Hackett Stevenson was the first woman member of the AMA, although her seating as a delegate caused controversy (Fishbein 1947). The AMA would not agree to separate Afro-American state medical societies, so by 1962 there was a separate National Medical Association in all fifty states (Gilb 1966).

Starting in 1916, the AMA began its long-term fight against "socialized medicine" with its participation in a debate over health insurance (Burrow 1977). In its early stages this fight took the form of opposition to government care for veterans, medical insurance, then compulsory medical insurance; in the 1930s there was AMA opposition to Social Security, while the 1940s saw its opposition to Truman's national health insurance plan; it initially fought Medicare in the 1960s (Duffy 1976). To the AMA, the underlying principle was opposition for any scheme that placed a physician on a contractual salary with no limitation on the amount of work to be done and that restricted a patient's right to choose a physician. Opposition to contract medical plans landed the AMA in legal difficulties in 1938, when antitrust charges were brought against it and the Medical Society of the District of Columbia for threatening to eject members who worked for a group health organization; the case went to the Supreme Court twice, and a guilty ruling, which resulted in small fines, was affirmed (Burrow 1963).

At every step in this fight, however, the AMA has avoided a totally disapproving attitude and has instead set forth its own alternative program (Fishbein 1947). During the 1930s it became less hostile toward voluntary health plans and after World War II became a participant in the Blue Cross and Blue Shield programs (Burrow 1963). This strategy continues through the 1990s as national health insurance and other health benefits are debated. The most feared aspect of these programs to the AMA would appear to be the loss of autonomy by the individual physician, who would either have medical practices dictated by a government bureaucracy or become an employee of the government.

Throughout the course of its existence, the AMA has followed the greater specialization of medicine by instituting separate boards for licensing and control of those specialties. The American Board of Ophthalmology, for example, was formed in 1917, and the American Board of Surgery in 1937

(Fishbein 1947). As specialization proceeded, the AMA began publishing additional journals, reaching a total of ten in 1991 (Burek 1991).

Other national medical organizations (date of formation/number of members in 1991) include American Academy of Allergy and Immunology (1943/4,100), American Society of Anesthesiologists (1905/27,000), American Association of Blood Banks (1947/10,000), American College of Cardiology (1949/17,300), American Chiropractic Association (1930/20,000), Academy of General Dentistry (1952/30,000), American Dental Association (1859/140,000), American Academy of Family Physicians (1947/66,000), American College of Healthcare Executives (1933/23,000), American Society of Internal Medicine (1956/20,000), Healthcare Financial Management Association (1946/27,000), Society of Nuclear Medicine (1954/12,200), American Nurses' Association (1896/188,000), American Academy of Ophthalmology (1896/16,000), American Academy of Optometry (1921/3,500), National Academy of Opticianry (1973/5,000), American Pharmaceutical Association (1852/40,000), American Psychiatric Association (1844/36,000), American Psychological Association (1892/70,000).

Bar Associations

Although one of the original professions, law has not always been considered the noblest. Building on an English tradition, the colonists in America were slow to recognize lawyers as persons of influence. This attitude followed the sentiment expressed by an unidentified author in England in 1677: "There was law before lawyers; there was a time when the Common Customs of the land were sufficient to secure Meum and Tuum." Seventeenth-century lawyers were still enmeshed with the rigidities of the feudal system and often enforced unpopular elements of the common law; early colonies specifically abjured any notion that the common law held in the New World (Warren [1911] 1980). The story of the legal profession and its associations is concerned with efforts of the practitioners of law to overturn this social attitude. To be sure, it is an ambivalent attitude. Americans have rarely given their complete trust to their attorneys (Bloomfield 1976), even as they hire them in numbers.

Many lawyers in the colonies were not formally educated but were merchants or traders who used the law to settle commercial disputes or to serve the needs of colonial rulers. The first recorded lawyer in Maryland, John Lewger, appears as counsel for the Lord Proprietor of the Colony in 1637; he was succeeded in his post in the 1640s by Mistress Margaret Brent of St. Mary's City, America's first female lawyer. When colleges were founded in the colonies, however, individuals began using their general education as a background for the study of law (Warren [1911] 1980). In New York in 1767, a person with a college degree had to serve a three-year apprenticeship at a law office, while others served seven years. A greater reliance on the common law to resolve disputes took place as the colonies moved away from the simple charters or proprietor's domination that marked their original settlement. In the period just prior to the Revolutionary War, lawyers became essential to defend against the rulings of the Crown, and their skill and prestige heightened. At the same time, the colonists sought to resolve conflict by obligatory arbitration and hindered professional lawyers by permitting nonattorneys to represent friends or relatives in court (Bloomfield 1976).

Several colonies began requiring licenses to practice law, with Virginia's statute of 1748 being typical. Bar associations were formed during this period to distinguish between the skilled lawyer and the hack. The Bar of New York was in existence by 1748, making it the earliest; the Bar Association of Boston was formed in 1770. The New York association fought the Stamp Act but vanished in 1770, and little is known about it. The Boston association tried to raise the standards of the profession by requiring a college education and an examination before entering legal training. At this time and for most of the next century, legal training consisted of a period of study under the tutelage of a member of the bar (Warren [1911] 1980).

The legal profession gained another boost in prestige and influence during the Revolutionary War and constitutional period, due to the impressive contributions made by leaders of those actions who were also lawyers. About half the signers of the Declaration of Independence and the Framers of the Constitution were lawyers, including Thomas Jefferson, James Madison, and Alexander Hamilton. A bar association was formed in Hartford County, Connecticut, in 1783, and the first professors of law in American colleges date from this period. The Litchfield Law School, an unaffiliated legal training institute, served 805 students during its operation from 1784 to 1833 (Warren [1911] 1980).

Still, there was concern that lawyers were gaining too much influence. In the early years of the United States, many of its citizens held strongly to democratic values, which saw laws as designed to protect a wealthy oligarchy. As part of the legal system and as framers of law, lawyers could readily be considered as opponents of revolutionary fervor, obstructing the installation of a true democracy. Some antilawyer elements, recognizing that expertise in lawmaking was essential to democracy, wanted to make all lawyers employees of the government to reduce the apparent conflict of those who wrote the laws they then profited from (Bloomfield 1976).

For the ensuing century, the prestige and influence of lawyers remained ambiguous. In the federal courts, the first half of the nineteenth century saw many landmark court decisions as the new Constitution was interpreted and made practical, and the lawyers arguing those cases—Daniel Webster and Henry Clay, for example—became justly prominent. Because lawyers at the local level dealt with unpopular property and tax law, the status of the profession did not prosper. Moreover, membership in the bar was not always required to plead cases in state and local courts (Warren [1911] 1980). In an effort to reduce public dependence on attorneys, the law was codified—the common and other law was formally adopted and written down in terms nonlawyers could understand (Haber 1991).

Legal associations dwindled, and bar associations were rare. In Massachusetts, which had the strongest bar associations—mainly social clubs—attempts to start a state bar association faltered. Requirements for membership in the bar, usually set and administered by state courts (Bloomfield 1976), were meager—by 1840 only eleven of thirty states had any training requisites, and in 1860 only nine of the thirty-nine states mandated any education (Matzko 1984).

As industrialization proceeded in the United States, prospects for the legal profession kept pace. The first corporate clients were railroads, which required a collection of legal talent to settle all the property, financial, and other legal issues connected with building and operating their systems. The burst of economic activity that followed the Civil War added to the demand for lawyers acquainted with corporate law. The American Legal Association was established in 1849, but it lasted only five years. Law journals, a sign of professionalism, increased from one in 1810, to ten in 1850, and seventeen in 1870 (Bloomfield 1976).

The Association of the Bar of the City of New York was founded in 1870, and by 1878 there were seven city and eight state bar associations scattered over twelve states. By 1900 half the states would have such organizations (Matzko 1984). The number of bar associations grew from 16 in 1880 to 600 in 1916 (Galambos 1983) as responsibility for examining prospective members of the bar shifted from state supreme courts to bar associations (Larson 1977).

The American Bar Association (ABA) was founded on August 21, 1878, in Saratoga, New York. The prime mover in the ABA was Simeon E. Baldwin (1840–1927), a lawyer and later Connecticut supreme court justice and governor; Baldwin was an advocate of professional associations and eventually served as president of the ABA, the American Historical Association, the American Social Science Association, the International Law Association, the American Political Science Association, and the Association of American Law Schools. Like most of the lawyers who formed the ABA, he was college-educated; he was professor of law at Yale for much of his career (Matzko 1984). Membership in the ABA was open to any five-year veteran of any state bar. Governance of the association was placed in the hands of a five-person executive committee (Sunderland 1953).

The constitution of the ABA listed as among its purposes "to advance the science of jurisprudence" and "uphold the honor of the profession of the law." Both of these purposes indicated a presumption toward higher educational standards for lawyers (Matzko 1984). There was also concern that lawyers who worked for corporations or were employed by large firms in corporate law were behaving more as hired hands than as professionals with clients (Hobson 1984). In its early years the ABA functioned as a social club, with its annual meetings continually held in the resort town of Saratoga Springs, New York. The membership grew slowly, reaching 750 in the first decade and about 1,500 at the turn of the century (Sunderland 1953).

During the ABA's first fifty years the legal profession underwent major changes. The growth of industry created a heightened demand for the services of corporate and business lawyers. At the same time, urbanization brought increasing crime rates and a new place for criminal law. Modern society also saw wider scope for civil law as accidents, negligence, and other torts became common. As a result, the legal profession stratified, with an elite of college-educated lawyers serving in corporations, government, and the judiciary and several layers of urban practitioners and country lawyers. The elite led the formation of bar associations in major cities and by 1910 were a major influence in the ABA. Country lawyers remained in charge of county and state bar associations and indifferent to the ABA (Auerbach 1976).

The leaders of the ABA took measures to unify the profession. In 1909 they established a membership committee to recruit lawyers, and membership tripled between 1909 and 1916 and doubled again by 1924. Steps were also taken to bring local bar associations into closer affiliation with the ABA. A subsidiary grouping of bar association delegates was started in 1916. In 1936 the ABA reorganized as a federation of local membership organizations, with governance vested in a house of delegates who represented a leading professional legal society (Sunderland 1953).

A vital issue among leaders of the ABA was the education of lawyers. Early law schools had been established at Harvard (1817) and Yale (1843), and individual law schools existed in most major cities (Warren [1911] 1980). In the last half of the nineteenth century, Harvard Law School became the standard in legal education—beginning in 1896 Harvard Law School required an undergraduate degree for admission. Around the country the number of law schools was increasing: 28 schools (1,600 students) in 1870; 100 schools (13,000 students) in 1900. Ten schools in 1890 offered evening programs for part-time students; the number had increased to 45 by 1910. In 1870, one-fourth of those admitted to the bar were law school graduates; by 1910, two-thirds.

Law school training was not homogeneous—night schools, for example, rarely required a college degree for admission. Leaders of the ABA expressed concern that these lax educational standards were hurting the professional standing of attorneys. To elevate educational standards, in 1900 the ABA organized the Association of American Law Schools (AALS), which began promoting educational selectiveness. In 1907 membership in AALS was limited to law schools with three-year programs; in 1912, primarily to day schools; by 1916 schools affiliated with AALS accounted for only 40 percent of law students (Larson 1977). These efforts were opposed by the night schools and by country lawyers who considered Abraham Lincoln the epitome of the self-educated lawyer.

Encouraged by the benefits of the Flexner report for the AMA, the ABA asked the Carnegie Foundation for a similar study of legal education: Alfred Z. Reed's *Training for the Public Profession of the Law* ([1921] 1986) had little impact—Reed's study did not have the effect on night schools that Flexner's had on proprietary medical schools (Auerbach 1976). Most lawyers believed academic training a poor substitute for practical instruction as an apprentice in a law office. Even the ABA stipulated merely a high school diploma as a condition of membership until 1921 and opposed the notion of "diploma privilege," which gave law school graduates immediate membership in the bar (Larson 1977). In the early 1920s, fifteen states had no educational requirements for admittance to the bar, and none subscribed to the ABA's recommendation of two years of college and a three-year law program (Auerbach 1976).

By the 1920s, however, the ABA and AALS agreed on the need for upgrading formal education requirements for lawyers and tried to eliminate night schools. An ABA Council on Legal Education gained the accrediting authority for law schools and started the profession on the path that has led to the law school's being the locus of training for all members of the profession (Larson 1977). Law school enrollments grew by 80 percent from 1919 to 1927 (Auerbach 1976).

In addition to protecting the legal profession's status, the ABA sought political influence. It opposed the nomination of Louis Dembitz Brandeis to the Supreme Court in 1916 (Auerbach 1976). It had previously formed a section on judicial affairs in 1913, and in 1939 this section was expanded into a Committee on Judicial Selection and Tenure. It also had a Conference of State Boards of Law Examiners, formed in 1898, with which it tried to foster standardization of state bar exams. A professional code of ethics was implemented in 1905 (Sunderland 1953) and revised in 1969 (Auerbach 1976). As part of attaining professional status, the ABA promoted the high standing of judges as the pinnacle of law. It campaigned for judicial recall in the early 1900s as a way of maintaining the integrity of judges and opposed Roosevelt's court-packing plan of the 1930s (Botein 1983).

Professionalization of law spurred ABA membership. Starting with 289 members in 1878, it grew slowly to 1,540 members in 1900 (1.4 percent of all lawyers); by 1910 it had 3,690 members (3.2 percent), increasing to 11,311 members (9.2 percent) in 1920. In the next decade, after its professional and educational reforms, the ABA had, in 1930, 28,667 members, nearly doubling its percentage of all lawyers to 17.8 percent (Sunderland 1953). By the 1960s it had over 100,000 members or nearly half of all lawyers (Auerbach 1976). In 1991, the ABA operated from headquarters in Chicago with 360,000 members, a staff of 750, and an annual budget of $50 million. It had twenty affiliated groups and published numerous journals (Burek 1991).

The ABA has not been as successful as the AMA. It has exerted influence over educational requirements and examinations for admittance to the bar but has not been effective in eliminating night schools catering to part-time students. As a result the number of lawyers in the United States continues to rise at rates surpassing those of physicians, with estimates of over 1 million lawyers by the end of the twentieth century. Lawyers have not gained the social status accorded physicians. ABA recommendations on Supreme Court nominations are not determinate, and public attacks on the legal profession are common. Although the ABA has elevated the status of the legal profession above its colonial origins, sensational events like the "monkey trial" at the beginning of the twentieth century and the O. J. Simpson affair at the end have kept lawyers in the social dunking chair despite the efforts of professional associations.

Engineering Societies

Engineering is tied to business because engineers, trained in science, are often the most likely to adapt technical knowledge to the production of marketable goods. Engineering societies help members balance the quest for knowledge with the attraction of profits.

Civil engineers worked on early American public works projects—military engineers worked on military projects. Although waterworks, bridges, roads, and public buildings employed U.S. civil engineers in the late eighteenth century, the nineteenth century gave civil engineers the challenges of canals and railroads. Most civil engineers received on-the-job training; those with academic training were mainly graduates of the U.S. Military Academy, military engineers entering civilian life, with a few being trained at fledgling engineering schools such as Rensselaer Polytechnic Institute, founded in 1824 (Calhoun 1960).

By 1840 civil engineering had become a settled occupation, which first attained official notice in the 1850 census with a count of 2,000 civil engineers (Layton 1986). The impetus for growth came from the railroads, which required civil engineers for construction of rail lines and fostered a need for development of methods for designing and building iron and steel bridges (Wisely 1974). As with most professional groups, civil engineering started to organize. While the Franklin Institute, founded in 1824, may be accorded the honors as the first engineering society, civil engineers soon became concerned with their own organization. In 1838 an attempt was made to form an Institution of Civil Engineers as an adjunct to the Franklin Institute, but apathy among wide-flung civil engineers scuttled it. The Boston Society of Civil Engineers lasted from 1848 to 1860, while the American Society of Civil Engineers, a local group in New York City, operated during 1852–1855. Finally, in 1867 a lasting national organization, the American Society of Civil Engineers (ASCE), was instituted (Calhoun 1960). It retained a narrow, elite view of itself, holding to very high standards of membership into the next century (Layton 1986).

Civil engineering included all aspects of engineering, even mechanical— railroad engineers not only built the roads and maintained the locomotives, but were employed to operate their creations for the owners (Chandler 1977). Eventually, the profession began to split into specialized fields. The American Institute of Mining Engineers (AIME) was created in 1871, partly in response to the high level of professionalism in ASCE; AIME admitted anyone who worked in mining, metallurgy, or metallurgical engineering. Nevertheless, its founders were concerned with professionalism and wanted a scientific approach attached to mining (Layton 1986).

The next group to split off was the mechanical engineers, who formed the American Society of Mechanical Engineers (ASME) in 1880; thirty important engineers took the lead, and the initial membership was 100 (Sinclair 1980). Mechanical engineers held a special place in industry and business. They designed and implemented industrial machinery that drove the mass-production industries of the late nineteenth century. Many mechanical engineers were owners of manufacturing plants or headed shops where machine tools were made. They were businessmen with practical training who saw ASME as a business club.

Colleges also trained mechanical engineers. Yale introduced courses in industrial mechanics in 1859, and the U.S. Naval Academy, to produce officers knowledgeable about steamships, set up a mechanical engineering program in the late 1860s; the passage of the Morrill Act of 1862 (also known as the College Land Grant Act of 1862) spurred the growth of public universities with mechanical engineering programs during 1868–1872. Most of the college-trained engineers went to work as salaried professionals in industry and looked to ASME to blend scientific and business interests (Calvert 1967).

Frederick W. Taylor, the father of scientific management, was a transitional figure between practical engineering and college engineering. From a wealthy family, Taylor used family contacts to get apprenticeship training in a machine shop but eventually took a college degree. Although employed at a number of manufacturing firms, Taylor developed his ideas independently (Stabile 1984). The founders of ASME set it up as an elite group, with an oligarchic council determining who could become members. In 1907 membership reached 2,957, about half being shop-trained. Elitism gave ASME financial problems. In 1906 Taylor was made president, and a group of his followers in the efficiency expert movement began reorganizing ASME on a more efficient basis. By 1910 local affiliates of ASME were being promoted (Sinclair 1980).

Electrical engineers started out as a division of ASME but in 1884 broke away as the American Institute of Electrical Engineers (AIEE). The membership organization of AIEE was less hierarchical than the ASME's, and more of its members were college-trained. They were employed in industry; most of them worked for either General Electric or Westinghouse (Calvert 1967). Nevertheless, AIEE required high professional experience on the part of its members (Layton 1986).

Professionalization created conflict in AIEE because many members were job-trained practitioners from the telegraph industry. Early officers of the organization included such practical thinkers as Thomas Edison and Alexander Graham Bell. As a result, a category of associate members was established for those not meeting regular standards. Electing as president of the AIEE engineers with a background in theoretical physics, such as Charles Steinmetz in 1901, emphasized high standards for membership and led to a uniform curriculum in education and adoption in 1912 of a code of ethics (McMahon 1984).

In 1912 a band of engineers in the new field of radio formed the Institute of Radio Engineers (IRE). As the electronics industry grew, IRE membership outstripped the AIEE. To strengthen both organizations and promote unity in the profession, the two merged in 1963 to form the Institute of Electrical and Electronic Engineers (McMahon 1984).

The four main engineering societies, ASCE, AIME, ASME, and AIEE, dominated the profession but did not have an open field. Smaller groups separated: American Electrochemical Society (1902), the Society of Automotive Engineers (1904), and the American Institute of Chemical Engineers (1908). The last named, abbreviated AIChE, has a special background. The chemical industry in the United States developed slowly. Much of the responsibility for the manufacturing process in industry fell to mechanical engineers. To avoid competing with chemists, who were longtime members of the American Chemical Society (formed in 1876), the AIChE restricted its membership to engineers; it grew slowly from forty charter members, to 344 members in 1920 and 872 in 1930. It relaxed the engineering requirement in the 1930s, and membership grew to 2,255 by 1940. Eventually, it was accorded status on par with the four founder societies (Reynolds 1983). In 1991 it had 55,000 members (Burek 1991).

Unification of engineering groups into a national conglomeration was an unfulfilled dream. As early as 1886 a proposal for an Academy of Engineering was made. In 1903 Andrew Carnegie gave the four main societies the money to build a common headquarters building in New York City, which was completed in 1906. The ASCE remained apart from the others, however, so all that came of the building was a joint tenancy. In the early

1920s, through the efforts of Herbert Hoover, in his guise as a prominent mining engineer and master organizer of associations, a Federation of Associated Engineering Societies was formed as part of the American Engineering Council. The federation soon disappeared, and the council disbanded in 1940 (Layton 1986).

Engineers gloried in their role as the purveyors of modern industrial civilization based on mass production; between 1880 and 1920 the number of engineers grew from 7,000 to 136,000 and reached 800,000 by 1960 (Layton 1986). As that civilization evolved, however, social critics observed that it was a mixed blessing. This attitude became especially strong in the United States with a Progressive Era that challenged large corporations during the 1900–1920 period. Engineers, seeking a bigger role for themselves in public policy, became part of this progressive movement (Stabile 1984). ASCE became concerned with conservation of resources, AIEE took up the cause of forest preservation, and some members of ASME began fighting the electric utility industry on issues of air pollution and pricing of services (Layton 1986). Despite these efforts, engineers as employees of large corporations were tainted in their efforts to serve as unbiased experts in service to society—witness the support of ASME for nuclear power in the 1970s (Sinclair 1980).

All of these efforts aimed at enhancing the prestige and influence of the engineering profession. In keeping with these efforts, all of the separate societies adopted codes of ethics and started setting standard practices and product specifications, such as the ASME boiler codes started in 1914 (Layton 1986). Much later this setting of standards would create antitrust problems for the ASME, when in the early 1980s the legal battle of *American Society of Mechanical Engineers, Inc. v. Hydrolevel Corp.* held that the ASME's determination that a firm's product did not meet its standard was unlawful (Sinclair 1980).

The Society for the Promotion of Engineering Education was formed in 1893 to help standardize the education of engineers; by the 1920s, with the help of the Carnegie Foundation, it had established curriculum guidelines, but no form of accreditation was established at a national level. During the 1920s a National Council of State Boards of Engineering Examiners started developing standards for professional licenses for engineers. The National Society of Professional Engineers was created in 1934 as a membership group for licensed engineers; its participants in 1959 were 43 percent civil engineers, 24 percent mechanical engineers, and 18 percent electrical engineers, not a very broad base of support and not corresponding to the national proportions of the profession. With their failure to attain national unity in membership or on other professional issues, engineers settled into a pattern of separate societies that has existed ever since, without attaining anything approaching the professional status of the AMA or the ABA (Calvert 1972).

In 1991 the original four engineering societies were still headquartered in the same building in New York City. The ASCE had 108,000 members, a staff of 166, and an annual budget of $17 million. The AIME had changed its name to the American Institute of Mining, Metallurgical and Petroleum Engineers and served as a transcendent group for members of the Society of Mining Engineers, the Metallurgical Society, the Iron and Steel Society, and the Society of Petroleum Engineers. ASME had nearly 120,000 members, and a staff of 320 and published twenty different journals. AIEE after its 1963 merger with IRE operated as the Institute of Electrical and Electronic Engineers and had 274,000 members and a staff of 500. The latest umbrella organization, the American Association of Engineering Societies, founded in 1979, had headquarters in Washington, twenty-two member societies, a staff of thirteen, and an annual budget of $1.5 million (Burek 1991). Other engineering societies (date founded/members in 1991) include American Association of Engineering Societies (1979/ 22), SPIE-The International Society for Optical Engineers (1955/10,500), Society of Petroleum Engineers (1922/51,000), ASM International (Metallurgy) (1922/54,000), American Society of Heating, Refrigerating and Air Conditioning Engineers (1894/55,000), Institute of Industrial Engineers (1948/42,000), Society of Manufacturing Engineers (1932/80,000), American Academy of Environmental Engineers (1955/2,400), SAE (Automotive) (1905/50,000), American Institute of Chemical Engineers (1908/ 55,000).

Scientific and Educational Societies

The rise of professional associations of scientists, scholars, and educators paralleled the flowering of institutions of higher learning in the United States in the second half of the nineteenth century. Prior to the Civil War, higher education was the province of small colleges—often of religious affiliation—that dotted the countryside. Harvard started an era of transformation in 1869, when it introduced elective courses; other institutions followed by the end of the century. The initiation of choice in course work by students required a broader diversity of specialized courses and permitted a similar specialization by faculty (Oleson and Voss 1979).

This period also saw the growth of universities as the site of graduate training. Previously, professors had been selected as knowledgeable advocates of the classics and the moral verities of the day. By the end of the century, the Ph.D. degree in a specialized discipline would become an accepted requisite for faculty status (Higham 1979). The first Ph.D. awarded in the United States was at Yale in 1869; the founding of Johns Hopkins University as a center for graduate education hastened the pace, and by 1900 Harvard, Columbia, and Chicago had attained prominence for their graduate programs (Hawkins 1979). Both these trends toward specialization resulted in colleges and universities that were divided into discipline-oriented departments, with the advanced degree serving as the only common denominator of those disciplines. The amateur scholar or scientist was replaced by the professional.

The evolution of professional societies in these disciplines followed a similar pattern. In the social sciences, for example, the American Social Science Association was formed in 1865 as an all-encompassing grouping for disciplines in the social sciences; its leaders stressed the interrelatedness of those disciplines rather than their distinctiveness. Over the next four decades, however, this organization went against the trends of professionalism based on unique authority accorded to specialists, and it ended in 1909 (Haskell 1977).

Of the branches of the social sciences, economics was the first to organize, and its society, the American Economic Association (AEA), has features in its motivation that shed light on problems faced by many academic disciplines. At the time of the formation of the AEA in 1885, economics was divided into two schools. An older school had been brought into teaching on the traditional path of profession of the accepted truths of the day, which in economics at the time centered on laissez-faire. The new school had been given doctoral training in Germany under the sway of a German Historical School with an emphasis on research. The research undertaken by the new school led to conclusions contrary to the received wisdom of laissez-faire.

The leader of this school, Richard T. Ely, pushed for the formation of the AEA as an organization of researchers and reformers with the potential for excluding members of the old school. Ely wanted to define professionalism in his own image and to use the AEA to promote it. In its formation, however, Ely and the AEA compromised on their terms to cast a wide membership net. The initial platform of the AEA favored by Ely went too far for many economists in its concerns with the unwholesome aspects of competition, and key members of the profession refused to join. For a time Ely was countered as a leader by more moderate members of the AEA and replaced as its secretary; by 1888 the membership voted to disdain any statement of general principles for the association. Thereafter, it became a more powerful voice for the discipline (Furner 1975).

A powerful voice was needed. In the 1890s faculty were threatened with dismissals that raised the issue of academic freedom. This troubling issue came from the professional research orientation of academics, especially in the social sciences. As scholarly research came to contradict the established verities previously handed down to students, nonprofessionals connected with colleges and universities became concerned that professors were undermining the pillars of society. Ely was one such victim of this attitude, and his experience may have led to his moderating his reformist position;

he went on to a successful, long career at the University of Wisconsin and a term as president of the AEA (Furner 1975).

The most celebrated academic freedom case addressed the firing of E. A. Ross from Stanford University after his comments on economics displeased the widow of Stanford's benefactor. As a former officer of the AEA and a respected scholar, Ross earned the sympathy of AEA members. Faculty at Stanford who could feasibly do so resigned in protest, and members of the AEA attempted to keep Stanford from filling those positions. An AEA committee was formed to investigate the case, but authorities at Stanford would not participate. The committee issued a report establishing Ross' competence as an economist and had fifteen prominent economists sign it. Although the effort failed to save Ross' job, it did much to eliminate the divisions that had marked the AEA at its formation and took the first step in the process that led to specialists being the only source for accreditation as professionals. By the 1890s the economists of the AEA had developed a strong sense of identity as a profession (Furner 1975). With 26,000 members in 1991 (Burek 1991), the AEA remains the largest and most influential body of professional economists.

Following in the path of the AEA, the American Political Science Association was formed in 1903; in 1991 it had 12,000 members. The American Anthropological Association (10,000 members in 1991) was founded in 1902, while the American Sociological Association was founded in 1905 (Burek 1991). An overall organization, the Social Sciences Research Council, was established in 1923 (Ross 1979).

Individuals affiliated with the natural sciences had formed one of the older scientific societies, the American Association for the Advancement of Science, in 1848 (Ross 1979). It served all scientists through the 1890s, when a rapid growth in doctorates in separate sciences resulted in the establishment of individual societies: the American Chemical Society in 1876 (as a local association made national in 1891), the American Mathematical Society in 1894, and the American Physical Society in 1891 (Kevles 1979). The growth of large corporations and their research and development divisions (Galambos 1979) gave scientific professional organizations a clientele outside academe—the American Chemical Society, for example, in 1991 had 138,000 members and a staff of 1,700 (Burek 1991).

Although the American Philosophical Society had been founded in 1743 with Benjamin Franklin as a founding member, the first truly professional associations in the humanities date from the 1880s. The Modern Language Association was inaugurated in 1883 to gain greater acceptability for the teaching of English, French, and German in place of classical Latin and Greek. The American Historical Association had its beginnings in 1884, mainly as a meeting ground between professional and amateur historians. In 1895 J. Franklin Jameson led a rebellion of academics that began moving the association in their direction, but it would be years before they would dominate it (Veysey 1979). It had 13,000 members in 1991 (Burek 1991).

Despite the organization of societies among academics, college professors remained in uneasy economic circumstances. As the disciplines separated, and the universities grew in size, faculty became more associated with hierarchical, fragmented institutions. Initially, they had filled administrative posts, but the organizational trends placed more power in the hands of the president of the institution, who mediated between faculty and governing boards; these leaders also came to place more of the responsibility for running the institution in the hands of professional administrators.

Faced with this environment as well as the still-unresolved issue of academic freedom, in 1915 academics formed the American Association of University Professors (AAUP) with 867 charter members. Its purpose was to strengthen the affiliations among its members and to have a direct impact on the relations between professors and their institutions. It especially aimed at setting standards for academic freedom and enforcing them through sanctions; during the years 1940–1977 it imposed sanctions against 119 university administrations. In 1972 there were 97,102 members of the AAUP. In that year its members voted to take on collective bargaining as part of its program—many members were alienated by the decision (Wilson 1979). By 1991 there were 50,000 members of the AAUP, which operated from headquarters in Washington with a staff of thirty-five and an annual budget of $2.8 million (Burek 1991).

Public school teachers are represented by the National Education Association (NEA), started in 1857 as the National Teachers Association, with the current name adopted in 1870. Earlier teachers' associations had been attempted, starting with the American Institute of Instructors in 1830, but none had survived. The NEA was the result of efforts by leaders of ten state teachers' associations to form a national group. Although the organization tried to improve employment conditions for teachers, the main efforts during its first half century were for educational reform and the promotion of higher educational requirements. When a study in 1905 revealed the low pay accorded to teachers, the emphasis shifted toward securing better salaries, academic freedom, tenure, and other employment practices beneficial to teachers. Membership grew from 10,000 in 1918, to 220,000 by 1931 and reached 700,000 in 1957 (Wesley 1957). In addition to serving the professional interests of teachers and lobbying for the cause of education, the NEA is a collective bargaining organization at all levels of education, including colleges and universities. In 1991 it had 1.6 million members, headquarters in Washington, a staff of 600, and an annual budget of $75 million (Burek 1991).

In service to all professions, librarianship also evolved as a profession. The American Library Association (ALA) was formally established as an organization in 1876, after over twenty years of conventions of librarians.

Prominent among its early members was Melvil Dewey, a library entrepreneur and originator of the book classification scheme that bears his name. Dewey also served as editor of the independent *American Library Journal*, which he used to promote the ALA. The ALA took as its charge to make quality books available to the public at low cost (Wiegand 1986). In its early years it had fewer than 500 members and only organized annual conferences. In the early 1900s it settled on a permanent headquarters and staff and began publishing its first journal, and membership began to expand. In addition to its professional services, ALA has often led the fight against censorship of books (Thomison 1978). In 1991 it had 49,483 members, headquarters in Chicago with a staff of 260, and an annual budget of $25 million.

Other scientific and educational organizations (year founded/membership in 1991) include American Accounting Association (1916/12,000), American Finance Association (1940/7,000), American Institute of Aeronautics and Astronautics (1963/42,000), Archaeological Institute of America (1879/7,500), American Society for Microbiology (1899/35,000), Flat Earth Research Society International (1800/2,800), American Geophysical Union (1919/32,000), Geological Society of America (1888/16,000), American Meteorological Society (1919/11,000), American Council on Education (1918/1,700), National Association of Elementary School Principals (1921/25,000), National Association of Secondary School Principals (1916/40,000), American Philological Association (1869/3,000), American Fisheries Society (1870/8,500), National Research Council (1916/9,500), American Institute of Architects (1857/54,000).

Business-Oriented Professionals

The rise of the large corporation in the beginning of this century brought with it the need for exacting standards of administration. At the same time, as these corporations began selling their stocks and bonds to the public, that public began demanding better information about the finances of the corporations. Both these trends created a need for business-oriented professionals to serve as internal managers and controllers of a firm's operations and as outside evaluators of a firm's performance. University programs of business at both undergraduate and graduate levels were developed in the first two decades of the twentieth century to meet the demand for professional business managers, controllers, and evaluators. Even with authoritative training, however, these business-oriented professionals found it necessary to form societies and institutes to further their interests and status.

Owing to its special nature, the field of public accounting provides a distinctive case of business professionalism. Accounting is among the oldest of occupations, as records of business dealing have been maintained since antiquity, and the development of the double-entry bookkeeping system has often been credited as a key factor in the development of capitalism. Under that system there came about a division of labor between the inside accountant who set up and monitored the books and the outside auditor who verified their accuracy, usually to the owner of the firm. The first recorded accounting audit took place with the books of the company involved with the South Sea Bubble of the eighteenth century (Chenok 1989).

As more firms in the United States became publicly owned at the end of the nineteenth century, this outside auditing function became unusually critical. Investors need assurances about the accuracy of financial statements. Outside auditors commonly operated as public accountants, with their services available to whoever hired them. Usually the hiring was done by management. Nevertheless, public accountants had to remain independent if their work was to carry authority with the public. This quest for independence and authority was the main feature in the formation of accounting associations.

The first, the American Association of Public Accountants (AAPA), was formed in 1886; its early membership was colored by British and Scottish accountants both in the United States and in the United Kingdom who served many investors overseas with money in American securities. It was soon rivaled by the New York Institute of Accountants, later the New York Society of Certified Public Accountants (NYSCPA); New York City, as a center of finance, made the NYSCPA a prominent group. Members of the New York group took the lead in efforts to make accounting a science, a claim the AAPA initially debunked. The two associations tried to cooperate in forming state licensing laws for public accounting, but their differences were not easily overcome. The first such law, enacted in New York in 1896, was mainly the work of the NYSCPA. By 1905 licensing laws had been passed in nine states through the efforts of accounting societies in those states (Miranti 1990).

In 1902 the state societies established the Federation of State Societies of Public Accountants in the United States, but it foundered from a reluctance of the AAPA and NYSCPA to consolidate with it. In 1905 an accord was reached whereby the AAPA absorbed the federation and become a national organization, leaving the NYSCPA as sole agent for New York accountants. The AAPA also took over publication of the *Journal of Accountancy* (Miranti 1990).

To keep its professional standing, for the next quarter century the AAPA worked to secure better educational requirements for public accountants and resisted efforts to use government regulations of accounting standards in place of the independent expertise of the public accountant. To enhance that status, the AAPA in 1916 reorganized into a stronger central instrument for accounting professionals and changed its name to the American Institute of Accountants (AIA); it began pushing for its own standards and qualifying examinations as a way of certifying public accountants. Many states adopted them by the early 1920s. This effort to have membership in the AIA supplant state licensing proved too much for many state societies, so in 1921 they formed the American Society of Certified Public Accountants (ASCPA). The AIA and ASCPA merged in 1936, with the AIA surviving as the official designation (Miranti 1990). In 1957 it adopted the current name of American Institute of Certified Public Accountants (AICPA) (Zeff 1972).

Through the period of their development, the various accounting associations aspired to set uniform accounting methods, what are today called generally accepted accounting principles (GAAP). During 1917–1918, the AIA issued a first suggested accounting practice. During the stock boom of the 1920s and especially after the crash of 1929, additional efforts in cooperation with the New York Stock Exchange were made to provide information useful to investors. The securities acts of the New Deal, particularly the formation of the Securities and Exchange Commission (SEC) in 1934, placed greater pressure on the accounting profession, because Congress gave the SEC the power to require annual reports from publicly held companies and to establish accounting procedures for those reports. This pressure reached a high point with the bankruptcy of the McKesson-Robbins Company, just after its certified public accountants (CPAs) had judged it solvent (Carey 1970).

The AIA responded with a research committee, which began issuing accounting research bulletins to recommend principles of accounting. It also set up a Committee on Cooperation to work with the SEC. Although this committee had some disagreements with the SEC, it was effective in getting AIA recommendations the authoritative backing of the SEC. In 1959 the AICPA set up an Accounting Principles Board, which issued opinions on GAAP. These opinions were not without controversy (Zeff 1972), and in 1973 the responsibility for devising GAAP was given to the newly formed Financial Accounting Standards Board (Solomons 1986). With the support of the SEC and through its own efforts in licensing, setting examination standards, and establishing educational requirements, the AICPA had gained a power and status for public accounting as a business profession analogous to that of the AMA and the ABA. In 1991 it had 280,000 members, headquarters in New York, and a staff of 700 (Burek 1991). About half of its members are engaged in public accounting, and 40 percent are employed by business. It also maintains offices in Washington, from which it initially offered learned counsel on tax law changes. Now it engages in more active efforts to influence legislation (Chenok 1989).

The National Association of Accountants (NAA) was formed in 1919 as the National Association of Cost Accountants to serve the needs of accountants working within a firm. It publishes a journal, *Management Accounting* (Zeff 1972). In 1972 it set up an Institute of Management

Accounting and began awarding a Certificate of Management Accounting on passage of a series of examinations; as of 1991 the institute had 9,000 members. During 1991 the NAA adopted the name of its subsidiary in an effort to enhance the dignity of its title and began operating as the Institute of Management Accounting. In 1991 the NAA had 85,000 members and a staff of 100 at its headquarters in Montvale, New Jersey (Burek 1991). The Financial Executives Institute was started in 1931 as the Controllers Institute of America (Zeff 1972). In 1991 it had 13,200 members and headquarters in Morristown, New Jersey (Burek 1991).

Other organizations of business professionals (date formed/members in 1991) include American Academy of Actuaries (1965/8,000), Institute of Certified Financial Planners (1973/7,500), Institute of Chartered Financial Analysts (1961/11,800), Society of Actuaries (1949/17,780), American Society of Chartered Life Underwriters (1927/33,000), American Institute of Real Estate Appraisers (1932/6,909), National Association of Purchasing Management (1915/32,000), Society for Human Resource Management (1948/42,000), American Marketing Association (1915/53,000), American Management Association (1923/75,000), Financial Analysts Federation (1947/17,300), American Society of Appraisers (1952/5,600).

BIBLIOGRAPHIC ESSAY

The sources on business and professional organizations are as diverse as the industry itself. The *Encyclopedia of Associations* (Burek 1991) provides a date of formation and traces reorganizations, mergers, and name changes, a good beginning point for the general history of organizations.

Organizational History

For a study of the forces leading to the development of organizations the best source is Kenneth E. Boulding's *Organizational Revolution* (1953). Mancur Olson has made a significant contribution to the theory of organizational development with his *Logic of Collective Action* (1971) and *Rise and Decline of Nations* (1982). Boulding and Olson are especially useful for establishing both the impulse for banding together as a group and the problems that make groups difficult to form. Few associations ever organized without strong leadership, and an entrepreneurial history of association leaders would be a useful area of research. Joseph F. Bradley (1965) gives an overview of both business and professional organizations and some brief historical information.

Any study of organizational history must make special mention of the work of Louis Galambos. He is the author of a major study of a trade association, and his survey article "Technology, Political Economy and Professionalization: Central Themes of the Organizational Synthesis" (1983) furnishes an excellent entry into the topic.

Trade Association Histories

The brief overview of "Organized Business Groups" by Albert K. Steigerwalt for the *Encyclopedia of American Economic History* (1980) is a starting point for any study of business organizations. Steigerwalt synthesizes the theories of business organizational development and uses them to give historical analyses of several major ones; he looks at peak associations such as NAM and the U.S. Chamber of Commerce in terms of their impact on national affairs and considers the impulse to cartel behavior of specific trade associations. Among peak organizations, much attention has been directed toward NAM because of its contentious stands against governmental policies and labor unions. Steigerwalt's *National Association of Manufacturers* (1964) traces its early years. Later studies of the NAM's efforts can be found in books dealing with the labor movement, with Howell John Harris' *Right to Manage* (1982) being among the best; Harris describes how business changed its approach to industrial relations to fend off unions and how the NAM led the way in inciting legal disputes that circumscribed the effectiveness of the National Labor Relations Board as a vehicle for maintaining the New Deal sympathy toward unions. Richard S. Tedlow's "National Association of Manufacturers and Public Relations during the New Deal" (1976) recounts the NAM's efforts to furnish Americans with a more positive image of business and to promote its version of responsible behavior by labor. The U.S. Chamber of Commerce has suffered neglect in comparison, but Werking (1978) is a useful study of its origins.

For specific trade associations, Galambos' *Competition and Cooperation: The Emergence of a National Trade Association* (1966) remains a paradigm. This study of trade association activity in the cotton textile industry supplies a thorough history of efforts to build a national trade association and recounts the problems encountered in attaining it. Those efforts are further placed in a context of industry conditions and of the politics involved with the association movement of the 1920s and the NIRA and the NRA of the 1930s. Honorable mention for trade association history goes to William H. Becker (1971) for his study of wholesale hardware trade associations, a solid, informative article.

Professional Organizations

Historical analysis of professional organizations in general has been greatly enhanced by the publication of Samuel Haber's *Quest for Authority and Honor in the American Professions, 1750–1900* (1991). This work contains a general analysis and interpretation of professions and traces the development of the major professions—medical doctors, lawyers, clergy, professors, and engineers. Haber contributes day-to-day detail on professional activities during the mid-nineteenth century and surrounds this with background data. Each chapter is documented, but there is no bibliography. A historical model of the development of professions and their associations forms the introductory chapter of *Accountancy Comes of Age* by Paul J. Miranti, Jr. (1990). Miranti argues that professions went through four stages in the development of their associations, and his brief analysis makes a good complement to the general theories of Boulding (1953) and Olson (1971, 1982). Magali Sarfatti Larson in *The Rise of Professionalism* (1977) takes a sociological perspective on professionals and their associationist tendencies, using histories of the AMA and ABA as prototypes.

Histories of individual professional organizations are more numerous than of business associations, perhaps because their members took a more professional attitude toward preserving their records and seeing that they were used. Besides, their activities had greater need of publicity and could more successfully stand the light of day than could the ventures of business organizations, which risked running afoul of the antitrust laws (Waters and Morse 1996). Regardless, histories of the prominent professions have been written; in the cases where the professional association was the sponsor of its history a wary eye should be turned to whether this resulted in an interpretation aimed at self-promotion.

Medical doctors stand at the pinnacle of professionalism in the United States, and the AMA is the model of an effective professional organization. In addition to Haber's efforts noted earlier, the books of James G. Burrow, *AMA: Voice of American Medicine* (1963) and *Organized Medicine in the Progressive Era* (1977) are essential to any understanding of the AMA and the inner and outer conflicts involved with the professionalization of medicine. Histories published by the AMA, such as Fishbein (1947) and Campion (1984), have useful information but reflect the official AMA point of view. The legal profession has produced many good studies of lawyers, with less attention given to the ABA. In addition to official ABA histories, the collection of essays in Gerard W. Gawalt, ed., *The New High Priests* (1984), has good accounts of how bar associations and the ABA shaped the legal profession. The engineering profession has been fortunate in having extensive coverage of its associations. *The Revolt of the Engineers* by Edwin T. Layton, Jr. (1986) is by far the most comprehensive, reporting on all the fields of engineering as they rose and formed separate societies. The story of civil engineers is told by Daniel Hovey Calhoun (1960), and William H. Wisely (1974) gives a comprehensive history of the ASCE; mechanical engineers have received the most attention owing to their role in implementing technology in mass production manufacturing, as recounted by Monte A. Calvert (1967) and Bruce Sinclair's history of ASME (1980); A. Michael McMahon (1984) provides a detailed history of the organizations related to electrical engineering. Miranti's work (1990) sets out the formation of the professional association of certified public accountants up to 1940; books related to accountancy after that period, Zeff (1972, 1988, [1966] 1991) and Carey (1970), are less satisfactory, as their authors are accountants and not historians.

BIBLIOGRAPHY

ABA Bankers Weekly: The Newspaper of the American Bankers Association. Washington, DC: American Bankers Association, 1986–1993. Weekly.

American Bankers Association. *Journal of the American Bankers Association.* New York: American Bankers Association, 1908–1924. Monthly.

American Bankers Association Banking Literature Index: Thesaurus. Washington, DC: American Bankers Association, 1992– . Annual.

American Bankers Association Journal. New York: American Bankers Association, 1924–1934. Monthly.

American Bar Association. *Centennial: A Century of Service.* Chicago: American Bar Association, 1979.

———. *The Complete Guide to ABA Publications: Author, Subject, and Title Guide to the ABA Archive.* Buffalo, NY: W. S. Hein, 1997.

———. *Promoting Professionalism: ABA Programs, Plans, and Strategies.* Chicago: American Bar Association, 1998.

"Associations and Liability." *Association Management* 50, no. 1 (January 1998): 7.

Auerbach, Jerold S. *Unequal Justice: Lawyers and Social Change in Modern America.* New York. Oxford University Press, 1976.

Banking's News Letter. New York: Banking-Journal of the American Bankers Association, –1942. Monthly. Continued by *Newsletter.*

Banking's Newsletter. New York: Banking, Journal of the American Bankers Association, 1953– . Monthly.

Becker, William. H. "American Wholesale Hardware Trade Associations, 1870–1900." *Business History Review* 45, no. 3 (Summer 1971): 179–200.

Bledstein, Burton J. *The Culture of Professionalism.* New York: W. W. Norton, 1976.

Bloomfield, Maxwell. *American Lawyers in a Changing Society, 1776–1876.* Cambridge: Harvard University Press, 1976.

Botein, Stephen. " 'What Shall We Meet Afterwards in Heaven': Judgeship as a Symbol for Modern American Lawyers." In *Professions and Professional Ideologies in America,* edited by Gerald L. Geison. Chapel Hill: University of North Carolina Press, 1983.

Boulding, Kenneth E. *The Organizational Revolution.* New York: Harper & Brothers, 1953.

Bradley, Joseph F. *The Role of Trade Associations and Professional Business Societies in America.* University Park: Pennsylvania University Press, 1965.

Brady, Robert A. *Business as a System of Power*. New York: Columbia University Press, 1943.

Bulletin. Chicago: American Medical Association, 1905–1936. 9 issues a year. Merged with the *Journal of the American Medical Association*, 1937.

Burek, Deborah M. *Encyclopedia of Associations*. Vol. 1, *National Organizations of the U.S.* Detroit: Gale Research, 1991.

Burrow, James G. *AMA: Voice of American Medicine*. Baltimore: Johns Hopkins Press, 1963.

———. *Organized Medicine in the Progressive Era*. Baltimore: Johns Hopkins University Press, 1977.

Calhoun, Daniel Hovey. *The American Civil Engineer: Origins and Conflict*. Cambridge: Harvard University Press, 1960.

Calvert, Monte A. *The Mechanical Engineer in America, 1830–1910: Professional Cultures in Conflict*. Baltimore: Johns Hopkins Press, 1967.

———. "The Search for Engineering Unity: The Professionalization of Special Interest." In *Building the Organizational Society: Essays on Associational Activities in Modern America*, edited by Jerry Israel. New York: Free Press, 1972.

Campion, Frank D. *The AMA and U.S. Health Policy since 1940*. Chicago: Chicago Review Press, 1984.

Carey, John L. *The Rise of the Accounting Profession to Responsibility and Authority, 1937–1969*. New York: American Institute of Certified Public Accountants, 1970.

Carson, Gerald. *A Good Day at Saratoga*. Chicago: American Bar Association, 1978.

Chandler, Alfred D., Jr. "The Beginnings of 'Big Business' in American History." *Business History Review* 33 (Spring 1959): 1–31.

———. *Strategy and Structure: Chapters in the History of the Industrial Enterprise*. Cambridge: MIT Press, 1962.

———. *The Visible Hand: The Managerial Revolution in American Business*. Cambridge: Harvard University Press, 1977.

———. *Scale and Scope: The Dynamics of Industrial Capitalism*. Cambridge: Harvard University Press, 1990.

Chenok, Philip B. *AICPA: Serving America's Business and Financial Needs*. New York: Newcomen Society in North America, 1989.

Corrigan, Janet M., and Paul B. Ginsburg. "Association Leaders Speak Out on Health System Change." *Health Affairs* 16, no. 1 (January/February 1997): 150–57.

Duffy, John. *The Healers: The Rise of the Medical Establishment*. New York: McGraw-Hill, 1976.

Edgerton, Charles E. "The Wire-Nail Association of 1895–96." In *Trusts, Pools, and Corporations*, edited by William Zebina Ripley. Rev. ed. Boston: Ginn, 1916.

Ernstthal, Henry L., and Bob Jones IV. *Principles of Association Management*. 3d ed. Washington, DC: American Society of Association Executives, 1996.

Facing the Future: A Report on the Trends and Issues Affecting Associations. Washington, DC: Foundation of the American Society of Association Executives, 1998.

Financial Age: Devoted to the Interests of the Members of the American Bankers' Association and State Associations. New York: Financial Age, 1898– . Weekly.

Fishbein, Morris. *A History of the American Medical Association, 1847 to 1947.* Philadelphia: W. B. Saunders, 1947.

Flexner, Abraham. *Medical Education in the United States and Canada.* Bulletin no. 4. New York: Carnegie Foundation for the Advancement of Teaching, 1910.

Foth, Joseph Henry. *Trade Associations: Their Service to Industry.* New York: Ronald Press, 1930.

Furner, Mary O. *Advocacy and Objectivity.* Lexington: University Press of Kentucky, 1975.

Galambos, Louis. *Competition and Cooperation: The Emergence of a National Trade Association.* Baltimore: Johns Hopkins Press, 1966.

———. "The Emerging Organizational Synthesis in Modern Economic History." *Business History Review* 44, no. 4 (Autumn 1970): 179–90.

———. "The American Economy and the Reorganization of the Sources of Knowledge." In *The Organization of Knowledge in Modern America, 1860–1920,* edited by Alexandra Oleson and John Voss. Baltimore: Johns Hopkins University Press, 1979.

———. "Technology, Political Economy and Professionalization: Central Themes of the Organizational Synthesis." *Business History Review* 57, no. 1 (Winter 1983): 471–93.

———. "The American Trade Association Movement." In *Trade Associations in Business History,* edited by Hiroaki Yamazaki and Matao Miyamoto. Tokyo: University of Tokyo Press, 1988.

Gawalt, Gerard W., ed. *The New High Priests: Lawyers in Post–Civil War America.* Contributions in Legal Studies, no. 29. Westport, CT: Greenwood Press, 1984.

Gilb, Corinne Lathrop. *Hidden Hierarchies: The Professions and Government.* New York: Harper & Row, 1966.

Haber, Samuel. *The Quest for Authority and Honor in the American Professions, 1750–1900.* Chicago: University of Chicago Press, 1991.

Harris, Howell John. *The Right to Manage: Industrial Relations Policies of American Business in the 1940s.* Madison: University of Wisconsin Press, 1982.

Haskell, Thomas L. *The Emergence of Professional Social Science.* Urbana: University of Illinois Press, 1977.

Hawkins, Hugh. "University Identity: The Teaching and Research Functions." In *The Organization of Knowledge in Modern America, 1860–1920,* edited by Alexandra Oleson and John Voss. Baltimore: Johns Hopkins University Press, 1979.

Higham, John. "The Matrix of Specialization." In *The Organization of Knowledge in Modern America, 1860–1920,* edited by Alexandra Oleson and John Voss. Baltimore: Johns Hopkins University Press, 1979.

Himmelberg, Robert F. *The Origins of the National Recovery Administration.* New York: Fordham University Press, 1976.

Hobson, Wayne K. "Symbol of the New Profession: Emergence of the Large Law Firm, 1870–1915." In *The New High Priests: Lawyers in Post–Civil War*

America, edited by Gerard W. Gawalt. Westport, CT: Greenwood Press, 1984.

———. *The American Legal Profession and the Organizational Society, 1890–1930*. American Legal and Constitutional History. New York: Garland, 1986.

Hope, C. C., Jr. *The American Bankers Association, Providing Unity and Leadership to the Banking Industry*. New York: Newcomen Society in North America, 1980.

Jacobs, Jerald A. *Association Law Handbook*. Washington, DC: American Society of Association Executives, 1996.

Jacobs, Jerald A., and David W. Ogden. *Legal Risk Management for Associations: A Legal Compliance Guide for Volunteers and Employees of Trade and Professional Associations*. Washington, DC: American Psychological Association, 1995.

JAMA: The Journal of the American Medical Association. Chicago: American Medical Association, 1960– . 48 issues a year.

Journal of the American Medical Association. Chicago: American Medical Association, 1883–1960. Continued by *JAMA*.

Kahn, Alfred E. "Cartels and Trade Associations." *International Encyclopedia of the Social Sciences*. New York: Macmillan, 1968.

Kastner, Michael E., ed. *Creating and Managing an Association Government Relations Program*. Washington, DC: American Society of Association Executives, 1998.

Kevles, Daniel. "The Physics, Mathematics and Chemistry Communities: A Comparative Analysis." In *The Organization of Knowledge in Modern America, 1860–1920*, edited by Alexandra Oleson and John Voss. Baltimore: Johns Hopkins University Press, 1979.

King, Lester S. *American Medicine Comes of Age*. Chicago: American Medical Association, 1984.

Larson, Magali Sarfatti. *The Rise of Professionalism: A Sociological Analysis*. Berkeley: University of California Press, 1977.

Layton, Edwin T., Jr. *The Revolt of the Engineers: Social Responsibility and the American Engineering Profession*. Baltimore: Johns Hopkins University Press, 1986.

Lowrey, Bill H. *The Beginning of the End of the ABA (American Bar Association)*. Sacramento, CA: B. H. Lowrey, 1994.

Lynn, Leonard H., and Timothy J. McKeown. *Trade Associations in America and Japan*. Washington, DC: American Enterprise Institute for Public Policy Research, 1988.

Martin, Clarence E., and William J. Donovan. *The American Bar, Its Past Leaders and Its Present Aim*. Chicago: University of Chicago Press, 1933.

Matzko, John A. " 'The Best Men of the Bar': The Founding of the American Bar Association." In *The New High Priests: Lawyers in Post–Civil War America*, edited by Gerard W. Gawalt. Westport, CT: Greenwood Press, 1984.

McMahon, A. Michael. *The Making of a Profession: A Century of Electrical Engineering in America*. New York: Institute of Electrical and Electronics Engineers, 1984.

Medical Education in the United States and Canada. Chicago: Council on Medical

Education and Hospitals of the American Medical Association, 1931–1960. Annual.

Meserve, Robert W. *The American Bar Association: A Brief History and Appreciation.* New York: Newcomen Society in North America, 1973.

Milner, Larry S., ed. *Business Associations for the 21st Century: A Blueprint for the Future.* Washington, DC: Center for International Private Enterprise, 1997.

Miranti, Paul J., Jr. *Accountancy Comes of Age: The Development of an American Profession, 1886–1940.* Chapel Hill: University of North Carolina Press, 1990.

National Trade and Professional Associations of the United States. Washington, DC: Columbia Books, 1982– . Annual.

Newsletter. New York: Banking, Journal of the American Bankers Association, 1943–1952. Monthly. Continues *Banking's News Letter.* Continued by *Banking's Newsletter.*

Oleson, Alexandra, and John Voss, eds. Introduction to *The Organization of Knowledge in Modern America, 1860–1920.* Baltimore: Johns Hopkins University Press, 1979.

Olson, Mancur. *The Logic of Collective Action.* Cambridge: Harvard University Press, 1971.

———. *The Rise and Decline of Nations.* New Haven, CT: Yale University Press, 1982.

Reed, Alfred Z. *Training for the Public Profession of the Law.* Carnegie Foundation for the Advancement of Teaching, no. 15. New York: C. Scribner's, 1921. Reprint. Historical Writings in Law and Jurisprudence, 2d ser., no. 2. Buffalo, NY: W. S. Hein, 1986.

Reynolds, Terry S. *75 Years of Progress: A History of the American Institute of Chemical Engineers.* New York: American Institute of Chemical Engineers, 1983.

Rogers, James Grafton. *The American Bar Association in Retrospect.* New York: New York University Press, 1937.

Rose, Nancy Ellen. *Put to Work: Relief Programs of the Great Depression.* New York: Monthly Review Press, 1994.

Rosenthal, Marilyn. "National Trade and Professional Associations of the United States/State and Regional Associations of the United States." *Library Journal* 122, no. 1 (January 1997): 90.

Ross, Dorothy. "The Development of the Social Sciences." In *The Organization of Knowledge in Modern America, 1860–1920,* edited by Alexandra Oleson and John Voss. Baltimore: Johns Hopkins University Press, 1979.

Ruud, Millard H. *The Role of the American Bar Association in Legal Education: Summary of the 1969 Chicago Symposium.* ABA Section of Legal Education and Admissions to the Bar, Monograph 1. Chicago: American Bar Association, 1970.

Schneider, Wilbert M. *The American Bankers Association, Its Past and Present.* Washington, DC: Public Affairs Press, 1956.

Schuyler, Philip N., ed. *Hundred Year Association of New York.* New York: A. S. Barnes, 1942.

Seavoy, Ronald E. *The Origins of the American Business Corporation, 1784–1855:*

Broadening the Concept of Public Service during Industrialization. Contributions in Legal Studies, no. 19. Westport, CT: Greenwood Press, 1982.

Shaiko, Ronald G. "Female Participation in Association Governance and Political Representation: Women as Executive Directors, Board Members, Lobbyists, and Political Action Committee Directors." *Nonprofit Management and Leadership* 8, no. 2 (Winter 1997): 121–39.

Sinclair, Bruce. A *Centennial History of the American Society of Mechanical Engineers.* Toronto, Canada: University of Toronto Press, 1980.

Sirkin, Arlene Farber, and Michael P. McDermott. *Keeping Members: The Myths and Realities; CEO Strategies for 21st Century Success.* Washington, DC: Foundation of the American Society of Association Executives, 1995.

Smith, Adam. *An Inquiry into the Nature and Causes of the Wealth of Nations.* London: W. Strahan & T. Cadell, 1776. Reprint. Chicago: University of Chicago Press, 1976.

Solomons, David. *Making Accounting Policy: The Quest for Credibility in Financial Reporting.* New York: Oxford University Press, 1986.

Solomons, David, and Stephen A. Zeff. *Accounting Research, 1948–1958.* 2 vols. New Works in Accounting History. New York: Garland, 1996.

Stabile, Donald R. *Prophets of Order: The Rise of the New Class, Technocracy and Socialism in America.* Boston: South End Press, 1984.

———. "New York Chamber of Commerce and Industry." *Encyclopedia of New York City.* New Haven, CT: Yale University Press, 1995.

———. "Mortgage Bankers and Brokers." In *Infrastructure and Services: A Historiographical and Bibliographical Guide,* vol. 3 of *Handbook of American Business History,* edited by David O. Whitten and Bessie E. Whitten. Westport, CT: Greenwood Press, 2000.

State and Regional Associations of the United States. Washington, DC: Columbia Books, 1989– . Annual.

Steeples, Douglas, and David O. Whitten. *Democracy in Desperation: The Depression of 1893.* Contributions in Economics and Economic History, no. 199. Westport, CT: Greenwood Press, 1998.

Steigerwalt, Albert K. *The National Association of Manufacturers 1895–1914: A Study in Business Leadership.* Ann Arbor: University of Michigan, Graduate School of Business Administration, Bureau of Business Research, 1964.

———. "Organized Business Groups." In *Encyclopedia of American Economic History: Studies of the Principal Movements and Ideas,* vol. 1, edited by Glenn Porter. New York: Scribners, 1980.

Sunderland, Edson R. *History of the American Bar Association and Its Work.* Ann Arbor, MI: American Bar Association, 1953.

Svevo-Cianci, Kimberly A. *Associations and the Global Marketplace: Profiles of Success.* Washington, DC: American Society of Association Executives, 1995.

Tedlow, Richard S. "The National Association of Manufacturers and Public Relations during the New Deal." *Business History Review* 50, no. 2 (Spring 1976): 25–45.

———. "Trade Associations and Public Relations." In *Trade Associations in Business History,* edited by Hiroaki Yamazaki and Matao Miyamoto. Tokyo: University of Tokyo Press, 1988.

Thomison, Dennis. *A History of the American Library Association, 1876–1972*. Chicago: American Library Association, 1978.

Transactions. Philadelphia: T. K. & P. G. Collins for the American Medical Association, 1848–1882. Continued by *Journal of the American Medical Association*.

Veysey, Laurence. "The Plural Organized Worlds of the Humanities." In *The Organization of Knowledge in Modern America, 1860–1920*, edited by Alexandra Oleson and John Voss. Baltimore: Johns Hopkins University Press, 1979.

Walker, David H. *Pioneers of Prosperity*. San Francisco: 1895. Washington, DC: Library of Congress Photoduplication Service, 1988. Microfilm.

Warren, Charles. *A History of the American Bar*. Boston: Little, Brown, 1911. Reprint. Historical Writings in Law and Jurisprudence, no. 3. Buffalo, NY: W. S. Hein, 1980.

Waters, Timothy J., and Robert H. Morse, eds. *Antitrust and Trade Associations: How Trade Regulation Laws Apply to Trade and Professional Associations*. Antitrust Practice Guide. Chicago: American Bar Association, Section of Antitrust Law, 1996.

Werking, Richard Hume. "Bureaucrats, Businessmen, and Foreign Trade: The Origins of the United States Chamber of Commerce." *Business History Review* 52, no. 4 (Autumn 1978): 321–44.

Wesley, Edgar B. *NEA: The First Hundred Years*. New York: Harper & Brothers, 1957.

Whitten, David O. *Emergence of Giant Enterprise, 1860–1914: American Commercial Enterprise and Extractive Industries*. Contributions in Economics and Economic History, no. 54. Westport, CT: Greenwood Press, 1983.

Wiegand, Wayne A. *The Politics of an Emerging Profession: The American Library Association, 1876–1917*. New York: Greenwood Press, 1986.

Wilson, Logan. *American Academics: Then and Now*. New York: Oxford University Press, 1979.

Wisely, William H. *The American Civil Engineer*. New York: American Society of Civil Engineers, 1974.

Wueschner, Silvano A. *Charting Twentieth-Century Monetary Policy: Herbert Hoover and Benjamin Strong, 1917–1927*. Contributions in Economics and Economic History, no. 210. Westport, CT: Greenwood Press, 1999.

Zeff, Stephen A. *American Accounting Association: Its First 50 Years, 1916–1966*. Sarasota, FL: American Accounting Association, 1991. Originally published in 1966.

———. *Forging Accounting Principles in Five Countries: A History and an Analysis*. Lecture Series/Arthur Andersen. Champaign, IL: Stipes, 1972.

———, ed. *The U.S. Accounting Profession in the 1890s and Early 1900s*. Foundations of Accounting. New York: Garland, 1988.

Part XVI

Public Administration
ESIC 90.0

CHAPTER 21

PUBLIC ADMINISTRATION, 90.0
DON M. COERVER

Public administration has played an important role in the evolution of American business since the colonial period. As a growing imperial power, England depended heavily on the Royal Navy for its security and an expanding merchant marine for its prosperity. The English government viewed colonies as a key element in the pursuit of imperial self-sufficiency. All of these factors came together in the philosophy of mercantilism, which England pursued along with the other European colonial powers (Magnusson 1994).

To implement mercantilism, England passed laws to regulate trade and prevent colonial industry from competing with English manufactures. The Trade and Navigation Acts imposed a number of restrictions aimed at channeling trade along lines believed to be beneficial to imperial interests. Under the acts, all trade between England and the colonies had to be in either English or colonial ships manned primarily by English or colonial sailors. Colonists were not permitted to import products directly from other European countries. Certain items produced in the colonies—the enumerated articles—could be sold only in the English market. The Woolens Act of 1699, the Hat Act of 1732, and the Iron Act of 1750 all restricted colonial manufacturing with a view to protecting English production. Given the overwhelmingly agricultural nature of the American economy, these acts had a limited impact on colonial business development (Perkins 1988).

The success of the American Revolution made the United States an independent country in an international trade market in which the major European powers were still following mercantilistic policies. While independence complicated trade, especially with England, it led to the virtual withdrawal of public administration from business. The new government under the Articles of Confederation had little power that impinged on the conduct of business affairs. The articles did not give the Confederation government the power to levy taxes or to regulate interstate or foreign commerce. The absence of central control did not give free rein to business enterprise; instead, it left the business community to confront thirteen different commercial codes and tax structures. Business and financial problems were key concerns in the mounting pressure to draft a new constitution (Jensen 1950; Crowley 1993).

The U.S. Constitution, drafted in 1787, marked a new phase in the public administration of business. The federal system assigned the central government the power both to levy taxes and to regulate interstate and foreign commerce. State governments were no longer permitted to issue paper money and could not take actions that would impair contracts. The federal government was given control of the western lands. The net effect of these provisions was to promote a national economy, improve financial stability, provide sources of revenue for the new government, and furnish an orderly basis for the exploitation of the public domain.

The disposition of the public finances under the new government had a major effect on the environment in which business–government relations developed. Alexander Hamilton, the first secretary of the treasury, put forward an ambitious program aimed at establishing the nation's credit, centralizing political power, and promoting manufacturing. Hamilton succeeded in refinancing and funding the national debt and in establishing the Bank of the United States. He enjoyed limited success in his efforts to pass a protective tariff and failed in an attempt to get the federal government directly involved in the financing of industrialization. Although politically controversial, Hamilton did much to restore business confidence in the central government, established government credit, and generally created a favorable atmosphere for the growing nonagricultural business interests in the country (Miller 1963; Whitten 1975).

In the early decades of the new nation, public administration was seen as promotional rather than restrictive. During the first half of the nineteenth century, public administration of business was devolving, with the federal government becoming less involved in the economy while the involvement of state and local governments increased. State governments simplified the incorporation process by passing general-incorporation legislation. Both state and local governments helped to finance the transportation revolution taking place by purchasing corporate stocks and bonds, guaranteeing business credit, and providing direct grants of money or land. Lower levels of government were heavily involved in the financing of canals and railroads, supplanting a federal government whose powers to act were increasingly circumscribed by sectional rivalries. The Panic of 1837 demonstrated that many governmental entities were overextended financially for internal improvements, and a withdrawal of government aid for such projects rapidly ensued (Goodrich 1960).

BUSINESS, GOVERNMENT, AND THE CIVIL WAR

The Civil War had a profound impact on the relationship between business and government, a product of a rapid increase in government spending coupled with the passage of new legislation—often blocked earlier by sectional differences—that influenced business operations. Federal spending in 1865 was twenty times what it had been in 1860; in financing the war, the North resorted to a blend of increased taxation, heavy borrowing, and the issuance of paper money. The increased federal spending had only a marginal impact on manufacturing due to the loss of southern markets and a reduction in exports (Engerman 1966).

The war years saw the passage of legislation that would have a long-term effect on public administration of business. The tariff—generally low from 1832 to 1861—was raised on three different occasions during the war, bringing rates to the highest level in U.S. history in 1865. The rates were not lowered once the wartime emergency was over but went on providing protection for American manufacturers. Congress also passed national banking legislation under wartime pressures, partially as a means of financing the war. Response to federal chartering of banks was initially weak owing to stricter regulations, but a federal tax on the circulation of state banknotes led to a rapid increase in the number of federal bank charters, with over 1,600 in operation by 1866. What had started out as an emergency wartime action was to be the basic federal legislation governing the financial system until 1913 (Studenski and Krooss 1963).

Federal land policy established during the Civil War did much to influence the administration of public lands in the postwar period. Of greatest importance was the Homestead Act (1862), a logical advance on the existing preemption system that provided for the transfer of federal lands to farmers without any cash payment. Federal land grants to railroads to help finance construction started on a large scale during the war and continued after 1865. The Morrill Land Grant Act of 1862 called for massive transfers of federal lands to state governments with the provision that proceeds from the sale of the lands should be used to finance higher education in agriculture, engineering, and military science (Carstensen 1963). The Morrill Act was extended to the southern states after the war.

THE RISE OF BIG BUSINESS AND PUBLIC ADMINISTRATION

One product of the Civil War was larger and more concentrated businesses. Fierce competition and the Panic of 1873 eroded laissez-faire values and opened the door to market regulation. As part of the reorganization of business that was taking place, cooperation—rather than competition—gained influence in decision making. In early efforts at cooperation, companies formed pools, informal agreements calling for production quotas, price-fixing, or market division. When pools proved unsatisfactory, trusts were formed by establishing a separate business entity with controlling interest in the formerly competitive companies. The first trust was established in the oil industry in 1879 by John D. Rockefeller. Rockefeller's success with Standard Oil led to the rapid spread of the trust as an organizational device. While men in big business viewed the trust as an efficient way of centralizing decision making and of rationalizing industrial activity, this rapid concentration of economic power soon aroused the public and led to an unprecedented effort at public administration of business (Chandler 1959, 1962, 1977, 1990; Porter 1973; Steeples and Whitten 1998; Whitten 1983).

The foundation for this new government involvement in business was a series of federal court decisions in the 1870s and 1880s. These decisions reflected the growing interstate nature of big business as well as the difficulties experienced by state governments in trying to regulate larger business entities. The Supreme Court established the basis for government regulation of business in its decision in *Munn v. Illinois* (1876), in which it reaffirmed the common-law principle that private property devoted to public use was subject to public regulation. The following year the Supreme Court ruled in the *Piek* case that state governments could regulate interstate commerce in the absence of federal regulation. Problems encountered in having state governments regulate interstate commerce caused some states to reduce their regulatory efforts; the option of state regulation disappeared completely in 1886, when the Supreme Court ruled in *Wabash v. Illinois* that state regulation of interstate trade was an unacceptable intrusion on the federal commerce power (Kelly et al. 1983).

State exclusion from the regulation of interstate commerce did not lead to an end to public demands to curb the growing power of the big corporations. The railroads in particular continued to be a target for reformers as they had been throughout the 1870s and 1880s. As recipients of government financing, many of the railroads had a public nature that other large enterprises lacked. As the first big business and the first substantial interstate business, the railroads attracted public attention in ways that other enterprises did not. With the states excluded from any significant role in railroad regulation by the *Wabash* decision and with some railroads seeing an advantage in federal regulation, the Congress quickly responded with the passage of the Interstate Commerce Act in 1887.

The act established the Interstate Commerce Commission (ICC) with the power to determine whether rates charged by the railroads were "reasonable and just." The act specifically outlawed the common railroad practices of rebates, pooling, and discriminatory pricing. Railroads had to publish their rate schedules and adhere to certain minimum accounting procedures. Efforts to implement the act encountered a series of problems that did much to undermine regulatory activity. There was no definition of what was meant by reasonable and just, opening the way to extensive litigation, with the ICC usually on the losing side. Federal court decisions prevented the ICC from actually setting rates. From the very beginning, there were charges that the commission had become a captive of the industry it was supposed to regulate—later, that charge that would be made against a number of other federal regulatory bodies. There was also criticism that the areas where the ICC enjoyed the most success—such as stabilizing the industry and rationalizing the rate structure—tended to benefit the industry rather than the public (Kolko 1965). Despite its many problems, the ICC represented a landmark in public administration of business.

While the Interstate Commerce Act dealt with the problem of concentration in the railroad industry, concentration was viewed as a growing problem in other industries as well. State governments led the way in general antitrust activity, just as they had in efforts to regulate the railroads. The interstate nature of big business frustrated these antitrust activities as it had state regulation of railroads. Most of the states with antitrust statutes were in the South and the West, where there were few large industrial firms. Thus, much the same scenario that led to the passage of the Interstate Commerce Act in 1887 also produced the Sherman Antitrust Act of 1890 (Gandy 1993).

The Sherman Act outlawed any kind of business arrangement in "restraint of trade." Violators of the measure were subject to a fine of up to $1,000 and a jail term of up to one year, while private parties injured by antitrust violations could sue for triple damages. No special commission was established to enforce the measure, responsibility for enforcement resting with the Department of Justice. Implementing the measure led to immediate problems. There was no definition of what constituted restraint of trade, and early court cases led to a series of defeats for the government. The federal courts further restricted the impact of the act by drawing an important distinction between commerce and manufacturing, ruling that the act applied only to commerce. More trusts were formed in the decade after 1890 than in the previous decade. That the Sherman Act was not considered a threat to big business can be seen from the actions in the Senate during its passage. Although business influence in the Senate was strong, only one vote was cast against the measure; even the measure's namesake—the respected Republican senator John Sherman—later denounced the act as "totally ineffective" in dealing with the problem of trusts (Letwin 1965; Freyer 1992; Steeples and Whitten 1998).

THE EXPANDING ROLE OF GOVERNMENT IN BUSINESS

The late nineteenth and early twentieth centuries saw an expanding role for public administration of business at all levels of government. This expansion was connected with what became imprecisely defined as the "Progressive movement," a reform movement aimed at introducing major political, social, and economic changes at all levels of government—in the 1990s a similar movement was called reinventing government. The drive for reform produced a situation where business was becoming more involved in government at the same time that government was becoming more involved in business. With increasing governmental intervention at all levels, business had to devote more attention to organizing for political action. The formation of such organizations as the Rotary Club, the Kiwanis, and the Lions Club represented not only an effort at civic service but also a method for promoting the business outlook in politics. The establishment of the National Association of Manufacturers and the U.S. Chamber of Commerce in the early twentieth century was aimed at strengthening business lobbying efforts at the national level. Confusing the situation was the fact that there was no monolithic business position on the issues of the day; it was difficult for the government to intervene on behalf of one business interest group without prejudicing the interests of some other business group.

At the municipal level, greater public administration of business involved the transformation of utilities into public utilities—the 1990s witnessed the privatization movement as city governments sought to escape the burdens of utility management by selling them to private operators. City governments increasingly exerted regulatory authority over such utilities as water, gas, electricity, telephones, and even transportation. This regulation took the form of granting municipal monopolies to private companies or sometimes even municipal ownership of the utility, as was frequently the case with water. Moreover, cities began regulating labor, housing, and public health (Rice 1977; Blackford 1993).

States also became more involved in the regulation of business, often under pressure from the public but sometimes at the urging of business interests that had failed at self-regulation and were looking to government intervention to rationalize business activity. Several states regulated labor, especially through restrictions on female and child labor and the passage of workmen's compensation legislation. A number of states established industrial commissions that typically featured an uneasy blend of administrative, judicial, and legislative functions. Often originally set up to deal with issues of safety and health, many of the commissions attempted to regulate working conditions (Blackford 1977).

The interstate nature of big business focused attention on the reform movement at the federal level, as state governments encountered legal and administrative restrictions in their efforts at regulation. Public administration of business at the national level took a new turn with the arrival of the first Progressive president, Theodore Roosevelt, in 1901. Roosevelt was limited in his ability to get new legislation through Congress owing to the strength of the conservative elements in his own Republican Party. Fearing a split in the Party, Roosevelt sidestepped tariff revision but did tackle antitrust enforcement. The Justice Department had compiled a dismal record in prosecutions under the Sherman Act during the 1890s. Roosevelt established an antitrust division in the Justice Department and launched a number of prosecutions against major trusts. Although Roosevelt gained a reputation as a trustbuster after the government's victory in the Northern Securities Company case in 1904, he was unable to get new antitrust legislation through Congress.

Roosevelt extended public administration over business in other ways: the Hepburn Act of 1906 gave the ICC the power to set aside rates upon complaint and establish a reasonable rate subject to judicial review; Congress established a Department of Commerce with a Bureau of Corporations—the department was viewed as an instrument for promoting business, but the bureau monitored interstate business activities and reported to the president. Roosevelt was moving in the direction of greater government involvement in business as his tenure neared its end, advocating an inheritance tax, an income tax, federal incorporation of interstate businesses, and federal regulation of working conditions. Although none of these reforms were enacted under Roosevelt, he had gone a long way toward establishing the Progressive business agenda for the future (Gould 1978).

Roosevelt's successor, William Howard Taft, nominally a Progressive but instinctively a conservative, grappled with tariff reform. Taft had called for a tariff revision, but the measure passed by Congress—the Payne-Aldrich bill of 1909—gave more protection to the manufacturing trusts. While the act failed as tariff reform, it had a major, long-range impact on business with its provision for a corporate income tax. Taft initiated more antitrust prosecutions than his more famous trustbusting predecessor despite obstacles to enforcement of the Sherman Act created by 1911 Supreme Court decisions that established the rule of reason, which interpreted the Sherman Act as prohibiting only unreasonable restraints of trade. The ICC received additional powers with the passage of the Mann-Elkins Act of 1910. Under the new law, the ICC had the power to initiate rates, not merely revise them upon complaint. The act also placed the burden of proof in rate disputes on the carrier. Regulation of interstate communications also became the responsibility of the ICC.

Woodrow Wilson in the presidency brought the greatest peacetime change in public administration of business to that time. Wilson's reform measures between 1913 and 1916 constituted the second wave in federal regulation of business. Wilson tackled the tariff issue with enthusiasm, bolstered by the support of a more reform-minded Congress. The Underwood Tariff of 1913 provided a substantial cut in the average tariff rate, in the process removing the protection afforded to the manufacturing trusts and imposing a personal income tax to help compensate for the loss of tariff revenue. Wilson addressed banking and currency reform, leading the fight for the Federal Reserve Act of 1913. The "Fed" legislation represented a compromise between Progressive forces demanding a banking system owned and controlled by the federal government and conservative elements that favored a system dominated by the major banking interests. The system was to be owned by its member banks but regulated by a board appointed by the president. The creation of the Federal Reserve gave the country a flexible currency and credit system as well as a mechanism for mobilizing bank reserves. National banks were required to join the system, but it was optional for state banks. Many state banks refused to join the system to avoid the regulation involved, laying the groundwork for major financial problems (White 1983).

Wilson extended public administration of business through the passage of the Clayton Antitrust Act and the Federal Trade Commission Act. The Clayton Act reflected the changing business practices that had developed in an effort to circumvent the Sherman Act. The act outlawed certain practices such as interlocking directorates and the purchase of stock in competing companies if these actions tended to "substantially lessen competition." The measure also exempted labor unions and farm cooperatives from prosecution under the Sherman Act. The Federal Trade Commission (FTC) Act gave broad powers to the commission it created to monitor interstate business for "unfair trade practices." When such practices were detected, the FTC could issue cease-and-desist orders and bring lawsuits if its orders were ignored. The Commerce Department's Bureau of Corporations, established under Roosevelt, was merged into the FTC in 1915. Both the Clayton Act and the FTC Act encountered difficulties with implementation, as had been the case with earlier efforts at regulation. These acts were indicative of a growing public administration of business at all levels of government—especially federal—on the eve of World War I (Wiebe 1962).

WORLD WAR AND BUSINESS–GOVERNMENT COOPERATION

The advent of World War I brought about major changes in the public administration of business even before the United States officially entered the war in April 1917. In an effort to maintain neutrality, the Wilson administration prohibited loans to the belligerent countries, which were eager to purchase American products but lacked the finances to do it. Amid doubts about the legality of the action and fears that it would inhibit an increase in trade, Wilson started the process of backing down from the policy, initially allowing the extension of commercial credit and eventually evolving to the point of encouraging American financial institutions to make loans to belligerent countries to purchase American products. In August 1916 the Council of National Defense was organized with a view toward planning for industrial mobilization. The Revenue Act of 1916 increased both personal and corporate income taxes to finance increased defense expenditures.

Turn-of-the-century changes were a prelude to business–government relations after the United States entered World War I in April 1917. The Council of National Defense proved inadequate to the task of mobilizing the economy, which led to the creation of the War Industries Board (WIB) in July 1917. The WIB initially encountered problems with internal friction between civilian and military elements, but the appointment of Bernard Baruch in the spring of 1918 as its chairman confirmed the WIB as the central agency in organizing and controlling the economy for the war effort. Rather than a case of government dictating to business, the WIB represented essentially an effort at self-regulation by business through government sanction, a goal sought by some business interests since the 1880s (Cuff 1973).

The government became more deeply involved in business in a number of other ways. The Lever Act of 1917 gave President Wilson broad controls over the production of fuel and foodstuffs, leading to the creation of the Fuel Administration and the Food Administration. These two agencies pursued conservation measures and encouraged production by manipulating price levels. An early effort at voluntary mobilization of the railroads came unraveled during the bitter winter of 1917–1918, leading to the establishment of the U.S. Railroad Administration, which coordinated and set priorities for rail transportation. Revenue acts passed in 1917 and 1918 produced substantial increases in personal and corporate income taxes, introduced the concept of an excess profits tax for business, and shifted the tax burden from the lower and middle classes to the upper class and corporations. World War I also saw the first successful use of wage-price controls to slow the rate of inflation without hurting productivity or causing the creation of a large enforcement bureaucracy (Rockoff 1984). The government also played a much more active role in labor relations during the war. Operating through the National War Labor Board, the federal government placed its support behind the right of workers to organize, an eight-hour day, and improved working conditions for women and children (Conner 1983).

Just as mobilization for the war effort had led to a dramatic increase in government involvement in business, so also did demobilization lead to an equally rapid retreat from intervention. The agencies created to extend public administration during the war quickly disappeared once the war ended in November 1918. There was talk of retaining the War Industries Board to deal with the "the postwar period's" changing real value of money—deflation in some industries and inflation in others—and to function as a mechanism for evading the antitrust laws. Instead, Wilson decreed that the agency would be completely disbanded no later than January 1, 1919 (Himmelberg 1965). There was talk of retaining the Railroad Administration and even of nationalizing the roads, but they returned to private operation in 1920. The Food and Fuel Administrations were also disbanded. The pro-labor policy followed during the war was strictly administrative, not legislative, and disappeared once the war ended. The removal of wage-price controls led to major postwar inflationary pressures (Rockoff 1981a, 1981b). Even the tax revolution produced by the Revenue Acts of 1916, 1917, and 1918 was largely undone by tax changes in the 1920s. While the changes in the public administration of business were primarily restricted to wartime and the immediate postwar period, they were to have long-term consequences when they served as examples for government intervention in the economy during the New Deal years of the 1930s.

BUSINESS AND GOVERNMENT IN BOOM AND BUST

The 1920s represented the peak of big business influence on government as wartime restrictions were dismantled during demobilization. The pro-business aspect of public administration showed itself in a number of ways. A conservative fiscal policy was the order of the day, with the emphasis on a balanced budget, tax breaks, and a sound dollar (Smiley and Keehn 1995). Treasury surpluses produced a substantial reduction in the federal debt, and enforcement of the antitrust laws was weak, leading to a second major phase in mergers and business concentration. The prevailing attitude was that businesses should cooperate with each other and with the government to promote economic growth. This attitude was personified in the career of Herbert Hoover, who followed his distinguished wartime service with a stint as secretary of commerce under Harding and Coolidge, then election to the presidency in 1928. Hoover tried to reconcile the technical and organizational changes affecting society and business in the 1920s with the traditional American values of individualism and voluntarism, the resulting blend being a peculiar brand of American corporatism characterized as the associative state (Hawley 1974).

The 1920s brought economic growth and an uneven prosperity that carried with it special perils of its own. The new era of prosperity started with a recession from 1920 to 1922 and ended with the stock market crash of 1929 and the first phase of the worst depression in the nation's history. Major areas of the economy like finance and agriculture were depressed despite national economic growth. Farmers could not stem overproduction, and the financial structure showed considerable instability throughout the period. The few federal agencies that could have addressed these problems—like the Federal Reserve—stayed on the administrative sidelines. Moreover, the profits of prosperity were accruing to the corporations and the upper class, creating in the process the underconsumption that would rock the economy at the end of the decade (Leuchtenberg 1958).

The stock market crash of 1929 brought a rapid end to the comfortable thoughts of a new era of perpetual prosperity. When the crash of 1929 became the Great Depression of the 1930s, politicians and economists— and historians of later generations—disagreed as to the causes of, and the cures for, the unprecedented economic downturn. Many people, including President Hoover, initially viewed the depression as a cyclical downturn in the economy and saw little cause for alarm or action. As the decline became more intense and prolonged, Hoover responded accordingly; his original approach based on voluntarism and reliance on the private sector increasingly gave way to a more activist public administration.

Even before the stock market crash, the federal government had intervened in agriculture with the Agricultural Marketing Act of 1929. Farm prices had been improving since the crisis of 1919–1923, but political pressure for federal aid to the farmers had been building for so long that action was taken nevertheless (Holt 1977). The act provided for federal loans to state-chartered commodity stabilization corporations to purchase and store crops in an effort to support prices; once the decreased supply had produced higher prices, the corporations could sell the crops and repay the loans. There was also a voluntary program of crop reduction but no direct federal financing for such activity. The act demonstrated the individualism, the corporatism, the voluntarism, and the decentralization that marked Hoover's early thinking; unfortunately, its failure to address financially the issue of overproduction led to its failure (Fausold 1977).

Hoover's growing activism led the federal government into new areas of public administration of business. While the president refused requests for direct federal relief programs, he supported a public works program of more than $300 million and the establishment of a public works administration to supervise the program. The program received approval, but a budget-minded Congress rejected the proposed agency on the grounds that it was too expensive. Hoover also supported a tax cut in an effort to stimulate the economy, an idea that he succeeded in selling to a highly skeptical Congress. Taxes were already so low and affected so few people that the cut had little impact. Of greater long-term significance was support for the establishment of the Reconstruction Finance Corporation, which made loans to financial institutions and to other businesses deemed critical to the economy. Hoover also backed the passage of the Federal Home Loan Bank Act, designed to ease liquidity pressures on financial institutions and reduce the rate of foreclosures. The act did relieve some of the growing financial pressures on lending institutions, but it came too late (July 1932) to aid many who had already lost their homes. While Hoover was not a do-nothing president as some of his critics said, it was unfortunately accurate that his efforts were often too little, too late, as other critics maintained (Joan Wilson 1975). Hoover—despite restrictions on his actions by his view of business–government relations—did more than any other president prior to 1933 to use the power of the federal government to promote business recovery and lay the foundation for broader government involvement in the economy under the New Deal.

NEW DEAL AND NEW REGULATION

When Franklin Roosevelt became president in 1933, the country was in the midst of a long-term depression and the biggest financial crisis in its history. Roosevelt, unencumbered by ideological baggage, addressed the depression with his New Deal, which had little that was new about it, calling for a balanced budget, a reduction in federal spending, a sound currency, and the removal of the federal government from most economic activities. It reflected the conventional economic wisdom of the time and deviated little from the Republican orthodoxy of the 1920s. Roosevelt, however, was an experimenter, and he was under tremendous public pressure to take some kind of action, particularly to bolster the financial structure.

Roosevelt launched short-term action and long-term reform. The Emergency Banking Act restricted gold transactions, authorized the Reconstruction Finance Corporation to support banks by buying their preferred stock, and directed treasury officials to supervise the reopening of banks as they returned to business after a four-day bank holiday proclaimed by Roosevelt. The Banking Act of 1933 separated commercial banks from their investment bank affiliates, with a view to restricting speculation, and established the Federal Deposit Insurance Corporation (FDIC), which would insure deposits in return for a small premium and additional regulation. The FDIC, in particular, did a great deal to reestablish public confidence in the financial system. There was considerable popular support for regulation of the stock market in view of the connection between the crash and the depression. The Federal Securities Act gave the Federal Trade Commission the power to supervise new security issues and to require full financial disclosure to accompany the new issue. This limited regulation was soon followed by a more comprehensive measure, the Securities Exchange Act of 1934, which placed all security transactions under federal regulation and established a new agency—the Securities and Exchange Commission—to monitor the measure (Myers 1970).

With 25 percent of the labor force unemployed in 1933, Roosevelt was under tremendous pressure to take rapid action to boost employment. His response—public works programs—was not original, but the scale on which these programs operated was unprecedented in American history. From the Civilian Conservation Corps to the Works Progress Administration, millions of Americans went back to work—at least temporarily—as employees of the federal government. Between 1934 and 1940 about 5 to 7 percent of the labor force was found in these types of jobs. Federal work programs required a level of spending that assumed a long-term commitment to large-scale deficit financing (Darby 1976).

Roosevelt's promotion of industrial recovery produced the most comprehensive effort at business–government planning during peacetime in American history. Under the National Industrial Recovery Act (NIRA), committees composed of representatives from labor, management, and government drafted detailed production codes for all branches of business and industry. The NIRA was influenced by the precedent of business–government cooperation during World War I. The codes were supposed to aid business by permitting cooperation among otherwise competitive firms while promoting labor by guaranteeing the right to organize, minimum wages, and maximum hours. Efforts to implement the codes soon became mired in administrative and legal controversy, which was not ended until the Supreme Court declared the NIRA unconstitutional in 1935.

The demise of NIRA was not the end of federal involvement with labor but the beginning. Section VIIA of NIRA was removed and passed as the National Labor Relations Act. With the NIRA codes inoperative, the right of labor to organize was once again without federal protection. The National Labor Relations Act reasserted federal protection for unionization, outlawed unfair management practices such as firing workers for joining unions, and established the National Labor Relations Board with the power to issue cease-and-desist orders to stop such practices. The passage of the Social Security Act represented the first major step in the country's uncertain march toward the welfare state. The United States, in fact, lagged behind most of the advanced industrial countries in terms of social insurance legislation; while the depression had helped to promote public support for some type of social security system, there was still major disagreement over how to finance such a system. The heart of the new act was a compromise: a national, compulsory system of old age insurance financed by equal contributions from employers and employees. The act also provided for a federal-state system of unemployment insurance that would be financed through a payroll tax on employers. While large numbers of workers were not covered by the Social Security Act, it was designed for future expansion (Hughes 1977; Gordon 1994; Rose 1994).

A combination of politics and economics dictated New Deal action to help farmers. The recovery of agricultural prices between 1923 and 1929 was undone quickly between 1929 and 1933. The failure of Hoover's Agricultural Marketing Act had convinced many government planners of the need for federal subsidies to promote crop reduction. The administration's response was the first Agricultural Adjustment Act (AAA) in 1933. The central theme of the AAA was to increase prices by reducing production through a variety of financial incentives. The most important was a direct, per acre subsidy for land taken out of production. The act also provided for export subsidies, loans to farmers to store crops, and last-resort purchases of surpluses by the Department of Agriculture. The system was financed by a tax on agricultural processors, a feature that ultimately led the Supreme Court to declare the act unconstitutional in 1936. A second AAA was passed in 1938, which continued the basic approaches of the earlier act without the objectionable financing. The AAAs helped to stop the disastrous decline in agricultural prices but proved unable to solve the basic problem of surplus production over the long term (Saloutos 1982).

The Roosevelt administration's antitrust policy was vague until Thurman Arnold was named head of the Antitrust Division of the Department of Justice in 1938, a political, not strategic, appointment. Arnold's vigorous trust-busting had the acquiescence, but not active support, of Roosevelt, who increasingly focused on foreign affairs (Miscamble 1982).

While the New Deal never demonstrated the capacity to promote full-scale economic recovery, it had a profound impact on business–government relations and the public administration of business. The most extreme example of this was agriculture, which had become the first federally subsidized business activity. Extensive federal regulation of the financial system had been introduced. The federal government had become the biggest employer and the biggest investor in the economy. While the inability of New Deal programs to restore prosperity led to a partial rehabilitation of business in the public mind, Americans increasingly looked to the central government, not business, to guide the economy and to guarantee a minimum standard of living. Only World War II would end the depression and lead to even more sweeping changes in business–government relations.

WORLD WAR II AND BUSINESS–GOVERNMENT RELATIONS

Before Pearl Harbor political considerations prevented U.S. formulation of any detailed mobilization plan, but the war in Europe and threatening war in Asia had already set afoot important changes in the economy and in public administration of business. Several wartime agencies such as the Office of Price Administration and the Supply Priorities and Allocation Board were established prior to December 1941, and the shift to a wartime economy was well under way by the summer of 1941.

Once the United States entered World War II, there was unprecedented business–government cooperation as well as government regulation of business. The practice of the Roosevelt administration was to add new agencies to those already in operation. Central direction of the economy was assumed successively by the War Production Board (1942), the Office of Economic Stabilization (1942), and the Office of War Mobilization (1943).

Unemployment problems quickly gave way to labor shortages, requiring the entry of over 2 million women into the workforce. The War Manpower Commission had the responsibility for directing the flow of workers into war industries. The National War Labor Board—composed of representatives from business, labor, and the public—had the dual responsibility of stabilizing wages and settling labor disputes so that war production would not be interrupted. Both the American Federation of Labor (AFL) and the Congress of Industrial Organizations (CIO) made no-strike pledges, which did not completely eliminate strikes but did have the effect of lessening the impact of those that did take place. The War Disputes Act of 1943 gave the president the power to seize plants that were struck (Keezer 1946).

Wartime financial policy reflected an effort to harmonize three goals: a desire to avoid war profiteering, a drive to curb inflation, and the need for a substantial increase in revenue. The United States would spend ten times as much ($320 billion) to fight World War II as it did to fight World War I. Although most of the revenue would come through deficit financing, there was another tax revolution as in World War I. Up until 1941 only a minority of Americans were affected by the personal income tax; the Revenue Act of 1942 drastically changed that. The act increased the personal income tax, imposed a surtax on incomes more than $200,000, lowered exemptions, and provided for a victory tax of 5 percent.

The same measure raised the corporate income tax and imposed an excess-profits tax. The act of 1942 brought so many additional persons under the income tax that subsequent wartime measures had to deal with the mechanics of collecting so much revenue from so many more people. The Revenue Act of 1943 introduced the withholding tax, while the Tax Act of 1944 provided for simplified returns for those with incomes under $5,000 (Studenski and Krooss 1963; Vernon 1994).

A combination of rationing and wage-price controls was used to curb inflation. Across-the-board controls went into effect in April 1942 but did not become effective until the spring of 1943. Rationing was effective despite a black market. Wage-price controls and rationing held price increases during the last two years of the war to less than 2 percent. This inflation rate was understated because it ignored indirect price increases such as quality deterioration, but the fight against inflation was, on balance, successful (Rockoff 1978).

New Deal programs of the 1930s had helped to expand agricultural production capacity and unintentionally to prepare agriculture to meet wartime demands. The war years were good times financially for the farmers, with prices up, net income up, and farm debt down. Unlike the industrial sector, there were no new major agencies set up to deal with agriculture during World War II. The federal government used a ceiling price-subsidy system to promote production and curb inflation (Wilcox 1947).

BUSINESS AND GOVERNMENT IN THE POSTWAR PERIOD

As the reconversion to a peacetime economy began, business–government relations were influenced by two great and seemingly contradictory factors: fear of inflation and fear of the economic depression. These fears came together uneasily in the Employment Act of 1946. The act reflected Keynesian countercyclical monetary and fiscal policy, confirmed a federal responsibility for the economy, and demonstrated the fear of inflation. Instead of committing the government to the pursuit of a policy of full employment as many Keynesians wanted—the Employment Act of 1946 grew out of the Full Employment Bill of 1945—the goal of maximizing employment was substituted (B. Jones 1972). Federal spending did not return to prewar levels after 1945 but instead showed a steady upward trend into the 1980s, reflecting growing outlays for social welfare and defense. While deficit-financing became a way of life, the national debt as a percentage of the gross national product (GNP) declined into the 1970s. From the mid-1970s onward, a series of planned and unplanned deficits led to a rapid increase in the ratio of national debt to GNP (Perkins and Walton 1985).

Postwar antitrust policy unfolded in an increasingly complicated and politicized environment. The overseas growth of American multinational corporations made it difficult for the federal government to monitor business activities. The growing use of the conglomerate as an organizational device beginning in the late 1950s led to a new wave of mergers but did not produce the traditional antitrust response of earlier decades. The growing popularity of franchising further confused the traditional antitrust approach. The only major change in antitrust legislation in the immediate postwar period was the passage of the Celler-Kefauver Act in 1950; the act introduced the concept of market-share as a test of anticompetitiveness but did not provide a specific figure. The increasingly politicized nature of the antitrust became evident with the oil crisis of the 1970s and the transition to the Reagan administration in 1981. The two major antitrust cases of the 1970s—AT&T and IBM—ended in the 1980s with no clear-cut indication of the future of antitrust activity.

Between 1945 and 1965 there were few new regulatory agencies established. The arrival of Lyndon Johnson in the presidency in 1963, however, represented the beginning of a new wave in federal regulation that would carry over into the 1970s. Johnson viewed his Great Society programs as the logical culmination of the New Deal of the 1930s. At the same time, consumerism and the environmental movement were having an increasing impact on the political structure. This new wave of regulation saw a shift in approach from telling business what had to be done to telling it how it must be done; the aim of the new regulation was not so much industrial control as social reform.

The Equal Employment Opportunity Commission (EEOC) was typical of Great Society regulation. The EEOC had broad responsibilities to monitor business for discriminatory personnel practices and soon became the center of political controversy. Environmental concerns culminated in the establishment of the Environmental Protection Agency (EPA) in 1970, with powers cutting across traditional business divisions. The complexity of environmental legislation coupled with the EPA's lack of attention to implementation costs and technical feasibility aroused political passions. By all odds the most disliked of the new agencies was OSHA—the Occupational Safety and Health Administration. OSHA represented an unprecedented federal involvement in the workplace that brought a growing crescendo of complaints from the business community. Other important new regulatory agencies included the Consumer Product Safety Commission, the Federal Energy Regulatory Commission, the Commodity Futures Trading Commission, and the National Transportation Safety Board (Congressional Quarterly 1982). One of the most telling points of the new regulation was that much of it was passed under an administration (Nixon) considered to be pro-business.

Enforcement efforts of these new agencies soon led to demands for modifications in their activities and even deregulation. The expansion of the regulatory bureaucracy came under increasing criticism as part of a growing public reaction against big government in general. Certain agencies, such as the EPA and OSHA, were repeatedly attacked for failing to weigh the costs of compliance against the benefits derived. This cost-benefits analysis soon spread to other regulatory activities (Weidenbaum 1977). Beginning with the Carter administration in 1977, the forces for deregulation launched a major effort to reform the regulatory system. Carter's greatest advances came in deregulation of the airlines (1978) and the financial services industry (1980). In both industries deregulation was followed by a period of fierce competition, which, in turn, led to a period of concentration.

The political agitation against regulation increased as it was linked to inflation and the decline in productivity during the 1970s. Regulation became a major issue in the presidential campaign of 1980, with Carter running on his record and the challenger, Ronald Reagan, calling for an even broader attack on regulation. The Reagan administration energetically attacked the problem of regulation by appointing a high-profile Task Force on Regulatory Relief to promote broad application of cost-benefit analyses and to review regulatory-impact reports from agencies proposing major new regulations. Reagan indirectly pursued deregulation by systematically cutting the budgets of enforcement agencies, with the FTC and the EPA particular targets. The president also used his power of appointment to regulatory bodies to place people in top positions who were sympathetic to deregulation; examples of this were his appointments to the FCC, the

SEC, and OSHA. By late 1982 the momentum of deregulation had already begun to slow. The president encountered declining congressional support for reform as well as the traditional problem of changing the federal bureaucracy. Congress refused the Reagan administration's request to close four of the ten regional offices of the Federal Trade Commission while bureaucrats unsympathetic to deregulation worked against efforts to speed up approval of new drugs by the Food and Drug Administration. By the mid-1980s deregulation had clearly slipped in political priorities (Congressional Quarterly 1985).

Public support for deregulation also waned in the mid- and late 1980s amid uncertainty about the effects of deregulation, especially in the airline and financial services industries. Airline deregulation led to a rapid proliferation of air carriers and fierce competition, which, in turn, led to bankruptcies, employee layoffs, and greater concentration in the industry. Even larger cities were often left with only one or two major carriers, as airlines tried to dominate particular hubs. Moreover, there was disagreement about the long-term effect of deregulation on air fares. While the immediate impact of deregulation was a reduction in air fares, consolidation and hub policies slowed the decline in air fares as early as the mid-1980s. By the early 1990s the airline industry was characterized by growing consolidation, declining profits, and a constantly changing fare structure.

Even more controversial was the national debate over the effect of deregulation on the financial services industry. The new competition among and between commercial banks and savings and loan associations led to a dramatic increase in financial services, an equally dramatic increase in bank failures, and the biggest crisis in the savings and loan sector since the Great Depression. Even the federal agency insuring the savings and loan associations—the Federal Savings and Loan Insurance Corporation (FSLIC)—technically went bankrupt and was terminated. Deregulation required a massive federal bailout of the thrifts industry—the full price of which is yet to be determined—and led to a rapid concentration in the financial services industry. Ironically, deregulation even led to an increase in the federal bureaucracy as a new agency, the Resolution Trust Corporation, was set up to deal with the S&L bailout.

American ambivalence about public administration continued into the 1990s. The momentum had gone out of the push for deregulation, but there was also little enthusiasm for expanding the government role in the economy and business. A major exception was the passage of the Americans with Disabilities Act of 1990, effective in 1992. Hailed as a civil rights law for the disabled, the new act came out of the type of environment that had produced the regulatory legislation of the 1960s and 1970s; the discussion focused on benefits, with limited attention to the costs of implementation. The act aimed at ensuring the disabled equal employment opportunities as well as access to programs, services, accommodations, transportation, and telecommunications. It affected all types and sizes of businesses. Although a sweeping and expensive—in terms of compliance—piece of legislation, the act was not part of a broad movement toward more regulation. Even calls for reregulation of the troubled airline and financial services industries attracted little support.

Public administration of business had evolved substantially from the mercantilist philosophy of the seventeenth century to the regulation-deregulation struggle of the late 1980s and 1990s. While some urged a continued retreat of government from business, still others called for reregulation, a new protectionism, and even a national industrial policy. The mercantilists of the colonial period would be amazed at the changes in business over the centuries; they would understand, however, the need to define the relationship between business and government (McQuaid 1994).

BIBLIOGRAPHIC ESSAY

Early historical evaluation attached a great deal of economic and political significance to mercantile restrictions, particularly their role in creating colonial discontent with British rule. More recent investigations have played down the economic impact and the political significance of mercantilism, particularly the classic work by Oliver Dickerson (1951). The growing use of the quantitative approach in history has focused attention on a burdens-versus-benefits analysis of mercantilism. While this approach confirmed the emerging view that mercantilism was not a major economic burden, it did not end the debate; instead, it merely pointed it in new directions over the impact and regional variations in burdens (Thomas 1965; Ransom 1968). Lars Magnusson (1994) stresses the evolution of mercantilist thinking and maintains that the mercantilist emphasis on trade and bullionism was justified in the context of the times.

The constitutional foundation for public administration of business has attracted considerable attention and provoked substantial controversy. Merrill Jensen (1950) provides a fundamental description of the business aspects of the Articles of Confederation. Business motives behind the drafting of the new Constitution were advanced by Charles A. Beard (1913). Beard's thesis led to a lengthy historical debate, with two of his most important critics being Robert E. Brown (1956) and Forrest McDonald (1958). D. W. Brogan (1965) provides a good review of the dispute over the economic interpretation of the Constitution.

John C. Miller (1963) furnishes a general overview of the 1790s, devoting considerable attention to business and economic affairs, including Hamilton's economic program. Hamilton's own views are set down in the edited work by Jacob E. Cooke (1964). John R. Nelson, Jr. (1979) reexamines the efforts of Hamilton to promote manufacturing, while E. James Ferguson (1961) surveys the financial situation of the nation. John E. Crowley

(1993) challenges the idea that the Revolution represented a victory for economic liberalism, maintaining that republican mercantilists in the United States clung to the mercantilist vision longer than English policymakers; Crowley maintains that Britain offered the same trade terms to former colonies that it did to all other sovereign nations.

The promotional aspects of public administration, especially in regard to internal improvements, have generated a body of literature. George Rogers Taylor (1951) still provides the best general study of the transportation revolution and its impact on the antebellum economy. Carter Goodrich (1960, 1967) has two excellent works on government involvement in the economy, especially the promotion of canals and railroads. For the devolving nature of public administration, see Bruchey (1968), especially Chapter 6. An excellent case study of state involvement is in Gunn (1988).

The traditional view that the Civil War stimulated northern industry is associated with the writings of Charles A. Beard and Mary R. Beard (1927) and Louis M. Hacker (1940). The Beard-Hacker thesis has been revised by quantitative historians Stanley Engerman (1966) and Claudia Goldin and Frank Lewis (1975), who maintain that the war slowed, rather than stimulated, economic development. The long-term impact of the war on the tariff and of the tariff on postwar developments is examined quantitatively by Jeffrey Williamson (1974). For more on the protective and revenue aspects of the tariff, see the financial survey by Paul Studenski and Herman Krooss (1963). Bray Hammond (1970) and Richard Timberlake (1978) examine the connection between the financial needs of the government and the passage of the new banking legislation. Good general treatments of government land policy are found in Carstensen (1963) and Gates (1973).

For general discussions of the rise of big business, see Kirkland (1961), Porter (1973), and Chandler (1977). James W. Hurst (1970) and Alfred H. Kelly et al. (1983) examine the interaction between the legal environment and big business. On the Interstate Commerce Act, Gabriel Kolko (1965) rejects the traditional public interest explanation for the origins of the act and offers the major work on the capture thesis, maintaining that railroad companies pressed for passage of the measure and viewed the ICC as a tool to promote railroad interests. For a critique of the Kolko thesis, see Harbeson (1967). Albro Martin (1971) revised the revisionists, arguing that the origins of the act were in a mercantile lobby and that both the railroads and the public were ultimately losers because of the misguided intervention of the ICC. William Letwin's *Law and Economic Policy in America* (1965) is a highly detailed account of the origins and implementation of the Sherman Antitrust Act. Christopher Gandy (1993) reviews the legislative history of the act and concludes that, in passing the measure, Congress had expressed more concern for producers than for consumers. Tony Freyer (1992) compares and contrasts antitrust enforcement in Britain and the

United States, concluding that antitrust efforts had the effect of facilitating managerial effectiveness in both countries (see also A. D. Neale, 1970).

Martin J. Schiesl (1977) and Bradley R. Rice (1977) examine the interaction between business and government at the municipal level, especially reform efforts aimed at making government more businesslike—more efficient and professional. Mansel G. Blackford (1993) explores how West Coast businessmen formed new associations and reorganized local governments to promote city planning to deal with rapid growth. Blackford (1977) also provides a good case study of the changing nature of public administration of business at the state level, especially the mixed motives behind greater regulation.

For general views of the interaction between business and government at the national level, see Lewis L. Gould (1978), Kolko (1963), and Robert H. Wiebe (1962). Gould provides a more traditional view of the period, especially in his treatment of the Wilson era. More controversial are the interpretations by Kolko and Wiebe. Kolko sees the growth in regulation as a product of business efforts to rationalize and stabilize the economy, which he describes as political capitalism. Wiebe provides an extended exposition of the capture thesis, maintaining that business captured the Progressive movement and used its influence to transform the regulatory agencies into instruments for promoting business interests. Eugene White (1983) and Robert C. West (1977) furnish excellent surveys of the events leading to the establishment of the Federal Reserve and its early years of operation. White places the establishment of the Fed in the context of a lengthy struggle between state and federal governments over control of banking and believes that the reformers tended to focus on peripheral issues rather than basic problems. West takes a similar approach, maintaining that the Fed began operations in an environment very different from the one envisioned by its creators. Silvano A. Wueschner (1999) details the conflict between Herbert Hoover and Benjamin Strong over monetary policy and Federal Reserve operations.

The interaction between business and government during World War I centers on the War Industries Board, for which Robert D. Cuff (1973) furnishes a detailed analysis of origins, operations, and dissolution. Also useful are the articles by Daniel R. Beaver (1965) and Robert F. Himmelberg (1965). Paul A. C. Koistinen (1967) sees the WIB as a key phase in the development of what would later be described as the military-industrial complex. Hugh Rockoff examines the problems of wage-price controls in three offerings (1981a, 1981b, 1984). The problems of financing the war are expertly covered in Chapter 23 of Studenski and Krooss (1963). Valerie Jean Conner (1983) covers the role of the National War Labor Board, emphasizing its importance in formulating the pro-labor policies of the wartime period and stressing its function as a model for the New Deal and

World War II actions. Himmelberg (1965) and Rockoff (1981a, 1981b) deal with major aspects of the demobilization.

William E. Leuchtenberg (1958) provides an excellent general survey of the 1920s, including political and social developments as well as economic and financial developments. Ellis W. Hawley (1974) discusses changing views on business–business and business–government relations as exemplified in the thoughts and actions of Herbert Hoover—Hawley wrote the Foreword to the Wueschner study (1999). Charles F. Holt (1977) and Robert T. Keller (1973) furnish quantitative answers to the question of how different groups shared in the prosperity of the 1920s; their conclusions generally support the traditional view that the corporations and the upper class preempted a disproportionate share of the profits of prosperity. Gene Smiley and Richard H. Keehn (1995) maintain that the tax cuts of the 1920s were not aimed at benefiting the wealthy but rather at reducing tax avoidance by the wealthier classes responding to earlier tax increases; although taxes were lowered, the effective burden of taxation was shifted from lower-income toward higher-income taxpayers. West (1977) and Elmus Wicker (1966) shed light on problems in the financial structure, while James Shideler (1957) examines the farm crisis of the early 1920s.

Arthur M. Schlesinger, Jr. (1957) and George Soule (1947) provide the traditional interpretation of the 1920s and the early depression as a time of monopoly power, technical change, maldistribution of income, and underconsumption. Holt (1977) and Keller (1973) confirm this traditional view of maldistribution in their quantitative studies. Joan Hoff Wilson (1975) provides a readable biography of Hoover, while the failure of Hoover's farm policies is examined and explained by Martin L. Fausold (1977).

The temporary changes and long-term reforms made by the New Deal in the financial structure are detailed in Myers (1970). The impact of New Deal fiscal policy is the topic of articles by E. Cary Brown (1956) and John J. Wallis (1984). Brown concludes that fiscal policy did not have a major influence on recovery—not because it failed but because it was not seriously tried. Wallis relates the changes in local and state expenditures to variations in federal spending. Michael Darby (1976) examines unemployment rates for the 1933–1941 period, concluding that they were greatly exaggerated due to a major conceptual error on the part of the Bureau of Labor Statistics.

Jonathan Hughes (1977) deals with the background, provisions, and impact of the labor legislation of the New Deal era, focusing on the National Labor Relations Act and the Social Security Act. Colin Gordon (1994) examines the use of labor unions to regulate costs and rationalize working practices (regulatory unionism); Gordon believes that the National Labor Relations Act and the Social Security Act grew out of this approach and were business-friendly. Theodore Saloutos (1982) traces the search for an agricultural policy between 1919 and 1933 and then examines the major

New Deal agencies aimed at aiding the farm sector: the Agricultural Adjustment Administration, the Resettlement Administration, and the Farm Security Administration. Saloutos sees mixed results coming from New Deal farm measures: the poorest farmers were essentially neglected; many family farmers were helped; but the large operators received disproportionate benefits. Richard S. Kirkendall (1966) describes the service intellectuals, or technical experts, who helped to frame and implement New Deal agricultural policy.

Hawley (1966) examines the New Deal's uncertain antitrust policy, which he sees as a function of three contending views: a group supporting legalization of a cartelized economy, a group that favored democratic planning for an integrated economy in which all major interest groups would have an input, and a group urging a Brandeisian policy of trust-busting and economic decentralization. No one view ever completely prevailed, but the trustbusters and the cartelizers were generally more influential than the planners. Wilson D. Miscamble (1982) analyzes the post-1938 increase in antitrust activity, maintaining that it reflected the personal interests of antitrust chief Thurman Arnold rather than a strategic policy decision by Roosevelt.

For the World War II period, Dexter M. Keezer (1946) provides an insider's view of the National War Labor Board. Serving as one of the public members of the board, Keezer recognizes the inefficiency and infighting that plagued the board but believes that the agency succeeded in its dual mission of reducing labor disputes and stabilizing wages. J. R. Vernon (1994) maintains that fiscal policy was the most important factor in economic recovery after 1940. For a general survey of wartime financing, see Studenski and Krooss (1963). Rockoff (1981b) examines the response of the giant corporations to wage-price controls, an especially important issue given the high degree of concentration taking place during the war. He concludes that compliance was generally good owing to a combination of fear of reprisal, a desire to maintain good public relations, constraints on allocation, and collective bargaining. Rockoff (1978) also explores the role of indirect price increases and their relation to real wages. Walter W. Wilcox (1947) provides a comprehensive account of wartime agricultural policy, which he sees as a financial success but a failure in terms of solving the basic problems of American farming.

Byrd L. Jones (1972) examines the influence of Keynesian thinking during World War II and how this led to the Employment Act of 1946. Edwin J. Perkins and Gary M. Walton (1985) and Hughes (1977) discuss the implications of the upward spiral in federal spending since World War II. Richard Hofstadter (1964) views postwar antitrust policy as "one of the faded passions of American reform"; the antitrust ideal became institutionalized, as ideology was transformed into technique.

The regulation-deregulation debate has produced an extensive literature in recent years. For a good nuts-and-bolts approach to the issue, see the two publications by the Congressional Quarterly (1982, 1985). Murray Weidenbaum (1977) was a key figure in applying cost-benefits analysis to regulation and later served as Reagan's first chairman of the Council of Economic Advisors and as an original member of the Task Force on Regulatory Relief. James Q. Wilson (1980) provides a collection of essays dealing with the politics of regulation. Martha Derthick and Paul J. Quirk (1985) use the airlines, trucking, and telecommunications as case studies in the politics of deregulation, explaining how the Congress and the regulatory agencies came to support deregulation, while the industries and labor unions affected were largely ineffective in their opposition. For a negative view on the results of airline deregulation, see Dempsey (1992). For an overview of airline regulation, see Richard H. K. Vietor (1990). Vietor (1994) also puts the regulation-deregulation contest into a broader context by examining case studies on airlines, energy, telecommunications, and financial services.

The extensive literature on the savings and loan (S & L) crisis is brought together by Pat L. Talley (1993). Ned Eichler (1989) directly links deregulation to the S & L crisis and advocates reregulation. The long-term effects of the Americans with Disabilities Act are yet to be examined; for a detailed overview of the act itself, see the publication by the Bureau of National Affairs (1990). Despite the political wrangling over regulation and deregulation, Kim McQuaid (1994) reminds us how, by downplaying ideology, the public and private sectors have worked together since World War II.

BIBLIOGRAPHY

American Review of Public Administration. Parkville, MO: Midwest Review of Public Administration, 1981– . Quarterly.

Aristigueta, Maria Pilar. *Managing for Results in State Government.* Westport, CT: Quorum Books, 1999.

Arnold, David S., and Jeremy F. Plant. *Public Official Associations and State and Local Government: A Bridge across One Hundred Years.* Fairfax, VA: George Mason University Press, 1994.

ASPA News and Views. Washington, DC: American Society for Public Administration, 1970–1977. Quarterly. Continued by *Public Administration Times.*

Bardach, Eugene. *Getting Agencies to Work Together: The Practice and Theory of Managerial Craftsmanship.* Washington, DC: Brookings Institution, 1998.

Barry, Donald D., and Howard R. Whitcomb. *The Legal Foundations of Public Administration.* 2d ed. St. Paul: West, 1987.

Beard, Charles A. *An Economic Interpretation of the Constitution.* New York: Macmillan, 1913.

Beard, Charles A., and Mary R. Beard. *The Rise of American Civilization.* Vol. 2, *The Industrial Era.* New York: Macmillan, 1927.

Beaver, Daniel R. "Newton D. Baker and the Genesis of the War Industries Board, 1917–1918." *Journal of American History* 52 (June 1965): 43–58.

Blackford, Mansel G. *The Politics of Business in California, 1890–1920.* Columbus: Ohio State University Press, 1977.

———. *The Lost Dream: Businessmen and City Planning on the Pacific Coast, 1890–1920.* Columbus: Ohio State University Press, 1993.

Bowen, Don L., ed. *Public Service Professional Associations and the Public Interest.* Philadelphia: American Academy of Political and Social Science, 1973.

Box, Richard C. *Citizen Governance Leading American Communities into the 21st Century.* Thousand Oaks, CA: Sage, 1998.

———. "Running Government like a Business: Implications for Public Administration Theory and Practice." *American Review of Public Administration* 29, no. 1 (March 1999): 19–43.

Bozeman, Barry, ed. *Public Management: The State of the Art.* Jossey-Bass Public Administration Series. San Francisco: Jossey-Bass, 1993.

Brogan, D. W. "The Quarrel over Charles Austin Beard and the American Constitution." *Economic History Review,* 2d ser., 18 (August 1965): 199–223.

Brown, E. Cary. "Fiscal Policy in the Thirties: A Reappraisal." *American Economic Review* 46, no. 4 (December 1956): 857–79.

Brown, Robert E. *Charles Beard and the Constitution.* Princeton, NJ: Princeton University Press, 1956.

Bruchey, Stuart. *The Roots of American Economic Growth, 1607–1861.* New York: Harper & Row, 1968.

Bureau of National Affairs. *The Americans with Disabilities Act: A Practical and Legal Guide to Impact, Enforcement, and Compliance.* Washington, DC: Bureau of National Affairs, 1990.

Carnevale, David G. *Trustworthy Government: Leadership and Management Strategies for Building Trust and High Performance.* Jossey-Bass Public Administration Series. San Francisco: Jossey-Bass, 1995.

Carstensen, Vernon R., ed. *The Public Lands: Studies in the History of the Public Domain.* Madison: University of Wisconsin Press, 1963.

Casper, Dale E. *Politics and Public Administration of State Affairs: A Historical Perspective, Journal Articles, 1982–1987.* Public Administration Series. Monticello, IL: Vance Bibliographies, 1988.

Cayer, N. Joseph, and Louis F. Weschler. *Public Administration: Social Change and Adaptive Management.* New York: St. Martin's Press, 1988.

Chandler, Alfred D., Jr. "The Beginnings of 'Big Business' in American History." *Business History Review* 33 (Spring 1959): 1–31.

———. *Strategy and Structure: Chapters in the History of the Industrial Enterprise.* Cambridge: MIT Press, 1962.

———. *The Visible Hand: The Managerial Revolution in American Business.* Cambridge: Harvard University Press, 1977.

———. *Scale and Scope: The Dynamics of Industrial Capitalism.* Cambridge: Harvard University Press, 1990.

Congressional Quarterly. *Regulation: Process and Politics.* Washington, DC: Congressional Quarterly, 1982.

———. *Federal Regulatory Directory, 1985–1986.* Washington, DC: Congressional Quarterly, 1985.

Conner, Valerie Jean. *The National War Labor Board: Stability, Social Justice, and the Voluntary State in World War I.* Chapel Hill: University of North Carolina Press, 1983.

Cook, Brian J. *Bureaucracy and Self-Government: Reconsidering the Role of Public Administration in American Politics.* Interpreting American Politics. Baltimore: Johns Hopkins University Press, 1996.

Cooke, Jacob E., ed. *The Reports of Alexander Hamilton.* New York: Harper & Row, 1964.

Cooper, Phillip J., and Chester A. Newland, eds. *Handbook of Public Law and Administration.* Jossey-Bass Nonprofit and Public Management Series. San Francisco: Jossey-Bass, 1997.

Cox, Raymond W. III, Susan J. Buck, and Betty N. Morgan. *Public Administration in Theory and Practice.* Englewood Cliffs, NJ: Prentice-Hall, 1994.

Crowley, John E. *The Privileges of Independence: Neomercantilism and the American Revolution.* Baltimore: Johns Hopkins University Press, 1993.

Cuff, Robert D. *The War Industries Board: Business-Government Relations during World War I.* Baltimore: Johns Hopkins University Press, 1973.

Daniels, Mark R. *Terminating Public Programs: An American Political Paradox.* Armonk, NY: M. E. Sharpe, 1997.

Darby, Michael. "Three and a Half Million U.S. Employees Have Been Mislaid: Or, an Explanation of Unemployment, 1934–1941." *Journal of Political Economy* 84, no. 1 (February 1976): 1–16.

Dempsey, Paul Stephen. *Airline Deregulation and Laissez Faire Mythology.* Westport, CT: Quorum Books, 1992.

Derthick, Martha, and Paul J. Quirk. *The Politics of Deregulation.* Washington, DC: Brookings Institution, 1985.

Dickerson, Oliver. *The Navigation Acts and the American Revolution.* Philadelphia: University of Pennsylvania Press, 1951.

DiIulio, John J., ed. *Deregulating the Public Service: Can Government Be Improved?* Washington, DC: Brookings Institution, 1994.

Dubnick, Melvin J., and Barbara S. Romzek. *American Public Administration: Politics and the Management of Expectations.* New York: Macmillan, 1991.

Eichler, Ned. *The Thrift Debacle.* Berkeley: University of California Press, 1989.

Engerman, Stanley. "The Economic Impact of the Civil War." *Explorations in Economic History* 3 (Spring 1966): 176–99.

Fausold, Martin L. "President Hoover's Farm Policies, 1929–1933." *Agricultural History* 51, no. 2 (April 1977): 362–77.

Ferguson, E. James. *The Power of the Purse: A History of American Public Finances, 1776–1790.* Chapel Hill: University of North Carolina Press, 1961.

Filipovitch, Tony. "Citizen Governance Leading American Communities into the 21st Century/Government Is Us: Public Administration in an Anti-Government Era." Review of *Citizen Governance Leading American Communities into the 21st Century,* by Richard C. Box, and *Government Is Us: Public Administration in an Anti-Government Era,* by Cheryl Simrell King and Camilla Stivers. *Journal of the American Planning Association* 65, no. 1 (Winter 1999): 118–19.

Fitch, Lyle C. *Making Democracy Work: The Life and Letters of Luther Halsey Gulick, 1892–1993.* Berkeley: University of California, Institute of Governmental Studies Press, 1996.

Frederickson, H. George. *The Spirit of Public Administration*. San Francisco: Jossey-Bass, 1997.

Frederickson, H. George, and Jocelyn M. Johnston, eds. *Public Management Reform and Innovation: Research, Theory, and Application*. Tuscaloosa: University of Alabama Press, 1999.

Freyer, Tony. *Regulating Big Business: Antitrust in Great Britain and America, 1880–1990*. Cambridge: Cambridge University Press, 1992.

Fry, Brian R. *Mastering Public Administration: From Max Weber to Dwight Waldo*. Chatham House Series on Change in American Politics. Chatham, NJ: Chatham House, 1989.

Gandy, Christopher. "Original Intent and the Sherman Antitrust Act: A Reexamination of the Consumer-Welfare Hypothesis." *Journal of Economic History* 53, no. 2 (June 1993): 359–76.

Garvey, Gerald. *Public Administration: The Profession and the Practice: A Case Study Approach*. New York: St. Martin's Press, 1997.

Gates, Paul W. *Landlords and Tenants on the Prairie Frontier: Studies in American Land Policy*. Ithaca, NY: Cornell University Press, 1973.

Goldin, Claudia, and Frank Lewis. "The Economic Cost of the American Civil War: Estimates and Implications." *Journal of Economic History* 35, no. 2 (June 1975): 299–326.

Goodrich, Carter. *Government Promotion of American Canals and Railroads, 1800–1890*. New York: Columbia University Press, 1960.

———. *The Government and the Economy, 1783–1861*. Indianapolis: Bobbs-Merrill, 1967.

Gordon, Colin. *New Deals: Business, Labor, and Politics in America, 1920–1935*. New York: Cambridge University Press, 1994.

Gordon, George J., and Michael E. Milakovich. *Public Administration in America*. 6th ed. New York: St. Martin's Press, 1998.

Gould, Lewis L. *Reform and Regulation: American Politics, 1910–1916*. New York: Wiley & Sons, 1978.

Gunn, L. Ray. *The Decline of Authority: Public Economic Policy and Political Development in New York, 1800–1860*. Ithaca, NY: Cornell University Press, 1988.

Hacker, Louis M. *The Triumph of American Capitalism*. New York: Columbia University Press, 1940.

Hammond, Bray. *Sovereignty and an Empty Purse: Banks and Politics in the Civil War*. Princeton: Princeton University Press, 1970.

Harbeson, Robert. "Railroads and Regulation, 1887–1916: Conspiracy or Public Interest?" *Journal of Economic History* 27, no. 2 (June 1967): 230–42.

Hawley, Ellis W. *The New Deal and the Problem of Monopoly*. Princeton, NJ: Princeton University Press, 1966.

———. "Herbert Hoover, the Commerce Secretariat, and the Vision of an 'Associative State.' " *Journal of American History* 61 (June 1974): 116–40.

Himmelberg, Robert F. "The War Industries Board and the Antitrust Question in 1918." *Journal of American History* 52 (June 1965): 59–74.

Hofstadter, Richard. "What Happened to the Antitrust Movement?" In *The Business Establishment*, edited by Earl F. Cheit. New York: Wiley, 1964.

Holden, Matthew, Jr. *Continuity and Disruption: Essays in Public Administration*.

Pitt Series in Policy and Institutional Studies. Pittsburgh: University of Pittsburgh Press, 1996.

Holt, Charles F. "Who Benefitted from the Prosperity of the Twenties?" *Explorations in Economic History* 14 (July 1977): 277–89.

Hughes, Jonathan. *The Governmental Habit*. New York: Basic Books, 1977.

Hurst, James W. *The Legitimacy of the Business Corporation in the United States, 1780–1970*. Charlottesville: University Press of Virginia, 1970.

Ingraham, Patricia W., James R. Thompson, and Ronald P. Sanders, eds. *Transforming Government: Lessons from the Reinvention Laboratories*. Jossey-Bass Nonprofit and Public Management Series. San Francisco: Jossey-Bass, 1998

"Integrity and Ethics in Public Administration." *PM, Public Management* 80, no. 10 (October 1998): 3–4.

Jensen, Merrill. *The New Nation: A History of the United States during the Confederation, 1781–1789*. New York: Knopf, 1950.

Johnson, William C. *Public Administration: Policy, Politics, and Practice*. Guilford, CT: Dushkin, 1992.

Jones, Byrd L. "The Role of Keynesians in Wartime Policy and Postwar Planning, 1940–1946." *American Economic Review* 62 (May 1972): 125–33.

Jones, Raymona A. *Human Relations in Public Administration: A Retrospective Bibliography*. Public Administration Series. Monticello, IL: Vance Bibliographies, 1990.

Jreisat, Jamil E. *Managing Public Organizations: A Developmental Perspective on Theory and Practice*. New York: Paragon House, 1992

Kaufman, Herbert. "Continuity and Disruption." Review of *Continuity and Disruption: Essays in Public Administration*, by Matthew Holden, Jr. *Public Administration Review* 58, no. 4 (July/August 1998): 368.

Keezer, Dexter M. "The National War Labor Board." *American Economic Review* 36 (June 1946): 233–57.

Keller, Robert T. "Factor Income Distribution in the United States during the 1920's: A Reexamination of the Fact and Theory." *Journal of Economic History* 33, no. 1 (March 1973): 252–73.

Kelly, Alfred H. et al. *The American Constitution: Its Origins and Development*. New York: W. W. Norton, 1983.

Kickert, Walter J. M., and Richard J. Stillman II, eds. *The Modern State and Its Study: New Administrative Sciences in a Changing Europe and United States*. Northampton, MA: Edward Elgar, 2000.

King, Cheryl Simrell, and Camilla Stivers, in collaboration with Richard C. Box et al. *Government Is Us: Public Administration in an Anti-Government Era*. Thousand Oaks, CA: Sage, 1998.

Kirkendall, Richard S. *Social Scientists and Farm Politics in the Age of Roosevelt*. Columbia: University of Missouri Press, 1966.

Kirkland, Edward C. *Industry Comes of Age: Business, Labor, and Public Policy, 1860–1897*. New York: Holt, Rinehart, Winston, 1961.

Koistinen, Paul A. C. "The Industrial-Military Complex in Historical Perspective: World War I." *Business History Review* 41, no. 4 (Winter 1967): 378–403.

Kolko, Gabriel. *The Triumph of Conservatism*. New York: Macmillan, 1963.

———. *Railroads and Regulation, 1887–1916*. Princeton, NJ: Princeton University Press, 1965.

Kramer, Robert. "Weaving the Public into Public Administration." Review of *Government Is Us: Public Administration in an Anti-Government Era*, by Cheryl Simrell King and Camilla Stivers. *Public Administration Review* 59, no. 1 (January/February 1999): 89–92.

Lawler, Peter Augustine, Robert Martin Schaefer, and David Lewis Schaefer, eds. *Active Duty: Public Administration as Democratic Statesmanship*. Lanham, MD: Rowman & Littlefield, 1998.

Letwin, William. *Law and Economic Policy in America: The Evolution of the Sherman Antitrust Act*. New York: Random House, 1965.

Leuchtenberg, William E. *The Perils of Prosperity, 1914–1933*. Chicago: University of Chicago Press, 1958.

Linden, Russell Matthew. *Seamless Government: A Practical Guide to Re-Engineering in the Public Sector*. Jossey-Bass Public Administration Series. San Francisco: Jossey-Bass, 1994.

Lynn, Laurence E., Jr. *Public Management as Art, Science, and Profession*. Chatham, NJ: Chatham House, 1996.

Lynn, Naomi B., and Aaron Wildavsky. *Public Administration: The State of the Discipline*. Chatham, NJ: Chatham House, 1990.

Magnusson, Lars. *Mercantilism: The Shaping of an Economic Language*. New York: Routledge, 1994.

Martin, Albro. *Enterprise Denied: Origins of the Decline of American Railroads*. New York: Columbia University Press, 1971.

Martin, Daniel. *The Guide to the Foundations of Public Administration*. Public Administration and Public Policy, 37. New York: Dekker, 1989.

Malone, Laurence J. *Opening the West: Federal Internal Improvements before 1860*. Contributions in Economics and Economic History, no. 196. Westport, CT: Greenwood Press, 1998.

McDonald, Forrest. *We the People: The Economic Origins of the Constitution*. Chicago: University of Chicago Press, 1958.

McQuaid, Kim. *Uneasy Partners: Big Business in American Politics, 1945–1990*. Baltimore: Johns Hopkins University Press, 1994.

McSwite, O. C. [Cynthia McSwain and Orion White]. *Legitimacy in Public Administration: A Discourse Analysis*. Advances in Public Administration. Thousand Oaks, CA: Sage, 1997.

Midwest Review of Public Administration. Parkville, MO: Midwest Review of Public Administration, 1967–1980. Quarterly. Continued by *American Review of Public Administration*.

Miller, John C. *The Federalist Era, 1789–1801*. New York: Harper & Row, 1963.

Miscamble, Wilson D. "Thurman Arnold Goes to Washington: A Look at Antitrust Policy in the Later New Deal." *Business History Review* 56, no 2 (Spring 1982): 1–15.

Myers, Margaret G. *A Financial History of the United States*. New York: Columbia University Press, 1970.

Namorato, Michael V., ed. *The Diary of Rexford G. Tugwell: The New Deal, 1932–1935*. Contributions in Economics and Economic History, no. 136. Westport, CT: Greenwood Press, 1992.

Neale, A. D. *The Antitrust Laws of the United States of America: A Study of Competition Enforced by Law*. New York: Cambridge University Press, 1970.

Nelson, John R., Jr. "Alexander Hamilton and American Manufacturing: A Reexamination." *Journal of American History* 65 (March 1979): 971–95.

Newland, Chester A. "A Document of These Times: The International Encyclopedia of Public Policy and Administration." Review of *International Encyclopedia of Public Policy and Administration*, edited by Jay M. Shafritz. *Public Administration Review* 58, no. 4 (July/August 1998): 361–67.

Ostrom, Vincent. *The Intellectual Crisis in American Public Administration*. 2d ed. Tuscaloosa: University of Alabama Press, 1989.

PA Times. Washington, DC: American Society for Public Administration, 1987– . Monthly.

Perkins, Edwin J. *The Economy of Colonial America*. 2d ed. New York: Columbia University Press, 1988.

———. *American Public Finance and Financial Services, 1700–1815*. Historical Perspectives on Business Enterprise Series. Columbus: Ohio State University Press, 1994.

Perkins, Edwin J., and Gary M. Walton. *A Prosperous People: The Growth of the American Economy*. Englewood Cliffs, NJ: Prentice-Hall, 1985.

Perry, James L., ed. *Handbook of Public Administration*. San Francisco: Jossey-Bass, 1997.

Porter, Glenn. *The Rise of Big Business, 1860–1910*. Arlington Heights, IL: Harlan Davidson, 1973.

Public Administration Quarterly. Randallstown, MD: Southern Public Administration Education Foundation, 1983– . Quarterly.

Public Administration Review. Washington, DC: American Society for Public Administration, 1940– . Quarterly.

Public Administration Times. Washington, DC: American Society for Public Administration, 1978–1987. Monthly. Continued by *PA Times*.

Public Productivity and Management Review. San Francisco: Jossey-Bass, 1989– . Quarterly.

Public Productivity Review. New York: Center for Productive Public Management, 1975–1989. Quarterly. Continued by *Public Productivity and Management Review*.

Raadschelders, Joseph C. N. *Handbook of Administrative History*. New Brunswick, NJ: Transaction Publishers, 1998.

Rabin, Jack, and James S. Bowman, eds. *Politics and Administration: Woodrow Wilson and American Public Administration*. Public Administration and Public Policy, 22. New York: Dekker, 1984.

Ransom, Roger. "British Policy and Colonial Growth: Some Implications of the Burden from the Navigation Acts." *Journal of Economic History* 28, no. 3 (September 1968): 427–35.

Rice, Bradley R. *Progressive Cities: The Commission Government Movement in America, 1901–1920*. Austin: University of Texas Press, 1977.

Rimmerman, Craig A. *The New Citizenship: Unconventional Politics, Activism, and Service*. Boulder, CO: Westview Press, 1997.

Rockoff, Hugh. "Indirect Price Increases and Real Wages during World War II." *Explorations in Economic History* 15 (October 1978): 407–20.

————. "Price and Wage Controls in Four Wartime Periods." *Journal of Economic History* 41, no. 2 (June 1981a): 381–401.

————. "The Response of the Giant Corporations to Wage and Price Controls in World War II." *Journal of Economic History* 41, no. 1 (March 1981b): 123–28.

————. *Drastic Measures: A History of Wage and Price Controls in the United States.* New York: Cambridge University Press, 1984.

Rohr, John A. *Public Service, Ethics, and Constitutional Practice.* Studies in Government and Public Policy. Lawrence: University Press of Kansas, 1998.

Rose, Nancy Ellen. *Put to Work: Relief Programs of the Great Depression.* New York: Monthly Review Press, 1994.

Rosenbloom, David H., and Rosemary O'Leary. *Public Administration and Law.* 2d ed. Public Administration and Public Policy, 61. New York: M. Dekker, 1997.

Rouse, John Edward. *Public Administration in American Society: A Guide to Information Sources.* Gale Information Guide Library. American Government and History Information Guide Series, vol. 11. Detroit: Gale Research, 1980.

Saloutos, Theodore. *The American Farmer and the New Deal.* Ames: Iowa State University Press, 1982.

Schachter, Hindy Lauer. *Frederick Taylor and the Public Administration Community: A Reevaluation.* SUNY Series in Public Administration. Albany: State University of New York Press, 1989.

————. *Reinventing Government or Reinventing Ourselves: The Role of Citizen Owners in Making a Better Government.* SUNY Series in Public Administration. Albany: State University of New York Press, 1997.

Schiesl, Martin J. *The Politics of Efficiency: Municipal Administration and Reform in America, 1880–1920.* Berkeley: University of California Press, 1977.

Schlesinger, Arthur M., Jr. *The Crisis of the Old Order, 1919–1933.* Boston: Houghton Mifflin, 1957.

Schneider, Saundra K. "Reinventing Public Administration: A Case Study of the Federal Emergency Management Agency." *Public Administration Quarterly* 22, no. 1 (Spring 1998): 35–57.

Schuman, David, and Dick W. Olufs III. *Public Administration in the United States.* 2d ed. Lexington, MA: D. C. Heath, 1993.

Shafritz, Jay M., ed. *International Encyclopedia of Public Policy and Administration.* 4 vols. Boulder, CO: Westview Press, 1998.

Sheeran, Patrick J. *Ethics in Public Administration: A Philosophical Approach.* Westport, CT: Praeger, 1993.

Shideler, James. *Farm Crisis, 1919–1923.* Berkeley: University of California Press, 1957.

Smiley, Gene, and Richard H. Keehn. "Federal Personal Income Tax Policy in the 1920s." *Journal of Economic History* 55, no. 2 (June 1995): 285–303.

Soule, George. *Prosperity Decade.* New York: Rinehart, 1947.

Spicer, Michael W. *The Founders, the Constitution, and Public Administration: A Conflict in Worldviews.* Washington, DC: Georgetown University Press, 1995.

————. "Frederick the Great on Government and Public Administration: An Examination of His Ideas and Their Significance for American Public Administration." *American Review of Public Administration* 28, no. 3 (September 1998): 287–304.

Stabile, Donald R. *The Origins of American Public Finance: Debates over Money, Debt, and Taxes in the Constitutional Era, 1776–1836.* Contributions in Economics and Economic History, no. 198. Westport, CT: Greenwood Press, 1998.

Steeples, Douglas, and David O. Whitten. *Democracy in Desperation: The Depression of 1893.* Contributions in Economics and Economic History, no. 199. Westport, CT: Greenwood Press, 1998.

Stillman, Richard Joseph II. *Creating the American State: The Moral Reformers and the Modern Administrative World They Made.* Tuscaloosa: University of Alabama Press, 1998.

———. *Preface to Public Administration: A Search for Themes and Direction.* 2d ed. Burke, VA: Chatelaine Press, 1999.

Studenski, Paul, and Herman Krooss. *Financial History of the United States: Fiscal, Monetary, Banking, and Tariff, including Financial Administration and State and Local Finance.* 2d ed. New York: McGraw-Hill, 1963.

Talley, Pat L., comp. *The Savings and Loan Crisis: An Annotated Bibliography.* Westport, CT: Greenwood Press, 1993.

Taylor, George Rogers. *The Transportation Revolution, 1815–1860.* New York: Rinehart, 1951.

Thomas, John Clayton. "Bringing the Public into Public Administration: The Struggle Continues." Review of *Citizen Governance: Leading American Communities into the 21st Century,* by Richard C. Box, and *The New Citizenship: Unconventional Politics, Activism, and Service,* by Craig A. Rimmerman. *Public Administration Review* 59, no. 1 (January/February 1999): 83–88.

Thomas, Robert Paul. "A Quantitative Approach to the Study of the Effects of British Imperial Policy upon Colonial Welfare." *Journal of Economic History* 25, no. 4 (December 1965): 615–38.

Timberlake, Richard H., Jr. *The Origins of Central Banking in the United States.* Cambridge: Harvard University Press, 1978.

U.S. General Accounting Office. *Improving Mission Performance through Information Management and Technology: Learning from Leading Organizations: Executive Guide.* Washington, DC: U.S. General Accounting Office, 1994.

Uveges, Joseph A., Jr., ed. *Public Administration, History and Theory in Contemporary Perspective.* Annals of Public Administration, no. 1. New York: M. Dekker, 1982.

Vernon, J. R. "World War II Fiscal Policies and the End of the Great Depression." *Journal of Economic History* 54, no. 4 (December 1994): 850–68.

Vietor, Richard H. K. "Contrived Competition: Airline Regulation and Deregulation, 1925–1988." *Business History Review* 64, no. 2 (Spring 1990): 61–108.

———. *Contrived Competition: Regulation and Deregulation in America.* Cambridge: Harvard University Press, 1994.

Waldo, Dwight. *The Administrative State: A Study of the Political Theory of American Public Administration.* 2d ed. New York: Holmes & Meier, 1984.

Wallis, John J. "The Birth of the Old Federalism: Financing the New Deal, 1932–1940." *Journal of Economic History* 44, no. 2 (March 1984): 139–59.

Wamsley, Gary L., and James F. Wolf, eds. *Refounding Democratic Public Administration*. Thousand Oaks, CA: Sage, 1996.

Weidenbaum, Murray. *Business, Government and the Public*. Englewood Cliffs, NJ: Prentice-Hall, 1977.

West, Robert C. *Banking Reform and the Federal Reserve, 1863–1923*. Ithaca, NY: Cornell University Press, 1977.

Whicker, Marcia Lynn. "Federalist Elitism vs. Confederationist Communitarianism as the Legitimacy Crisis in Public Administration." Review of *Legitimacy in Public Administration: A Discourse Analysis*, by O. C. McSwite. *Public Productivity & Management Review* 22, no. 2 (December 1998): 259–64.

White, Anthony G. *Military Officership as a Public Administration Career: A Selected Bibliography*. Public Administration Series. Monticello, IL: Vance Bibliographies, 1986.

White, Eugene. *The Regulation and Reform of the American Banking System, 1900–1929*. Princeton, NJ: Princeton University Press, 1983.

Whitten, David O. "An Economic Inquiry into the Whiskey Rebellion of 1794." *Agricultural History* 49, no. 3 (Summer 1975): 491–504.

———. *Emergence of Giant Enterprise, 1860–1914: American Commercial Enterprise and Extractive Industries*. Contributions in Economics and Economic History, no. 54. Westport, CT: Greenwood Press, 1983.

Wicker, Elmus R. *Federal Reserve Policy, 1917–1933*. New York: Random House, 1966.

Wiebe, Robert H. *Businessmen and Reform: A Study of the Progressive Movement*. Cambridge: Harvard University Press, 1962.

Wilcox, Walter W. *The Farmer in the Second World War*. Ames: Iowa State College Press, 1947.

Williamson, Jeffrey. "Watersheds and Turning Points: Conjectures on the Long-Term Impact of Civil War Financing." *Journal of Economic History*, 34, no. 3 (September 1974): 636–61.

Wilson, James Q., ed. *The Politics of Regulation*. New York: Basic Books, 1980.

Wilson, Joan Hoff. *Herbert Hoover: Forgotten Progressive*. Boston: Little, Brown, 1975.

Wueschner, Silvano A. *Charting Twentieth-Century Monetary Policy: Herbert Hoover and Benjamin Strong, 1917–1927*. Contributions in Economics and Economic History, no. 210. Westport, CT: Greenwood Press, 1999.

INDEX

Health Insurance Association of America
(HIAA), 270, 340
*Health Insurance: How Health Care Re-
form May Affect State Regulation*, 274
"Health Insurance Movement in the United
States," 268
Health Insurance Plan (HIP) of Greater
New York, 353
*Health Insurance Portability and Accounta-
bility Act of 1996*, 274
*Health Insurance Purchasing Cooperative
Act*, 273
*Health Insurance Reform Act of 1995:
Hearing . . . on S 1028*, 273
*Health Maintenance Organization: Subject
Analysis with Reference Bibliography*,
364
Health Maintenance Organizations, 363
health maintenance organizations (HMOs),
9, 259, 265, 267, 351–58
*Health Maintenance Organizations: A
Guide to Planning and Development*, 359
*Health Maintenance Organizations and Pre-
paid Group Practices*, 360
"Health Maintenance Organizations and the
Market for Health Services," 362
*Health Maintenance Organizations: A Re-
search Report*, 363
*Health Maintenance Organizations as an
Instrument for Cost Containment Policy*,
360
*Health Maintenance Organizations: Dimen-
sions of Performance*, 362
*Health Maintenance Organizations: Empiri-
cal Evidence*, 363
*Health Maintenance Organizations: Indus-
try Characteristics*, 362
"Health Maintenance Strategy," 356, 361
Health Marketing Quarterly, 412
Health Plans and Collective Bargaining, 269
*Health Policies, Health Politics . . . British
and American . . . 1911–1965*, 269
Health Policy and the Disadvantaged, 360
*Health Policy in the United States: Issues
and Options*, 360
*Health Policy in Transition: A Decade of
Health Politics, Policy, and Law*, 360
*Health Progress in the United States, 1900–
1960*, 362
Health Services Administration, 360
*Health Services and Health Hazards: The
Employee's Need to Know*, 361

*Health Services as a Growth Enterprise in
the United States Since 1875*, 359
*Health Services Continuum in Democratic
States*, 359
*Health Services in the United States: A
Growth Enterprise Since 1875*, 268, 359
Health Services Research, 348, 349
*HealthAmerica Legislation. Hearings on S.
1227*, 273
healthcare, 253–67, 400–403
Healthcare Blue Book, 358, 362
healthcare finance, 253–67
Healthcare Financial Management, 362
Healthcare Financial Management Associa-
tion, 440
Healthcare policy, 334, 335
Healthplan, 358, 362
Healy, Tom, 247
"Hear It Now," 71
*Hearings on H.R. 995, the ERISA Targeted
Health Insurance Reform Act*, 273
*Hearing on H.R. 1415, the Patient Access
to Responsible Care Act* (PARCA), 273
*Hearing on H.R. 1515 . . . Health Insurance
Coverage Act* (EPHIC), 273
hearse, 299
Heatter, Gabriel, 70, 71
Hebrews, 298
Hechinger, Fred M., 377
Heinen, LuAnn, 361
Heinz, Donald, 297, 306, 308
Heirich, Max, 270
Helberg, Kristin, 287
Helbing, Charles, 347
"Hello, Western Union? First Data Call-
ing," 53
*Helmsleys: The Rise and Fall of Harry and
Leona*, 280, 286
Helping the Federal Reserve Work Smarter,
205
hemimorphite, 16
Henderson, John A., 362
Hendrickson, Anthony, 249
Henkins, Leon, 377
Henry, David Ford, 287
Henry E. Sigerist Supplements to the Bulle-
tin of the History of Medicine, 271
Henry O'Rielly Papers, 38, 47
*Heralds of Science . . . the Dibner Library,
Smithsonian Institution*, 40
Herbert, John H., 146
Herbert Hoover as Secretary of Commerce,
79, 89

ABOUT THE EDITORS AND CONTRIBUTORS

KLAUS G. BECKER, Associate Professor of Economics at Texas Tech University and Senior Utility Rate Auditor of the Kansas Corporation Commission, researches the economics of regulation, public enterprise pricing, and market structure.

MARGARET S. BOND is Professor Emerita of Economics, University of Alabama in Huntsville.

DON M. COERVER, Professor and Chairman of the Department of History at Texas Christian University, is the coauthor with Linda B. Hall of *The United States and Latin America* (1999).

ANDREA C. DRAGON, Associate Professor of Business Administration at the College of Saint Elizabeth, Morristown, New Jersey, is the author of "Rubber" in *Extractives, Manufacturing, and Services: A Historiographical and Bibliographical Guide*, volume II of *Handbook of American Business History*, and associate editor (management and business) for *Business Library Review International*.

JOSEPH FINKELSTEIN, Professor Emeritus, Graduate Management Institute, Union College, Schenectady, New York, is associate editor (economics, management, and business) for *Business Library Review International*; author of "Joseph Finkelstein on Quality Management," *Business Library Review* 18, no. 4 (November 1993): 261–64; coauthor with Alfred L. Thimm of *Economists and Society: The Development of Economic*

Thought from Aquinas to Keynes (1981); and editor of *Windows on a New World: The Third Industrial Revolution* (1989).

NADIA EHRLICH FINKELSTEIN, a Child and Family Services Management Specialist in private practice, is a certified social worker and member of the Academy of Certified Social Workers and the author of *Children and Youth in Limbo: A Search for Connections* (1991).

MARVIN N. FISCHBAUM, Professor of Economics, Indiana State University, Terre Haute, wrote "Drugs" for *Manufacturing: A Historiographical and Bibliographical Guide*, volume I of *Handbook of American Business History*.

JOSEPH A. GIACALONE is Associate Professor of Economics and Finance at St. Johns University, Jamaica, New York.

K. PETER HARDER, Professor of Economics at Western Washington University, Bellingham, wrote "Forestry" for *Extractives, Manufacturing, and Services: A Historiographical and Bibliographical Guide*, volume II of *Handbook of American Business History*, and is the author of *Environmental Factors of Early Railroads: A Comparative Study of Massachusetts and the German States of Baden and Pfalz (Palatinate) Before 1870* (1981).

JOHN L. NEUFELD is Professor of Economics, University of North Carolina at Greensboro.

SPIRO G. PATTON is an independent consultant for retail and tourism development. His chapter "Blast Furnaces and Steel Mills" appeared in *Manufacturing: A Historiographical and Bibliographical Guide*, volume I of *Handbook of American Business History*, followed by "Local and Suburban Transit" in *Extractives, Manufacturing, and Services: A Historiographical and Bibliographical Guide*, volume II of *Handbook of American Business History*.

R. D. PETERSON, Professor Emeritus of Economics at Colorado State University, is the author of *Political Economy and American Capitalism* (1991), *Economic Organization in Medical Equipment and Supply* (with C. R. MacPhee 1973), *Economic Structure of Idaho: A Provisional Input-Output Study* (1968), and *Idaho's Minerals Industry: A Flow-of-Product Analysis* (with Merle L. Newell 1968).

HUGH T. ROCKOFF, Professor of Economics at Rutgers University, is author of *History of the American Economy* (with Gary M. Walton 1998), *Drastic Measures: A History of Wage and Price Controls in the United*

States (1984), and *The Free Banking Era: A Re-Examination* (1975) and editor of *The Sinews of War: Essays on the Economic History of World War II* (with Geofrey T. Mills 1993) and *Strategic Factors in Nineteenth Century American Economic History: A Volume to Honor Robert W. Fogel* (with Claudia Golden 1992).

RICHARD C. SCHIMING, Professor of Economics at Minnesota State University, Mankato, is associate editor (economics) for *Business Library Review International*.

CAROLE E. SCOTT, Professor of Economics at West Georgia State University, is founder and editor of *B→QUEST*, an electronic journal.

DONALD R. STABILE, Professor of Economics at St. Mary's College, Maryland, is associate editor (economics) for *Business Library Review International* and the author of *The Origins of American Public Finance: Debates over Money, Debt, and Taxes in the Constitutional Era, 1776–1836* (1998) and *Work and Welfare: The Social Costs of Labor in the History of Economic Thought* (1996). Stabile contributed the chapter titled "Bakery Products" in *Manufacturing: A Historiographical and Bibliographical Guide*, volume I of *Handbook of American Business History*, and the Introduction to *Extractives, Manufacturing, and Services: A Historiographical and Bibliographical Guide*, volume II of *Handbook of American Business History*.

MARTIN A. STROSBERG, Associate Professor in the Graduate Management Institute at Union College in Schenectady, New York, was Senior Program Analyst at the U.S. Department of Health and Human Services in Washington, D.C., from 1979 to 1981.

H. BRUCE THROCKMORTON is Professor of Economics at Tennessee Technological University in Cookeville, Tennessee.

ELEANOR T. VON ENDE, Research Associate at the Institute for Public Policy and Business Research at the University of Kansas, is a scholar of nineteenth-century American economic history.

SUSAN DuBROCK WENDEL, former chief of training for the Chicago District Internal Revenue Service and recipient of the Zeggar Memorial Award for "President Herbert Hoover and Banking Reform," teaches history and economics.

BESSIE E. WHITTEN is editor, with David O. Whitten, of *Business Library Review International*.

DAVID O. WHITTEN, Professor of Economics, Auburn University, Auburn, Alabama, is author of *Andrew Durnford: A Black Sugar Planter in the Antebellum South* (1995) and *A History of Economics and Business at Auburn University* (1992) and coauthor with Douglas Steeples of *Democracy in Desperation: The Depression of 1893* (1998).

JAMES L. WILES, Professor Emeritus of Economics, Stonehill College, North Easton, Massachusetts, was codirector of the Bridgewater State College-Stonehill College Regional Research Institute. He is the author of "Leather and Leather Products," in *Extractives, Manufacturing, and Services: A Historiographical and Bibliographical Guide*, volume II, *Handbook of American Business History*.